Good Jobs for All in a Changing World of Work

THE OECD JOBS STRATEGY

OECD
BETTER POLICIES FOR BETTER LIVES

This work is published under the responsibility of the Secretary-General of the OECD. The opinions expressed and arguments employed herein do not necessarily reflect the official views of OECD member countries.

This document, as well as any data and any map included herein, are without prejudice to the status of or sovereignty over any territory, to the delimitation of international frontiers and boundaries and to the name of any territory, city or area.

Please cite this publication as:
OECD (2018), *Good Jobs for All in a Changing World of Work: The OECD Jobs Strategy*, OECD Publishing, Paris.
https://doi.org/10.1787/9789264308817-en

ISBN 978-92-64-30880-0 (print)
ISBN 978-92-64-30881-7 (pdf)

The statistical data for Israel are supplied by and under the responsibility of the relevant Israeli authorities. The use of such data by the OECD is without prejudice to the status of the Golan Heights, East Jerusalem and Israeli settlements in the West Bank under the terms of international law.

Photo credits: www.leondelmonte.cl

Corrigenda to OECD publications may be found on line at: *www.oecd.org/publishing/corrigenda*.

Foreword

Times were very different when the Reassessed OECD Job Strategy was launched in 2006. We had just witnessed more than a decade of sustained growth, record low unemployment rates, and relatively robust wage growth. Then the global financial crisis hit, and ten years later, the world has once again changed. While the global economy has been recovering from the financial crisis for several years now, wage growth remains sluggish in most OECD countries. Additionally, productivity growth has fallen from about 2.5% before the crisis to about half this rate over the past five years, and inequalities have reached unprecedentedly high levels: the average disposable income of the richest 10% of the population is now around nine and a half times that of the poorest 10% across the OECD, up from seven times three decades ago. Rapid digital transformation, globalisation and population ageing, are deeply rooted trends changing the very nature of jobs and the functioning of the labour market, thus raising new policy challenges.

In this context, in January 2016, OECD Employment and Labour Ministers called for a new OECD Jobs Strategy that fully reflects this new reality. The result is a profoundly revised OECD Jobs Strategy. While the 2006 Reassessed Strategy already recognised that good labour market performance could be achieved with different models, the new OECD Jobs Strategy goes beyond job quantity and considers job quality and inclusiveness as central policy priorities. It is an essential part of our broader strategy for Inclusive Growth, and seeks to address the fact that some groups, including the low income and the low skilled, youth and older workers, are even more at risk of exclusion now than a decade ago. This is not just unfair, but also economically and politically very challenging. The new Jobs Strategy recognises that flexibility-enhancing policies in product and labour markets are important but certainly not sufficient. It stresses the need for policies and constructive social dialogue that protect workers, foster inclusiveness and allow workers and firms to make the most of ongoing challenges and opportunities. The Strategy also emphasises that, in a fast changing world of work, we need to foster resilience and adaptability of the labour market to achieve good economic and labour market performance.

The key policy recommendations of the new OECD Jobs Strategy are organised around three broad principles that provide guidance on reforms across a broad range of public policy areas:

i. ***Promoting an environment in which high-quality jobs can thrive.*** Good labour market performance requires a sound macroeconomic framework, a growth-friendly environment and skills evolving in line with market needs. Adaptability in product and labour markets is also needed, and the costs and benefits of this should be fairly shared between workers and firms, as well as among workers on different contracts by avoiding an over-reliance on temporary (often precarious) contracts through balanced employment protection schemes.

ii. ***Preventing labour market exclusion and protecting individuals against labour market risks.*** Supporting the quick (re)integration of job seekers in employment remains a top priority, but the new strategy also highlights the importance of addressing challenges *before* they arise by promoting equality of opportunities and preventing the accumulation of disadvantages over the life-course.

iii. ***Preparing for future opportunities and challenges in a rapidly changing economy and labour market.*** People will need to be equipped with the right skills in a context of rapidly changing skills demands. Workers also need to remain protected against labour market risks in a world where new forms of work may arise.

The big challenge now is to translate these general policy prescriptions into actionable policy packages that can promote better jobs for everyone in a fast-changing world of work. The OECD is committed to assisting countries in this process by developing solid diagnoses, well-tailored recommendations and by providing guidance for their effective implementation through the *OECD Economic Surveys*. We look forward to working with OECD member and partner countries on the implementation of the new OECD Jobs Strategy.

Angel Gurría,
Secretary-General,
Organisation for Economic Co-operation
and Development

Acknowledgements

This report is the outcome of a collaboration between the Directorate for Employment, Labour and Social Affairs (ELS) and the Economics Department (ECO).

The publication was coordinated and edited by Alexander Hijzen (ELS) and Cyrille Schwellnus (ECO). The main authors were Andrea Bassanini (Chapters 1, 3-6 and 9), Stijn Broecke (Chapters 1, 3-7 and 12), Oliver Denk (Chapters 11 and 15), Alexander Hijzen (Chapters 1-10, 13, 14, 16, 17), Cyrille Schwellnus (Chapters 1-6, 13, 14, 17) as well as Willem Adema (Chapter 11), Ruediger Ahrend (Chapter 14), Stéphane Carcillo (Chapter 9), Elena Crivellaro (Chapter 17), Emily Farchy (Chapter 11), Andrea Garnero (Chapter 8), Sebastian Königs (Chapter 10), Fabio Manca (Chapter 14), Christopher Prinz (Chapters 9 and 11), Glenda Quintini (Chapter 10), Veerle Miranda (Chapter 11), Anne Saint-Martin (Chapter 11), Stéphane Sorbe (Chapter 14), Stefan Thewissen (Chapter 16). Agnès Puymoyen provided statistical assistance for all chapters. Brigitte Beyeler, Natalie Corry, Liv Gudmundson, Lucy Hulett and Sarah Michelson prepared the manuscript for publication. Steve Whitehouse and Kate Lancaster contributed to the editing of the report. The senior management, including Gabriela Ramos (Chief of Staff and G20 Sherpa), Stefano Scarpetta (Director of ELS), Luiz De Mello (Director of ECO), Mark Pearson, Alain de Serres, Stéphane Carcillo, Mark Keese and Giuseppe Nicoletti, provided guidance and extensive comments on various versions of the report.

The report has benefited from the strong support and fruitful exchanges with the delegates of the Working Party on Employment, the Employment Labour and Social Affairs Committee, the Economic Policy Committee of the OECD and representatives of the Trade Union Advisory Committee and the Business and Industry Advisory Committee throughout the process. Useful comments and suggestions were provided by colleagues from various OECD Directorates, including the Office of the Secretary-General, the Directorate for Education and Skills, the Directorate for Science, Technology and Innovation, the Public Affairs Directorate, the Centre for Tax Policy and Administration and the Statistics Directorate, and the Centre for Entrepreneurship, SMEs, Regions and Cities. Last but not least, recognition is due to the members of the Advisory Group on the new Jobs Strategy: Torben Andersen (Aarhus University, Denmark), Michael Burda (Humboldt University, Germany), Jason Furman (Peterson Institute for International Economics, United States), Lesley Giles (Work Foundation, United Kingdom), Lisa Lynch (Brandeis University, United States), Selma Mahfouz (DARES, France), Alan Manning (London School of Economics, United Kingdom) and Stephen Nickell (Oxford University, United Kingdom).

The German Federal Ministry of Labour and Social Affairs and the French Ministry of Labour provided special support to the new OECD Jobs Strategy, including by hosting respectively the High-Level Policy Forum in Berlin (13 June 2017) and the High-Level Policy Forum and Launch of the new OECD Jobs Strategy in Paris (4 December 2018).

Table of contents

Tables

Figures

Boxes

Chapter 1. Key messages and recommendations

The new OECD Jobs Strategy provides guidance to policy makers on policies that enable workers and firms to make the most of emerging challenges and opportunities and ensure that the fruits of growth are broadly shared. The key policy recommendations are organised around three broad principles: i) promote an environment in which high-quality jobs can flourish; ii) prevent labour market exclusion and protect individuals against labour market risks; iii) prepare for future opportunities and challenges in a rapidly changing labour market. To support countries in building stronger and more inclusive labour markets, the new OECD Jobs Strategy goes beyond general policy recommendations by providing guidance on the implementation of reforms.

Introduction

Since the publication of the OECD's *Reassessed Jobs Strategy* in 2006 (OECD, 2006[1]), OECD and emerging economies have undergone major structural changes and faced deep shocks: the worst financial and economic crisis since the Great Depression and continued weak productivity growth; unprecedentedly high levels of income inequality in many countries; and substantial upheaval linked to technological progress, globalisation, and demographic change. In light of these major changes, and the central role of labour policies in addressing them, OECD Employment and Labour Ministers in January 2016 called for a new Jobs Strategy that fully reflects new challenges and opportunities to continue to provide an effective tool to guide policy makers.

The new OECD Jobs Strategy is more comprehensive in scope and forward looking in outlook than previous OECD Jobs Strategies, putting a well-functioning labour market at the centre stage of inclusive growth. The original OECD Jobs Strategy of 1994 (OECD, 1994[2]) emphasised the role of flexible labour and product markets for tackling high and persistent unemployment – the main policy concern at the time. Providing a growth-friendly environment, including through flexible product and labour markets, was seen as the key to promoting job creation and good labour market performance more generally. The 2006 Reassessed Jobs Strategy placed more emphasis on promoting labour force participation and improving job quality. The main message was that there are "several roads to Rome", i.e. good labour market performance is consistent with more market-reliant models that emphasise labour and product market flexibility, but also with models that involve a stronger role of public policies, generally coupled with strong social dialogue and a combination of stronger protection for workers with flexibility for firms.

Building on these previous jobs strategies, the new OECD Jobs Strategy provides guidance to policy makers on labour market and other policies that enable workers and firms to harness the opportunities provided by new technologies and markets, while helping them to cope with the required adjustments and ensuring that the fruits of growth are broadly shared. The new Jobs Strategy continues to stress the links between strong and sustained economic growth and the quantity of jobs, but also recognises job quality, in terms of both wage and non-wage working conditions, and labour market inclusiveness as central policy priorities. Resilience and adaptability are placed at the heart of the new Jobs Strategy as in a rapidly evolving economy and labour market, policy needs to foster economic dynamism and be forward-looking to allow individuals and firms to absorb, adapt and make the most of challenges and opportunities related to changes in macroeconomic conditions and the megatrends affecting the future of work.

The main message of the new OECD Jobs Strategy is that while policies to support flexibility in product and labour markets are needed for growth, they are not sufficient to simultaneously deliver good outcomes in terms of job quantity, job quality and inclusiveness. This also requires policies and institutions to promote job quality and inclusiveness, which are often more effective when supported by the social partners. In this sense, the new OECD Jobs Strategy represents a significant evolution from the 2006 strategy, and even more from the original 1994 strategy. It is based on new evidence that shows that countries with policies and institutions that promote job quality, job quantity and greater inclusiveness perform better than countries where the focus of policy is predominantly on enhancing (or preserving) market flexibility. In other words, it is necessary to combine policies that encourage economic growth with policies and work practices agreed by the social partners that foster inclusiveness and protect workers. Thus, a whole-of-government approach is needed, embedding the new OECD Jobs Strategy in the OECD Inclusive Growth Initiative and making appropriate linkages to other OECD strategies.[1]

1.1. Key policy principles

The key policy recommendations of the new OECD Jobs Strategy are organised around three broad principles: i) promote an environment in which high-quality jobs can flourish; ii) prevent labour market exclusion and protect individuals against labour market risks; iii) prepare for future opportunities and challenges in a rapidly changing labour market.

Promote an environment in which high-quality jobs can flourish

High-quality employment requires a sound macroeconomic policy framework, a growth-friendly environment and skills evolving in line with market needs. This is broadly consistent with previous strategies, but with some important nuances.

- The recent global economic and financial crisis was a stark reminder of the importance of counter-cyclical macroeconomic policies for stabilising economic and labour market outcomes and preventing temporary downturns in activity from turning into low-growth traps. When monetary policy is constrained, letting automatic fiscal stabilisers operate freely and complementing them with additional fiscal measures in response to large economic shocks becomes particularly effective. This requires a fiscal policy framework that creates sufficient fiscal space during upturns to allow for a stimulating fiscal policy response during downturns and rapidly scaling up income support and active labour market programmes as needed. An important nuance with respect to the Jobs Strategy of 2006 is that the new strategy recognises that it can be useful during sharp economic downturns to channel fiscal resources to well-designed short-time work programmes that seek to preserve vulnerable jobs that are viable in the long term, while scaling them down quickly as conditions return to normal.
- Flexibility in product and labour markets is essential to create high-quality jobs in an ever more dynamic environment. Barriers in product and labour markets to the entry of new firms, the expansion of high-performing firms and the orderly exit of underperforming firms need to be reduced. However, some forms of flexibility are better than others. For example, partial labour market reforms that liberalise the use of temporary contracts, but maintain high levels of employment protection for workers on open-ended contracts can be counter-productive. This can result in an excessive use of temporary contracts, leading to low overall job quality, high levels of inequality and low resilience, without a clear benefit for the overall number of jobs. Similar issues can arise in emerging economies where overly strict employment protection for employees in the formal sector, alongside a range of other factors such as high non-wage labour costs, contribute to high levels of informal work without providing effective protection to workers.
- Moreover, policies need to strike the right balance between employment flexibility and stability. The challenge is to ensure that resources can be reallocated to more productive uses while providing a level of employment stability that fosters learning and innovation in the workplace. Employment stability can be promoted by having moderate and predictable employment protection provisions that provide security to all workers and by strengthening the

link between employers' unemployment insurance contributions and the cost of unemployment insurance benefits for displaced workers (e.g. partially experience-rated contributions). Moreover, by facilitating flexibility in earnings, in particular through adjustments in working time, collective bargaining and social dialogue can also support employment stability by helping to preserve good-quality jobs during difficult times.

- High-quality employment also depends crucially on having an effective education and training system, which equips workers with the skills needed by employers and offers opportunities and incentives for education and training throughout their working lives. To better match skills with labour market needs, it is important to develop stronger links between the world of education and the world of work and have robust systems and tools for assessing and anticipating skills needs.

Prevent labour market exclusion and protect individuals against labour market risks

The best way of promoting an inclusive labour market is by addressing problems before they arise. This means that a shift in emphasis is required from remedial to preventive policies. This enables workers to avoid many of the social and financial costs associated with labour market risks (such as unemployment, sickness and disability); it contributes directly to economic growth by expanding opportunities for workers; and alleviates fiscal pressures by reducing the overall costs of social programmes. Such an approach could therefore boost efficiency and equity at the same time.

- The core of a preventive approach to labour market inclusiveness is to strengthen equality of opportunities so that socio-economic background does not act as a key determinant of success in the labour market. This key policy priority crucially hinges on tackling barriers to the acquisition of adequate levels of education and labour market skills by individuals from disadvantaged backgrounds, through targeted interventions during (pre-)school years and in the transition from school to work.
- A preventive approach also requires a life-course perspective, to avoid an accumulation of individual disadvantages that require costly interventions at a later stage. To reduce the risk of workers becoming trapped in low-quality jobs or joblessness, they should have continuous opportunities to develop, maintain and upgrade skills through learning and training at all ages. This would help them navigate a labour market that will increasingly require frequent changes of jobs and activities throughout a career. Similarly, working conditions should be adapted to workers' needs over the life course. By making it easier to combine work, care and social responsibilities and preventing the development of work-related health problems, this increases labour force participation over a working life among both men and women, narrows gender gaps and reduces the risk of poverty and exclusion. But, as new forms of work are emerging, such policy instruments must be extended beyond those in dependent employment.
- A preventive approach cannot avoid that some people fall through the cracks. As suggested by the 2006 OECD Jobs Strategy, activation measures, wage-setting rules and the tax-and-benefits system can be combined to make work pay and handle individual shocks by protecting workers rather than jobs, so that the required adaptability of the labour market is not jeopardised. In this way, the

protection of workers against labour market risks and exclusion can be achieved by supporting and accompanying job-seekers towards new economic activities, conditional on individual commitment and job-search efforts (the so-called "mutual-obligations" framework).

- Previous *Jobs Strategies* have pointed to the need to ensure that unemployment, disability and other social benefits do not unduly discourage active job search. Recent evidence suggests, however, that reaching a high coverage of unemployment, disability and social assistance benefits, conditional on the rigorous enforcement of mutual obligations, plays a pivotal role in the success of activation strategies: by providing a key instrument for connecting with jobless people it allows addressing barriers to employment related to the employability of workers, the availability of suitable job opportunities and worker motivation. This also means extending the reach of social protection to new forms of work as much as possible.

Prepare for future opportunities and challenges in a rapidly changing labour market

Product and labour market dynamism will be essential to deal with the rapid transformation of economies resulting from technological progress, globalisation and demographic change. However, helping workers move from declining businesses, industries and regions to those with the highest growth prospects should be accompanied by policies to help individuals maintain and upgrade their skills, assist lagging regions, strengthen social safety nets and enhance the role of social dialogue in shaping the future world of work. Skills policies, social protection and labour market regulations will need to be adapted to the new world of work to achieve greater job quality and inclusiveness. In some cases, this may require a fundamental rethink of current policies and institutions.

- A first challenge is to equip workers with the right skills in a context where the demand for skills is likely to evolve rapidly and people continue working at a higher age, with an increased emphasis on Science, Technology, Engineering and Mathematics (STEM) as well as soft skills, and incentives for the acquisition of non-transferable skills may be eroded. The increased fragmentation of production processes and the likelihood that workers will move between jobs more frequently may reduce incentives for firms and workers to invest in firm-specific skills. The policy challenge lies in: i) designing novel tools that reduce barriers to lifelong learning by linking education and training to individuals rather than jobs, while updating existing ones like grants and loans to make them more accessible to all adults; ii) strengthening work-based learning programmes (e.g. apprenticeships). More generally, existing infrastructures for lifelong learning may need to be scaled up, for example by fully exploiting the opportunities afforded by new technologies.
- A further challenge is to ensure that workers remain protected against labour market risks in a world where flexible forms of work may increase. This includes ensuring that everybody has access to social protection and is covered by basic labour market regulations. Workers on 'flexible' labour contracts often have limited or no access to certain forms of social protection, such as workplace accident and unemployment insurance, and they may not be covered by basic labour market regulations. To some extent, it might be possible to address this concern by extending or adapting existing social security schemes and by

clarifying and effectively enforcing existing labour market regulations. In other cases, innovative solutions need to be found to ensure adequate wages and working conditions.

- Possible approaches for extending social protection coverage include: creating new, specially designed benefit schemes; expanding the role of non-contributory schemes; implementing minimum floors to social benefits; and making social protection more portable. A more radical solution would be to introduce a universal basic income (UBI), although it is unlikely that such a scheme could provide effective protection to all workers without significantly raising fiscal pressure or making some people worse off because of the need to cut other, well-targeted benefits to finance the UBI. In terms of labour market policies and institutions, policy makers should experiment with new instruments to fight in-work poverty and put in place a legal framework that allows labour relations to adapt to new emerging challenges.

1.2. Policy implementation

To support countries in building stronger and more inclusive labour markets, the new OECD Jobs Strategy goes beyond general policy recommendations by providing guidance for the implementation of reforms:

- Policy reform strategies need to be adapted to a country's specific characteristics in terms of its institutional set-up, social preferences, administrative capacity and social capital. While sub-par performance in an area of the labour market suggests the need for policy reform, countries should adapt their reform strategies to their specific situation. For instance, where social capital is low and administrative capacity lacking, policy action should aim at being simple, transparent and easily accountable.
- Policies are also often more effective when combined into coherent packages that enhance synergies and limit the potential cost of reforms in the short-run or for specific groups. For example, interventions targeted at specific groups should simultaneously address all barriers to employment through co-ordinated actions concerning the design of tax-and-benefits policies and the provision of employment, health and social services.
- Packaging and sequencing reforms in effective ways – acting first on those that are a prerequisite for the success of others – minimises trade-offs between individual policies and can broaden support among the electorate. For example, product market and employment protection reforms tend to be less costly in the short term when the former precede the latter.
- Building support for reforms is vital for their success. This requires winning a mandate for reform, effective communication including through the use of new technologies, and complementary reforms and policy actions to cushion short-term costs, including appropriate use of macroeconomic policy levers.
- Once reforms are passed, ensure that they are fully implemented, effectively enforced and rigorously evaluated. This requires investing in data collection if suitable data for monitoring compliance and outcomes are not available and strengthening evaluation mechanisms into policy actions to allow assessing their effects.

- Building strong and inclusive labour markets also requires proactive policy making. This requires innovative systems that help identifying potential challenges and opportunities ahead of time, rather than firefighting problems when they arise and recognising opportunities when they have long been missed. Anticipating future challenges and opportunities, finding solutions, managing change proactively, and shaping the future world of work can be achieved more easily and effectively if employers, workers and their representatives work closely together with the government in a spirit of co-operation and mutual trust.

1.3. Roadmap

Part I of this volume provides an overview of the new OECD Jobs Strategy. Chapter 2 presents the main motivation as the dual challenge of reviving productivity growth and making labour markets more inclusive in a rapidly changing world of work. Chapter 3 introduces the OECD Jobs Strategy framework for assessing labour market performance that focuses on three key dimensions through which the labour market contributes to inclusive growth and well-being: i) the quantity and quality of jobs; ii) labour market inclusiveness; and iii) resilience and adaptability. It is operationalised by the OECD Jobs Strategy dashboard that can be used to assess labour market performance and identify country-specific reform priorities. Chapter 4 provides an overview of the role of policies and institutions in promoting good labour market performance, with the underlying evidence and background analysis being discussed in Parts II – IV of this Volume. Going beyond the general policy principles of the Jobs Strategy, Chapter 5 provides concrete guidance to countries regarding implementation based on Part V of this Volume. Chapter 6 presents the detailed policy recommendations of the new OECD Jobs Strategy.

Part II of the Volume discusses in depth how policies and institutions can contribute to the **quantity and quality of jobs**. Since productivity growth is a pre-condition for better wages and working conditions in the long-term, Chapter 7 provides a comprehensive discussion of the role of policies and institution for worker productivity. However, productivity growth does not automatically translate into higher wages, better working conditions and sufficient job opportunities. Chapter 8, therefore, discusses the role of wage-setting institutions and labour taxes in ensuring that productivity gains translate into higher wages and better working conditions while maintaining high employment. Chapter 9 emphasises the need to combine high-quality job creation with measures to support labour supply by ensuring that work is accessible, attractive and sustainable over the life-course.

Part III focuses on promoting **labour market inclusiveness** so that everybody benefits from increased prosperity. The OECD Jobs Strategy emphasises the importance of promoting equal opportunities, but also recognises that excessive inequalities in outcomes are incompatible with equal opportunities and could in many cases be reduced without unduly reducing employment and growth. Chapter 10 discusses how policies and institutions can tackle deep and persistent inequalities in the labour market by promoting equal opportunities and containing excessive income inequalities. A number of groups, e.g. workers with low skills, persons with caring responsibilities or disabilities and migrants, face particular barriers to accessing good quality jobs and require specific support. Chapter 11 discusses the role of measures tailored to the needs of each of these groups and distils a number of common lessons. Chapter 12 considers a range of policies that can help policy makers balance innovation in work arrangements with the concern that new forms of work – including those related to the emergence of the platform economy – may push vulnerable workers into jobs with limited worker protections.

Part IV of the Volume discusses the role of resilience and adaptability in ensuring good quality jobs in a rapidly changing world of work. Chapter 13 emphasises the role of labour market resilience in limiting the social costs of economic downturns, with a particular focus on the potential role of state-dependent employment and social policies to provide effective support to workers while reinforcing the stabilising role of social expenditures for aggregate demand. Chapter 14 discusses how labour markets can be made more adaptable to structural change by promoting: i) the efficient reallocation of workers across jobs, firms, industries and regions; ii) responsive, effective and worker-centred adult learning systems; and iii) effective employment and social policies to support displaced workers.

Part V of this Volume goes beyond the general policy principles of the new Jobs Strategy by providing concrete guidance to countries on the implementation of reforms. Chapter 15 discusses factors that make reform happen and support the reform process. Chapter 16 translates the general recommendations of the new Jobs Strategy to the specific context of emerging economies that need to address the challenge of broadly shared productivity gains with limited fiscal and administrative capacity. Chapter 17 identifies country-specific reform priorities and a range of contextual factors that need to be taken into account for developing country-specific recommendations using the OECD Jobs Strategy dashboard.

Box 1.1. The main policy recommendations of the new OECD Jobs Strategy

This Box summarises the main policy recommendations of the new OECD Jobs Strategy. The full policy recommendations can be found in Chapter 6 at the end of Part I "Overview" of this Volume. These policy recommendations are a key pillar of the OECD Inclusive Growth Initiative. In the implementation of the new Jobs Strategy, it will be important to exploit synergies among different policy areas and ensure consistency with the OECD Going for Growth recommendations, the OECD Skills Strategy, the OECD Innovation Strategy and the OECD Green Growth Strategy. Thus, a whole-of-government approach is necessary.

A. Promote an environment in which high-quality jobs can flourish

1. Implement a sound macroeconomic policy framework that ensures price stability and fiscal sustainability while allowing for an effective counter-cyclical monetary and fiscal policy response during economic downturns.
2. Boost investment and productivity growth, and promote quality job creation by removing barriers to the creation and expansion of successful businesses, the restructuring or exit of underperforming ones, and by creating an entrepreneurship-friendly environment.
3. Ensure that employment protection legislation generates dismissal costs that are predictable, balanced across contract types and not overly restrictive, while protecting workers against possible abuses and limit excessive turnover.
4. Facilitate the adoption of flexible working-time arrangements to help firms adjust to temporary changes in business conditions, while helping workers to reconcile work and personal life.

5. Reduce non-wage labour costs, especially for low-wage workers, and differences in fiscal treatment based on employment status.
6. Consider using a statutory minimum wage set at a moderate level as a tool to raise wages at the bottom of the wage ladder, while avoiding that it prices low-skilled workers out of jobs.
7. Promote the inclusiveness of collective bargaining systems while providing sufficient flexibility for firms to adapt to aggregate shocks and structural change.
8. Foster the development of suitable skills for labour market needs, while promoting the use of these skills and their adaptation during the working life to respond to evolving skills needs.
9. Promote formal employment by enhancing the enforcement of labour market rules, making formal work more attractive for firms and workers and promoting skills development to enhance worker productivity.

B. Prevent labour market exclusion and protect individuals against labour market risks

1. Promote equal opportunities to avoid that socio-economic background determines opportunities in the labour market through its influence on the acquisition of relevant labour market skills or as a source of discrimination.
2. Adopt a life-course perspective to prevent that individual disadvantages cumulate over time, requiring interventions at a later stage, which are usually less effective and involve larger fiscal costs.
3. Develop a comprehensive strategy to activate and protect workers, by combining adequate and widely accessible out-of-work benefits with active programmes in a mutual-obligations framework.
4. Adopt specific policies for underrepresented and disadvantaged groups, ensuring that they simultaneously address all barriers to employment.
5. Support lagging regions through coordinated policies at the national, regional and local levels that promote growth and competitiveness based on their specific assets and tackle social problems associated with local concentrations of labour market exclusion and poverty.

C. Prepare for future opportunities and challenges in a rapidly changing labour market

6. Promote the reallocation of workers between firms, industries and regions, while supporting displaced workers.
7. Enable displaced workers to move quickly into jobs, using a mixture of general and targeted income support and re-employment assistance, combined with prevention and early intervention measures.
8. Accompany innovation in new forms of employment with policies to safeguard job quality by avoiding abuse, creating a level-playing field between firms, and providing adequate protection for all workers regardless of employment contract.
9. Plan for the future by anticipating change; facilitating inclusive dialogue with the social partners and other relevant stakeholders on the future of work; and where necessary, adapting today's labour market, skills and social policies to the emerging needs in the changing world of work.

D. Implementation

10. Make reforms successful by adapting them to country specificities, carefully packaging and sequencing them to limit their potential cost in the short-run or for specific groups and building support for them.
11. Ensure that reforms are fully implemented effectively enforced and rigorously evaluated; invest in data collection if suitable data are not available.

Note

[1] The OECD Inclusive Growth Initiative was launched in 2012. It has resulted in the OECD Framework for Policy Action on Inclusive Growth as well as the development of Inclusive Growth dashboard (OECD, 2018[3]). The Framework is organised around four pillars: i) shared prosperity; ii) inclusive markets; iii) equality of opportunities; and iv) inclusive growth governance. For a discussion of the links between the Inclusive Growth Initiative and the new Jobs Strategy see Chapter 3 of this Volume.

References

OECD (2018), *The Framework for Policy Action on Inclusive Growth*, https://www.oecd.org/mcm/documents/C-MIN-2018-5-EN.pdf. [3]

OECD (2006), *OECD Employment Outlook 2006: Boosting Jobs and Incomes*, OECD Publishing, Paris, https://doi.org/10.1787/empl_outlook-2006-en. [1]

OECD (1994), *The OECD Jobs Study: Facts, Analysis, Strategies*, OECD Publishing, Paris, https://www.oecd.org/els/emp/1941679.pdf (accessed on 25 September 2018). [2]

Part I. Overview

Chapter 2. The challenge: Broadly shared productivity gains

Reviving productivity growth and ensuring that productivity gains are broadly shared through higher wages and better employment opportunities are key to raising well-being for all members of society. This chapter discusses the role of the labour market as an engine of a dynamic economy sustained by strong productivity growth whose benefits are shared with all workers through enhanced employment opportunities, higher wages and better working conditions.

The statistical data for Israel are supplied by and under the responsibility of the relevant Israeli authorities. The use of such data by the OECD is without prejudice to the status of the Golan Heights, East Jerusalem and Israeli settlements in the West Bank under the terms of international law.

Introduction

A well-functioning labour market is crucial for sustaining gains in productivity which underpin high and inclusive growth and rising levels of well-being. Yet productivity growth has tended to slow in practically all advanced and emerging market economies over the past two decades. At the same time, median real wages have failed to keep up with even this diminished productivity growth in many countries, making growth less inclusive. Thus, not only have productivity gains become smaller, but the share transmitted to low-wage and middle-wage workers through real wage increases has also declined, resulting in real wage stagnation for workers in the bottom half of the wage distribution.

In this light, this chapter discusses how a well-functioning labour market can foster a dynamic economy sustained by strong productivity growth that benefits all workers through enhanced employment opportunities, higher wages and better working conditions. Labour markets are crucial for the efficient re-allocation of resources in the economy, providing workers with opportunities to acquire and upgrade their skills and ensuring decent working conditions for all workers, including those in a weak bargaining position. The tax and benefits system also has an important role to play in improving workers' well-being, but on its own it cannot raise living standards for all or provide the sense of gratification that work potentially offers through economic engagement, social interaction and personal accomplishment.

The remainder of this chapter is structured as follows. Section 2.1 describes the twin challenge of achieving high productivity growth and ensuring that the gains of productivity growth are transmitted to all workers through better employment opportunities and higher wages. It also outlines trends in productivity, wages and employment over the past two decades and links these trends to underlying drivers. Section 2.2 discusses the role of the labour market in promoting: high productivity growth; a good transmission from productivity to wages; and the availability and accessibility of good employment opportunities.

2.1. The challenge

Over the past two decades, productivity growth in the OECD has slowed, raising concerns about growth in living standards and the creation of high-quality job opportunities. The productivity slowdown reflects both slower capital deepening (growth in capital per worker) and lower multi-factor productivity growth (Figure 2.1). The slowdown in capital deepening was particularly pronounced after the global crisis of 2008-09, suggesting that economic downturns can have long-lasting effects. By contrast, low growth in multi-factor productivity appears to be a structural development that pre-dates the global crisis. In conjunction with the projected decline in overall labour force participation due to population ageing, a structural slowdown in productivity growth could significantly reduce growth in living standards (Guillemette and Turner, 2018[1]).

Figure 2.1. Productivity growth has declined over the past 20 years

OECD average

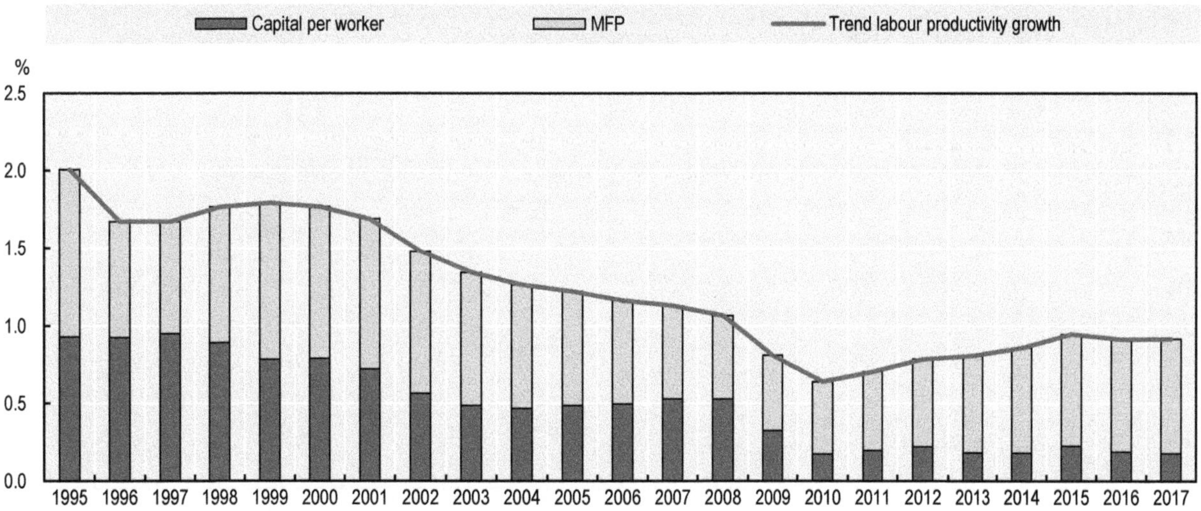

Source: OECD (2018), "OECD Economic Outlook No. 103" (Edition 2018/1), *OECD Economic Outlook: Statistics and Projections* (database), https://doi.org/10.1787/494f29a4-en (accessed on 22 November 2018).

StatLink http://dx.doi.org/10.1787/888933880945

In many OECD countries, real wage growth has been even lower than the growth in labour productivity (Figure 2.2). In many OECD countries, real average wages have decoupled from labour productivity, i.e. there has been a decline labour shares (the share of national income accounted for by labour compensation in the form of wages, salaries and other benefits).[1] Moreover, real median wages have grown at an even lower rate than real average wages in the overwhelming majority of OECD countries, which means that wage inequality has increased.[2] Consequently, in many OECD countries, productivity gains are no longer translating into broadly shared wage gains for all workers (OECD, 2018[2]; Schwellnus, Kappeler and Pionnier, 2017[3]; Sharpe and Uguccioni, 2017[4]).

Figure 2.2. Real median wages have decoupled from labour productivity

Total economy excluding primary, housing and non-market industries, 1995=100

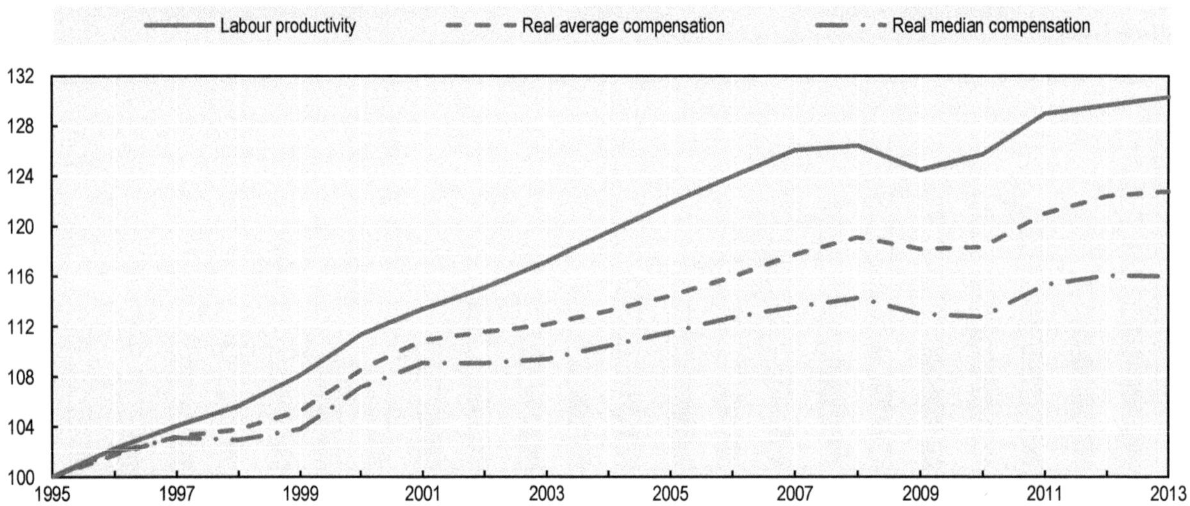

Note: Employment weighted average of 24 countries (two-year moving averages ending in the indicated years). 1995-2013 for Finland, Germany, Japan, Korea, United States; 1995-2012 for France, Italy, Sweden; 1996-2013 for Austria, Belgium; United Kingdom; 1996-2012 for Australia, Spain; 1997-2013 for Czech Republic, Denmark, Hungary; 1997-2012 for Poland; 1996-2010 for Netherlands; 1998-2013 for Norway; 1998-2012 for Canada, New Zealand; 1999-2013 for Ireland; 2002-11 for Israel; 2003-13 for Slovak Republic. All series are deflated by the value added price index excluding the primary, housing and non-market industries. The industries excluded are the following (ISIC rev. 4 classification): (1) Agriculture, Forestry and Fishing (A), (2) Mining and quarrying (B), (3) Real estate activities (L), (4) Public administration and defence, compulsory social security (O), (5) Education (P), (6) Human health and social work activities (Q), (7) Activities of households as employers (T), and (8) Activities of extraterritorial organisations and bodies (U).
Source: OECD (2018[5]), "Decoupling of wages from productivity: What implications for public policies?", in *OECD Economic Outlook, Volume 2018 Issue 2*, https://doi.org/10.1787/eco_outlook-v2018-2-en.

StatLink http://dx.doi.org/10.1787/888933880964

The slowdown in aggregate productivity growth and the decoupling of real median wages (the wages of "typical" workers) from productivity have gone hand in hand with growing divergences between firms in both productivity and wages (Box 2.1). While firms at the technological frontier (firms belonging to the global top 5% in terms of productivity) have recorded robust productivity growth since the early 2000s, the productivity of non-frontier firms has stagnated, weighing on aggregate productivity (Andrews, Criscuolo and Gal, 2016[6]). Divergence in productivity between firms in turn has been accompanied by divergence in wages (Berlingieri, Blanchenay and Criscuolo, 2017[7]), which in many countries explains a large part of developments in wage inequality.[3] Moreover, in a number of countries, there are growing signs that in firms at the technological frontier wages have decoupled from productivity while their market shares were increasing. Irrespective of whether decoupling at the technological frontier reflects increases in profit margins or higher capital intensity, these developments have contributed to the aggregate decoupling of wages from observed productivity.

Box 2.1. Productivity and wage dispersion: The role of "winner-takes-most" dynamics

Growing productivity and wage divergence between firms could reflect "winner-takes-most" dynamics, in which a few firms reap outsized rewards. While the relevant market for the best manufacturing firms used to be primarily national or regional, the fall in transport costs and tariffs mean that these firms can now serve significant shares of the global market, strengthening economies of scale (Autor et al., 2017[8]; Frank and Cook, 1995[9]; Rosen, 1981[10]). The trend toward larger market size has been reinforced by rapid progress in information and communication technologies (ICT) that allow the matching of sellers and buyers across geographically distant locations. Rapid progress in ICT has also facilitated the emergence of markets with a global scale in a number of traditional services industries, such as retail and transport, as well as new ICT services for which the marginal cost of scaling up operations is near zero. In some of these industries, including ICT services, retail and transport, network externalities that favour the emergence of a dominant player have become more important. Consistent with "winner-takes-most" dynamics, emerging evidence suggests that trade integration and digitalisation have contributed to the divergence of wages between the most successful firms and the rest (Berlingieri, Blanchenay and Criscuolo, 2017[7]).

The aggregate decoupling of median wages from productivity partly reflects declines in labour shares at the technological frontier (defined as the top 5% of firms in terms of labour productivity within each country group in each industry and year). In countries where aggregate labour shares have declined, real wages in firms at the technological frontier have decoupled from productivity, whereas this has not been the case in the remaining firms (Figure 2.3). This could indicate the presence of "winner-takes-most" dynamics, as frontier firms take advantage of technology- or globalisation-related increases in economies of scale and scope to reduce the value added share of fixed labour costs (e.g. related to research and development, product design or marketing) and/or gain a dominant position that allows them to raise their mark-ups (Autor et al., 2017[11]; Calligaris, Criscuolo and Marcolin, 2018[12]; Philippon, 2018[13]) By contrast, there has been no such decoupling of wages from productivity in frontier firms in countries where labour shares have increased, which suggests that "winner-takes-most" dynamics have been less pronounced in these countries.

The decoupling of wages from productivity at the technological frontier coincides with increasing market shares of frontier firms. In principle, this could indicate a rise in anti-competitive forces as superstar firms increase their markups. However, the evidence thus far supports a more benign view that considers the rise in market concentration as a temporary development related to technological dynamism. Schwellnus et al. (2018[14]) find evidence that the decoupling of wages from productivity at the technological frontier primarily reflects the entry of firms with low labour shares into the technological frontier. Autor et al. (2017[8]) find evidence that growing market concentration in the United States occurs primarily in industries with rapid technological change. Nevertheless, there is a risk that over time incumbent technological leaders could hamper market entry through anti-competitive practices (Furman, 2018[15]).

Figure 2.3. Average wages and productivity for leading firms and others

(2001–100)

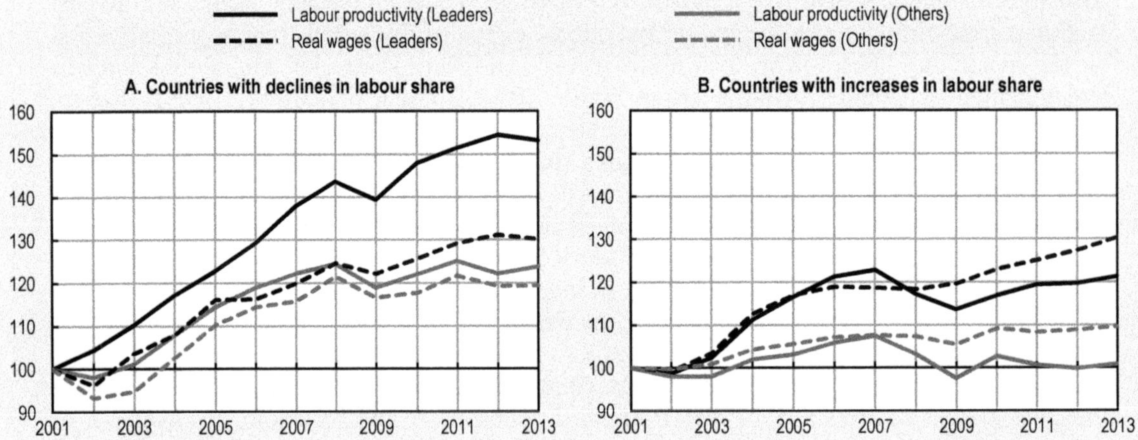

Note: Labour productivity and real wages are computed as the unweighted mean across firms of real value added per worker and real labour compensation per worker. Leaders are defined as the top 5% of firms in terms of labour productivity within each country group in each industry and year. The countries with a decline in the labour share excluding the primary, housing, financial and non-market industries over the period 2001-13 are: Belgium, Denmark, Germany, Ireland, Japan, Korea, Sweden, United Kingdom and United States. The countries with an increase are: Austria, Czech Republic, Estonia, Finland, France, Italy, Netherlands and Spain.

Source: Schwellnus et al. (2018[14]), "Labour share developments over the past two decades: The role of technological progress, globalisation and "winner-takes-most" dynamics", OECD Economics Department Working Papers, No. 1503, https://doi.org/10.1787/3eb9f9ed-en.

StatLink http://dx.doi.org/10.1787/888933880983

The decoupling of wages from productivity is not limited to the median worker but extends to all workers in the bottom half of the wage distribution (Figure 2.4). Low-wage workers at the 10th percentile of the wage distribution fared no better than workers in the middle of the distribution, whereas workers at the top of the distribution experienced high wage growth, with one of the most striking developments over the past two decades being the divergence of wages of the top 1% from the rest (Alvaredo et al., 2017[16]; Schwellnus, Kappeler and Pionnier, 2017[3]). This decoupling of low- and middle-wages from productivity has been accompanied by polarisation in terms of jobs, i.e. the gradual disappearance of middle-wage and middle-skill jobs (Box 2.2).

Figure 2.4. Wage growth in the bottom half of the distribution has decoupled from the top

(1995=100)

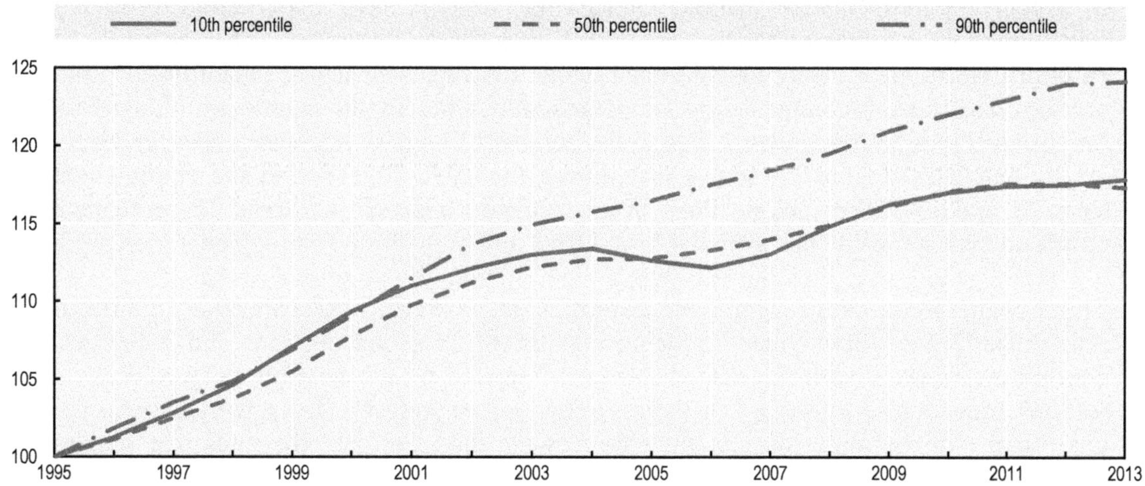

Note: GDP weighted average of 24 countries (two-year moving averages ending in the indicated years). 1995-2013 for Finland, Germany, Japan, Korea, United States; 1995-2012 for France, Italy, Sweden; 1996-2013 for Austria, Belgium; United Kingdom; 1996-2012 for Australia, Spain; 1997-2013 for Czech Republic, Denmark, Hungary; 1997-2012 for Poland; 1996-2010 for Netherlands; 1998-2013 for Norway; 1998-2012 for Canada, New Zealand; 1999-2013 for Ireland; 2002-11 for Israel; 2003-13 for Slovak Republic. All series are deflated by the same total economy value added price index.
Source: *OECD Earnings Distribution Database*, www.oecd.org/employment/emp/employmentdatabase-earningsandwages.htm.

StatLink http://dx.doi.org/10.1787/888933881002

Box 2.2. Polarisation and automation

In recent decades, labour markets across the OECD have experienced profound transformations in their occupational and industrial structures. The process of de-industrialisation – involving significant shifts of employment from manufacturing to services – has been accompanied by job polarisation, whereby the number of middle-pay, middle-skill jobs has declined relative to the number of high-skilled and to a lesser extent low-skilled ones. Figure 2.5 shows that during the 1995-2015 period the employment share of middle-skilled jobs declined in all countries analysed by about 10 percentage points on average, while the shares of low-skilled and high-skilled employment increased.

These changes can cause significant disruption in workers' lives and raise significant policy challenges. Employment is being reshuffled across occupations and industries, confronting workers with the risk of job loss followed by the possible need to make a difficult transition to a job in a different occupation or industry. Even workers who are able to stay in the same job are often faced with changing skill demands that require retraining (Battisti, Dustmann and Schönberg, 2017[17]). Moreover, different changes in skill demands, driven by changing industrial structures, can affect trends in wage inequality over time (Acemoglu and Autor, 2010[18]).

The increasing ability of technology to perform easy-to-codify routine tasks has been singled out as a key driver of job polarisation (Goos, Manning and Salomons, 2014[19]). At the same time, the offshoring of production to countries with lower labour costs has contributed to growing concerns about the negative impacts of globalisation in developed countries. The emergence of new players, including China's transition to a market economy and its entry into the World Trade Organization, has heightened these concerns and been linked to the decline in manufacturing employment in advanced economies (Autor, Dorn and Hanson, 2016[20]), and to job polarisation in particular (Keller and Utar, 2016[21]). Using industry-level data for 22 OECD countries over two decades, the OECD (2017[22]) shows that technology in the form of more widespread use of ICT contributed to job polarisation while no such evidence is found for globalisation, whether related to a country's involvement in global value chains or the penetration of imports from China.

Further progress in digitalisation and automation is likely to further widen job polarisation in advanced countries and has even raised concerns that the number of routine jobs destroyed could outweigh the non-routine ones created, resulting in technological unemployment (Acemoglu and Restrepo, 2018[23]; Brynjolfsson and McAfee, 2011[24]; Mokyr, Vickers and Ziebarth, 2015[25]). In their seminal contribution, Osborne and Frey (2017[26]) estimate that up to almost half of jobs in the United States could be subject to automation. Recent OECD research by Nedelkoska and Quintini (2018[27]) paints a less radical picture, suggesting that only one-in-seven jobs across the 32 OECD countries analysed are at risk of automation, but also that (OECD, 2015[28])about one-in-three are at risk of significant change. Whether jobs are destroyed altogether or their contents radically change, in both cases this presents significant challenges to policy and to lifelong learning and training systems in particular.

Figure 2.5. Jobs have become more polarised

Changes in employment shares by skill content of occupation (percentage points), 1995-2015

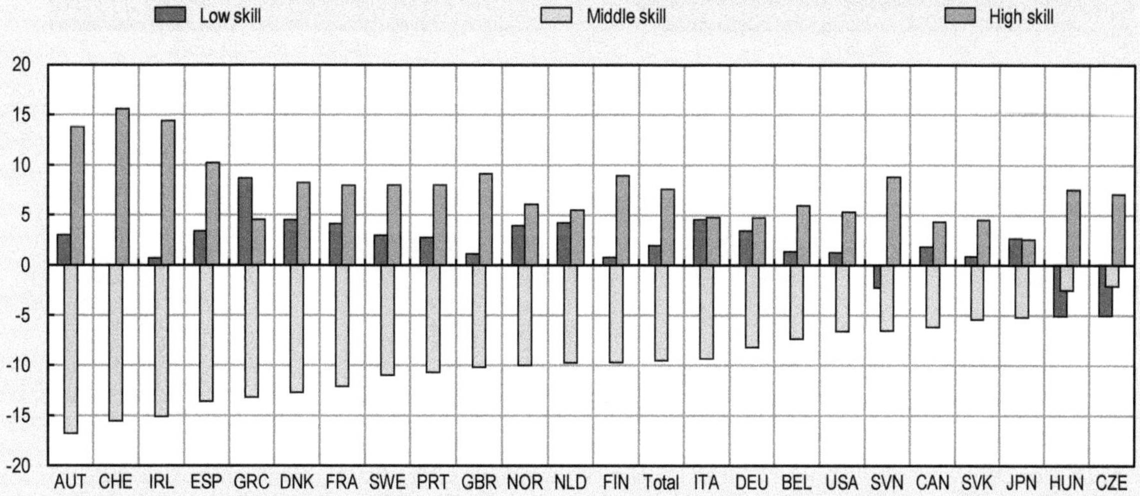

Note: High-skill occupations include jobs classified under the ISCO-88 major groups 1, 2, and 3. That is, legislators, senior officials, and managers (group 1), professionals (group 2), and technicians and associate professionals (group 3). Middle-skill occupations include jobs classified under the ISCO-88 major groups 4, 7, and 8 i.e. clerks (group 4), craft and related trades workers (group 7), and plant and machine operators and assemblers (group 8). Low-skill occupations include jobs classified under the ISCO-88 major groups 5 and 9: workers and shop and market sales workers (group 5), and elementary occupations (group 9).
Source: OECD (2017[22]), "How technology and globalisation are transforming the labour market", in *OECD Employment Outlook 2017*, https://doi.org/10.1787/empl_outlook-2017-7-en.

StatLink http://dx.doi.org/10.1787/888933881021

High employment can support the broad sharing of productivity gains by ensuring that wage gains benefit as many people as possible. While employment gaps (the share of jobless people among the working-age population) have tended to decline, more than a quarter of people not in education or training still do not have any paid form of employment (Figure 2.6), with employment gaps being particularly large for the young, women and older people. Moreover, in many countries, an important share of the workforce is underemployed, either working less than they would like to or not fully using their skills in their jobs (OECD, 2016[29]). Despite good progress in many countries, employment gaps remain particularly large for groups who are under-represented in the workforce (e.g. the young, women and older people): their employment rate is about 20 % lower than that of prime-age males. Integrating under-represented groups into the labour market is not only important to ensure that no groups are left behind but also represents a key way of improving overall employment performance, particularly in countries where employment rates for prime-age males are already very high.

Figure 2.6. Employment gaps remain large, particularly for underrepresented groups

1995-2017

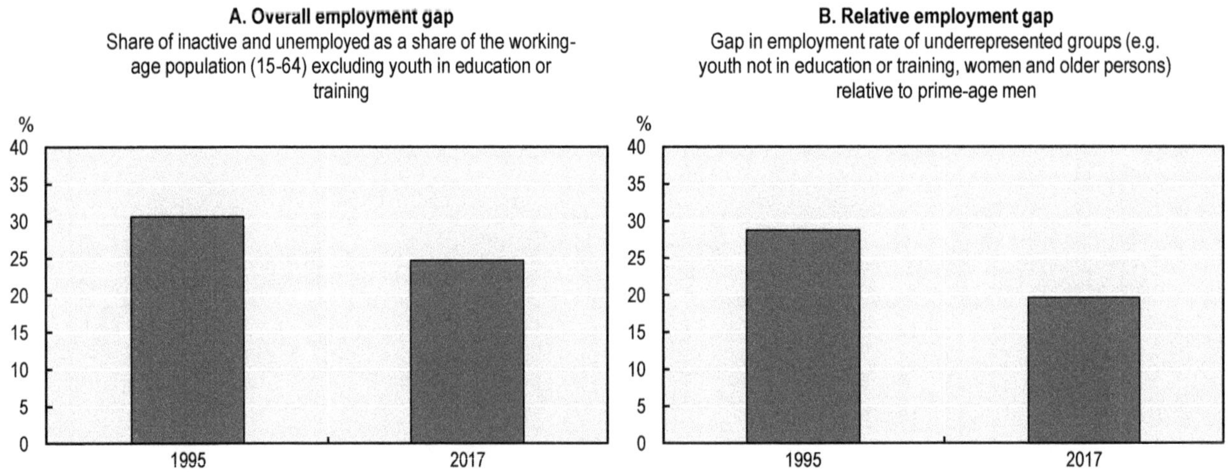

Note: Unweighted average across 25 OECD countries (excluding Chile, Estonia, Finland, Iceland, Israel, Japan, Korea, Latvia, Lithuania, New Zealand and Slovenia). Panel B: Difference between the employment rate of prime age men (30-54) and the rest (women, youth men and older men), expressed as a percentage of the employment rate of prime age men (30-54).

Source: *OECD Employment Database* (www.oecd.org/employment/database); OECD (2018[30]), *Education at a Glance 2018: OECD Indicators*, https://doi.org/10.1787/eag-2018-en.

StatLink http://dx.doi.org/10.1787/888933881040

To some extent, the tax and benefits system can correct the market distribution of income and ensure that gains from productivity growth are broadly shared with workers and their families. However, recent OECD evidence shows that redistribution through the tax and benefits system has tended to become less effective since the mid-1990s. To an important extent this reflects a shift of income support from workless households to working households (OECD, 2015[28]; Causa and Hermansen, 2017[31]). As a result of growing inequalities in market income inequality (pre-tax income excluding income from government sources) and the weakening of redistribution, inequalities in households' disposable incomes have reached unprecedented levels in many OECD countries. This raises concerns about fairness, social cohesion and the sustainability of economic growth (OECD, 2015[28]; Cingano, 2014[32]).

Summing up, in most countries productivity gains from technological change and globalisation have not been broadly shared with workers. Productivity growth at the technological frontier remains high, suggesting that only a small group of innovative firms are able to fully take advantage of technological advances and globalisation, while many others trail further and further behind, weighing on aggregate productivity growth. At the same time, the distribution of income has become more tilted towards capital at the expense of labour income and the distribution of income and wealth has become increasingly unequal. Higher employment rates have mitigated but not prevented the rise in income inequality, and more remains to be done to better integrate those excluded from the labour market and to raise the effectiveness of redistribution through the tax and benefits system.

2.2. The central role of the labour market for broadly shared productivity gains

Alongside product and financial markets, the labour market is a central element of a well-functioning market economy that delivers: 1) high productivity growth; 2) a broad sharing of the gains from productivity growth through wages; and 3) ensuring accessible job opportunities for all.

The labour market as an engine of productivity growth

High productivity growth requires constant reallocation, in the sense that highly productive firms enter the market and expand while less productive ones downsize and eventually exit if they do not manage to upgrade their production processes. Empirical studies for OECD countries suggest that entry and exit alone contribute 15-45% to industry-level productivity growth (Bartelsman, Haltiwanger and Scarpetta, 2009[33]). The evidence also suggests that job reallocations between existing firms raise productivity growth further as firms with high initial productivity levels gain market shares at the expense of lower-productivity firms (OECD, 2009[34]).

The labour market is a key facilitator of productivity-enhancing reallocation that allows workers to move from downsizing firms to new and expanding ones. Empirical studies suggest that in OECD countries job reallocation – firm-level job creation and destruction – affects around 20% of employment every year (OECD, 2009[34]).[4] Worker reallocation – the sum of hires and separations – is even higher at around 30%. Although not all reallocation necessarily enhances productivity, these figures imply that small changes in net employment mask large gross worker flows between firms.

Achieving productive matches between workers and firms requires some degree of labour market fluidity, especially during periods of rapid structural change. Technological development, globalisation and demographic change require the reallocation of labour to its most productive uses while limiting transition costs. In a well-functioning labour market, workers are able to switch jobs to seize higher-paid job opportunities elsewhere while firms adopting new technologies and business models are able to rapidly expand employment, thereby raising aggregate productivity.

A fluid labour market may also support the diffusion of technological advances across firms, helping to improve productivity at firms that are lagging behind. The adoption of new general-purpose technologies for production typically requires workers with the relevant technical expertise and some degree of reorganisation (David, 1990[35]; Bresnahan, 2003[36]). The evidence suggests that one channel for the diffusion of this expertise is the movement of workers between firms, including job switchers and consultants (Draca, Sadun and Van Reenen, 2009[37]; Tambe and Hitt, 2014[38]).

High productivity growth also requires the constant development of workers' skills. Skills raise worker productivity by allowing them to produce more at a given level of technology (Lucas, 1988[39]) and promote innovation and the adoption of new technologies (Aghion et al., 1998[40]; Stokey, 2018[41]). Empirical studies suggest that there is a close causal link between cognitive skills and economic growth (Hanushek and Woessmann, 2015[42]) and that human capital is a key factor in influencing the speed of technology adoption (Andrews, Nicoletti and Timiliotis, 2018[43]).

The labour market is a key determinant of workers' skill development. While the education system lays the foundations for the acquisition of cognitive and non-cognitive skills, the labour market plays a crucial role in maintaining and developing them. A well-functioning labour market promotes the development of relevant skills by: providing strong incentives for investment in human capital; facilitating the school-to-work transition; and offering opportunities for lifelong learning. It also allows workers to seek out and develop their comparative advantage through job-to-job transitions.

Rapid structural change in the form of technological progress, globalisation and population ageing puts a premium on continuous skill development in the labour market. Automation, digitalisation and the rapid development of artificial intelligence broaden the range of tasks that can potentially be carried out by machines, while declines in the cost of offshoring will lead to changes in the mix of tasks carried out domestically. At the same time, population ageing is likely to lead to longer careers. Maintaining the skills acquired in youth will not be sufficient for workers to adapt to these developments. Instead, workers will need to acquire and develop skills in the labour market that will allow them to transition to new and more productive tasks throughout their (longer) working lives.

The labour market also plays an important role in providing strong incentives for innovation and the adoption of technology and high-performance management and work practices within firms. Firms' capacity to innovate depends on how much flexibility they have to adjust the organisation of work, including employment levels and the definition of tasks (Griffith and Macartney, 2014[44]; Bartelsman, Gautier and De Wind, 2016[45]). But high-performance work and management practices are to an important extent geared towards building long-term employer-employee relationships to foster learning and innovation. More generally, incentives for human capital accumulation and workers' propensity to innovate depend on job security, with higher job security implying a higher return on their innovation effort (Acharya, Baghai and Subramanian, 2013[46]). High rates of innovation and technology adoption within firms therefore require the right balance to be struck between sufficient flexibility for firms and sufficient job security for workers.

The labour market as a transmission channel of productivity gains to wages

By supporting workers' skills the labour market is not only crucial for raising productivity growth but also for determining the extent to which the benefits of technological developments are shared with workers. Automation and digitalisation are likely to have important implications for the kind of available jobs and the tasks required to perform them (see Box 2.2). For workers to make the most of these developments they will need to upgrade their skills, especially those required to carry out non-routine tasks that cannot easily be substituted by new technology.

The degree to which productivity gains are shared with workers also depends on their bargaining position. An emerging literature suggests that employer market power (labour market monopsony) is substantial and may be increasing (Dube et al., 2018[47]; Benmelech, Bergman and Kim, 2018[48]; Azar, Marinescu and Steinbaum, 2017[49]). Such employer market power may reflect high costs for workers of switching jobs because of natural barriers to job mobility (such as search costs or costs of geographical relocation) or regulation (e.g. limited portability of social security entitlements, professional licencing rules, non-compete clauses). The potential emergence of dominant players in industries with strong network effects could further re-inforce this tendency toward labour market monopsony (Autor et al., 2017[8]; Schwellnus et al., 2018[14]). In addition, the emergence of non-standard forms of work, declining trade union membership and weaker collective bargaining institutions can further reduce workers' voice and their bargaining position, and in doing so increase the role of monopsony in the labour market (OECD, 2018[50]).

The labour market as a transmission channel of productivity gains to employment

The broad sharing of productivity gains requires high employment, which in turn requires a good alignment of average wages and productivity to support labour demand, low barriers to employment to promote labour supply and an efficient matching process between firms and workers.

While a broad sharing of productivity gains requires that wage growth does not fall short of productivity growth, it is also important that in the medium term aggregate labour costs do not grow more quickly than productivity to avoid undermining job creation. A good alignment of average wages and productivity at the aggregate level does not preclude the use of statutory or collective agreed wage floors that can play a useful role in supporting the earnings of workers and ensuring minimum labour standards in firms. However, they should not be set so high that they price low-productivity workers out of the market.

The job opportunities that are available should also be accessible. Jobless people and those marginally attached to the labour market often face one or several barriers to labour force participation and quality employment (Fernandez et al., 2016[51]). They may have weak incentives to work because of a combination of poor job quality and ill-designed tax and benefit schemes. Alternatively, jobless people may simply lack the skills or experience needed for paid employment or may be unavailable for work because they have caring responsibilities, health and other social problems or because of weak hiring by employers. While some jobless people will be able to find work by themselves, many will need targeted support to overcome these specific barriers to paid employment. This highlights the importance of effective policies that connect people to work for a well-functioning labour market in which the gains from growing prosperity are shared as widely as possible.

An efficient matching process between job vacancies and jobseekers is also key for good employment performance. Systematic imbalances between jobseekers and vacancies in terms of educational qualifications and requirements (skills mismatch), the supply and demand for occupation-specific or industry-specific skills (occupational or sectoral mismatch), or the supply and demand for labour in different regions (geographical mismatch) reduces the efficiency of the matching process.

Mismatch results from barriers to job mobility due to cost of obtaining information on vacancies and jobseekers, the cost of moving between regions and the cost of retraining. It also may reflect deeper factors such as a disconnect between the world of education and the world of work or the lack of attention of country-wide policies and institutions for regional disparities.

Conclusions

Although it is conceptually useful to separate the labour market's roles in promoting high productivity growth, transmitting productivity gains to workers and strengthening economic inclusion, these objectives are closely interrelated. The key challenge is to develop a labour market that sustains high productivity growth and economic dynamism while at the same time fostering a broad sharing of productivity gains through higher wages and employment opportunities for all. Country evidence suggests that there can be synergies between high productivity growth and the broad sharing of productivity gains. For example, episodes of high productivity growth, such as the second half of the 1990s in the United States, have often been associated with increasing labour shares, declining wage inequality and growing employment (Stansbury and Summers, 2017[52]).

One mechanism through which the labour market can foster synergies between high and broadly shared productivity gains is the development of workers' skills. A labour market that provides opportunities for continual skill development not only raises productivity growth, but also contributes to a broader sharing of productivity gains. Increases in human capital contribute directly to productivity growth (Fernald and Jones, 2014[53]). But they also help to alleviate barriers to finding work and reduce the risk of being displaced and staying unemployed as a result of technological change and globalisation. Promoting the skill development of low-wage and middle-wage workers is particularly important since it improves their employment opportunities, wages and productivity and so contributes to a more inclusive labour market.

Labour market dynamism is another mechanism that supports both high productivity growth and a broad sharing of productivity gains in the form of higher wages and employment, especially for disadvantaged groups. The efficient allocation of workers to jobs, firms and regions contributes to high productivity and raises wages and employment, especially of relative outsiders in the labour market, by making job offers more abundant (Moscarini and Postel-Vinay, 2016[54]). Job switching is typically associated with significant increases in both wages and productivity as high-wage firms poach from low-wage firms (Haltiwanger et al., 2018[55]). This mechanism is particularly important for the wage progression of young workers as it is unlikely that workers find the best possible match in their first job. A dynamic labour market thus prevents them from becoming trapped in low-productivity and low-wage firms (Haltiwanger, Hyatt and McEntarfer, 2018[56]) or lagging regions with limited prospects for career advancement.

Keeping the economy close to full employment is crucial to achieve high and broadly shared productivity growth. The experience of the global crisis of 2008-09 suggests that it contributed to a further slowing of productivity growth as weak business expectations reduced investment (Ollivaud, Guillemette and Turner, 2018[57]).This highlights the importance of stabilising aggregate demand and keeping the economy close to full employment for long-term productivity growth. At the same time, a vibrant labour market strengthens workers' bargaining position and allows workers to climb the job ladder within the same firm and by moving from low-wage to high-wage firms (Haltiwanger et al., 2018[55]).

Notes

[1] Algebraically, the labour share is equivalent to the ratio of labour productivity to the real wage, with the real wage expressed in terms of the value added deflator.

[2] The positive gap between average and median wage growth implies a widening of wage inequality since medium- and lower-paid workers have experience lower wage growth than those in the upper part of the wage distribution.

[3] Recent evidence on the role of cross-firm divergence in wages on overall wage inequality developments exists for Brazil (Helpman et al., 2017[56]), Denmark (Bagger, Sørensen and Vejlin, 2013[57]), Germany (Baumgarten, Felbermayr and Lehwald, 2016[58]; Card, Heining and Kline, 2013[59]; Goldschmidt and Schmieder, 2015[60]), Italy (Card, Devicienti and Maida, 2014[61]),

Portugal (Card, Cardoso and Kline, 2016[62]), Sweden (Skans, Edin and Holmlund, 2009[66]), the United Kingdom (Faggio, Salvanes and Van Reenen, 2010[67]) and the United States (Dunne et al., 2004[63]; Barth et al., 2016[64]; Song et al., 2015[65]).

[4] Job creation is defined as the sum of net employment growth at all entering and expanding firms; job destruction as the total number of jobs lost at exiting and contracting firms; and job reallocation as the sum of job creation and destruction.

References

Acemoglu, D. and D. Autor (2010), "Skills, Tasks and Technologies: Implications for Employment and Earnings", *NBER Working Paper*, No. 16082, National Bureau of Economic Research, Cambridge, MA, http://dx.doi.org/10.3386/w16082. [18]

Acemoglu, D. and P. Restrepo (2018), "The Race between Man and Machine: Implications of Technology for Growth, Factor Shares, and Employment", *American Economic Review*, Vol. 108/6, pp. 1488-1542, http://dx.doi.org/10.1257/aer.20160696. [23]

Acharya, V., R. Baghai and K. Subramanian (2013), "Labor Laws and Innovation", *The Journal of Law and Economics*, Vol. 56/4, pp. 997-1037, http://dx.doi.org/10.1086/674106. [46]

Aghion, P. et al. (1998), *Endogenous growth theory*, MIT Press, https://mitpress.mit.edu/books/endogenous-growth-theory. [40]

Alvaredo, F. et al. (2017), "Global Inequality Dynamics: New Findings from WID.world", *American Economic Review*, Vol. 107/5, pp. 404-409, http://dx.doi.org/10.1257/aer.p20171095. [16]

Andrews, D., C. Criscuolo and P. Gal (2016), "The Best versus the Rest: The Global Productivity Slowdown, Divergence across Firms and the Role of Public Policy", *OECD Productivity Working Papers*, No. 5, OECD Publishing, Paris, http://dx.doi.org/10.1787/63629cc9-en. [6]

Andrews, D., G. Nicoletti and C. Timiliotis (2018), "Digital technology diffusion: A matter of capabilities, incentives or both?", *Economics Department Working Papers*, No. 1476, OECD Publishing, Paris, http://dx.doi.org/10.1787/7c542c16-en. [43]

Autor, D., D. Dorn and G. Hanson (2016), "The China Shock: Learning from Labor-Market Adjustment to Large Changes in Trade", *Annual Review of Economics*, Vol. 8/1, http://dx.doi.org/10.1146/annurev-economics-080315-015041. [20]

Autor, D. et al. (2017), "Concentrating on the Fall of the Labor Share", *NBER Working Paper*, No. 23108, National Bureau of Economic Research, Cambridge, MA, http://dx.doi.org/10.3386/w23108. [8]

Autor, D. et al. (2017), "Concentrating on the Fall of the Labor Share", *NBER Working Paper*, No. 23108, National Bureau of Economic Research, Cambridge, MA, http://dx.doi.org/10.3386/w23108. [11]

Azar, J., I. Marinescu and M. Steinbaum (2017), "Labor Market Concentration", *NBER Working Paper*, No. 24147, http://dx.doi.org/10.3386/w24147. [49]

Bagger, J., K. Sørensen and R. Vejlin (2013), "Wage sorting trends", *Economics Letters*, Vol. 118/1, pp. 63-67, http://dx.doi.org/10.1016/J.ECONLET.2012.09.021. [59]

Bartelsman, E., P. Gautier and J. De Wind (2016), "Employment protection, technology choice, and worker allocation", *International Economic Review*, Vol. 57/3, pp. 787-826, http://dx.doi.org/10.1111/iere.12176. [45]

Bartelsman, E., J. Haltiwanger and S. Scarpetta (2009), "Measuring and Analyzing Cross-country Differences in Firm Dynamics", in Dunne, T., J. Jensen and M. Roberts (eds.), *Producer Dynamics: New Evidence from Micro Data*, University of Chicago Press, http://www.nber.org/chapters/c0480. [33]

Barth, E. et al. (2016), "It's Where You Work: Increases in the Dispersion of Earnings across Establishments and Individuals in the United States", *Journal of Labor Economics*, Vol. 34/S2, pp. S67-S97, http://dx.doi.org/10.1086/684045. [66]

Battisti, M., C. Dustmann and U. Schönberg (2017), *Technological and Organizational Change and the Careers of Workers* *, https://www.technologyreview.com/s/515926/how-technology-is-destroying-jobs/ (accessed on 06 November 2018). [17]

Baumgarten, D., G. Felbermayr and S. Lehwald (2016), "Dissecting between-plant and within-plant wage dispersion Evidence from Germany Dissecting between-plant and within-plant wage dispersion: Evidence from Germany", *Ifo Working Paper*, No. 216, Ifo Institute – Leibniz Institute for Economic Research at the University of Munich, https://www.cesifo-group.de/DocDL/wp-2016-216-baumgarten-felbermayr-lehwald-wage-dispersion.pdf. [60]

Benmelech, E., N. Bergman and H. Kim (2018), "Strong Employers and Weak Employees: How Does Employer Concentration Affect Wages?", *NBER Working Paper*, No. 24307, http://dx.doi.org/10.3386/w24307. [48]

Berlingieri, G., P. Blanchenay and C. Criscuolo (2017), "The great divergence(s)", *OECD Science, Technology and Industry Policy Papers*, No. 39, OECD Publishing, Paris, http://dx.doi.org/10.1787/953f3853-en. [7]

Bresnahan, T. (2003), "The mechanisms of information technology's contribution to economic growth", in Touffut, J. (ed.), *Institutions, Innovation and Growth: Selected Economic Papers*, Edward Elgar Publishing, https://www.elgaronline.com/view/1843765276.00013.xml. [36]

Brynjolfsson, E. and A. McAfee (2011), *Race Against The Machine: How the Digital Revolution is Accelerating Innovation, Driving Productivity, and Irreversibly Transforming Employment and the Economy*, Digital Frontier Press, Lexington. [24]

Calligaris, S., C. Criscuolo and L. Marcolin (2018), "Mark-ups in the digital era", *OECD Science, Technology and Industry Working Papers*, No. 2018/10, OECD Publishing, Paris, http://dx.doi.org/10.1787/4efe2d25-en. [12]

Card, D., A. Cardoso and P. Kline (2016), "Bargaining, Sorting, and the Gender Wage Gap: Quantifying the Impact of Firms on the Relative Pay of Women", *The Quarterly Journal of Economics*, Vol. 131/2, pp. 633-686, http://dx.doi.org/10.1093/qje/qjv038. [64]

Card, D., F. Devicienti and A. Maida (2014), "Rent-sharing, Holdup, and Wages: Evidence from Matched Panel Data", *The Review of Economic Studies*, Vol. 81/1, pp. 84-111, http://dx.doi.org/10.1093/restud/rdt030. [63]

Card, D., J. Heining and P. Kline (2013), "Workplace Heterogeneity and the Rise of West German Wage Inequality", *The Quarterly Journal of Economics*, Vol. 128/3, pp. 967-1015, http://dx.doi.org/10.1093/qje/qjt006. [61]

Causa, O. and M. Hermansen (2017), "Income redistribution through taxes and transfers across OECD countries", *OECD Economics Department Working Papers*, No. 1453, OECD Publishing, Paris, http://dx.doi.org/10.1787/bc7569c6-en. [31]

Cingano, F. (2014), "Trends in Income Inequality and its Impact on Economic Growth", *OECD Social, Employment and Migration Working Papers*, No. 163, OECD Publishing, Paris, http://dx.doi.org/10.1787/5jxrjncwxv6j-en. [32]

David, P. (1990), "The Dynamo and the Computer: An Historical Perspective on the Modern Productivity Paradox", *The American Economic Review*, Vol. 80/2, pp. 355-361, http://www.dklevine.com/archive/refs4115.pdf. [35]

Draca, M., R. Sadun and J. Van Reenen (2009), "Productivity and ICTs: A review of the evidence", in Avgerou, Chrisanthi Mansell, R., D. Quah and R. Silverstone (eds.), *The Oxford Handbook of Information and Communication Technologies*, Oxford University Press, http://dx.doi.org/10.1093/oxfordhb/9780199548798.003.0005. [37]

Dube, A. et al. (2018), "Monopsony in Online Labor Markets", *NBER Working Paper*, No. 24416, http://dx.doi.org/10.3386/w24416. [47]

Dunne, T. et al. (2004), "Wage and Productivity Dispersion in United States Manufacturing: The Role of Computer Investment of the Census", *Journal of Labor Economics*, Vol. 22/2, pp. 397-429, http://www.jstor.org/stable/3653629. [65]

Faggio, G., K. Salvanes and J. Van Reenen (2010), "The evolution of inequality in productivity and wages: panel data evidence", *Industrial and Corporate Change*, Vol. 19/6, pp. 1919-1951, http://dx.doi.org/10.1093/icc/dtq058. [69]

Fernald, J. and C. Jones (2014), "The Future of US Economic Growth", *American Economic Review*, Vol. 104/5, pp. 44-49, http://dx.doi.org/10.1257/aer.104.5.44. [53]

Fernandez, R. et al. (2016), "Faces of Joblessness: Characterising Employment Barriers to Inform Policy", *OECD Social, Employment and Migration Working Papers*, No. 192, OECD Publishing, Paris, http://dx.doi.org/10.1787/5jlwvz47xptj-en. [51]

Frank, R. and P. Cook (1995), *The winner-take-all society : how more and more Americans compete for ever fewer and bigger prizes, encouraging economic waste, income inequality, and an impoverished cultural life*, Free Press. [9]

Frey, C. and M. Osborne (2017), "The future of employment: How susceptible are jobs to computerisation?", *Technological Forecasting and Social Change*, Vol. 114, pp. 254-280, http://dx.doi.org/10.1016/J.TECHFORE.2016.08.019. [26]

Furman, J. (2018), *Market concentration*, https://one.oecd.org/document/DAF/COMP/WD(2018)67/en/pdf. [15]

Goldschmidt, D. and J. Schmieder (2015), "The Rise of Domestic Outsourcing and the Evolution of the German Wage Structure", *NBER Working Paper*, No. 21366, http://www.nber.org/papers/w21366. [62]

Goos, M., A. Manning and A. Salomons (2014), "Explaining Job Polarization: Routine-Biased Technological Change and Offshoring", *American Economic Review*, Vol. 104/8, pp. 2509-2526, http://dx.doi.org/10.1257/aer.104.8.2509. [19]

Griffith, R. and G. Macartney (2014), "Employment protection legislation, multinational firms, and innovation", *The Review of Economics and Statistics*, Vol. 96/1, pp. 135-150, http://dx.doi.org/10.1162/REST_a_00348. [44]

Guillemette, Y. and D. Turner (2018), "The Long View : Scenarios for the World Economy to 2060", No. 22, OECD Publishing, Paris, http://dx.doi.org/10.1787/b4f4e03e-en. [1]

Haltiwanger, J. et al. (2018), "Cyclical Job Ladders by Firm Size and Firm Wage", *American Economic Journal: Macroeconomics*, Vol. 10/2, pp. 52-85, http://dx.doi.org/10.1257/mac.20150245. [55]

Haltiwanger, J., H. Hyatt and E. McEntarfer (2018), "Who Moves Up the Job Ladder?", *Journal of Labor Economics*, Vol. 36/S1, pp. S301-S336, http://dx.doi.org/10.1086/694417. [56]

Hanushek, E. and L. Woessmann (2015), *The knowledge capital of nations : education and the economics of growth*, MIT Press, https://mitpress.mit.edu/books/knowledge-capital-nations. [42]

Helpman, E. et al. (2017), "Trade and Inequality: From Theory to Estimation", *Review of Economic Studies*, Vol. 84, pp. 357-405, http://dx.doi.org/10.1093/restud/rdw025. [58]

Keller, W. and H. Utar (2016), *International Trade and Job Polarization: Evidence at the Worker-Level*, National Bureau of Economic Research, Cambridge, MA, http://dx.doi.org/10.3386/w22315. [21]

Lucas, R. (1988), "On the mechanics of economic development", *Journal of Monetary Economics*, Vol. 22/1, pp. 3-42, http://dx.doi.org/10.1016/0304-3932(88)90168-7. [39]

Mokyr, J., C. Vickers and N. Ziebarth (2015), "The History of Technological Anxiety and the Future of Economic Growth: Is This Time Different?", *Journal of Economic Perspectives*, Vol. 29/3, pp. 31-50, http://dx.doi.org/10.1257/jep.29.3.31. [25]

Moscarini, G. and F. Postel-Vinay (2016), "Wage Posting and Business Cycles", *American Economic Review*, Vol. 106/5, pp. 208-213, http://dx.doi.org/10.1257/aer.p20161051. [54]

Nedelkoska, L. and G. Quintini (2018), "Automation, skills use and training", *OECD Social, Employment and Migration Working Papers*, No. 202, OECD Publishing, Paris, http://dx.doi.org/10.1787/2e2f4eea-en. [27]

OECD (2018), "Decoupling of wages from productivity: What implications for public policies?", in *OECD Economic Outlook, Volume 2018 Issue 2*, OECD Publishing, Paris, https://doi.org/10.1787/eco_outlook-v2018-2-en.. [5]

OECD (2018), *Education at a Glance 2018: OECD Indicators*, OECD Publishing, Paris, https://dx.doi.org/10.1787/eag-2018-en. [30]

OECD (2018), *OECD Employment Outlook 2018*, OECD Publishing, Paris, http://dx.doi.org/10.1787/empl_outlook-2018-en. [2]

OECD (2018), "The role of collective bargaining systems for good labour market performance", in *OECD Employment Outlook 2018*, OECD Publishing, Paris, http://dx.doi.org/10.1787/empl_outlook-2018-7-en. [50]

OECD (2017), "How technology and globalisation are transforming the labour market", in *OECD Employment Outlook 2017*, OECD Publishing, Paris, http://dx.doi.org/10.1787/empl_outlook-2017-7-en. [22]

OECD (2016), *Skills Matter - Further Results from the Survey of Adult Skills*, OECD Publishing, https://doi.org/10.1787/9789264258051-en. [29]

OECD (2015), *In It Together: Why Less Inequality Benefits All*, OECD Publishing, Paris, http://dx.doi.org/10.1787/9789264235120-en. [28]

OECD (2009), *OECD Employment Outlook 2009: Tackling the Jobs Crisis*, OECD Publishing, Paris, http://dx.doi.org/10.1787/empl_outlook-2009-en. [34]

Ollivaud, P., Y. Guillemette and D. Turner (2018), "Investment as a transmission mechanism from weak demand to weak supply and the post-crisis productivity slowdown", *OECD Economics Department Working Papers*, No. 1466, http://www.oecd.org/eco/workingpapers.. [57]

Philippon, T. (2018), *A Primer On Concentration, Investment and Growth,* https://www.kansascityfed.org/~/media/files/publicat/sympos/2018/papersandhandouts/824180819philipponhandout.pdf?la=en. [13]

Rosen, S. (1981), "The Economics of Superstars", *The American Economic Review*, Vol. 71/5, pp. 845-858, http://dx.doi.org/10.2307/1803469. [10]

Schwellnus, C., A. Kappeler and P. Pionnier (2017), "The Decoupling of Median Wages from Productivity in OECD Countries", *International Productivity Monitor*, Vol. 32, http://www.csls.ca/ipm/32/Schwellnus_Kappeler_Pionnier.pdf. [3]

Schwellnus, C. et al. (2018), "Labour share developments over the past two decades: The role of technological progress, globalisation and "winner-take-most" dynamics", *OECD Economics Department Working Papers*, No. 1503, OECD Publishing, Paris, https://doi.org/10.1787/3eb9f9ed-en. [14]

Sharpe, A. and J. Uguccioni (2017), "Decomposing the Productivity- Wage Nexus in Selected OECD Countries, 1986-2013", *International Productivity Monitor*, Vol. 32, pp. 25-43, http://www.csls.ca/ipm/32/Uguccioni_Sharpe.pdf. [4]

Skans, O., P. Edin and B. Holmlund (2009), "Wage Dispersion Between and Within Plants: Sweden 1985-2000", in Lazear, E. and K. Shaw (eds.), *The Structure of Wages: An International Comparison*, University of Chicago Press, http://www.nber.org/chapters/c2372. [68]

Song, J. et al. (2015), "Firming Up Inequality", *NBER Working Paper*, No. 21199, http://www.nber.org/papers/w21199.pdf. [67]

Stansbury, A. and L. Summers (2017), "Productivity and Pay: Is the link broken?", No. 24165, National Bureau of Economic Research, Cambridge, MA, http://dx.doi.org/10.3386/w24165. [52]

Stokey, N. (2018), *Technology and Skill: Twin Engines of Growth*, National Bureau of Economic Research, Cambridge, MA, http://dx.doi.org/10.3386/w24570. [41]

Tambe, P. and L. Hitt (2014), "Job Hopping, Information Technology Spillovers, and Productivity Growth", *Management Science*, Vol. 60/2, pp. 338-355, http://dx.doi.org/10.1287/mnsc.2013.1764. [38]

Chapter 3. A new framework for assessing labour market performance

This chapter presents the conceptual and operational framework of the new OECD Jobs Strategy for assessing labour market performance. The conceptual framework distinguishes between three outcome dimensions through which the labour market contributes to inclusive growth and well-being: i) the quantity and quality of jobs; ii) labour market inclusiveness; and iii) resilience and adaptability. The framework is operationalised by means of a dashboard that allows an easy comparison of labour market performance along these different dimensions and the identification of possible reform priorities.

The statistical data for Israel are supplied by and under the responsibility of the relevant Israeli authorities. The use of such data by the OECD is without prejudice to the status of the Golan Heights, East Jerusalem and Israeli settlements in the West Bank under the terms of international law.

Introduction

A well-functioning labour market is a key condition for achieving inclusive growth – that is, a strong and sustained process of economic growth whose benefits are widely shared – and rising levels of well-being. As discussed in Chapter 2, the main challenge for policy makers is to reconcile the ability of an economy to sustain aggregate productivity gains with the capacity to generate jobs with good working conditions (both monetary and non-monetary) as well as ensuring that the gains from growth are fairly shared.

Since the publication of the OECD's *Reassessed Jobs Strategy* in 2006 (OECD, 2006[1]), the challenge of achieving inclusive growth has acquired renewed urgency: many OECD and emerging economies have experienced continued low productivity growth, unprecedentedly high levels of inequality and dislocations related to technological progress, globalisation, demographic change as well as the global economic and financial crisis of 2008-09.

In light of this, the new OECD Jobs Strategy develops a new conceptual and operational framework for assessing labour market performance. The conceptual framework distinguishes between three dimensions through which the labour market contributes to inclusive growth and well-being: i) the quantity and quality of jobs; ii) labour market inclusiveness; and iii) the resilience and adaptability of the labour market to absorb and adjust to economic shocks and make the most of new opportunities. The framework is put into operation through the new OECD Jobs Strategy dashboard that allows assessing labour market performance and identifying reform priorities based on a number of selected indicators for each of the dimensions of the framework.

The remainder of this chapter is structured as follows. Section 3.1 presents the new OECD Jobs Strategy's framework for assessing labour market performance. Section 0 puts the framework into practice by using selected indicators to provide a broad assessment of labour market performance in OECD countries and emerging economies.[1] The conclusions emphasise that a well-functioning labour market that promotes economic and social progress requires a combination of labour and non-labour market policies in a whole-of-government approach.

3.1. The OECD Jobs Strategy framework

A well-functioning labour market is a key condition for achieving inclusive growth and rising levels of well-being.[2] It promotes prosperity by matching workers to productive and rewarding jobs and facilitating the adoption of new technologies and new ways of organising work, including by providing workers with opportunities to acquire and update relevant skills in a rapidly changing economic environment. A well-functioning labour market further ensures that increased prosperity is reflected in increased well-being and job quality, in both monetary and non-monetary terms, by creating good job opportunities for all, ensuring productivity gains are transmitted to wages, and protecting and improving the living standards of the most vulnerable. Thus, the new OECD Jobs Strategy recognises that policies that improve the functioning of the labour market are crucial for raising economic growth and its inclusiveness in a socially sustainable way.

Recent policy concerns have focused on reconciling the ability of an economy to sustain aggregate productivity gains with the capacity to generate jobs that are fairly remunerated and associated with good non-wage working conditions as well as ensuring that the gains from growth are broadly shared (Chapter 2). In light of this, the framework of the new

Jobs Strategy has been broadened compared with previous versions of the OECD Jobs Strategy (1994, 2006) and now encompasses three over-arching policy objectives that together define good labour market performance and are each necessary for inclusive growth and well-being more generally (Figure 3.1):

- **More and better jobs.** This captures the labour market situation in terms of both the quantity of jobs (e.g. unemployment, labour force participation, working time) as well the quality of jobs by taking account of the three dimensions of the OECD Job Quality Framework that are key for worker well-being: i) earnings; ii) labour market security; and iii) the quality of the work environment.
- **Labour market inclusiveness**. This dimension focuses on the distribution of opportunities and outcomes across individuals. Ensuring equal opportunities to succeed in the labour market for all reduces the risk that people are excluded from fully participating in the labour market and fall into poverty. Labour market inclusiveness therefore relates to both dynamic aspects of inequality such as the prospects for social mobility and career advancement, as well as static ones such as the distribution of individual earnings and household incomes, and differences in access to quality jobs between different socio-economic groups.
- **Adaptability and resilience**. This dimension relates to the effectiveness with which individuals, institutions and societies absorb and adapt to economic shocks, and make the most out of the new opportunities arising from megatrends such as technological change (including automation and digitalisation), climate and demographic change and globalisation.

The first two dimensions focus on current outcomes of individuals and their distribution. The third dimension contains a forward-looking element that focuses on the ability of workers and labour markets to withstand future shocks and seize new opportunities. Adaptability and resilience are essential to ensure the sustainability of *good labour market* and *economic performance* in a constantly evolving world.

Figure 3.1. The conceptual framework of the OECD Jobs Strategy

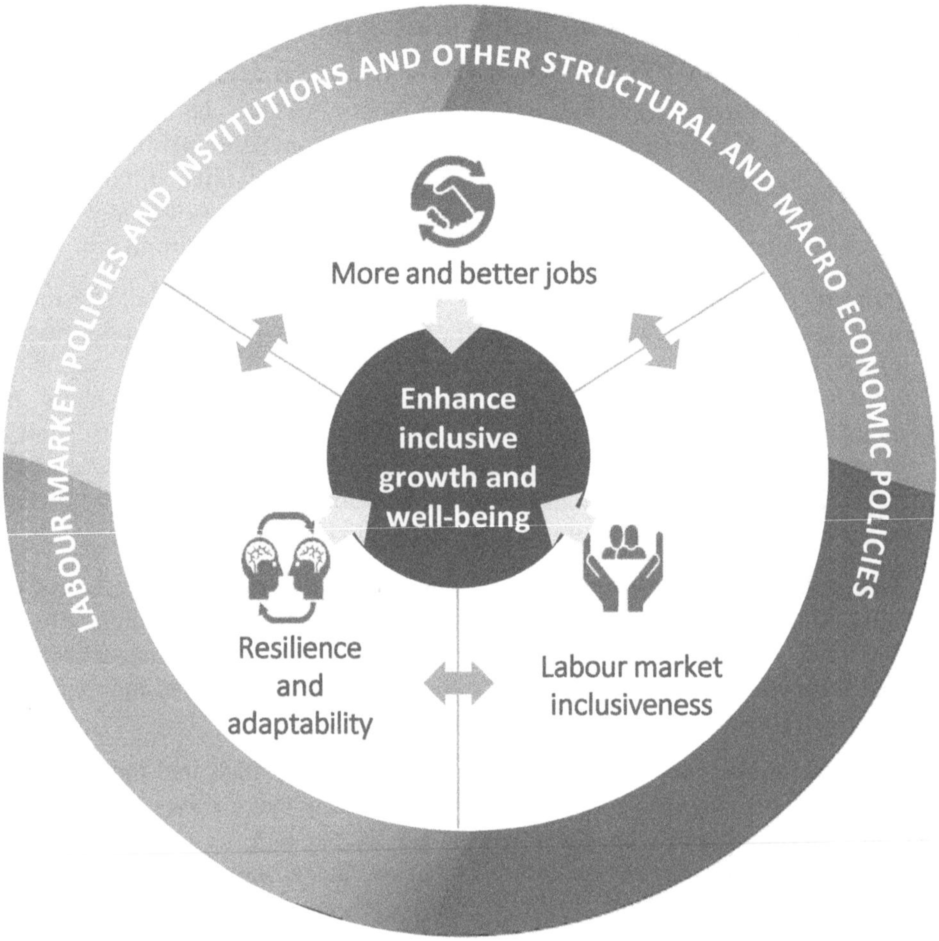

Good labour market performance along these dimensions does not depend on labour market policies alone but also on a range of other policies, including sound macroeconomic and financial policies, productivity-enhancing policies in product, financial, and housing markets, education and skill policies, tax policies, entrepreneurship policies, regional policies, as well as the protection of property rights and the rule of law. In turn, labour market policies do not only affect labour market performance but also other dimensions of economic performance, well-being and social progress. Thus, a whole-of-government approach is needed to ensure that the new OECD Jobs Strategy is well embedded in the OECD Inclusive Growth Initiative (see Box 3.1 for details). Such whole-of-government approach recognises that there are synergies between effective labour market and social policies, a conducive macroeconomic environment and other key strategies of the Organisation, including *Going for Growth*, the OECD Skills Strategy, the OECD Innovation Strategy, the OECD Green Growth Strategy and the OECD *Recommendations on Gender Equality, Mental Health, and Ageing.*[3]

Box 3.1. The OECD Inclusive Growth Initiative

Persistently high inequalities of income, wealth and well-being and the slowdown in productivity growth are undermining social mobility, holding back progress in living standards and threatening political stability. The OECD is seeking to address these trends through the Inclusive Growth Initiative that was launched in 2012. The work on inclusive growth is organised along four pillars: i) shared prosperity; ii) inclusive markets; iii) equality of opportunities; and iv) inclusive growth governance. The new Jobs Strategy relates closely to each of these pillars:

- ***Shared prosperity recognises*** that the measurement of economic performance and social progress needs to go beyond gross domestic product (GDP) by taking account of both material and non-material living conditions as well as their distribution in society. This is reflected in the new Jobs Strategy which seeks to promote good quality jobs for all. This requires not only promoting the availability and access to jobs, but also ensuring that job quality is consistent with a healthy working life. It further emphasises the importance of labour market resilience and adaptability to ensure that labour market performance can be sustained in an uncertain future.
- ***Inclusive markets recognise*** the importance of well-functioning markets as well as the need for additional measures to ensure that everybody can participate fully in society. The new Jobs Strategy incorporates the key insight that inclusive markets require more than flexibility. It recognises that flexible markets are necessary to achieve good economic and labour market performance, but that supporting public policies are needed to promote more and better jobs for all.
- ***Equality of opportunities*** recognises equality of opportunity as the foundation of future prosperity. Similarly, the new Jobs Strategy emphasises the importance of equality of opportunity and social mobility for reducing the depth and persistence of economic inequalities, while raising long-term economic growth. Equality of opportunity is seen as a key component of the inclusiveness dimension of the new Jobs Strategy framework.
- ***Inclusive growth governance*** recognises the need for coordination and integration of policy actions using a whole-of-government approach. The new Jobs Strategy also recognises that winning the twin challenge of high inequality and low productivity growth requires comprehensive and integrated policy actions that reduce inequality while minimising potential adverse effects on economic growth, embedding the new Jobs Strategy as a key pillar of the Inclusive Growth Initiative.

Source: OECD (2018[21]) "The Framework for Policy Action on Inclusive Growth", Meeting of the Council at Ministerial Level, 30-31 May 2018, https://www.oecd.org/mcm/documents/C-MIN-2018-5-EN.pdf *(accessed 25 August 2018).*

3.2. The OECD Jobs Strategy dashboard

To what extent can policy improve labour market performance along each of the three dimensions of the new Jobs Strategy? Can synergies be developed or are trade-offs inevitable? How do policy priorities differ across countries? A good way of getting a first idea about the answers to these important questions is to review key indicators as presented in a dashboard that allows comparisons of labour market performance across OECD countries and major emerging market economies along each of its dimensions. Table 3.1, Panel A uses the employment rate, the unemployment rate, and the broad labour utilisation rate (defined as the share of inactive, unemployed and involuntary part-timers in the non-student working-age population) to measure job quantity; earnings quality, labour market security[4] and the incidence of job strain[5] for job quality; and the share of persons in low-income households, a general measure of gender inequality in the labour market and the typical employment gap of disadvantaged groups for inclusiveness (youth, older workers, mothers with children, people with disabilities and migrants).[6]

The main conclusion from the dashboard presented in Table 3.1, Panel A is that **policies can be combined into coherent packages that enhance synergies across policies and minimise possible trade-offs**. More specifically:

- *It is possible to combine good outcomes in terms of job quantity, job quality and inclusiveness.* Many countries that have relatively high employment rates tend to do relatively well with respect to the different components of job quality and inclusiveness. For example, the Nordic countries, such as Iceland, Denmark, Norway and Sweden, as well as Germany are among the best performing countries across at least two-thirds of the dimensions of the dashboard, while they are absent from the bottom third of low performers. At the other end of the spectrum, a number of Southern European and emerging economies score relatively low on the majority of indicators. This suggests that there are few systematic trade-offs, and crucially, that it is possible to design policies that simultaneously raise job quantity, job quality and inclusiveness.[7,8]
- *While more affluent countries tend to perform better along most outcomes, other factors – including sound employment and social policies – also play an important role.* After accounting for the role of economic development most Nordic countries, as well as Czech Republic, Estonia, Latvia, and New Zealand rank among the top performing countries in the OECD in terms of average performance (see Annex Table 3.A.3).[9] By contrast, Mediterranean countries (except France and Israel), as well as Ireland and the United States are among the least performing countries in the OECD. These differences in average performance are likely to reflect the role of various factors, including that of policies, institutions and social capital.
- *Changes in performance over time reflect a combination of policy developments, structural changes and the legacy of the global financial crisis.* A decade after the onset of the global financial crisis labour market insecurity and low-income rate remain elevated in several countries compared with their levels in 2006. Earnings quality has remained more or less stable. At the same time, however, most countries managed to improve the quality of the work environment, narrow the gender labour income gap and better integrate disadvantaged groups into the labour market (cf. Table 3.1 and Annex Table 3.A.1). Moreover, most countries

have improved job quantity over the past two decades, largely thanks to the rise in female and older-worker employment rates (cf. Annex Table 3.A.2).

- *Performance has been uneven across countries.* Those European countries that were badly hit by the financial crisis and had to undergo significant fiscal restraint experienced worsening performance in many indicators over the past decade.[10] By contrast, Chile, Czech Republic, Germany, Japan, Israel and Poland stand out for having achieved significant improvements along at least four of the nine performance dimensions, while being stable along the other dimensions. Finally, many English-speaking countries are characterised by a striking stability of their performance over the past two decades, though often at intermediate-to-low levels of job quality and inclusiveness.[11]

Are countries prepared for the opportunities and challenges posed by the future of work? Table 3.1, Panel B provides descriptive evidence on these issues by comparing framework conditions for resilience and adaptability across OECD and a number of emerging market economies.[12] Resilience is measured by the estimated average increase in the unemployment rate in the three years following a negative shock to GDP of 1%, i.e. the capacity to limit fluctuations in unemployment and to quickly rebound in the wake of an aggregate shock.[13] Framework conditions for adaptability are measured by the following indicators:

- the *rate of labour productivity growth* as a key pre-condition for high growth of output, employment and wages;
- the *ability of productive firms to attract workers* and grow as a key component of labour productivity and therefore wages;
- the *decoupling or real median wage growth from productivity growth*, as a measure of the extent to which productivity gains are transmitted to the wages of the typical worker during periods of rapid structural change;
- *adult skills*, as higher skills promote learning, innovation and higher wages; *student skills*, as an indication of the readiness of the next generation to respond to future challenges; as well as the *share of non-standard workers in total employment* - defined in terms of self-employed and temporary workers - since non-standard work can contribute to adaptability by providing flexibility to workers and firms, but may pose challenges in terms job quality and inclusiveness;
- *regional disparities in unemployment rates* within countries as a measure of the extent to which countries adapt to the uneven regional impact of mega-trends such as technological change, globalisation and demographic change.

The key message from Table 3.1, Panel B is that framework conditions for resilience and adaptability are closely related to labour market outcomes in terms of job quantity, job quality and inclusiveness.[14] In most cases, framework conditions for resilience and adaptability are complementary to all dimensions of good labour market performance. However, in some cases there can be potential trade-offs in the sense that some framework conditions may raise labour market performance along some dimensions but reduce it along others.

- *Countries with more resilient labour markets and a higher share of skilled workers do better across all dimensions of labour market performance.*

  - Labour market resilience is crucial not only to contain the short-term social costs of economic downturns but also to support labour market and economic performance in the medium to long term by avoiding that cyclical downturns translate into structurally lower growth of output, employment and wages. In fact, the unemployment rate and the low-income rate are generally lower while labour market security is higher in countries with more resilient labour markets. Labour market resilience is high in countries such as Japan and a number of Nordic countries (Finland, Iceland, Norway and Sweden), whereas it is low in a number of Mediterranean countries and the United States.
  - A skilled workforce promotes innovation and the adoption of new technologies and work organisation practices, thereby boosting productivity, employment and wages. In fact, countries with a highly skilled workforce perform better across all dimensions of labour market performance. Countries with particularly low shares of low-skilled individuals include the Scandinavian countries, Germany, Japan and the Netherlands, but on average around one fifth of adults and one third of students in OECD countries do not have the basic skills required to succeed in a rapidly changing labour market.
- *Countries in which productive firms can more easily attract workers and grow also perform relatively better on job quantity.* A number of countries, such as Germany, the Netherlands and Norway, in which labour markets allocate workers efficiently – in the sense that employment growth is higher in more productive firms than in less productive ones – are also among the best-performing ones on most indicators of job quantity. However, a high ability of productive firms to attract workers is not sufficient to perform well on job quantity, as illustrated by a number of Mediterranean countries and the United States.
- *Countries in which real wage growth follow more closely labour productivity growth have generally done well on both job quantity and inclusiveness*. A large number of countries have experienced very low productivity growth over the past two decades, with productivity growth only partly transmitted to the real wage of the typical worker. Consequently, real median wages have stagnated in a large number of countries. Countries in which real median wage growth has closely tracked productivity growth, such as Denmark and New Zealand, have generally done well on both job quantity and inclusiveness. By contrast, countries in which real median wage growth has exceeded productivity growth, especially in the run-up to the crisis, such as Greece, Italy and Spain, have experienced large increases in unemployment. This suggests that large positive deviations of wage growth from productivity growth are unsustainable and may harm employment prospects in the long run. Countries in which real median wage growth has fallen short of productivity growth, such as Ireland, Poland and the United States, have typically experienced sub-par performance in terms of inclusiveness without any clear benefits in terms of job quantity.
- *Countries with high shares of non-standard workers and high regional disparities do worse than other countries on job quality and inclusiveness,* without apparent benefits in terms of job quantity. Around one fifth of workers in OECD countries are employed on non-standard contracts, which raises flexibility for employers and workers – including on working time – but may also pose challenges for skills development, job quality and inclusiveness. In fact, job quality and inclusiveness are lower in countries with high-shares of non-standard workers,

such as most Mediterranean countries. A similar pattern emerges for countries with high regional disparities that typically do worse than other countries in terms of job quality and inclusiveness but do not systematically do better on job quantity.

A whole-of-government approach is needed to make framework conditions for resilience and adaptability conducive to good overall economic and labour market performance. Labour market policies can influence most framework conditions for resilience and adaptability. For instance, well-designed and adequately funded education and training policies could improve adult skills and productivity growth while providing workers with the right tools to navigate change, thereby reducing skill mismatch and improving the ability of productive firms to attract qualified workers. However, labour market policies alone cannot achieve framework conditions for resilience and adaptability. Key non-labour market policies are:

- *Sound macroeconomic policies* smooth business cycle fluctuations in aggregate demand and can have longer-term effects by reducing the scope for hysteresis-type mechanisms that turn temporary downturns in activity into sustained periods of low economic activity. This may, for instance, happen if cyclical increases in unemployment translate into increases in structural unemployment or reduced labour force participation, or if cyclical declines in investment reduce growth expectations, resulting in a low-growth trap characterised by low investment and low growth in productivity and wages.
- *Productivity-enhancing policies and institutions* not directly related to the labour market are key to promote a vibrant economic environment that is conducive to innovation and the efficient re-allocation of factors of production. Business dynamism could be promoted by facilitating the entry of new firms, the reallocation of workers towards the most productive firms and the restructuring (or orderly exit) of the weakly productive ones. Raising the efficiency of tax systems; providing a sound legal and judicial infrastructure; enhancing the robustness of financial markets that serve the real economy; continuing efforts to strengthen the rule of law and fight corruption; and creating a level playing field and improving the governance of state-owned enterprises are other policy areas that will be key to sustainably raise productivity, employment and wages.
- In accordance with the OECD Skills Strategy, the challenge for ***skills policies*** is to provide learning opportunities from early childhood throughout the working life. A high-quality initial education and training system will be crucial to give individuals the best possible start in the labour market by providing them with strong basic skills, socio-emotional skills and specific skills required by employers, as well as the capacity for lifelong learning and to make education, training and occupational choices throughout their working lives.

Table 3.1. OECD Jobs Strategy dashboard for labour market performance

Panel A. Dashboard of job quantity, job quality and inclusiveness

	Quantity			Quality			Inclusiveness		
	Employment	Unemployment	Broad labour underutilisation	Earnings quality	Labour market insecurity	Quality of working environment	Low-income rate	Gender labour income gap	Employment gap for disadvantaged groups
	Share of working-age population (20-64 years) in employment (%) (2017)	Share of persons in the labour force (15-64 years) in unemployment (%) (2017)	Share of inactive, unemployed or involuntary part-timers (15-64) in population (%), excluding youth (15-29) in education and not in employment (2016)	Gross hourly earnings in USD adjusted for inequality (2015)	Expected monetary loss associated with becoming and staying unemployed as a share of previous earnings (%) (2016)	Share of workers experiencing job strain (%) (2015)	Poverty rate after taxes and transfers, poverty line 50%, working-age population (18-64) (%) (2015)	Difference between average annual earnings of men and women divided by average earnings of men (%) (2015)	Average employment gap as a percentage of the benchmark group (prime-age male workers) (2016)
OECD countries									
Iceland	87.2	2.9	12.6	22.7	2.2	23.8	6.5	35.3	9.2
Switzerland	82.1	5.0	18.3	28.4	1.7	..	6.4	48.3	14.6
Sweden	81.8	6.8	19.5	20.3	3.8	23.6	8.4	25.6	13.3
New Zealand	81.3	4.9	21.4	16.8	4.4	21.6	9.7	..	17.7
Japan	80.3	3.0	24.0	16.1	1.6	31.2	14.5	57.7	24.7
Germany	79.2	3.8	21.0	25.0	1.9	28.5	10.0	42.6	20.2
Estonia	78.7	5.9	21.9	7.5	5.2	23.0	12.9	30.4	22.1
Czech Republic	78.5	2.9	20.7	9.0	1.8	25.4	5.8	44.3	30.3
Norway	78.3	4.3	19.2	29.0	1.9	13.8	9.3	35.0	16.0
United Kingdom	78.1	4.5	23.5	17.7	2.7	20.7	10.1	42.6	22.9
Netherlands	78.0	4.9	22.9	28.7	1.9	23.4	8.8	46.2	22.2
Denmark	76.9	5.9	21.0	29.8	3.1	18.2	7.0	29.8	16.7
Canada	76.3	6.4	26.0	19.6	3.8	..	14.1	38.7	19.3
Lithuania	76.0	7.3	23.5	7.5	..	30.8	14.7	26.9	17.6
Australia	76.0	5.8	28.5	21.9	3.8	25.6	10.2	41.5	21.4
Israel	75.5	4.3	24.0	8.7	3.5	25.1	14.3	..	14.6
Austria	75.4	5.6	25.4	23.0	2.6	28.5	8.7	47.8	21.6
Latvia	74.7	8.9	26.8	6.4	..	30.3	13.0	24.9	17.7
Finland	74.3	8.8	26.6	21.2	2.0	16.3	6.8	21.4	18.6
United States	73.6	4.4	25.7	17.7	3.7	25.8	15.5	39.5	25.4
Slovenia	73.4	6.7	27.6	14.2	3.5	31.8	8.7	22.8	27.4
Portugal	73.4	9.2	29.8	8.7	7.0	33.2	12.3	29.0	22.0
Hungary	73.3	4.2	26.8	7.2	3.2	36.4	10.0	29.3	33.6
Ireland	72.7	7.0	33.5	19.3	3.1	23.9	9.9	39.9	26.3
Korea	71.6	3.8	..	9.9	2.4	..	8.5	61.0	31.8
Luxembourg	71.5	5.5	27.5	28.8	2.2	23.1	10.9	31.9	24.0
Slovak Republic	71.1	8.2	29.7	8.8	6.4	32.0	7.6	31.7	33.5
France	71.0	9.2	32.7	21.9	4.4	25.8	8.3	34.6	27.8
Poland	70.9	5.0	29.4	7.6	4.0	30.0	11.0	35.5	31.5
Chile	69.1	7.0	33.2	6.6	7.1	28.2	14.2	46.4	27.5
Belgium	68.5	7.1	30.0	29.3	2.4	25.8	9.5	33.3	30.0
Mexico	66.6	3.6	..	4.6	4.0	28.9	13.9	54.5	40.4
Spain	65.5	17.3	39.3	17.5	17.5	35.0	15.9	34.0	27.5
Italy	62.3	11.4	42.9	19.1	10.7	29.6	14.7	44.3	34.0
Greece	57.8	21.7	44.8	10.0	22.7	47.9	16.0	49.1	38.2
Turkey	55.3	11.2	44.2	5.8	13.0	42.9	13.5	..	47.1
OECD	**72.1**	**5.9**	**27.2**	**16.6**	**4.9**	**27.6**	**10.9**	**38.1**	**24.7**
Non-OECD countries									
Colombia	73.1	9.7	30.2	3.7	11.0	..	..	42.5	34.3
Costa Rica	66.6	9.2	37.8	5.5	7.2	..	17.5	48.5	44.9
Argentina	69.0	8.5	36.2	7.4	7.5	..	..	45.1	38.8
Brazil	65.9	13.0	32.7	4.8	6.6	..	17.3	48.2	39.2
China	79.0	2.9	..	..	5.8	28.9	26.0	..	32.0
India	59.5	3.7	..	2.7	3.6	30.7	17.1	78.1	50.1
Indonesia	72.6	5.6	29.6	1.6	8.2	..	..	62.7	40.1
Russian Federation	74.9	5.2	23.3	6.8	5.1	33.4	12.8	33.2	35.4
Saudi Arabia	60.0	5.7	..	..	..	..	..	..	..
South Africa	49.8	27.4	50.2	2.5	22.6	26.7	23.9	50.1	50.3

Above average performers (Top-third) | About average performers (Mid-third) | Below average performers (Bottom-third)

Note: Countries are ordered in descending order by the employment rate. Dark blue stands for better performance, light blue for worse one. Youth, aged 15-29 years, in education and not in employment are excluded from both the numerator and the denominator of broad labour underutilisation. The groups considered in the last columns are youth, older workers, mothers with children, people with disabilities and non-natives. Data refer to the latest available data for each group. Data on job quantity refer to 2017 (2016 for broad labour utilisation) except for China (2010), India (2011-12) and Saudi Arabia (2016). Data on earnings quality refer to 2015, except for Argentina, Japan and the Russian Federation (2013) and India (2011-12). Data on earnings quality for non-OECD countries are provisional estimates. Data on labour market insecurity refer to 2016 except for Israel (2015) and non-OECD countries (2013). Data for job strain are preliminary estimates for 2015. Data on low-income rate refer to 2015 except for Costa Rica, Finland, Israel, Latvia, the Netherlands, Sweden and the United States (2016); Australia, Hungary, Iceland, Mexico and New Zealand (2014); Brazil (2013); Japan (2012), China, India and the Russian Federation (2011). Data on labour income gap per capita refer to 2015 except for Argentina, Chile, Colombia, Indonesia and the United States (2016); Canada, Iceland, Ireland, Italy, Luxembourg, the Russian Federation and Switzerland (2014); Korea (2013) and India (2011-12).

Source: OECD (2016[3]), "Recent labour market developments and the short-term outlook", in *OECD Employment Outlook 2016*, https://dx.doi.org/10.1787/empl_outlook-2016-5-en; OECD (2017[4]) "How are we doing? A broad assessment of labour market performance", in *OECD Employment Outlook 2017*, https://doi.org/10.1787/empl_outlook-2017-5-en; OECD (2018[5]), "Still out of pocket: Recent labour market performance and wage developments", in *OECD Employment Outlook 2018*, https://doi.org/10.1787/empl_outlook-2018-5-en; *OECD Employment Database* http://www.oecd.org/employment/database; *OECD Job Quality Database*, http://www.oecd.org/statistics/job-quality.htm and *OECD Income Distribution Database*, http://www.oecd.org/social/income-distribution-database.htm.

Panel B. Framework conditions for resilience and adaptability

	Resilience	Adaptability						
	Unemployment cost of a decline in GDP	Labour productivity growth	Ability of productive firms to attract workers	Wage-productivity decoupling	Adult skills	Student skills	Non-standard workers	Regional disparities
	Average increase in unemployment rate over three years after a negative shock to GDP of 1% (pp) (2000-16)	Average annual labour productivity growth (%) (2000-16)	Cross-firm employment growth differential associated with 10 pp productivity differential (2003-13)	Difference between annual real median wage growth and labour productivity growth (pp) (2000-13)	Share of adults with numeracy skills below level 2 in PIAAC (%) (2012, 2015)	Share of 15-year-olds not in secondary school or scoring below Level 2 in PISA (%) (2015)	Own-account self-employed and temporary workers in % of total employment (2013)	Coefficient of variation in regional unemployment rates (2000, 2016)
OECD countries								
Iceland	0.1	1.5 o	..	..	..	28.8	20.6	Low ↑
Switzerland	0.4	0.4 ↓	Low o	..	..	19.0	18.7	Low ↑
Sweden	0.3	1.3 o	Average o	0.4 ↑	14.7	25.9	19.0	Average ↓
New Zealand	0.4	0.7 o	..	0.3 o	18.9	29.3	..	Low o
Japan	0.2	0.7 ↑	Average ↑	-0.5 ↑	8.1	15.4	20.2	Low o
Germany	0.4	0.6 o	High o	-0.4 o	18.4	20.6	18.1	High ↓
Estonia	0.7	2.8 ↓	Average o	..	14.3	17.6	8.4	Average ↑
Czech Republic	0.3	2.1 o	..	0.3 o	12.9	26.8	21.2	High o
Norway	0.2	0.5 ↑	High o	-0.5 o	14.6	24.3	11.8	Low o
United Kingdom	0.4	0.8 o	Low o	-0.2 ↓	24.2	34.4	16.1	Average o
Netherlands	0.4	0.7 ↑	High ↓	-0.7 ..	13.2	20.8	25.9	Average o
Denmark	0.6	0.6 o	Low o	0.1 ↓	14.2	23.1	13.6	Low o
Canada	0.5	0.6 o	..	-0.6 o	22.4	28.5	21.2	High ↓
Lithuania	0.5	4.2 ↓	..	..	17.4	32.7	..	Low ↑
Australia	0.4	1.0 o	..	-1.0 ↑	20.1	29.3	32.1	High o
Israel	0.6	0.7 o	..	-0.6 ..	30.9	36.4	..	Low o
Austria	0.1	0.4 o	High o	-0.0 o	14.3	34.8	15.4	Average ↑
Latvia	0.8	3.9 ↓	High ↓	..	..	30.2	..	Low ↑
Finland	0.2	0.6 o	Average o	1.0 o	12.8	15.9	21.8	High ↓
United States	0.7	1.3 ↓	High ↑	-1.5 ↑	28.7	41.0	..	Average o
Slovenia	0.3	1.0 o	Average o	..	25.8	22.2	18.6	Low o
Portugal	0.3	0.8 ↓	Low o	0.5 ↓	..	33.2	31.0	High ↓
Hungary	0.3	1.7 ↓	Average o	-0.6 o	..	35.5	15.9	Average ↑
Ireland	0.3	3.0 ↑	Low o	-1.1 ↓	25.2	18.0	19.5	Average ↓
Korea	0.2	2.5 ↓	Average ↑	-1.1 ↑	18.9	22.5	32.7	Low o
Luxembourg	0.1	0.0 ↑	Low o	..	..	35.0	11.9	..
Slovak Republic	0.5	3.2 ↓	..	-0.8 ↑	13.8	35.5	22.3	High o
France	0.4	0.6 o	Average o	0.7 o	28.0	30.4	20.8	Average ↓
Poland	0.6	2.7 ↓	Average ↑	-1.3 ↓	23.5	24.7	37.4	Low o
Chile	0.3	1.4 ↓	..	..	61.9	59.6	..	Average o
Belgium	0.3	0.6 o	Low o	-0.2 ↑	13.4	25.7	16.9	High o
Mexico	0.2	0.2 ↑	..	..	..	73.2	..	Average o
Spain	0.9	0.7 o	High o	0.5 ↓	30.6	29.3	32.1	High ↓
Italy	0.5	-0.4 o	High ↓	1.0 ↓	31.7	38.4	27.9	High ↓
Greece	0.8	0.2 ↓	Low ↑	1.4 ↓	28.5	41.5	35.6	Average o
Turkey	0.2	2.6 o	..	..	50.2	66.0	30.2	High ↓
OECD	**0.4**	**1.2 o**		**-0.2 o**	**22.7**	**32.4**	**22.0**	
Non-OECD countries								
Colombia	0.2	1.9 o	..	..	..	**74.8**	..	Average o
Costa Rica	0.6	2.1 o	..	..	..	76.2	..	..
Argentina	..	0.7 o	..	..	..	75.9	..	..
Brazil	0.3	1.5 ↓	..	..	..	79.0	..	Average o
China	0.0	2.1 o	..	..	..	46.2	..	High -
India	..	6.5 o	..	..	..	..	..	..
Indonesia	..	3.7 o	..	..	..	78.6	..	..
Russian Federation	0.1	2.8 ↓	..	..	..	22.8	..	High ↑
Saudi Arabia	..	-1.8 ↓	..	..	..	..	..	..
South Africa	0.3	0.6 ↓	..	..	..	..	..	Low o

Note: Countries are ordered in descending order of the employment rate. OECD unweighted average. The signs ↑, o, ↓ indicate differences in the most recent period (see Annex Table 3.A.4 for the details) relative to the overall period, with ↑ denoting an increase, o indicating approximate stability and ↓ indicating a decline. For instance, ↑ for the decoupling indicator means that over 2010-13 real median wage growth accelerated relative to labour productivity growth. Changes in indicators are considered to be significant when they are at least as large as one-half of the standard deviation of that indicator across OECD countries.
Source: Resilience: OECD calculations based on OECD (2017[6]), *OECD Employment Outlook 2017*, http://dx.doi.org/10.1787/empl_outlook-2017-en; Labour productivity growth: OECD Economic Outlook database (labour productivity measured in per worker terms); Wage-productivity decoupling: OECD calculations based on OECD National Accounts Database and OECD Earnings Database (labour productivity measured in per hour terms); Ability of productive firms to attract workers: OECD calculations based on the 2013 ORBIS vintage; Low-skilled adults: OECD (2016[7]), *Skills Matter: Further Results from the Survey of Adult Skills*, http://dx.doi.org/10.1787/9789264258051-en; Low-performing students in mathematics: OECD (2016[8]), *PISA 2015 Results (Volume I): Excellence and Equity in Education*, http://dx.doi.org/10.1787/9789264266490-en. Non-standard workers: OECD (2015[9]), *In It Together - Why Less Inequality Benefits All*, http://dx.doi.org/10.1787/9789264232662-en. Regional disparities: OECD (2018), *OECD Regional Statistics Database*, https://dx.doi.org/10.1787/region-data-en.

StatLink http://dx.doi.org/10.1787/888933881059

Conclusions

The conceptual framework of the new Jobs Strategy introduced in this chapter distinguishes between three broad performance areas: i) the quantity and quality of jobs; ii) labour market inclusiveness; and iii) the resilience and adaptability of the labour market. This framework is then applied by using the OECD Jobs Strategy dashboard to assess labour market performance and identify reform priorities.

The multidimensional approach to labour market performance adopted by the new Jobs Strategy potentially raises difficult questions for policy-makers as a result of possible trade-offs between different outcomes. Evaluating such trade-offs is difficult as social preferences may well differ significantly and across countries. In that sense, evaluating trade-off involves inherently political choices. The new OECD Jobs Strategy does not take a stance on the relative importance of the different dimensions beyond recognising that all are important in their own right.

A key insight of this chapter is that, while trade-offs between the performance areas of the framework are likely to be important in some cases, there are also important synergies. For instance, it is possible to design policy packages that simultaneously raise job quantity, job quality and inclusiveness. To some extent this reflects the role of economic development which not only tends to be associated with higher incomes, but also better public institutions and more resources for education, employment and social policies. However, it also suggests that coherent policy packages can go a long way towards mitigating possible trade-offs.

The remainder of Part I consists of three chapters that respectively consider the role of policies and institutions for labour market performance (Chapter 4), discuss their effective implementation in specific countries (Chapter 5), and contain the detailed policy recommendations of the new OECD Jobs Strategy (Chapter 6).

Notes

[1] Chapter 17 will develop this further to identify to challenges and priorities in specific countries.

[2] The OECD measures well-being as a multi-dimensional construct capturing material conditions, the quality of life and the sustainability of well-being in the future (OECD, 2017$_{[10]}$).

3 Recommendation of the Council on Gender Equality in Public Life (OECD, 2015$_{[11]}$), Recommendation of the Council on Gender Equality in Education, Employment and Entrepreneurship (OECD, 2013$_{[14]}$), Recommendation of the Council on Integrated Mental Health, Skills and Work Policy (OECD, 2015$_{[13]}$) and the Recommendation of the Council on Ageing and Employment Policies (OECD, 2015$_{[14]}$).

[4] Because of data availability, the measure of labour market insecurity considered here – that is the expected monetary loss associated with becoming and staying unemployed as a percentage of previous earnings – does not incorporate the broader issue of "earnings insecurity" due to unpredictable hours or extremely low pay, which is equally important for economic security, particularly in emerging economies.

[5] Job strain measures the risk that work impairs peoples' health due to the combination of excessive job demands and insufficient job resources to meet work requirements. Job demands relate to physical demands, work intensity and the flexibility of working time. Job resources relate to task discretion and work autonomy, training and learning opportunities and scope for career advancement. For further details, please visit: http://www.oecd.org/statistics/job-quality.htm.

[6] More specifically, the three dimensions of inclusiveness considered in the scoreboard are: i) the share of the working-age population with disposable income substantially below that of a typical working-age person; ii) the gender gap in labour income per capita; and iii) the gap in employment rates between prime-age men and selected disadvantaged groups – youth, older workers, mothers with children, people with disabilities and migrants (i.e. the foreign-born). The reason for including these measures is threefold: i) labour income – along with out-of-work transfers and the taxation of employment-related income – is a key determinant of household disposable income for the working-age population, particularly in the lower range of the distribution, which implies that an economy with an inclusive labour market is one in which relatively few working-age persons have disposable income that lies far below the median income; ii) an inclusive labour market means that opportunities to develop a successful career should not differ by gender; and iii) an inclusive labour market should ensure that potentially disadvantaged groups are not left behind. A more exhaustive discussion of these choices and the robustness of the scoreboard to their measurement is available in OECD (2017$_{[4]}$).

[7] While the tendency for performance to go together across different outcomes reflects to some extent the role of economic development, accounting for this does not change the message that it is possible to do well in terms of each of the dimensions of labour market performance at the same time.

[8] Of course, higher employment rates do not necessarily imply better quality jobs or greater inclusiveness and vice versa. Policy priorities and effectiveness can differ significantly across countries.

[9] The role of economic development is accounted for by regressing each of the indicators of labour market performance on GDP per capita across OECD countries (excluding Luxembourg), retrieving and standardising residuals and when necessary multiplying by minus one so that positive values are associated with better performance. The results are reported in Annex Table 3.A.3.

[10] A few of them have however significantly improved their job quantity performance in the past two decades (e.g. Ireland and Spain).

[11] The United States, where the employment rate has fallen by 1.7 percentage points and broad labour underutilisation has increased by 2.5 percentage points in the past decade, represents a notable exception to this pattern of stability.

[12] See Chapter 13 and 14 of this Volume for a detailed policy discussion of these issues and Annex Table 3.A.4 for further information on framework conditions for resilience and adaptability and their measurement.

[13] An alternative indicator using the employment rate instead of the unemployment rate has also been calculated and provides a qualitatively similar picture. The pairwise rank correlation between the indicators of unemployment and employment resilience is 0.7.

[14] The conclusions in this paragraph are based on rank correlations between the levels of the indicators in Panel B and the levels/changes of the indicators in Panel A. Changes of the indicators in Panel A are computed over the period 2006-16.

References

OECD (2018), "Still out of pocket: Recent labour market performance and wage developments", in *OECD Employment Outlook 2018*, OECD Publishing, Paris, https://dx.doi.org/10.1787/empl_outlook-2018-5-en. [5]

OECD (2018), *The Framework for Policy Action on Inclusive Growth*, https://one.oecd.org/document/C/MIN(2018)5/en/pdf (accessed on 25 September 2018). [2]

OECD (2017), "How are we doing? A broad assessment of labour market performance", in *OECD Employment Outlook 2017*, OECD Publishing, Paris, https://dx.doi.org/10.1787/empl_outlook-2017-5-en. [4]

OECD (2017), *How's Life? 2017: Measuring Well-being*, OECD Publishing, Paris, http://dx.doi.org/10.1787/how_life-2017-en. [10]

OECD (2017), *OECD Employment Outlook 2017*, OECD Publishing, Paris, https://dx.doi.org/10.1787/empl_outlook-2017-en. [6]

OECD (2016), *PISA 2015 Results (Volume I): Excellence and Equity in Education*, PISA, OECD Publishing, Paris, https://dx.doi.org/10.1787/9789264266490-en. [8]

OECD (2016), "Recent labour market developments and the short-term outlook", in *OECD Employment Outlook 2016*, OECD Publishing, Paris, https://dx.doi.org/10.1787/empl_outlook-2016-5-en. [3]

OECD (2016), *Skills Matter: Further Results from the Survey of Adult Skills*, OECD Skills Studies, OECD Publishing, Paris, https://dx.doi.org/10.1787/9789264258051-en. [7]

OECD (2015), *Draft Recommendation of the Council on Ageing and Employment Policies*, https://one.oecd.org/document/C(2015)172/CORR1/en/pdf. [13]

OECD (2015), *Draft Recommendation of The Council on Gender Equality in Public Life*, https://one.oecd.org/document/C(2015)164/CORR1/en/pdf. [11]

OECD (2015), *Draft Recommendation of the Council on Integrated Mental Health, School and Work Policy*, https://one.oecd.org/document/C(2015)173/CORR1/en/pdf. [12]

OECD (2015), *In It Together: Why Less Inequality Benefits All*, OECD Publishing, Paris, http://dx.doi.org/10.1787/9789264232662-en. [9]

OECD (2013), *Recommendation of the Council on Gender Equality in Education, Employment and Entrepreneurship*, https://one.oecd.org/document/C/MIN(2013)5/FINAL/en/pdf. [14]

OECD (2006), *OECD Employment Outlook 2006: Boosting Jobs and Incomes*, OECD Publishing, Paris, https://doi.org/10.1787/empl_outlook-2006-en. [1]

Annex 3.A. Additional information

Annex Table 3.A.1. Dashboard of job quantity, job quality and inclusiveness, 2006 or closest available date

	Quantity			Quality			Inclusiveness		
	Employment	Unemployment	Broad labour underutilisation	Earnings quality	Labour market insecurity	Quality of working environment	Low-income rate	Gender labour income gap	Employment gap for disadvantaged groups
	Share of working-age population (20-64 years) in employment (%) (2006)	Share of persons in the labour force (15-64 years) in unemployment (%) (2006)	Share of inactive, unemployed or involuntary part-timers (15-64) in population (%), excluding youth (15-29) in education and not in employment (2007)	Gross hourly earnings in USD adjusted for inequality (2006)	Expected monetary loss associated with becoming and staying unemployed as a share of previous earnings (%) (2007)	Share of workers experiencing job strain (%) (2005)	Poverty rate after taxes and transfers, Poverty line 50% Working-age population (18-64) (%) (2006)	Difference between average annual earnings of men and women divided by average earnings of men (%) (2005)	Average employment gap as a percentage of the benchmark group (prime-age male workers) (2006)
OECD countries									
Iceland	87.0	3.0	10.6	21.2	1.1	..	5.2	41.2	10.4
Switzerland	80.5	4.1	18.6	26.6	1.4	..	..	..	18.8
Norway	79.6	3.5	17.5	25.3	0.7	21.8	8.6	38.6	20.0
Denmark	79.4	4.0	20.6	27.1	1.8	23.2	5.3	31.6	21.5
Sweden	78.8	7.1	23.1	18.5	2.5	21.2	7.5	32.3	16.8
New Zealand	78.4	3.9	21.8	14.9	3.1	24.8	8.3	..	21.1
Canada	75.8	6.4	24.6	16.9	3.2	30.1	12.8	41.2	20.8
Estonia	75.6	6.1	21.7	5.7	4.0	30.7	11.2	37.2	22.6
United States	75.3	4.7	23.2	18.0	3.4	28.1	14.1	44.2	26.0
United Kingdom	75.0	5.4	24.9	17.6	3.1	28.4	10.4	46.3	25.5
Ireland	74.7	5.0	24.4	16.4	1.8	27.6	9.4	49.3	29.7
Netherlands	74.6	4.3	22.8	27.5	1.1	27.8	6.6	56.0	28.8
Australia	74.5	4.9	27.3	20.1	2.7	27.3	10.7	46.7	24.3
Japan	74.5	4.3	26.0	15.0	1.8	37.8	13.4	64.3	29.5
Finland	74.0	7.7	24.5	19.9	2.6	20.3	7.1	27.5	19.4
Latvia	73.2	7.2	24.1	4.2	..	37.5	11.9	..	21.3
Portugal	72.6	8.1	27.1	8.6	5.5	46.8	10.5	..	23.0
Austria	71.6	5.3	26.7	20.9	2.1	31.0	..	50.3	28.6
Slovenia	71.5	6.1	24.6	13.4	2.1	41.1	5.9	23.3	25.4
Lithuania	71.3	5.8	27.6	6.1	..	46.1	10.4	27.2	22.7
Czech Republic	71.2	7.2	25.1	8.4	2.2	37.8	5.0	46.7	35.9
Germany	71.1	10.4	28.2	22.8	3.4	44.8	8.7	51.8	28.6
Korea	69.6	3.6	..	8.0	2.2	38.7	11.1	67.9	35.1
France	69.4	8.5	31.0	20.8	3.1	34.1	7.4	38.7	30.7
Luxembourg	69.1	4.7	27.0	28.3	1.3	29.1	..	58.3	30.7
Spain	69.0	8.5	30.8	15.6	5.5	49.2	11.3	..	28.4
Israel	68.1	10.8	34.0	8.6	5.4	35.8	14.4	..	21.6
Belgium	66.5	8.3	31.7	27.4	3.1	30.0	8.3	47.9	36.7
Mexico	66.1	3.7	..	4.8	3.8	31.5	15.2	..	41.1
Slovak Republic	66.0	13.3	30.4	7.3	8.1	37.4	5.3	34.7	39.2
Greece	65.6	9.1	32.6	11.4	7.5	49.8	11.3	..	35.2
Chile	64.0	9.2	..	4.1	8.1	..	16.3	59.0	37.9
Hungary	62.6	7.5	35.0	7.0	4.0	49.8	6.7	33.5	38.4
Italy	62.4	6.9	38.0	18.5	5.0	35.6	10.7	..	37.8
Poland	60.1	14.0	35.0	6.3	4.8	39.1	10.8	32.7	40.6
Turkey	48.2	10.5	51.8	6.0	9.7	57.2	12.2	..	52.3

	Quantity			Quality			Inclusiveness		
	Employment	Unemployment	Broad labour underutilisation	Earnings quality	Labour market insecurity	Quality of working environment	Low-income rate	Gender labour income gap	Employment gap for disadvantaged groups
	Share of working-age population (20-64 years) in employment (%) (2006)	Share of persons in the labour force (15-64 years) in unemployment (%) (2006)	Share of inactive, unemployed or involuntary part-timers (15-64) in population (%), excluding youth (15-29) in education and not in employment (2007)	Gross hourly earnings in USD adjusted for inequality (2006)	Expected monetary loss associated with becoming and staying unemployed as a share of previous earnings (%) (2007)	Share of workers experiencing job strain (%) (2005)	Poverty rate after taxes and transfers, Poverty line 50% Working-age population (18-64) (%) (2006)	Difference between average annual earnings of men and women divided by average earnings of men (%) (2005)	Average employment gap as a percentage of the benchmark group (prime-age male workers) (2006)
OECD	70.3	6.3	27.0	15.3	3.6	34.9	9.8	43.4	28.5
Non-OECD countries									
Colombia	66.8	11.5	..	2.9	..	..	..	51.3	..
Costa Rica	69.3	5.8	..	..	..	..	..	..	..
Argentina	68.8	10.3	36.0	5.6	..	..	..	54.3	35.1
Brazil	71.9	8.6	31.7	3.5	..	..	17.6	54.2	36.8
China	83.8	3.7	..	..	..	..	..	..	..
India	63.4	4.5	..	..	..	..	17.4	..	46.4
Indonesia	67.5	10.6	..	..	..	..	..	..	43.6
Russian Federation	74.2	7.1	..	5.5	..	42.7	..	..	..
Saudi Arabia	56.9	5.8	..	..	..	..	..	..	..
South Africa	53.1	22.6	..	..	..	38.0	..	58.9	..

Above average performers (Top-third) | About average performers (Mid-third) | Below average performers (Bottom-third)

Note: Countries are ordered in descending order by the employment rate. Dark blue stands for better performance, light blue for worse one. The groups considered in the last columns are youth, older workers, mothers with children, people with disabilities and non-natives. Data on job quantity refer to 2006 except for Colombia and Saudi Arabia (2007); China (2000). Data on job strain are preliminary revised estimates for 2005. Data on low-income rate refer to 2006 except for Israel and the United States (2005); Hungary, Spain and Turkey (2007); Australia, Mexico, Norway, New Zealand and Sweden (2008); India (2004). Data on gender labour income gap refer to 2006 except for Japan (2005).

Source: OECD (2016[3]), "Recent labour market developments and the short-term outlook", in *OECD Employment Outlook 2016*, https://dx.doi.org/10.1787/empl_outlook-2016-5-en; OECD (2017[4]) "How are we doing? A broad assessment of labour market performance", in *OECD Employment Outlook 2017*, https://doi.org/10.1787/empl_outlook-2017-5-en; *OECD Employment Database*, www.oecd.org/employment/database, *OECD Job Quality Database*, http://www.oecd.org/statistics/job-quality.htm and *OECD Income Distribution Database*, http://www.oecd.org/social/income-distribution-database.htm.

StatLink http://dx.doi.org/10.1787/888933881078

Annex Table 3.A.2. Dashboard of job quantity, 1995 or closest available date

	Quantity	
	Employment	Unemployment
	Share of working-age population (20-64 years) in employment (%) (1995)	Share of persons in the labour force (15-64 years)in unemployment (%) (1995)
OECD countries		
Iceland	86.0	5.0
Switzerland	79.4	3.4
Norway	77.0	5.0
Sweden	76.0	9.2
Czech Republic	75.6	4.0
Denmark	75.3	7.0
United States	75.2	5.6
Japan	75.1	3.3
New Zealand	72.6	6.5
Estonia	71.4	9.7
Austria	71.3	3.7
Korea	70.9	2.1
United Kingdom	70.7	8.7
Canada	70.5	9.6
Australia	70.1	8.6
Israel	68.3	8.9
Portugal	67.8	7.4
Netherlands	67.6	7.1
Germany	67.6	8.2
Slovak Republic	67.4	13.1
Finland	66.3	15.4
France	65.1	11.6
Poland	64.3	13.7
Luxembourg	62.4	2.9
Chile	62.2	7.5
Belgium	61.4	9.4
Mexico	61.1	7.1
Ireland	60.7	12.4
Greece	59.9	9.3
Hungary	58.9	10.2
Turkey	55.9	7.8
Italy	55.2	11.7
Spain	51.8	22.8
Latvia	..	..
Lithuania	..	..
Slovenia	..	..
OECD	**68.3**	**7.6**
Non-OECD countries		
Colombia	..	..
Costa Rica	63.6	5.2
Argentina	..	..
Brazil	..	..
China	..	..
India	..	..
Indonesia	..	..
Russian Federation	70.2	9.5
Saudi Arabia	57.2	4.4
South Africa	..	..

Above average performers (Top-third) | About average performers (Mid-third) | Below average performers (Bottom-third)

Note: Countries are ordered in descending order by the employment rate. Dark blue stands for better performance, light blue for worse one. Data refer to 1995 except for Chile (1996) and Saudi Arabia (1999).
Source: OECD Employment Database, www.oecd.org/employment/database.

StatLink http://dx.doi.org/10.1787/888933881097

Annex Table 3.A.3. Dashboard of job quality, job quantity and inclusiveness after adjusting for the role of economic development

2017 or latest available year, taking in account GDP per capita using the residuals of regressing each indicator on GDP per capita, standardised

	Quantity			Quality			Inclusiveness		
	Employment	Unemployment	Broad labour underutilisation	Earnings quality	Labour market insecurity	Quality of working environment	Low-income rate	Gender labour income gap	Employment gap for disadvantaged groups
Iceland	1.9	0.8	1.8	0.3	0.3	0.1	1.2	0.3	1.7
New Zealand	1.4	0.6	1.0	0.4	0.2	1.2	0.5	..	1.1
Estonia	1.3	0.5	1.2	-0.7	0.4	1.4	-0.4	0.7	0.8
Japan	1.1	1.0	0.4	-0.1	0.8	-0.7	-1.3	-1.9	-0.1
Czech Republic	1.1	1.2	1.2	-0.9	1.0	0.7	2.0	-0.6	-0.5
Sweden	1.0	-0.2	0.8	-0.1	0.0	0.2	0.6	1.3	1.2
Lithuania	0.8	0.1	0.9	-0.8	..	0.0	-1.0	1.1	1.5
Latvia	0.8	-0.2	0.6	-0.5	..	0.3	-0.2	1.3	1.7
United Kingdom	0.6	0.6	0.5	0.1	0.5	1.1	0.2	-0.4	0.1
Germany	0.6	0.6	0.7	1.1	0.5	-0.6	0.1	-0.4	0.3
Switzerland	0.6	0.0	0.6	0.5	0.0	..	0.9	-0.9	0.5
Israel	0.5	0.8	0.7	-1.0	0.6	0.7	-1.0	..	1.7
Hungary	0.4	1.0	0.5	-0.5	0.9	-0.9	0.8	0.8	-0.6
Portugal	0.4	-0.4	0.0	-0.5	-0.1	-0.4	-0.1	0.9	0.9
Slovenia	0.2	0.2	0.2	0.4	0.7	-0.3	1.0	1.5	0.0
Netherlands	0.2	0.3	0.2	1.4	0.3	0.1	0.3	-0.8	-0.2
Canada	0.1	0.0	0.0	0.0	0.0	..	-1.4	0.0	0.4
Denmark	0.1	0.0	0.6	1.9	0.1	1.1	1.0	0.9	0.7
Poland	0.0	0.8	0.1	-0.5	0.7	0.3	0.4	0.2	-0.4
Australia	0.0	0.1	-0.5	0.2	0.0	-0.2	-0.1	-0.3	0.0
Finland	0.0	-0.6	0.0	0.8	0.6	1.8	1.4	1.7	0.7
Chile	0.0	0.4	-0.2	0.0	0.2	0.9	-0.5	-0.9	0.5
Austria	-0.1	0.2	0.0	0.6	0.3	-0.6	0.5	-0.9	0.1
Slovak Republic	-0.1	-0.2	-0.1	-0.7	0.0	-0.3	1.4	0.6	-0.8
Mexico	-0.3	1.4	..	0.0	1.1	1.0	-0.3	-1.7	-1.1
Korea	-0.3	0.8	..	-1.2	0.7	..	0.9	-2.3	-0.9
Norway	-0.3	0.1	0.3	-0.1	-0.2	0.9	-0.3	0.4	0.0
France	-0.5	-0.6	-0.8	1.2	0.1	0.3	0.9	0.4	-0.4
United States	-0.8	0.2	-0.4	-1.7	-0.4	-0.7	-2.3	-0.1	-0.9
Belgium	-1.1	-0.2	-0.6	2.3	0.4	0.0	0.3	0.5	-1.0
Spain	-1.2	-2.7	-1.6	0.7	-2.8	-1.1	-1.6	0.4	-0.2
Ireland	-1.6	-0.8	-2.0	-2.9	-0.8	-1.2	-0.8	0.0	-1.7
Italy	-1.8	-1.2	-2.1	1.0	-1.2	-0.2	-1.2	-0.6	-1.1
Greece	-2.1	-3.6	-2.0	0.3	-3.6	-2.8	-1.3	-1.1	-1.2
Turkey	-2.6	-0.8	-2.0	-0.7	-1.4	-2.0	-0.5	..	-2.5
Correlation with column (1)	**1.0**	**0.7**	**1.0**	**0.0**	**0.7**	**0.6**	**0.4**	**0.2**	**0.8**

Above average performers (Top-third) | About average performers (Mid-third) | Below average performers (Bottom-third)

Note: The role of economic development is accounted for by regressing each of the indicators of labour market performance on GDP per capita across OECD countries (excluding Luxembourg), retrieving and standardising residuals and, when necessary, multiplying by minus one so that positive values are associated with better performance. Countries are ordered in descending order by the employment rate. Dark blue stands for better performance, light blue for worse one. For details on variable definitions see Table .
Source: See Table .

StatLink http://dx.doi.org/10.1787/888933881116

Annex Table 3.A.4. Extended information on framework conditions for resilience and adaptability

	Resilience	Adaptability										
	Unemployment cost of a decline in GDP	Labour productivity growth		Ability of productive firms to attract workers		Wage-productivity decoupling		Adult skills: low-skilled adults	Student skills	Non-standard workers	Regional disparities	
	Average increase in unemployment rate over three years after a negative shock to GDP of 1% (pp)	Average annual labour productivity growth (%)		Cross-firm employment growth differential associated with 10 pp productivity differential (%)		Difference between annual real median wage growth and labour productivity growth (pp)		Share of adults with numeracy skills below level 2 in PIAAC (%)	Share of 15-year-olds not in secondary school or scoring below Level 2 in PISA (%)	Share of Own-account self-employed and temporary workers in total employment (%)	Coefficient of variation in regional unemployment rates (%)	
	2000-16	2000-16	2010-16	2003-13	2010-13	2000-13	2010-13	2012, 2015	2015	2013	2000	2016
OECD countries												
Iceland	0.1	1.5	1.4	..	..	..	..	..	28.8	20.6	15.0	22.3
Switzerland	0.4	0.4	-0.1	0.1	0.1	..	..	..	19.0	18.7	23.6	31.7
Sweden	0.3	1.3	0.9	0.2	0.3	0.4	1.9	14.7	25.9	19.0	30.9	12.2
New Zealand	0.4	0.7	0.9	..	..	0.3	-0.4	18.9	29.3	..	19.2	24.3
Japan	0.2	0.7	0.6	0.3	0.4	-0.5	0.5	8.1	15.4	20.2	18.6	13.9
Germany	0.4	0.6	0.7	0.8	0.9	-0.4	0.1	18.4	20.6	18.1	51.7	30.1
Norway	0.2	0.5	0.5	0.6	0.5	-0.5	0.0	14.6	24.3	11.8	20.5	16.7
United Kingdom	0.4	0.8	0.7	0.1	0.0	-0.2	-1.0	24.2	34.4	16.1	28.9	20.2
Denmark	0.6	0.6	0.8	0.1	0.2	0.1	0.8	14.2	23.1	13.6	13.0	6.6
Netherlands	0.4	0.7	0.8	1.1	0.3	-0.7	..	13.2	20.8	25.9	26.5	20.0
Czech Republic	0.3	2.1	1.2	..	..	0.3	0.3	12.9	26.8	21.2	42.9	36.2
Estonia	0.7	2.8	1.2	0.4	0.4	..	..	14.3	17.6	8.4	26.2	38.5
Canada	0.5	0.6	1.0	..	..	-0.6	-0.5	22.4	28.5	21.2	42.3	29.3
Australia	0.4	1.0	1.3	..	..	-1.0	0.9	20.1	29.3	32.1	39.7	46.0
Israel	0.6	0.7	0.8	..	..	-0.6	..	30.9	36.4	..	15.1	17.3
Austria	0.1	0.4	0.2	0.7	0.7	0.0	0.4	14.3	34.8	15.4	32.8	46.3
Finland	0.2	0.6	0.1	0.2	0.3	1.0	0.7	12.8	15.9	21.8	62.2	13.1
Latvia	0.8	3.9	2.5	0.5	0.3	..	..	..	30.2	..	23.6	40.7
United States	0.7	1.3	0.5	0.5	0.7	-1.5	-1.0	28.7	41.0	..	23.9	21.1
Hungary	0.3	1.7	0.1	0.4	0.3	-0.6	-0.3	..	35.5	15.9	34.8	43.9
Korea	0.2	2.5	1.3	0.3	0.5	-1.1	0.8	18.9	22.5	32.7	23.7	20.1
Portugal	0.3	0.8	0.3	0.2	0.3	0.5	-1.2	..	33.2	31.0	36.0	15.0
Luxembourg	0.1	0.0	0.3	0.1	0.0	..	..	..	35.0	11.9	..	..
France	0.4	0.6	0.6	0.3	0.4	0.7	0.9	28.0	30.4	20.8	35.7	17.2
Slovenia	0.3	1.0	0.9	0.2	0.1	..	..	25.8	22.2	18.6	22.7	15.9
Ireland	0.3	3.0	5.5	0.1	0.1	-1.1	-3.1	25.2	18.0	19.5	26.5	13.6
Slovak Republic	0.5	3.1	1.5	..	..	-0.8	0.5	13.8	35.5	22.3	41.6	38.5
Poland	0.6	2.7	2.3	0.2	0.5	-1.3	-2.0	23.5	24.7	37.4	20.0	24.8
Chile	0.3	1.4	1.2	..	..	..	..	61.9	59.6	..	31.3	25.2
Belgium	0.3	0.6	0.4	0.1	0.0	-0.3	0.9	13.4	25.7	16.9	54.8	56.1
Mexico	0.2	0.2	1.3	..	..	..	..	..	73.2	..	29.6	28.7
Spain	0.9	0.7	0.9	0.5	0.4	0.5	-0.6	30.6	29.3	32.1	35.9	28.9
Italy	0.5	-0.4	-0.4	0.4	0.3	1.0	-0.4	31.7	38.4	27.9	73.6	46.8
Greece	0.8	0.2	-1.0	0.2	0.6	1.4	-1.4	28.5	41.5	35.6	26.3	19.7
Turkey	0.2	2.6	2.6	..	..	..	..	50.2	66.0	30.2	42.0	50.3
Lithuania	0.5	4.2	2.0	..	..	..	..	17.4	32.7	..	13.1	29.6
OECD	**0.4**	**1.3**	**0.8**	**0.3**	**0.3**	**-0.2**	**-0.1**	**22.5**	**31.3**	**22.0**	**31.6**	**27.4**
Non-OECD countries												
Colombia	0.2	1.9	1.7	..	..	..	..	..	74.8	..	29.7	21.9
Costa Rica	0.6	2.1	2.7	..	..	..	..	..	76.2	..	..	..
Argentina	..	0.7	-0.3	..	..	..	..	..	75.9	..	..	..
Brazil	0.3	1.5	-0.2	..	..	..	..	..	79.0	..	33.7	33.6
China	0.0	2.1	2.0	..	..	..	..	..	46.2	..	53.9	..
India	..	6.5	5.6	..	..	..	..	..	..	..	..	..
Indonesia	..	3.6	3.8	..	..	..	..	..	78.6	..	..	..
Russian Federation	0.1	2.8	0.6	..	..	..	..	..	22.8	..	38.2	63.2
Saudi Arabia	..	-1.8	-2.7	..	..	..	..	..	..	..	..	..
South Africa	0.3	0.6	-0.3	..	..	..	..	..	..	..	14.0	20.0

Note: OECD unweighted average. Resilience: The indicator of labour market resilience measures the estimated average increase in the unemployment rate over the three years following a 1% decline in GDP. The indicator is obtained from estimating the following model: $U_{t+s} - U_{t-1} = \beta_0^s + \beta_1^s dlnGDPV_t + \beta_2^s dU_{t-1} + \beta_3^s dlnGDPV_{t-1} + \beta_4^s dU_{t-2} + \beta_5^s dlnGDPV_{t-2} + \sum_{j=1}^{s} \beta_4^j \, dlnGDP_{t+j} + \varepsilon_{t+s}$, where U_t is the unemployment rate, $GDPV_t$ is real GDP in period t and s indicates the number of periods after the GDP shock. The model is estimated separately for each country and each s, with the estimated β_1^s denoting the impulse-response function of unemployment to a 1% increase in GDP. The average change in unemployment is computed as the average of β_1^s over the three years following a 1% reduction in GDP. Data refer to the period 2000-16 for all countries. Labour productivity growth: Labour productivity is measured in per worker terms. Data refer to the period 2000-16 for all countries except Colombia (2001-16). Ability of productive firms to attract workers: The efficiency of labour re-allocation measures the elasticity of firm-level employment growth to lagged labour productivity. The baseline estimated equation is: $\Delta lnL_{i,j,c,t} = \sum_{c=1}^{26} \beta_c \, C_c lnLP_{i,j,c,t-1} + \theta x'_{i,j,c,t-1} + \gamma_{jct} + \varepsilon_{ijct}$, where $\Delta lnL_{i,j,t}$ denotes employment growth in firm i, industry j and country c; C_c are country dummies; $lnLP_{i,j,c,t-1}$ is labour productivity in gross output terms; $x_{i,j,t-1}$ are employment and age of the firm; and γ_{jct} are industry-country-year fixed effects to control for unobserved time-varying country-industry specific determinants of employment growth. The country-specific β_c parameters provide a measure of dynamic allocative efficiency. Data refer to the period 2003-13 for all countries except Portugal (2006-08) and Hungary (2009-13). To control for effects of the business cycle on the efficiency of labour re-allocation, over the sample period 2003-2013 the baseline specification is augmented with an interaction term of lagged labour productivity with a dummy variable taking the value 1 if the lagged change in the output gap is below 0. Countries omitted from the table do not have sufficient coverage of firms in the ORBIS dataset. Wage-productivity decoupling: The indicator of decoupling measures the percentage point difference between real median wage growth and labour productivity growth. Using the notation $\Delta\% \, X$ to denote the per cent growth rate of X, macro-level decoupling is defined as follows: $Decoupling \equiv \Delta\% \left(\frac{W^{med}}{P^Y}\right) - \Delta\% \left(\frac{Y/P^Y}{L}\right)$, where W^{med} denotes the nominal median wage, Y denotes nominal value added, P^Y denotes the value added price and L denotes hours worked. Data refer to the period 2000-13 for all countries except Australia, Canada, France, Italy New Zealand, Poland, Spain and Sweden (2000-12); Greece and Portugal (2004-13); Israel (2001-11); the Slovak Republic (2001-12). Low skills adults: Data refer to 2012 for all countries except Chile, Greece, Israel, Lithuania, New Zealand, Slovenia, Turkey and Jakarta (Indonesia). Data for Belgium refer to Flanders; data for the United Kingdom are the weighted average (2/3 and 1/3) of the data for England and the Northern Ireland; data for Indonesia refer to Jakarta. Low-performing students in mathematics: Data for China refer to Beijing-Shanghai-Jiangsu-Guangdong. Argentina: Coverage is too small to guarantee comparability. Non-standard workers: Workers on temporary contracts and self-employed (own account) workers aged 15-64, excluding employers, student workers and apprentices. Regional disparities: Data refer to the Territorial Level 2 (TL2) classification except for Australia, Estonia, Latvia and Lithuania (TL3), and to 2000 and 2016 except for Denmark (2007, 2016); Estonia, Chile, Israel., Mexico and the Russian Federation (2000, 2014); Spain (2002, 2014); Latvia and Lithuania (2000, 2015); Slovenia (2001, 2016); Turkey (2004, 2016); Brazil (2004, 2013); China (2008); Colombia (2001, 2014) and South Africa (2008, 2014).

Source: Resilience: OECD calculations based on OECD (2017[6]), *OECD Employment Outlook 2017*, http://dx.doi.org/10.1787/empl_outlook-2017-en; Labour productivity growth: *OECD Economic Outlook Database* and WEO-IMF; Wage-productivity decoupling: OECD calculations based on *OECD National Accounts Database* and *OECD Earnings Database*; Ability of productive firms to attract workers: OECD calculations based on the 2013 ORBIS vintage; Low-skilled adults: OECD (2016[7]), *Skills Matter: Further Results from the Survey of Adult Skills*, http://dx.doi.org/10.1787/9789264258051-en; Low-performing students in mathematics: OECD (2016[8]), *PISA 2015 Results (Volume I): Excellence and Equity in Education*, http://dx.doi.org/10.1787/9789264266490-en; Non-standard workers: OECD (2015[9]), *In It Together - Why Less Inequality Benefits All*, http://dx.doi.org/10.1787/9789264232662-en; Regional disparities: OECD (2018), *OECD Regional Statistics Database*, https://dx.doi.org/10.1787/region-data-en.

StatLink http://dx.doi.org/10.1787/888933881135

Chapter 4. Policies and institutions to enhance labour market performance

This chapter provides an overview of the role of policies and institutions for good labour market performance. The discussion is organised according to the three principal dimensions of the new Jobs Strategy framework: i) job quantity and quality; ii) labour market inclusiveness; and iii) resilience and adaptability. A more detailed discussion and the supporting evidence are presented in Parts II to IV of this Volume.

Introduction

Combining good labour market performance in terms of employment with good levels of job quality and inclusiveness is very important, but it is straightforward. A pre-condition for good performance along these dimensions is that labour markets are resilient (i.e. they limit employment losses during downturns and ensure a rapid rebound after economic shocks) and adapt to the challenges and opportunities resulting from mega-trends, such as rapid technological developments, globalisation and demographic change. It is also essential that policies and institutions are coherent so that the promotion of better outcomes along one specific dimension does not undermine other economic and labour market outcomes. A whole-of-government approach is therefore crucial.

This chapter provides an overview of the role played by policies and institutions in good labour market performance. The discussion is organised according to the three principal dimensions of the Jobs Strategy framework: i) job quantity and quality; ii) labour market inclusiveness; and iii) resilience and adaptability. In general, the discussion takes into account the broad impact of policy levers along different dimensions to avoid a fragmented approach and the drawing of misleading conclusions. A more detailed discussion along with the supporting evidence are presented in Parts II to IV of this Volume.

The remainder of the chapter is organised as follows. Section 4.1 discusses the roles of productivity growth, the broad sharing of productivity gains and access to work for in increasing the quantity and quality of jobs. Section 4.2 analyses policies to promote labour market inclusiveness, including policies aimed at weakening the link between socio-economic background and labour market success, policies to promote opportunities for career progression and tax and benefit policies. Section 4.3 discusses how policies and institutions can promote resilience and adaptability to ensure that labour markets are able to absorb and adjust to economic shocks and structural change and make the most any resulting opportunities.

4.1. Raising the quantity and the quality of jobs

This section discusses the role of policies and institutions for raising the quantity and quality of jobs by placing particular emphasis on how synergies between these two outcomes can be achieved while mitigating possible trade-offs. It first discusses the role of policies and institutions for creating an environment in which quality jobs can flourish. It then switches to the supply side of the labour market by discussing policies and institutions that enhance the effective supply of labour and job quality by making work more accessible, attractive and sustainable.

Promote an environment in which high quality jobs can thrive

Good labour market performance in terms of both job quantity and job quality requires that labour demand is sufficiently strong to ensure that enough good quality jobs are available for everyone who wants to work. This can be achieved by fostering skills and productivity, while ensuring that the gains from productivity growth are broadly shared with workers and non-wage labour costs are kept down.

Better and well-matched skills are key for both job quantity and job quality

Policies should ensure that workers are equipped with the right skills to thrive in the labour market. Individuals with the right skills are more likely to be employed and, when in employment, tend to have better jobs. A skilled workforce also makes it easier to innovate and adopt new technologies and work organisation practices, thereby boosting productivity and growth. To ensure that the skills acquired through the education and training system correspond to labour market needs, and hence avoid major issues with poor school-to-work transitions and skill mismatch (including shortages), it is important to develop stronger links between the world of education and training on the one hand and the world of work on the other. This can be achieved inter alia by promoting work based learning, the involvement of social partners in the development and delivery of curricula that match market needs, and by cost-sharing in skills funding. The relevance of skills formation can also be improved by having in place robust systems and tools for assessing and anticipating skills needs, combined with effective mechanisms and procedures that ensure that such information feeds into policy-making as well as into lifelong guidance and the design of education and training programmes. Skills policies should also account for regional variations in the supply and demand for skills. This requires close collaboration between employers and the education sector at the regional and local levels.

Promote worker productivity within firms and through the effective reallocation of resources across firms

Productivity growth is the main driving force of higher wages and incomes, and hence rising living standards. Good wages and working conditions, in turn, can promote productivity growth as they enhance motivation, worker effort, skills use and incentives for learning and innovation. A positive dynamic between the performance of labour markets and that of the economy as a whole requires policies that provide sufficient flexibility to allow for the efficient reallocation of workers across firms and sectors along with policies that promote the conditions for learning and innovation in the workplace. In emerging economies, a major challenge is also to design policies and institutions that address the problem of widespread labour informality, as this is associated with both low productivity and poor job quality outcomes (see Box 4.1).

Providing good working conditions and opportunities for career development can foster learning and innovation in the workplace. Good working conditions and opportunities for career development are not only important for employee well-being directly, but can also contribute to productivity by strengthening the commitment of workers to their firm, reduce excessive worker turnover, promote the use of skills in the workplace and strengthen the incentives of firms and workers to invest in training and skill acquisition. Firms therefore often have a strong interest in providing good working conditions since this provides long-term gains in terms of higher productivity and profitability. In practice, the combination of good working conditions with high performance is often associated with the presence of high-quality management and so-called High-Performance Work Practices (HPWP), which tend to emphasise the importance of team work, autonomy, task discretion, mentoring, job rotation and the use of new tools and technologies. The adoption of HPWP depends to an important extent on the production technology of firms, and particularly the importance of skills, but also their size since this determines in large part the resources that firms have at their disposal to implement such practices.

A sound regulatory framework combined with effective social dialogue and targeted information services can help support the conditions for learning and innovation in the workplace. A sound regulatory framework includes adequate standards for working conditions based on occupational health and safety regulations to reduce physical and mental health risks. It also includes working time regulations that limit excessive working hours and the use of night shifts, while establishing the right to rest breaks and paid leave. There also needs to be balanced employment protection provisions that protect workers against possible abuses but which do not prevent required job reallocation. It may also include a minimum wage set at a level that avoids pricing low-wage workers out of jobs. Well-functioning collective bargaining institutions, particularly when associated with high coverage, can also be useful. They allow for more differentiation in terms of wages and working conditions than statutory rules, can foster skills development and skills use in the workplace, and allow for the effective dissemination of good working practices. Finally, governments can indirectly promote high-performance management and working practices through information dissemination and advice on best-practice, as well as facilitating access to management training.

The efficient reallocation of resources depends on the flexibility of firms and the mobility of workers. This includes the ease with which entrepreneurs can start or liquidate a business, firms adjust their workforce in response to changing business conditions and workers move across firms and places in search of better matches for their skills and ambitions to enhance their career opportunities. The efficiency of reallocation is to an important extent determined by the functioning and regulation of financial, housing and product markets, including through policies that affect entry and exit of firms. Labour market policies and institutions also play an important role by determining the flexibility with which firms can adjust their workforces (e.g. employment protection) and the ease with which workers can move across firms. The latter depends to an important extent on the transferability of skills and the portability of benefits, availability of effective employment services and active labour market programmes to facilitate job transitions. Worker mobility also depends on wage incentives for workers to move from low to high-productivity firms, highlighting the importance of allowing sufficient scope to adjust wages to business conditions at the firm level, especially in countries where collective bargaining predominantly takes places at the sector or national level.

Employment protection legislation plays a key role in preventing abuses and avoiding inefficient dismissals but excessive and/or uncertain termination costs hinder efficient labour reallocation. Regulations concerning dismissal and termination of contracts are designed to protect workers against unfair hiring and firing practices and can reduce excessive turnover by preserving worker-firm matches that are viable in the longer term by making firms take account of the social cost in their dismissal decisions (i.e. the social and budgetary consequences of greater joblessness). Regulations that limit the gap in protection between workers on open-ended and fixed-term contracts can further reduce excessive turnover by preventing an undue reliance on temporary contracts. This is likely to spur learning and innovation in the workplace by strengthening incentives for investment in firm-specific human capital. However, excessively high and uncertain termination costs discourage hiring on open-ended contracts and hinder efficient resource reallocation and skill matching, thereby affecting productivity growth and efficiency. In addition, large statutory disparities in termination costs by type of contract trigger differences in job security and generate persistent divides between non-regular and regular workers, in particular because restrictive definitions of fair termination cannot be effectively applied to non-regular workers. This suggests that a narrow definition of unfair dismissal that focuses on false reasons, reasons unrelated to work, discrimination and prohibited grounds should be used. Predictable advance notice, ordinary severance pay and layoff taxes - whose level might depend on the reason for dismissal – can be used to avoid inefficient dismissals and compensate workers for involuntary separations that are not related to their performance.

Box 4.1. Reducing the incidence of low-quality jobs by curbing informality

The high incidence of informality in the labour market is one of the most salient features of labour markets in many emerging economies. Informal jobs are typically characterised by lower levels of productivity, partly as a consequence of lower investment in human capital, worse management practices and credit constraints. They also tend to be of much lower quality than formal jobs and reduce labour market inclusiveness. Promoting quality jobs and increasing labour productivity in emerging economies requires effective action in several areas:

- *Firms and workers need to clearly see the benefits of formalisation.* Governments should improve the quality of the public services they deliver and, where appropriate, strengthen the link between contributions and benefits in social insurance schemes.
- *The costs of formality should be lowered for employers and the self-employed.* Simplified tax and administrative systems, streamlined registration processes and a reduction in red tape are crucial steps in the right direction.
- *Enforcement methods should be improved.* The labour inspectorate should be given sufficient resources and labour inspectors should be adequately qualified. Importantly, enforcement should be transparent and strict, but not be overly harsh, to avoid worsening the situation of vulnerable workers even further.
- *Skills development should be promoted.* By raising the productivity of workers, skills can compensate for the higher cost of formal jobs and enhance access to formal-sector employment.

Ensure that productivity gains are shared with workers, particularly those with low skills

Real wages are the most direct mechanism for transmitting the benefits of productivity growth to workers and their families. Over the past two decades, however, real median wage growth in most OECD countries has decoupled from aggregate labour productivity growth. This reflects both declines in labour shares (decoupling of average wages from productivity) and increases in wage inequality (decoupling of median wages from average wages). Productivity gains no longer appear to translate into broadly shared wage gains for all workers.

The decoupling of real median wages from productivity partly reflects global megatrends, but large cross-country heterogeneity in decoupling suggests that national policies and institutions also matter. The evidence suggests that capital-enhancing technological change and the rise of global value chains have contributed to this decoupling by reducing labour shares (decoupling or real average wages from productivity) and raising wage inequality (decoupling of median wages from average wages). However, the evidence also suggests that national policies in the areas of skills, product markets and labour markets are not only key to raising productivity but can also ensure that the dividend from higher productivity is broadly shared. Skills policies can support the broader sharing of productivity gains by limiting capital-labour substitution in response to global megatrends while pro-competitive product market policies limit the size of product market rents appropriated by capital. Labour market policies and institutions can support a fairer sharing of productivity gains both by affecting the relative cost of labour – and thereby the degree to which capital is substituted for some types of labour – and by influencing the distribution of product market rents.

A statutory minimum wage can help ensure that workers at the bottom of the wage ladder also benefit from growing economic prosperity, particularly in the absence of encompassing collectively agreed wage floors. The latter can be considered a functional equivalent of a minimum wage set by law insofar as most, if not all, workers, especially the weakest ones, are covered by them. Nevertheless, several OECD countries complement collective wage agreements with a statutory minimum wage. When minimum wages are moderate and well designed, adverse employment effects can be avoided. The following principles can help to enhance the design of minimum wage systems. First, make minimum wages pay while avoiding that they price low-skilled workers out of jobs by carefully considering their interactions with the tax-benefit system. For example, by reducing social security contributions around the minimum wage, it is possible to enhance the effectiveness of the minimum wage as a tool to reduce low pay and fight poverty while limiting the rise in labour costs for employers. Second, ensure that minimum wages are revised regularly, based on accurate, up-to-date and impartial information and advice that carefully considers current labour market conditions and the views of social partners and experts (e.g. independent commissions). Third, allow minimum wages to vary by group (if differences in productivity or employment barriers between groups are large) and/or by region (if differences in economic conditions are large). Fourth, improve coverage of, and compliance with, minimum wage legislation.

Collective bargaining institutions and social dialogue can help promote a broad sharing of productivity gains, including with those at the bottom of the job ladder, provide voice to workers and endow employers and employees with a tool for addressing common challenges. To promote good quality jobs for all in a changing world of work, collective bargaining systems have to have wide coverage, while providing sufficient flexibility to firms.

The best way of ensuring the inclusiveness of collective bargaining is by having well-organised social partners based on broad memberships. This allows social dialogue to be widespread at the firm-level among worker organisations and employers and to be based on representative social partners at higher levels (e.g. sector, country). To extend social dialogue to all segments of the economy, including small firms and non-standard forms of employment, governments should put in place a legal framework that promotes social dialogue in large and small firms alike and allows labour relations to adapt to emerging challenges. In the absence of broad-based social partners, another way of promoting the inclusiveness of collective bargaining is through the use of administrative extensions that extend the coverage of collective agreements beyond the members of the signatory unions and employer organisations to all workers and firms in a sector. To avoid that extensions harm the economic prospects of start-ups, small firms or vulnerable workers, it is important that the parties negotiating the agreements represent the collective interest of all groups of firms and workers. This can be achieved by subjecting extension requests to reasonable representativeness criteria, a meaningful test of public interest and providing well-defined procedures for exemptions and opt-outs of firms in case of economic hardship.

Collective bargaining systems characterised by predominantly sector-level bargaining need to allow for sufficient economic flexibility at the firm and country levels. The introduction of flexibility in predominantly sector-level systems has often been considered as requiring a shift from sector to firm-level bargaining. While such a shift would indeed provide more flexibility to firms, it is also likely to induce a decline in bargaining coverage, undermining the inclusiveness of the system. Experience in a number of OECD countries has shown that less radical options are also available, based on the use of controlled opt-outs or sectoral framework agreements that explicitly leave space for further adaptation at the firm or individual level. In principle, these instruments preserve the integrity of sector-level bargaining, while at the same time enabling a closer link between productivity and working conditions at the firm-level. However, their effectiveness in providing additional flexibility for firms largely depends to an important extent on having high levels of collective worker representation across firms. Flexibility with respect to macroeconomic conditions can be fostered through the effective coordination of bargaining outcomes across bargaining units (e.g. industries or firms). Recent OECD analysis suggests that coordination can promote better labour market outcomes by providing more flexibility with respect to macroeconomic conditions (see Chapters 8 and 13 of this Volume). Effective coordination can be achieved through *peak-level bargaining* based on the presence of national confederations of unions and employers that provide guidance to bargaining parties at lower levels. Another possibility is *pattern bargaining* where a leading sector sets the targets - usually the manufacturing sector exposed to international trade - and others follow.

Collective bargaining systems differ widely across countries in terms of their coverage, the flexibility that they provide to firms and their specific institutional set-up and these differences tend to be deeply rooted in the sociocultural fabric of countries. National traditions in collective bargaining are important. Yet, this does not imply that collective bargaining systems cannot and should not adapt to a changing economic context. Indeed, one of the most salient features of successful collective bargaining systems may be their ability to adapt gradually to changing economic conditions within their national industrial-relations tradition. This depends crucially on the quality of industrial relations, but also on a government that provides space for collective bargaining and social dialogue, while setting the boundaries.

Promote job quantity and job quality by keeping non-wage labour costs down

Labour taxes in the form of personal income taxes and social security contributions represent a key source of revenue to governments, but can have an adverse impact on employment, earnings and inclusiveness if excessively high. On average across the OECD, labour taxation accounts for about one third of labour costs.

Changes in the composition of labour taxation that broaden the tax base and increase tax progressivity can contribute to better labour market performance. This could for example take the form of a partial shift away from social security contributions towards personal income taxes, when there is already a weak link between individual contributions and entitlements (e.g. health insurance, family allowances). A partial shift to personal income taxes would reduce the burden of taxation on labour by broadening the tax base since the application of personal income taxes is not limited to labour earnings from dependent employees. It would further reduce differences in fiscal treatment based on labour market status and income source, thereby weakening possible unintended tax incentives for self-employment or employment in the informal sector. If personal incomes taxes are more progressive than social security contributions, as is typically the case, this is likely to increase the overall progressivity of labour taxation, with beneficial implications for inclusiveness. Moreover, in contrast to social security contributions, personal income tax systems in many countries have credits or deductions that make effective rates close to zero or even negative at low income levels, which could benefit employment as well. Such a move also has the potential to strengthen the effectiveness of other policy instruments. For example, a partial shift to personal income taxes could help make the statutory minimum wage more effective in supporting pay for low-productivity workers (job quality), while mitigating any potential adverse effects on employment (job quantity). A similar argument applies to collectively agreed wage floors.[1]

Reducing the overall burden of labour taxation by switching to taxes that weigh less directly on labour can promote employment and take-home pay. One example could be real estate taxes. This would not only be efficient, given the immobile nature of real estate, but also promote inclusiveness since low income households tend to own less property than higher income and more wealthy households. There are also arguments for strengthening the taxation of capital income at the individual level and increasing the reliance on consumption and environmental taxes.

Building secure labour markets by protecting workers and removing barriers to work

Since high-quality job creation and strong productivity growth require a sufficiently flexible labour market, which exposes workers to the risk of job loss, good labour market performance also requires building secure labour markets by providing workers with income support in the event of job loss and removing barriers to work. More generally, high-quality job creation needs to be combined with measures to support an effective labour supply by ensuring that work is accessible, attractive and sustainable.

Effective safety nets against labour market shocks improve job quality

Effective social safety nets alleviate concerns about job security among the employed, with important consequences for worker well-being. Moreover, adequate unemployment insurance and other social benefits – including sickness, disability, lone parent and social assistance benefits – enhance job quality by effectively insuring workers against individual labour market shocks (such as job loss) and smoothing consumption between joblessness and employment spells. While moderate employment protection also has a role to play unemployment insurance coupled with effective re-employment support is generally more effective in providing security to workers. Moderate layoff taxes or some degree of experience rating of employer contributions to finance active and passive labour market policies can then be used to provide employers' with incentives to reduce the use of layoffs and take greater responsibility for the social cost of unemployment, sickness and disability (in terms of greater public spending, lower tax revenues, loss of human capital, health consequences, etc.). However, care should be taken not to unduly penalise certain types of firms and workers and to minimise any unintended consequences on the hiring and firing behaviour of firms, for example by introducing exemptions for employers hiring sick, disabled or long-term unemployed workers.

Adequate safety nets should be accompanied by complementary policies to minimise work disincentives and promote effective job search. In most advanced economies, adequate safety nets consist of multiple layers, including: i) unemployment insurance benefits for those who meet certain minimum contribution requirements; and ii) universal but modest unemployment and social assistance benefits that are available to all non-employed persons subject to a means test. Yet, benefits should be accompanied by strong incentives for effective job search to avoid the risk of benefit dependence and thus increased joblessness and higher costs for the public purse. Mutual obligation principles supported by effective employment services, including job-search assistance and skill development opportunities, active programmes and strictly-enforced job-search requirements are key.

In emerging economies, the provision of effective social safety nets is particularly challenging due to the presence of widespread informal employment (see Box 4.1). In the case of unemployment insurance, for example, the requirement of not being in formal employment for receiving benefits provides potentially strong incentives for working informally while receiving benefits. Moreover, workers who do not perceive the potential benefits of social insurance may "opt out" by taking up informal employment. This can be detrimental to workers' well-being in the longer term and undermines economic growth and the financial sustainability of social protection systems. To address both issues a number of emerging economies have introduced mandatory self-insurance schemes based on individual savings accounts for unemployment, while ensuring that some form of income support is available to those with insufficient savings. In principle, such a system could also be used to provide unemployment insurance to self-employed workers.

In order to strengthen incentives to work, employability and opportunities, a comprehensive activation strategy is needed...

An effective activation strategy must deal with all barriers to employment through the coordination of a range of policies and services. Jobless persons and individuals marginally attached to the labour market often face multiple barriers to labour force participation and quality employment. Some of these may result from the effect of ill-designed benefit schemes on recipients' incentives to engage in active job search. However, jobless persons and individuals marginally attached to the labour market typically face other barriers that can cause them to refrain from actively seeking work and/or prevent them from finding suitable jobs. These barriers are particularly important for a number of groups – including older workers, mothers with young children, discouraged workers and people with disabilities. Therefore, raising labour force participation and improving employment performance – in terms of both job quantity and job quality – require a comprehensive activation strategy that makes work more accessible. This means addressing the different barriers to employment through the coordination, at both national and regional levels, of employment, health and social services, the administration of active labour market programmes and the design of tax and benefits policies. An effective activation strategy must combine measures to ensure that jobless people have the motivation to search actively and accept suitable jobs (e.g. through appropriate tax and benefit incentives) with actions to expand opportunities (e.g. job-search assistance, direct referrals, subsidised employment) and interventions to increase the employability of the least employable (e.g. training and work-experience programmes).

Efficient employment services and active labour market programmes are crucial for the success of such an activation strategy. For harder-to-place workers, the provision of these services may require intensive counselling and skilled case managers, the effectiveness of which is typically enhanced by a low client-to-staff caseload ratio. In order to cope with scarce resources, effective profiling tools must therefore be used sufficiently early in the jobless spell as a way to efficiently allocate jobseekers to less or more intensive service streams. It is also important to ensure that local employment offices have sufficient local labour market expertise to effectively place people into jobs. Private providers could play a useful supporting role to improve the delivery and targeting of employment services or alleviate capacity constraints, conditional on adequate performance management. Moreover, active programmes must be rigorously evaluated and ineffective ones must be swiftly terminated.

... which combines active policies with appropriate taxes and transfers by enforcing a system of "mutual obligations"

Employment services and active labour market programmes must be combined with tax and transfer policies. Effective activation needs to be accompanied by moderately generous and high coverage unemployment and social-assistance benefit systems. There are two reasons for this. First, where effective monitoring and sanction systems are in place within a "mutual-obligations" framework – in which governments have the duty to provide jobseekers with benefits and effective services to enable them to find work and, in turn, beneficiaries have to take active steps to find work or improve their employability – the threat of potential sanctions in terms of benefit withdrawal significantly increases the financial incentive for seeking and taking up gainful employment as well as seriously participating in active programmes.[2] Second, unemployment and social-assistance benefits provide the principal instrument for linking jobless people to employment services and active labour market programmes. Within a "mutual obligations" framework, benefit recipients are referred to employment services, which provide job-search assistance or, depending on the unemployed person's profile, direct them towards more intensive programmes, while monitoring their job-search effort or rehabilitation progress. By contrast, in the absence of unemployment and social assistance benefits, it is often difficult to reach out to those facing multiple barriers to employment, who risk being left behind. While moderately generous and comprehensive social benefits strengthen the effectiveness of activation policies, in the absence of effective active labour market policies, there is a risk that such benefits reduce work incentives and deepen labour market exclusion. Passive and active policies should therefore be conceived together rather than in isolation.

Well-targeted, permanent in-work benefits can be effective to make work pay. Combined with active policies and social safety nets, well-targeted, permanent in-work benefits can be effective to set up the right incentives for low-pay workers to both work and climb the earnings ladder, while supporting the living standards of low-income families. Yet, incentives must be properly understood by potential recipients, implying that simple and transparent in-work benefit systems are typically more effective. Since these schemes tend to exert downward pressure on wages, their effectiveness can be enhanced by combining them with binding wage floors that are set at an appropriate, not-too-high level. Finally, in-work benefit schemes are more effective if combined with individual-based taxation, since family-based tax systems often create an important work disincentive for second earners. Since second earners are often women, this has a tendency to further reinforce existing gender inequalities in the labour market.

Enhance the sustainability of work by providing good-quality, productive and healthy work environments

A comprehensive activation approach also implies making work sustainable over the life-cycle through policies that enhance the quality of the work environment. A healthy working environment can be promoted through policies preventing and addressing work-related health and safety risks. While work-related physical hazards are often well-addressed by existing policies in most advanced economies, they remain a source of concern in many emerging economies. Moreover, health and safety legislation and incentives have been slow in most OECD countries in recognising that physical health risks are on the decline and mental health risks are rising fast: psychosocial expertise is limited in labour inspectorates and equally so in occupational health services, where such services exist. As emphasised in the OECD Recommendation of the Council on Integrated Mental Health, Skills and Work Policy (OECD, 2015$_{[11]}$), mental health risks can be minimised over the life-cycle through a comprehensive approach. This involves: the implementation and enforcement of rigorous legislation for psycho-social risk assessment and risk prevention; the introduction of appropriate financial incentives to promote high-performance work organisation and management practices that reduce the risk that work impairs one's health; and more effective leverage of market incentives by making the business case for models of work organisation and management practices that result in better working conditions.[3] The involvement of the social partners is crucial to ensure the effective implementation of incentives, regulation and guidelines. Initiatives to improve the quality of the work environment will also help people to prolong their working lives, which is particularly important in the context of rapid population ageing.

4.2. Promoting labour market inclusiveness

High levels of inequality can undermine social cohesion by reducing trust in institutions and can also become an obstacle to economic growth and well-being, including by undermining the ability of the less well-off to invest adequately in their children's human capital. However, high inequality in income and opportunities is not inevitable and indeed, despite a widespread increase, there remain large differences across countries. Governments have a range of instruments at their disposal that can be used to tackle inequality or promote equal opportunities. The way they choose to address these challenges depends on the national context, including societal values regarding the importance of solidarity, redistribution and equality. Consistent with the OECD *Inclusive Growth initiative and framework*, this section discusses the key policy choices to address inequality by fostering the inclusiveness of the labour market, while also considering their implications for economic growth. Particular emphasis is given to policies that can enhance the position of low-income earners and their families. This not only reflects social concerns associated with low incomes, but also the recognition that low incomes typically result from a number of specific labour market challenges. Addressing these problems not only increases inclusiveness and social cohesion but can also promote economic growth.

Promote equal opportunities

The depth and persistence of economic inequalities reflect the degree of social mobility across generations as well as over the life-course. Low social mobility reflects the importance of people's socio-economic background for the way they enter the labour market (inter-generational mobility) and the presence of different barriers to career development once in the labour market (intra-generational mobility). Tackling deep and persistent inequalities therefore requires policies that provide access to quality education, health and labour market opportunities for disadvantaged people.

Foster social mobility between generations

The importance of socio-economic background for future labour market performance derives largely from the difficulty that individuals from poor socio-economic backgrounds and/or poor neighbourhoods have in acquiring solid labour market skills. This is also a key channel through which high income inequality can lower economic growth. By opening new opportunities, social mobility can also strengthen incentives for innovation and entrepreneurship, reinforcing its potential impact on economic growth.

Public investments to improve the educational outcomes of those from lower socio-economic backgrounds are key for promoting social mobility. The evidence suggests that early interventions are the most cost-effective, such as improving the access to high quality pre-school programs for children from disadvantaged backgrounds. But measures targeting older students are also needed, such as reducing early school leaving. This requires effective mechanisms for the early detection of youth at risk of dropping out, combined with remedial education interventions. Governments can reduce school failure and dropout by eliminating system-level practices that undermine equity, such as grade repetition and early tracking, by ensuring that school choice does not exacerbate economic or spatial inequities, and by designing alternative upper secondary education pathways to ensure that students complete their education. For individuals who leave education with very low levels of skills, second-chance options for education can provide a way out of a low-skills/poor-economic-outcome trap. Countries should also ensure equal access to post-secondary education. Funding mechanisms can be instrumental in mitigating inequities, particularly after compulsory education, by ensuring that financial considerations are not a barrier to skills development.

Reforms in the tax and benefits system can also help reduce the role of socio-economic background on the educational and health outcomes of children. Cash transfers or tax rebates targeted at poor households or households with children (such as family or child benefits/allowances) can improve the future labour market outcomes of their children. To increase their effectiveness, receipt of these benefits can be made conditional on the behaviour of beneficiaries with respect to education (e.g. school attendance) and health (e.g. medical check-ups), as in the conditional cash transfer (CCTs) programmes developed in many emerging economies as well as some advanced economies. To make conditional cash transfers work, it is important that they are combined with investments in the quality of education and health.

Enhance upward mobility and career development over the life-course

More must be done to help youth make a good start in the labour market, avoiding poor careers characterised by intermittent spells of low-paid work and unemployment. The OECD Action Plan for Youth recommends a set of measures to tackle high youth unemployment, including: strengthening the education system and preparing all young people for the world of work; encouraging employers to expand work-based and work integrated learning programmes (including quality apprenticeships or internship programmes); expanding active labour market strategies to enhance employability and job opportunities; and removing barriers to stable and rewarding work. Governments should also ensure that the cost of hiring youth reflects their productivity through the use of wage-subsidies, the design of non-wage labour costs or a sub-minimum wage. There should also be strong incentives for employers to convert temporary contracts into open ended ones so that they provide a useful stepping stone into more stable employment rather than become a dead end to career progression.

Workers should also be provided with opportunities to develop, maintain and upgrade their skills at all ages to reduce the risk of becoming trapped in low-quality jobs and joblessness, as well as to be able to respond to the rapidly changing demand for skills in existing and new jobs. While there are significant benefits from investing in adult learning for firms and individuals, there are various reasons why such investments tend to be sub-optimal in practice in many countries – particularly among the low-skilled and the disadvantaged, as well as in small and medium-sized enterprises. The lowest skilled are only a third as likely as the highest skilled to participate in adult education and training in most OECD countries. Governments at the national and the local levels, therefore, play a critical role in helping individuals and firms overcome these barriers. Specifically, policies should focus on: i) increasing and promoting the benefits of adult learning (e.g. by strengthening the recognition of acquired skills during the working life and not just those during the training programme); ii) helping individuals and firms overcome any financial constraints they might face (e.g. by offering co-financing arrangements) as well as non-financial constraints (e.g. through flexible provision); iii) helping individuals make good vocational education and training choices by providing high-quality information, advice and guidance; and iv) fostering stronger business-education partnerships which ensure that training programmes are well aligned with the needs of employers. Such efforts should focus in particular on the least-skilled as well as SME's. The social partners also have an important role to play in fostering greater participation in training of under-represented groups.

Good working conditions are essential for long, productive and healthy working lives. Working conditions must not impinge negatively on workers' health, and work organisation should adapt to workers' strengths and needs, making the most of a diverse workforce, including age and gender diversity (see Box 4.2). For example, this means taking into account how specific obligations in terms of family commitments vary across working lives and individual situations, and individual differences across workers in terms of maturity, experience and aptitude to carry out more physically and mentally demanding work. A working environment that is conducive to career development, work-life balance and good physical and mental health will help avoid that difficulties cumulate over the working life. Indeed, health problems and the difficulty of combining work and family life are among the main reasons for withdrawing from the labour force, especially for older workers and women. While working conditions and work organisation are primarily determined by employers, often together with trade unions or other forms of worker representation, policies and institutions can provide employers with incentives and tools to improve them.

Box 4.2. Reducing gender inequalities in the labour market

Gender inequality is not only bad for labour market inclusiveness, it also harms economic performance. OECD analysis has shown that if the proportion of households with a working woman had remained at around 1990 levels, income inequality on average in the OECD – measured in terms of the Gini coefficient – would have been almost 1 percentage point higher than it is now. Similarly, if the share of women working full-time and the gender pay gap had remained constant at their 1990 levels, this would have added another percentage point to income inequality. Enhanced educational outcomes for women, increased female labour force participation, and improved opportunities for career development for women also contribute to better economic performance and higher living standards. Despite significant progress, important gender gaps remain. As emphasised by the Recommendation of the Council on Gender Equality in Public Life (OECD, 2015[21]), Recommendation of the Council on Gender Equality in Education, Employment and Entrepreneurship (OECD, 2013[31]), countries must step up their efforts to ensure that public policy truly reflects inclusive labour markets in which both men and women can reach their full potential.

- Gender stereotyping needs to be addressed in educational choices at school from a young age since it has important implications for education and career choice of girls. As a result, girls are still much less likely to study in STEM areas (science, technology, engineering and mathematics) and women are less likely to be employed in, typically high-paid, occupations using STEM skills. Career guidance initiatives and information campaigns to promote gender equality in STEM areas should focus on parents, teachers and students.
- Measures supporting the reconciliation of work and family life are critical for men and women to participate in the labour market on an equal footing. The difficulty of combining work and family responsibilities very often results in women working part-time or dropping out of the labour force altogether. Policies that can help parents with young children include parental leave, childcare, out-of-school-hours care and flexible working arrangements. A better sharing of parental care can be achieved by instituting leave arrangements for the exclusive use of fathers, or provide "bonus" months when couples share leave entitlements.
- While working part-time facilitates the combination of work and family responsibilities, it can come at a cost to long-term career and earnings prospects. This also contributes to the glass ceiling that women face in getting through to the top of their professions. To increase women's representation in decision-making positions, countries have introduced mandatory quotas, target-setting, disclosure initiatives and monitoring processes.
- Female entrepreneurship can be promoted by reducing gender gaps in access to finance and entrepreneurial skills and networks and skills through, for example, entrepreneurship training, coaching and mentoring programmes.
- Gender gaps in labour market performance tend to be larger in most emerging economies than in the OECD average. In these countries, additional policy challenges for reducing gender gaps in labour market performance are closing remaining gaps in education, facilitating access to credit for women, fighting labour market discrimination and curbing informal employment.

Promote more equal outcomes without undermining employment and growth

More equal opportunities lead to more equal outcomes, but more equal outcomes also lead to more equal opportunities by levelling the playing field. Indeed, it is the feedback effect of inequality in outcomes to inequality in education and health that is driving a negative relationship between inequality and economic growth. As a result, there is a strong argument for policies that seek to reduce inequality in outcomes directly, provided they do not unduly undermine incentives to invest in skills, work and entrepreneurship. Apart from the role of education and skills, which already has been discussed above, this mainly concerns the tax-benefit system and, to a more limited extent, wage-setting policies.

Appropriately designed wage-setting institutions can be part of a broader strategy to reduce poverty and labour market exclusion

Wage-setting policies in the form of statutory minimum wages or collective wage bargaining reduce wage inequality, but their effectiveness in reducing poverty is likely to be modest. While in-work poverty is associated with low wage levels, a substantial number of minimum-wage workers live in households with incomes above the poverty line and a number of poor people have earnings above the minimum wage but live in relatively large households without other earners. However, a moderate minimum wage can help to enhance the effectiveness of in-work benefits, designed to tackle low in-work incomes. Collective wage bargaining potentially affects a greater number of low-wage workers at risk of poverty, but also tends to have a greater impact on workers in households with incomes above the poverty line, especially in the context of a statutory minimum wage. Moreover, if not well designed, there is a risk that the benefits of reducing in-work poverty as a result of statutory or collectively agreed minimum wages are offset by greater poverty among jobless households when they reduce the employment prospects of low-productivity workers. The main features of well-designed minimum wage policies and collective bargaining systems are discussed in the context of creating high-quality jobs above.

Redistribution through the tax-benefit system is crucial for limiting financial hardship

Redistribution through the tax-benefit system can play a crucial role in making labour markets more inclusive by ensuring that the gains from economic growth are broadly shared in the population, including among families with low incomes. Most of its redistributive effect reflects the role of cash transfers – accounting for around two thirds on average across OECD countries – with progressive taxation accounting for the remaining part. Redistribution also takes place through the provision of public services, notably in the form of education and health. Efforts to strengthen the scope and effectiveness of redistribution should bear in mind possible adverse effects on work incentives, particularly among low-income families. The design of such policies is key for their effectiveness in reducing inequality and overcoming trade-offs with employment and economic growth.

At the lower end of the income spectrum, government transfers have an important role to play in lifting low-income households from financial hardship, but they need to be paired with measures to promote self-sufficiency and prevent long-term benefit dependency. Even in the context of constant budgets, policies to address growing inequality could be made more efficient, for example by making greater use of in-work relative to out-of-work benefits to encourage people to take up paid work and give additional income support to low-income households. Unemployment insurance can also contribute significantly to redistribution since the risk of unemployment tends to be highly concentrated at the bottom of the wage distribution. Increasing the coverage of unemployment insurance is a promising avenue for promoting labour market security and inclusiveness, provided it is carried out together with the rigorous enforcement of a "mutual-obligations" framework to preserve work incentives. This is especially important for non-standard workers who may not be eligible for unemployment benefits and the long-term unemployed who have exhausted the maximum duration of their benefit entitlements.

There is also scope to strengthen the role of taxation for redistribution to ensure that everyone contributes a fair share, especially those at the top end of the income distribution. Over the past decades, incomes of top earners have risen much faster than those of other earners in most OECD countries while effective marginal tax rates on high incomes have remained stable or declined. Governments therefore should ensure that wealthier individuals contribute their fair share of the tax revenue, including by improving tax compliance, scaling back tax deductions and reassessing the role of property and inheritance taxes, while taking account of the impact of possible reform options on incentives for work, effort and skills development. A particular effort should be made to ensure that profits of companies, in particular multinationals, are taxed where revenues are generated (OECD, 2017[4]).

Reduce spatial inequalities and support lagging regions

Large regional labour market and income divides in many OECD countries and emerging economies can partly be addressed by promoting growth and competitiveness in lagging regions. At a minimum, this requires that high-quality public services, including public education, public health, public transport and public employment services, are maintained in lagging regions. However, unlocking these regions' growth potential may in some cases require additional public investments in education, transport and infrastructure that could – if well designed – strengthen a region's competitiveness and facilitate the diffusion of innovation and good practices across regions, industries and firms. Policies may also be needed to provide special support to firm and job creation in regions hit by technology or trade shocks, including by adequate innovation support, improving access to finance and supporting well-designed business incubators.

But preventing lagging regions from falling behind further also requires specific policies to help displaced workers and disadvantaged groups. While trade liberalisation and technological progress bring important benefits to countries, some regions can be hard hit because of their industrial structure. Place-based employment and social policies should tackle the social problems associated with the local concentration of unemployment, social exclusion and poverty through: the provision of easily accessible anti-poverty programmes; the establishment of community centres and the use of urban regeneration projects; and retraining, work experience or entrepreneurship programmes that help displaced workers move into new activities or towards other regions with suitable job opportunities. Some regions may need to raise specific support for linguistic minorities and promote the acquisition of new skills and trades for indigenous people whose traditional ways for maintaining their livelihoods are being eroded in an increasingly modern and interconnected world.

Addressing the needs of lagging regions requires a good coordination between national, regional and local policies. Sub-national governments play an important role in the selection of public investment projects, the development of local infrastructure and the design of regional education, employment and social policies. But all levels of government, including the central government, should work together in a coordinated way to effectively promote regional development. Given the limited capacity of lagging regions to collect taxes to finance basic public services and the need for additional measures to support workers in lagging regions, some degree of inter-regional fiscal redistribution is required. A coordinated approach should also involve efforts to enhance the capacity of regional and local governments to effectively administer and implement large-scale investment projects, education and employment programmes.

Specific policies are needed to ensure that underrepresented and disadvantaged groups are not left behind

Policy should also ensure that groups at greater risk of labour market disadvantage are not excluded. A number of groups are fully integrated in the labour market and do not equally share the benefits of economic growth. For example, in OECD countries, the employment rate of people with disabilities is on average 44% lower than that of prime-age men. Also, the low-income rate in households with a migrant head is 21% higher than in the average household. And mothers in couples with young children are often not in work or working as secondary earners, bringing home less than 30% of household earnings in many countries.

Supporting disadvantaged groups requires, in some cases, adapting policy interventions to their specific needs and employment barriers, which often are quite heterogeneous not only between groups but also within groups. For example, increasing the integration of women with caring responsibilities requires encouraging men to take care leave, increasing access to affordable child-care, and enhancing the availability of flexible working arrangements (see Box 4.2), as well as removing fiscal disincentives to work for second earners. However, in the case of sole parents, a comprehensive activation strategy should be put in place by promoting a mutual-obligations framework in which employment and childcare support (including out-of-school support) are combined with work and effective job-search effort. Childcare support should be designed to ensure that work pays once taxes, transfers and childcare costs are taken into account, without heightening the risk of poverty. Similarly, a more inclusive labour market policy for migrants implies tackling discrimination, ensuring equal access to active labour market policies, assessing and recognising qualifications and skills acquired abroad as well as providing migrants with specific training opportunities corresponding to their needs, including language courses. In the case of migrant mothers with children, however, equal access to childcare and social services (which includes effective provision of information on these services) plays a paramount role. And fostering the inclusion of people with disabilities requires organising disability policy around removing each person's specific barrier(s) to his/her employability and making the incentives of all actors involved – sickness and disability benefit recipients, employers, authorities, service providers and medical professionals – consistent with this strategy.

Entrepreneurship policies can also play a role in opening up opportunities for disadvantaged groups. Entrepreneurship policies should therefore be designed so as to be inclusive and ensure that everyone, including disadvantaged groups, have opportunities to start up and operate a business or be self-employed. This requires policy measures that are tailored to the specific challenges faced by the different disadvantaged groups, possibly bundled into packages to allow addressing all barriers simultaneously, and that rely on specialist agencies to ensure policy effectiveness. Key policies to promote and support inclusive entrepreneurship include entrepreneurship training, coaching and mentoring, facilitating access to finance, and building entrepreneurial networks.

4.3. Fostering resilient and adaptable labour markets for the future of work

Economies and labour markets are in a constant state of flux, which reflects the creative destruction process inherent to well-functioning market economies as well as swings in the business cycle. Creative destruction involves the efficient reallocation of labour and capital to their most productive uses, which supports aggregate productivity, higher wages and better job quality. Policies can support the adaptability of labour markets by promoting efficient reallocation, which becomes particularly important when economies are subject to longer-term secular changes, such as technological progress, globalisation and demographic change. Policies, especially a sound macroeconomic policy framework, can also make economies more resilient to large swings in the business cycle (i.e. promote the ability to limit fluctuations in employment or unemployment and to quickly rebound in the wake of aggregate shocks). Beyond efficient reallocation and sound macroeconomic policies, resilience and adaptability also require an additional set of policies in the areas of skills, social protection, activation and social dialogue to maintain, if not enhance, labour market performance in the face of changing economic conditions. Such policies not only help improve labour reallocation, which boosts productivity and avoids the individual and social losses associated with prolonged unemployment, but also promote other objectives in their own right, such as job quality and labour market inclusiveness. Having the right combination of policies in place will be particularly important for shaping the future of work, ensuring that potential threats arising from secular trends are turned into opportunities, and that opportunities are shared fairly among all actors in society.

Macro-economic and structural policies and institutions can strengthen labour market resilience and enhance long-term labour market performance

The Great Recession of 2008-09 and the slow pace of the subsequent recovery in many countries have highlighted that large economic downturns can have long-lasting negative economic and social effects. Public policies that enhance labour market resilience, i.e. an economy's capacity to limit fluctuations in employment and to quickly rebound in the wake of aggregate shocks, are key not only to limit the short-term social cost of economic downturns but also to support labour market and economic performance in the medium- to long-term. In particular, public policies can reduce the degree to which increases in cyclical unemployment translate into structural unemployment, lower labour force participation and lower wage and productivity growth.

Macroeconomic policies play an important role in stabilising the labour market and preventing hysteresis in the wake of aggregate shocks. Monetary policy can be deployed rapidly and may have immediate effects on the real interest rate and aggregate demand by affecting inflation expectations. Even when interest rates cannot be reduced further during large economic downturns, monetary easing can be provided by unconventional measures and should be accompanied by a forceful fiscal policy response. Allowing automatic stabilisers to operate freely and complementing them by discretionary measures – preferably with a focus on high-quality public investment that crowds in private investment and raises the long-term growth potential of the economy – during deep economic downturns is crucial in this respect. The evidence indicates that fiscal policy is particularly effective during economic downturns and when initial levels of public debt are low. This suggests that adverse effects on fiscal sustainability of an effective forceful fiscal policy response during economic downturns may be limited, especially when sufficient fiscal space is built up during economic upturns. Keeping public debt at prudent levels during good times and building sufficient flexibility into fiscal rules is crucial in this respect.

Labour market policies need to be sufficiently responsive to changes in the need for public support. Having a system of adequate income support for the unemployed coupled with an effective activation strategy even before an economic downturn occurs is key. However, in countries where the maximum duration of unemployment benefits is low and unemployed workers have limited access to second-tier benefits (e.g. social assistance), there may be a case for temporarily extending their maximum duration during a recession. Moreover, resources for active labour market policies need to respond sufficiently strongly to cyclical increases in unemployment to promote a rapid return to work and preserve the mutual-obligations ethos of activation regimes. This would also strengthen automatic fiscal stabilisers. A major challenge in this context is to scale up capacity quickly, while maintaining service quality. Another is to maintain effectiveness in a context where the number of job opportunities is depressed. This may require temporarily shifting the emphasis of activation from work-first to train-first, in particular for hard-to-place jobseekers.

Short-time work schemes can promote resilience by preserving vulnerable jobs that are viable in the long-term. Short-time work schemes have played an important role in limiting job losses during the Great Recession in a number of OECD countries. To ensure that short-time work schemes are operational before job losses materialise, it is desirable to establish them during normal times so that they can rapidly be activated and scaled up at the start of recessions. However, short-time work schemes should be kept small or dormant during normal times as they risk undermining the efficient reallocation of resources across firms, and hence productivity growth. Factors that can help ensure that take-up does not persist for too long in a recovery are to require firms to participate in the cost of these schemes and limit their maximum duration.

Structural labour market policies and institutions that do not vary over the course of the business cycle also affect labour market resilience. Employment protection provisions for regular workers, if set at an adequate level, can promote labour market resilience by preserving job matches that are at risk of being suppressed but are viable in the medium term. However, excessively strict employment protection risks becoming counter-productive by increasing incentives for the use of temporary contracts in good times that are also more easy to terminate in a downturn, thereby amplifying job cuts in the wake of economic downturns, and slowing the creation of jobs associated with regular contracts in a recovery. Well-designed collective bargaining systems are also found to promote labour market resilience by facilitating adjustments in wages and working time. This can be achieved through the effective coordination of bargaining outcomes across firms and industries and by allowing for sufficient flexibility at the firm level to align wages with productivity, including through the use of opt-out clauses in the case of economic hardship.

Labour market and macroeconomic policies that promote labour market resilience may also have beneficial effects for long-run growth, employment performance and inclusiveness. Stabilising labour market outcomes during large economic downturns not only reduces the social cost of economic downturns, but also reduces the risk that transitory increases in unemployment translate into structural increases in unemployment and structural declines in labour force participation. Moreover, the benefits of higher labour market resilience are likely to accrue disproportionately to the most vulnerable workers, including youth, those at risk of long-term unemployment and workers with temporary contracts.

Rapid structural change places a premium on efficient labour re-allocation and on measures to help displaced workers back into work quickly

Globalisation, technological progress and demographic change are having a profound impact on both labour demand and supply – creating new jobs in emerging areas and destroying some in declining ones. These trends are also changing the nature of jobs, the way they are being carried out, and by whom. Thus, labour markets will need to be adaptable to turn the potential threats posed by these trends into opportunities and ensure that productivity gains are passed on to workers while limiting the risk of technological unemployment, a deterioration in job quality, increases in skills mismatches, and the rise of long-term inequalities.

Adapting to globalisation, technological progress and demographic change will require more than ever policies that promote the efficient redeployment of workers from low-performing to higher-performing businesses, industries and regions – while also helping lagging regions to catch up. These include labour and product market policies that do not constrain the entry and exit of firms and the mobility of workers across businesses and regions. If flexible forms of work, and particularly those associated with the platform economy, experience a rapid expansion, ensuring the portability of accrued rights and protections for all forms of work becomes particularly important to avoid that the loss of accrued rights becomes a barrier to job mobility. Housing policies could further promote geographical mobility of workers to help people move to the regions where the best jobs are available. This could be achieved by making the allocation of public housing more responsive to the needs of people moving from areas in decline and reducing constraints on the development of private rental markets. Reducing transaction costs – including by raising competition among intermediaries –would also help to support the mobility of home owners, especially in countries where the share of homeownership is high. Providing unemployed workers with subsidies to cover the costs of relocating can be a cost-effective way to enhance labour mobility and help displaced workers back into employment. In some countries, occupational licensing has acted as a barrier to mobility, without clear benefits in terms of better service quality, consumer health or safety. Such licensing should be used judiciously and standards should be harmonised across regions as much as possible. More generally, the mobility of workers across firms, industries and regions should be accompanied by effective skills policies, adequate social protection and constructive social dialogue.

Adaptability also requires targeted policies that help displaced workers get back to work quickly. Standard activation policies may not be sufficient to help displaced workers back into work quickly. Intervening early is particularly important, since it has been found to be the most cost-effective way to provide support to displaced workers. New OECD analysis highlights the importance of rules that require advance notice of redundancy (Chapter 14). This allows the affected workers and relevant labour market authorities to start early in preparing for a smooth adjustment. In some countries, this may require a shift in workers' protection from severance pay to advance notice to prevent the lack of advance notice from becoming an obstacle to job reallocation. While many displaced workers may not need much additional help apart from being rapidly oriented/motivated towards active jobs search, some will be at risk of long-term unemployment and benefit exhaustion. Profiling tools are therefore needed to identify those workers early and target dedicated support at them – thereby avoiding that unnecessarily intensive (and expensive) special assistance services are provided to jobseekers not needing them. Systematic early needs assessments are particularly helpful, especially when the outcome is formalised in an individual action plan that can lead to early intervention when specific barriers to re-employment have been identified. It is also important that services are available to all displaced workers, and not just those affected by collective dismissal in large firms.

Non-standard forms of work contribute to the adaptability of labour markets, but also raise concerns about job quality

In all advanced and emerging economies, different types of non-standard forms of work (temporary and self-employment) already coexist with more traditional permanent contracts. In addition, technological advances are promoting the emergence of new forms of work such as "crowd work", "gig work", and other forms of on-demand, independent jobs which, despite currently representing only a small share of employment, may expand significantly in the near future.

Non-standard forms of work can help labour markets be more adaptable but, in some cases, also raise concerns about job quality. Non-standard forms of work can offer an important source of flexibility for both workers and employers, which enhances the development of new business models, innovation and productivity. They may also facilitate the labour market integration of under-represented groups (and therefore promote inclusiveness) by helping individuals overcome barriers to participation. In some cases, they can promote a better work-life balance. For many individuals, non-standard employment is therefore a choice. However, labour market outcomes vary greatly across workers in non-standard jobs, in particular in terms of pay, job security and social protection. In addition, workers may be less likely to be covered by collective bargaining arrangements and/or some labour regulation, and may not be eligible for labour market programmes and support. They may also get low pay, receive less training and suffer more job strain. Given that certain population groups are over-represented in non-standard forms of work (typically women, youth, the least-skilled and workers in small firms as well as migrants), such forms of work risk generating a source of inequality in access to good jobs (with some groups confined to less attractive types of work) resulting in labour market segmentation. Concerns about low job quality and labour market segmentation are more prevalent when non-standard work is involuntary and results from a weak position in the labour market.

The challenge for governments is to accompany innovation in the creation and use of non-standard employment arrangements while avoiding abuse, creating a level playing field between companies, and providing adequate protection for all workers. Differences in tax and regulatory treatment between standard employees and those in other forms of employment can promote inefficient arbitrage, with employers and workers choosing non-standard contracts solely to circumvent taxes and regulations on regular contracts. Such arbitrage may be exacerbated by regulatory gaps and ambiguities that result in the "misclassification" of workers. Not only does this unfairly transfer risks and costs from employers onto workers, but it also distorts competition. Businesses should succeed and expand on the basis of their superior technology, efficiency and/or quality of service, and not because of regulatory arbitrage. Governments therefore need to reduce differences in treatment across different forms of work, remove loopholes and ambiguity in regulation, and ensure effective enforcement of existing regulation (including the use of appropriate penalties where necessary) – while preserving those flexibility-enhancing features of alternative employment arrangements that are beneficial for individuals and employers. Governments should also endeavour to provide adequate protection for all workers. In the area of social protection, and depending upon circumstances, this may require: adapting or extending existing social insurance schemes to cover previously excluded categories of workers; complementing social insurance with non-contributory schemes; implementing minimum floors for social benefits; and/or making social protection portable (i.e. linking entitlements to individuals rather than jobs). But governments should also try and extend other forms of protection to non-standard workers, including: the minimum wage (to protect against low-pay); and protection from arbitrary dismissal, discrimination, and health and safety risks, among others. Finally, while employers and workers themselves will have to find ways to reconcile flexibility with protection through collective bargaining, governments can help promote an environment conducive to constructive dialogue. This includes putting in place a legal framework that facilitates the adaptation of social partnerships to give a voice to workers in non-standard forms of work. These issues are likely to become more important as on-demand work expands.

The challenges posed by the future of work may require a more fundamental shake-up of labour market, skills and social policies, rather than just incremental changes to the systems in place.

Job losses associated with previous episodes of major technological upheaval have tended to be short-lived and have, in the long-term, made room for the creation of more productive and rewarding jobs. However, the expected speed and breadth of the changes occurring in the labour market, as well as evidence from a number of OECD countries that productivity gains are no longer broadly shared with workers, have raised concerns that this time might be different. If this is the case, then tinkering with existing systems may not offer an answer to the skills, labour market and social challenges of the future, and a more fundamental paradigm shift may be required. In fact, some challenges are already evident in the available data, and will require immediate action. For example, many non-standard workers have no access to old age, accident, unemployment or health insurance. A majority of individuals lack the basic digital skills to function in a technology-rich work environment. The number of workers who are member of trade unions has declined dramatically in several countries making it more difficult for collective bargaining to be effective. At the same time, labour markets are polarising and inequality is at its highest level for the past half century. Other challenges lie further ahead and the implications for policy remain uncertain. This means that labour market policy needs to be forward-looking and have a certain agility to allow for learning, experimentation and adaptation. Learning from other countries becomes particularly important in this context, as some may be better prepared for the changes that lie ahead than others.

Social protection systems will need to be extended and adapted, but a more fundamental re-think may be required. While many countries are already struggling to provide adequate social protection for workers on non-standard work contracts, the advent of the platform economy is adding to these difficulties as an increasing number of workers only work occasionally and/or have multiple jobs and income sources, with frequent transitions between dependent employment, self-employment and work-free periods. Many of them do not even have worker status. These new ways of working are therefore bringing additional challenges for existing social security systems, which are often still largely predicated on the assumption of a full-time, regular, open-ended contract with a single employer. As a result, some workers risk falling through the cracks – although the scale of the problem that lies ahead is difficult to predict at this stage. In some cases, employment regulation will need to be clarified or adapted to take into account new forms of employment. At the same time, tax and benefit systems themselves would need to be extended and or adapted to the new forms of work so that all workers are provided with a minimum form of protection. Portability of social security entitlements should be promoted where this is not already the case to prevent the loss of benefit entitlements when workers move between jobs. And governments may also need to expand the role of non-contributory schemes. Several countries are experimenting with various forms of basic income schemes that, besides being simple, have the advantage of not leaving anyone without support. However, an unconditional payment to everyone at meaningful but fiscally sustainable levels would require tax hikes as well as reductions in existing (often targeted) benefits, and would often not be an effective tool for reducing poverty. In addition, some disadvantaged groups would lose out when existing benefits are replaced by a basic income, illustrating the downsides of social protection without any form of targeting at all.

Extending social protection should go hand in hand with measures that strengthen activation frameworks. The new forms of work that are emerging may hinder the ability of countries to enforce the principle of mutual obligations given that monitoring work activity may become more difficult. Activation strategies more generally might be weakened if a growing share of the unemployed are no longer eligible for unemployment benefits and will therefore slip under the radar of the authorities. In many ways, this parallels the challenges that many emerging economies already encounter due to the existence of large informal sectors, and more advanced countries may therefore have much to learn from the experience of emerging ones. One particular area where emerging economies have taken the lead is in establishing job guarantees – i.e. the promise of a job to anyone willing and able to work at some minimum wage rate. Compared to basic income schemes, job guarantees fit better with the principle of "mutual obligations", whereby society's responsibility to support those in need is matched by the individual's duty to contribute something in return. Job guarantees also have the advantage over basic income schemes that they go beyond the provision of income and, by providing a job, help individuals to (re)connect with the labour market, build self-esteem, as well as develop skills and competencies. By establishing and maintaining a buffer of employed workers (which would grow during recessions and shrink during booms), a job guarantee would also contribute to labour market resilience. In more advanced economies, however, past experience with public sector employment programmes has shown that they have negligible effects on the post-programme outcomes of participants, and therefore are best considered as a form of income-support rather than a policy to promote self-sufficiency.

The future of work could also raise important challenges for existing labour market regulation, including employment protection legislation, minimum wage laws, working time regulations and regulations to safeguard occupational health and safety. A rise of non-standard work would be accompanied by a reduction in job security for many workers as they would not be protected by the standard rules for hiring and firing that have been defined for open-ended contracts. Oftentimes, less strict rules would apply (e.g. in cases of temporary employment, temporary work agency work or dependent self-employment) while in others, workers would be excluded from employment protection legislation altogether (e.g. the self-employed). For some of the emerging new forms of work, it is not even clear what the status of workers is, who the employer is, and what rules should apply to them. It will therefore be critical that countries examine their legal framework to determine whether it needs to be updated and/or adjusted in order to provide some form of minimum employment protection for all workers. The usefulness of minimum wage policy might also be challenged in the future world of work. Existing minimum wage legislation may not be applicable to many of the new forms of employment where workers become independent contractors, work for multiple clients and are often paid on a piece-rate basis. Countries also face policy challenges with regards to regulations that seek to improve workplace safety and health. New forms of employment, particularly crowd sourcing, tend to transfer responsibilities for occupational health and safety away from the employer and into the hands of individual workers, who often lack the training or resources to take appropriate measures to ensure that working conditions and the working environment are safe. Sometimes, strong competition between workers may result in corners being cut and unnecessary risks being taken while, at the same time, labour inspectorates are often not adequately prepared to deal with these new forms of employment. Regulations may therefore need to be adapted/clarified, and monitoring and control mechanisms strengthened and improved.

An increase in non-standard forms of employment would also present a major challenge for collective bargaining systems. The new forms of work add to the challenge of organising worker voice since individuals are increasingly working alone, separated by geography, language and legal status. In some cases, there are also important regulatory challenges to overcome. For example, in some countries, it is illegal for independent workers to unionise since this would be considered forming a cartel and therefore against competition laws. Some innovative solutions are nevertheless emerging: non-standard workers are setting up new unions and "traditional" unions are trying to improve the coverage of non-standard forms of work. In some cases, companies voluntarily extend the terms set in collective agreements for standard workers to non-standard workers and/or engage in collective bargaining. What is needed from governments is a favourable regulatory environment that allows effective forms of worker representation to emerge so that both workers and firms benefit from the flexibility afforded by non-standard forms of work.

Future skills challenges will require a significant upscaling of adult learning opportunities as well as the development of new tools for incentivising skills investments. A key challenge lies in the fact that large numbers of workers lack the basic digital skills required to survive in a technologically-rich work environment. Addressing this challenge will require a rapid and massive upscaling of adult learning opportunities. The rise in non-standard forms of work further compounds the challenge, since workers in such types of employment are less likely to receive training (and, in the case of the self-employed, bear responsibility for their own training). Addressing this challenge might require the development of new instruments for incentivising investments in training (such as personal training accounts, or lifelong training rights) as well as mechanisms to allow the portability of training rights between employers. But adjustments may also be needed to more traditional financial measures that promote access to learning opportunities, such as grants and loans, to make them accessible to adults of all ages; and provision of education and training should be made more flexible such that adults can overcome time constraints and care responsibilities which act as barriers to participation. More generally, existing infrastructures for lifelong learning may not be geared up for the significant changes that lie ahead. A key challenge lies in the facts that: i) the majority of workers exposed to deep and rapid changes in the labour market has already left initial education; ii) the skills of these workers will become obsolete rather quickly as a result of rapid technological change; and iii) they will be required to stay in the labour force for longer. A significant upscaling of adult learning may therefore be required. In doing so, countries should fully exploit the opportunities presented by new technologies that allow access to courses to be scaled up massively at only a fraction of the cost of traditional courses, but care must be taken in avoiding marginalising those lacking basic digital skills.

Conclusions

To promote more and better-quality jobs and greater access to the labour market for under-represented groups, the new Jobs Strategy identifies a whole-of-government action around three broad principles:

Promoting an environment in which high-quality jobs can flourish

This requires a sound macroeconomic framework, a growth-friendly environment and skills evolving in line with market needs. A key new insight is that during sharp economic downturns it can be beneficial to channel resources to short-term work programmes that seek to preserve vulnerable jobs that are viable in the long term. Moreover, it is important to provide a good balance in employment protection for workers in different contracts. Liberalising temporary contracts while maintaining high levels of employment protection for workers on open-ended contracts can lead to the excessive use of the former and low job quality, high levels of inequality and low resilience, without clear gains in overall employment.

Preventing labour market exclusion and protecting individuals against labour market risks

Supporting job seekers for a quick (re)integration in employment remains essential, including by unemployment benefit and social assistance schemes that provide high coverage with rigorous enforcement of mutual obligations. At the same time, the new Jobs Strategy emphasises the importance of addressing problems before they arise by promoting equality of opportunities and taking a life-course perspective that prevents the accumulation of individual disadvantages that require costly interventions at a later stage. This requires ensuring that social background is not a major determinant of success in the labour market and investing in life-course policies that promote adult learning, enhance work-life balance and reduce the risk of work-related health problems.

Preparing for future opportunities and challenges in a rapidly changing economy and labour market.

Product and labour market dynamism will be key to deal with rapid economic change. However, workers need to be equipped with the right skills in a context where the demand for skills is evolving rapidly. Workers also need to remain protected against labour market risks in a world where flexible forms of work may increase. This includes social protection and labour market regulations but possibly also expanding the role of non-contributory schemes, minimum floors to social benefits, and making social protection more portable.

Notes

[1] In the case of insurance for unemployment, sickness and disability, there may be an argument for increasing the financial responsibility of employers for the cost of social protection by strengthening the link between employer contributions and expenditures (see "Building secure labour markets" below for further details).

[2] A rigorous "mutual-obligations" framework should as much as possible be applied to any kind of benefit, to avoid substitution across benefits with different degree of conditionality.

[3] For example, by specifying employer obligations with regard to psychosocial risk assessment and risk prevention, defining the role of workers' representatives, providing tools and supports to enable employers to adjust the psychosocial work environment. Action is also needed to improve management's responses to workers' stress and mental health issues – e.g. by providing stress prevention and mental health training for managers and other stakeholders while offering toolkits and guidelines to line managers on how to deal with health issues when they emerge.

Reference

OECD (2017), *OECD/G20 Inclusive Framework on BEPS*, http://www.oecd.org/tax/beps/inclusive-framework-on-beps-progress-report-july-2017-june-2018.pdf (accessed on 02 November 2018). [4]

OECD (2015), *Draft Recommendation of the Council on Gender Equality in Public Life*, https://one.oecd.org/document/C(2015)164/CORR1/en/pdf. [2]

OECD (2015), *Draft Recommendation of the Council on Integrated Mental Health, School and Work Policy*, https://one.oecd.org/document/C(2015)173/CORR1/en/pdf. [1]

OECD (2013), *Recommendation of the Council on Gender Equality in Education, Employment and Entrepreneurship*, https://one.oecd.org/document/C/MIN(2013)5/FINAL/en/pdf. [3]

Chapter 5. Implementing reforms

To provide more concrete support for countries it is important to accompany the general policy principles of the new Jobs Strategy with concrete guidance for: i) identifying reform priorities and developing country-specific recommendations; ii) building support for successful reforms and iii) evaluating the effectiveness of reforms. These issues are developed in more detail in Part V of the Volume.

Introduction

This chapter goes beyond the general policy principles of the new OECD Jobs Strategy by providing concrete guidance for their implementation and evaluation. More specifically, Section 5.1 makes use of the Jobs Strategy dashboard to identify countries with the same challenges based on their relative scores for the different dimensions of labour market performance and sets out the factors that need to be taken into account when developing country-specific recommendations. To assist countries with their implementation, Section 5.2 outlines some key elements that can help build support for reforms. Section 5.3 briefly discusses the importance of evaluating reforms.

5.1. Identifying policy priorities and country-specific recommendations

Developing country-specific recommendations requires identifying policy priorities based on labour market performance, while taking account of a country's specific economic and social circumstances and starting point in terms of existing policy and institutional settings.

Identifying policy priorities

Apart from assessing labour market performance, the OECD Jobs Strategy dashboard can also be used to identify policy challenges based on *relative* performance (a given country's performance on one outcome *relative* to other outcomes). As discussed in more detail in Chapter 17, identifying priorities based on *relative* performance allows setting policy priorities for all countries. Even when a given country tends to perform well or poorly across all/most dimensions of the dashboard, it is possible to identify one or several outcomes for which performance is weak relative to other outcomes.

As an illustration, in Figure 5.1 countries are grouped according to their relative performance on labour market outcomes (Panel A of the dashboard, job quantity, job quality, inclusiveness) and on framework conditions (Panel B, resilience, labour productivity growth and skills). For simplicity, one main challenge is chosen for each of the two areas. It should be stressed that while this procedure allows establishing performance challenges for all countries, there may be large differences in *absolute* performance even among countries sharing the same challenge. For instance, countries with job quantity as the main challenge may include countries with below-average performance in job quantity as well as countries with above-average performance (if they are performing even better on job quality and inclusiveness).

On average, countries with job quantity as the main challenge also do worse than the OECD average in terms of job quality and inclusiveness (Figure 5.1). Countries with inclusiveness as the main challenge perform around the OECD average in terms of job quantity and job quality, whereas countries with job quality as the main challenge typically outperform the OECD average in job quantity and inclusiveness. Regarding the performance areas of Panel B, countries with weak *relative* performance in one area tend to outperform the OECD average in other areas.

Figure 5.1. Broad performance challenges

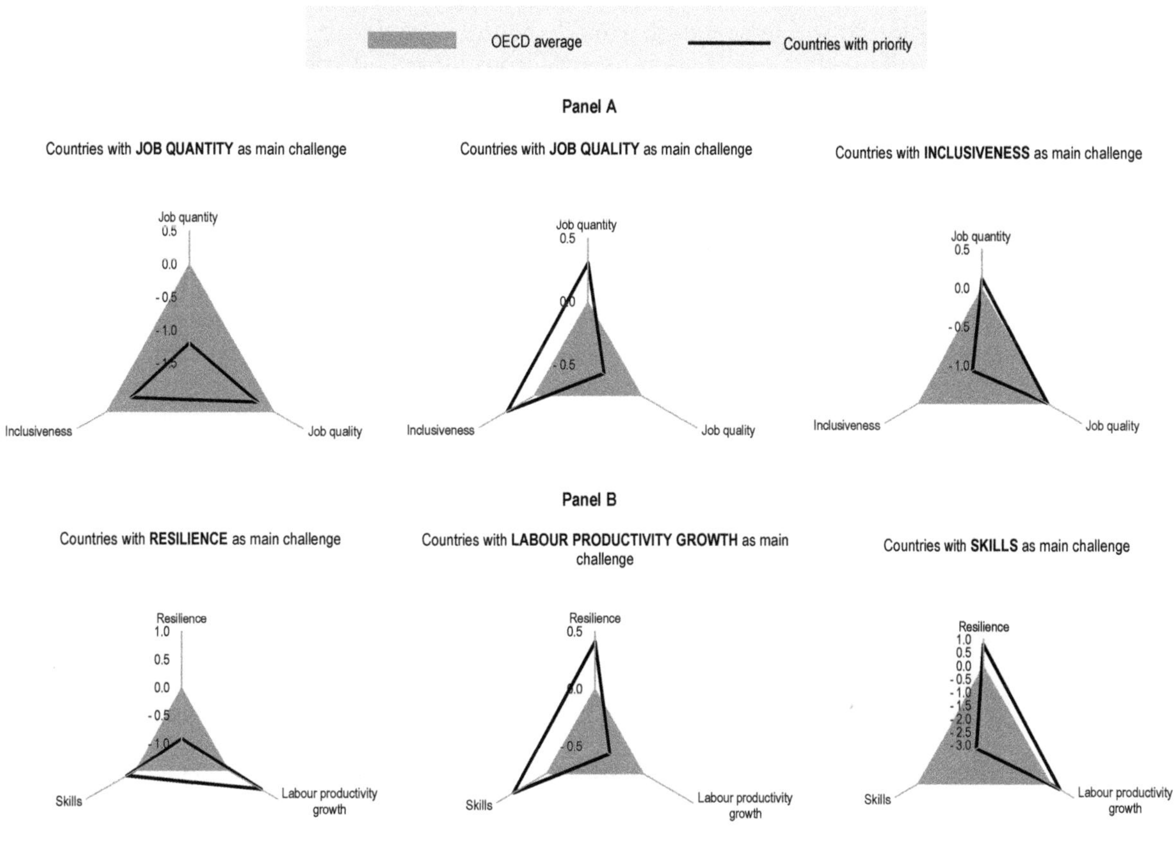

Note: The blue triangle indicates the average performance of OECD countries (see Chapter 3, Table 3.1 for details on the indicators). The black line indicates the average performance of countries with the same performance challenge. All indicators have been standardised and rescaled so that a higher score indicates better outcomes.
Source: Chapter 17.

StatLink http://dx.doi.org/10.1787/888933881154

Developing country-specific recommendations

Once countries have identified their main broad performance challenges, the development of specific policy priorities requires taking account of countries' specific challenges, institutional capacity and reform preferences. This acknowledges not only that countries differ in terms of their starting points but also that improving labour market performance is necessarily a gradual process and one that can take different forms in different countries.

Country-specific policy recommendations should reflect global good practices as well as the country's level of institutional capacity. For example, in emerging economies, where the institutional capacity of the state tends to be relatively weak and informal work is widespread, providing effective social protection is a major challenge. In these countries, a mandatory system of self-insurance based on individual savings accounts for unemployment complemented with a small collective component for those without sufficient savings may be an appropriate first step to improve coverage and effectiveness of social protection. More generally, where social capital is low and administrative capacity lacking, policy action should aim at being particularly simple, transparent and easily accountable. Its implementation would require combining further investment in civil servants' skills with the definition of a rigorously-applied code of conduct and the setting up of independent bodies for internal control and audit that have enforcement powers.

Policy recommendations may also differ across countries depending on the degree of interventionism of social systems. More market-reliant countries may want to place more emphasis on measures to prevent labour market exclusion and poverty by promoting equality of opportunity – for example, by improving equal access to quality education – relative to measures that seek to promote equality of outcomes ex post– for example, by enhancing the redistribution role of the tax and benefits system. This allows taking some account of reform preferences without calling into question the importance of inclusiveness as a policy objective or compromising in terms of policy effectiveness.

Finally, policy challenges will differ significantly across countries with different demographic developments even when performance gaps are similar. Countries with rapidly ageing populations may need to prioritise policies promoting working at older age and female labour force participation, whereas countries with younger populations may need to prioritise initial training and the school-to-work transition. Similarly, in a number of countries, the labour market integration of migrants may require specific policies.

5.2. Implementing reforms

Broad-based support for welfare-enhancing reforms may be low because their benefits often take time to materialise and may not be equally distributed. In most cases, the benefits of reforms materialise gradually through firm entry, hiring and productivity growth. By contrast, negative effects in terms of job and income losses may be immediate. For example, reforms reducing dismissal costs, while encouraging hiring in viable jobs in the long-run, would make it convenient to swiftly terminate inefficient positions. In some cases, specific groups of workers may lose from the reforms even if most people gain. For example, trade liberalisation, while benefiting consumers through more and better products at lower prices, often induces downsizing in unskilled-labour intensive sectors and regions.

By combining policy reforms into coherent packages, it is possible to broaden support and make reforms more successful. Coherent reform packages can be used to strengthen the long-term benefits by exploiting synergies, minimise the short-term costs and foster a more equal sharing of long-term gains and short-term burden across a large number of stakeholders. This implies that reforms with potential short-term or distributional costs could be accompanied by complementary actions in terms of macroeconomic and other structural policies. If job losses are concentrated in specific regions, policies at the national level need to be coordinated with policies at the regional level to be effective. This requires coordination across levels of government and a fiscal system that can compensate for revenue shortfalls that regional governments are likely to suffer during times of crisis.

Macroeconomic policy can offset the short-term costs of structural reforms. Monetary policy would typically react to a fall in aggregate demand and inflation expectations and stabilise the economy. However, room to intervene may be limited when interest rates are already very low. Resorting to unconventional monetary policy for prolonged periods of time raises issues of effectiveness, financial stability and possibly an inefficient allocation of credit. In such cases, a growth-enhancing fiscal initiative can offset the short-term costs of structural reform if there is sufficient fiscal space. Depending on country specificities, such an initiative could take the form of an increase in productive public investment or a reduction in taxes that are most harmful to economic growth.

Other structural policies can help minimising short-term costs. The recent experience of reforming countries suggests that short-term adverse effects of costly structural reforms can be reduced if they are accompanied by changes in collective bargaining, policy actions to enhance firm-level flexibility or, in some cases, designing reforms in ways to preserve acquired workers' rights. For example, recent experiences suggest that, in countries with national, regional or branch-level collective bargaining, allowing scope for individual firms to adapt wages and working conditions to their individual situation can limit any short-term job losses resulting from the relaxation of dismissal regulations. More flexibility in working conditions and wage setting allows firms to make use of variables other than employment when adjusting to the required restructuring. Alternatively, more flexible dismissal legislation could be introduced and applied only to new hires. There is evidence that such "grandfather clauses" more than offset short-term employment costs of reforms of dismissal legislation.

Sequencing reforms in effective ways – advancing those that are pre-requisite for the success of others – can play a key role in ensuring reform success. For example, short-term costs of some structural reforms tend to be smaller in countries with an effective activation strategy to support jobseekers. Yet, if efficient programmes are not already in place, there are limits to how rapidly active labour market policies can be scaled up when unemployment rises, since fine-tuning of these institutions typically takes several years. This suggests that building up an effective activation strategy should precede reforms that likely involve short-term labour market side effects. Similarly, product market and employment protection reforms are less costly in the short term when the former precede the latter. This is because when barriers to entry are lowered in industries with dominant incumbents, the latter react to the reform by reorganising and downsizing to deter entry of potential competitors, but this reaction is less likely when dismissals are more costly. On the other hand, greater competition and greater entry accelerates the positive effect of reforms reducing dismissal costs on hiring, thereby improving the net short-term effects induced by such a reform. Last but not least, undertaking reforms when the fiscal position is sound makes it easier to accompany them with an expansionary macroeconomic policy stance.

Reforms are most often successful when governments are able to build support for them. Evidence suggests that this typically implies: i) winning an electoral mandate for the reform; ii) effective communication of the reform rationale and the consequences of inaction based on rigorous evidence; and iii) intensive tripartite discussions involving the government and the social partners, provided that the government has a strong bargaining position and that negotiations take place in a spirit of trust and cooperation. This typically occurs in the presence of strong government cohesion and the willingness to exchange support for the reforms against action aimed at minimising the short-term and distributional costs, including boosting aggregate demand (e.g. by enhancing productive public investment) or compensating losers.

5.3. Evaluating reforms

While existing good practices provide evidence-based guidance for action, country specificities make each reform unique. For this reason, new policies and programmes need to be assessed regularly and rigorously and inefficient ones need to be swiftly adjusted or terminated. This requires investing in data collection to allow monitoring programme participation and the outcomes of firms and workers over time, including by mobilising administrative data in a way that respects confidentiality. It also requires building evaluation mechanisms into the design of policy reforms. In particular, small-scale experimentation of new measures – where possible based on a random-assignment design – before implementing them on a large scale could represent an effective tool to avoid mistakes and/or build up the evidence base required to win consensus.

Conclusions

This chapter has provided some general guidelines for the implementation of the new OECD Jobs Strategy and the evaluation of reforms, all of which are developed in more detail in Part V of the Volume. In particular, it has explained how policy challenges can be identified using the new Jobs Strategy dashboard based on *relative* performance. However, specific policy recommendations need to take account of the challenges faced by individual countries, the means available and national reform preferences. Policy measures may also vary with the degree of intervention of social systems and demographic developments.

The chapter also found that reforms are more successful if they benefit from broad support and identified key elements that can help build such support. These include combining policy reforms into coherent packages, which exploit synergies, minimise the short-term costs and foster a more equal sharing of the long-term gains and short-term burden across a large number of stakeholders. An effective sequencing of reforms, a clear electoral mandate for policies, the effective communication of their rationale and of the consequences of inaction, as well as constructive negotiations with stakeholders are further vital ingredients for successful reforms.

Reforms should be evaluated rigorously, so that inefficient policies can be swiftly adjusted or ended. Investments in data collection and building evaluation mechanisms into programmes are essential to monitor their success. It can also be useful to test new measures on a small scale before implementing them more widely.

Chapter 6. Detailed policy recommendations

This chapter contains the detailed policy recommendations of the new OECD Jobs Strategy. These policy recommendations are organised around three broad principles: i) promote an environment in which high-quality jobs can flourish; ii) prevent labour market exclusion and protect individuals against labour market risks; and iii) prepare for future opportunities and challenges in a rapidly changing labour market. The chapter ends with recommendations on the implementation of reforms, in order to provide countries guidance in building stronger and more inclusive labour markets.

Introduction

This chapter presents the detailed policy recommendations of the new OECD Jobs Strategy. These policy recommendations are a key pillar of the OECD Inclusive Growth Initiative.

The detailed policy recommendations are organised around three broad principles: i) promote an environment in which high-quality jobs can flourish; ii) prevent labour market exclusion and protect individuals against labour market risks; and iii) prepare for future opportunities and challenges in a rapidly changing labour market. To further assist countries in building stronger and more inclusive labour markets, the chapter also includes recommendations on the implementation of reforms.

In the implementation of the new Jobs Strategy, it will be important to exploit synergies among different policy areas and ensure consistency with the OECD Going for Growth recommendations, the OECD Skills Strategy, the OECD Innovation Strategy and the OECD Green Growth Strategy. Thus, a whole-of-government approach is necessary.

A. Promote an environment in which high-quality jobs can flourish

1. Implement a sound macroeconomic policy framework that ensures price stability and fiscal sustainability while allowing for an effective counter-cyclical monetary and fiscal policy response during economic downturns

- Monetary policy should pursue medium-term price stability by reacting to both inflationary and dis-inflationary shocks and aim to stabilise economic activity, including through non-conventional measures when interest rates cannot be lowered further during large economic downturns.
- Automatic fiscal stabilisers should be allowed to fully operate, possibly supported by additional discretionary measures in response to particularly large economic shocks. Discretionary increases in public investment, including well-designed infrastructure projects and maintenance of the existing capital stock, can be particularly effective in containing unemployment pressure during prolonged economic downturns.
- The use of fiscal policy for macroeconomic stabilisation is particularly effective when monetary policy is over-burdened and where monetary policy cannot be used for this purpose.
- A sound fiscal policy framework should create sufficient fiscal space during upturns to allow for a stabilising fiscal policy response during downturns, including in the form of increased public investment and spending on labour market programmes.

2. Promote growth and quality job creation by removing barriers to the creation and growth of new businesses, the restructuring or exit of underperforming ones, and by creating an entrepreneurship-friendly environment

- Promote business dynamism and competition in both manufacturing and especially services to revive productivity growth, by implementing labour market and other policies that facilitate entry of new firms, reallocation of workers towards the most productive firms and the restructuring or orderly exit of the weakly productive ones.

- Create an entrepreneurship-friendly environment to raise investment, innovation and job creation by raising the efficiency of tax systems; providing a sound legal and judicial infrastructure; enhancing the robustness of financial markets that serve the real economy; continuing efforts to strengthen the rule of law and fight corruption; and by improving the governance of state-owned enterprises.

3. Ensure that employment protection legislation yields dismissal costs which are predictable, balanced across contract types and not overly restrictive, while protecting workers against possible abuses and limiting excessive turnover.

- Reduce differences, and to the extent possible, equalise advance notice, ordinary severance pay and layoff taxes across types of contract, but keeping them at a level that does not hinder efficient labour reallocation.
- Clarify the conditions that firms are expected to meet to dismiss workers on open-ended contracts for economic reasons and make worker compensation predictable. The latter may be achieved by adopting a comprehensive definition of fair economic dismissal while setting different notice periods and ordinary severance pay depending on the reason.
- In the case of dismissal for personal motives, restrict, and if needed clarify, the definition of unfair dismissal, for which remedial action can be sought in courts, to abuses, including false reasons, reasons unrelated to work, discrimination, harassment and prohibited grounds.

4. Facilitate the adoption of flexible working-time arrangements to help firms adjust to temporary changes in business conditions, while helping workers to reconcile work and personal life.

- Enhance work-life balance by removing legal impediments and discriminatory tax and social security provisions against the use of voluntary part-time work and flexible work schedules, while promoting the use of teleworking arrangements.
- Increase the flexibility of working time to temporary changes in business conditions through the use of working-time accounts and overtime, collectively-agreed working-time adjustments and publicly provided short-time work schemes to provide additional flexibility to firms and reduce excessive turnover.
- Use short-time work schemes as a tool to preserve jobs in times of crisis, but limit their use in good times to avoid that that they undermine the efficient reallocation of resources across firms, and hence productivity growth.
    - Prepare for economic downturns by establishing a short-time work scheme that can be scaled up or activated in times of crisis, if no such scheme exists, while providing clear and easily accessible information on the modalities for their use.
    - Ensure that the use of short-time work schemes is largely limited to economic downturns, by requiring firms to participate in the cost of

short-time work, limiting the maximum duration of short-time work schemes and targeting them at firms in temporary difficulties.

5. Reduce non-wage labour costs, especially for low-wage workers, and differences in fiscal treatment based on employment status.

Consistent with the OECD's recommendations on *Tax Policy Design for Inclusive Growth*, the following principles can help to improve the design of labour taxation for good labour market performance:

- Broaden the tax base of labour taxation to reduce non-wage labour costs as well as differences in fiscal treatment based on employment status, with a particular focus on low-wage workers. This can be done by switching to taxes that weigh less heavily on labour or by adjusting the composition of labour taxation.
- For a given level of labour taxation, consider increasing its progressivity by relying more heavily on progressive personal income taxes for the financing of social protection when there is already a weak link between individual contributions and entitlements, removing exemptions and deductibles from personal income taxation that are regressive and treating all forms of remuneration evenly (e.g. wage earnings, fringe benefits, stock options).
- Provide clear incentives to firms for minimising labour market risks by strengthening the link between employer social security contributions and expenditures in the context of existing insurance-based sickness, disability and unemployment benefit schemes, while avoiding penalising certain types of firms and workers and minimising any unintended consequences on the hiring and firing behaviour of firms.

6. Consider using a statutory minimum wage set at a moderate level as a tool to raise wages at the bottom of the wage ladder, while avoiding that it prices low-skilled workers out of jobs.

- Accompany minimum wages with tax and benefit measures to ensure that measures to make work pay have their intended effects for workers, while limiting the impact of minimum wages on the cost of labour for firms.
- Ensure that minimum wages are revised regularly, based on accurate, up-to-date and impartial information and advice that carefully considers current labour market conditions and the views of social partners.
- Where appropriate, allow minimum wages to vary by age group (to reflect differences in productivity or employment barriers) and/or by region (to reflect differences in economic conditions).

7. Promote the inclusiveness of collective bargaining systems while providing sufficient flexibility for firms to adapt to aggregate shocks and structural change.

Collective bargaining systems differ widely across countries in terms of their coverage and the flexibility that they provide to firms. Moreover, these differences tend to be deeply rooted in their socio-cultural fabric. The challenge is to adapt collective bargaining systems to a changing world of work within the broad terms of the existing national industrial-relations tradition. Systems characterised by predominantly sector-level bargaining tend to be associated with high coverage, but also risk undermining employment and productivity growth if not well-designed. In countries characterised by predominantly firm-level bargaining, coverage tends to be limited to large firms and their workers, the main question is how the reach of collective bargaining and social dialogue can be extended.

- The best way of fostering an inclusive collective bargaining system is through well-organised social partners based on broad memberships. To extend social dialogue to all segments of the economy, including small firms and non-standard forms of employment, governments should put in place a legal framework that promotes social dialogue in large and smalls firms alike and allows labour relations to adapt to new emerging challenges.
- In the absence of broad-based social partners, administrative extensions of sectoral agreements can help make collective bargaining systems more inclusive by achieving higher coverage, but need to be well-designed to ensure their representativeness, and avoid undermining the economic prospects of start-ups, small firms or vulnerable workers. This could be done by subjecting extension requests to reasonable representativeness criteria, a meaningful test of public interest or requiring well-defined procedures for exemptions and opt out.
- Collective bargaining systems should provide sufficient flexibility to allow wages and working conditions to adjust to difficult economic conditions. In the case of predominantly sector-level collective bargaining, this can be promoted through organised decentralisation which preserves the integrity of sector-level bargaining while providing the possibility of controlled opt-outs or, by leaving space in sector-level agreements through the use of framework agreements for bargaining at the firm or individual level. To engage effectively in organised decentralisation, it is important to have high levels of local representation of workers in firms. Flexibility to macroeconomic conditions can be fostered through the effective co-ordination of collective bargaining outcomes across bargaining units through peak or pattern bargaining.
- Promote the quality of labour relations by: fostering broad, representative and well-organised employer and worker associations; creating built-in incentives for the regular re-negotiation of collective agreements; providing high quality and objective statistics on the state of the economy; and supporting mechanisms that enhance the accountability of the social partners for the effective implementation of collective agreements.

8. Foster the development of suitable skills for labour market needs, while promoting the use of these skills and their adaptation during the working life to respond to evolving skills needs.

Consistent with the OECD Skills Strategy:

- Put in place a high-quality initial education and training system, from early childhood education through school and beyond, which gives individuals the best possible start in the labour market by providing them with strong basic skills, socio-emotional skills and specific skills required by employers, as well as the capacity for lifelong learning and to make education, training and occupational choices throughout their working lives.

- Develop strong links between the world of education and the world of work to ensure that the skills acquired through the education and training system correspond to labour market needs, and hence avoid major issues with skill mismatch. Policies to foster closer links between education and work include: work-based learning; the involvement of social partners in the development and delivery of curricula matching market needs; and an element of cost-sharing in skills funding.
- Encourage better skills use in the workplace, including through collective bargaining and the promotion of good management and high-performance management and working practices.
- Adapt education and training programmes in different regions to meet the specific needs of the regional economy.

9. Promote formal employment by enhancing the enforcement of labour market rules, making formal work more attractive for firms and workers and promoting skills development to enhance worker productivity

- In countries where there are many informal jobs, tackle informality by improving the efficiency of public spending and the quality of the public services and, where they exist, strengthening the link between contributions and benefits in social insurance schemes; by simplifying tax and administrative systems; by increasing resources for labour inspectorates and making the enforcement process transparent and strict; and by promoting skill development to compensate for the higher cost of formal jobs and enhance access to formal-sector employment.

B. Prevent labour market exclusion and protect individuals against labour market risks

1. Promote equal opportunities to avoid that socio-economic background determines opportunities in the labour market through its role for the acquisition of relevant labour market skills or as a source of discrimination.

- Promote access to quality education for disadvantaged children and youth. Promoting access to pre-school programmes for children from disadvantaged backgrounds is particularly important, but countries should also ensure equal access to post-secondary education.
- Tackle the problem of school dropout through early identification and targeting of at-risk students. For individuals who leave education with very low levels of skills, second-chance options for education can provide a way out of a low skills/poor-economic-outcome trap.
- Develop policies to tackle discrimination in the labour market against women, older workers, LGBT, ethnic minorities, migrants and disabled through enforced regulations, suitable incentives and information campaigns encouraging employers to hire, promote and/or retain these workers.
- Following the Recommendation of the Council on Gender Equality in Public Life (OECD, 2015[1]), Recommendation of the Council on Gender Equality in Education, Employment and Entrepreneurship (OECD, 2013[2]), countries must step up efforts to ensure that public policy truly reflects inclusive labour markets

in which both men and women can reach their full potential. This includes, among other things, tackling gender stereotyping in education choice, promoting a more equal sharing of caring responsibilities between men and women and addressing glass-ceiling effects.

2. Adopt a life course perspective to prevent that individual disadvantages cumulate over time, requiring interventions at a later stage, which are usually less effective and involve larger fiscal costs.

- Use policy and social dialogue to encourage and enable people to develop, maintain and upgrade skills at all ages, making sure that the appropriate skill mix of vocational education and training opportunities vary according to workers' barriers and evolve throughout the working life.
- Provide workers with the right incentives to avoid early withdrawal from the labour force, consistent with the Recommendation of the Council on Ageing and Employment Policies (OECD, 2015[3]).
- Consistent with the Recommendation of the Council on Mental Health, Skills and Work Policy (OECD, 2015[4]), shape incentives, define regulations and provide guidance to adapt working conditions to workers' strengths and needs over the life cycle, including enhancing reconciliation of work and family life, thereby avoiding impinging on workers' physical and mental health. This can be done by: i) developing a rigorous legislative framework for physical and psycho-social risk assessment and risk prevention; ii) using appropriate financial incentives; and iii) making the business case for management and organisational practices that result in better working conditions.

3. Develop a comprehensive strategy to activate and protect workers, by combining adequate and widely accessible out-of-work benefits with active programmes in a mutual-obligations framework.

- Develop a comprehensive activation strategy that makes work more accessible by dealing with all barriers simultaneously by combining measures to ensure that jobless people have the motivation to search actively and accept suitable jobs with actions to expand opportunities and interventions to increase the employability of the least employable.
    - Develop and implement effective profiling tools early in the jobless spell so that intensive counselling and tailored case-management are targeted to harder-to-place jobless individuals and staff caseload is contained.
    - Make work pay through tax-benefit reforms and by providing targeted in-work benefits, while making sure that schemes are sufficiently simple and transparent to be understood by potential recipients.
    - Spending on active labour market policies needs to respond to cyclical increases in unemployment to allow for a rapid return to work and preserve the mutual-obligations ethos of activation regimes.
- Combine activation measures with adequate and widely accessible unemployment, disability and social- assistance benefits to provide income support to jobless people.

  - To help ensure that activation measures reach all people facing barriers to work it is important that income support in the form of unemployment, disability and social assistance benefits cover a large part of the potential target population.
  - Consider temporarily extending the maximum duration of unemployment benefits during a recession in countries where the maximum duration of unemployment benefits is short and unemployed workers have limited access to second-tier benefits (e.g. social assistance). Complement these extensions with enhanced access to training programmes.
- Embed activation and income-support measures in a rigorous mutual-obligations framework which makes income support and effective re-employment services conditional on beneficiaries taking active steps to find work or improve their employability. This requires making sure that job seekers efforts are strictly monitored and that warnings and sanctions are articulated in a balanced way.

4. Adopt specific policies for underrepresented and disadvantaged groups, ensuring that they simultaneously address all barriers to employment.

- Identify and analyse the barriers to quality employment faced by specific groups and jobless individuals using a comprehensive approach through coordinated actions concerning the design of tax-and-benefit policies and the provision of employment, education, training, health, childcare, housing, transport and other social services.
- Promote the labour market inclusion of people with caring responsibilities, by developing flexible working-time arrangements, removing fiscal disincentives to full-time work for second earners, encouraging sharing responsibilities between adults in the family as well as securing availability of and access to affordable and good-quality childcare and elderly care.
- Ensure that work is rewarding for lone parents, older workers and people with health issues by putting in place a comprehensive activation strategy based on the principle of mutual obligations in which employment, transfers and support services are exchanged for work and effective job-search or rehabilitation effort, while ensuring that work pays once taxes, transfers and other costs are taken into account, without heightening the risk of poverty.
- Organise disability policy around the principle of promoting ability, removing each person's specific barrier(s) to his/her employability, where this is possible, but taking care of avoiding increasing the poverty risk. Take steps to make the incentives of all actors involved – sickness and disability benefit recipients, employers, service providers as well as gate-keeping authorities and medical professionals – consistent with this strategy.
- Assess and recognise qualifications and skills acquired abroad and provide migrants with accessible language and training opportunities corresponding to their needs.

5. Support lagging regions through coordinated policies at the national, regional and local levels that promote growth and competitiveness based on their specific assets and tackle social problems associated with local concentrations of labour market exclusion and poverty.

- Promote regional growth and competitiveness by ensuring high-quality basic public services complemented with well-designed public investments to strengthen a region's competitiveness and facilitate the diffusion of innovation and good practices across regions, industries and firms.
- Use place-based policies to tackle social problems related to the local concentration of unemployment, social exclusion and poverty by alleviating financial hardship, supporting local communities and promoting employability.
- Coordinate regional and local development policies with national policies to foster policy coherence and effectiveness; to ensure sufficient financial resources for local and regional policies are available; and to strengthen the capacity of local and regional government to administer and implement them.
- Remove impediments to geographical mobility, including by making the allocation of public housing more responsive to the needs of people moving away from areas in decline and by considering the provision of subsidies to cover the costs of relocating in case people are unlikely to find employment in their region of residence, e.g. after a plant closure.

C. Prepare for future opportunities and challenges in a rapidly changing labour market

1. Promote the reallocation of workers between firms, industries and regions, while supporting displaced workers.

- Promote the reallocation of workers between firms, industries and regions through product, labour market and housing policies.
- Support displaced workers through effective skills policies (including the accreditation of informal and formal learning), adequate social protection and constructive social dialogue.

2. Enable displaced workers to move quickly into jobs, using a mixture of general and targeted income support and re-employment assistance, combined with prevention and early intervention measures.

- Provide adequate income support to displaced workers, ensuring that delays in access to unemployment benefits as a result of severance payments do not delay access to re-employment support, and being mindful that higher benefits for displaced workers might create inequities.
- In countries with low unemployment insurance coverage and spending on ALMPS, provide targeted re-employment assistance to displaced workers in the form of counselling, job search assistance and retraining.

- Minimise post-displacement costs by beginning the adjustment process during the notification period through early interventions by the public employment service and/or initiatives by the social partners to provide counselling and training before workers are laid-off. In order to make early intervention possible, countries should allow for at least a short advance notice period, while taking care that this does not undermine job reallocation and hiring on permanent contracts, and provide firms and workers with incentives to cooperate and connect with employment services as early as possible.
- Partner effectively with other actors who have the requisite contacts and expertise, such as private labour market intermediaries and public and private vocational training providers as well as employers and trade unions.

3. Accompany innovation in new forms of employment with policies to safeguard job quality by avoiding abuse, creating a level-playing field between firms, and providing adequate protection for all workers regardless of employment contract.

- Minimise abuse and the misclassification of workers by: reducing differences in regulatory and tax treatment across different forms of work; removing regulatory gaps and ambiguities; providing companies with adequate guidance on how (and based on what criteria) an employment relationship will be presumed; and guaranteeing the effective enforcement of existing regulation.
- Address tax evasion and under-reporting, while bringing new types of workers into the tax system.
- Provide adequate social protection for all workers by: extending existing social insurance schemes to previously excluded categories of workers or adapting them to non-standard forms of work (e.g. by revising thresholds on earnings or contributory periods that limit workers' receipts of benefits); making social protection more portable (i.e. linking entitlements to individuals rather than jobs); and strengthening non-contributory social assistance schemes.

4. Plan for the future by anticipating change; facilitating inclusive dialogue with the social partners and other relevant stakeholders on the future of work; and where necessary, adapting today's labour market, skills and social policies to the emerging needs in the changing world of work..

- Adopt robust systems and tools for assessing and anticipating change, combined with effective mechanisms and procedures which ensure that such information feeds into policy-making as well as into lifelong guidance.
- Ensure that all relevant stakeholders are involved in discussions around the future of work, aiming for consensus around the challenges that lie ahead and the possible solutions which could be implemented.
- Prepare for a possible paradigm shift in skills, labour market and social policy by considering new options to replace old ones, and piloting and evaluating such schemes were feasible.

). Implementation

1. Make reforms successful by adapting them to country specificities, carefully packaging and sequencing them to limit their potential cost in the short-run or for specific groups and building support for them.

- Where social capital is low and administrative capacity lacking, opt for particularly simple, transparent and easily-accountable policy actions. Combine their implementation with further investments in civil servants' skills, the definition of a rigorously-applied code of conduct and the establishment of independent bodies for internal control and audit that have enforcement powers.
- When structural reforms involve short-term or distributional costs, offset these adverse effects – through appropriately expansionary monetary or – if fiscal space exists – fiscal policy and/or by accompanying costly reforms with appropriate reforms of collective bargaining, policy actions to enhance firm-level flexibility or, in some cases, designing reforms in ways to preserve workers' entitlements as they have been acquired at the reform date (e.g. grandfathering).
- Get the sequence of reforms right by ensuring that effective activation schemes are already well functioning when reforms potentially involving short-term employment costs are implemented and by having product market reforms preceding the loosening of employment protection legislation.
- Build support for reforms by seeking an electoral mandate for them, communicating effectively on their rationale, and negotiating constructively with stakeholders.

2. Ensure that reforms are fully implemented, effectively enforced and rigorously evaluated; invest in data collection if suitable data are not available.

- Invest in data collection, including by mobilising administrative data in a way that respects confidentiality, to allow monitoring regulatory compliance, programme participation and tracking worker and firm outcomes over time.
- Ensuring compliance requires well-resourced labour inspectorates, both in terms the number of staff and their qualifications, as well as a transparent and strict enforcement process.
- Ensure that policies and programmes are regularly assessed in a rigorous way and that inefficient ones are swiftly amended or terminated.
- Build evaluation mechanisms into policy actions. Consider small-scale experimentation of new measures before implementing them on a large scale.

References

OECD (2015), *Draft Recommendation of the Council on Ageing and Employment Policies*, https://one.oecd.org/document/C(2015)172/CORR1/en/pdf. [3]

OECD (2015), *Draft Recommendation of The Council on Gender Equality in Public Life*, https://one.oecd.org/document/C(2015)164/CORR1/en/pdf. [1]

OECD (2015), *Draft Recommendation of the Council on Integrated Mental Health, School and Work Policy*, https://one.oecd.org/document/C(2015)173/CORR1/en/pdf. [4]

OECD (2013), *Recommendation of the Council on Gender Equality in Education, Employment and Entrepreneurship*, https://one.oecd.org/document/C/MIN(2013)5/FINAL/en/pdf. [2]

Part II. More and better jobs

Chapter 7. Fostering worker productivity

Productivity growth is a precondition for promoting better wages and working conditions and hence achieving high quality jobs for all. This chapter therefore discusses the main drivers of worker productivity and the role of policies and institutions to foster it. To this end, it focuses on the role of skills development, the performance of firms, with an emphasis on work and management practices, and the process through which workers are allocated to jobs in different firms.

The statistical data for Israel are supplied by and under the responsibility of the relevant Israeli authorities. The use of such data by the OECD is without prejudice to the status of the Golan Heights, East Jerusalem and Israeli settlements in the West Bank under the terms of international law.

Introduction

Productivity growth is the main driving force of better wages and working conditions in the long-term, and hence rising living standards. As such, it is also a necessary, albeit not sufficient, condition for achieving high quality jobs for all. Hence, good economic and labour market performance are inextricably linked.

The objective of this chapter is to discuss the main sources of worker productivity and the role of policies and institutions. To this end, it starts by discussing the role of skills since this is one key determinant of worker productivity. At the same time, however, employers' decisions and strategies also matter. The chapter therefore also focuses on the role of good working conditions for learning and innovation in the workplace and, more specifically, the use of high-performance work and management practices. Moreover, to ensure that good performance is rewarded and translates into high-quality job creation a fluid labour market is needed that promotes an efficient allocation of workers to firms and skills to jobs.

The chapter is structured as follows. Section 7.1 provides a brief discussion of the role of skills. Section 7.2 discusses the role of public policies for promoting the conditions for learning and innovation in the workplace. Section 7.3 discusses the role of policies and institutions for promoting a more efficient allocation of workers across jobs and firms. The final section concludes.

7.1. Boosting performance through a better supply and use of skills

Good skills are crucial for the success of both workers and firms. By increasing worker productivity, skills can strengthen incentives for firms to create jobs, offer higher wages and provide better non-wage working conditions. Skills can also make work more attractive to individuals as a result of better productivity, wages and working conditions. And a greater attractiveness of work in turn will increase labour force participation. Consequently, investing in workforce skills throughout the working life is critical for achieving better labour market outcomes in terms of both job quantity and job quality. Moreover, it is important to achieve a good match between the skills acquired by workers and those needed by employers and to ensure that the skills that workers possess are fully used in their jobs.

Skills are a key determinant of worker productivity and wages

Adults with higher proficiency in literacy, numeracy and digital problem-solving tend to have better outcomes in the labour market than their less proficient peers: they have greater chances of being employed and, when employed, are more productive in their jobs and earn higher wages. Across the countries participating in the Survey of Adult Skills, an adult who scores one standard deviation higher than another on the literacy test is 0.8 percentage point more likely to be employed and has a 6% higher wage, on average, after accounting for other factors, including educational attainment (OECD, 2016[1]). But literacy, numeracy and problem-solving only capture a subset of the skills that individuals possess. Educational attainment, beyond its impact on cognitive skills, further boosts labour market outcomes: an additional year of completed formal education is associated with an increase in the likelihood of being employed of about one percentage point and increases wages by 12% (OECD, 2016[1]).

A different way to assess the relative influence of skills on wages is to determine the extent to which worker characteristics predict differences in wages (Figure 7.1). According to the Survey of Adult Skills, on average across countries, one third of the variation in wages is explained by factors such as experience, years of education and skills proficiency. Educational attainment accounts for 13% of the variation, work experience for 9%, proficiency in literacy and numeracy for 5% and field of study for 1%. Individual characteristics, such as gender, immigrant background, marital status and language spoken at home, account for a further 4% of the variation. The unobserved component of wages partly reflects unobserved worker characteristics (e.g. unobserved ability). Indeed, the evidence summarised in OECD (2015[2]) suggests that the bulk of the variation in wages – about three quarters – can be traced to the (observable or unobservable) characteristics of workers, with the remainder being determined by their job or employer. In summary, adult skills are the main determinant of wages and productivity and are acquired through education and training as well as on-the-job learning.

Figure 7.1. Contribution of education, literacy and numeracy to the variation in wages

Contribution of each factor to the explained variance in hourly wages

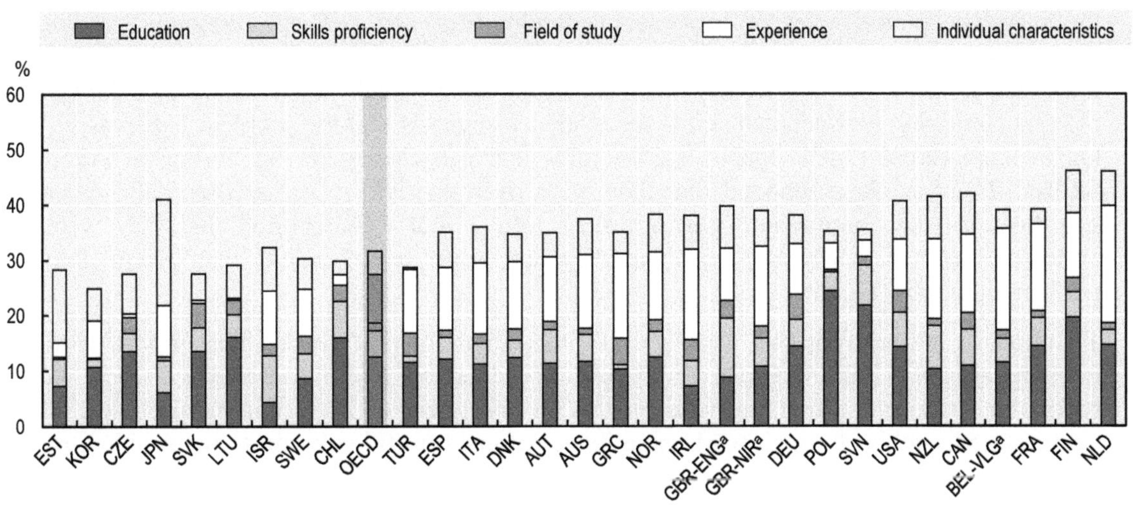

Note: Each bar summarises the results from one regression on the log of real hourly wages. Its height represents the explained share of the variance of that regression (R-squared). The sub-components of each bar show the contribution of each factor (or set of regressors) to the total R-squared. The regressors for each factor are: years of working experience and its squared term for "Experience"; proficiency in literacy and numeracy for "Skills proficiency"; years of education for "Education"; and gender, marital status, migration status and language spoken at home for "Individual characteristics".

a) The Survey of Adult Skills only covers England (GBR-ENG), Northern Ireland (GBR-NIR) and Flanders (BEL-VLG).

Source: OECD (2016[1]), *Skills Matter: Further Results from the Survey of Adult Skills*, https://doi.org/10.1787/9789264258051-en.

StatLink http://dx.doi.org/10.1787/888933881173

Consequently, providing high-quality initial education is critical to give individuals the best possible start in the labour market. Investing in high-quality early childhood education and initial schooling, particularly for children from disadvantaged socio-economic backgrounds, has proved to be an efficient strategy to ensure that all children are well positioned and become effective learners. This is discussed in detail in the *OECD Skills Strategy* (OECD, 2012[3]). However, people also need opportunities to maintain their skills, up-skill and/or re-skill throughout their working lives. At the country level, there is a clear relationship between the extent of participation in organised adult learning activities and average proficiency in key information-processing skills. In addition, much learning takes places outside formal education and training. It is therefore also important to recognise and certify skills proficiency to facilitate and encourage adult learners to undertake continued education and training. The design of life-long learning systems will be discussed in more detail in Chapters 10 and 14 of this Volume.

To reap the full potential of skills for worker productivity they need to be well-matched to job demands and fully used

While developing a better supply of skills is a necessary condition for achieving good labour market outcomes, it is not sufficient. It is equally important that the skills provided by the education and training system correspond to the skills that are required by firms and that the labour market matches workers to jobs in which they can put their skills to the best use. Indeed, a mismatch between the skills of workers and the demands of their jobs can have adverse economic implications: at the individual level, it affects job satisfaction and wages; at the firm level, it increases the rate of job turnover and may reduce productivity; at the macro-economic level, it increases unemployment and reduces economic growth through the waste of human capital and the implied reduction in productivity. While some mismatch is inevitable in a rapidly evolving economy in which new technologies disrupt old ones requiring new/adapted skills, the evidence suggests that the problem is pervasive. On average across OECD countries/economies that participated in the Survey of Adult Skills, 17% of workers reported that they were overqualified – i.e. that they had higher qualifications than required to perform their jobs – and 19% reported that they were underqualified for their jobs – i.e. that they had lower qualifications than required to perform their jobs (Figure 7.2).

To improve the relevance of worker skills for labour market needs, it is important to develop stronger links between the world of education and the world of work. In particular, work-based learning (whether this be structured, such as in apprenticeships, or unstructured, such as through work experience) offers a useful solution to the problem of skills matching since provision adjusts more or less automatically to the (immediate) needs of the labour market. More generally, employers and trade unions can play an important role in shaping education and training to make them more relevant to current needs of the labour market, for instance, by being involved in curriculum design. The social partners can also help in assessing and anticipating skills needs, another important tool to ensure that the skills produced by the education and training system are in line with labour market needs. Such information then needs to be translated into impartial, accurate and accessible information designed to help people make learning decisions, based on a good understanding of their abilities, skills, interests and values, as well as of the options available to them (OECD, 2011[4]). This will be particularly important for addressing skill shortages, but also will help to reduce the issue of overskilling by prioritising educational investments in line with the skills required in the labour market. Such involvement of the social partners requires a constant and effective dialogue between employers and the world of education – schools, universities, and other training institutions –, to adapt curricula to changing skills needs.

Figure 7.2. Qualification mismatch in OECD countries

Percentage of mismatched workers, 2016

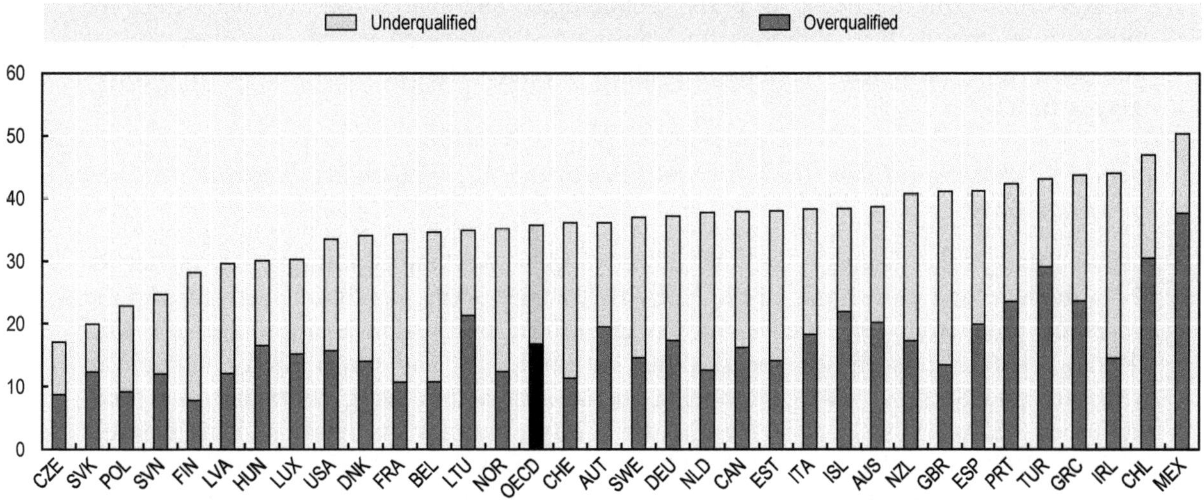

Note: Data refer to 2015 for Canada, Chile and Turkey 2015 and to 2013 for Germany. Countries are ranked in descending order of the prevalence of total mismatch (underqualification and overqualification). OECD is the unweighted average of the countries shown.

Source: OECD Skills for Jobs Database, 2018, https://stats.oecd.org/Index.aspx?DataSetCode=MISMATCH.

StatLink http://dx.doi.org/10.1787//888933881192

One way of addressing the problem of overskilling in particular is to promote a better use of skills by currently employed workers in the workplace.[1] Workers who use skills more intensely in their jobs tend to be more productive, earn higher wages and be more satisfied with their job, reducing staff turnover (UKCES, 2014[5]; OECD, 2016[11]). For example, in the Survey of Adult Skills, the intensity of use of reading skills at work correlates strongly with output per hour worked at the country level – a link which remains strong even after accounting for average proficiency scores in literacy and numeracy (OECD, 2016[6]). Put simply, the intensity with which workers use information-processing skills is important in accounting for differences in labour productivity, beyond workers' level of proficiency. Using skills at work is also important for their maintenance and, hence, avoiding atrophy. Adults who engage more often in literacy- and numeracy-related activities and use information and communication technology more – both at and outside of work – have greater proficiency in literacy, numeracy and problem-solving skills, even after accounting for educational attainment (OECD, 2016[11]). The use of skills in the workplace depends to an important extent on work and management practices and the role of policies and institutions. This is discussed more fully in Section 7.2.

Finally, to ensure that workers are well-matched to firms in terms of skills, it is equally important that firms have the means to attract, retain and, if necessary, let go of workers, and workers can move freely between firms in the pursuit of better job opportunities (see Section 7.3).

7.2. Promoting the conditions for learning and innovation in the workplace

While a good supply and use of skills are key for worker productivity, it also matters for which firm one works. This section focuses on the role of good wages and working conditions for firm performance and high-performance work and management (HPWM) practices. It is argued that good working conditions contribute to long-term employer-employee relationships, and by doing so, strengthen incentives for both workers and firms to invest in skills, technologies and innovation. The challenge for policy is to provide the conditions for learning and innovation in the workplace and, at the same time, sufficient flexibility to allow for the efficient reallocation of workers across firms.

Good working conditions not only matter for worker well-being but also for firm performance

Among many other factors – see OECD (2015[7]) – working conditions may matter for both the level and growth rate of productivity. Better working conditions may support the *level* of productivity by increasing worker effort, motivation and morale (Akerlof, 1982[8]), reducing incentives for shirking by employees and the need for monitoring (Shapiro and Stiglitz, 1984[9]), reducing recruitment and training costs due to worker turnover (Salop, 1979[10]) strengthening the ability to attract and retain suitable workers (Weiss, 1980[11]) and promoting health at work (Box 7.1).[2] Working conditions may further affect the *growth rate* of productivity by providing the conditions for learning and innovation. Indeed, the main virtue of providing relatively good working conditions may be to foster long-term employer-employee relationships that create incentives for both workers and firms to invest in skills, technologies and innovation. This logic is at the heart of so-called high-performance work and management (HPWM) practices, which include aspects of work organisation – team work, autonomy, task discretion, mentoring, job rotation, applying new learning – as well as management practices – employee participation, group-based incentive pay, training practices and flexibility in working hours (Johnston et al., 2002[12]). Apart from promoting incentives for learning and innovation, they typically seek to make work more responsive to emerging challenges and opportunities by facilitating the adoption of innovative production technologies and the experimentation with new ideas.[3]

The available empirical evidence tends to support the view that HPWM practices can help promote productivity (Bloom and Reenen, 2011[13]). While the evidence typically relates to the level of productivity rather than its growth rate and causality is not always reliably established, it provides a number of plausible insights. First, individual practices that are associated with higher productivity include group-based incentive pay, decentralised decision-making and employee voice (Bloom and Reenen, 2011[13]). Second, the overall coherence of HR practices may be more important for firm performance than the use of individual practices on their own (Ichniowski, Shaw and Prennushi, 1997[14]). For example, the combination of group-based incentive pay and teamwork tends to be more effective than either measure on its own. Third, HPWM practices encourage a better use of skills in the workplace. For example, OECD (2016[6]) finds that HPWM practices explain about a fifth of the variation in the intensity with which workers use information-processing skills.

Despite the potentially important benefits of HPWM practices, there are large differences in their use across firms, industries and countries – e.g. Ichniowski and Shaw (2003[15]), Lazear and Shaw (2007[16]), Bloom and Van Reenen (2011[13]). For instance, the share of jobs in HPWM workplaces ranges from about 10% in Greece to about 40% in Denmark, Finland and Sweden (Figure 7.3). One possible explanation for these differences is that their benefits differ across firms, depending on their production technology, the availability of other input factors (e.g. skills, capital), consumer preferences and the wider institutional context. Consequently, a more widespread use of such practices may not be optimal for firms given the environment in which they operate. Another is related to the presence of information or transaction costs. Information or transaction costs may relate to the acquisition of management expertise, the introduction of new management systems and the adjustment of the workforce to new tasks and work practices. This could explain why HPWM practices spread more easily among firms with a certain size or a strong ICT infrastructure (Bresnahan, Brynjolfsson and Hitt, 2002[17]; Bartel, Ichniowski and Shaw, 2007[18]).

Figure 7.3. High-performance work and management practices

Share of jobs with HPWM practices

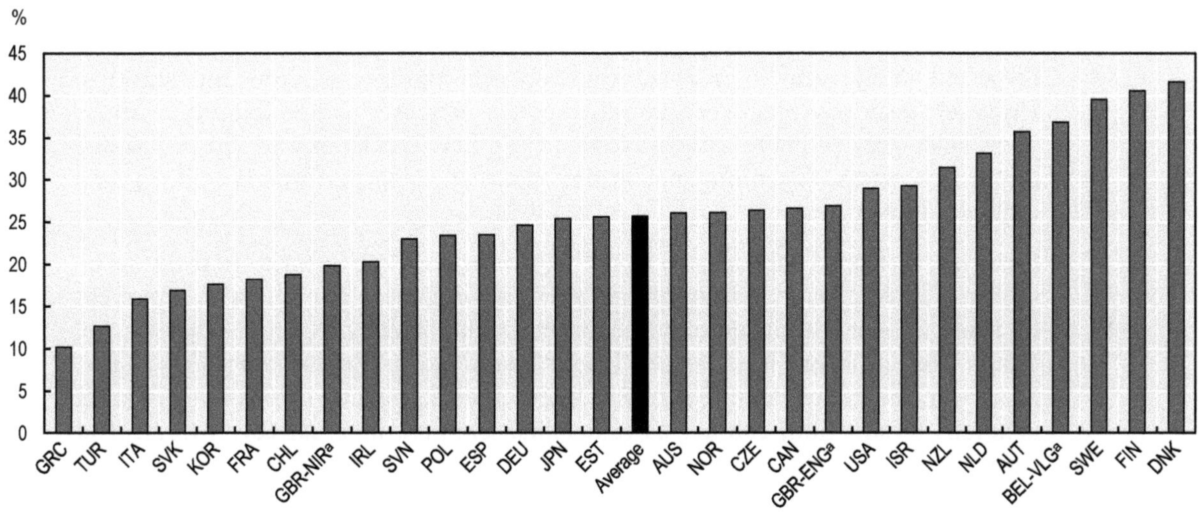

Note: Share of workers in jobs where the summary HPWM practices is above the top 25th percentile of the pooled distribution.

a) The Survey of Adult Skills only covers England (GBR-ENG), Northern Ireland (GBR-NIR) and Flanders (BEL-VLG).

Source: OECD (2016[6]), "Skills use at work: Why does it matter and what influences it?", in *OECD Employment Outlook 2016*, https://doi.org/10.1787/empl_outlook-2016-6-en.

StatLink http://dx.doi.org/10.1787/888933881211

Box 7.1. High-performance work and management practices and the OECD Job Quality framework

High-performance work and management (HPWM) practices are likely to affect many aspects of job quality. They tend to place a particularly strong emphasis on the intrinsic value of work by investing in people and the organisation of work. This box briefly reviews some of the links between HPWM practices and the key dimensions of job quality as defined in the *OECD Job Quality framework* – e.g. OECD (2014[19]), Cazes et al. (2015[20]).

1. **Earnings**. In firms characterised by HPWM practices, reward packages are likely to be: i) relatively generous to attract and retain good workers; ii) closely aligned with firm performance to maintain strong group incentives; and iii) not too dispersed within firms to promote teamwork and harmonious work relationships. However, such pay practices may also induce increased wage dispersion across firms since they promote assortative matching between firms and workers based on the presence of complementarities between high-performance firms and high-ability workers.
2. **Security.** In firms characterised by HPWM practices, job security is likely to be higher. The emphasis on training and skills development requires a commitment of firms to longer-term employer-employee relationships. Among other things, this is likely to result in increased labour hoarding during temporary downturns. Moreover, the use of flexible forms of work organisation can help finding internal solutions to structural challenges rather than external ones based on hiring and firing.
3. **Work environment.** HPWM practices are likely to be particularly important for the quality of the work environment. The OECD measures the quality of the work environment in terms of the balance between job demands and job resources. Job demands relate to physical demands, work intensity and the flexibility of working time. Job resources include various HPWM practices and relate to task discretion and work autonomy, training and learning opportunities and the scope for career advancement. By investing in job resources, HPWM practices allow workers to cope with greater job demands, reduce psycho-social health risks and boost worker and firm performance (Arends, Prinz and Abma, 2017[21]).

The role of policies and institutions for good firm performance

Work and organisational practices are ultimately decided by employers. But public policies have also a role to play by promoting the conditions for learning and innovation in the workplace and the adoption of HPWM practices.[4] Beyond the key role of developing and adapting skills, which has already been discussed above, this could involve setting standards to rule out unsustainable work practices, while preserving incentives for good performance of firms. Social dialogue in the workplace between management and worker representatives also has a potentially important role to play.

Work and organisational practices are set by firms subject to legal standards and social norms

Policies and institutions can rule out unsustainable work practices that undermine worker well-being as well as business performance in the medium to longer-term by setting legal working standards. Despite being in the long-term interest of firms themselves, not all firms might meet minimum standards in the absence of regulation due to the role of poor management, liquidity constraints or an excessive focus on short-term outcomes. Working standards may relate to: occupational health and safety to reduce physical and mental health risks; working time to limit excessive working hours and the use of night shifts, while establishing the right to rest breaks and paid leave; work-life balance policies in the form of parental leave, as well as; a balanced employment protection that strengthens incentives for learning, without undermining experimentation or job reallocation. It may also include a moderate minimum wage that strikes a balance between strengthening incentives for the adoption of more efficient organisation and management practices, including a better use of skills, and maintaining good employment prospects for low-skilled workers.

But governments should also leave sufficient space to provide incentives for good performance and reap the benefits of HPMW practices. High performance firms need flexibility to allow experimenting with new ideas and adapting to emerging challenges and opportunities. Moreover, product market competition typically strengthens incentives for more efficient work and management practices. Simple cross-country correlations provide some indication that firms are more likely to adopt HPMW practices the more flexible the institutional environment – e.g. Hall and Soskice (2001[22]), Frege and Godard (2014[23]), Bloom and Van Reenen (2011[13]).[5] This, however, does not necessarily mean that more market-oriented policies are required for stronger productivity growth within firms. OECD (2007[24]) shows that countries with more interventionist, but coherent employment and social policies, recorded similar levels of economic growth as more market-reliant countries. These countries tend to be characterised by government policies that focus on the protection of workers rather than their jobs and a strong reliance on the social partners for the determination of working conditions.

Governments can also actively promote HPWM practices by setting clear expectations on the behaviour of business through the establishment of social norms. While compliance with norms is voluntary, firms often prefer to abide by them when they can. Norms can be particularly important in emerging and developing economies where regulatory standards can be weak or enforcement lax. The impact of norms can be reinforced through information dissemination and advice on best practices, as well as through the provision of management training. There exist a number of multilateral initiatives that seek to promote responsible business conduct in the area of employment and industrial relations. The OECD Guidelines for Multinational Enterprises are the most comprehensive government-supported corporate responsibility instrument (see Box 7.2). A unique feature of the Guidelines is that they come with a system of National Contact Points (NCPs) to disseminate them, provide training and offer mediation in specific instances.

Box 7.2. The OECD Guidelines for Multinational Enterprises

The OECD Guidelines for Multinational Enterprises, adopted in 1976 and revised in 2000 and 2011, are the most comprehensive government-supported corporate responsibility instrument in existence today. Their forty-six adhering governments – 35 OECD countries and 11 non-OECD countries – are committed to encourage enterprises in their country to observe a set of widely recognised principles and standards for responsible business conduct in their business operations and supply chains. In the area of employment and industrial relations, it commits government to encourage enterprises and their supply chains amongst others to:

- Contribute to the effective abolition of child and forced labour, non-discrimination and equality of opportunity, respect the right to worker representation and ensure the health and safety of workers in their operations.
- In the event of collective lay-offs, provide reasonable notice to worker representatives and co-operate with the worker representatives and appropriate governmental authorities so as to mitigate to the maximum extent practicable adverse effects.
- In the context of *bona fide* negotiations with workers' representatives on conditions of employment, not threaten to transfer activities from the country concerned to other countries in order to influence those negotiations unfairly.
- Refrain from seeking or accepting exemptions to labour and other regulatory standards.

Adhering countries take up the obligation to set up national contact points (NCPs), with the general aim of furthering the effectiveness of the guidelines. NCPs undertake promotional activities, handle enquiries and contribute to the resolution of grievances related to the non-observance of the Guidelines in specific instances. Most specific instances relate to human rights, employment and industrial relations. NCPs may be organised as tripartite, government or independent agencies.

Source: OECD (2008[25]), "Do Multinationals Promote Better Pay and Working Conditions?", in *OECD Employment Outlook 2008*, https://doi.org/10.1787/empl_outlook-2008-7-en; and OECD (2017[26]), Annual Report on the OECD Guidelines for Multinational Enterprises 2016, http://mneguidelines.oecd.org/2016-Annual-Report-MNE-Guidelines-EN.pdf.

Social dialogue in the workplace has the potential to promote better outcomes for firms and workers

Social dialogue and collective bargaining not only contribute to better conditions for workers, but may also affect productivity. Their impact on firm productivity depends in theory on two potentially opposing channels (Freedom and Medoff, 1984[27]). By providing a voice to workers, collective worker representation can help overcome common challenges (e.g. adoption of new technologies or the prevention of work-related health problems) and promote productivity ("voice" channel). At the same time, by strengthening the bargaining power of workers, collective bargaining can lead to a larger share of rents for workers, induce a more compressed wage structure and stronger worker protections, with potentially adverse effects for resource allocation, profitability, investment and human capital accumulation, as well as productivity ("monopoly" channel).

The empirical evidence on social dialogue and collective bargaining in the workplace tentatively suggests either no or small positive net effects on firm productivity, with considerable heterogeneity across workplaces, industries and countries – e.g. Hirsch (2004[28]), Addison (2016[29]), Doucouliagos et al. (2018[30]).[6] The effects are likely to be more positive the better the quality of the labour relations (Krueger and Mas, 2004[31]; OECD, 2016[6]),[7] the higher the degree of product market competition (Freedom and Medoff, 1984[27]) and when collective worker representation in the workplace is present (OECD, 2018[32]). It may also help if the voice and monopoly channels are clearly separated as is the case in dual systems that combine sector-level collective bargaining with works councils in the workplace (Marsden, 2015[33]; Freeman and Lazear, 1995[34]).

In principle, collective worker representation in the workplace could strengthen the use and effectiveness of HPWM practices, by promoting the use of skills in the workplace, facilitating the flow of information, encouraging the participation of workers in management decisions and building employee support for organisational change. However, the evidence on the role of collective worker representation for either the use or effectiveness of HPWM practices tends to be relatively weak, albeit mostly positive e.g. Addison (2016[29]), OECD (2016[6]), Laroche and Salesina (2017[35]).

7.3. Promoting an efficient allocation of workers across jobs and firms

Providing the conditions for learning and innovation in the workplace also requires that good performance is rewarded by allowing high-performing firms to thrive and grow and ensuring that workers are employed in firms that fit their skills. This not only would strengthen incentives for good performance and skill acquisition, but also would amplify their benefits by increasing the contribution of high-performing firms and human capital to overall economic growth. However, the extent to which good performance is rewarded differs importantly across countries due to differences in the efficiency and effectiveness of job reallocation across firms. There are also important differences in the extent to which the skills of workers match those required by the firms for which they work.

An efficient allocation of jobs is needed to ensure that high-performance firms create high-quality jobs

All modern economies are characterised by sizeable labour reallocation across firms, industries and regions. Each year, more than 20% of jobs, on average, are created and/or terminated, and around one-third of all workers are hired and/or separate from their employer, with most of these flows occurring within industries (OECD, 2009[36]). There are large differences in job reallocation rates across countries, ranging from 15% of jobs being created or destroyed in a number of continental European countries to 25% in countries such as the United Kingdom and the United States.

Labour reallocation is an important driver of aggregate productivity growth (OECD, 2009[36]; OECD, 2010[37])[8] and differences in its efficiency can account for sizeable differences in productivity performance across countries (Hsieh and Klenow, 2009[38]; Bartelsman, Haltiwanger and Scarpetta, 2013[39]). Moreover, OECD research suggests that skill mismatch reduces productivity as a result of inefficiencies in the process of job reallocation across firms (McGowan and Andrews, 2015[40]).[9] For policy, this implies that aggregate productivity can be promoted and skills mismatch reduced by removing barriers to the efficient reallocation of workers across firms, provided this is not offset by weaker incentives for learning and innovation within continuing firms.

The efficiency of job reallocation depends on the ease with which firms adjust their workforce in response to changing business conditions, entrepreneurs can start or liquidate a business and workers move across firms and places in search of better career opportunities. This section focuses mainly on the role of employment protection for reallocation, but also discusses some issues in relation to the regulation of product markets and worker mobility. A more in-depth discussion of entry and exit barriers in product market markets and geographical mobility is presented in Chapter 14 of this Volume.

To allow for efficient job reallocation employment protection should not be overly strict

Employment protection legislation defines the rules that govern the hiring and firing of workers (see Box 7.3 for a general introduction to employment protection). It is generally justified by the need to protect workers from unfair behaviour on the part of their employers, to internalise some of the social cost of labour turnover and to preserve firm-specific human capital by preventing the destruction of jobs that are viable in the longer-term (Pissarides, 2010[41]). However, overly restrictive regulations hinder productivity growth by reducing job turnover and the efficient reallocation of resources. It can also have a negative impact on the employment opportunities of outsiders. The inclusiveness aspects of employment protection will be discussed in Chapter 10.

Employment protection has raised concerns over labour market fluidity and duality

Employment protection for workers on open-ended contracts reduces job dismissals, but in doing so, also reduces incentives for hiring on open-ended contracts by employers and on-the-job search by workers. As a result, employment protection tends to have either no or a small negative effect on employment – see OECD (2006[42]) and Kemperer (2016[43]) for surveys. Its main effect is therefore to reduce overall labour market fluidity in terms of worker and job flows (Micco and Pagés, 2006[44]; OECD, 2010[37]; Bartelsman, Haltiwanger and Scarpetta, 2013[39]).[10] A detailed look at the impact of different employment-protection provisions suggests that this is mainly driven by high severance pay, long trial periods and strict reinstatement rules (Bassanini and Garnero, 2013[45]).

The productivity effects of employment protection tend to be mostly negative, suggesting that its adverse effects on job reallocation tend to dominate any potentially positive effects on learning and innovation. Using cross-country industry data, Bassanini, Nunziata and Venn (2009[46]) show that dismissal regulations depress productivity growth in industries where layoff restrictions are most likely to be binding.[11] These effects may reflect the role of employment protection for the efficiency of job reallocation, the engagement of firms and entrepreneurs in risky activities such as innovation (Bartelsman, Gautier and De Wind, 2016[47]; Griffith and Macartney, 2014[48]), or the excessive use of temporary contracts (Dolado, Ortigueira and Stucchi, 2016[49]).

Box 7.3. The regulation of employment protection in OECD and key emerging economies

The OECD employment protection indicators measure the costs and procedures involved in dismissing workers on open-ended contacts – either individually or collectively – (Figure 7.4, Panel A) or hiring workers on fixed-term contracts or temporary-agency workers (Figure 7.4, Panel B). The regulation of individual dismissals of workers on open-ended contracts consists of three key aspects: i) procedural inconveniences for employers engaging in a dismissal process, such as notification and consultation requirements; ii) notice periods and severance pay in the case of fair dismissal; and iii) difficulty of dismissal, which relates to the permissible grounds for dismissal and the repercussions for the employer if a dismissal is found to be unfair. Most countries further impose additional restrictions for collective dismissals of a large group of workers at the same time. The regulation of the use of fixed-term contracts or temporary-agency workers relates to the circumstances where they can be used, the number of times they can be renewed and their cumulative duration.

As of 2013, the employment protection rules for the individual dismissal of workers on open-ended contracts were most stringent in a number of key emerging economies and also tended to be rather stringent in countries such as Czech Republic, Germany, the Netherlands and Portugal (before recent reforms in some of these countries). They are least strict in the United States, Canada and the United Kingdom. The use of fixed-term and temporary contracts is least stringent in common-law countries where employment protection for workers on open-ended contacts is relatively weak, but also in some countries that maintain relatively strict rules for workers on open-ended contracts such as the Netherlands and Sweden. With few exceptions, countries with more stringent rules for the use of temporary contracts also tend to have more stringent rules for temporary-agency work.

Firing and hiring regulations across countries exhibit a number of patterns (OECD, 2013[50]). First, one can distinguish two broad classes of employment protection systems across countries: i) countries where the definition of unfair dismissal is very narrow but workers are usually compensated, no matter whether termination was fair or not; ii) countries where compensation for fair dismissals tends to be low or zero, but the definition of unfair dismissal is broad and compensation high. Second, beyond common-law countries, there is no obvious relationship between the difficulty of dismissing workers on open-ended contracts and the ease of using fixed-term contracts or temporary-agency workers.

Over the past decade, there has been a clear tendency towards reducing the strictness of employment protection in relation to workers on open-ended contracts. Reforms have tended to focus on limiting the possibility of reinstatement in the case of unfair dismissal and the extension of the probation period. At the same time, there has also been some tendency to restrict the use of temporary contracts and temporary-agency work, albeit reforms have tended to be modest and some went in the opposite direction (e.g. Mexico). The recent convergence in the protection of open-ended and fixed-term contracts stands in marked contrast with developments during the 1990s, when many countries deregulated hiring on temporary contracts, while maintaining stringent rules for regular contracts.

Figure 7.4. Employment protection in OECD and key emerging economies

2013

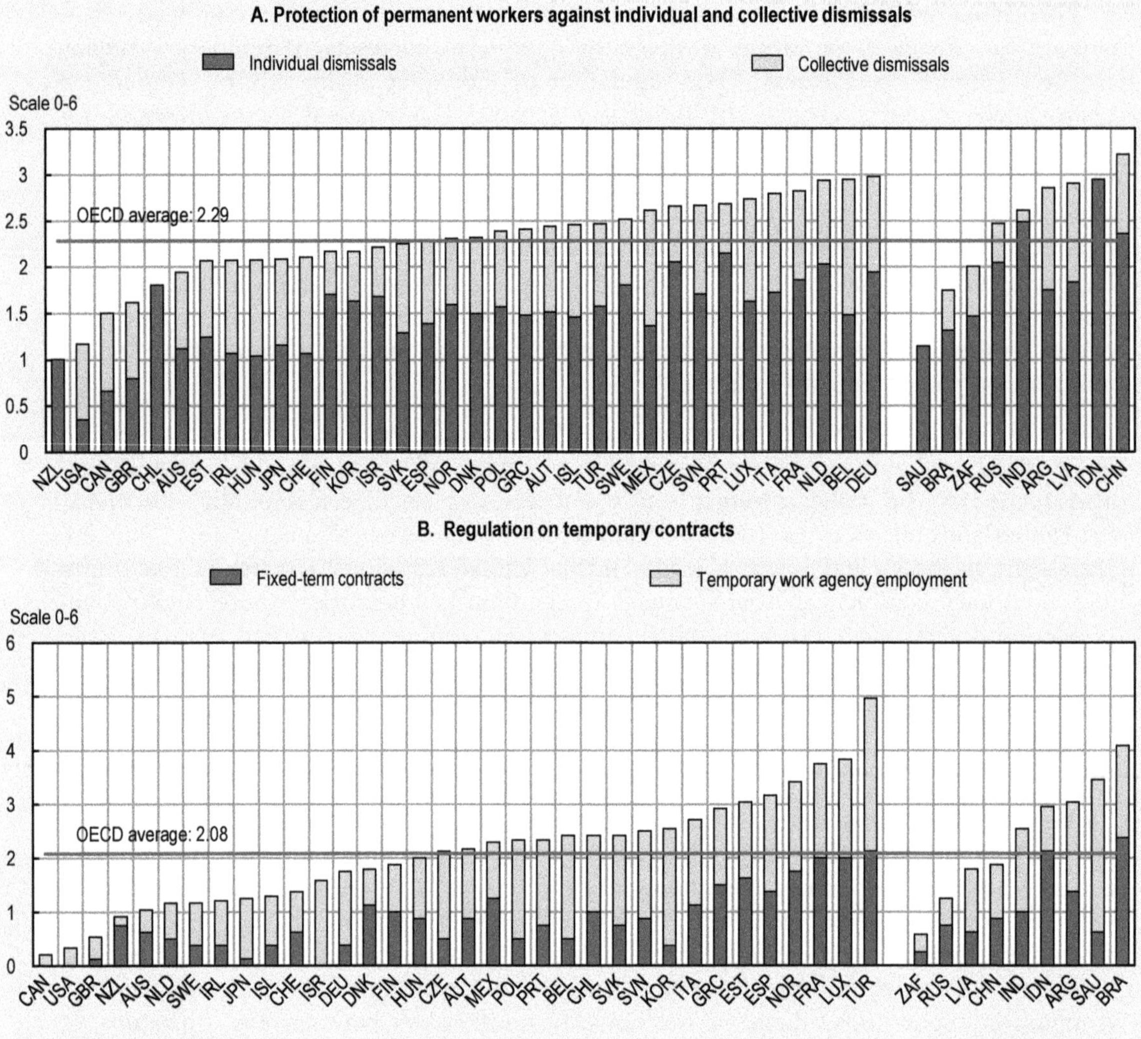

Source: OECD (2013[50]), "Protecting jobs, enhancing flexibility: A new look at employment protection legislation", in *OECD Employment Outlook 2013*, https://doi.org/10.1787/empl_outlook-2013-6-en.

StatLink http://dx.doi.org/10.1787/888933881230

There is little indication that strict employment protection contributes to better job quality. While employment protection reduces the risk of involuntary job loss, and hence objective concerns over job security, it also reduces the probability of finding another job. Aghion et al. (2016[51]) and Hijzen and Menyhert (2016[52]) suggest that, for a given level of unemployment, the speed of job reallocation tends to be positively related to well-being, suggesting that its impact on job-finding dominates that on job loss. This also may explain the apparent paradox documented in Postel-Vinay and Saint-Martin (2005),

Clark and Postel-Vinay (2009[53]) and Saucier-Lepage and Wasmer (2016[54]) that, across countries, more stringent employment protection is associated with weaker perceived job security, lower life satisfaction, and increased stress levels. Apart from affecting labour market security, employment protection may also affect earnings. It may lower wages to the extent that expected dismissal costs are passed on from employers to employees[12] or, alternatively, increase them by strengthening the bargaining position of workers (Leonardi and Pica, 2013[55]).

Beyond the direct effects of employment protection on workers with open-ended contracts, employment protection can also have consequences for the composition of open-ended and fixed-term contracts. More specifically, when employment protection is rather strict employers can circumvent employment-protection provisions by substituting open-ended contracts by fixed-term or service contracts, with potentially important adverse consequences for job quality, inclusiveness and productivity performance. This will be discussed in more detail in Chapter 10.

Employment protection needs to balance flexibility for firms with security for workers

Well-designed employment-protection rules protect workers against abuse, limit excessive layoffs, while supporting a dynamic business environment. This requires a balanced employment-protection framework that provides flexibility for firms and protection for workers, while avoiding excessive differences in legal treatment by reason of dismissal and type of contract. Large differences in compensation by reason of dismissal increase the risk that this becomes a source of conflict between employer and employee that needs to be resolved in court. Large differences by contract generate incentives for firms to circumvent provisions for open-ended contracts by relying more heavily on fixed-term contracts (OECD, 2014[56]).

This first of all requires that workers are effectively protected against unfair dismissals, i.e. dismissals that relate to false reasons and reasons unrelated to work, including discrimination, harassment and prohibited grounds. However, to avoid harming the economic flexibility of firms, it is important that the definition of unfair dismissal is restricted to those reasons alone and that dismissals for serious economic and personal reasons are considered fair. While such a restrictive definition of unfair dismissal already exists in most common-law countries, implementing this in civil-law countries could be challenging in practice. To an important extent, this reflects the difficulty of unambiguously defining the boundary between fair and unfair dismissal in the law. This is particularly an issue in the case of dismissals for personal reasons since it can be difficult to establish whether they are work-related or not.[13]

At the same time, the conditions for economic dismissals in terms of advance notice and severance pay should strike the right balance between containing excessive layoffs, insuring workers against the risk of job loss and providing flexibility to firms.[14] While it is difficult to determine the optimal levels of severance pay and advance notice, the predominantly negative productivity effects of employment protection in the empirical literature suggest that they should not be too high.[15] Since this would imply limited insurance against the risk of unemployment, it is important that high-coverage unemployment benefits are available to unemployed workers as part of a broader activation strategy based on mutual obligations (see Chapter 9).[16]

Regulations that limit the gap in protection between workers on open-ended and fixed-term contracts can further help to strengthen incentives for learning and innovation without undermining the efficient reallocation of resources.[17] Importantly, having balanced employment-protection regulations across contract types would also help to reduce labour market segmentation and related concerns about low quality jobs with poor opportunities for career advancement (see Chapter 10). Full convergence in termination costs could be achieved through the introduction of either a single contract – with termination costs increasing with job tenure and applied to all workers, while suppressing fixed-term contracts – or a unified contract – with the same termination costs applying to all contracts, independently of whether they are permanent or temporary. However, their effective implementation would require extending the definition of fair dismissal and restricting that of unfair dismissal.[18]

The cost and effectiveness of employment protection also depend on the efficiency of the system for dispute resolution. For employers, costly, complex or time-consuming legal processes can add significantly to the effective costs of dismissing workers. But equally, if it is difficult or costly for employees to pursue cases of unfair dismissal, they might be exposed to arbitrary actions from employers. More than half of OECD countries have specialised courts or procedures to handle unfair dismissal cases, making courts more accessible, reducing the time taken to deal with cases and improving satisfaction with outcomes. In addition, alternative dispute resolution mechanisms are often in place (OECD, 2013[50]). Resolving disputes early (either through pre-court dispute resolution mechanisms or pre-trial conciliation) saves time and money compared with waiting for a court decision (Knight and Latreille, 2000[57]; Montes Rojas and Santamaría, 2007[58]; Hayward, 2004[59]).

Reduce barriers to firm entry and exit

Supressing anti-competitive product market regulations can spur productivity growth by promoting entry, enhancing market discipline and facilitating access to intermediate inputs. Product market regulations also shape the diffusion of existing technologies from the national frontier to laggard firms. Reducing the stringency of product market regulations, particularly entry barriers, is associated with higher productivity growth, stronger catch-up of firms to the national frontier (Andrews and Gal, 2015[60])) and higher investment and job creation (Gal and Hijzen, 2016[61]). While much progress has been made in opening up markets in energy, transport, and communications since the 1990s, substantial scope for reform remains in retail and professional services in many countries (Gal and Hijzen, 2016[61]). Restrictions in retail have tended to slow the transition from small-scale, low productivity, often family-owned businesses to larger, more productive businesses using more sophisticated management and work practices, with adverse consequences for the creation of quality jobs. Restrictions in professional services typically relate to the recognition of qualifications and occupational licencing. In some countries, occupational licensing has acted as a barrier to mobility, without clear benefits in terms of service quality, consumer health or safety.

Bankruptcy regimes make it less likely that inefficient firms with low growth potential will continue to operate, underpinning the reallocation of capital and labour toward high-performing firms. In principle, it can also foster experimentation with risky technologies, technology diffusion and innovation. However, this is less likely if credit conditions are tightened as a result of reduced loss recovery in case of bankruptcy. Striking the right balance between these two forces makes the design of bankruptcy provisions complicated. Adalet McGowan, Andrews and Millot (2017[62]) show that there is much scope to improve the design of insolvency regimes in order to reduce the barriers to the restructuring of weak firms and the personal costs associated with entrepreneurial failure. Since the survival of low productivity firms that would typically exit in a competitive market may partly stem from bank forbearance, complementary reforms to insolvency regimes are essential to ensure that a more aggressive policy to resolve non-performing loans is effective.

The ability of high-performing firms to create high quality jobs also hinges on their access to credit (Aghion, Fally and Scarpetta, 2007[63]). Financing constraints tend to be more acute for young firms to the extent that they have limited internal funds and lack a track record to signal their "quality" to investors. This financing gap is partly bridged by venture capitalists or business angels, who address informational asymmetries by intensively scrutinising firms before providing capital and subsequent monitoring (Hall and Lerner, 2010[64]). Empirical evidence suggests that venture capital has a sizeable positive impact on innovation and growth (Andrews and Gal, 2015[60]).

Promote the mobility of workers across jobs

The policy discussion on job reallocation typically focuses on the role of flexibility on the employer side, with less attention being paid to the role of barriers to and incentives for mobility on the worker side. This section briefly reviews some of the elements that are important for worker mobility.

Efficiency-enhancing job reallocation can be costly for both firms and workers, particularly when associated with involuntary worker movements, due to the role of dismissal and displacement costs. Voluntary worker mobility, where workers quit their job for another one in a different firm, induces downsizing in low-productivity firms even if firm flexibility is limited. Davis, Faberman and Haltiwanger (2006[65]) show for the United States that small reductions in employment – which account for a very large part of overall job destruction – are largely accommodated through quits rather than layoffs. Voluntary worker mobility is to an important extent driven by the ability of high-performing firms to offer higher wages, provide better working conditions and more appealing career perspectives than their less productive competitors. This highlights the role of wage-setting for job reallocation (Haltiwanger et al., 2018[66]).

Wage-setting institutions, such as statutory minimum wages and collective bargaining, are mainly motivated by concerns about fair pay and working conditions, but can also have implications for the cost and effectiveness of job reallocation. By compressing the distribution of wages across firms for similar jobs, they potentially reduce worker incentives for job-to-job mobility, while increasing the risk that low-productivity workers are displaced, with potentially important implications for the cost and effectiveness of labour reallocation. OECD (2018[32]), for instance, suggests that centralised bargaining systems tend to be associated with lower productivity growth if coverage of collective agreements is high. In the same vein, McGowan and Andrews (2015[40]) suggest that flexible wage-setting policies reduce skills mismatch. Concerns about the adverse effects of centralised bargaining on productivity growth have motivated calls for more decentralised forms of collective bargaining that provide more space to firms for setting wage and working conditions according to business conditions (see Chapter 8 for more details).[19]

While wage incentives are important for job-to-job mobility they are not sufficient. Workers also should have the right skills required for the job. In general, skills barriers to job mobility tend to be less important when skills are transferable across jobs (Montt, 2015[67]). Skills transferability can be promoted by placing more emphasis on the provision of general or cognitive skills in the education and training system while relying more on the job-learning for the acquisition of additional job-specific skills. To limit the adverse effects of occupational licensing on job mobility, one possibility may be to rely more heavily on occupational competences rather than formal qualifications for the attribution of licenses. The portability of accrued rights and protections related to, for example, severance pay, unemployment insurance or training across jobs also matters. To address the role of limited portability for job-to-job mobility a number of countries have introduced mandatory individual saving accounts. For example, Austria and Brazil have mandatory individual saving accounts for the purpose of severance pay, while France has made training rights portable by making use of individual training accounts. The portability of entitlements for social protection is particularly important given the increasing prevalence of new forms of work, such as those associated with the platform economy.

Additional measures to reduce the costs of job transitions may also be needed. These could include targeted policies for displaced workers or policies to help people move to the regions where the best jobs are available (see Chapter 14). Policies targeted at displaced workers typically complement standard activation policies with specific measures to intervene early during the advance-notice period and address specific barriers to re-employment through, for example, retraining or the use of financial incentives. In some countries, sector-level initiatives between the social partners also exist with the aim of facilitating job transitions and ensure that the skills of workers remain up-to-date. Geographical mobility can be promoted through housing policies that do not impede residential mobility (e.g. transaction costs on buying property and stringent planning regulations) or the use of financial incentives for relocation. In some countries, occupational licensing has acted as a barrier to mobility. Such licensing should be used judiciously and standards should be harmonised across regions as much as possible.

Conclusions

This chapter discussed the main sources of worker productivity and the role of policies and institutions. To this end, it focused on the role of skills development, the performance of firms, with an emphasis on high-performance work and management practices, and the process through which workers are allocated to jobs in different firms.

Skills are paramount for worker productivity and success in the labour market more generally. Skills do not only allow workers to be more effective in their jobs, but they also promote learning, innovation and the adoption of new technologies. However, just having a skilled workforce is not enough. It is equally important that the skills of workers are effectively matched to the needs of employers. This highlights the importance of education and training systems that equip workers with the skills that are required by employers, the use of high-performance work and management practices built around long-term employer-employee relationships and an efficient matching process that allocates workers to firms and skills to jobs according to their most productive use.

To promote both learning and innovation in the workplace and an efficient job reallocation process, policies need to strike the right balance between stability – to promote incentives for human capital accumulation – and flexibility – to allow for efficient job reallocation. While this may suggest a possible trade-off for policy, in practice, stability is best achieved by human-resources policies that seek to promote firm performance by investing in the workforce. Indeed, high-performance work and management practices rely to an important extent on the flexibility of such practices to adapt to emerging challenges. The main focus of regulation should therefore be to protect workers against exploitation and abuse (and entrepreneurs against the personal cost of failure), while leaving employers, along with social partners, sufficient space to manage their business. The next chapter will discuss the role of regulation in more detail by focusing on the role of wage-setting institutions for achieving a broader sharing of productivity gains.

Looking ahead, in a rapidly changing world of work, it will be increasingly important to ensure that workers can move easily across jobs according to their skills and opportunities. This will put a premium on policies that support flexible product and labour markets, but also on policies that facilitate job transitions related to skills, social protection and social dialogue. Chapter 14 will provide a deeper discussion of policies that can help the labour market become more adaptable in a context of rapid structural change.

Notes

[1] There is also a need to make better use of the skills of those out of employment. The importance of "activating" those skills and the policies required to do so are discussed in the Chapter 9.

[2] Early studies emphasised that if all firms act alike, the benefits of efficiency wages in terms of productivity disappear and their main consequence will be to depress employment by increasing labour costs. This is known as the "efficiency-wage" explanation for unemployment. Similar to the standard competitive model of the labour market, this yields a negative relationship between job quality and job quantity. The relevance of efficiency wages as an explanation for unemployment may nevertheless be limited. In practice, different human-resource practices are likely to co-exist due to differences in the benefits of efficiency wages across firms or the availability of other, more tailored, instruments for motivating and selecting workers, such as performance pay (Lazear and Shaw, 2007[16]).

[3] This way, HPWM practices help to transform firms in effective learning organisations (Senge, 1990[69]).

[4] Barriers derive from the lack of management skills and expertise as well as the need for significant upfront investments in organisational capital. Incentives are shaped by the context in which firms operate.

[5] Bloom and Van Reenen (2010[70]), for example, show that firms in countries with more flexible employment protection rules tend to invest more in people management. This may reflect the possibility that in such countries worker turnover tends to be higher and that this increases the importance of investing in people management.

[6] While there is no evidence of a negative effect of social dialogue or collective bargaining within firms, there are number of studies that have found negative effects at the sector or country level (OECD, 2018[32]).

[7] OECD (2016[6]) shows that strong collective bargaining institutions are found to be positively associated with a higher utilisation of workers' skills in the workplace. It is argued that this reflects the role of good industrial relations, institutions and practices for encouraging the participation of workers in firm decisions and facilitating the buy-in of employees to changes in work organisation and management practices associated with higher skills use.

[8] The link between job reallocation and productivity is typically investigated using dynamic accounting decompositions. This entails decomposing aggregate productivity growth into the contribution of firm entry and exit – which is positive if entrants are more productive than exiting firms – and, for continuing firms, the contribution of within-firm productivity growth at a given

employment level and that of job reallocation between firms. The evidence tends to suggest large positive contributions of within-firm productivity growth independent of labour reallocation, but also a positive contribution of firm entry and exit and job reallocation between continuing firms.

[9] Further analysis shows that the impact of skills mismatch on productivity mainly reflects overskilling, suggesting there is a close connection between skills mismatch and skills use.

[10] Reduced worker flows tend to be mainly associated with reduced job-to-job mobility, at least in normal times, while job-to-non-employment mobility is largely unaffected (Bassanini and Garnero, 2013[46]).

[11] Autor, Kerr and Kugler (2007[68]) provide tentative evidence for the United States suggesting that wrongful-discharge protections reduce productivity growth.

[12] However, this should not affect overall job quality to the extent that the reduction of wages reflects the value of employment protection to workers.

[13] However, worker incentives for filing a legal complaint in the case of dismissal also play a role, since this increases the number of cases in which the courts need to establish the precise nature of dismissal. Incentives for filing legal complaints tend to be larger in countries where the level of compensation for unfair dismissals is much higher than that of fair dismissals and the costs of court cases to workers are small or non-existent (Venn, 2009[71]).

[14] An alternative way of limiting excessive layoffs is to make use of experience-rated unemployment insurance contributions as in the United States.

[15] Progressive tenure profiles are typically considered most appropriate for striking the right balance between providing incentives for worker investment in their job on the one hand and experimentation and hiring on the other.

[16] To insure workers specifically against the *risk of severance* (as opposed to unemployment) one could envisage the use of employer-funded insurance accounts (e.g. Ireland) or individual savings accounts (e.g. Austria, Brazil) which can be accessed upon dismissal.

[17] While temporary contracts can help in principle facilitate job matching and reallocation, such contracts tend to be disproportionately used by low-productivity firms, and particularly those with business models that place little weight on learning and innovation. Firms with HPWM practices are in general less inclined to make use of temporary contracts.

[18] Moreover, suppressing fixed-term contracts in the case of a single contract runs the risk of promoting alternative and potentially more vulnerable forms of independent work (see also Chapter 12 on new forms of work).

[19] However, it should be noted that other interpretations are possible as well and additional research is needed to better understand the relationship between wage-setting, job mobility and reallocation.

References

Adalet MacGowan, M., D. Andrews and V. Millot (2017), "Insolvency Regimes, Zombie Firms and Capital Reallocation", *OECD Economics Department Working Papers*, OECD Publishing, Paris, https://doi.org/10.1787/5a16beda-en (accessed on 09 November 2018). [62]

Addison, J. (2016), "Collective bargaining systems and macroeconomic and microeconomic flexibility: the quest for appropriate institutional forms in advanced economies", http://dx.doi.org/10.1186/s40173-016-0075-8. [29]

Aghion, P. et al. (2016), "Creative Destruction and Subjective Well-Being", *American Economic Review*, Vol. 106/12, pp. 3869-3897, http://dx.doi.org/10.1257/aer.20150338. [51]

Aghion, P., T. Fally and S. Scarpetta (2007), "Credit constraints as a barrier to the entry and post-entry growth of firms", *Economic Policy*, Vol. 22/52, pp. 732-779, http://dx.doi.org/10.1111/j.1468-0327.2007.00190.x. [63]

Akerlof, G. (1982), "Labor contracts as partial gift exchange", *The Quarterly Journal of Economics*, Vol. 97/4, https://doi.org/10.2307/1885099 (accessed on 16 May 2018). [8]

Andrews, D. and N. Gal (2015), *OECD Productivity Working Papers*, https://www.oecd-ilibrary.org/docserver/5jrql2q2jj7b-en.pdf?expires=1541327689&id=id&accname=ocid84004878&checksum=C72587FE87CC6D341272F6BCF935834B (accessed on 04 November 2018). [60]

Arends, I., C. Prinz and F. Abma (2017), "Job quality, health and at-work productivity", *OECD Social, Employment and Migration Working Papers*, No. 195, OECD Publishing, Paris, http://dx.doi.org/10.1787/43ff6bdc-en. [21]

Autor, D., W. Kerr and A. Kugler (2007), "Does Employment Protection Reduce Productivity? Evidence From US States*", *The Economic Journal*, Vol. 117/521, pp. F189-F217, http://dx.doi.org/10.1111/j.1468-0297.2007.02055.x. [68]

Bartel, A., C. Ichniowski and K. Shaw (2007), "How does information technology affect productivity? Plant-level comparisons of product innovation, process improvement, and worker skills", https://www0.gsb.columbia.edu/faculty/abartel/papers/info_tech.pdf (accessed on 30 October 2018). [18]

Bartelsman, E., P. Gautier and J. De Wind (2016), "Employment protection, technology choice, and worker allocation", *International Economic Review*, Vol. 57/3, pp. 787-826, http://dx.doi.org/10.1111/iere.12176. [47]

Bartelsman, E., J. Haltiwanger and S. Scarpetta (2013), "Cross-Country Differences in Productivity: The Role of Allocation and Selection", *American Economic Review*, Vol. 103/1, pp. 305-334, http://dx.doi.org/10.1257/aer.103.1.305. [39]

Bassanini, A. and A. Garnero (2013), "Dismissal protection and worker flows in OECD countries: Evidence from cross-country/cross-industry data", *Labour Economics*, Vol. 21, http://dx.doi.org/10.1016/j.labeco.2012.12.003. [45]

Bassanini, A., L. Nunziata and D. Venn (2009), "Job protection legislation and productivity growth in OECD countries", *Economic Policy*, Vol. 24/58, pp. 349-402, http://dx.doi.org/10.1111/j.1468-0327.2009.00221.x. [46]

Bloom, N. and J. Reenen (2011), "Human Resource Management and Productivity", *Handbook of Labor Economics*, Vol. 4, pp. 1697-1767, http://dx.doi.org/10.1016/S0169-7218(11)02417-8. [13]

Bloom, N. and J. Van Reenen (2010), "Why Do Management Practices Differ across Firms and Countries?", *Journal of Economic Perspectives*, Vol. 24/1, pp. 203-224, http://dx.doi.org/10.1257/jep.24.1.203. [70]

Bresnahan, T., E. Brynjolfsson and L. Hitt (2002), "Information Technology, Workplace Organization, and the Demand for Skilled Labor: Firm-Level Evidence", *The Quarterly Journal of Economics*, Vol. 117/1, pp. 339-376, http://dx.doi.org/10.1162/003355302753399526. [17]

Cazes, S., A. Hijzen and A. Saint-Martin (2015), "Measuring and Assessing Job Quality: The OECD Job Quality Framework", *OECD Social, Employment and Migration Working Papers*, No. 174, OECD Publishing, Paris, http://dx.doi.org/10.1787/5jrp02kjw1mr-en. [20]

Clark, A. and F. Postel-Vinayy (2009), "Job security and job protection", *Oxford Economic Papares*, http://dx.doi.org/10.1093/oep/gpn017. [53]

Davis, S., R. Faberman and J. Haltiwanger (2006), *American Economic Association The Flow Approach to Labor Markets: New Data Sources and Micro-Macro Links*, https://www.jstor.org/stable/pdf/30033664.pdf?refreqid=excelsior%3Ad1b759ea695b88c54e7c5a8370ba8f7a (accessed on 30 October 2018). [65]

Dolado, J., S. Ortigueira and R. Stucchi (2016), "Does dual employment protection affect TFP? Evidence from Spanish manufacturing firms", *SERIEs*, Vol. 7/4, pp. 421-459, http://dx.doi.org/10.1007/s13209-016-0150-9. [49]

Doucouliagos, H. et al. (2018), "How Credible Is Trade Union Research? Forty Years of Evidence on the Monopoly–Voice Trade-Off", *ILR Review*, Vol. 71/2, pp. 287-305, http://dx.doi.org/10.1177/0019793917751144. [30]

Freedom and Medoff (1984), *What Do Unions Do? by Richard B. Freeman, James L. Medoff, 1984 | Online Research Library: Questia*, https://www.questia.com/library/100894663/what-do-unions-do (accessed on 30 October 2018). [27]

Freeman, R. and E. Lazear (1995), "An Economic Analysis of Works Councils", *NBER Chapters*, pp. 27-52, https://ideas.repec.org/h/nbr/nberch/11555.html (accessed on 30 October 2018). [34]

Frege, C. and J. Godard (2014), "Varieties of Capitalism and Job Quality", *American Sociological Review*, Vol. 79/5, pp. 942-965, http://dx.doi.org/10.1177/0003122414548194. [23]

Gal, P. and A. Hijzen (2016), "The short-term impact of product market reforms: A cross-country firm-level analysis", *OECD Economics Department Working Papers*, No. 1311, OECD Publishing, Paris, http://dx.doi.org/10.1787/5jlv2jm07djl-en. [61]

George Mason University. Department of Economics., B., Hirsch and Barry (2004), *Journal of Labor Research.*, Transaction Publishers, https://econpapers.repec.org/article/trajlabre/v_3a25_3ay_3a2004_3ai_3a3_3ap_3a415-456.htm (accessed on 30 October 2018). [28]

Griffith, R. and G. Macartney (2014), "Employment Protection Legislation, Multinational Firms, and Innovation", *Review of Economics and Statistics*, Vol. 96/1, pp. 135-150, http://dx.doi.org/10.1162/REST_a_00348. [48]

Hall, B. and J. Lerner (2010), "The Financing of R&D and Innovation", http://dx.doi.org/10.1016/S0169-7218(10)01014-2. [64]

Hall, P. and D. Soskice (2001), *Varieties of capitalism : the institutional foundations of comparative advantage*, Oxford University Press. [22]

Haltiwanger, J. et al. (2018), "Cyclical Job Ladders by Firm Size and Firm Wage", *American Economic Journal: Macroeconomics*, Vol. 10/2, pp. 52-85, http://dx.doi.org/10.1257/mac.20150245. [66]

Hayward (2004), "Findings from the Survey of Employment Tribunal Applications 2003", *Employment Relations Research Series,*, Vol. 33. [59]

Hijzen, A. and B. Menyhert (2016), "Measuring Labour Market Security and Assessing its Implications for Individual Well-Being", *OECD Social, Employment and Migration Working Papers*, No. 175, OECD Publishing, Paris, http://dx.doi.org/10.1787/5jm58qvzd6s4-en. [52]

Hsieh, C. and P. Klenow (2009), "Misallocation and manufacturing tfp in china and india", *QUARTERLY JOURNAL OF ECONOMICS* Issue 4, http://klenow.com/MMTFP.pdf (accessed on 30 October 2018). [38]

Ichniowski, C. and K. Shaw (2003), "Beyond Incentive Pay: Insiders' Estimates of the Value of Complementary Human Resource Management Practices", *Journal of Economic Perspectives*, Vol. 17/1, pp. 155-180, http://dx.doi.org/10.1257/089533003321164994. [15]

Ichniowski, C., K. Shaw and G. Prennushi (1997), *The Effects of Human Resource Management Practices on Productivity: A Study of Steel Finishing Lines*, American Economic Association, http://dx.doi.org/10.2307/2951347. [14]

Johnston, R. et al. (2002), *Case studies of organisations with established learning cultures*, NCVER, http://www.voced.edu.au/content/ngv%3A15219 (accessed on 16 May 2018). [12]

Kemper, J. (2016), "Resolving the Ambiguity: A Meta-Analysis of the Effect of Employment Protection on Employment and Unemployment ETH Library", http://dx.doi.org/10.3929/ethz-a-010719179. [43]

Knight, K. and P. Latreille (2000), "How Far Do Cases Go? Resolution in Industrial Tribunal Applications", *Manchester School*, Vol. 68/6, pp. 723-744, https://ideas.repec.org/a/bla/manchs/v68y2000i6p723-44.html (accessed on 30 October 2018). [57]

Krueger, A. and A. Mas (2004), "Strikes, Scabs, and Tread Separations: Labor Strife and the Production of Defective Bridgestone/Firestone Tires", *Source: The Journal of Political Economy*, Vol. 112/2, pp. 253-289, http://dx.doi.org/10.1086/381479. [31]

Laroche, P. and M. Salesina (2017), "The Effects of Union and Nonunion Forms of Employee Representation on High-Performance Work Systems: New Evidence from French Microdata", *Human Resource Management*, Vol. 56/1, pp. 173-189, http://dx.doi.org/10.1002/hrm.21784. [35]

Lazear, E. and K. Shaw (2007), "Personnel Economics: The Economist's View of Human Resources", *Journal of Economic Perspectives*, Vol. 21/4, pp. 91-114, http://dx.doi.org/10.1257/jep.21.4.91. [16]

Leonardi, M. and G. Pica (2013), "Who Pays for it? The Heterogeneous Wage Effects of Employment Protection Legislation", *The Economic Journal*, Vol. 123/573, pp. 1236-1278, http://dx.doi.org/10.1111/ecoj.12022. [55]

Lepage-Saucier, N. and E. Wasmer (2016), "Does Employment Protection Raise Stress? A Cross-Country and Cross-Province Analysis", *Journal of Human Capital*, https://www.journals.uchicago.edu/doi/pdfplus/10.1086/684510 (accessed on 13 April 2018). [54]

Marsden, D. (2015), "The future of the German industrial relations model", *Journal for Labour Market Research*, Vol. 48/2, pp. 169-187, http://dx.doi.org/10.1007/s12651-015-0188-3. [33]

McGowan, M. and D. Andrews (2015), "The Future of Productivity: Main Background Papers Skill Mismatch and Public Policy in OECD Countries", https://www.oecd.org/eco/growth/Skill-mismatch-and-public-policy-in-OECD-countries.pdf (accessed on 06 June 2018). [40]

Micco, A. and C. Pagés (2006), "The Economic Effects of Employment Protection: Evidence from International Industry-Level Data", *IZA Discussion Papers*, https://ideas.repec.org/p/iza/izadps/dp2433.html (accessed on 13 April 2018). [44]

Montes Rojas, G. and R. Santamaría (2007), "The Burden of Labour Costs in Mexico", *Labour*, Vol. 21, http://gabrielmontes.com.ar/Montes-Rojas%20Santamaria%20LABOUR%202007.pdf (accessed on 08 November 2018). [58]

Montt, G. (2015), "The causes and consequences of field-of-study mismatch: An analysis using PIAAC", *OECD Social, Employment and Migration Working Papers*, No. 167, OECD Publishing, Paris, http://dx.doi.org/10.1787/5jrxm4dhv9r2-en. [67]

OECD (2018), "The role of collective bargaining systems for good labour market performance", in *OECD Employment Outlook 2018*, OECD Publishing, Paris, http://dx.doi.org/10.1787/empl_outlook-2018-7-en. [32]

OECD (2017), *Annual Report on the OECD Guidelines for Multinational Enterprises 2016*, http://mneguidelines.oecd.org/2016-Annual-Report-MNE-Guidelines-EN.pdf. [26]

OECD (2016), *Skills Matter: Further Results from the Survey of Adult Skills*, OECD Skills Studies, OECD Publishing Paris, https://doi.org/10.1787/9789264258051-en. [1]

OECD (2016), "Skills use at work: Why does it matter and what influences it?", in *OECD Employment Outlook 2016*, OECD Publishing, Paris, http://dx.doi.org/10.1787/empl_outlook-2016-6-en. [6]

OECD (2015), "Enhancing job quality in emerging economies", in *OECD Employment Outlook 2015*, OECD Publishing, Paris, http://dx.doi.org/10.1787/empl_outlook-2015-9-en. [2]

OECD (2015), *The Future of Productivity*, OECD Publishing, Paris, http://dx.doi.org/10.1787/9789264248533-en. [7]

OECD (2014), "How good is your job? Measuring and assessing job quality", in *OECD Employment Outlook 2014*, OECD Publishing, Paris, http://dx.doi.org/10.1787/empl_outlook-2014-6-en. [19]

OECD (2014), *Non-regular employment, job security and the labour market divide*, OECD Publishing, Paris, https://doi.org/10.1787/empl_outlook-2014-7-en.. [56]

OECD (2013), "Protecting jobs, enhancing flexibility: A new look at employment protection legislation", in *OECD Employment Outlook 2013*, OECD Publishing, Paris, http://dx.doi.org/10.1787/empl_outlook-2013-6-en. [50]

OECD (2012), *Better Skills, Better Jobs, Better Lives: A Strategic Approach to Skills Policies,*, OECD Publishing, Paris, https://doi.org/10.1787/9789264177338-en.. [3]

OECD (2011), *OECD Employment Outlook 2011*, OECD Publishing, Paris, https://doi.org/10.1787/empl_outlook-2011-en.. [4]

OECD (2010), *Institutional and Policy Determinants of Labour Market Flows*, http://www.oecd.org/els/emp/48806733.pdf (accessed on 30 October 2018). [37]

OECD (2009), *How Do Industry, Firm and Worker Characteristics Shape Job and Worker Flows?*, http://www.oecd.org/els/emp/45219606.pdf (accessed on 30 October 2018). [36]

OECD (2008), *Do Multinationals Promote Better Pay and Working Conditions?*, OECD Publishing, Paris, https://doi.org/10.1787/empl_outlook-2008-7-en.. [25]

OECD (2007), "More Jobs but Less Productive? The Impact of Labour Market Policies on Productivity", http://www.oecd.org/els/emp/40776638.pdf (accessed on 16 May 2018). [24]

OECD (2006), "General Policies to Improve Employment Opportunities for All", in *OECD Employment Outlook 2006: Boosting Jobs and Incomes*, OECD Publishing, Paris, https://doi.org/10.1787/empl_outlook-2006-5-en. [42]

Pissarides, C. (2010), "Why Do Firms Offer 'Employment Protection'?", *Economica*, Vol. 77/308, pp. 613-636, http://dx.doi.org/10.1111/j.1468-0335.2010.00861.x. [41]

Salop, S. (1979), "American Economic Association A Model of the Natural Rate of Unemployment A Model of the Natural Rate of Unemployment", *Source: The American Economic Review*, Vol. 69/1, pp. 117-125, http://www.jstor.org/stable/1802502 (accessed on 16 May 2018). [10]

Senge, P. (1990), *The fifth discipline : the art and practice of the learning organization*, Doubleday/Currency. [69]

Shapiro, C. and J. Stiglitz (1984), *Equilibrium Unemployment as a Worker Discipline Device*, American Economic Association, http://dx.doi.org/10.2307/1804018. [9]

UKCES (2014), *The Labour Market Story: Skills Use at Work*, https://assets.publishing.service.gov.uk/government/uploads/system/uploads/attachment_data/file/343457/The_Labour_Market_Story-_Skills_Use_at_Work.pdf (accessed on 27 June 2018). [5]

Venn (2009), *Legislation, Collective Bargaining and Enforcement: Updating the OECD Employment Protection Indicators*, https://ideas.repec.org/p/oec/elsaab/89-en.html (accessed on 30 October 2018). [71]

Weiss, A. (1980), "Job Queues and Layoffs in Labor Markets with Flexible Wages", *Journal of Political Economy*, Vol. 88/3, pp. 526-538, http://dx.doi.org/10.1086/260884. [11]

Chapter 8. Promoting fair wages and labour taxes

While productivity growth is a pre-condition for rising standards of living it does not automatically translate into higher wages and better working conditions for workers. This chapter discusses the role of minimum wages, collective bargaining and labour taxation for promoting a broad sharing of productivity gains. Wage-setting institutions can help avoid that the proceeds of productive labour disproportionately go to capital, but also risk pricing low-productivity workers out of the market. To increase their effectiveness and mitigate any potentially adverse employment effects, a good coordination of wage-setting institutions with the system of labour taxation is crucial. This will also help to limit the adverse effects of labour taxation on labour market outcomes.

The statistical data for Israel are supplied by and under the responsibility of the relevant Israeli authorities. The use of such data by the OECD is without prejudice to the status of the Golan Heights, East Jerusalem and Israeli settlements in the West Bank under the terms of international law.

Introduction

Productivity growth is a pre-condition for higher living standards. Yet, productivity growth does not automatically translate into higher wages and better working conditions, nor does it necessarily lead to the creation of more quality jobs. The challenge for policy-makers is to promote a broad sharing of productivity gains without undermining employment.

This chapter discusses the role of policies and institutions for promoting a broad sharing of productivity gains, with a focus on wage-setting institutions and labour taxation. Labour market institutions such as a minimum wage or collective bargaining can help, by setting minimum standards for employment and avoid that the proceeds of productive labour disproportionately go to capital. This is particularly important for workers with a weak bargaining position such as those with low skills and precarious contracts. Moreover, the coordination of wage-setting institutions with the system of labour taxation can enhance their effectiveness in ensuring a broad sharing of productivity gains, while containing the risk that they undermine the employment opportunities of the workers they seek to help. Policy coordination is equally important from the perspective of labour taxation since wage-setting institutions determine to an important extent the effects of labour taxation on labour market outcomes.

The remainder of the chapter is structured as follows. Section 8.1 discusses the role of the statutory minimum wage for ensuring that work is rewarding for everyone. Section 8.2 discusses the role of collectively-agreed wages and working conditions for a broader sharing of productivity gains while maintaining a good alignment between labour costs and productivity. Section 8.3 discusses the role of labour taxation for wages and employment, with a particular focus on those in the bottom of the distribution.[1] The final section concludes.

8.1. Minimum wages can help ensure that work is rewarding for everyone

Statutory minimum wages are the most direct policy lever governments have for influencing wage levels, especially at the bottom of the distribution. More specifically, minimum wages have been justified for: i) ensuring fair pay and preventing exploitation; ii) making work pay; iii) boosting tax revenue and/or tax compliance by limiting the scope of wage under-reporting; and iv) anchoring wage bargaining, particularly for vulnerable workers with a weak bargaining position.

Currently, 28 out of 36 OECD countries have statutory minimum wages in place. Minimum wages also exist in most non-OECD emerging economies.[2] Statutory minimum wages may exist alongside collectively agreed wage floors and can sometimes substitute for them when collective bargaining coverage is low. In the eight OECD countries without statutory minimum wages (Austria, Denmark, Finland, Iceland, Italy, Norway, Sweden and Switzerland), a large part of the workforce is, at least formally, covered by wage floors specified in sector- or occupation-level collective agreements. The role of collectively-agreed minimum wages is discussed in the next section.

Minimum wages, as a stand-alone policy, can be useful but tend to have limits

A long-standing debate exists around the impact of minimum wages on employment. There are theoretical explanations for both a negative or a positive effect of minimum-wage increases on employment, and thus the question is ultimately an empirical one. Based on a review of the evidence, OECD (2015[1]) concludes that the impact of moderate minimum-wage increases on employment tends to be small in both advanced and emerging economies, although effects on some vulnerable groups – such as youth – may be more negative. Yet, this conclusion remains controversial.[3] While on average across OECD countries, gross minimum wages are set at around 50% of the median, what exactly defines an appropriate level of the minimum wage, i.e. a minimum wage that supports workers' earnings, without undermining employment, is not clear and inevitably depends on country-specific factors, including the behavioural response of employers, the degree of competition in product and labour markets and its interaction with other policies, in particular taxes and benefits.[4]

High minimum wages reduce wage inequality, particularly in the presence of ripple effects higher up in the wage distribution.[5] Ripple effects (or knock-on/spill-over effects) reflect the situation where increases in the minimum wage result in wage adjustments higher up in the wage distribution. Wage increases above the minimum wage may be needed to maintain incentive structures in the workplace based on wage differences between lower and higher-paid workers, while wage reductions in the top may be needed to compensate for mandated wage increases in the bottom. Ripple effects have been documented for some countries, such as France, the United States and several emerging economies, but not in others.[6] When inequality is assessed over the long-run, the inequality-reducing effect of minimum wages may be more modest due to the possibility of mobility in and out of employment and up and down the wage ladder (OECD, 2015[1]).

Minimum wages only have a rather limited effect on reducing poverty – see Card and Krueger (1995[2]); Neumark and Wascher (2008[3]); MaCurdy (2015[4]). This reflects several factors: i) poor households often have no one working; ii) minimum-wage workers often live in non-poor households; and iii) in-work poverty is often the result of low working hours and household composition, rather than low hourly wages (OECD, 2009[5]). The level of the minimum wage is of course also critical: it may be too low to have a significant impact on poverty headcounts, or too high so that the positive effects of higher hourly wages on poverty are more than offset by their adverse impacts on employment and working hours among low-paid workers. All in all, minimum wages are a relatively blunt instrument for reducing poverty.

Coordinating minimum wages with the tax and benefit systems is key to make them more effective

Gross minimum-wage levels expressed as a share of median wages vary significantly across OECD countries and emerging economies (Figure 8.1). In the OECD area, they range from below 40% of median wages in the Czech Republic, Mexico, the United States, Estonia and Japan, to 60% and over in Turkey, Chile, France and Slovenia and a minimum-to-median-wage ratio of nearly 1 in Colombia.[7]

Gross values of the minimum wage neither give an accurate picture of workers' take-home pay, nor of the costs of employing minimum-wage workers for firms due to the role of taxes and transfers. To lower employers' costs and the risk of employment losses following minimum-wage hikes, some countries, most notably France, have introduced sizeable reductions in employer social security contributions for workers at around the minimum wage, thereby lowering the ratio of minimum-to-median labour costs below that of the minimum-to-median wage. Other countries have attempted to increase the effectiveness of the minimum wage to "make work pay" using targeted reductions in income taxes and/or employee social contributions for low-wage workers.

Some countries offer tax credits or in-work benefits targeted at low-wage workers (e.g. Belgium, Mexico, United Kingdom, United States), while others rely on progressive income taxes to keep the tax burdens of low-wage earners well below those applicable to the typical worker (e.g. New Zealand).

A good coordination between minimum wages and the tax and benefits system is key to mutually reinforce their impact. As discussed above, such a coordination helps to make minimum wages more effective in ensuring that work pays and addressing poverty, without significant employment losses. But minimum wages can also enhance the effectiveness and affordability of in-work benefits and tax credits in supporting the incomes of workers and their families. By imposing a wage floor, they limit the risk that employers lower wages in an effort to "pocket" in-work benefits and tax credits, thereby neutralising their impact on the take-home pay of workers.[8] At the same time, for in-work benefits or tax concessions to remain well targeted and affordable, wage floors should be set at moderate levels and reliable information on wages and working time should be available to the authorities for means-testing.

Figure 8.1. Gross and net minimum wages and labour cost at the minimum wage

% of gross median wage, net median wage and median labour cost respectively, 2016

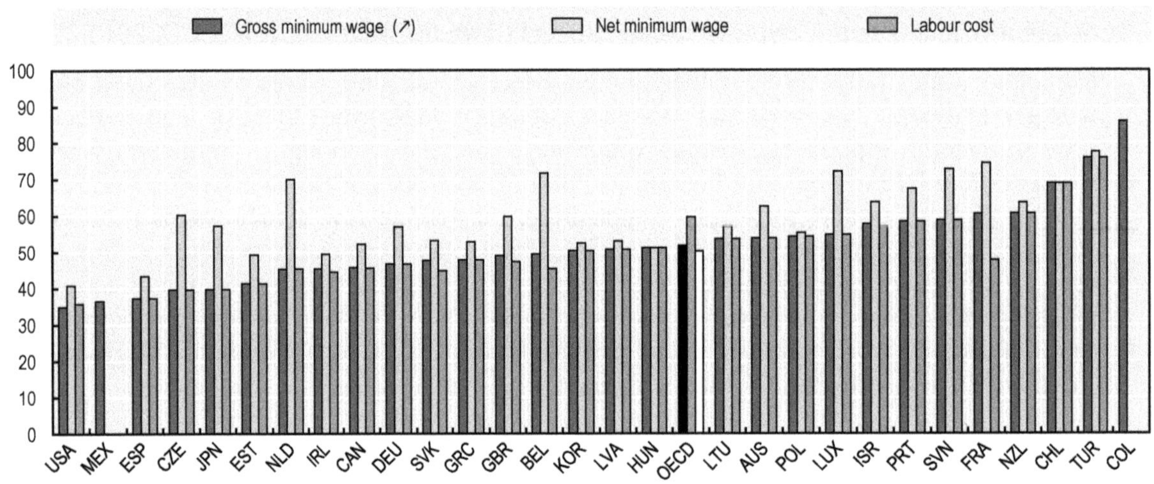

Note: Labour cost is calculated as the gross minimum wage + employer social security contributions. Data refer to a single person without children aged 40 working full-time. Social assistance and cash housing supplements are assumed to be available where relevant. Countries are ordered in ascending order of the gross minimum wage.

Source: *OECD Database on Minimum Wages* (https://stats.oecd.org/Index.aspx?DataSetCode=MIN2AVE) and OECD Tax-Benefit Models (http://www.oecd.org/social/benefits-and-wages.htm). Net minimum wages and labour costs are not provided for Colombia and Mexico as these countries are not currently included in the OECD Tax-Benefit Model.

StatLink http://dx.doi.org/10.1787/888933881249

Another way to minimise any possible dis-employment effect of the minimum wage is to apply different rates across regions, economic activities or workforce groups to reflect differences in economic conditions and productivity. While in most countries, minimum wages are set at the national level, in Canada, Japan, Mexico, the United States and several emerging economies, they are set at sub-national level, while in Costa Rica, Japan and Mexico rates differ by sector or occupation. Around half of OECD countries with a statutory minimum set lower rates for youth. Lower rates are also set in some cases for workers on training/apprenticeship contracts, for workers with disabilities as well as for long-term unemployed – for details, see OECD (2015[1]).

Regularly revise minimum wages based on accurate information, impartial advice and the views of the social partners

Minimum wages need to be regularly revised to ensure that they maintain their usefulness as a policy instrument and need to be set based on accurate information and a wide range of views. Most OECD countries review and adjust minimum wages every year. Not revising the minimum wage regularly can result in a significant erosion of its value in real terms. Irregular revisions may also heighten the risk of the minimum wage being adjusted for political reasons, with insufficient consideration of current and future labour market effects. However, rather than revising minimum wages mechanically (e.g. by linking them to average wage growth), this should be done carefully by taking due account of labour market conditions for the intended beneficiaries based on accurate, impartial and up-to-date information.

The process of setting the minimum wage varies significantly across countries, e.g. OECD (2015[1]), Boeri (2012[6]). Minimum wages may be: i) legislated by the government or parliament (e.g. the United States); ii) set by government following a formal, but non-binding, consultation process with the social partners (the majority of OECD countries, including France, Japan, Portugal, Spain and the United Kingdom); iii) the outcome of a bargaining process between social partners, with or without the involvement of government (e.g. Belgium and Mexico); or iv) set by an independent body (e.g. Australia).

Independent commissions are particularly well placed to give objective recommendations, based on a wide range of economic and social factors. The operation of these bodies varies from country to country in terms of the advisory (e.g. France) or legally-binding (e.g. Australia) nature of their recommendations, the extent to which the view of the social partners are taken into account and their independence.[9] When the advice of these commissions is taken seriously and social partners support the process, it may be less important who ultimately sets the minimum wage.

8.2. Collective bargaining can contribute to a broader sharing of productivity gains

Governments can further promote a broad sharing of productivity gains by supporting collective bargaining and social dialogue. Collective bargaining and social dialogue contribute to the determination of wages and non-wage working conditions and help ensure that workers with a weak bargaining position share in the benefits of productivity growth. Collective bargaining and social dialogue can operate alongside statutory rules for wages and working conditions or act as a substitute, provided that coverage is high. In addition, collective bargaining and social dialogue provide voice to workers, while endowing employers and employees with a tool for addressing common challenges. Indeed, collective bargaining and social dialogue play a potentially central role for most, if not all, aspects of labour market performance. This crucially rests on the ability of workers and firms to associate and the coverage of collective agreements negotiated. However, since the 1980s, collective bargaining has been confronted with serious challenges in the face of global competition, technological change and a long-running trend towards decentralisation of bargaining.

Collective bargaining has increasingly come under pressure

On average across OECD countries, trade union density almost halved during the past 30 years, falling from 30% in 1985 to 17% in 2016 (Figure 8.2, Panel A). As of 2016, less than 10% of the workforce is unionised in countries such as Estonia, France and Turkey and considerably more than half in countries such as Denmark, Finland, Iceland and Sweden. Union members tend to be predominantly male, middle-aged, and medium to highly skilled, tend to work in large firms, and typically have a permanent contract.

Trade unions either engage directly with employers or bargain with employer organisations. Membership to employer organisations varies considerably across countries, but, in contrast to union density, has been relatively stable over time (Figure 8.2, Panel B). In countries characterised by predominantly firm-level bargaining (e.g. Central and Eastern European countries, OECD countries outside Europe), employer organisations typically do not engage in collective bargaining and employer organisation tends to be low. By contrast, employer association membership is high in Belgium, Luxembourg, the Netherlands, Sweden, as well as in Austria where membership is compulsory. Employer organisations tend to be most important in manufacturing and construction and more likely to represent the interests of employers in large firms.

The number of workers covered by collective bargaining has tended to decline in tandem with trade union density in countries predominantly characterised by firm-level bargaining, but has been relatively stable in others, except Germany and, more recently, Greece. On average across OECD countries, it decreased from 45% in 1985 to 32% in 2016 (Figure 8.2, Panel C). Collective bargaining coverage is above 50% only in countries with sector-level bargaining based on either high employer organisation density or a widespread use of administrative extensions that expand the reach of collective agreements beyond the signatory parties in a sector. Collective bargaining coverage tends to be highest in manufacturing and construction as well as in larger firms. In the presence of multi-employer bargaining at sectoral or national level, collective bargaining coverage of small firms tends to be much higher.

All in all, the weakening of labour relations in many OECD countries has put collective bargaining systems under strong pressure and concerns have been growing about their ability to contribute to better labour market outcomes, notably when coverage has declined significantly or when social partners' representativeness and strength have declined following shrinking membership rates.

Figure 8.2. Trade union density and collective bargaining coverage have trended to fall

Trade union density, employer organisation density, and collective bargaining coverage by country and year, 1980-2016

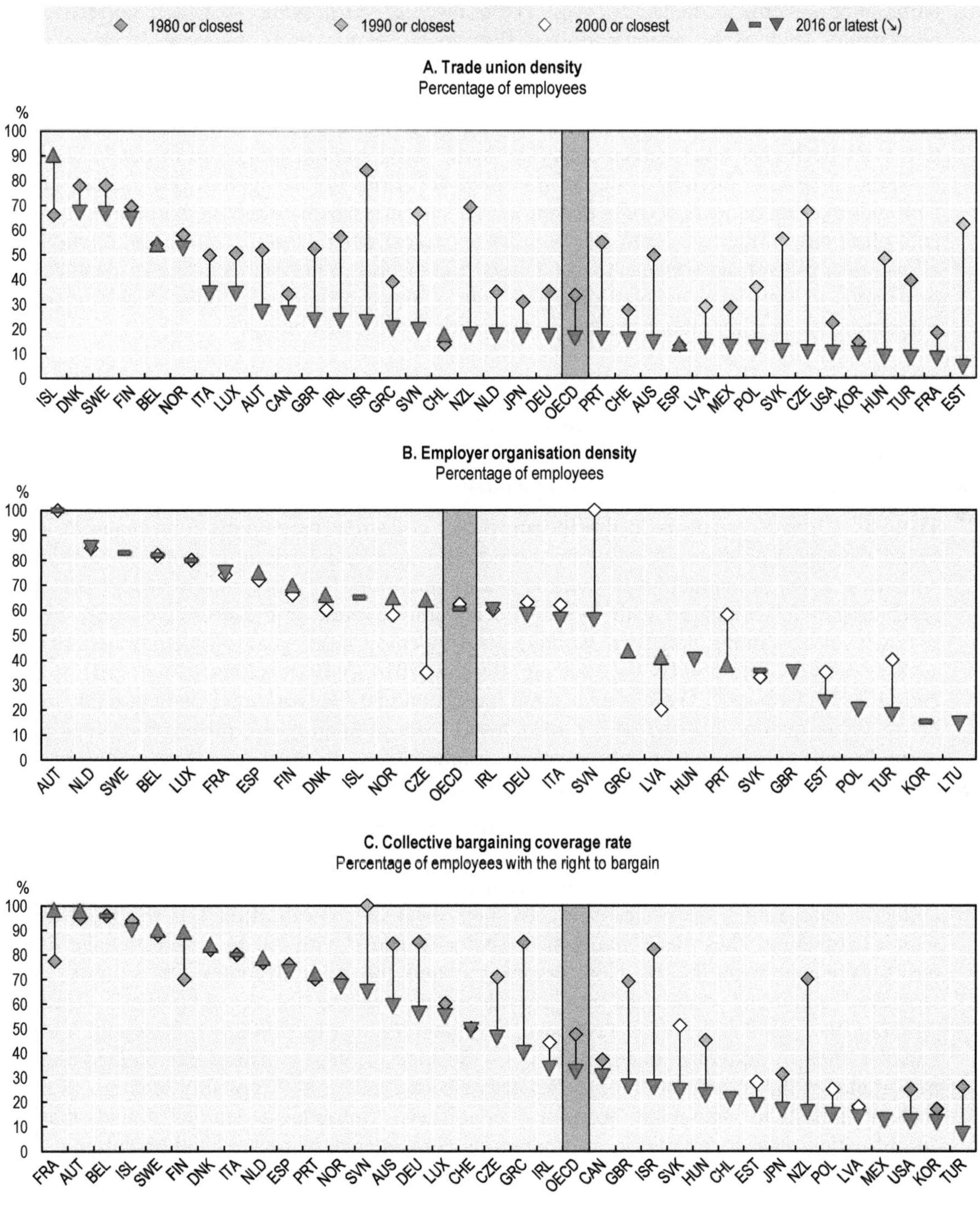

Note: OECD are employee-weighted averages across countries shown.

Source: *OECD Trade Unions and Collective Bargaining Database*, (www.oecd.org/employment/collective-bargaining.htm).

StatLink http://dx.doi.org/10.1787/888933881268

To assess the role of collective bargaining for labour market performance, it is important to go beyond the membership rates of the social partners and collective bargaining coverage by also taking account of other key features that characterise collective bargaining systems (OECD, 2017[7]): i) the *level of bargaining* at which collective agreements tend to be negotiated (e.g. firm level, sector level, national level or a combination of different levels); ii) the role of *wage co-ordination* between sector-level (or firm-level) agreements, such as the setting of common wage targets, to take account of macroeconomic conditions; and iii) the *degree of flexibility* for firms to modify the terms set by higher-level agreements. The level of bargaining ranges from *centralised* systems, in which there is little or no room for firms to derogate from sector- or national-level agreements, to *fully decentralised* systems, where collective bargaining can take place only at the firm level. Between these two extremes, *organised decentralisation* allows sector-level agreements to set broad framework conditions but leaves detailed provisions to firm-level negotiations. The role of these different features of collective bargaining systems for labour market performance is discussed below.

Collective bargaining can contribute to better labour market performance

Collective bargaining has the potential to play a central role in all aspects of labour market performance, including: i) wages and non-wage working conditions; ii) employment and unemployment; iii) inequality; and iv) productivity.

There is a broad consensus in the literature that collective bargaining contributes to a broad sharing of productivity gains by promoting wages and working conditions. Within countries, at the individual level, there is a wage premium for workers covered by firm-level bargaining compared with those who are not covered or those covered only by sector-level bargaining and such workers tend to enjoy more generous fringe benefits such as pensions and holiday pay, see e.g. Bryson (2014[8]), Ferracci and Guyot (2015[9]) and OECD (2018[10]).[10] There is also some indication that the work environment tends to be of higher quality in firms with a recognised form of employee representation (e.g. a union or works council), thanks to lower work intensity, more training options and higher prospects for career advancement (OECD, 2018[10]).

By contrast, the role of collective bargaining for employment and unemployment has been the subject of a long-standing and intense debate. Comparing collective bargaining systems across countries, Calmfors and Driffill (1988[11]) conjectured that the effect of collective bargaining varies according to their level of centralisation (i.e. the level at which bargaining takes place, national or sector or firm), with the best performance in terms of employment in the most centralised and the most decentralised systems.[11] However, empirical studies did not provide much backing for this hypothesis – see OECD (1997[12]), Traxler et al. (2001[13]), Aidt and Tzannatos (2002[14]), Bassanini and Duval (2006[15]) and Eurofound (2015[16]).[12] Soskice (1990[17]) instead highlighted the importance of the co-ordination of wages across bargaining units – typically sectors – as a tool to adjust to aggregate economic conditions. Subsequent studies found that co-ordination plays a key role in improving the performance of sector-level bargaining – e.g. Elmeskov et al. (1998[18]), Aidt and Tzannatos (2002[14]), OECD (2004[19]), Bassanini and Duval (2006[15]), OECD (2012[20]), Eurofound (2015[16]).[13]

Building on a more granular characterisation of national collective bargaining systems that takes account not just of the degree of bargaining coverage but also the level of bargaining, the use of wage co-ordination and the degree of flexibility for firms, OECD (2018[10]) finds that co-ordinated systems are linked with better employment and unemployment outcomes than fully decentralised systems. Moreover, co-ordinated systems are associated with lower unemployment for vulnerable groups, including youth and low-skilled workers as well as women than fully decentralised systems. There is therefore no indication that such systems deliver good labour market outcomes for "insiders" (e.g. skilled prime-age males) at the expense of jobs for "outsiders" (e.g. youth, women and low skilled) – see Saint-Paul (1996[21]) and Bertola (1999[22]). Predominantly centralised systems with no co-ordination hold an intermediate position, with somewhat better employment outcomes than in fully decentralised ones but similar outcomes in terms of unemployment.

Collective bargaining also matters for wage dispersion, with greater dispersion in settings with no collective bargaining, e.g. OECD (2011[23]), Jaumotte and Buitron (2015[24]) and OECD (2018[10]).[14] Wage dispersion tends to be lowest among workers who are covered by sector-level bargaining. The lower dispersion in wages associated with sector-level bargaining in part reflects lower returns to education, seniority and potential experience for workers covered by collective agreements (OECD, 2018[10]).

The effect on wages is also reflected in the relationship of collective bargaining with productivity growth. By its nature, sector-level bargaining tends to focus on the typical firm in a sector, and as a result, tends to reduce average wage differences between firms in the same sector. Similarly, co-ordinated systems place more emphasis on macro-economic conditions and have a tendency to reduce average wage differences between sectors. In this sense, lower wage flexibility at the sub-national level and lower wage dispersion across firms could be seen as two sides of the same coin. This has raised concerns about efficient job reallocation and productivity growth. OECD (2018[10]) shows that centralised bargaining systems tend to be associated with lower productivity growth if coverage of agreements is high. This result suggests that the lack of flexibility at the firm level, which characterises centralised bargaining systems, may come at the expense of lower productivity growth. By contrast, higher coordination in decentralised systems is not found to have adverse effects on productivity.

Many OECD countries have taken steps towards decentralisation in the past two decades. Overall, the analysis in OECD (2018[10]) suggests that *organised* decentralisation which allows sector-level agreements to set broad framework conditions but leaves detailed provisions to firm-level negotiations tends to deliver good employment performance, better productivity outcomes and higher wages for covered workers. By contrast, other forms of decentralisation that simply replace sector- with firm-level bargaining tend to be associated with somewhat poorer labour market outcomes.

Balancing inclusiveness and flexibility in collective bargaining systems

The main challenge for social partners and governments is to make collective bargaining work better in terms of employment, job quality and inclusiveness, while avoiding that it becomes a straitjacket for firms. The exact nature of this challenge and the way it is addressed will differ from country to country and depend to an important extent on the existing national collective bargaining traditions. Systems characterised by predominantly sector-level bargaining tend to be associated with high coverage and lower inequality, but also risk undermining employment and productivity growth if not well-designed. In contrast, systems characterised by predominantly firm-level bargaining allow for a better alignment of wages and productivity, but coverage tends to be low, limiting the potential benefits of collective agreements mainly to workers in large firms.

The best way of ensuring the inclusiveness of collective bargaining is by having well-organised social partners based on broad memberships (OECD, 2018[10]). This allows social dialogue to be widespread at the firm-level among worker organisations and employers and to be based on representative social partners at higher levels (e.g. sector, country). Governments should therefore promote social dialogue in large and small firms alike and allow labour relations to adapt to emerging challenges, including in relation to non-standard forms of work. In systems with sector-level bargaining, administrative extensions are another way of promoting the inclusiveness of collective bargaining by extending the coverage of collective agreements beyond the members of the signatory unions and employer organisations to all workers and firms in a sector. To avoid that extensions harm the economic prospects of start-ups, small firms or vulnerable workers – see Haucap, Pauly and Wey (2001[25]), Magruder (2012[26]) and Hijzen and Martins (2016[27]) –, they need to be well-designed to ensure that the parties negotiating the agreements represent the collective interest of all groups of firms and workers. This can be achieved by subjecting extension requests to reasonable representativeness criteria, a meaningful test of public interest and providing well-defined procedures for exemptions and opt-outs of firms in case of economic hardship (OECD, 2017[7]).[15]

Collective bargaining systems characterised by predominantly sector-level bargaining need to allow for sufficient economic flexibility at the firm and country levels. The introduction of flexibility in predominantly sector-level systems has often been considered as requiring a shift from sector to firm-level bargaining. While such a shift would indeed provide more flexibility to firms, it is also likely to induce a decline in bargaining coverage, undermining the inclusiveness of the system. Experience in a number of OECD countries has shown that less radical options are also available, based on the use of controlled opt-outs or sectoral framework agreements that explicitly leave space for further adaptation at the firm or individual level (Ibsen and Keune, 2018[28]). In principle, these instruments preserve the integrity of sector-level bargaining, while at the same time enabling a closer link between productivity and working conditions at the firm-level. However, their effectiveness in providing additional flexibility for firms largely depends on having high levels of collective worker representation across firms.

Flexibility to macroeconomic conditions can be fostered through the effective co-ordination of bargaining outcomes across bargaining units (e.g. industries or firms). Effective wage co-ordination can be achieved through peak-level bargaining based on the presence of national confederations of unions and employers that provide guidance to bargaining parties at lower levels. Another possibility is pattern bargaining where a leading sector sets the targets – usually the manufacturing sector exposed to international trade – and others follow. A precondition for a well-functioning co-ordination of wage bargaining is to have strong and representative employer and employee organisations as well as effective mediation bodies (Ibsen, 2016[29]).

Collective bargaining systems differ widely across countries in terms of their coverage, the flexibility that they provide to firms and their specific institutional set-up and these differences tend to be deeply rooted in the sociocultural fabric of countries. National traditions in collective bargaining are important and need to be respected. Yet, this does not imply that collective bargaining systems cannot and should not adapt to a changing economic context. Indeed, one of the most salient features of successful collective bargaining systems may be their ability to adapt gradually to changing economic conditions, while considering their national industrial-relations tradition. This depends crucially on the quality of industrial relations (Blanchard and Philippon, 2006[30]), but also on a government that provides space for collective bargaining and social dialogue, while setting the boundaries.[16]

8.3. Designing labour-market friendly tax policies

The effectiveness of wage floors – whether statutory or collectively agreed – can be enhanced, and any potentially adverse employment effects mitigated, through their coordination with the system of labour taxation. By the same token, the wage and employment effects of labour taxation depend to an important extent on the nature of wage-setting institutions. This section provides a detailed discussion of the role of labour taxation for labour market performance. While the argument for policy coordination is similar in the context of in-work benefits, this discussion is relegated to Chapter 9 as part of a comprehensive discussion on social protection and activation.

Labour taxes differ significantly in terms of their level and composition across countries

Labour taxes represent a key source of revenue for governments. A considerable part is used to fund social protection. However, as not all labour taxes are earmarked, they cannot always be linked to specific public social expenditures. Even if they are, the link between individual contributions and expenditures tends to be relatively weak due to the redistributional nature of social protection systems in most countries. This means that individual contributions are best considered as a tax on work rather than a form of mandatory savings by employers or employees. It also implies that the way social protection systems are financed can have important implications for labour market performance.[17]

Labour taxes drive a wedge between the cost of labour to employers and the value of work to employees in terms of labour incomes. This is called the tax wedge. It is calculated by expressing the sum of personal income taxes, payroll taxes, and employee and employer social security contributions, minus benefits as a percentage of labour costs.[18] Figure 8.3 documents the statutory tax wedge averaged across eight different family types in 2015 across OECD countries. Note that the statutory tax wedge does not take account of contributions for private social insurance which are very important in some countries.

On average across OECD countries, the tax wedge amounted to almost one third of labour costs in 2015. However, it varies considerably across countries, from less than 20% in New Zealand, Czech Republic, Ireland and emerging economies except Turkey, to over 40% in Austria, Belgium and France. These differences reflect to an important extent the importance of public social expenditures. Social security contributions, which are earmarked for social protection, account for over two-thirds of the tax wedge on average across countries. While personal income taxes are not earmarked, a large share of their revenues is generally used to finance social protection (OECD, 2007[31]). Social security contributions tend to be more relatively important in countries where personal income taxes are very low such as Chile as well as in several Central and Eastern European countries, while they tend to be less important in countries where social security benefits are means-tested such as Australia and New Zealand, as well as in Denmark and Iceland.

While the average tax wedge for the OECD has been largely stable between 2005 and 2015, this hides significant changes in a number of countries. Significant decreases are observed in the Netherlands, New Zealand, Sweden and Turkey, while significant increases are observed in Mexico and Luxembourg. In a number of countries, there have also been substantial changes in the composition of the tax wedge. In Denmark and the Netherlands, there has been a substantial shift from social security contributions to personal income taxes. In Hungary, social security contributions have been shifted from the employer to the employee.

Figure 8.3. The tax wedge and its principal components

Average statutory tax wedge as % of total labour costs, 2015

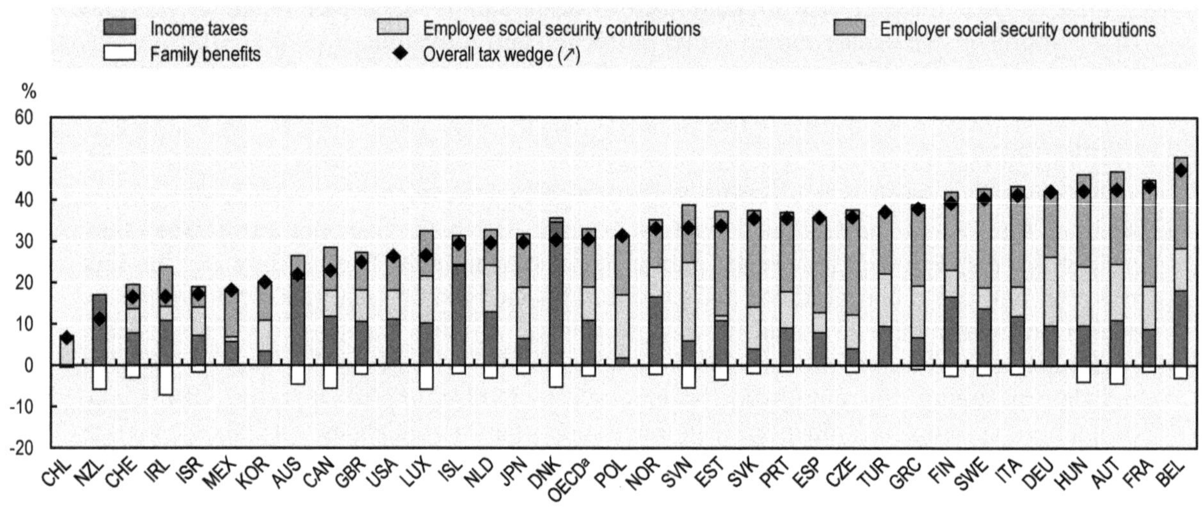

Note: Average over eight different household types characterised by marital status, number of children, earnings levels expressed as proportion of average wages and whether there are one or two earners.
a) Unweighted average of countries shown.
Source: OECD (2016[32]), *Taxing Wages 2016*, https://doi.org/10.1787/tax_wages-2016-en.

StatLink http://dx.doi.org/10.1787/888933881287

The tax wedge has potentially important consequences for employment and wages

Labour taxes can have potentially important consequences for both job quantity and job quality, particularly in the case of low-productivity workers. In a labour market without frictions, labour taxes reduce employment and wages. By increasing the cost of labour to employers and reducing the take-home pay for employees, it reduces both labour demand and supply, resulting in lower employment and wages, without creating any involuntary unemployment. The relative importance of wage and employment effects depends on the bargaining position of employees.[19] To the extent that workers have a relatively weak bargaining position, particularly those with low skills and precarious contracts, they disproportionately bear the economic burden of labour taxes – in the form of lower net wages –, irrespective of their statutory incidence on employers or employees. In a labour market with frictions, labour taxes also affect the unemployment rate when the burden of labour taxation differs between in-work and out-of-work income, i.e. when unemployment benefits are not taxed at the same level as wages (Pissarides, 1998[33]) or when the scope of shifting them onto workers in terms of lower wages is limited due to the presence of statutory or collectively-agreed minimum wages. This is particularly relevant for low-skilled workers.

Cross-country evidence suggests that the average tax wedge tends to increase unemployment and, to a lesser extent, reduce labour force participation (Bassanini and Duval, 2006[34]).[20] The effect of the tax wedge on unemployment differs importantly across countries due to its dependence on wage-setting institutions. The tax wedge tends to have a more negative impact on unemployment in countries with a high minimum wage (Bassanini and Duval, 2006[34]) or high union membership and a low or intermediate degree of centralisation/coordination (Daveri and Tabellini, 2000[35]). By contrast, in countries with low union membership (e.g. mostly English-speaking countries) or countries where collective bargaining is strongly coordinated (e.g. the Nordic countries) the costs of higher labour taxes tend to be largely shifted to workers in the form of lower take-home pay, while the effects on labour costs and employment tend to be limited.[21]

Micro-economic evidence, which typically provides more attention to the specific nature of reforms and the context in which they take place, generally supports cross-country findings. There is some indication that wages adjust more strongly to labour taxes and employment effects tend to be smaller in countries with flexible wage-setting institutions such as such as Canada, Chile and the United States (Gruber and Jonathan, 1994[36]; Gruber and Jonathan, 1997[37]; Anderson and Meyer, 2000[38]; Deslauriers et al., 2018[39]) than in countries with more rigid wage-setting institutions such as Colombia (Kugler and Kugler, 2009[40]).[22] The importance of wage shifting also depends on the extent to which contribution payments and benefit entitlements are linked. Based on a series of reforms in France, Bozio, Breda and Grenet (2017[41]) show that wage shifting is more important when there is a strong tax and benefit linkage. Moreover, wage shifting appears to be less important when reforms are targeted at specific age groups or are implemented gradually for different groups of workers.[23] Finally, using matched employer-employee data for Norway, Stokke (2016[42]) shows that wage shifting tends to be more important for workers with low skills, presumably because of their weaker bargaining position.

There is some indication that the composition of the tax wedge also matters. OECD (2007[31]) finds that the negative effect of the tax wedge on unemployment is entirely driven by social security contributions. This may reflect the possibility that personal income taxes do not depend on employment status and highlights the value of using a broad tax base. Alternatively, it may reflect the possibility that the negative unemployment effects of the tax wedge are mitigated by the degree of tax progressivity (Lehmann et al., 2016[43]).[24] Since personal income taxes are typically more progressive than social-security contributions, this may explain why the adverse effect of the tax wedge on employment is concentrated among social security contributions. This also would imply that the adverse unemployment effects of the average tax wedge are concentrated among low-wage workers.

The design of the tax wedge should therefore take account of the possible adverse employment effects of overall labour taxes, particularly for low-productivity workers. This is all the more important in the current context of population ageing in many OECD countries, widening inequality and the rising prevalence of non-standard forms of work. However, attention also needs to be paid to the composition of overall labour taxation, its progressivity as well as the link between social security contributions and entitlements. These elements not only matter for employment, but also for job quality, in terms of the take-home pay of employees and the ability to provide security to workers through social protection, as well as labour market inclusiveness. The remainder of this sub-section develops these issues in more detail by building on the *OECD Principles for Tax Policy Design for Inclusive Growth* (Brys et al., 2016[44]).[25]

Broaden the base and increase the progressivity of labour taxation, while strengthening the responsibility of employers for labour market risks

A major advantage of broadening the tax base for the purpose of financing of social protection is that it reduces the average burden of taxation on labour. A second advantage is that broadening the tax base has the potential to reduce differences in fiscal treatment based on employment status or income source. Such differences in fiscal treatment may provide incentives for workers to move from dependent employment into self-employment, tax evasion based on the under-declaration of earnings per employee or working in the informal sector. This can have potentially important consequences for the level of social protection for the individuals involved and may undermine the fiscal sustainability of the social protection system as a whole.

The tax base can be broadened by adjusting the composition of labour taxation, removing inefficiencies in labour taxation or relying more heavily on other forms of taxation. The tax base can be broadened by shifting the composition of labour taxes away from social security contributions to other forms of labour taxation with a broader tax base such as personal income or consumption taxes. While social security contributions mainly weigh on payrolls, personal income taxes typically do not depend on labour market status (employed, or non-employed) or income source (dependent or self-employment) and consumption taxes apply equally to all individuals.[26] A second possibility would be to remove inefficiencies in labour taxation by scaling back poorly targeted forms of income tax relief and reduced value-added tax (VAT) rates. These include, for example, the deductibility of mortgage interest from personal income taxes or preferential VAT rates on expenditures that disproportionately benefit rich households. To the extent that this reduces the tax burden on workers with lower incomes this is likely to promote their job prospects and earnings potential. A third possibility would be to increase the reliance on alternative sources of financing. From the perspective of tax efficiency, measures that increase the emphasis of taxation on immobile sources of income are most promising. Real estate taxes provide one example. This would not only be efficient, given the immobile nature of real estate, but also promote inclusiveness since low income households tend to own less property than higher income and more wealthy households. There are also arguments for strengthening the taxation of capital income at the individual level and increasing the reliance on consumption and environmental taxes.

There is also a case to be made for more progressivity in labour taxation. Labour tax progressivity has a tendency to reduce the adverse unemployment effects of labour taxes in general, but particularly for low-skilled workers. By increasing access to work and the take-home pay of low-skilled workers, tax progressivity also increases inclusiveness.[27] Moreover, in contrast to social security contributions, personal income tax systems in many countries have credits or deductions that make effective rates close to zero or even negative at low income levels, which could benefit employment as well. But the benefits of increased tax progressivity in terms of unemployment and inclusiveness need to be weighed against its potential costs in terms of incentives for work, effort, skills development and tax compliance. While there is considerable uncertainty about the optimal degree of tax progressivity – see Boadway (2012[45]) and Piketty and Saez, (2013[46]) for recent reviews –, taking account of unemployment and equity considerations in addition to the traditional labour-supply considerations will tend to shift the balance in favour of more labour tax progressivity.

The most obvious way of increasing the progressivity of labour taxation is to shift away from the current emphasis on social security contributions by placing more emphasis on personal income taxes. The benefits of tax progressivity therefore provide an additional argument for shifting towards personal income taxes in addition to its role for broadening the tax base. A partial shift from social security contributions to personal income taxes makes most sense for social programmes that are highly redistributive, such as social assistance, or social expenditures that seek to cover "risks" that are largely independent of the labour market behaviour of employers and employees such as health care, old-age and family allowances. Since health care, old-age pensions, family allowances and social assistance account for a sizeable share of total social expenditures, there is considerable room for such a shift in many OECD countries.

Finally, increasing the responsibility of employers for labour market risks in the context of sickness, disability and unemployment can also be considered. This can be achieved by strengthening the link between employer contributions and expenditures for those components of social protection. In practice, this can be done by giving employers direct responsibility for the cost of certain labour market risks during a time-limited period in combination with a waiting period for benefit entitlements (this is fairly common in the case of sickness, see Chapter 9) or by increasing their responsibility indirectly by linking employer contributions to the firm's benefit history through experience-rating (e.g. Netherlands in the case of disability, United States in the case of unemployment insurance). Experience-rating social security contributions allows taking account of both benefit inflows and outflows, but also tends to be difficult to administer. Systems based on direct responsibility are easier to administer than systems based on experience-rating, but act primarily on the inflow margin (when time-bound) and, in the case of unemployment insurance, may be of limited effectiveness when a firm's decision to lay off workers reflects its financial situation and, hence, its ability to take direct responsibility for the cost of unemployment. On the part of employees, increasing the link between entitlements and contributions moderates wage claims and supports labour supply by making labour taxes less distortionary. This logic is most readily applied to pensions.

Conclusion

This chapter has discussed the role of minimum wages, collective bargaining and labour taxation for promoting a broad sharing of productivity gains. The overall message of the chapter is that wage-setting institutions can contribute to a broader sharing of productivity benefits without undermining employment or the basis for productivity itself. However, for this to be the case, their design is crucial as well as their articulation with other policies and institutions.

The minimum wage represents a useful albeit limited tool for promoting broadly shared productivity gains by ensuring fair pay and preventing exploitation. It may also have implications for wages further up the wage distribution, but the evidence on such "ripple" effects is rather mixed. A good coordination with the tax-and-benefits system is key to the design of minimum wages since this can help increase their effectiveness in boosting take-home pay, while limiting their potential adverse side effects on employment.

Collective bargaining allows for a potentially broader sharing of productivity gains by affecting the wages and working conditions of all workers covered by collective agreements, but has come increasingly under pressure as a result of global competition, technological change and a long-running trend towards decentralisation of bargaining. Moreover, the world of work is changing rapidly, with workers moving more easily between employers, sometimes combining several jobs at the same and the emergence of new forms of work. These challenges require rethinking the role of collective bargaining and collective action in a changing world of work.

To further facilitate a broader sharing of productivity gains, it is important to limit non-wage labour costs, particularly for low-wage workers. This can be achieved by broadening the base for labour taxation, while increasing its progressivity. Of course, the prime reason for having labour taxes in the first place is to finance social expenditures which themselves are an important instrument for a broad sharing of productivity gains. This will be discussed in Chapters 9 and 10.

While wage-setting institutions have a role to play, it is also important to caution against excessive expectations. Wage-setting institutions can correct for poor wage outcomes as a result of a weak bargaining position of workers, but they cannot correct for a very unequal distribution of productivity across firms or workers. This requires different measures related to, for example, technology diffusion and skills development (see Chapters 7, 10 and 14).

Notes

[1] The role of social benefits, including in-work benefits, will be discussed in detail in Chapters 9 and 10.

[2] Including in the OECD's six key partner countries (Brazil, China, India, Indonesia, Russian Federation and South Africa) and Costa Rica (currently seeking membership) and Colombia (invited to become a member)

[3] See for example the recent debate in the United States between Dube, Lester and Reich (2010[51]), Allegretto, Dube and Reich (2011[52]), Allegretto et al. (2017[53]) on the one hand, and Neumark, Salas and Wascher (2014[54]) on the other.

[4] Firms may mitigate the impact of minimum wages on labour costs by adopting more efficient work practices to raise productivity – e.g. Riley and Rosazza-Bondibene (2017[55]); Hirsch et al. (2015[56]), – reducing non-wage labour costs – e.g. Kaminska and Lewandoski (2015[57]) or in the absence of an effective enforcement, firms do not fully comply with the legislation – e.g. Bhorat, Kanbur and Rayet (2012[58]); Rani et al. (2013[59]); Garnero (2018[50]) – or employ workers informally (Comola and De Mello, 2011[60]). Weak competition in product and labour markets has a tendency to reduce the impact of minimum-wage increases on employment and may even render them positive. When product market competition is weak, i.e. firms can increase profits by setting prices above the competitive level, employers can shift part of the increase in labour costs that results from a higher minimum wage to consumers through higher product prices (Allegretto and Reich, 2018[61]) or, alternatively, absorb some of the increase in labour costs by accepting lower profits (Draca, Machin and Van Reenen, 2011[62]). When labour market competition is weak, firms may be in a position to increase profits by offering wages below the competitive level. This situation may arise when there is only a single firm active in a labour market or when there are significant search frictions on the part of workers that limit competition for workers between firms, leading to cases of "monopsony". In this case, a minimum wage can help to increase wages and employment at the same time.

5. A significant number of papers have associated minimum wages with lower wage inequality - e.g. DiNardo et al. (1996[64]), Lee (1999[63]), Autor, Manning and Smith (2016[65]) for the United States, DiNardo and Lemieux (1997[66]) for Canada, Machin (1997[67]) for the United Kingdom and Koeniger, Leonardi and Nunziata (2007[68]) for 11 OECD countries.

6. E.g. Koubi and L'Hommeau (2007[69]) and Goarant and Muller (2011[70]) for France and Card and Krueger (1995[2]), Lee (1999[63]), Neumark, Salas and Wascher (2014[54]) (2004), Autor, Manning and Smith (2016[65]) for the United States and Dickens and Manning (2004[71]) (2004) and Stewart (2012[72]) for the United Kingdom.

7 The median includes workers in informal employment where wages tend to be much lower than in the formal sector and compliance is weak. However, even when the index is restricted to formal workers the minimum wage in Colombia remains very high by OECD standards.

8 This is one of the stated aims of introducing the UK National Minimum Wage. This is also a concern in the United States where significant parts of the Earned Income Tax Credit (EITC) fail to reach low-paid workers – see Rothstein (2010[73]); Lee and Saez (2012[74]).

9 In France, the commission has only an advisory role on the discretionary increase that the government can add to the automatic increase due to price and productivity increases. In Ireland and the United Kingdom, the commissions are composed of experts and representatives of the social partners and the government has to justify in parliament the decision not to follow their advice. In Germany, the government can refuse the recommendation of the minimum wage commission, which is composed by social partners and two experts without voting rights, but cannot change it. Finally, in Australia, the *Fair Work Commission* is entirely independent and its decisions are legally binding

10 Evidence using microdata for the US and for the UK points to an average union membership wage premium of between 10% and 15%.

11 This motivated the critical stance of the 1994 OECD Jobs Strategy on sector-level bargaining and its recommendation to decentralise collective bargaining. In the original Jobs Strategy, centralised or co-ordinated bargaining arrangements were viewed more positively than sector-level bargaining but not explicitly supported. While countries with such systems typically managed to sustain relatively high employment levels, the empirical evidence based on country panels was judged to be weak. More fundamentally, the ability to foster fully centralised bargaining systems or systems that are effectively co-ordinated so as to promote resilience and contain wage spirals was put in doubt.

12 In part, this reflects the fact that seemingly similar systems differ importantly in the way they operate in practice due to the role of institutional details and the broader socio-economic context (OECD, 2017[7]; Hijzen, Martins and Parlevliet, 2018[79]).

13 The Reassessed OECD Jobs Strategy in 2006 embraced this "augmented" version of the Calmfors-Driffill hypothesis which entailed that decentralised and centralised or co-ordinated bargaining systems result in better employment performance than sectoral bargaining systems.

14 See also Blanchflower and Freeman (1993[47]), Card, Lemieux and Riddell (2004[48]) and DiNardo and Lee (2004[49]).

15. The case of Australia, where a government body determines minimum standards for each sector, represents an alternative approach for ensuring basic terms of employment among all firms in a sector in the presence of firm-level bargaining (OECD, 2018[10]).

16 Governments can promote the quality of labour relations by: fostering broad, representative and well-organised employer and worker associations; creating built-in incentives for the regular re-negotiation of collective agreements; providing high quality and objective statistics on the state of the economy; and supporting mechanisms that enhance the accountability of the social partners for the effective implementation of collective agreements.

[17] To the extent that labour taxes represent a form of mandatory savings, and hence can be considered as part of the compensation package of employees, they should affect neither the utility from work to employees (which matters for labour supply) or the cost of labour to employers (which matters for demand) and leave employment and wages unaffected. However, since in practice the link between contributions and entitlements is imperfect, they can reduce the net take-home pay of the employee, and hence job quality, with negative consequences for labour supply and/or increase the cost of labour to employers and reduce labour demand.

[18] Ideally, consumer taxes would also be included because they create a wedge between the total labour costs faced by the employer and the return to work by the employee. However, this is not done here as this requires taking account of detailed expenditure patterns which is not obvious in practice.

[19] This depends in turn on the relative responsiveness ("elasticity") of labour demand and supply to wages. If labour demand is perfectly inelastic and labour supply is not, the burden of taxation falls entirely on firms. On the contrary, if labour supply is perfectly inelastic and labour demand is not, the burden of taxation falls entirely on workers. Since labour demand tends to be considerably more elastic than labour supply, the conventional wisdom is that the burden of labour taxation is mostly borne by workers in the form of lower take-home wages.

[20] These results appear to be broadly representative for macroeconomic studies, with similar results found in OECD (2007[31]), Murtin, De Serres and Hijzen (2014[76]) and Gal and Theising (2015[75]). Note that these studies typically identify short-run effects. To the extent that wages adjust only slowly to changes in labour taxes one might expect these employment effects to (partially) dissipate with time.

[21] Because of the interaction of labour taxation with wage-setting institutions, it also has been suggested that it can undermine labour market resilience by amplifying the unemployment effects of aggregate shocks (Blanchard and Wolfers, 2000[77]).

[22] However, apart from labour market frictions, these differences may also reflect the nature of reforms and particularly, the extent to which contribution payments and benefit entitlements are linked.

[23] Evidence from permanent social security reductions by respectively Saez, Schoefer and Seim (2018[78]) and Saez, Matsaganis and Tsaklogou (2012[80]) targeted respectively at new hires in Greece and youth in Sweden point at limited wage shifting (and more important employment effects). This may reflect the role of fairness considerations (and legal constraints) that prevent employers from wage discriminating between employees in the same firm based on age or cohort.

[24] Labour tax progressivity may reduce unemployment through three different channels. First, progressivity implies rising marginal tax rates and higher marginal tax rates moderate wage claims (Pissarides, 1998[33]). Second, shifting the burden of taxation to high-wage workers reduces the role of interactions between labour taxation and institutional features that create wage floors for low-wage workers. Third, unemployment is reduced because of a composition effect that results from the greater responsiveness of low-wage employment to taxation relative to that of higher-wage workers (Lehmann et al., 2016[43]).

[25] These are: broadening tax bases; strengthening the overall progressivity of the tax system; nudging pre-tax behaviours and opportunities; and enhancing tax policy and administration. The discussion here focuses on the first three, with a specific focus on financing social protection.

[26] OECD (2007[31]) shows that the required increase in personal income or consumption tax rates to compensate for the loss in revenue of a reduction in the social security contribution rate are much smaller. This is even the case under constant employment.

[27] Not surprisingly, the arguments for in-work benefits are very similar. This is discussed in detail in Chapter 9.

References

Aidt, T. and Z. Tzannatos (2002), *Unions and Collective Bargaining : Economic Effects in a Global Environment.*, The World Bank, Washington, DC, http://documents.worldbank.org/curated/en/831241468740150591/Unions-and-collective-bargaining-economic-effects-in-a-global-environment (accessed on 15 January 2018). [14]

Allegretto, S., A. Dube and M. Reich (2011), "Do Minimum Wages Really Reduce Teen Employment? Accounting for Heterogeneity and Selectivity in State Panel Data", *Industrial Relations: A Journal of Economy and Society*, Vol. 50/2, pp. 205-240, http://dx.doi.org/10.1111/j.1468-232X.2011.00634.x. [52]

Allegretto, S. et al. (2017), "Credible Research Designs for Minimum Wage Studies", *ILR Review*, Vol. 70/3, pp. 559-592, http://dx.doi.org/10.1177/0019793917692788. [53]

Allegretto, S. and M. Reich (2018), "Are Local Minimum Wages Absorbed by Price Increases? Estimates from Internet-Based Restaurant Menus", *ILR Review*, Vol. 71/1, pp. 35-63, http://dx.doi.org/10.1177/0019793917713735. [61]

Anderson, P. and B. Meyer (2000), *The effects of the unemployment insurance payroll tax on wages, employment, claims and denials*, http://www.elsevier.nl/locate/econbase (accessed on 02 November 2018). [38]

Autor, D., A. Manning and C. Smith (2016), "The Contribution of the Minimum Wage to US Wage Inequality over Three Decades: A Reassessment", *American Economic Journal: Applied Economics*, Vol. 8/1, pp. 58-99, http://dx.doi.org/10.1257/app.20140073. [65]

Bassanini, A. and R. Duval (2006), "Employment Patterns in OECD Countries: Reassessing the Role of Policies and Institutions", *OECD Social, Employment and Migration Working Papers* , http://www.oecd.org/els/workingpapers (accessed on 30 October 2018). [34]

Bassanini, A. and R. Duval (2006), "Employment Patterns in OECD Countries: Reassessing the Role of Policies and Institutions", *OECD Social, Employment and Migration Working Papers*, No. 35, OECD Publishing, Paris, http://dx.doi.org/10.1787/702031136412. [15]

Ashenfelter, O. and D. Card (eds.) (1999), *Microeconomic perspectives on aggregate labor markets*, Elsevier. [22]

Bhorat, H., R. Kanbur and N. Mayet (2012), "Minimum wage violation in South Africa", *International Labour Review*, Vol. 151/3, pp. 277-287, http://dx.doi.org/10.1111/j.1564-913X.2012.00149.x. [58]

Blanchard, O. and T. Philippon (2006), "The Quality of Labor Relations and Unemployment", *NYU Working Paper No. FIN-06-038.* [30]

Blanchard, O. and J. Wolfers (2000), "The Role of Shocks and Institutions in the Rise of European Unemployment: the Aggregate Evidence", *The Economic Journal*, Vol. 110/462, pp. 1-33, http://dx.doi.org/10.1111/1468-0297.00518. [77]

Blanchflower, D. and R. Freeman (1993), "Did the Thatcher Reforms Change British Labour Performance?", *NBER Working Papers*, https://ideas.repec.org/p/nbr/nberwo/4384.html (accessed on 15 January 2018). [47]

Boadway, R. (2012), *From optimal tax theory to tax policy : retrospective and prospective views*, MIT Press, https://mitpress.mit.edu/books/optimal-tax-theory-tax-policy (accessed on 30 October 2018). [45]

Boeri, T. (2012), "Setting the minimum wage", *Labour Economics*, Vol. 19/3, pp. 281-290, http://dx.doi.org/10.1016/j.labeco.2012.01.001. [6]

Bozio, A., T. Breda and J. Grenet (2017), "Incidence and Behavioural Response to Social Security Contributions: An Analysis of Kink Points in France", *De Economist*, Vol. 165/2, pp. 141-163, http://dx.doi.org/10.1007/s10645-017-9297-4. [41]

Brys, B. et al. (2016), "Tax Design for Inclusive Economic Growth", *OECD Taxation Working Papers*, No. 26, OECD Publishing, Paris, http://dx.doi.org/10.1787/5jlv74ggk0g7-en. [44]

Bryson, A. (2014), "Union wage effects", *IZA World of Labor*, Vol. 35, http://dx.doi.org/10.15185/izawol.35. [8]

Calmfors, L. and J. Driffill (1988), "Bargaining Structure, Corporatism and Macroeconomic Performance", *Economic Policy*, Vol. 3/6, p. 13, http://dx.doi.org/10.2307/1344503. [11]

Card, D. and A. Krueger (1995), *Myth and measurement. The new economics of the minimum wage*, Princeton University Press, Princeton. [2]

Card, D., T. Lemieux and W. Riddell (2004), "Unions and wage inequality", *Journal of Labor Research*, Vol. 25/4, pp. 519-559, http://dx.doi.org/10.1007/s12122-004-1011-z. [48]

Comola, M. and L. De Mello (2011), "How does decentralized minimum wage setting affect employment and informality? The case of Indonesia", *Review of Income and Wealth*, Vol. 57, pp. S79-S99, http://dx.doi.org/10.1111/j.1475-4991.2011.00451.x. [60]

Daveri, F. and G. Tabellini (2000), "Unemployment, growth and taxation in industrial countries", *Economic Policy*, Vol. 15/30, pp. 48-104, http://dx.doi.org/10.1111/1468-0327.00057. [35]

Deslauriers, J. et al. (2018), *Estimating the Impacts of Payroll Taxes: Evidence from Canadian Employer-Employee Tax Data*, http://www.iza.org (accessed on 02 November 2018). [39]

Dickens, R. and A. Manning (2004), "Has the National Minimum Wage Reduced UK Wage Inequality?", *Journal of the Royal Statistical Society. Series A (Statistics in Society)*, Vol. 167, pp. 613-626, http://dx.doi.org/10.2307/3559879. [71]

DiNardo, J. et al. (1996), "Labor Market Institutions and the Distribution of Wages, 1973-1992: A Semiparametric Approach", *Econometrica*, Vol. 64/5, pp. 1001-44, https://econpapers.repec.org/article/ecmemetrp/v_3a64_3ay_3a1996_3ai_3a5_3ap_3a1001-44.htm (accessed on 23 August 2018). [64]

DiNardo, J. and D. Lee (2004), "Economic Impacts of New Unionization on Private Sector Employers: 1984-2001", *The Quarterly Journal of Economics*, Vol. 119/4, pp. 1383-1441, http://dx.doi.org/10.1162/0033553042476189. [49]

Dinardo, J. and T. Lemieux (1997), "Diverging Male Wage Inequality in the United States and Ganada, 1981–1988: Do Institutions Explain the Difference?", *ILR Review*, Vol. 50/4, pp. 629-651, http://dx.doi.org/10.1177/001979399705000405. [66]

Draca, M., S. Machin and J. Van Reenen (2011), "Minimum Wages and Firm Profitability", *American Economic Journal: Applied Economics*, Vol. 3/1, pp. 129-151, http://dx.doi.org/10.1257/app.3.1.129. [62]

Dube, A., T. Lester and M. Reich (2010), "Minimum Wage Effects Across State Borders: Estimates Using Contiguous Counties", *Review of Economics and Statistics*, Vol. 92/4, pp. 945-964, http://dx.doi.org/10.1162/REST_a_00039. [51]

Elmeskov, J., J. Martin and S. Scarpetta (1998), "Key lessons for labour market reforms: Evidence from OECD countries' experience", *Swedish Economic Policy Review*, Vol. 5/2. [18]

Eurofound (2015), *Pay in Europe in different wage-bargaining regimes*, Publications Office of the European Union, Luxembourg. [16]

Ferracci, M. and F. Guyot (2015), *Dialogue social et performance économique*, Presses de Sciences Po. [9]

Gal, P. and A. Theising (2015), "The macroeconomic impact of structural policies on labour market outcomes in OECD countries: A reassessment", *OECD Economics Department Working Papers*, No. 1271, OECD Publishing, Paris, http://dx.doi.org/10.1787/5jrqc6t8ktjf-en. [75]

Garnero, A. (2018), "The dog that barks doesn't bite: coverage and compliance of sectoral minimum wages in Italy", *IZA Journal of Labor Policy*, Vol. 7/1, http://dx.doi.org/10.1186/s40173-018-0096-6. [50]

Goarant, C. and L. Muller (2011), "Les effets des hausses du Smic sur les salaires mensuels dans les entreprises de 10 salariés ou plus de 2006 à 2009 – Emploi et salaires | Insee", in *Emploi et salaires*, INSEE, Paris, https://www.insee.fr/fr/statistiques/1373824?sommaire=1373833 (accessed on 23 August 2018). [70]

Gruber and Jonathan (1997), "The Incidence of Payroll Taxation: Evidence from Chile", *Journal of Labor Economics*, Vol. 15/3, pp. 72-101, https://ideas.repec.org/a/ucp/jlabec/v15y1997i3ps72-101.html (accessed on 02 November 2018). [37]

Gruber and Jonathan (1994), "The Incidence of Mandated Maternity Benefits", *American Economic Review*, Vol. 84/3, pp. 622-641, https://ideas.repec.org/a/aea/aecrev/v84y1994i3p622-41.html (accessed on 02 November 2018). [36]

Haucap, J., U. Pauly and C. Wey (2001), "Collective wage setting when wages are generally binding An antitrust perspective", *International Review of Law and Economics*, Vol. 21/3, pp. 287-307, http://dx.doi.org/10.1016/S0144-8188(01)00061-8. [25]

Hijzen, A. and P. Martins (2016), "No Extension Without Representation? Evidence from a Natural Experiment in Collective Bargaining", *IZA Discussion Paper*, No. 10204. [27]

Hijzen, A., P. Martins and J. Parlevliet (2018), "Collective bargaining through the magnifying glass: A comparison between the Netherlands and Portugal", *OECD Social, Employment and Migration Working Papers*, No. 199, OECD Publishing, Paris, http://dx.doi.org/10.1787/06b8e7dd-en. [79]

Hirsch, B., B. Kaufman and T. Zelenska (2015), "Minimum Wage Channels of Adjustment", *Industrial Relations: A Journal of Economy and Society*, Vol. 54/2, pp. 199-239, http://dx.doi.org/10.1111/irel.12091. [56]

Ibsen, C. (2016), "The role of mediation institutions in Sweden and Denmark after centralized bargaining", *British Journal of Industrial Relations*, Vol. 54/2, pp. 285-310. [29]

Ibsen, C. and M. Keune (2018), "Organized Decentralization: Case studies of Germany, Netherlands and Denmark", *OECD Social, Employment and Migration Working Papers*, forthcoming, OECD Publishing, Paris. [28]

Jaumotte, F. and C. Buitron (2015), "Inequality and Labor Market Institutions", *Staff Discussion Note*, No. 15/14, IMF, https://www.imf.org/external/pubs/ft/sdn/2015/sdn1514.pdf (accessed on 26 January 2018). [24]

Koeniger, W., M. Leonardi and L. Nunziata (2007), "Labor Market Institutions and Wage Inequality", *ILR Review*, Vol. 60/3, pp. 340-356, http://dx.doi.org/10.1177/001979390706000302. [68]

Koubi, M. and B. Lhommeau (2007), "Les effets de diffusion de court terme des hausses du Smic dans les grilles salariales des entreprises de dix salariés ou plus sur la période 2000-2005", in *Les salaires en France*, INSEE, Paris. [69]

Kugler, A. and M. Kugler (2009), "Labor Market Effects of Payroll Taxes in Developing Countries: Evidence from Colombia", *Economic Development and Cultural Change*, Vol. 57/2, pp. 335-358, http://dx.doi.org/10.1086/592839. [40]

Lee, D. (1999), "Wage Inequality in the United States During the 1980s: Rising Dispersion or Falling Minimum Wage?", *The Quarterly Journal of Economics*, Vol. 114/3, pp. 977-1023, http://dx.doi.org/10.1162/003355399556197. [63]

Lee, D. and E. Saez (2012), "Optimal minimum wage policy in competitive labor markets", *Journal of Public Economics*, Vol. 96/9-10, pp. 739-749, http://dx.doi.org/10.1016/J.JPUBECO.2012.06.001. [74]

Lehmann, E. et al. (2016), "Beyond the labour income tax wedge: the unemployment-reducing effect of tax progressivity", *International Tax and Public Finance*, Vol. 23/3, pp. 454-489, http://dx.doi.org/10.1007/s10797-015-9377-9. [43]

Lewandowski, P. et al. (2015), "The effects of minimum wage on a labour market with high temporary employment", *IBS Working Paper*, No. 07, https://econpapers.repec.org/paper/ibtwpaper/wp072015.htm (accessed on 23 August 2018). [57]

Machin, S. (1997), "The decline of labour market institutions and the rise in wage inequality in Britain", *European Economic Review*, Vol. 41/3-5, pp. 647-657, http://dx.doi.org/10.1016/S0014-2921(97)00027-5. [67]

MaCurdy, T. (2015), "How Effective Is the Minimum Wage at Supporting the Poor?", *Journal of Political Economy*, Vol. 123/2, pp. 497-545, http://dx.doi.org/10.1086/679626. [4]

Magruder, J. (2012), "High Unemployment Yet Few Small Firms: The Role of Centralized Bargaining in South Africa", *American Economic Journal: Applied Economics*, Vol. 4/3, pp. 138-166, http://dx.doi.org/10.1257/app.4.3.138. [26]

Murtin, F., A. De Serres and A. Hijzen (2014), "Unemployment and the coverage extension of collective wage agreements", *European Economic Review*, Vol. 71, http://dx.doi.org/10.1016/j.euroecorev.2014.06.010. [76]

Neumark, D., J. Salas and W. Wascher (2014), "Revisiting the Minimum Wage—Employment Debate: Throwing Out the Baby with the Bathwater?", *ILR Review*, Vol. 67/3_suppl, pp. 608-648, http://dx.doi.org/10.1177/00197939140670S307. [54]

Neumark, D. and W. Wascher (2008), *Minimum wages*, The MIT Press. [3]

OECD (2018), "The role of collective bargaining systems for good labour market performance", in *OECD Employment Outlook 2018*, OECD Publishing, Paris, http://dx.doi.org/10.1787/empl_outlook-2018-7-en. [10]

OECD (2017), "Collective bargaining in a changing world of work", in *OECD Employment Outlook 2017*, OECD Publishing, Paris, http://dx.doi.org/10.1787/empl_outlook-2017-8-en. [7]

OECD (2016), *Taxing Wages 2016*, OECD Publishing, Paris, http://dx.doi.org/10.1787/tax_wages-2016-en. [32]

OECD (2015), "Recent labour market developments with a focus on minimum wages", in *OECD Employment Outlook 2015*, OECD Publishing, Paris, http://dx.doi.org/10.1787/empl_outlook-2015-5-en. [1]

OECD (2012), "What Makes Labour Markets Resilient During Recessions?", in *OECD Employment Outlook 2012*, OECD Publishing, Paris, http://dx.doi.org/10.1787/empl_outlook-2012-3-en. [20]

OECD (2011), *Divided we stand: Why inequality keeps rising*, OECD Publishing, Paris, http://dx.doi.org/10.1787/9789264119536-en. [23]

OECD (2009), "Is Work the Best Antidote to Poverty?", in *OECD Employment Outlook 2009: Tackling the Jobs Crisis*, OECD Publishing, Paris, http://dx.doi.org/10.1787/empl_outlook-2009-4-en. [5]

OECD (2007), "Financing Social Protection: The Employment Effect", in *OECD Employment Outlook 2007*, OECD Publishing, Paris, https://doi.org/10.1787/empl_outlook-2007-en. [31]

OECD (2004), *OECD Employment Outlook 2004*, OECD Publishing, Paris, http://dx.doi.org/10.1787/empl_outlook-2004-en. [19]

OECD (1997), *OECD Employment Outlook 1997*, OECD Publishing, Paris, http://dx.doi.org/10.1787/empl_outlook-1997-en. [12]

Piketty, T. (2013), "Optimal Labor Income Taxation", *Handbook of Public Economics*, Vol. 5, pp. 391-474, http://dx.doi.org/10.1016/B978-0-444-53759-1.00007-8. [46]

Pissarides, C. (1998), "The impact of employment tax cuts on unemployment and wages; The role of unemployment benefits and tax structure", https://ac.els-cdn.com/S0014292197000901/1-s2.0-S0014292197000901-main.pdf?_tid=2eece62f-8f9b-4142-b0f5-81ebbc4482f9&acdnat=1529670679_30b750816fa72ad85a74ec19411996d9 (accessed on 22 June 2018). [33]

Rani, U. et al. (2013), "Minimum wage coverage and compliance in developing countries", *International Labour Review*, Vol. 152/3-4, pp. 381-410, http://dx.doi.org/10.1111/j.1564-913X.2013.00197.x. [59]

Riley, R. and C. Rosazza Bondibene (2017), "Raising the standard: Minimum wages and firm productivity", *Labour Economics*, Vol. 44, pp. 27-50, http://dx.doi.org/10.1016/J.LABECO.2016.11.010. [55]

Rothstein, J. (2010), "Is the EITC as Good as an NIT? Conditional Cash Transfers and Tax Incidence", *American Economic Journal: Economic Policy*, Vol. 2/1, pp. 177-208, http://dx.doi.org/10.1257/pol.2.1.177. [73]

Saez, E., M. Matsaganis and P. Tsaklogou (2012), "EARNINGS Earnings Determination and Taxes: Evidence From a Cohort-Based Payroll Tax Reform in Greece", *The Quarterly Journal of Economics*, Vol. 127/1, pp. 493–533, https://doi.org/10.1093/qje/qjr052. [80]

Saez, E., B. Schoefer and D. Seim (2018), *Payroll Taxes, Firm Behavior, and Rent Sharing: Evidence from a Young Workers' Tax Cut in Sweden* *, https://eml.berkeley.edu/~saez/saez-schoefer-seimAER18sweden.pdf (accessed on 04 November 2018). [78]

Saint-Paul, G. (1996), *Dual labor markets: A macroeconomic perspective*, MIT Press. [21]

Soskice, D. (1990), "Reinterpreting Corporatism and Explaining Unemployment: Co-ordinated and Non-co-ordinated Market Economies", in Brunetta, R. and C. Dell'Aringa (eds.), *Labour Relations and Economic Performance*, Palgrave Macmillan UK, London, http://dx.doi.org/10.1007/978-1-349-11562-4_7. [17]

Stewart, M. (2012), "Wage inequality, minimum wage effects, and spillovers", *Oxford Economic Papers*, Vol. 64/4, pp. 616-634, http://dx.doi.org/10.1093/oep/gps003. [72]

Stokke, H. (2016), *Regional payroll tax cuts and individual wages: Heterogeneous effects across education groups* *, https://www.sole-jole.org/16217.pdf (accessed on 02 November 2018). [42]

Traxler, F., S. Blaschke and B. Kittel (2001), *National Labour Relations in Internationalized Markets*, Oxford University Press, Oxford, http://dx.doi.org/10.1093/acprof:oso/9780198295549.001.0001. [13]

Chapter 9. Protecting and supporting workers

This chapter focuses on the role of policies and institutions for promoting an effective labour supply by ensuring that work is accessible, attractive and sustainable over the life-course. This first of all requires tackling barriers to employment through the use of a comprehensive activation strategy that combines measures to enhance motivation with measures to promote employability and foster job opportunities. However, it also requires measures to make work more attractive and sustainable by ensuring that work pays, workers are protected against the risk of unemployment and workers can enjoy a healthy work environment.

The statistical data for Israel are supplied by and under the responsibility of the relevant Israeli authorities. The use of such data by the OECD is without prejudice to the status of the Golan Heights, East Jerusalem and Israeli settlements in the West Bank under the terms of international law.

Note by Turkey:
The information in this document with reference to "Cyprus" relates to the southern part of the Island. There is no single authority representing both Turkish and Greek Cypriot people on the Island. Turkey recognises the Turkish Republic of Northern Cyprus (TRNC). Until a lasting and equitable solution is found within the context of the United Nations, Turkey shall preserve its position concerning the "Cyprus issue".

Note by all the European Union Member States of the OECD and the European Union:
The Republic of Cyprus is recognised by all members of the United Nations with the exception of Turkey. The information in this document relates to the area under the effective control of the Government of the Republic of Cyprus.

Introduction

To promote quality jobs for all in a changing world of work, policies and institutions to promote productivity growth and job creation need to be combined with policies and institutions to support an effective supply of labour. Yet, many jobless and marginally attached individuals face various barriers to good quality employment, relating to their individual situation as well as the quality of the jobs available. Addressing these barriers is crucial to prevent that a sizeable share of the working-age population is effectively excluded from the labour market.

Promoting an effective labour supply requires a mix of policies that stimulate both job quantity and job quality. It includes policies that primarily relate to job quantity, i.e. employment and social policies that address employment barriers related to work motivation, worker employability and job opportunities. If designed well, such measures can also improve job quality through enhanced job matching, with potentially important implications for earnings and job stability. However, an effective labour supply also requires policies that ensure that work is attractive and sustainable over the life-cycle through improvements in job quality. This includes, amongst others, measures to ensure that work pays, to protect workers against the risk of joblessness and to support a healthy working environment.

The remainder of this chapter is structured as follows. Section 9.1 discusses the role of in-work and out-of-work benefits to make labour markets more secure by protecting workers against the risk of unemployment and in-work poverty, while preserving and promoting good work incentives. Section 9.2 presents the main elements of a comprehensive activation strategy based on a mutual-obligations framework that seeks to make work accessible for all by tackling employment barriers. Section 9.3 discusses how governments can support a quality work environment to ensure that work is attractive and sustainable over the life-course. The last section concludes.

9.1. Protecting workers against the risk of unemployment and in-work poverty

This section focuses on the role of out-of-work benefits for protecting workers against income losses in the case of joblessness and in-work benefits for protecting workers against the risk of in-work poverty. Apart from supporting the incomes of poor working families, in-work benefits also play an important role in alleviating the potentially negative impact of unemployment benefits on work incentives.

Insuring workers against joblessness

Public income support for the unemployed, either in the form of unemployment insurance or assistance programmes, serve two main policy objectives. First, these programmes protect individual workers against the risk of income loss during joblessness, smoothing consumption between unemployment and employment spells. This also acts as an automatic stabiliser at the aggregate level (see Chapter 13), while ensuring a fair distribution of income and containing poverty (see Chapter 10). Second, by alleviating liquidity constraints and allowing more time for workers to look for a suitable position, unemployment benefits can enhance the quality of job matches in terms of both earnings and job stability, with potentially important implications for aggregate efficiency.

There is considerable variation across countries in the design of unemployment benefit systems, and hence, the extent to which they support incomes during joblessness and facilitate job search. Figure 9.1 summarises some of the key institutional details by means of net benefit replacement rates - which express the net income of a beneficiary as a percentage of net income in the previous job – for different unemployment durations. On average across countries, the replacement rate declines from 64% at the start of the unemployment spell to 53 % during the first year and just 28% on average during the first five years. In countries with universal unemployment benefit systems such as Australia, New Zealand and the United Kingdom, modest unemployment benefits are available to all non-employed persons subject to a means test. Most other countries operate mixed systems with unemployment insurance benefits for those who meet certain contribution requirements and means-tested social-assistance benefits for those who do not receive unemployment benefits. In those countries, the generosity of income support tends to decrease over the unemployment spell due to the role of declining benefit schedules or limits to the maximum duration of receiving unemployment insurance benefits.

Figure 9.1. Unemployment benefit schemes protect workers against the income losses during joblessness

Net replacement rates for an average-income earner in % of previous income, 2015

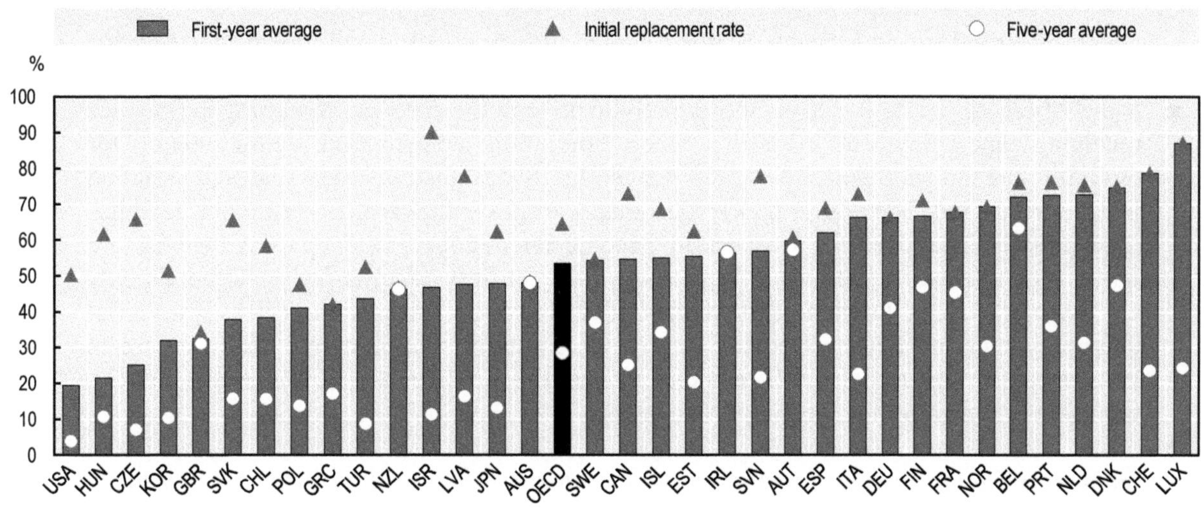

Note: The net replacement rate is the ratio of net income out-of-work to net income while in-work. Unemployment benefits include unemployment insurance, unemployment assistance as well as family benefits. Social assistance and housing- related benefits are not included. Calculations consider cash income as well as income taxes and mandatory social security contributions paid by employees. They are averages over four different stylised family types (single parents and one- earner couples, with and without children) and two earnings levels on the lost job (67% and 100% of average full- time wages). OECD is the unweighted average of the countries shown.
Source: OECD Tax- Benefit Models, www.oecd.org/els/social/workincentives.

StatLink http://dx.doi.org/10.1787/888933881306

Unemployment benefits smooth consumption and can also contribute to better post-unemployment outcomes if well designed

Unemployment-insurance and assistance programmes are indeed effective in smoothing consumption between job spells. While unemployed persons who are not eligible to income support dramatically reduce their level of consumption, the drop is usually very limited among those who are eligible (Gruber, 1997[1]; Kroft and Notowidigdo, 2016[2]).

These positive effects on consumption tend to be larger among unemployment-benefit recipients, who have no assets and those whose spouse is not employed (Browning and Crossley, (2001[3]). Unemployment insurance can also play an important role in supporting aggregate demand during economic downturns. For example, evidence for the United States suggests that the effects of adverse economic shocks on aggregate consumption are larger in counties with less generous unemployment insurance (Di Maggio and Kermani, 2016[4]).

Evidence on the ability of income-support schemes to improve the quality of job matches is mixed. While unemployment-benefit recipients can take more time and be more demanding in terms of the job offers to accept, their employability tends to decline over the unemployment spell as a result of human capital depreciation and discrimination among recruiters against long-term unemployed (Schmieder and Von Wachter, 2016[5]). Recent studies detect no or only small positive impacts of the generosity of unemployment insurance on post-unemployment earnings.[1] The effects on post-unemployment earnings may depend on the characteristics of workers as, for instance, financially constrained workers benefit more from generous benefits than other recipients (Centeno, Centeno and Novo, 2009[6]) or the design of unemployment insurance systems.

Poorly designed unemployment benefits can contribute to job instability if they provide incentives for alternating between short-duration jobs and unemployment (Boeri, Cahuc and Zylberberg, 2015[7]). This is more likely to arise in the absence of waiting periods for receiving unemployment benefits, when minimum contribution requirements for eligibility are too short, and when rules are implicitly designed to cover seasonal variation in labour demand. Moreover, poorly designed partial unemployment insurance schemes may provide incentives for workers to become unemployed when partial benefits are withdrawn after some period of time and rights for full benefits are restored quickly e.g. Kyyrä (2010[8]), Fontaine and Malherbet (2016[9]), Le Barbanchon (2016[10]). Partial unemployment insurance associated with low eligibility requirements can also create incentives for firms to lay off workers or make excessive use of flexible contracts, increasing the cost of income-support schemes.

Generous unemployment benefits may discourage job-search efforts and increase joblessness

More generous unemployment insurance may lengthen unemployment spells and the overall level of unemployment through its impact on job-search incentives and the acceptance rate of job offers (Chetty, 2008[11]). The usual argument is that unemployment insurance reduces incentives for job search by distorting the relative price of leisure and consumption. This is the "moral hazard effect" and reduces social welfare. However, it may also reduce job-search intensity by reducing the pressure on cash-strapped unemployed persons to find a job. This "liquidity effect" follows from the consumption-smoothing role of unemployment insurance and is intended.

In normal times, more generous unemployment benefits tend to reduce job-search intensity and increase the duration of unemployment spells, with varying intensity across countries and groups (Tatsiramos and van Ours, 2014[12]; Schmieder and Von Wachter, 2016[5]). Rigorous impact evaluations of reforms reveal that a 1% increase in the replacement ratio raises the duration of unemployment between 0.4% and 1.6%. Moreover, the elasticity of unemployment duration to benefit levels is greater than its elasticity to the maximum duration of entitlements: a one-month increase in the duration of benefit entitlements leads on average to an increase in unemployment duration of a bit less than one week.

Job-seekers tend to search more intensively around the time unemployment-insurance rights expire. Empirical studies for Austria, France, Germany and the United States highlight a significant spike in the exit rate from unemployment to employment in the period immediately preceding the exhaustion of rights. In the case of France, this behaviour turned out to be stronger among medium to high skilled workers than among the low skilled who benefit from fewer job opportunities and have less leeway in deciding when to exit unemployment (Dormont, Fougère and Prieto, 2001[13]). The peak is even more pronounced when all types of transitions are taken into account, i.e. not only exits to employment but also the exits to training and inactivity (Card, Chetty and Weber, 2007[14]).[2]

The aggregate impact of unemployment insurance is likely to be smaller than that measured at the individual level due to spill-over effects. A reduction in the generosity of benefits increases competition for jobs among jobs-seekers and reduces the effectiveness of job search.[3] This in turn reduces the time it takes for firms to fill vacancies, leading to higher job creation and aggregate employment (Landais, 2015[15]; Landais, Michaillat and Saez, 2018[16]). For instance, the extension of the maximum duration of unemployment benefits in Austria in the late 1980s increased the job-finding rate among non-eligible workers (Lalive, Landais and Zweimüller, 2015[17]). As a result, the elasticity of unemployment duration to the generosity of benefits at the aggregate level tends to be smaller than that at the individual level (Schmieder and Von Wachter, 2016[5]).

The design of unemployment benefit systems needs to strike a careful balance between their costs and benefits

Since income support is essential to smooth consumption over job spells but can also reduce job search effort if too generous, policy makers need to strike a balance. The optimal level of income support is primarily an empirical problem which requires rich country-specific micro-data sets that allow comparing the social welfare gains stemming from smoothed consumption and the behavioural costs due to reduced search efforts. This is an avenue for future research and the available evidence is still scattered at this stage – e.g. Schmieder and von Wachter (2016[5]). However, since the duration of unemployment tends to be more sensitive to the level of benefits than to its maximum duration, countries with very short benefit durations could improve welfare by extending them. Similarly countries featuring long unemployment duration and high replacement rates could benefit from lowering replacement rates.

There are a number of further design issues that can help to strengthen work incentives during the unemployment spell and limit overuse by workers and employers. First, it is possible to increase the responsibility of workers and employers for the use of unemployment benefits. The responsibility of workers can be increased by relying at least to some extent on mandatory self-insurance as is the case in some emerging economies (see Chapter 16).[4] The responsibility of employers can be increased through the experience-rating of employer social security contributions for unemployment insurance based on the recent dismissal behaviour of individual employers, as is done in the United States. This forces firms to internalise the social cost of their workforce policies.[5] Second, one can strengthen work incentives by reducing the participation tax associated with moving from benefits to work. This can be done explicitly through the use of in-work benefits as discussed in the next sub-section or by embedding income-support schemes in an effective activation strategy based on the principle of mutual obligations which links benefit receipt to active job search and the right and duty to participate in training and other employment-support programmes (Section 9.2).

Making work pay

The marginal effective tax rate of moving into work from unemployment benefits (participation tax) amount to 77% on average across OECD countries, but can be close to 100% in a few countries such as Austria, Luxembourg and Norway (Figure 9.2).[6] Participation taxes tend to be smaller in the case of means-tested social assistance benefits but remain sizeable, amounting to 66% on average across OECD countries.[7] The financial incentives to take up gainful opportunities at the bottom of the distribution can be enhanced through in-work benefits (IWB) or tax credits. In the case of second-earners, work incentives can be strengthened by relying on individual rather than family-based taxation.

Well-targeted, permanent in-work benefits can make work pay and support living standards of low-income families, provided incentives are properly understood

IWB schemes are designed to create a significant gap between the incomes of people in work as compared with the income that they would get if they were out of work, thereby making work pay, while supporting the incomes of the most vulnerable in or out of work. They pursue, therefore, the twin goal of, on the one hand, enhancing employment and the movement of workers up the earnings ladder and, on the other hand, ensuring a greater inclusiveness of the labour market. In order to avoid creating new disincentives higher up the earnings ladder, IWB must avoid threshold effects by maintaining a sufficiently large phase-out region over which benefits are withdrawn gradually.

The effectiveness of IWB depends on their targeting, the duration for which they are provided and the way they are operated. First, the effects of in-work benefits on work incentives are more pronounced when targeted at groups that are more sensitive to financial incentives such as lone parents (Immervoll and Scarpetta, 2012[18]).[8] Moreover, in-work benefits are more effective when they are provided permanently, i.e. as long as needed, rather than for a limited maximum duration. The evidence suggests that temporary in-work benefits have limited effects on poverty in the longer-term (van der Linden, 2016[19]). Finally, IWB systems tend to be more effective when they are operated in a simple and transparent way. If potential beneficiaries do not understand the IWB system, the desired labour-supply response tends to be smaller (Chetty, Friedman and Saez, 2013[20]). This is more likely when the interaction with other taxes and benefits is complex.

The effectiveness of in-work benefits further depends on the institutional settings of each country. If earnings distributions are compressed at the bottom, it is more difficult to accentuate work incentives in a meaningful way. IWB in these cases either would be very expensive, – because their phase-out region would include many workers resulting in a high fiscal burden –or largely ineffective, – because they would make little difference to recipients (Immervoll and Pearson, 2009[21]). Furthermore, their effectiveness in reducing in-work poverty can be enhanced by complementing them with binding wage floors in the form of statutory minimum wages, or negotiated wage floors set by collective bargaining (see Chapter 8). By providing a minimum level below which wages cannot fall, they help avoiding that employers capture most of the programme benefits through lower wages, thereby achieving the intended redistribution to low-wage workers (OECD, 2009[22]; Nichols and Rothstein, 2015[23]).[9]

Figure 9.2. Work incentives for unemployment-benefit recipients vary significantly across OECD countries

Average participation tax rate, % of gross earnings, 2016

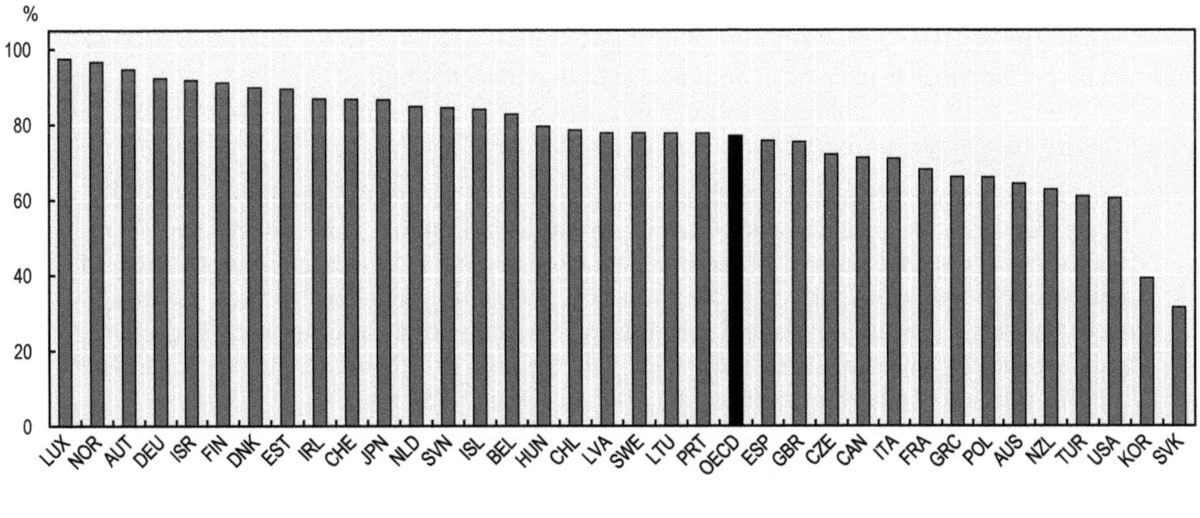

Note: Marginal effective tax rate of taking up work at 67% of the average wage for recipients of unemployment benefits in one-earner couple with two children. This shows how much of the new gross earnings are 'taxed away' through the payment of taxes and the loss of benefits. Transitional 'into work' benefits are included where applicable, on an annualised basis. Supplements are included.
Source: *OECD Tax-Benefit Database*, http://www.oecd.org/social/benefits-and-wages.htm.

StatLink http://dx.doi.org/10.1787/888933881325

Participation tax rates for second earners can be lowered by moving to individual taxation

Participation tax rates may also be very high for second-earners as a result of family-based taxation. A few OECD countries operate family-based systems of labour income taxation – where the family rather than the individual is the unit of taxation –, on a either compulsory or optional basis (Thomas and O'Reilly, 2016[24]). Family-based tax systems often create important work disincentives for second earners, when marginal tax rates are progressive and/or tax credits means-tested. In this case, second earners are effectively taxed at higher marginal tax rates than a single individual would be, because the primary earner has already "used up" the lower tax brackets and any tax credit available to the family. Moving to individual-based systems usually improves the work incentives for second earners. This would also leave more space for targeting in-work benefits on low-income families (instead of individuals) without jeopardising work incentives (Immervoll and Pearson, 2009[21]).

9.2. Tackling all employment barriers simultaneously

This section discusses the need for, and key requirements of, a comprehensive activation strategy to tackle all employment barriers effectively. In order to be comprehensive, an activation strategy should combine measures to ensure that jobless people are motivated to search actively and accept suitable jobs, with measures that increase the employability of those that are least employable. Therefore, the activation strategy is consistent with a mutual-obligations framework that makes income support and effective re-employment services conditional on beneficiaries taking active steps to find work or improve their employability. The cost-effectiveness of employment services can be improved through sound performance management and the use of digital technologies.

A comprehensive activation strategy is needed

Jobless and marginally attached individuals face various barriers to quality employment. These barriers may include lack of adequate education, skills and/or work-experience, health problems (see Box 9.1), care responsibilities, lack of transportation, lack of suitable information on job vacancies and how to qualify for them as well as lack of access to new job search tools and technology, discrimination, or other social problems, and insufficient financial incentives due to the impact of labour income on taxes and benefits (CEA, 2016[25]; Fernandez et al., 2016[26]; OECD, 2015[27]).

Importantly, recent research – e.g. Sundaram et al. (2014[28]); Fernandez et al. (2016[26]) – shows that only a small fraction of those persistently unemployed face high benefit-induced participation tax rates – i.e. the net marginal tax on labour income associated with the transition from joblessness to employment, taking into account all taxes and transfers – and that, in general, other barriers play an equally or more important role.[10] This suggests that a comprehensive activation strategy, going beyond the strengthening of work incentives, is needed to promote successful transitions into stable jobs and overall employment levels more generally.[11]

Re-employment services and active policies provide help to the unemployed (and other inactive groups) with finding work and seek to improve the quality of job matches. Countries spend on average 0.5% of gross domestic product (GDP) on active policies, with a large cross-country variation ranging from 2.1% in Denmark to 0.1% in the United States and even less in Mexico (Figure 9.3). Typical services include the provision of labour market information, job search assistance (e.g. guidance for finding jobs, help drafting a resume), direct placement or active job brokering (e.g. collecting job vacancies, making job referrals), training and rehabilitation services, subsidised employment opportunities, and in certain cases, direct job-creation measures.

An effective activation strategy requires combining measures to ensure that jobseekers have the *motivation* to search actively and accept suitable jobs with actions to expand job *opportunities* – for example, by addressing demand-side barriers through actively engaging and assisting employers in hiring and retaining workers and addressing high non-wage labour costs, as well as reaching out to employers to utilise new recruitment tools – and interventions to increase the *employability* of those who are less employable – for example, by offering intensive case-management and placement services, participation in training and subsidised employment programmes, as well as lifting supply-side barriers to participation related to for example transportation, childcare, or social problems.

A holistic approach is needed to address all employment barriers through coordinated actions concerning the provision of employment services and the administration of active programmes as well as the design of tax and benefits policies (OECD, 2015[27]). For example, even in the presence of aggressive job brokering strategies by the public employment service (PES), workers may not succeed in gaining or maintaining jobs in the absence of access to suitable transportation or if they lack the necessary competences. Similarly, workers who enrol in training and re-employment programmes may lack the motivation for making the most out of them.

Figure 9.3. Public spending on active labour market policies

Total spending on active measures[a] as a percentage of GDP in OECD countries, 2015[b]

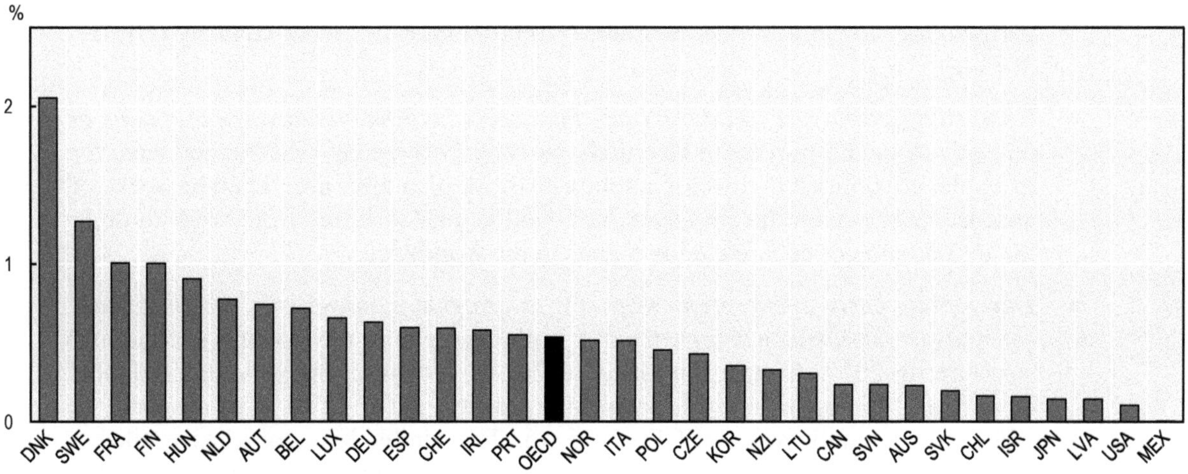

Note: OECD is the unweighted average of the countries shown. Countries are ranked by decreasing order of public expenditure in active measures.

a) Data cover administration, training, employment incentives, sheltered and supported employment and rehabilitation, direct job creation, start-up incentives.

b) Data refer to active measures and to 2014 for Estonia, to 2011/12 for the United Kingdom, to FY 2014/15 for New Zealand and to FY 2015/16 for Australia, Canada, Japan and the United States.

Source: *OECD/Eurostat Labour Market Programme Database*, http://dx.doi.org/10.1787/data-00312-en.

StatLink http://dx.doi.org/10.1787/888933881344

Box 9.1. Fostering effective return-to-work policies for people with health problems

Preventing long-term sickness absence and disability-benefit claims is a major challenge in many OECD countries, calling for specific return-to-work measures for people with health problems. Data for a number of OECD countries demonstrate that after a period of around three months, return to work becomes very difficult for people off-work for health reasons (OECD, 2013[29]; OECD, 2013[30]). Effective policies to control sickness and disability caseloads typically focus on the start of a sickness spell, with special attention for people with stress and mental health-related problems. Promising return-to-work policies include:

- *Moving towards more informative, capacity-oriented sickness certificates from doctors*. For example, the United Kingdom has shifted from providing "sick notes" to preparing "fit notes" which focus on the work a patient can still do and describe in some detail what tasks he or she can reasonably perform and what workplace adjustments may be necessary (OECD, 2014[31]). Some countries, including Sweden, also developed better sickness absence guidelines for doctors, with for example information about the typical duration for sickness for a particular illness to prevent the certification of unreasonably long absences (OECD, 2013[30]).

- *Promoting a gradual return-to-work instead of allowing workers to stay away sick until they are fully recovered.* Norway recently made partial sick leave the default option for certifying physicians, compelling them to justify why they may have prescribed full sick leave. At the same time, it introduced tools to support physicians through online feedback about their certification behaviour (OECD, 2013[32]). More recently, Finland and Austria have also started to promote a partial return to work for sick workers to rebuild their full work capacity (OECD, 2015[33]).
- *Compelling employers to address an employee's health-related work problems at an early stage.* Employers in Denmark, Norway, Sweden and the Netherlands, for example, are obliged to develop a return-to-work plan after around eight weeks of absence, jointly with the employee, and facilitate an early return to work through the introduction of concrete adjustments in the workplace.
- *Developing early-intervention services to provide counselling and treatment referrals to sick-listed workers,* thereby bridging a gap in the existing institutional structure. In 2013, Austria introduced fit2work, a counselling service to support employees with mental health problems (typically after 40 days of absence) as well as their employers (OECD, 2015[34]). The United Kingdom has trialled a similar programme, Fit for Work, providing occupational assessments for employees (typically after 4-12 weeks of absence) also with a particular focus on mental health issues (OECD, 2014[31]).

Address all employment barriers related to motivation, employability and opportunities

Universal and moderately-generous benefits increase the scope and effectiveness of a mutual-obligations approach to activation

Unemployment and social-assistance benefits provide the principal instrument for linking jobless people to employment services and active labour market programmes. By contrast, those not receiving income support can find accessing employment services significantly more difficult: they may be excluded by design or lack the information or motivation to register with the public employment services (Immervoll, 2012[35]; OECD, 2015[27]). Indeed, the "mutual-obligations" framework – in which governments commit to providing jobseekers with benefits and effective employment services and, in turn, beneficiaries have to take active steps to find work or improve their employability by participating in employment services – is based on the premise that workers receive benefits. Where monitoring and enforced sanction systems are in place, its effectiveness tends to increase with the generosity of benefits by raising the cost of sanctions and strengthening financial incentives for taking up gainful employment. Consequently, the accessibility and adequacy of benefits plays a crucial role in determining the scope and effectiveness of a mutual-obligations approach that is supported with the threat of benefit sanctions.

Despite the importance of high benefit coverage for providing effective re-employment support to the most vulnerable, only a minority of unemployed workers receive unemployment benefits in most OECD countries (Figure 9.4), often because of stringent eligibility criteria for initial benefit entitlements or short maximum durations, curtailing continued benefit recipiency. In most countries, jobseekers who do not receive unemployment benefits have access to means-tested social benefits – see OECD (2018[36]). However, in this case, "mutual obligations" are often less strictly enforced. To the extent that employment services find it difficult to reach out to potential clients that receive social-assistance benefits or no benefits at all, unemployment insurance should be designed so as to maximise coverage, while maintaining work incentives.

However, improving coverage is challenging to the extent that unemployment-benefit entitlements are still largely based on the notion of a unique employment relationship at any point in time. Many countries are struggling to provide adequate coverage for workers on non-standard work contracts such as self-employed, multi-employer employees and various forms of crowd workers, who only work occasionally and/or combine multiple income sources, with no statutory working hours. These issues are developed in Chapter 12.

Figure 9.4. Only a minority of unemployed workers receive unemployment benefits

Share of unemployed persons receiving unemployment benefits, selected countries, 2016

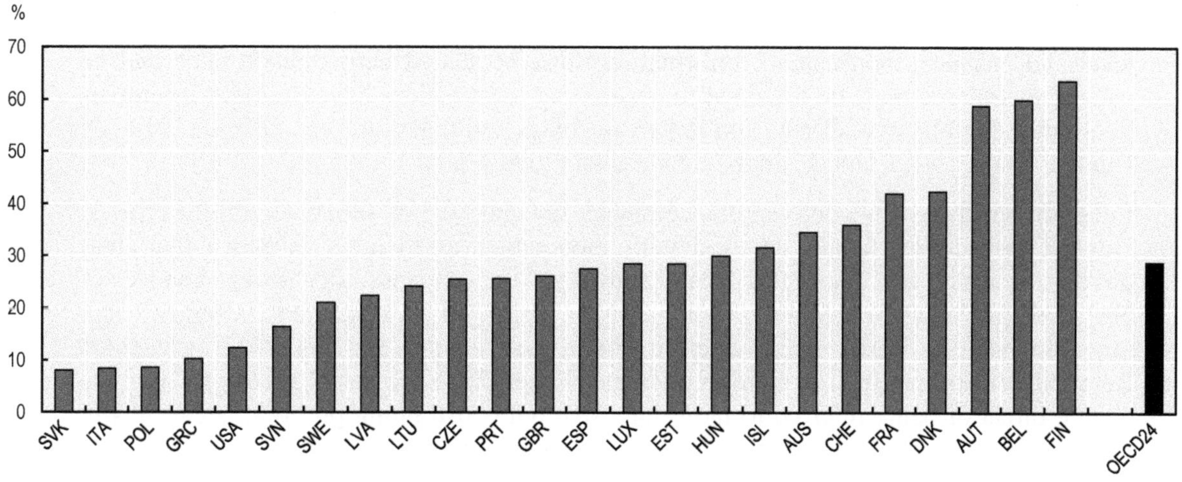

Note: Some European countries are excluded due to missing information in EU-LFS data. OECD-24 corresponds to the unweighted average of the countries shown. 2015 figures for Australia. Unemployed workers are identified according to the definition of the International Labour Organization.
Source: OECD (2018[36]), *OECD Employment Outlook 2018*, https://doi.org/10.1787/empl_outlook-2018-en, based on: Household, Income and Labour Dynamics in Australia (HILDA) for Australia; European Union Labour Force Survey (EU-LFS) for European countries; and Current Population Survey (CPS) for the United States.

StatLink http://dx.doi.org/10.1787/888933881363

Strictly-enforced eligibility criteria for benefits can motivate jobseekers to look for jobs, but require a balanced articulation of warnings and sanctions

An effective activation strategy must define strict eligibility criteria, involving the suitability of job offers, requirements to report on the outcomes of independent job-search efforts, the obligation to participate in active programmes and the determination of benefit sanctions for non-compliance with these rules. If suitably designed, these rules help ensure that new benefit recipients, who are relatively employable, return to work quickly, while maintaining the motivation of benefit recipients who require longer-term measures, such as training, to restore their employability. Frequent interviews with caseworkers and effort verification based on documented actions are usually found to yield positive employment outcomes. However, excessive monitoring based on bureaucratic procedures may be counterproductive, while inducing a shift from informal to formal job-search methods, particularly for the most-qualified (van den Berg and van der Klaauw, 2006[37]; OECD, 2015[27]). Flexible individual action plans developed by caseworkers can be better tailored on the characteristics of the client.

Benefit provision and employment services work best if they are either integrated into a single service provider (one-shop agency) or strictly coordinated. The UK experience suggests that merging the public employment service and benefit agency has improved employment outcomes and services for clients and has been cost-effective (OECD, 2014[31]). Experience from other countries, such as Australia, Finland, Ireland and Switzerland, suggests partnership approaches between organisations and agencies (including those in the private and not-for-profit sector) can improve the co-ordination of service delivery, especially for disadvantaged client groups or in high-unemployment areas (OECD, 2013[38]). The problem of coordination typically arises where employment services are decentralised, while the administration of benefits takes place at the national level. To enhance coordination, information must be shared across institutions and an incentive structure must be designed to ensure that local offices have the right incentives to monitor eligibility conditions and impart warnings and sanctions, e.g. OECD (2014[39]); Duell et al. (2010[40]); Duell, Singh and Tergeist (2009[41]).

Enforced sanctions for non-compliance are an integral part of sound eligibility criteria. However, sanctions should be used with moderation as there is evidence that their positive impact on exit rates may come at the expense of lower quality of post-unemployment outcomes, with higher risk of subsequent re-entry into unemployment or overall exit to inactivity (Arni, Lalive and Van Ours, 2013[42]; van den Berg and Vikström, 2014[43]; Card, Kluve and Weber, 2015[44]; Busk, 2016[45]). Often the simple threat of being referred to more intensive but constraining programmes results in increased search effort and job finding (Graversen and van Ours, 2008[46]; Røed, 2012[47]; Bredgaard, 2015[48]), and so do early warnings of benefit sanctions (Arni, Lalive and Van Ours, 2013[42]; Lachowska, Meral and Woodbury, 2016[49]). In the case of assistance-benefit recipients, safeguards must be included in the system to prevent that excessive sanctions result in severe loss of child welfare or increases in poverty among vulnerable groups (Griggs and Evans, 2010[50]). In practice, the graduation of warnings and sanctions is likely to require some discretion from decision-makers. Overall, the overarching principle should be to intensify and maintain engagement rather than cutting links with the jobseeker altogether.

Effective job-search assistance and other active programmes require intensive counselling, personalised services as well as skilful case management

Early and frequent counselling interviews have been identified as an efficient way of assisting jobseekers (OECD, 2015[27]). However, individualisation of content is key: highly-tailored counselling and employment services (e.g. in-depth review of skills and experience, development of individual search plans, direct referral to vacancies matching the jobseeker's competences) tend to be associated with improved employment prospects and post-unemployment outcomes. By contrast, low-intensity counselling interventions do not seem to have substantial impact on labour market outcomes – e.g. van den Berg and van der Klaauw (2006[37]).

More personalised services and better case management require sufficiently low client-staff ratios. Recent small-scale experiments in Germany suggest that the hiring of additional, suitably qualified, caseworkers can substantially improve the performance of local public employment services thanks to increased monitoring and enhanced job-brokering. Such investments may even pay for themselves, as the increase in staff expenses may be more than offset by the reduction in benefit dependency (Hainmueller et al., 2016[51]). Similarity in social background between caseworker and jobseeker can contribute to successful performance, possibly as a result of enhanced communication, motivation, and trust (Behncke, Frölich and Lechner, 2010[52]), provided that this does not lead to softer attitudes by the caseworker (OECD, 2015[27]).[12] Lower caseloads also allow for a better diversification of competences within the public employment service and, hence, more effective and tailored responses to the specific needs of clients.

Profiling tools are an effective way to target costly interventions

Profiling tools have been used by many countries, sometimes very early in the jobless spell, as a way to efficiently allocate jobseekers to less or more intensive service streams in a context of limited resources. Effective profiling tools typically involve an initial questionnaire or interview, the use of a regularly-evaluated statistical matching model and adjustments based on feedback from clients and service providers. The need for formal categorisation of clients is greater where resources constraints are stronger (OECD, 2015[27]) and clients are very heterogeneous in their needs for support (Lechner and Smith, 2007[53]). Profiling tools may be particularly useful in the assignment of jobseekers to more intensive and expensive programmes, such as training.

Training and rehabilitation programmes have been shown to produce better and more stable effects on long-term individual performance than strategies based only on job-search assistance and sanctions – e.g. Card, Kluve and Weber (2015[44]). Yet, lock-in effects due to missed job opportunities during training may reduce effective labour supply in the short-run (Kluve, 2010[54]). This underlines the importance of "mixed strategies" characterised by selective referrals to training for those in most need (i.e. for whom lock-in effects are less important and potential gains greater), with job-search assistance remaining the key tool for other jobseekers. Such strategies crucially require adequate profiling tools and skilful case-management.

Effective out-placement services require reaching out to employers

Expanding available and accessible job opportunities requires that public employment services act as competent job brokers with the trust of employers. Actively developing contacts with employers is a major factor in reducing unemployment duration (Hainmueller et al., 2016[51]). Instead of only passively registering vacancies, PES staff may actively solicit employers for new job offers or even apply reverse-marketing techniques when this makes particular sense (OECD, 2012[55]). PES placement can also be enhanced by proposing career development and training services to small and medium enterprises that often do not have the capacity to provide these in-house (OECD, 2014[56]).

More generally, monitoring labour demand with respect to the skill requirements of job vacancies is essential for the PES to ensure efficient matching of jobseekers to prospective employers. In this respect, it is crucial that countries develop effective systems and tools for assessing and anticipating skills needs (OECD, 2017[57]) and that these are used to inform PES actions.

The provision of subsidised employment opportunities could be part of a comprehensive activation strategy if done cautiously

Direct job creation and employment/hiring incentives represent additional instruments that can be used to promote opportunities within a comprehensive activation policy. Compulsory referrals of the long-term unemployed to direct job creation measures are often costly but are easily implementable, tend to increase job finding in the months ahead of programme participation thanks to a threat effect and can promote the integration of disadvantaged groups, at least in the short-term. The scheduling of job-creation measures several months ahead, combined with intensive counselling and training measures to promote market work helps to maximise the threat effect and minimise programme costs. This provides some support in favour of the use of job-creation measures as one element of a comprehensive activation strategy. However, they must be used with great caution because their effects in fostering self-sufficiency in the long-term are uncertain (OECD, 2015[27]; Card, Kluve and Weber, 2015[44]).

By contrast, hiring subsidies, that is, wage subsidies or tax rebates granted for a limited period of time, can be cost-effective in the case of temporary lack of demand (Cahuc, Carcillo and Le Barbanchon, forthcoming[58]) or to provide relevant work experience to specific groups (Brown, 2015[59]). To minimise deadweight costs, they should be conditioned on net job creation, while taking account of the administrative costs of monitoring eligibility requirements on take-up. Targeting hiring subsidies on the most disadvantaged (e.g. the long-term unemployed) can further help to reduce deadweight costs, while contributing to a more inclusive labour market through a more equal sharing of employment opportunities, albeit at the cost of potentially greater displacement and substitution effects. Targeted discretionary recruitment incentives can be an effective tool for caseworkers to promote trial hires of jobseekers with significant employability barriers, in particular if efforts are made to ensure that they provide valuable work experience and at least some prospect of being retained in their job beyond the subsidy period (OECD, 2015[27]).

Enhancing the cost-effectiveness of employment services through sound performance management and the use of digital technologies

The cost-effectiveness of employment services, whether provided publicly or privately, can be improved through sound performance management. This requires measuring and evaluating performance in terms of job placements and, especially for harder-to-help groups, longer-term employment outcomes. A few countries rate local employment office performance in terms of outcomes with adjustments for jobseeker and local labour market characteristics, based on rigorous and tested statistical methods. When well developed, this approach encourages the robust measurement of outcomes, helps identifying further factors influencing performance and generates relatively accurate and objective ratings of local office performance (OECD, 2013[38]).

Several OECD countries have experimented with the outsourcing of employment services to private providers. Contracting out job-placement and training services appears an attractive option to the extent that it opens up the market for these services to competition, which might decrease costs as compared to public delivery and stimulate innovative ways of responding to client needs. Experiences with outsourcing of employment services in Australia and the United Kingdom, the countries which have gone furthest in this regard, are very informative (OECD, 2012[55]; OECD, 2014[56]).[13] One challenge is that contracting out requires the capacity to design an appropriate incentive contract for private providers and to effectively monitor service delivery. This requires building up a number of skills that are not necessarily within the core competences of the PES. In the absence of appropriate incentive contracts, private service providers may have incentives to engage in "cream-skimming", i.e. focussing on easy-to-place individuals, or "parking", i.e. paying less attention to hard-to-place jobseekers (Finn, 2011[60]).

To implement an effective activation strategy with the involvement of private service providers, a number of conditions must be met (OECD, 2015[27]). First, the size of the market for private services must be large enough. This allows for effective competition between local providers and facilitates benchmarking provider performance. Second, relative provider performance must be outcome-based and measured accurately with a fee structure that varies by client group, depending on their distance to the labour market. This requires effective profiling tools to support client categorisation and ensure that also the hard-to-employ receive adequate services. Third, inefficient providers should have their contracts terminated to avoid poor performance affecting service quality to clients (OECD, 2015[27]). Finally, contracts should be prescriptive with a detailed specification of service requirements, without undermining competition. However, striking the balance between prescription and competition can be challenging in practice.[14]

Programme evaluation is a crucial component of sound performance management. To make rigorous evaluation possible, the initial design of policy measures should be adapted, where feasible through the use of randomisation. Evaluations can cover various aspects of the implementation of new policies and programmes and give insights into what effects the policies and programmes had, for whom and why. More generally, evaluations allow for a continuous improvement of policies and programmes, but unsuccessful ones need to be adjusted or terminated. It is also advisable to test new programmes locally, possibly on the basis of random trials, and implement them on a larger scale only after rigorous evaluation. Care must be taken in comparing different types of programmes since certain measures are conceived to pay off over a longer time horizon than others, e.g. training and requalification against work-first strategies (Card, Kluve and Weber, 2015[44]).

Digital technologies are transforming the way the PES operates while making it easier to exploit information about vacancies and jobseekers. By automating a number of tasks such as benefit applications and vacancy registration, digitalisation allows the PES to concentrate resources on activities requiring personal interactions (e.g. counselling, certain types of training). However, safeguards must be introduced in digitalised systems to avoid creating a digital divide handicapping more disadvantaged jobseekers, in particular displaced older workers that lack basic IT skills (OECD, 2017[61]).

9.3. Supporting workers by securing healthy work environments

Protecting and supporting workers goes beyond the provision of adequate benefits and effective employment services in case of job loss. Equally important are policies that prevent unemployment and non-employment in the first place by making work more attractive and sustainable over the life course (European Foundation for the Improvement of Living and Working Conditions, 2015[62]).[15] One key element of the prevention of joblessness is adult learning policies that help ensure workers remain employable throughout the lifecycle (see Chapters 10 and 14). Another critical element is the quality of the work environment which makes it not only attractive for people to become or stay employed, but also makes work more sustainable by preventing the risk that work impairs one's health and people are forced to leave the labour force prematurely.

The quality of the work environment is key for the sustainability of work

According to the *OECD Job Quality Framework*, the quality of the work environment is one of the three keys dimensions through which work affects well-being (OECD, 2014[63]; Cazes, Hijzen and Saint-Martin, 2015[64]). A poor work environment – characterised by intensive job demands with insufficient job resources (e.g. feedback and support) – reduces worker well-being, weakens worker engagement and productivity[16] and increases the risk of physical and mental health problems (Saint-Martin, Inanc and Prinz, 2018[65]). A poor quality working environment can not only cause burnout, but also increase the risk of coronary heart disease, musculoskeletal disorders and common mental disorders (Harvey et al., 2018[66]; Kivimäki et al., 2012[67]; Hauke et al., 2011[68]).

Data from the European Working Conditions Survey for 2015 show a strong correlation between the quality of the work environment and self-reported health and well-being outcomes (Figure 9.5). For instance, almost 40% of workers facing a poor work environment say that work affects their health negatively compared to less than 15% of those with good working conditions. Similarly, work-related sickness absence is more than three times as frequent for workers reporting a poor work environment as for those reporting a good one. Job satisfaction and work engagement is also significantly higher for those in jobs with high quality work environments.

Work-related health problems can lead to prolonged periods of not working and often, particularly among older workers, result in permanent withdrawal from the labour market. Moreover, as emphasised by Arends, Prinz and Abma (2017[69]), a good quality work environment is not only key for preventing work-related health problems with long-term consequences for workers' careers, but also for allowing people with health problems to return to work more quickly after an illness and to remain economically active for longer. Therefore, the quality of the work environment is key for sustaining an effective labour supply over the life course.

Figure 9.5. The quality of the work environment affects health and well-being

Share of workers in Europe reporting that the work environment affects their health, 2015

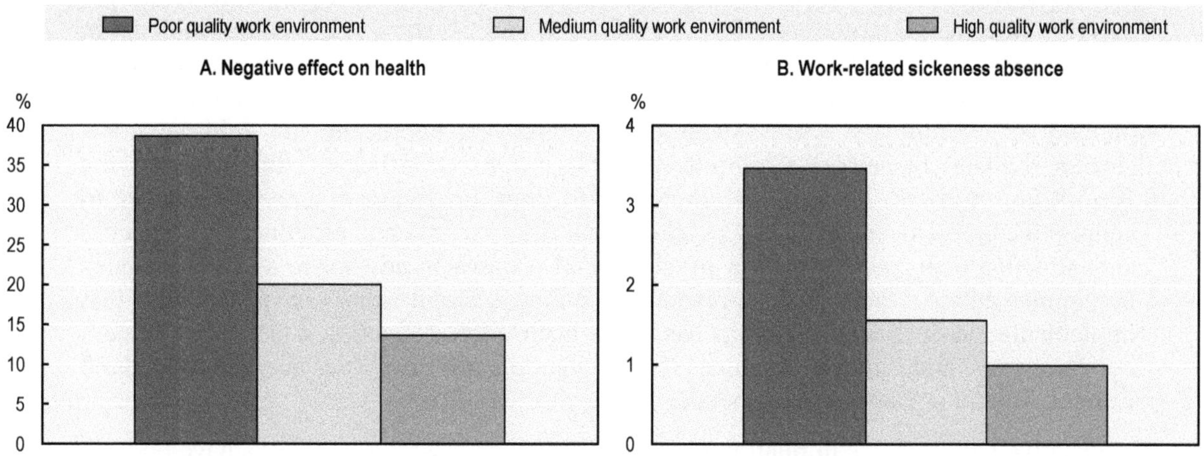

Note: In a poor quality work environment, there are more job demands than job resources; in a high quality work environment, there are more job resources than job demands; and in a medium quality work environment job demands equal job resources.
Source: OECD calculations based on the *6th European Working Conditions Survey* (2015).

StatLink http://dx.doi.org/10.1787/888933881382

Despite its importance, the quality of the work environment has received little attention in national and international policy debates to promote long-term labour market performance. Two recent OECD initiatives have sought to address this issue. The first is the OECD Framework for the Measurement and Assessment of Job Quality (OECD, 2014[63]; Cazes, Hijzen and Saint-Martin, 2015[64]) which defines the quality of the work environment as one of the three main dimensions through which job quality affects well-being and contributes to the mainstreaming of quality-of-the-work-environment issues in the broader policy debate on labour market performance. The second is the 2016 *Recommendation of the Council on Integrated Mental Health, Skills and Work Policy* which seeks to promote better policies to improve the work environment, to safeguard labour productivity and job retention, and enhance the inclusion of people with mental health problems in the labour market (OECD, 2015[33]).[17]

Legislative measures, financial incentives and management practices

Effective policies to promote the quality of the work environment require a mix of legislative measures, financial incentives and actions to promote good workplace practices.

Promote and enforce legislation for psychosocial risk assessment and prevention

Over the past decade, a number of OECD countries have put in place more effective legislative frameworks for the prevention of psychosocial risks. Such legislation requires employers to routinely assess, prevent and control psychosocial risks at work, in addition to any physical workplace hazards, such as noise or dust, which have long been the only focus of health and safety regulations and labour inspection authorities. In some countries, legislation merely provides guidelines for employers, while others compel employers to engage occupational health specialists.

Denmark and Belgium provide two interesting, far-reaching examples. The *Working Environment Act* in Denmark includes 24 sector- and job-specific guidance tools that describe in concrete terms both the risks of stress and psycho-social health problems in the workplace and the instruments that companies can use to address them. Inspectors from the *Working Environment Authority* have been trained to support employers in their obligations. Preliminary results suggest that employers appreciate the guidance tools (Senior Labour Inspectors Committee, 2008[70]; OECD, 2013[71]). In Belgium, the *Well-Being at Work Act* requires employers to draw up five-year prevention plans to address the problems identified by psycho-social risk assessments; establish more specific annual action plans; and appoint a psycho-social prevention advisor to assist companies in implementing their risk prevention policy. Evaluations have shown that implementation of these obligations has so far been weak, reflecting a lack of awareness by employers and limited resources for prevention advisors (Service public fédéral Emploi, Travail et Concertation sociale, 2011[72]; OECD, 2013[29]).

Legislative requirements in relation to the prevention of psycho-social risks have boosted the development of professional support and tools available to employers and fostered greater public awareness of psycho-social workplace risks. But the use of psycho-social prevention tools by companies remains uneven, especially because the vast majority of small and medium-sized enterprises struggle to comply with the stricter regulations and because occupational health services, which support companies in the prevention of health risks, still tend to concentrate their attention mainly on physical rather than psycho-social risks.

New legislation to prevent work-related health problems will only be effective if properly implemented and enforced. Ways to improve the implementation and enforcement of legislation to prevent psycho-social risks include: i) specifying compulsory employer obligations in regard to psycho-social risk assessment and risk prevention; ii) providing targeted tools and support mechanisms that enable employers of all sizes to make adjustments to the work environment; iii) directing resources in the labour inspectorate and occupational health service to psycho-social issues; and iv) involving worker and employer organisations in the enforcement and sharing of good practices.

Provide adequate financial incentives to employers to promote good working conditions

The effective implementation of more comprehensive and stricter regulations can be enhanced by matching legal obligations with financial incentives. In most OECD countries, employers pay for workers' compensation insurance, which covers the costs of work-*caused* health problems, i.e. work accidents and occupational injuries. However, the general taxpayer rather than the employer bears the main responsibility for the costs of all other diseases or injuries, many of which are also work-*related* to a certain degree.[18] As a result, employers tend to invest less in the quality of the working environment than would be desirable from an economic point of view. Governments should ensure that firms face the right incentives to internalise the social cost of poor working conditions by increasing the responsibility of employers for the costs of work-related health problems, beyond work accidents and occupational diseases. In principle, this can be achieved by requiring employers to cover part of wage-costs during sickness for a certain period; by experience-rating employer social security contributions for disability insurance against long-term illness; and, by making the cost of workers' compensation schemes for the employer dependent on the presence of health risks in the workplace.

In many OECD countries, employers are obliged, by law or through collective agreement, to cover sick-pay costs for a certain period. The length of this period and the share of the wage to be paid, however, differ drastically across countries. In the Netherlands, employers are legally obliged to cover 70% of wage costs during the first two years of sickness.[19] Moreover, employers face an obligation to facilitate and promote the return to work of sick employees, enforced with financial measures.[20] In the United Kingdom, employers have to cover a part of the wage costs during the first six months and have only limited re-employment obligations. Other countries including Austria (6-12 weeks), Germany (six weeks), Italy (up to 180 days), Luxembourg (13 weeks for white-collar workers), and Switzerland (up to six months, varying with tenure) also impose several months of continued wage payments in the case of sickness.[21]

While employer-provided sick pay is common across OECD countries, only a few countries operate longer-term disability insurance schemes with experience-rated employer contributions, where contributions are higher for employers whose employees were more likely to end up claiming disability in the past. In the Netherlands, public disability insurance is experience-rated by taking account of past benefit claimants with a partial earnings incapacity. Similarly, Finland operates a public disability insurance system with experience rating for large firms. Moreover, in countries where private disability insurance plays an important role such as Switzerland and Canada, experience-rating has also become more common (OECD, 2006[73]; OECD, 2010[74]).

While employer co-payments are the exception for disability benefits, employer premiums to workers' compensation schemes, which compensate the cost of work-caused health problems, are more frequently varied by actual risk. In most countries, the risk relates to an entire sector rather than an individual employer, according to the occurrence of work injuries and occupational diseases in the sector. In some OECD countries, however, there is no compensation-differentiation across sectors and employers. As a result, low-risk sectors effectively subsidise compensation payments in high-risk sectors and firms face no financial incentives to invest in the prevention of work-related health risks.

Rigorous scientific evidence on the impact of financial incentives for employers on the incidence of sickness and disability is scarce. However, there is some indication that countries imposing obligations for continued wage payments during sickness experience lower levels of sickness absence and that increasing that period has tended to reduce it (OECD, 2008[75]; OECD, 2010[76]). Moreover, experience-rated disability insurance in Finland and the Netherlands appears to have reduced disability benefit inflows (Koning, 2004[77]; Korkeamäki and Kyyrä, 2009[78]). Similar moderately positively findings are also available for risk-rated premiums for workers' compensation schemes (Tompa, Trevithick and McLeod, 2007[79]; Elsler et al., 2010[80]). While these results suggest that financial incentives for employers can contribute to the prevention of both work-related and work-caused health risks, they may also have potentially important side effects by providing incentives for discriminatory hiring practices against population groups facing higher health risks (e.g. older workers). Further research and policy experimentation is necessary to better understand how financial incentives can be designed to reduce sickness and disability claims, while minimising any unintended consequences related to the hiring and firing behaviour of firms.

Improve management's responses to workers' stress and mental health issues

While risk assessment and prevention can ensure a healthier work environment, not all health risks can be avoided. Enabling management to deal with (mental) health problems when they arise is equally critical, not only for workers, but also for business, because of the massive impact such health problems can have on economic performance.[22] This is particularly important for small and medium-sized enterprises that tend to be unaware of the need for better information and support to deal with workplace stress, workplace conflicts and mental health complaints, which can weigh heavily on the work environment and significantly heighten the risk of recurrent sickness absences (Arends et al., 2014[81]; OECD, 2015[33]).

Ambitious policy changes have to be introduced to assist employers in dealing with mental health problems at work and improving the quality of the work environment more generally. Measures for improving managers' ability to respond to workers' mental health issues include providing stress prevention and mental health training for managers, worker representatives and workers; developing the health competence in human-resource departments to support managers and workers; and offering guidelines and toolkits that help line managers in dealing with workers' mental health problems.

Especially in English-speaking OECD countries, many big companies have put in place *Employee Assistance Programmes*, which offer short-term counselling to employees with personal problems that affect work performance, whether or not those problems originate in the workplace. These programmes often provide support for mental health, drug and alcohol issues; counselling for divorce and parenting problems; services targeting wellness and health promotion; and work-related supports such as career counselling. These services are often provided free of charge and have been shown to contribute to decreased absenteeism, greater employee retention and reduced medical costs through early identification and treatment (Hargrave et al., 2008[82]; Lam and Walker, 2012[83]).

Conclusions

An effective labour supply requires policies that ensure that work is accessible, attractive and sustainable over the life-course. This calls for policies that ensure that work pays, protect workers against the risk of joblessness, and support a safe and healthy working environment. It also requires that quality work is accessible to all by effectively tackling all barriers to employment simultaneously through measures that promote work incentives, worker employability and job opportunities.

The chapter provides three key insights:

- Public income-support programmes for the unemployed alleviate concerns about job security among the employed and mitigate financial hardship among the jobless, with important consequences for worker well-being. The design of unemployment-benefit systems should strike a balance between the potential costs associated with reduced work incentives and the benefits in terms of greater consumption smoothing and enhanced job matching. The balance between costs and benefits can be enhanced by increasing the responsibility of employers and employees for the use of unemployment benefits, combining out-of-work benefits with well-designed in-work benefits, and embedding income-support policies in effective activation strategies based on a rigorous mutual-obligations framework.

- Tackling all barriers to employment requires a comprehensive activation strategy that combines measures to enhance motivation with measures to promote employability and foster job opportunities. Jobless persons typically face various barriers to employment at the same time and consequently activation strategies should go beyond strengthening work incentives to be effective. Unemployment and social-assistance benefits are crucial for the effective implementation of comprehensive activation strategies since they provide the principle instrument for linking jobless people to employment services and provide substance to the threat of benefit sanctions that underpins the mutual-obligations framework. This highlights the importance of high-coverage social protection systems for overcoming employment barriers.
- High-quality work environments are critical for the health and wellbeing of workers but also contribute to the sustainability of work up to an older age, thereby helping to deal with the challenges of population ageing. While employers are the first actors for providing good quality working conditions, governments also have an important role to play. Where appropriate, they should modernise legislative frameworks with respect to health and safety to go beyond the prevention of physical health hazards by requiring firms to take appropriate actions for the assessment and prevention of psycho-social risks. Legislative action could be supported with innovative financial incentives that increase the responsibility of employers for work-related health risks. However, further research is needed on their design, effectiveness and unintended side effects.

Notes

[1] No or small positive effects are found in Card, Chetty and Weber (2007[14]) for Austria, van Ours and Vodopivec (2008[89]) for Slovenia, Caliendo, Tatsiramos and Uhlendorff (2013[95]) for Germany and Centeno, Centeno and Novo (2009[6]) for Portugal, while Schmieder, von Wachter and Bender (2016[90]) find negative effects for Germany.

[2] There is no exception for older workers: an extension of the duration of potential entitlements also increases the duration of unemployment, especially as the retirement age is approaching (Lalive, 2008[91]). However, some of the outflows observed at the time benefits expire could reflect exits from the labour market and not returns to employment.

[3] The number of unemployed persons may also increase because it induces inactive persons to look for work as employment is associated with better social protection.

[4] Self-insurance can take the form of individual unemployment saving accounts from which workers can make withdrawals to support their income and job-search. They are typically funded though mandatory contributions on wages and, in some circumstances, can benefit from public subsidies notably when savings are insufficient to cover minimum withdrawal amounts (e.g. Chile).

[5] However, to be effective, this system must rely on rules simple enough for employers to able to predict the cost of their separation decisions, which can be a challenge in practice (Krueger and Meyer, 2002[88]).

[6] These figures refer to a one-earner couple with two children taking up work at 67% of the average wage. Supplements are included.

[7] These figures become even greater when additional expenditures incurred by the working household are taking into account, such as transport and childcare (OECD, 2018[36]).

[8] Yet, as these groups often incur additional costs upon raising their hours of work (e.g. childcare costs), systems providing an immediate payment are preferable with respect to those providing only an end-of-year tax rebate.

[9] The critical issue is, however, setting the minimum wage at an appropriate level, as overly high minimum wages tend to compress the earnings distribution at the bottom of the wage ladder, so that, as discussed above, IWBs are likely to become either very expensive or ineffective.

[10] For instance, in Italy, less than 10% of people with no or limited labour-market attachment would face significant benefit losses when taking up a job (Browne and Pacifico, 2016[94]).

[11] This chapter focusses on general activation of the labour force. Specific policy actions concerning group-specific barriers are discussed in Chapter 11.

[12] Yet, the effect of tougher caseworkers is concentrated on easier-to-employ clients, for which monitoring and sanctions are likely to be the most effective – see e.g. Huber, Lechner and Mellace (2017[84]); Lagerström (2011[85]).

[13] There are very few success stories and experiments typically took several years of fine-tuning (OECD, 2015[27]; Stephan, 2016[86]). In Australia, the outsourcing framework was introduced in 1998, but significantly revised in 2003, with further changes in 2009 and 2015 (OECD, 2012[55]).

[14] The Australian experience shows that excessively prescriptive contracts may induce providers to become bureaucratic, thereby promoting the use of standardised actions plans and undermining innovation, a key advantage of increased competition (Fowkes, 2011[87]). However, rigorous evaluations have shown that the lack of prescriptive contracts tends to end up in inefficient

programmes, casting doubts on the feasibility of effectively outsourcing employment services to private providers (Stephan, 2016[86]).

15 Several chapters of this Volume address this question directly or indirectly, e.g. looking at labour demand, labour regulations or product market flexibility.

16 The relationship between the quality of the work environment and productivity is discussed in more detail in Chapter 7 of this Volume as well as in (Arends, Prinz and Abma, 2017[69]).

17 https://legalinstruments.oecd.org/en/instruments/334

18 Worker compensation schemes only provide limited incentives for employers to prevent work-related health problems because: i) the costs of compensations tends to be partially socialised; ii) presenteeism, typically considered more costly to employers than absenteeism, is not addressed; and iii) mental health problems are poorly covered, because the link with work is difficult to establish.

19 This can even increase to 100% depending on the applicable collective agreement and may extend to a third year if the employer has not fulfilled his/her reintegration obligations.

20 Dutch employers have to make every reasonable effort to make it possible for the sick worker to return to the previous job, another job in the company or a job in another company. During this period, workers cannot be dismissed unless they fail to comply with their co-operation obligation and refuse to accept another position in the company.

21 In some countries, employers can reinsure their sick-pay risk with a private insurer. The role of continued wage-payment obligations for the incentives of firms to invest in the quality of the work environment may depend on the ability of firms to re-insure and the extent to which fees for private insurance have an element of experience-rating. Far-ranging re-integration obligations are not easily insurable and, hence, can have potentially important financial consequences, further strengthening incentives for the prevention of work-related health risks.

22 Businesses that invest in better work environments and high-performance work practices see improvements in the quality of products and services and equally in customer satisfaction and loyalty (Saint-Martin et al., 2018). Improved productivity outcomes also translate into stronger financial performance and higher rates of business survival. The impact on economic performance can be sizable, with convincing evidence for causality (Bryson, Forth and Stokes, 2017[92]; Sadun, Bloom and Reenen, 2017[93]).

References

Arends, I., C. Prinz and F. Abma (2017), "Job quality, health and at-work productivity", *OECD Social, Employment and Migration Working Papers*, No. 195, OECD Publishing, Paris, http://dx.doi.org/10.1787/43ff6bdc-en. [69]

Arends, I. et al. (2014), "Predictors of recurrent sickness absence among workers having returned to work after sickness absence due to common mental disorders", *Scandinavian Journal of Work, Environment & Health*, Vol. 40/2, pp. 195-202, http://dx.doi.org/10.5271/sjweh.3384. [81]

Arni, P., R. Lalive and J. Van Ours (2013), "How effective are unemployment benefit sanctions? Looking beyond unemployment exit", *Journal of Applied Econometrics*, Vol. 28/7, pp. 1153-1178, http://dx.doi.org/10.1002/jae.2289. [42]

Behncke, S., M. Frölich and M. Lechner (2010), "A caseworker like me - Does the similarity between the unemployed and their caseworkers increase job placements?", *The Economic Journal*, Vol. 120/549, pp. 1430-1459, http://dx.doi.org/10.1111/j.1468-0297.2010.02382.x. [52]

Boeri, T., P. Cahuc and A. Zylberberg (2015), "The costs of flexibility-enhancing structural reforms: A literature review", *OECD Economics Department Working Papers*, No. 1264, OECD Publishing, Paris, http://dx.doi.org/10.1787/5jrs558c5r5f-en. [7]

Bredgaard, T. (2015), "Evaluating what works for whom in active labour market policies", *European Journal of Social Security*, Vol. 17/4, pp. 436-452, http://dx.doi.org/10.1177/138826271501700403. [48]

Brown, A. (2015), "Can hiring subsidies benefit the unemployed?", *IZA World of Labor*, http://dx.doi.org/10.15185/izawol.163. [59]

Browne, J. and D. Pacifico (2016), *Faces of joblessness in Italy: Anatomy of employment barriers*, OECD Publishing, Paris, http://www.oecd.org/els/soc/Faces-of-Joblessness-in-Italy.pdf (accessed on 23 July 2018). [94]

Browning, M. and T. Crossley (2001), "Unemployment insurance benefit levels and consumption changes", *Journal of Public Economics*, Vol. 80/1, pp. 1-23, https://doi.org/10.1016/S0047-2727(00)00084-0. [3]

Bryson, A., J. Forth and L. Stokes (2017), "Does employees' subjective well-being affect workplace performance?", *Human Relations*, Vol. 70/8, pp. 1017-1037, http://dx.doi.org/10.1177/0018726717693073. [92]

Busk, H. (2016), "Sanctions and the exit from unemployment in two different benefit schemes", *Labour Economics*, Vol. 42, pp. 159-176, http://dx.doi.org/10.1016/j.labeco.2016.09.001. [45]

Cahuc, P., S. Carcillo and T. Le Barbanchon (forthcoming), "The effectiveness of hiring credits", *The Review of Economic Studies*, http://dx.doi.org/10.1093/restud/rdy011. [58]

Caliendo, M., K. Tatsiramos and A. Uhlendorff (2013), "Benefit duration, unemployment duration and job match quality: A regression-discontinuity approach", *Journal of Applied Econometrics*, Vol. 28/4, pp. 604-627, http://dx.doi.org/10.1002/jae.2293. [95]

Card, D., R. Chetty and A. Weber (2007), "The spike at benefit exhaustion: Leaving the unemployment system or starting a new job?", *American Economic Review*, Vol. 97/2, pp. 113-118, http://dx.doi.org/10.1257/aer.97.2.113. [14]

Card, D., J. Kluve and A. Weber (2015), "What Works? A Meta Analysis of Recent Active Labor Market Program Evaluations", *IZA Discussion Paper*, No. 9236, http://ftp.iza.org/dp9236.pdf (accessed on 23 July 2018). [44]

Cazes, S., A. Hijzen and A. Saint-Martin (2015), "Measuring and Assessing Job Quality: The OECD Job Quality Framework", *OECD Social, Employment and Migration Working Papers*, No. 174, OECD Publishing, Paris, http://dx.doi.org/10.1787/5jrp02kjw1mr-en. [64]

CEA (2016), "Active labor market policies: Theory and evidence for what works", *Council of Economic Advisers issue brief*, No. December 2016. [25]

Centeno, L., M. Centeno and Á. Novo (2009), "Evaluating job-search programs for old and young individuals: Heterogeneous impact on unemployment duration", *Labour Economics*, Vol. 16/1, pp. 12-25, http://dx.doi.org/10.1016/J.LABECO.2008.02.004. [6]

Chetty, R. (2008), "Moral Hazard versus Liquidity and Optimal Unemployment Insurance", *Journal of Political Economy*, Vol. 116/2, pp. 173-234, http://dx.doi.org/10.1086/588585. [11]

Chetty, R., J. Friedman and E. Saez (2013), "Using Differences in Knowledge Across Neighborhoods to Uncover the Impacts of the EITC on Earnings", *American Economic Review*, Vol. 103/7, pp. 2683-2721, http://dx.doi.org/10.1257/aer.103.7.2683. [20]

Di Maggio, M. and A. Kermani (2016), "The Importance of Unemployment Insurance as an Automatic Stabilizer", *NBER Working Paper No. 22625*, http://dx.doi.org/10.3386/w22625. [4]

Dormont, B., D. Fougère and A. Prieto (2001), "L'effet de l'allocation unique dégressive sur la reprise d'emploi", *Economie et statistique*, Vol. 343/1, pp. 3-28, http://dx.doi.org/10.3406/estat.2001.7457. [13]

Duell, N., S. Singh and P. Tergeist (2009), "Activation Policies in Norway", *OECD Social, Employment and Migration Working Papers*, No. 78, OECD Publishing, Paris, http://dx.doi.org/10.1787/226388712174. [41]

Duell, N. et al. (2010), "Activation Policies in Switzerland", *OECD Social, Employment and Migration Working Papers*, No. 112, OECD Publishing, Paris, http://dx.doi.org/10.1787/5km4hd7r28f6-en. [40]

Elsler, D. et al. (2010), "A review of case studies evaluating economic incentives to promote occupational safety and health.", *Scandinavian journal of work, environment & health*, Vol. 36/4, pp. 289-98, http://dx.doi.org/10.5271/sjweh.3018. [80]

European Foundation for the Improvement of Living and Working Conditions (2015), *Sustainable work over the life course concept paper*, European Foundation for the Improvement of Living and Working Conditions, https://www.eurofound.europa.eu/publications/report/2015/working-conditions/sustainable-work-over-the-life-course-concept-paper (accessed on 08 October 2018). [62]

Fernandez, R. et al. (2016), "Faces of Joblessness: Characterising Employment Barriers to Inform Policy", *OECD Social, Employment and Migration Working Papers*, No. 192, OECD Publishing, Paris, http://dx.doi.org/10.1787/5jlwvz47xptj-en. [26]

Finn, D. (2011), *Sub-contracting in Public Employment Services: Review of Research Findings and Literature on Recent Trends and Business Models*, The European Commission Mutual Learning Programme for Public Employment Services. [60]

Fontaine, F. and F. Malherbet (2016), *CDD vs CDI : les effets d'un dualisme contractuel*, Presses de Sciences Po, Paris. [9]

Fowkes, L. (2011), "Rethinking Australia's employment services", *Perspectives*, No. 6, Whitlam Institute, http://www.whitlam.org. [87]

Graversen, B. and J. van Ours (2008), "How to help unemployed find jobs quickly: Experimental evidence from a mandatory activation program", *Journal of Public Economics*, Vol. 92/10-11, pp. 2020-2035, http://dx.doi.org/10.1016/j.jpubeco.2008.04.013. [46]

Griggs, J. and M. Evans (2010), *Sanctions within conditional benefi t systems A review of evidence*, Joseph Rowntree Foundation, http://www.jrf.org.uk (accessed on 23 July 2018). [50]

Gruber, J. (1997), "The Consumption Smoothing Benefits of Unemployment Insurance", *The American Economic Review,*, Vol. 87/1, pp. 192-205, https://www.jstor.org/stable/pdf/2950862.pdf?refreqid=excelsior%3Ad5ee7870eec052a71859 1a4b10acb805 (accessed on 05 October 2018). [1]

Hainmueller, J. et al. (2016), "Do Lower Caseloads Improve the Performance of Public Employment Services? New Evidence from German Employment Offices", *The Scandinavian Journal of Economics*, Vol. 118/4, pp. 941-974, http://dx.doi.org/10.1111/sjoe.12166. [51]

Hargrave, G. et al. (2008), "EAP Treatment Impact on Presenteeism and Absenteeism: Implications for Return on Investment", *Journal of Workplace Behavioral Health*, Vol. 23/3, pp. 283-293, http://dx.doi.org/10.1080/15555240802242999. [82]

Harvey, S. et al. (2018), "The role of job strain in understanding midlife common mental disorder: a national birth cohort study", *The Lancet Psychiatry*, Vol. 5/6, pp. 498-506, http://dx.doi.org/10.1016/S2215-0366(18)30137-8. [66]

Hauke, A. et al. (2011), "The impact of work-related psychosocial stressors on the onset of musculoskeletal disorders in specific body regions: A review and meta-analysis of 54 longitudinal studies", *Work & Stress*, Vol. 25/3, pp. 243-256, http://dx.doi.org/10.1080/02678373.2011.614069. [68]

Huber, M., M. Lechner and G. Mellace (2017), "Why Do Tougher Caseworkers Increase Employment? The Role of Program Assignment as a Causal Mechanism", *Review of Economics and Statistics*, Vol. 99/1, pp. 180-183, http://dx.doi.org/10.1162/rest_a_00632. [84]

Immervoll, H. (2012), "Reforming the Benefit System to 'Make Work Pay': Options and Priorities in a Weak Labour Market", *IZA Policy Papers*, No. 50, IZA, Bonn. [35]

Immervoll, H. and M. Pearson (2009), "A Good Time for Making Work Pay? Taking Stock of In-Work Benefits and Related Measures across the OECD", *OECD Social, Employment and Migration Working Papers*, No. 81, OECD Publishing, Paris, http://dx.doi.org/10.1787/225442803245. [21]

Immervoll, H. and S. Scarpetta (2012), "Activation and employment support policies in OECD countries. An overview of current approaches", *IZA Journal of Labor Policy*, Vol. 1/1, p. 9, http://dx.doi.org/10.1186/2193-9004-1-9. [18]

Kivimäki, M. et al. (2012), "Job strain as a risk factor for coronary heart disease: a collaborative meta-analysis of individual participant data", *The Lancet*, Vol. 380/9852, pp. 1491-1497, http://dx.doi.org/10.1016/S0140-6736(12)60994-5. [67]

Kluve, J. (2010), "The effectiveness of European active labor market programs", *Labour Economics*, Vol. 17/6, pp. 904-918, http://dx.doi.org/10.1016/j.labeco.2010.02.004. [54]

Koning, P. (2004), "Estimating the impact of experience rating on the inflow into disability insurance in the Netherlands", *CPB Discussion Paper*, https://ideas.repec.org/p/cpb/discus/37.html (accessed on 22 October 2018). [77]

Korkeamäki, O. and T. Kyyrä (2009), *Institutional rules, labour demand and disability programme participation*, Finnish Centre for Pensions, Working Papers, 2009: 5, https://www.julkari.fi/bitstream/handle/10024/129136/Institutionalruleslabourdemandanddisabilityprogrammeparticipation.pdf?sequence=1 (accessed on 22 October 2018). [78]

Kroft, K. and M. Notowidigdo (2016), "Should Unemployment Insurance Vary with the Unemployment Rate? Theory and Evidence", *The Review of Economic Studies*, Vol. 83/3, pp. 1092-1124, http://dx.doi.org/10.1093/restud/rdw009. [2]

Krueger, A. and B. Meyer (2002), "Labor supply effects of social insurance", in *Handbook of Public Economics (Volume 4)*, Elsevier, https://ac.els-cdn.com/S157344200280012X/1-s2.0-S157344200280012X-main.pdf?_tid=7b72bb8a-0225-47b3-a4e9-cafe566e50ff&acdnat=1538668179_8c527d15bb10d845b03d0abad2c40272 (accessed on 04 October 2018). [88]

Kyyrä, T. (2010), "Partial unemployment insurance benefits and the transition rate to regular work", *European Economic Review*, Vol. 54/7, pp. 911-930, http://dx.doi.org/10.1016/J.EUROECOREV.2010.02.005. [8]

Lachowska, M., M. Meral and S. Woodbury (2016), "Effects of the unemployment insurance work test on long-term employment outcomes", *Labour Economics*, Vol. 41, pp. 246-265, http://dx.doi.org/10.1016/j.labeco.2016.05.015. [49]

Lagerström, J. (2011), "How important are caseworkers - and why? New evidence from Swedish employment offices", *IFAU Working Papers*, No. 2011:10, IFAU, http://www.ifau.se (accessed on 23 July 2018). [85]

Lalive, R. (2008), "How do extended benefits affect unemployment duration? A regression discontinuity approach", *Journal of Econometrics*, Vol. 142/2, pp. 785-806, http://dx.doi.org/10.1016/J.JECONOM.2007.05.013. [91]

Lalive, R., C. Landais and J. Zweimüller (2015), "Market Externalities of Large Unemployment Insurance Extension Programs", *American Economic Review*, Vol. 105/12, pp. 3564-3596, http://dx.doi.org/10.1257/aer.20131273. [17]

Lam, R. and A. Walker (2012), “The Prevalence and Impact of Depression in Self-Referred Clients Attending an Employee Assistance Program”, *Journal of Occupational and Environmental Medicine*, Vol. 54/11, pp. 1395-1399 , http://dx.doi.org/10.1097/JOM.0b013e3182611a69. [83]

Landais, C. (2015), “Assessing the welfare effects of unemployment benefits using the regression kink design”, *American Economic Journal: Economic Policy*, Vol. 7/4, http://dx.doi.org/10.1257/pol.20130248. [15]

Landais, C., P. Michaillat and E. Saez (2018), “A Macroeconomic Approach to Optimal Unemployment Insurance: Theory”, *American Economic Journal: Economic Policy*, Vol. 10/No. 2, pp. 152-81, http://dx.doi.org/10.1257/pol.20150088. [16]

Le Barbanchon, T. (2016), “Optimal Partial Unemployment Insurance: Evidence from Bunching in the U.S.”, *Mimeo*, Bocconi University, https://www.dropbox.com/s/9okyit1gxpzb2ss/draft_partial_UI_LeBarbanchon.pdf?dl=0 (accessed on 13 March 2018). [10]

Lechner, M. and J. Smith (2007), “What is the value added by caseworkers?”, *Labour Economics*, Vol. 14/2, pp. 135-151, http://dx.doi.org/10.1016/j.labeco.2004.12.002. [53]

Nichols, A. and J. Rothstein (2015), “The Earned Income Tax Credit (EITC)”, *NBER Working Papers*, No. 21211, National Bureau of Economic Research, Cambridge, MA, http://dx.doi.org/10.3386/w21211. [23]

OECD (2018), “Unemployment-benefit coverage: Recent trends and their drivers”, in *OECD Employment Outlook 2018*, OECD Publishing, Paris, https://doi.org/10.1787/empl_outlook-2018-9-en. [36]

OECD (2017), *Getting Skills Right: Skills for Jobs Indicators*, Getting Skills Right, OECD Publishing, Paris, http://dx.doi.org/10.1787/9789264277878-en. [57]

OECD (2017), *Preventing Ageing Unequally*, OECD Publishing, Paris, http://dx.doi.org/10.1787/9789264279087-en. [61]

OECD (2015), *Fit Mind, Fit Job: From evidence to practice in mental health and work.*, OECD Publishing, Paris. [33]

OECD (2015), *Mental Health and Work: Austria*, Mental Health and Work, OECD Publishing, Paris, http://dx.doi.org/10.1787/9789264228047-en. [34]

OECD (2015), *OECD Employment Outlook 2015*, OECD Publishing, Paris, http://dx.doi.org/10.1787/empl_outlook-2015-en. [27]

OECD (2014), *Connecting People with Jobs: Activation Policies in the United Kingdom*, Connecting People with Jobs, OECD Publishing, Paris, https://dx.doi.org/10.1787/9789264217188-en. [56]

OECD (2014), “How good is your job? Measuring and assessing job quality”, in *OECD Employment Outlook 2014*, OECD Publishing, Paris, http://dx.doi.org/10.1787/empl_outlook-2014-6-en. [63]

OECD (2014), *Mental Health and Work: United Kingdom*, Mental Health and Work, OECD Publishing, Paris, http://dx.doi.org/10.1787/9789264204997-en. [31]

OECD (2014), *The 2012 Labour Market Reform in Spain: A Preliminary Assessment*, OECD Publishing, Paris, http://dx.doi.org/10.1787/9789264213586-en. [39]

OECD (2013), *Mental Health and Work: Belgium*, Mental Health and Work, OECD Publishing, Paris, http://dx.doi.org/10.1787/9789264187566-en. [29]

OECD (2013), *Mental Health and Work: Denmark*, Mental Health and Work, OECD Publishing, Paris, http://dx.doi.org/10.1787/9789264188631-en. [71]

OECD (2013), *Mental Health and Work: Norway*, Mental Health and Work, OECD Publishing, Paris, http://dx.doi.org/10.1787/9789264178984-en. [32]

OECD (2013), *Mental Health and Work: Sweden*, Mental Health and Work, OECD Publishing, Paris, https://dx.doi.org/10.1787/9789264188730-en. [30]

OECD (2013), *OECD Employment Outlook 2013*, OECD Publishing, Paris, https://doi.org/10.1787/empl_outlook-2013-en. [38]

OECD (2012), *Activating Jobseekers: How Australia Does It*, OECD Publishing, Paris, http://dx.doi.org/10.1787/9789264185920-en. [55]

OECD (2010), *Sickness, Disability and Work: Breaking the Barriers: Canada: Opportunities for Collaboration*, OECD Publishing, Paris, https://dx.doi.org/10.1787/9789264090422-en. [74]

OECD (2010), *Sickness, Disability and Work: Breaking the Barriers: A Synthesis of Findings across OECD Countries*, OECD Publishing, Paris, https://dx.doi.org/10.1787/9789264088856-en. [76]

OECD (2009), *OECD Employment Outlook 2009: Tackling the Jobs Crisis*, OECD Publishing, Paris, https://doi.org/10.1787/empl_outlook-2009-en. [22]

OECD (2008), *Sickness, Disability and Work: Breaking the Barriers (Vol. 3): Denmark, Finland, Ireland and the Netherlands*, OECD Publishing, Paris, http://dx.doi.org/10.1787/9789264049826-en. [75]

OECD (2006), *Sickness, Disability and Work: Breaking the Barriers (Vol. 1): Norway, Poland and Switzerland*, OECD Publishing, Paris, http://dx.doi.org/10.1787/9789264026322-en. [73]

Røed, K. (2012), “Active social insurance”, *IZA Journal of Labor Policy*, Vol. 1/1, p. 8, http://dx.doi.org/10.1186/2193-9004-1-8. [47]

Sadun, R., N. Bloom and J. Reenen (2017), "Why Do We Undervalue Competent Management?", *Harvard Business Review*, Vol. 95/5, pp. 120-127, https://www.hbs.edu/faculty/Pages/item.aspx?num=53203 (accessed on 22 October 2018). [93]

Saint-Martin, A., H. Inanc and C. Prinz (2018), "Job quality, health and productivity: An evidence-based framework for analysis", *OECD Social, Employment and Migration Working Papers*, forthcoming. [65]

Schmieder, J. and T. Von Wachter (2016), "The Effects of Unemployment Insurance Benefits: New Evidence and Interpretation", *SSRN*, http://dx.doi.org/10.1146/annurev-economics-080614-115758. [5]

Schmieder, J., T. von Wachter and S. Bender (2016), "The Effect of Unemployment Benefits and Nonemployment Durations on Wages", *American Economic Review*, Vol. 106/3, pp. 739-777, http://dx.doi.org/10.1257/aer.20141566. [90]

Senior Labour Inspectors Committee (2008), *Report on the Evaluation of the Danish Working Environment Authority in 2008*. [70]

Service public fédéral Emploi, Travail et Concertation sociale (2011), *Évaluation de la législation relative à la prévention de la charge psychosociale occasionnée par le travail, dont la violence et le harcèlement moral ou sexuel au travail*. [72]

Stephan, G. (2016), "Public or private job placement services—Are private ones more effective?", *IZA World of Labor*, http://dx.doi.org/10.15185/izawol.285. [86]

Sundaram, R. et al. (2014), *Portraits of labor market exclusion*, http://documents.worldbank.org/curated/en/837771468246370480/Portraits-of-labor-market-exclusion (accessed on 23 July 2018). [28]

Tatsiramos, K. and J. van Ours (2014), "Labor Market Effects of Unemployment Insurance Design", *Journal of Economic Surveys*, Vol. 28/2, pp. 284-311, http://dx.doi.org/10.1111/joes.12005. [12]

Thomas, A. and P. O'Reilly (2016), "The Impact of Tax and Benefit Systems on the Workforce Participation Incentives of Women", *OECD Taxation Working Papers*, No. 29, OECD Publishing, Paris, http://dx.doi.org/10.1787/d950acfc-en. [24]

Tompa, E., S. Trevithick and C. McLeod (2007), "Systematic review of the prevention incentives of insurance and regulatory mechanisms for occupational health and safety.", *Scandinavian journal of work, environment & health*, Vol. 33/2, pp. 85-95, http://dx.doi.org/10.5271/sjweh.1111. [79]

van den Berg, G. and B. van der Klaauw (2006), "Counseling and Monitoring of Unemployed Workers: Theory and Evidence from a Controlled Social Experiment", *International Economic Review*, Vol. 47/3, pp. 895-936, http://dx.doi.org/10.1111/j.1468-2354.2006.00399.x. [37]

van den Berg, G. and J. Vikström (2014), "Monitoring Job Offer Decisions, Punishments, Exit to Work, and Job Quality", *The Scandinavian Journal of Economics*, Vol. 116/2, pp. 284-334, http://dx.doi.org/10.1111/sjoe.12051. [43]

van der Linden, B. (2016), "Do in-work benefits work for low-skilled workers?", *IZA World of Labor*, http://dx.doi.org/10.15185/izawol.246. [19]

van Ours, J. and M. Vodopivec (2008), "Does reducing unemployment insurance generosity reduce job match quality?", *Journal of Public Economics*, Vol. 92/3-4, pp. 684-695, http://dx.doi.org/10.1016/J.JPUBECO.2007.05.006. [89]

Part III. Labour market inclusiveness

Chapter 10. Tackling deep and persistent inequalities in the labour market

This chapter discusses the role of policies and institutions for tackling deep and persistent inequalities in the labour market. To this end, it discusses the role of policies and institutions for ensuring that workers are not at a disadvantage in the labour market because of their socio-economic background and, once in the labour market, all workers have good prospects for accessing quality employment and moving up the earnings ladder. The chapter also considers the role of the taxes-and-benefits system for ensuring that everybody benefits from increased prosperity.

The statistical data for Israel are supplied by and under the responsibility of the relevant Israeli authorities. The use of such data by the OECD is without prejudice to the status of the Golan Heights, East Jerusalem and Israeli settlements in the West Bank under the terms of international law.

Introduction

Not only have wages tended to decouple from productivity and inequalities in earnings and incomes tended to increase in many countries (Chapter 2), there are also growing concerns that people do not get a fair chance in the labour market due to a lack of social mobility (OECD, 2018[1]). In many countries, socio-economic background is an important determinant for labour market success and the possibility of improving one's socio-economic position over the life-course (OECD, 2018[2]). In other words, concerns about the depth and persistence of inequality have gone hand-in-hand.

While there is no consensus on the acceptable – or desirable – level of inequality, very large and persistent inequalities in the labour market can have significant adverse social and economic consequences. First, they tend to reduce well-being as people do not only care about their own success in the labour market but also that of others (Clark, Frijters and Shields, 2008[3]; OECD, 2014[4]). Second, high inequality can reduce human capital accumulation by limiting the ability of low-income people to invest in their skills (Cingano, 2014[5]), with adverse consequences for social mobility and long-term growth. Third, inequality can reduce mutual trust as well as trust in economic and institutional processes , with potentially important consequences for social cohesion, economic growth and mainstream politics (Gould and Hijzen, 2016[6]; Alesina and Giuliano, 2015[7]).[1]

Yet, deep and persistent inequalities in the labour market are not inevitable as illustrated by the large differences observed across countries. Governments have a range of instruments at their disposal that can be used to tackle inequality or promote equal opportunities. The way they choose to address these challenges depends to an important extent on societal values regarding the importance of solidarity, redistribution and equality, as well as many other factors related to the national context (e.g. demographic structure, macroeconomic situation, the fiscal and administrative capacity of the state).

After a short section to set the scene (Section 10.1), this chapter discusses three broad and complementary policy approaches that can be used to tackle deep and persistent inequalities in the labour market: i) policies and institutions to promote equality of opportunity through greater social mobility across generations (Section 10.2); ii) policies and institutions to promote better career opportunities for those already in the labour market (Section 10.3); iii) tax-and-benefit policies to contain excessive inequalities and ensure that nobody is left behind (Section 10.4). The last section concludes.

10.1. Setting the scene

Inequality of earnings is not only high in many countries, but also tends to persist over the life-course and across generations (OECD, 2015[8]; OECD, 2018[2]; Garnero, Hijzen and Martin, 2019[9]). Figure 10.1 provides an indication of the degree of earnings inequality in a given year (short-term inequality) as well as over the entire working life (life-time inequality). Life-time inequality tends to be lower than inequality in a given year. This reflects the role of earnings mobility during the life-course that results from movements into and out of employment or up and down the earnings ladder. However, the difference between life-time and short-term inequality is modest in most countries, suggesting that the equalising effect of earnings mobility over the life-course is fairly small and most inequality is permanent: on average across countries, life-time inequality is only about 20% lower than short-term inequality. Moreover, earnings mobility is not sufficiently different across countries to bring about significant changes in the cross-country ranking of inequality. Life-time inequality tends to be high in countries where wage inequality is high (e.g. Japan and the United States), earnings mobility is low (e.g. Japan and Portugal) or unemployment is high and unemployment insurance limited (e.g. Greece and Italy).

Figure 10.1. Inequality is not only high by historical standards but also very persistent

Gini coefficients of earnings in 2010 (short-term inequality) and cumulative earnings over the working life (life-time inequality)

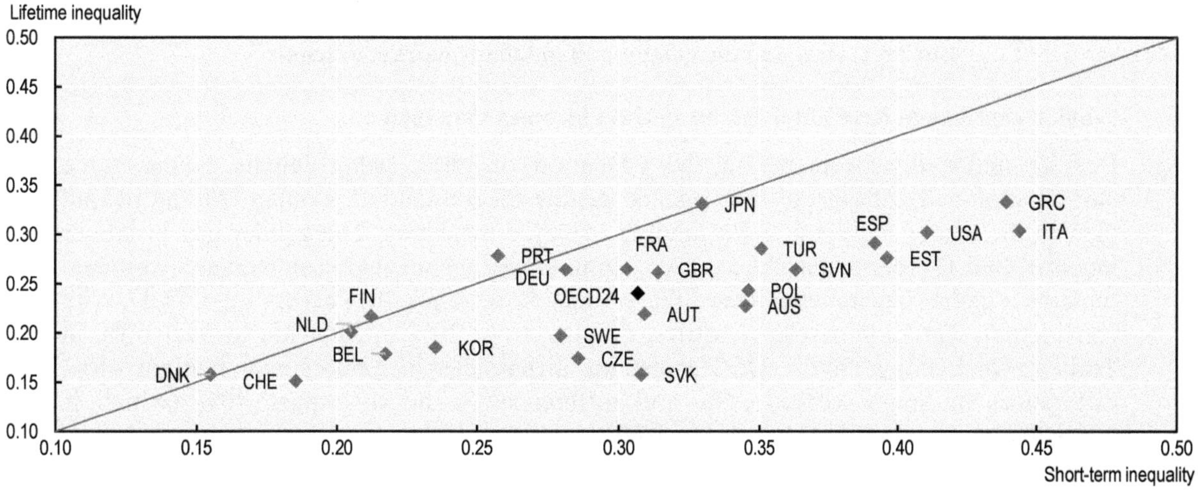

Note: Earnings inequality is measured across all active persons of working age and reflects hourly wages, working time and unemployment benefits when unemployed. Since data that allow following persons over their working lives are not available on a cross-country basis, life-time inequality is estimated using statistical simulation methods rather than directly observed in the data.

Source: Garnero, A., A. Hijzen and S. Martin (2019[9]), "More unequal, but more mobile? Earnings inequality and mobility in OECD countries", *Labour Economics*, https://doi.org/10.1016/j.labeco.2018.08.005.

StatLink http://dx.doi.org/10.1787//888933881401

Tackling deep and persistent inequalities requires addressing three important policy priorities:

- *Reducing the impact of socio-economic background on labour market outcomes.* This requires making sure that all children have access to quality education and health services irrespective of their parents' income. It also requires ensuring that socio-economic background, related to gender, ethnicity, religion, age or LGBTI status, does do not become a source of discrimination in the labour market. Box 10.1 provides a discussion of the gender gap in the labour market and the role of policies.

- *Promoting access to quality employment and prospects for career advancement.* Promoting the outcomes of those already in the labour market requires measures that enhance workers' employability and earnings potential by investing in adult learning and making adult learning systems more inclusive by promoting participation among vulnerable workers with limited basic skills. However, it also requires ensuring that sufficient opportunities are available and workers have good opportunities for career progression. This requires policies that facilitate job transitions towards better-paid and more stable employment.

- *Providing effective redistribution.* This requires designing tax-and-benefit systems that contain excessive inequalities, protect individuals and households from negative income shocks and prevent financial hardship, without undermining work incentives and, as a result, the long-term career prospects of those involved. Taxes-and-benefits policies can also contribute to more equal opportunities by alleviating financial constraints that limit access to quality education and health services of children in poor households.

Box 10.1. Bridging the gender gap in labour market outcomes

Women continue to have lower labour market incomes than men

Despite major improvements in the education of girls, rising female labour force participation and widespread laws against gender discrimination, women still lag behind men in the labour market along a number of key dimensions. The gender gap in labour income (GGLI) – defined as the average gap in labour income between men and women – remains a global phenomenon (see Figure 10.2). It averages 40% across the OECD, with considerable variation across countries, ranging from 20% in Slovenia to over 60% in Turkey. On average in the OECD, gender differences in employment explain 40%, differences in hours worked 20% and differences in hourly wages 40% (which is consistent with an hourly wage gap of 16%).

Gender disparities tend to widen over the life course

The GGLI tends to widen over the working life, with most of it arising in the first half of the career. On average across the OECD, the GGLI amounts to around 25% for people in their 20s, widens to 40% for those in their 30s and early 40s, but increases only little after that. The evolution of the GGLI over the life-cycle reflects different labour market mobility patterns for men and women. Most importantly, childbirth often has long-lasting effects on women's careers, in terms of time spent out of employment, limited hours of work, earnings and career progression. Part-time work can help to avoid that women withdraw from the labour market after childbirth, but also may limit opportunities for career progression within their firm. Women also experience fewer job-to-job transitions, partly reflecting the role of family commitments. Weaker job mobility, within and between firms, harms career progression and earnings growth (Barth and Kerr, 2017[10]).

Targeted measures can reduce gender inequalities

Effective strategies to promote gender equality consist of a number of key elements: i) family policies that improve access to childcare, correct disincentives to work for second earners and move towards gender-neutral taxes-and-benefit systems; ii) measures to encourage behavioural changes, including combating long hours, getting fathers more involved in caring, and promoting more equal forms of paid leave; and iii) inducing changes in the workplace, including increased take-up of part time and flexible working-time arrangements. The relative importance of these different elements varies from country to country. In countries where women are less likely to enter the labour market at any stage (e.g. Greece, Italy and Spain), policies should focus on ensuring high female labour participation at young ages. By contrast, in countries where women tend to withdraw from the labour market following childbirth (e.g. Australia, Austria and several Eastern European countries) and those where women tend to spend large parts of their careers in part-time work (e.g. Germany, the Netherlands and Switzerland) attention should focus on policies promoting the reconciliation of parental care responsibilities with work and an equal sharing of care responsibilities in the household.

Figure 10.2. The gender gap in labour income

Decomposition of the gender gap in labour income (20-64 years old), 2013-15, percentages

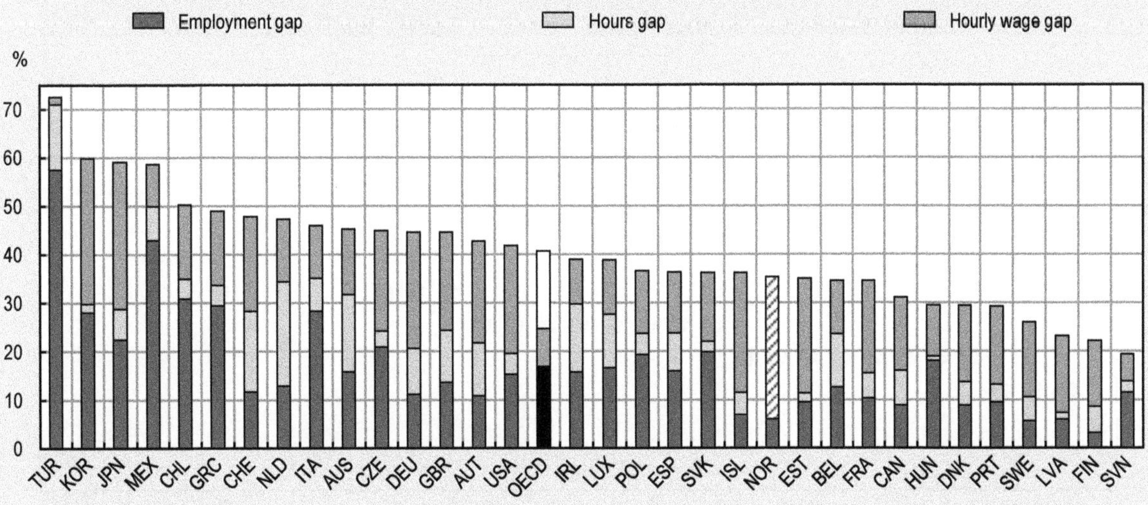

Note: For Canada and Turkey, data on earnings refer to wage and salary only. For Norway, the breakdown of hourly wage gap and hours gap is not available.
Source: OECD (2018[11]), *OECD Employment Outlook 2018*, https://doi.org/10.1787/empl_outlook-2018-en.

StatLink http://dx.doi.org/10.1787/888933881420

10.2. Promoting social mobility across generations

Most people agree that democratic societies should promote equality of opportunities – i.e. try to ensure that all people have similar chances to succeed in the labour market regardless of their socio-economic background. Inequalities in outcomes and opportunities, however, are inherently linked: in the absence of equal opportunities, today's inequalities transmit into inequalities for the next generation. High inequality in outcomes in turn undermines equality of opportunity – or "social mobility" across generations – as children from well-off backgrounds get a substantial head start in life. Indeed, empirical evidence shows that social mobility across generations tends to be higher in societies where outcomes are less unequal (a relationship described by the so-called "Great Gatsby Curve" (Corak, 2006[12])).

Intergenerational mobility is low in many OECD countries

People's socio-economic outcomes tend to be strongly related to those of their parents, i.e. intergenerational mobility tends to be low (OECD, 2018[2]). About 40% of the differences in fathers' earnings carry over to the next generation in the OECD on average. The degree of earnings persistence between generations varies substantially across countries, from below 20% in the Nordic countries to 60% in Hungary, Luxembourg and some emerging economies.[2] These figures imply that, in an "average OECD country", it could take about five generations for the offspring of a family in the bottom decile of the income distribution to reach the average income (Figure 10.3). In the Nordic countries, this process could only take two generations, while in some emerging economies, it could take around ten.

Figure 10.3. Intergenerational mobility tends to be low

Expected number of generations for the offspring from a family at the bottom 10% of the income distribution to reach the mean income

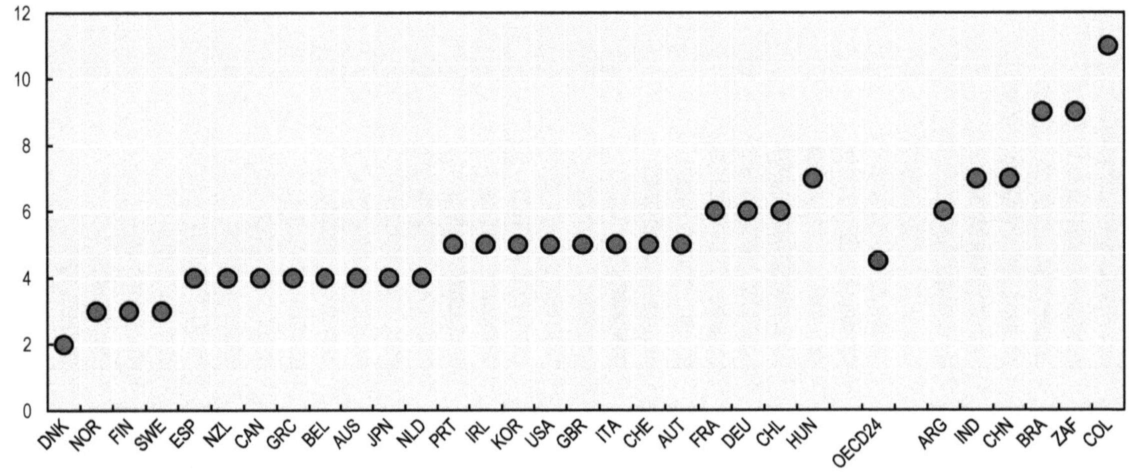

Note: These estimates are simulation-based and intended to be illustrative. They are based on estimates of earnings persistence (elasticities) between fathers and sons and the current level of household incomes of the bottom decile and the mean, assuming constant elasticities.
Source: OECD (2018[2]), *A Broken Social Elevator? How to Promote Social Mobility*, https://doi.org/10.1787/9789264301085-en.

StatLink http://dx.doi.org/10.1787/888933881439

The strong persistence in earnings across generations reflects various factors, including low educational mobility, the inter-generational transmission of health outcomes and the role of parental social networks. Educational attainment is highly persistent across generations: 42% of people with low-educated parents – i.e. those without an upper-secondary qualification – do not finish high school, while only 12% complete tertiary education. By contrast, people whose parents have completed tertiary education nearly always obtain at least a high school degree (only 7% do not) and 63% obtain a tertiary degree. Health outcomes also tend to be transmitted from one generation to the next. Having grown up in a family with little or no wealth and having ill parents are two main predictors of poor health, and young people with poor health are four times more likely to be NEET than their peers (OECD, 2016[13]). Parental social networks also play a role in sustaining earnings inequalities across generations, particularly for those from high-income backgrounds, e.g. Narayan et al. (2018[14]), Corak and Piraino (2011[15]).

Improving social mobility

There is nothing inevitable about socio-economic privilege or disadvantage being passed on from one generation to another. Large differences in social mobility across countries indicate that there is room for policies to make societies more mobile. Improving social mobility requires investments in education and health as well as effective family and regional policies.

Public investment in quality education, from early childhood education and care through tertiary education

For the youngest, good-quality childcare and pre-primary school attendance can have large beneficial effects for all, but in particular for children from more disadvantaged backgrounds with long-term consequences for educational attainment and labour market outcomes.[3] In the United States, for instance, the Infant Health and Development Program (IHDP), which provided free full-day early education with a focus on language development, was found to substantially boost cognitive ability, particularly for children from low-income households.[4] Similarly, children attending a French pre-school (*école maternelle*) from the age of two showed significantly improved cognitive and non-cognitive skills at age six and better literacy and numeracy from grades three to nine (Filatriau, Fougère and Tô, 2013[16]). Good-quality childcare and pre-primary school attendance can also have beneficial effects in the long-run, particularly for disadvantaged children (Van Huizen and Plantenga, 2015[17]; Ruhm and Waldfogel, 2012[18]). The introduction of universal childcare in Norway, for instance, was found to have strong positive effects on labour market participation and to reduce welfare dependency later in life (Havnes and Mogstad, 2011[19]). Many countries offer pre-primary education as a statutory right to all children from the age of three, and attendance is frequently subsidised or free. In most OECD countries, 80% or more of 3-5 year-olds are enrolled in pre-primary education or primary schools.

At compulsory-schooling level, policies to support social mobility need to address the often large performance gap for students from disadvantaged backgrounds and fight early school leaving. PISA mathematics scores are about 20% lower for 15-year-olds with parents of lower socio-economic status than for those with parents of a high status. Young people with less-educated parents and those from workless households are also much more likely to leave school without an upper-secondary degree. These early school leavers are strongly overrepresented among young people who are not in employment, education or training (NEETs), accounting for about one third of all NEETs across OECD countries (OECD, 2016[20]). Effective strategies to support students from disadvantaged backgrounds include targeted investments in low-performing schools and those located in marginalised communities (e.g. for smaller classes, better educational material and physical infrastructure and the recruitment and training of teachers and support staff),[5] eliminating grade repetition, avoiding early tracking and deferring student selection to upper-secondary education (OECD, 2012[21]). The *OECD Action Plan for Youth* (OECD, 2013[22]) recommends a set of educational measures to tackle high youth unemployment. It places particular emphasis on second-chance programmes for young people who quit school without an upper-secondary degree and quality apprenticeships and internship programmes that help smooth the school-to-work transition.

Students from disadvantaged socio-economic backgrounds also tend to be under-represented in higher education, especially at prestigious institutions. At the most competitive U.S. colleges, for instance, the large majority of students come from households in the top income quartile, while the bottom half accounts for only a tiny portion e.g. Carnevale and Strohl (2010[23]), Chetty et al. (2017[24]). Targeted outreach in upper-secondary schools and counselling/tutoring services during tertiary education can be effective at increasing tertiary-level educational enrolment and completion rates of young people from underprivileged backgrounds. Differential admission policies, such as class-based affirmative action, can help high-potential candidates from disadvantaged backgrounds pass the initial admissions screening.

Early health support, notably for children and young people from lower socio-economic backgrounds

Targeted investments in health support for children and young people from low socio-economic backgrounds can help to address low social mobility related to health. Pre- and post-natal homecare for low-income families has been shown to increase child well-being (Greenberg and Shroder, 2004[25]). Pre-natal and childhood health in turn are significant predictors of adult health and employment status (Case, Fertig and Paxson, 2005[26]). Moreover, many governments are taking steps to promote a culture of healthy eating and regular physical activity in schools (OECD, 2017[27]). Direct health support for young people should be part of an effective effort to reduce early school leaving and promote a successful school-to-work transition. To tackle the rapidly growing share of young people diagnosed with mental health problems easily, accessible mental health services are needed.[6] More generally, the absence of universal health coverage, high privately-financed out-of-pocket payments and the lack of public screening programmes are associated with greater income-related health inequalities (Devaux and de Looper, 2012[28]).

Family policies that address early disadvantage

Policies that provide financial support to low-income parents and help them invest in their children's human capital can also help to promote social mobility. There is ample evidence of a strong causal impact of parental income on children's health, school performance and future success in the labour market. Financial support that effectively targets low-income parents, such as child benefits or earned income tax credits, can therefore contribute to reducing the achievement gap of children from disadvantaged backgrounds.[7] Similarly, policies that promote the labour market participation of both parents – such as generous parental leave entitlements, especially for fathers, the availability of affordable childcare, flexible working-time arrangements and fiscal incentives for second-earners to participate in the labour market – can help improve the financial situation of families and hence promote intergenerational mobility. In emerging economies, conditional cash transfer programmes that provide income support to poor households conditional on children's school attendance or health check-ups have had positive effects on educational attainment, health and future labour market outcomes (OECD, 2015[29]).

Tackling spatial segregation and strengthening lagging regions

The geographical concentration of disadvantaged families in low-income neighbourhoods and large economic differences across regions tend to reinforce some of the mechanisms responsible for the transmission of disadvantage across generations. Low-income urban neighbourhoods and less developed regions tend to suffer from poorer-quality public services (notably in education and healthcare), a weaker transport infrastructure and fewer employment opportunities. This creates additional hurdles for children and young people from disadvantaged backgrounds. Urban planning and regional development policies that support equal access can help address these. This could include housing policies that promote the geographical mobility of families to help them move to regions with better economic prospects (see Chapter 14). It could also involve measures that limit school choice – to avoid that large differences in school quality in urban areas induce social segregation – and facilitate a more equitable allocation of children to schools in terms of their socio-economic background.[8] It may further involve measures to improve the quality of education and health services in low-income communities, for example by offering more attractive pay packages for education and health professionals.

10.3. Bridging the labour market divide

Deep and persistent inequalities in the labour market reflect the growing imbalance between relative skill supplies and demands, partly driven by globalisation and technological change. However, segmentation in product and labour markets – as reflected by significant differences in firm and contract-specific pay – can also play an important role when labour markets are imperfectly competitive. This section first discusses the role of adult learning policies for vulnerable workers ("the supply side of the labour market divide") and then turns to the discussion of segmentation in product and labour markets ("the demand side of the labour market divide").[9]

Adult learning systems need to become more inclusive

Adult learning is key for addressing labour market inequality, particularly for persons with low skills. Taking part in training provides adults with the opportunity to up-skill and re-skill in line with changing labour market demands. It also supports positive labour market transitions and promotes upward mobility to better-paid jobs.

Participation in adult learning tends to be weak, particularly among those who need it most

According to data from the OECD Survey of Adult Skills (PIAAC), only 41% of adults in the surveyed countries participate in adult learning in any given year. This varies markedly across countries, ranging from over one half in countries such as New Zealand, the Netherlands and the Nordic countries to less than a quarter in countries such as Greece, Italy and Turkey. Importantly, participation in adult learning and training is much lower among low-skilled workers, i.e. those most in need of upskilling and reskilling. On average across countries, the participation gap in job-related training between low-skilled and more skilled persons is 23 percentage points.

Engaging adults who currently do not participate in training is a major task for all stakeholders involved, as most of them (82%) have no interest or motivation to do so, according to data from the Survey of Adult Skills (PIAAC). This implies that across OECD countries participating in the PIAAC survey, about half of adults neither participate nor want to participate in adult learning. With adult learning being a key lever to improve labour market outcomes of low-skilled workers and prepare workers for changing skill needs, it will be crucial to find effective ways to motivate this part of the population to take part in education and training.

Promoting adult learning among disadvantaged groups

A comprehensive strategy for improving the inclusiveness of adult learning systems focuses on those most in need of up- and re-skilling, but least likely to participate in adult training and consists of the following features: i) providing good quality information and guidance; ii) tackling participation barriers; and iii) engaging employers and unions in the provision and financing of adult learning.[10]

Providing information and guidance

Policy should enable adults to make good education and training choices. Yet, there is evidence to suggest that adults, in particular those with low skills, are not particularly good at recognising the need to develop their skills further (Windisch, 2015[30]). Hence, engaging adults in learning must go beyond providing training opportunities and involve raising public awareness, providing high-quality individualised advice and guidance services and developing on-line databases to inform workers of re-training opportunities and labour market needs.

Public awareness campaigns are a good way to promote the benefits of adult learning and reach out to underrepresented groups (Kowalczyk et al., 2016[31]). The Institute for Adult Education in Slovenia, for example, has been organising an annual life-long learning week since 1996, which today includes more than 1 500 events implemented in cooperation with partner organisations across the country. Portugal launched its adult learning program Qualifica in 2016/2017 with a large-scale public awareness campaign titled "Get yourself together and invest in your future!". In 2017, the city of Brussels, Belgium, launched a mobile information centre Formtruck to engage job-seekers, the low-qualified and young people not in employment, education and training in adult learning.

Career guidance helps individuals understand their skill set and development needs and navigate available learning opportunities. To be effective, it must take into account timely labour market and skill needs information. Career guidance is typically delivered through a range of channels, including public employment services (PES), specialised guidance services, education providers and social partners. Dedicated services tend to be the most effective as they are specifically set up to provide in-depth and timely skill-needs information drawn from effective skills anticipation systems. *Career New Zealand* provides a wealth of services, increasingly available online, ranging from tools that allow users to explore careers and find jobs that match their skills and qualifications. Also in New Zealand, the *Occupation Outlook* is a mobile phone app that allows exploring study and career options, with extensive information on labour supply and demand in over 100 occupations. Some countries have developed one-stop shops to ensure individuals get all the information they need to make informed decisions. The House of Orientation (*Maison de l'Orientation*) in Luxembourg provides a one-stop shop for education and labour market orientation.[11]

Online databases can also be useful for end-users (workers, prospective students) as well as trainers, counsellors and other adult learning experts. Australia's national directory of vocational education and training providers and courses (www.myskills.gov.au) allows users to search VET qualifications by industry and to access information about average course fees, course duration, available subsidies and average employment outcomes. While employment outcomes are currently available by qualification, a plan exists to make them available at provider level.

Reducing barriers to participation

Policy efforts must also focus on those individuals who want to take up or continue adult learning opportunities, but face a variety of obstacles to doing so. 18% of people who do not take part in job-related adult learning would like to do so. Equally, 34% of people who take part in job-related adult learning would like to continue, but do not do so. Barriers to participation are diverse and include a lack of time due to work (29% of those indicating they would like to participate or continue in adult learning but do not do so), a lack of time due to family commitments, a lack of financial resources (both 16%), inconvenient time or location of the learning opportunity (12%) and a lack of employer support (7%), according to PIAAC data. For low-skilled adults, an additional barrier to participation is the lack of basic skills, which are often set as pre-conditions for participation in adult learning.

Most adult learning opportunities require individuals to have a basic level of literacy and numeracy and some have specific skills or qualifications as a pre-condition for entry. As some skills are acquired through labour market experience, validating and certifying existing skills can help to re-engage individuals in formal learning (OECD, 2019[32]). Effective recognition of prior learning must be transparent, streamlined and ensure the buy-in of all relevant stakeholders, including employers and education and training providers. In Portugal, the launch of Qualifica programme in 2017 included the creation of a credit-based system for professional training in line with European frameworks, an online tool for the recording of qualification and competences ('*Passaporte Qualifica*'), and the establishment of a network of 300 Qualifica centres which provide free services related to information and guidance, as well as the recognition, validation and certification of skills (OECD, 2018[33]).[12]

In many countries, several forms of flexible learning provision exist that facilitate combining training with work and family commitments, including on a part-time basis, in the evenings, weekends, distance learning, or in a modular and/or credit-based format. Modular approaches are especially helpful in allowing adult learners to focus on developing the skills they currently lack, complete self-contained learning modules on these skills and combine these modules to eventually gain a full (formal) qualification. Research suggests that such provisions can broaden access to formal qualifications, in particular for disadvantaged groups (Kis and Windisch, 2018[34]). The Danish adult learning system allows students a high degree of flexibility by enabling them to combine modules from different providers and across different subjects. For example, individuals working towards a vocational qualification in Labour Market Training Centres (*Arbejdsmarkedsuddannelse*) can select from a wide range of vocational training courses but also tap into subjects provided by the general education system.

Statutory education and training leave – i.e. the right to take time off during working hours to participate in education and training – is typically regulated in national legislation or set out in collective agreements and can be universal or targeted at specific groups such as the low-skilled or small and medium-sized enterprises (OECD, 2017[35]). In order to ensure its uptake, many countries provide financial incentives for learners and employers alongside statutory leave. In Belgium, full-time private-sector employees participating in recognised training and education programmes are entitled to training leave for up to 180 hours per year. During training leave, workers receive full-pay (up to a ceiling), while employers can be compensated for the wages paid during training leave by the Federal Public Service for Employment, Labour and Social Dialogue.

Financial incentives are used widely to encourage adults' participation in education and training and they often include specific provisions targeted at the low-skilled. An equitable system of financial incentives should focus on addressing cases of under-investment in adult learning. A range of tools can be mobilised including wage or training subsidies (also voucher-based), tax incentives, subsidised loans or training/time account schemes (OECD, 2017[35]). For example, the Austrian city of Vienna supports its employed and unemployed inhabitants with below tertiary education through education accounts (*Bildungskonto*), which co-finance the costs of recognised education and training programmes or that of recognition procedures for prior learning. To promote equity and avoid deadweight loss – financial support to persons who would have participated in training anyway – financial incentives are often targeted at under-represented groups, such as the low-skilled, by limiting entitlements to such groups or allowing for more generous support (as in the Vienna initiative described above). In France, the *Compte Personnel de Formation* is a personal account that provides individuals with training credits based on the time spent in employment during the year. Entitlements are transferable between employers. Low-skilled individuals receive double the credits of their higher-skilled counterparts (48 hours per year as opposed to 24 hours) and the ceiling for the accumulated credits is also significantly higher (400 hours compared with 150 hours).

Engaging employers and unions

With much learning taking place in the workplace, the engagement of employers and unions in the design, implementation and financing of skill development opportunities is critical to raising participation in job-related training.

While employers play a key role in providing and financing job-related adult learning, underinvestment in training and education is common, particularly among small and medium enterprises. This often reflects a lack of information, capacity and/or resources. Many governments therefore actively seek to engage employers in adult learning activities through awareness campaigns, tailored support and financial incentives. For example, the Japanese System to Support Human Resource Development (*Jinzai Kaihatsu Shien Joseikin*) co-funds business expenses for training, with higher subsidies available for small and medium-sized enterprises.

Trade unions can also play a key role, building on their involvement in job design, work organisation, and the application of new technologies at work. Indeed, in many countries, unions engage in the promotion and management of training provisions. In the United Kingdom, Unionlearn – the skills and learning branch of Trade Union Confederation – assists its members in the delivery of learning opportunities and the management of the Union Learning fund. This initiative has been particularly successful in recruiting low-skilled workers into training courses.

In some countries with sector-level bargaining, unions and employer organisations collaborate to invest in the skills of the workforce. In the Netherlands, the sectoral training and development funds (*Opleidings- en Ontwikkelingsfondsen*) are social partner initiatives that are financed primarily through payroll levies, fixed in collective agreements. They provide learning possibilities to workers to maintain their skills and anticipate future skills needs. Similarly, the Finish social partners administer an education and training fund *(Koulutusrahasto*), which provides education and training grants to employed and self-employed adults, who meet certain eligibility criteria.[13]

Tackling labour market segmentation

When labour markets are imperfectly competitive, inequalities do not just depend on the skill structure of labour demand and supply, but also on the composition of firms and contracts. Moreover, the persistence of inequalities depends on the extent to which workers can take advantage of the different opportunities offered by firms and progress from fixed-term to open-ended contracts. The role of firms for labour market inequality is discussed in Box 10.2.

Contractual segmentation has tended to increase before the global financial crisis

Temporary contracts tend to be associated with lower wages, even after controlling for the characteristics of workers and their jobs (OECD, 2015[36]). Moreover, people on temporary contracts are less likely to receive bonuses (Venn, 2011[37]) and typically experience lower levels of labour market security and lower quality working environments (OECD, 2014[4]). The wage penalty associated with temporary contracts most likely reflects the weaker bargaining position of people employed on such contracts. People employed on temporary contracts also tend to experience weaker earnings growth over time, possibly due to more limited in human capital accumulation, further reinforcing pre-existing wage gaps (OECD, 2015[36]). Given the weaker outcomes associated with temporary contracts, it is particularly important that they enhance access to permanent jobs in the future. Indeed, to the extent that temporary contracts help workers gain access to stable jobs, a short-lived period of weaker employment conditions may well be worth the investment in the long-term.

In the late 1990s and early 2000s, many OECD countries engaged in reforms to tackle persistent unemployment and promote labour market flexibility. These reforms in many cases involved easing the use of flexible contracts, while maintaining a relatively strict employment protection for open-ended contracts (and are often referred to as "partial labour market reforms"). Today's evidence, however, suggests that such reforms did little to promote overall employment, but increased the incidence of temporary contracts (Kahn, 2010[38]), with adverse consequences for job quality and inclusiveness.[14] The positive effect of partial labour market reforms on the probability of finding work was probably offset by an increase in the risk of losing one's job, as a result of the substitution of permanent contracts by temporary ones (Cahuc, Charlot and Malherbet, 2016[39]). As suggested by Panel A of Figure 10.4, this substitution effect tends to be stronger and the use of temporary contracts more important, the stricter the employment protection of permanent contracts. This is consistent with econometric findings in Bassanini and Garnero (2013[40]) for a large number of OECD countries as well as Hijzen, Mondauto and Scarpetta (2017[41]) for Italy and Centeno and Novo (2012[42]) for Portugal.

Moreover, an increase in temporary employment at the expense of permanent employment tends to slow the transition from temporary to permanent work. Panel B of Figure 10.4 shows that a higher use of temporary work is associated with a significantly lower probability that a person with a fixed-term contract will have an open-ended contract three years later. In other words, a higher incidence of temporary contracts increases labour market segmentation. This may seem to contradict findings from a literature showing that temporary jobs provide a stepping stone to permanent work, see e.g. Booth et al. (2002[43]), Ichino et al. (2008[44]), Jahn and Rosholm (2014[45]) and OECD (2015[36]). However, these studies adopt an individual perspective in which the structure of employment is taken as given and hence do not shed light on the consequences of an *increase* in the number of temporary jobs on the career opportunities of workers.[15] In fact, there is growing evidence that an excessive use of temporary work can have adverse consequences for individual pathways. For example, the liberalisation of the use of temporary contracts in Spain in 1984 reduced life-time earnings among the low-skilled as a result of weaker job stability and increased non-employment spells (García-Pérez, Castelló and Marinescu, 2018[46]).

In sum, reforms that promote the use of temporary work in a context of strict protection employment for workers on open-ended contracts risk being counterproductive by inducing an excessive use of fixed-term work. A widespread use of temporary work tends to have only a limited impact on improving employment opportunities for disadvantaged groups, while at the same time, tends to come at the expense of permanent employment, reducing job quality, slowing the transition of temporary to permanent work and reinforcing long-term inequalities in the labour market. Reforms in recent years have therefore tended to follow a different pattern, by focusing on ways to reduce the regulatory gap in employment protection between permanent and temporary contracts (see Box 7.3 in Chapter 7 for details).

Figure 10.4. Employment protection, temporary work and contractual segmentation

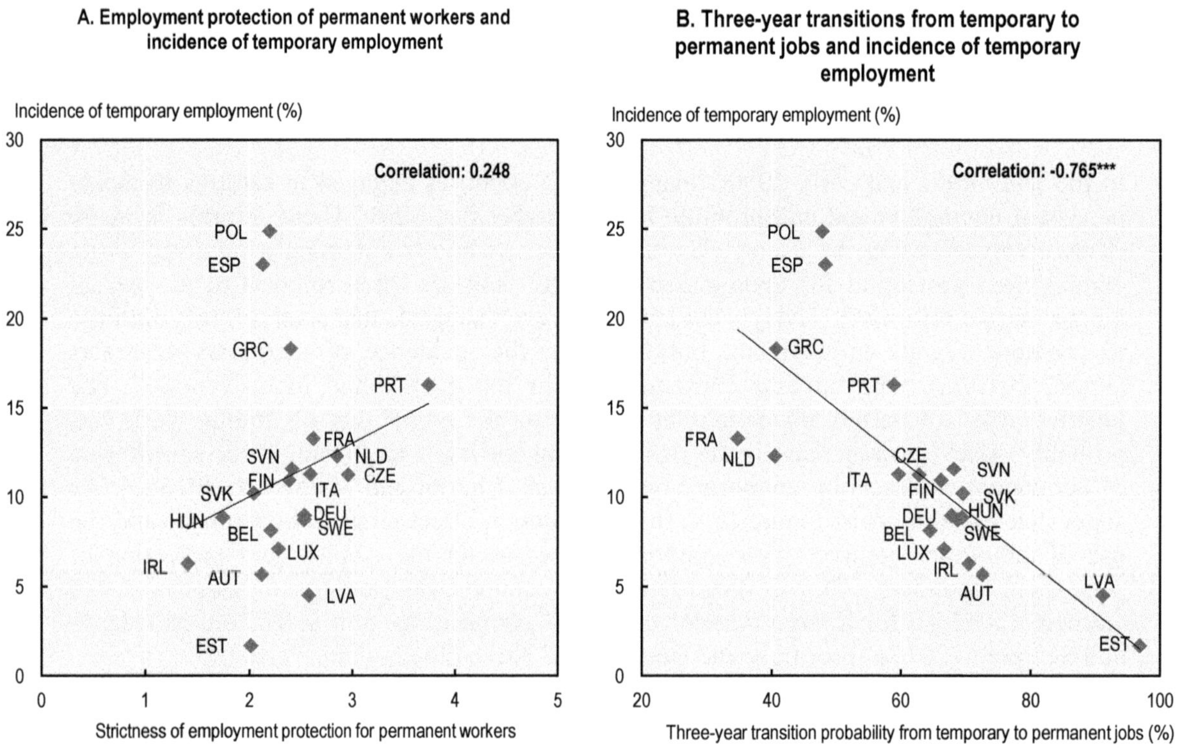

Note: *** Statistically significant at the 1% level.
Source: OECD estimates based on the European Union Statistics on Income and Living Conditions (EU-SILC), the German Socio-Economic Panel (SOEP) for Germany and OECD Indicators of employment protection, www.oecd.org/employment/protection.

StatLink http://dx.doi.org/10.1787/888933881458

Tackling contractual segmentation

One possible strategy to reduce contractual segmentation is to make hiring on temporary contracts more difficult and costly, while leaving unchanged or simultaneously reducing dismissal costs for permanent workers. Reforms along these lines typically take the form of restricting renewals of temporary contract, their cumulative duration or their scope. One concern with such reforms is that restricting the use of temporary contracts tends to be difficult to enforce in practice. The enforcement of employment protection is mainly dependent on legal complaints of employees who consider themselves wrongfully treated. In the context of temporary contracts, employees often benefit from non-enforcement, at least in the short-run, and therefore have little incentive to lodge a case (Muñoz-Bullón, 2004[47]).[16]

Another strategy is to ease the employment protection of permanent workers in countries where this is overly restrictive. Reforms of this type have been relatively common in recent years and typically focus on extending or clarifying the conditions for economic dismissal and limiting the costs of unfair dismissal. An early assessment of such a reform in Spain suggested that this reduced the reliance of temporary work by increasing the share of permanent contracts among new hires (OECD, 2013[48]). However, by making it easier to dismiss workers for economic reasons, such reforms also increase the risk of job displacement and financial hardship for incumbents. They should, therefore, be accompanied by the provision of adequate unemployment benefits as part of a comprehensive activation strategy (see Chapter 9). Recent labour market reforms in Italy and Portugal that increased the ease with workers on open-ended contracts can be dismissed also involved measures to strengthen the effectiveness of their unemployment benefit and activation systems.[17]

A third strategy is to focus on the convergence in termination costs across contract types. Full convergence would effectively imply moving to a single or unified contract. Under a *single* contract all existing contracts are replaced by a single open-ended contract, with the level of protection increasing in tenure.[18] This option therefore does not provide an explicit instrument for time-limited activities beyond dismissal. This is problematic when compensation costs for unfair dismissal costs are high and their grounds wide-ranging or unclear.[19] Under a *unified* contract, all contracts types are preserved, but tenure-dependent termination costs are harmonised across contracts. To the extent that the costs for unfair dismissal are high and uncertain, this option may still leave strong incentives for substituting permanent by temporary contracts. The effective operation of a single or unified contract, therefore, requires that the grounds for unfair dismissal are limited to discrimination and prohibitive grounds (see Chapter 7).

To evaluate these different reform options, it is useful to recall why temporary contracts exist in the first place. Temporary contracts provide employment flexibility to employers for dealing with product demand shocks, overcoming information asymmetries about worker productivity, and organising time-limited activities. Introducing employment protection entitlements (e.g. severance pay) from the start of a job spell for everyone reduces the risk of labour market segmentation, but also increases the cost of uncertainty and engaging in truly time-limited activities, with potentially important implications for job creation (or the use of alternative work arrangements such as self-employment). The challenge for policy-makers is to limit the statutory divide between contract types in terms of employment protection, while allowing for sufficient employment flexibility for firms, particularly at the start of the job spell.

Box 10.2. Segmentation across firms

While rising wage inequality reflects to an important extent growing returns to skills, recent evidence suggests firms are increasingly contributing to rising inequality as well. Indeed, a significant share of the rise in wage inequality has been linked to increased wage dispersion between firms, e.g. Song et al. (forthcoming[49]) for the United States and references therein. Rising wage dispersion across firms may reflect growing differences in firms' compensation policies, the tendency for good workers to sort into good firms as well as that of similar workers to cluster in the same firm.

Firm performance. The growing dispersion in firm's compensation policies in many countries is likely to reflect a growing variation in the ability of firms to offer more generous compensation packages due to growing productivity dispersion (Berlingieri, Blanchenay and Criscuolo, 2017[50]), or growing product market concentration (Diez, Leigh and Tambunlertchai, 2018[51]). Productivity dispersion has tended to rise as frontier firms have pulled away from the rest, possibly because they were better placed to take advantage of the opportunities presented by globalisation and technological change, while technology diffusion from the frontier to the rest of the economy has stalled. Globalisation and technological change are also likely to have contributed to growing market concentration, resulting in rising market shares and mark-ups at the technological frontier. To tackle high and persistent inequalities in the labour market it is therefore not enough to invest in skills development. It is equally important to invest in policies that can revive productivity growth in lagging firms or promote the reallocation of resources to more efficient firms (OECD, 2016[52]).

Sorting. A growing variation in the ability of firms to provide generous compensation packages does not necessarily explain why compensation packages have grown more diverse; firms also need to have an interest in doing so. One possibility is that firms use more generous compensation packages to attract better workers in the presence of complementarities in production between technologically advanced firms and skilled workers. High-performance work and management practices are one example since they tend to be more effective in the presence of skilled workers. The increased importance of information and communication technology may be another. The greater role of such production complementarities may have increased the dispersion in average pay across firms and reinforced the sorting of better workers into better firms. Sorting may also have increased as a result of reduced "frictions" in the labour market, i.e. the ease with which firms can create or terminate jobs and workers can move between jobs. While increased sorting may be good for economic efficiency, it also contributes to the depth and persistence of labour market inequality (OECD, 2015[8]).[1]

Segregation. Rising wage dispersion across firms also reflects the clustering of workers with similar workers in the same firm, so-called "segregation".[2] Increased segregation in terms of skills or occupations may reflect the growing importance of outsourcing. Human-resource practices may be most effective when tailored to the specific nature of work activities, but at the same time, there may be limited scope for differentiating HR practices within a single firm. This provides incentives for firms to concentrate on "core" activities and outsource non-core activities. Consistent with this argument, Goldschmidt and Schmieder (2017[53]) find, using data for Germany, that outsourcing is associated with lower wages for workers in outsourced activities. The resulting segregation of the workforce has raised concerns about increased competition on the basis of labour standards and reduced opportunities for career advancement (Weil, 2004[54]). Possible policy responses involve protecting workers through minimum standards related to for example wages, health and safety (statutory or collectively agreed) or establishing social norms that increase the responsibility of firms for labour standards in their supply chain.

Notes:

1 As mentioned in Box 10.1, the increased importance of sorting may have reinforced existing gender inequalities as men are typically better positioned to take advantage of evolving job opportunities in the labour market than women who, in many cases, place a greater emphasis on family considerations when making career choices.

2 As opposed to the sorting described above, this is not driven by firm-specific wage premia and hence does not contribute to efficiency. Segregation also does not contribute to inequality in a given year since an increase in between-firm wage dispersion as a result of segregation is exactly offset by a reduction in inequality within firms. However, segregation is likely to reduce mobility over the life-course, and hence increase the persistence of inequality.

10.4. Fair and efficient redistribution

Redistribution through the taxes-and-benefits system can play a crucial role in making labour markets more inclusive by ensuring that the gains from economic growth are broadly shared in the population, including among families with low incomes.

Redistribution has an important role to play but has weakened over time

The redistributive effects of taxes and transfers among the working-age population can be quantified by comparing market income inequality among working-age households before taxes and transfers with disposable income inequality after taxes and transfers.[20] On average across OECD countries, taxes and benefits reduce market income inequality among the working-age population by about one quarter (Figure 10.5). However, there is considerable variation across countries. The inequality-reducing effect of taxes and transfers amounts to about 40% in countries such as Finland, Ireland and Slovenia and less than 10% in countries such as Chile and Korea.[21]

Redistribution mainly reflects the role of cash transfers, which account for about two- thirds to three-quarters of the total inequality-reducing effect of taxes and transfers on average across OECD countries (Immervoll and Richardson, 2011[55]; Causa and Hermansen, 2017[56]). When measuring inequality in terms of the Gini, the redistributive impact of cash transfers is strongly associated with their size and less so with their targeting (Causa and Hermansen, 2017[56]). This explains why social insurance benefits – which account for a much larger share of public social expenditures than social assistance benefits – play a much larger role for redistribution than social assistance benefits, despite being less targeted.[22]

Personal income taxes account for the remainder of redistribution. In countries with relatively little redistribution, the role of personal income taxes tends to be relatively more important for redistribution (Japan, Korea, Israel and the United States). Social security contributions tend to be distribution-neutral and even are regressive in some countries. However, they are used to finance highly progressive benefits, implying that the social security system as a whole tends to be strongly redistributive.[23]

Figure 10.5. The equalising effect of taxes and transfers

Difference between the Gini coefficient of market income and disposable income as a share of the Gini of market income, working-age population (18-65), 2014 or latest available year

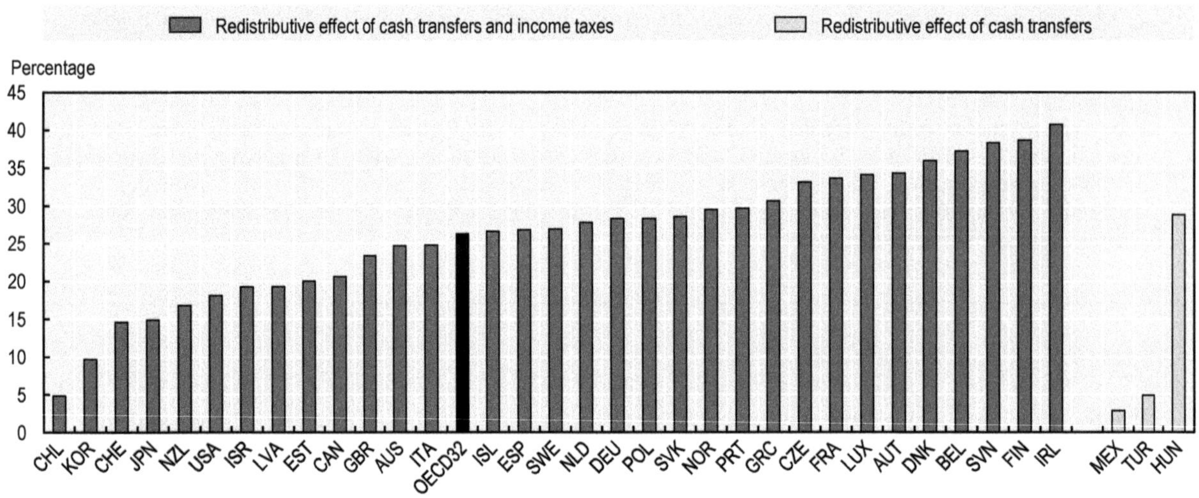

Note: The Gini index measures the extent to which the distribution of incomes among households deviates from perfect equal distribution. A value of zero represents perfect equality and a value of 100 extreme inequality.

Source: Causa and Hermansen ($2017_{[56]}$), "Income redistribution through taxes and transfers across OECD countries", *OECD Economics Department Working Papers*, No. 1453, https://doi.org/10.1787/bc7569c6-en.

StatLink http://dx.doi.org/10.1787/888933881477

Over the last two decades, redistribution through taxes and benefits has fallen in the majority of OECD countries (Causa and Hermansen, $2017_{[56]}$).[24] This reflects a fairly pervasive decline in the redistributive effect of cash transfers, driven by a reduction in their overall importance as well as their reduced targeting on the poor. The latter results from a shift in emphasis away from social insurance benefits for workless households to less generous social assistance benefits and a greater use of in-work benefits among working households to strengthen work incentives among poor families (Causa, Vindics and Akgun, $2018_{[57]}$). By contrast, the redistributive effect of taxes has changed only modestly on average across countries: a shift towards more progressivity in personal income taxes in the bottom end of the distribution in some countries was compensated by a slight decline in progressivity at the top end.

Making redistribution fairer and more efficient

Efforts to promote labour market inclusiveness by strengthening the importance of redistribution policies should bear in mind the possible adverse effects on work incentives, particularly among low-income families. Indeed, the design of such policies is key for their effectiveness in reducing inequality and overcoming short-term trade-offs between inequality, on the one hand, and employment and economic growth, on the other. Taking a long-term perspective can help overcome such short-term trade-offs since this requires taking account not only of the impact of taxes and transfers on financial hardship at a given time, but also of the extent to which they help or hinder worker careers.

Consequently, the impacts of well-designed redistribution policies on different economic outcomes are likely to be more aligned in the long-term.

Government transfers are needed to address financial hardship

At the lower end of the income spectrum, government transfers have an important role to play in lifting low-income households from financial hardship, but they need to be sufficiently large to make a significant difference and be paired with measures to re-establish self-sufficiency and prevent long-term benefit dependency. In most advanced economies, social transfers consist of multiple components, including: i) primary out-of-work benefits (e.g. unemployment insurance benefits) for those who meet certain minimum contribution requirements; ii) secondary out-of-work benefits (e.g. unemployment assistance or minimum-income benefits such as social and housing assistance) that are available to all non-employed persons subject to a means test; and iii) means-tested in-work benefits (e.g. partial unemployment insurance or social assistance for individuals who are working) for those working but with low incomes.

High-coverage unemployment insurance benefits tend to play an important role in absorbing the financial costs of unemployment as well as for the importance of redistribution. If the risk of unemployment were to be evenly distributed across the workforce and unemployment spells relatively short-lived, the role of unemployment risk and unemployment insurance for life-time inequality would be limited. However, in practice, the risk of unemployment tends to be highly concentrated among workers with low-paid jobs and, hence, tends to contribute significantly to life-time inequality (OECD, 2015[8]). In countries, where informal employment is pervasive or eligibility criteria for receiving benefits are very tight, unemployment-insurance benefits tend to be limited to workers with relatively well-paid stable jobs and may even be regressive. Ensuring high coverage of unemployment benefits therefore is not only important for making labour markets more secure (Chapter 9), but also for making them more inclusive, provided that systems are designed to preserve work incentives through the enforcement of a "mutual-obligations" framework.

Last-resort social safety nets play a crucial role for preventing financial hardship, especially for those who are not eligible for unemployment insurance or have exhausted their benefit entitlements. Such benefits are particularly important for out-of-work youth or persons with a history of non-standard work, since they often do not meet minimum contribution requirements for unemployment insurance (OECD, 2016[58]). They are also key in many countries for alleviating the social costs of economic downturns. Due to the decline in hiring during such periods, the typical duration of unemployment tends to increase, increasing the number of unemployed persons that exhaust their unemployment benefit entitlements (OECD, 2011[59]). One concern with last-resort benefits is that, even when combined with housing benefits, they are often not sufficiently generous to lift recipient households out of poverty. Moreover, social assistance benefits are typically associated with considerable duration dependence, i.e. the extent to which benefit receipt in one period increases the probability of benefit receipt in the future. This "state dependence" mainly reflects persistence in the structural drivers of low income (e.g. being a lone parent, having weak socio-economic skills) rather than the role of benefit receipt on work incentives (Immervoll, Jenkins and Königs, 2015[60]).

In some countries, it may be possible to enhance the efficiency of social assistance by making greater use of in-work benefits. This encourages people to take up paid work and gives additional income support to poor working households.[25] The effectiveness of in-work benefits in reducing in-work poverty depends importantly on the design and the context in which they are used (Immervoll and Pearson, 2009[61]). For example, they tend to be more effective when they are simple, transparent and well understood by potential recipients. This is more likely when they are permanent rather than temporary or when they are means-tested on family incomes rather than individual earnings, given the importance of household composition for the risk of poverty. Moreover, they tend to be more effective in reducing in-work poverty when combined with a binding minimum wage at a moderate level – by law or collective agreement – since this reduces the extent to which in-work benefits can be appropriated by employers (Chapter 8). However, in-work benefits work less well in the context of compressed wage structures in the bottom of the distribution since this prevents a proper targeting, making them either ineffective or very expensive.

The design of tax systems should ensure that everyone contributes fairly

In addition to government transfers, there is also scope for strengthening the role of taxation, so that everyone contributes a fair share, including those at the top end of the income distribution. More specifically, tax systems can be made more efficient and more inclusive by broadening the tax base, increasing their fiscal progressivity, while taking account of the impact of possible reform options on incentives for working, effort at work and skills development (Brys et al., 2016[62]).

A broadening of the tax base levels the playing field and allows charging lower tax rates. The tax base can be broadened by improving tax compliance and removing or capping tax expenditures that are not well targeted at redistributive goals such as tax exemptions that disproportionately benefit high income groups related to items such as mortgage interests, pension savings or capital gains from secondary residences. Moreover, and as discussed in Chapter 8, when the link between social contributions and expenditures is not strong, levying contributions through progressive personal incomes taxes or other taxes that do not bear exclusively on labour can help to reduce the cost of labour, particularly for low-skilled workers, and increase their employment.

The overall progressivity of the tax system could also be strengthened through a better alignment of capital and labour income for tax purposes and reassessing the role of property and inheritance taxes. The presence of significant tax differentials across income and asset classes distorts compensation, investment and saving decisions, with adverse implications for efficiency and equity (Aghion et al., 2017[63]). Progressive personal income rates do not have to be limited to labour income but can also be applied to capital income, although possibly at a lower and less progressive rate.[26] Taxes on immovable property, such as real estate taxes, can promote both efficiency and equity since poor households are less likely to own property (Akgun, Cournède and Fournier, 2017[64]). Reforming inheritance taxes, by raising rates, reducing exemptions and fighting avoidance, can also contribute to greater overall tax progressivity, labour market inclusiveness as well as intergenerational mobility.[27]

Conclusions

Countries differ importantly in the depth and persistence of inequalities in the labour market. This variation suggests that there is nothing inevitable about deep and persistent inequalities and policy has an important role to play in limiting excessive inequalities in the labour market while fostering equality of opportunities.

Tackling deep and persistent inequalities in the labour market requires a comprehensive policy strategy that simultaneously seeks to promote: i) equal opportunities to avoid that socio-economic background determines success in the labour market; ii) access to quality jobs for vulnerable workers by encouraging their participation in adult learning and tackling labour market segmentation; and iii) an appropriate sharing in prosperity through fair and inclusive tax and benefits policies.

The presence of important policy complementarities across these three elements means that the best strategy for promoting labour market inclusiveness is to consider all three at the same time. In large part, this is due to the interdependence between inequality in outcomes and inequality in opportunities. Excessive inequalities in outcomes typically reflect inequalities in opportunities, but also contribute to their persistence due to the role of family income for investments in the education and health of children.

Yet, strategies for labour market inclusiveness may differ in their emphasis across policy priorities. For example, some countries may opt for placing education and adult learning at the centre of their inclusiveness strategy, with only a limited role for redistribution through the taxes and benefits system. Others may choose to place more emphasis on solidarity and redistribution, recognising the limits of a strongly merit-based model in a world where not everyone is born alike and luck remains an important factor for success.

Finally, taking a long-term perspective can help focussing the public debate on inclusiveness and the development of an effective policy strategy. It allows focusing on persistent differences in inequality, which should be the prime focus of redistribution, while abstracting from public insurance issues related to temporary income shocks. Moreover, it can help overcome possible short-term trade-offs between different policy objectives since long-term inequalities do not just take account of wages at a point in time, but also employment and wage growth during the working life.

Notes

1 Alternatively, high inequality, low mobility and weak economic growth may be reflections of deeper underlying problems related to, for example, labour market segmentation, informality or corruption.

2 These figures give the earnings persistence from fathers to sons. Earnings elasticities for daughters are more difficult to estimate because women have lower employment rates. Daughters' decisions to participate in the labour market, moreover, depend on factors that also determine earnings, such as age or educational attainment.

3 In addition to formal early childhood education and care, home education programmes can help to improve parenting skills and children's socio-emotional skills. Effective interventions include support for maternal health during the perinatal period and parenting support programmes targeted at high-risk groups.

4 Indeed, an impact evaluation projected that – if systematically implemented – intensive early childhood education programmes like the IHDP could essentially eliminate income-based IQ gaps among three-year-olds (Duncan and Sojourner, 2013[78]).

5 OECD evidence based on PISA further suggests that school autonomy in relation to the recruitment of teaching staff can be help to improve the quality of teachers, notably in disadvantaged areas (OECD, 2018[84]).

[6] The Australian National Youth Mental Health Foundation *headspace*, for instance, operates centres in which young people can confidentially seek mental health support and treatment outside their immediate social and educational environment (OECD, 2016[80]).

[7] Evidence for the United States further suggests that both the level of social expenditures and the progressivity of taxation are correlated with greater levels of intergenerational mobility across localities (Chetty et al., 2015[79]).

[8] For instance, the system of parallel waiting lists in Rotterdam permits oversubscribed schools to give preference to children from a minority background (OECD, 2016[77]). Some countries, such as Chile and the Netherlands, moreover, offer financial incentives to schools to enrol disadvantaged students in order to offset the costs of additional teaching and support staff.

[9] These are not independent issues. Investing in worker skills is more challenging in an environment in which work is organised based on fixed-term contractual arrangements and firms are poorly managed. Similarly, incentives for providing stable contractual arrangements may be weaker when worker skills are poor and firm productivity is low.

[10] High and broad participation are not the only features of an effective adult learning system. Other important aspects include the use of good quality labour market information on skill needs, the responsiveness to change, a sound quality assurance system and mechanisms for the recognition of prior learning. These aspects are discussed in Chapter 14.

[11] While initially targeted at younger persons, there has been an increasing focus on adult learners since 2017.

[12] In 2017, almost 30 000 adults enrolled in recognition processes and over 10 000 gained recognition.

[13] In a somewhat similar manner, Austria's Outplacement Labour Foundations and Sweden's Job Security Councils provide a range of services targeted at displaced workers to foster re-employment, including in the form of career guidance and training services.

[14] Consequently, in recent years the tendency has been to reverse these partial labour market reforms by reducing differences in regulatory protection across contract types (see Box 7.3 in Chapter 7).

[15] These studies ask whether from the perspective of an unemployed person accepting a temporary job offer increases the chance of obtaining a stable job or whether it is better to stay unemployed, keep searching for a permanent job and avoid the risk of getting locked in a "temporary work trap". Note that not all studies find evidence of stepping-stone effects. Zijl et al. (2011[83]) do not find evidence for this except in the case of immigrants, while Autor and Housemann (2010[84]) find that temporary-agency work harms future employment and earnings outcomes.

[16] Another option would be to increase social security contributions for the use of temporary contracts as in, for example, France. This would go in the direction of experience-rating unemployment benefits to the extent that temporary work is associated with higher unemployment.

[17] This could also make it more difficult to implement such reforms since it would impose significant extra costs on public budgets and requires having the capacity to administer such systems effectively. This may be particularly an issue in emerging economies (see Chapter 16).

[18] Tenure-dependent employment protection can be justified on efficiency grounds in the presence of job-specific investments by workers (Boeri, Garibaldi and Moen, 2017[74]).

[19] There is also a risk that it provides too little employment flexibility when a prolonged period of relative stability is followed by a severe economic downturn (OECD, 2014[49]).

[20] Moreover, redistribution is measured in a given year and not over the life-course. This means that the measured extent of redistribution reflects the role of taxes and benefits for stabilising incomes over time (insurance) as well as that for redistribution in terms of life-time incomes.

[21] This does not take account of *in-kind* social transfers. While the primary objective of in-kind social transfers is to provide access to good-quality education and healthcare, they are likely to have significant implications for redistribution given their size and declining importance along the income distribution (OECD, 2011[82]).

[22] However, the relative importance of size and targeting depends crucially on the measure on inequality used, with the role of targeting being more important the more weight is placed on the bottom of the distribution.

[23] Consumption and environmental taxes and excise duties are not taken into account for the purposes of this decomposition.

[24] This is all the more notable since in a context of rising market inequality measured redistribution typically increases, everything else equal.

[25] Countries differ substantially in the relative importance of in-work relative to out-of-work benefits, with many English-speaking countries placing more emphasis on in-work benefits and many Southern European countries on jobless households (OECD, 2009[81]).

[26] A more equal treatment of capital and labour income also would reduce the role of labour market status (e.g. self-employed versus dependent employee) for tax purposes and hence reduce incentives for employers to replace dependent employees with independent contractors.

[27] Wealth is distributed much more unequally than income (OECD, 2015[37]; Balestra and Tonkin, 2018[75]). Policies that limit wealth concentration and help low-income households accumulate wealth can therefore promote inclusiveness and contribute to social mobility across generations. However, revenues from taxes on wealth transfers have been very low and declining, from 1.1% of total tax revenues in 1965 to 0.4% today across the OECD on average (OECD, 2018[76]).

References

Aghion, P. et al. (2017), *Tax Simplicity and Heterogeneous Learning* *, https://scholar.harvard.edu/files/aghion/files/tax_simplicity.pdf (accessed on 02 November 2018). [63]

Akgun, O., B. Cournède and J. Fournier (2017), *The Effects of the Tax Mix on Inequality and Growth*, http://www.oecd.org/eco/workingpapers. (accessed on 02 November 2018). [64]

Alesina, A. and P. Giuliano (2015), "Culture and Institutions", *Journal of Economic Literature*, Vol. 53/4, pp. 898-944, http://dx.doi.org/10.1257/jel.53.4.898. [7]

Autor, D. and S. Houseman (2010), "Do Temporary-Help Jobs Improve Labor Market Outcomes for Low-Skilled Workers? Evidence from "Work First"", *American Economic Journal: Applied Economics*, Vol. 2/3, pp. 96-128, http://dx.doi.org/10.1257/app.2.3.96. [75]

Balestra, C. and R. Tonkin (2018), "Inequalities in household wealth across OECD countries: Evidence from the OECD Wealth Distribution Database", *Statistics and Data Working Paper*, No. 2018/01, OECD, Paris. [66]

Barth, E. and S. Kerr (2017), "The Dynamics of Gender Earnings Differentials: Evidence from Establishment Data*", http://fmwww.bc.edu/EC-P/wp923.pdf. [10]

Bassanini, A. and A. Garnero (2013), "Dismissal protection and worker flows in OECD countries: Evidence from cross-country/cross-industry data", *Labour Economics*, Vol. 21, http://dx.doi.org/10.1016/j.labeco.2012.12.003. [40]

Berlingieri, G., P. Blanchenay and C. Criscuolo (2017), "The great divergence(s)", *OECD Science, Technology and Industry Policy Papers*, No. 39, OECD Publishing, Paris, http://dx.doi.org/10.1787/953f3853-en. [50]

Boeri, T., P. Garibaldi and E. Moen (2017), "Inside severance pay", *Journal of Public Economics*, Vol. 145, pp. 211-225, http://dx.doi.org/10.1016/J.JPUBECO.2016.11.003. [65]

Booth, A., M. Francesconi and J. Frank (2002), "Temporary Jobs: Stepping Stones Or Dead Ends?", *Economic Journal*, Vol. 112/480, pp. 189-213, https://ideas.repec.org/a/ecj/econjl/v112y2002i480pf189-f213.html (accessed on 04 November 2018). [43]

Brys, B. et al. (2016), "Tax Design for Inclusive Economic Growth", *OECD Taxation Working Papers*, No. 26, OECD Publishing, Paris, http://dx.doi.org/10.1787/5jlv74ggk0g7-en. [62]

Cahuc, P., O. Charlot and F. Malherbet (2016), "Explaining the spread of temporary jobs and its impact on labor turnover", *International Economic Review*, Vol. 57/2, pp. 533-572, http://dx.doi.org/10.1111/iere.12167. [39]

Carnevale, A. and J. Strohl (2010), "How Increasing College Access Is Increasing Inequality, and What to Do About It", in Kahlenberg, R. (ed.), *Rewarding Strivers: Helping Low-Income Students Succeed in College*, Century Foundation Books, New York, https://vtechworks.lib.vt.edu/handle/10919/83054. [23]

Case, A., A. Fertig and C. Paxson (2005), "The lasting impact of childhood health and circumstance", *Journal of Health Economics*, Vol. 24/2, pp. 365-389, http://dx.doi.org/10.1016/J.JHEALECO.2004.09.008. [26]

Causa, O. and M. Hermansen (2017), "Income redistribution through taxes and transfers across OECD countries", *OECD Economics Department Working Papers*, No. 1453, OECD Publishing, Paris, http://dx.doi.org/10.1787/bc7569c6-en. [56]

Causa, O., A. Vindics and O. Akgun (2018), "An empirical investigation on the drivers of income redistribution across OECD countries", *OECD Economics Department Working Papers*, No. 1488, OECD Publishing, Paris, http://dx.doi.org/10.1787/5cb47f33-en. [57]

Centeno, M. and Á. Novo (2012), "Excess worker turnover and fixed-term contracts: Causal evidence in a two-tier system", *Labour Economics*, Vol. 19/3, pp. 320-328, http://dx.doi.org/10.1016/J.LABECO.2012.02.006. [42]

Chetty, R. et al. (2017), "Mobility Report Cards: The Role of Colleges in Intergenerational Mobility", No. 23618, NBER, Cambridge, MA, http://dx.doi.org/10.3386/w23618. [24]

Chetty, R. et al. (2015), "The Economic Impact of Tax Expenditures: Evidence from Spatial Variation Across the U.S.", https://www.irs.gov/pub/irs-soi/14rptaxexpenditures.pdf. [70]

Cingano, F. (2014), "Trends in Income Inequality and its Impact on Economic Growth", *OECD Social, Employment and Migration Working Papers*, No. 163, OECD Publishing, Paris, http://dx.doi.org/10.1787/5jxrjncwxv6j-en. [5]

Clark, A., P. Frijters and M. Shields (2008), "Relative Income, Happiness, and Utility: An Explanation for the Easterlin Paradox and Other Puzzles", *Journal of Economic Literature*, Vol. 46/1, pp. 95-144, http://dx.doi.org/10.1257/jel.46.1.95. [3]

Corak, M. (2006), "Do Poor Children Become Poor Adults? Lessons from a Cross-Country Comparison of Generational Earnings Mobility", in Creedy, J. and G. Kalb (eds.), *Research on Economic Inequality, Volume 13, Dynamics of Inequality*, Emerald Publishing, http://dx.doi.org/10.1016/S1049-2585(06)13006-9. [12]

Corak, M. and P. Piraino (2011), "The Intergenerational Transmission of Employers", *Journal of Labor Economics*, Vol. 29/1, pp. 37-68, http://dx.doi.org/10.1086/656371. [15]

de Graaf-Zijl, M., G. van den Berg and A. Heyma (2011), "Stepping stones for the unemployed: the effect of temporary jobs on the duration until (regular) work", *Journal of Population Economics*, Vol. 24/1, pp. 107-139, http://dx.doi.org/10.1007/s00148-009-0287-y. [74]

Devaux, M. and M. de Looper (2012), "Income-Related Inequalities in Health Service Utilisation in 19 OECD Countries, 2008-2009", *OECD Health Working Papers*, No. 58, OECD Publishing, Paris, http://dx.doi.org/10.1787/5k95xd6stnxt-en. [28]

Diez, F., D. Leigh and S. Tambunlertchai (2018), "Global Market Power and its Macroeconomic Implications", *IMF Working Paper*, https://www.imf.org/~/media/Files/Publications/WP/2018/wp18137.ashx. [51]

Duncan, G. and A. Sojourner (2013), "Can Intensive Early Childhood Intervention Programs Eliminate Income-Based Cognitive and Achievement Gaps?", *Journal of Human Resources*, Vol. 48/4, pp. 945-968, http://dx.doi.org/10.3368/jhr.48.4.945. [69]

Filatriau, O., D. Fougère and M. Tô (2013), "Will Sooner Be Better? The Impact of Early Preschool Enrollment on Cognitive and Noncognitive Achievement of Children", *Discussion Paper No. 9480*, No. 9480, Centre for Economic Policy Research, https://cepr.org/active/publications/discussion_papers/dp.php?dpno=9480#. [16]

García-Pérez, J., J. Castelló and I. Marinescu (2018), "Can Fixed-Term Contracts Put Low Skilled Youth on a Better Career Path? Evidence from Spain", *Economic Journal*, https://onlinelibrary.wiley.com/doi/epdf/10.1111/ecoj.12621 (accessed on 12 June 2018). [46]

Garnero, A., A. Hijzen and S. Martin (2019), "More unequal, but more mobile? Earnings inequality and mobility in OECD countries", *Labour Economics*, Vol. 56, pp. 26-35, http://dx.doi.org/10.1016/j.labeco.2018.08.005. [9]

Goldschmidt, D. and J. Schmieder (2017), "The Rise of Domestic Outsourcing and the Evolution of the German Wage Structure", *The Quarterly Journal of Economics*, Vol. 132/3, pp. 1165–1217, https://academic.oup.com/qje/article/132/3/1165/3746069. [53]

Gould, E. and A. Hijzen (2016), "WP/16/176 Growing Apart, Losing Trust? The Impact of Inequality on Social Capital Growing Apart, Losing Trust? The Impact of Inequality on Social Capital", *IMF Working Paper* 16176, https://www.imf.org/external/pubs/ft/wp/2016/wp16176.pdf (accessed on 12 June 2018). [6]

Greenberg, D. and M. Shroder (2004), *The digest of social experiments*, The Urban Institute Press, Washington DC. [25]

Havnes, T. and M. Mogstad (2011), "No Child Left Behind: Subsidized Child Care and Children's Long-Run Outcomes", *American Economic Journal: Economic Policy*, Vol. 3/2, pp. 97-129, http://dx.doi.org/10.1257/POL.3.2.97. [19]

Hijzen, A., L. Mondauto and S. Scarpetta (2017), "The impact of employment protection on temporary employment: Evidence from a regression discontinuity design", *Labour Economics*, Vol. 46, pp. 64-76, http://dx.doi.org/10.1016/j.labeco.2017.01.002. [41]

Ichino, A., F. Mealli and T. Nannicini (2008), "From temporary help jobs to permanent employment: what can we learn from matching estimators and their sensitivity?", *Journal of Applied Econometrics*, Vol. 23/3, pp. 305-327, http://dx.doi.org/10.1002/jae.998. [44]

Immervoll, H., S. Jenkins and S. Königs (2015), "Are Recipients of Social Assistance 'Benefit Dependent'? Concepts, Measurement and Results for Selected Countries", http://ftp.iza.org/dp8786.pdf (accessed on 02 July 2018). [60]

Immervoll, H. and M. Pearson (2009), "A Good Time for Making Work Pay? Taking Stock of In-Work Benefits and Related Measures across the OECD", http://ftp.iza.org/pp3.pdf (accessed on 29 June 2018). [61]

Immervoll, H. and L. Richardson (2011), "Redistribution Policy and Inequality Reduction in OECD Countries: What Has Changed in Two Decades?", *OECD Social, Employment and Migration Working Papers*, No. 122, OECD Publishing, Paris, http://dx.doi.org/10.1787/5kg5dlkhjq0x-en. [55]

Jahn, E. and M. Rosholm (2014), "Looking beyond the bridge: The effect of temporary agency employment on labor market outcomes", *European Economic Review*, Vol. 65, pp. 108-125, http://dx.doi.org/10.1016/j.euroecorev.2013.11.001. [45]

Kahn (2010), "Employment protection reforms, employment and the incidence of temporary jobs in Europe: 1996-2001", *Labour Economics*, Vol. 17/1, pp. 1-15, https://ideas.repec.org/a/eee/labeco/v17y2010i1p1-15.html (accessed on 14 June 2018). [38]

Kis, V. and H. Windisch (2018), "Making skills transparent: Recognising vocational skills acquired through workbased learning", *OECD Education Working Papers*, No. 180, OECD Publishing, Paris, http://dx.doi.org/10.1787/5830c400-en. [34]

Kowalczyk, K. et al. (2016), "„Arbeitsplatzorientierte Alphabetisierung und Grundbildung Erwachsener",", *Evaluation des BMBF-Förderschwerpunkts*, http://www.ramboll.de/management-consulting. [31]

Muñoz-Bullón, F. (2004), "Training Provision and regulaton: An Analysis of the Temporary Help industry", *International Journal of Manpower*, Vol. 25/7, pp. 656-682. [47]

Narayan, A. et al. (2018), *Fair Progress? Economic Mobility across Generations around the World*, World Bank Group, Washington DC, https://openknowledge.worldbank.org/bitstream/handle/10986/28428/211210ov.pdf?sequence=9 (accessed on 05 July 2018). [14]

OECD (2019), *Getting Skills Right: Future-ready adult learning systems*, OECD Publishing, Paris. [32]

OECD (2018), *A Broken Social Elevator? How to Promote Social Mobility*, OECD Publishing, Paris, https://dx.doi.org/10.1787/9789264301085-en. [2]

OECD (2018), *Effective Teacher Policies: Insights from PISA*, PISA, OECD Publishing, Paris, https://dx.doi.org/10.1787/9789264301603-en. [77]

OECD (2018), *OECD Employment Outlook 2018*, OECD Publishing, Paris, http://dx.doi.org/10.1787/empl_outlook-2018-en. [11]

OECD (2018), *Skills Strategy Implementation Guidance for Portugal: Strengthening the Adult-Learning System*, OECD Skills Studies, OECD Publishing, Paris, http://dx.doi.org/10.1787/9789264298705-en. [33]

OECD (2018), *The Framework for Policy Action on Inclusive Growth*, https://one.oecd.org/document/C/MIN(2018)5/en/pdf (accessed on 25 September 2018). [1]

OECD (2018), *The Role and Design of Net Wealth Taxes in the OECD*, OECD Tax Policy Studies, No. 26, OECD Publishing, Paris, http://dx.doi.org/10.1787/9789264290303-en. [67]

OECD (2017), *Financial Incentives for Steering Education and Training*, Getting Skills Right, OECD Publishing, Paris, http://dx.doi.org/10.1787/9789264272415-en. [35]

OECD (2017), *Obesity Update 2017*, http://www.oecd.org/health/obesity-update.htm. [27]

OECD (2016), *Investing in Youth: Australia*, Investing in Youth, OECD Publishing, Paris, http://dx.doi.org/10.1787/9789264257498-en. [71]

OECD (2016), *Making Cities Work for All: Data and Actions for Inclusive Growth*, OECD Publishing, Paris, http://dx.doi.org/10.1787/9789264263260-en. [68]

OECD (2016), *OECD Employment Outlook 2016*, OECD Publishing, Paris, http://dx.doi.org/10.1787/empl_outlook-2016-en. [20]

OECD (2016), "Society at a Glance 2016 OECD SOCial inDiCatOrS a spotlight on youth", http://pac-files.oecd.org/acrobatebook/8116131e.pdf (accessed on 02 July 2018). [58]

OECD (2016), *Society at a Glance 2016: OECD Social Indicators*, OECD Publishing, Paris, http://dx.doi.org/10.1787/9789264261488-en. [13]

OECD (2016), *The Future of Productivity*, https://doi.org/10.1787/9789264248533-en. [52]

OECD (2015), *Health at a Glance 2015: OECD Indicators.*, OECD Publishing, Paris, https://doi.org/10.1787/19991312. [29]

OECD (2015), *In It Together: Why Less Inequality Benefits All*, OECD Publishing, Paris, http://dx.doi.org/10.1787/9789264235120-en. [36]

OECD (2015), "The quality of working lives: Earnings mobility, labour market risk and long-term inequality", in *OECD Employment Outlook 2015*, OECD Publishing, Paris, https://dx.doi.org/10.1787/empl_outlook-2015-8-en. [8]

OECD (2014), "How good is your job? Measuring and assessing job quality", in *OECD Employment Outlook 2014*, OECD Publishing, Paris, http://dx.doi.org/10.1787/empl_outlook-2014-6-en. [4]

OECD (2014), *Non-regular employment, job security and the labour market divide*, https://www.oecd-ilibrary.org/docserver/empl_outlook-2014-7-en.pdf?expires=1541325804&id=id&accname=ocid84004878&checksum=519CFDAA792DD22D44A442BA1BE4A6B7 (accessed on 04 November 2018). [76]

OECD (2013), *The 2012 Labour Market Reform in Spain: A Preliminary Assessment*, https://www.oecd.org/els/emp/SpainLabourMarketReform-Report.pdf (accessed on 04 November 2018). [48]

OECD (2013), *The OECD Action Plan for Youth: Giving youth a better start in the labour market*, https://www.oecd.org/newsroom/Action-plan-youth.pdf. [22]

OECD (2012), *Equity and Quality in Education: Supporting Disadvantaged Students and Schools*, OECD Publishing, Paris, http://dx.doi.org/10.1787/9789264130852-en. [21]

OECD (2011), *Divided We Stand: Why Inequality Keeps Rising*, OECD Publishing, Paris, http://dx.doi.org/10.1787/9789264119536-en. [73]

OECD (2011), *OECD Employment Outlook 2011 Income Support for the Unemployed: How Well Has the Safety-Net Held Up During the "Great Recession"?*, http://www.oecd.org/els/emp/EMO%202011%20Chap%201%20ENG.pdf (accessed on 02 November 2018). [59]

OECD (2009), "Is Work the Best Antidote to Poverty?", *Employment Outlook*, https://www.oecd.org/els/emp/45219514.pdf (accessed on 29 June 2018). [72]

Ruhm, C. and J. Waldfogel (2012), "Long-term effects of early childhood care and education", *Nordic Economic Policy Review*, Vol. 1/2012, pp. 23-51, http://dx.doi.org/10.6027/TN2012-544. [18]

Song, J. et al. (forthcoming), "Firming Up Inequality", *The Quarterly Journal of Economics*, https://fguvenendotcom.files.wordpress.com/2018/09/fui_qje_accepted.pdf (accessed on 04 November 2018). [49]

Van Huizen, T. and J. Plantenga (2015), "Universal Child Care and Children's Outcomes: A Meta-Analysis of Evidence from Natural Experiments", *U.S.E. Discussion Paper Series*, No. 15-13, Utrecht University School of Economics, https://www.uu.nl/sites/default/files/rebo_use_dp_2015_15-13.pdf (accessed on 26 June 2018). [17]

Venn, D. (2011), "Earnings Volatility and its Consequences for Households", *OECD Social, Employment and Migration Working Papers*, No. 125, OECD Publishing, Paris, http://dx.doi.org/10.1787/5kg3v00zgslw-en. [37]

Weil, D. (2004), *The fissured workplace : why work became so bad for so many and what can be done to improve it*. [54]

Windisch, H. (2015), "Adults with low literacy and numeracy skills: A literature review on policy intervention", *OECD Education Working Papers*, No. 123, OECD Publishing, Paris, http://dx.doi.org/10.1787/5jrxnjdd3r5k-en. [30]

Chapter 11. Enhancing the prospects of disadvantaged workers in the labour market

Employment and job vacancies are high in many OECD countries. However, some people tend to find it more difficult than others to be hired. This chapter focuses on those population groups (low-skilled young people, persons with care responsibilities, migrants, persons with disabilities and older workers) facing disadvantages in the labour market and on policies that could help improve their situation. The right policies are often different from one group to another, but several common lessons can be drawn. First, the participation of disadvantaged workers in the labour market can be enhanced by making policy support more employment-oriented. Second, early intervention is usually better than costly interventions at a late stage. Third, policies to reduce discrimination in hiring and retaining of workers are important. And fourth, a coherent set of policies, not only a single policy, is needed to deliver broad progress.

Introduction

Fostering social cohesion and inclusive growth requires a labour market that provides access and equal opportunities to all and leaves no-one behind. Yet, labour market inequalities have been widening, with persistent difficulties to participate fully in the labour market for some groups and large disparities in pay, working conditions and career prospects.

Governments use a wide range of labour market and other policies that influence the performance of labour markets. This chapter focuses on specific policies aimed at helping people with disadvantages in the labour market. While general policies also affect disadvantaged groups, additional support that targets them may, or in some cases may not, be warranted.

This chapter defines five groups of workers as disadvantaged in the labour market because, in most countries, they have comparatively low employment rates. Low employment rates often go hand-in-hand with social exclusion and low levels of well-being.

The five groups are:

- low-skilled young people
- people with care responsibilities
- migrants
- people with disabilities
- older workers.

The employment rates of each of these five groups are lower than for prime-age men in almost every country of the OECD (Figure 11.1). On average, the employment gap (i.e. the difference between the employment rate of prime-age men and that of the group, as a per cent of the employment rate of prime-age men) is 9% for youth not in education and training,[1] 22% for mothers with young children, 23% for migrants, 45% for people with disabilities and 32% for workers aged 55-64.

Over the past ten years, employment gaps for disadvantaged workers have declined on average, but many people who could work remain jobless. The sheer size of the current employment gaps and their differences across countries suggest that further policy action has the potential to improve the labour market performance of these workers.

As the policy challenges are often specific to a group of disadvantaged workers, the chapter discusses the issues group by group: low-skilled young people (Section 11.1); persons with care responsibilities (Section 11.2); migrants (Section 11.3); persons with disabilities (Section 11.4); and older workers (Section 11.5). The conclusion draws common lessons for policy design to enhance the economic prospects of disadvantaged workers.

As will become clear in the chapter, policy considerations often overlap, especially when workers cumulate several disadvantages, as is the case for low-skilled young migrants or older persons with partial work capacity. Commonly, it is also different members of the same family who encounter disadvantages at the same time, for example when young parents have children with difficulties at school. People's lives can rarely be classified neatly into simple categories, and a major challenge is to make policy responsive to the actual, often multiple, problems that people face. The focus must be on matching help to the needs of people, not matching people to the schemes that providers are offering.

Figure 11.1. Employment gaps for disadvantaged groups with respect to prime-age men

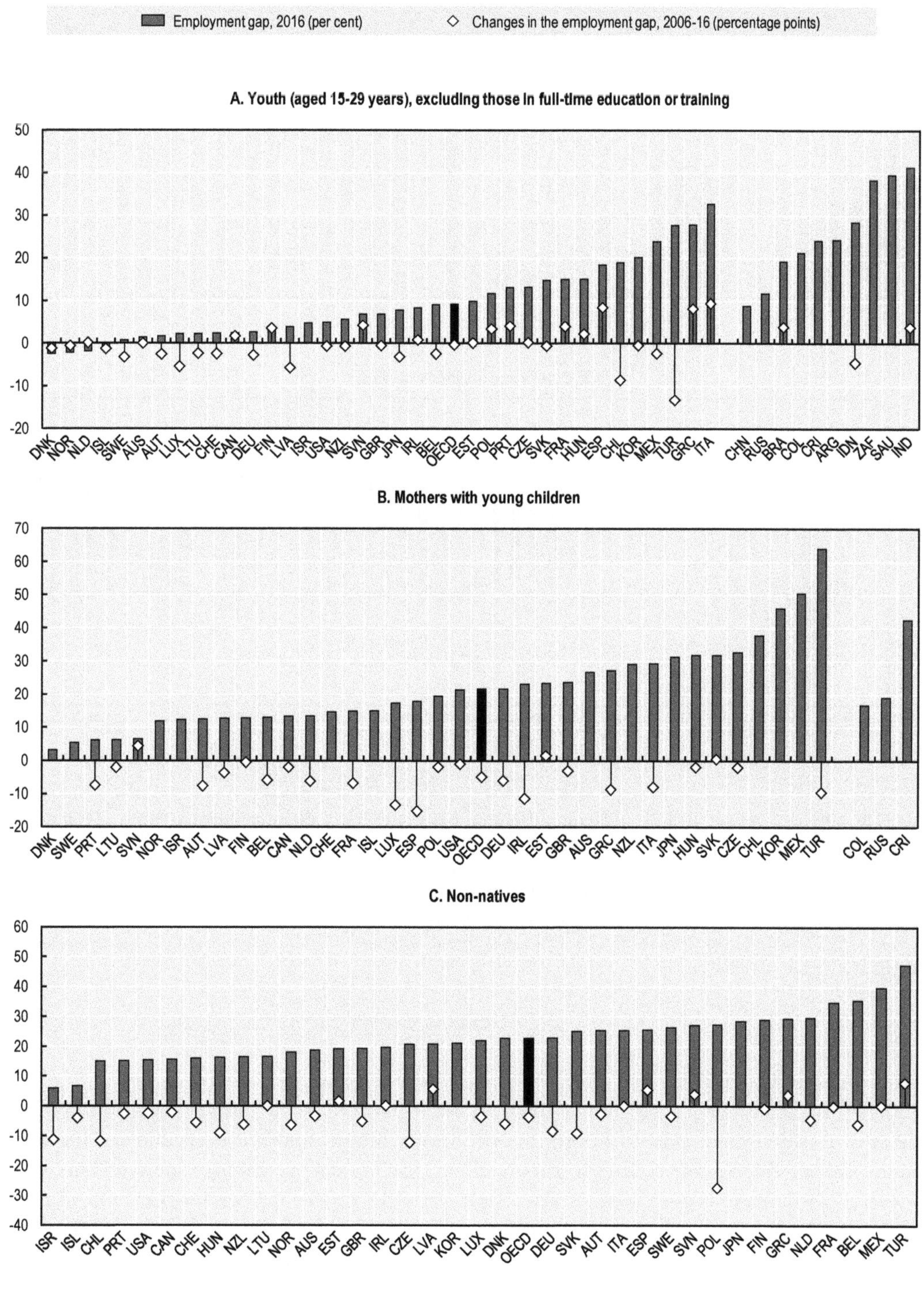

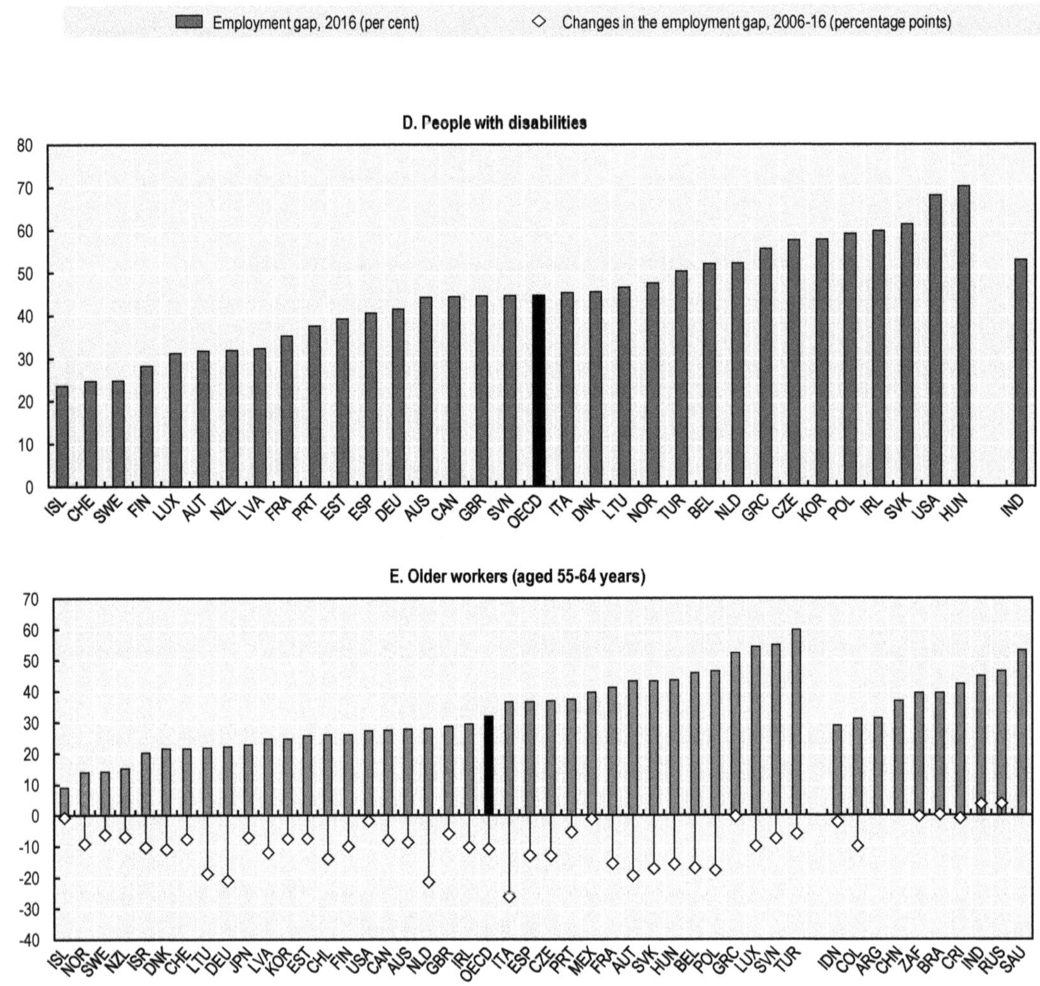

Note: The employment gap is defined as the difference between the employment rate of prime-age men (aged 25-54 years) and that of the group, expressed as a percentage of the employment rate of prime-age men. "Mothers with young children" refers to working-age mothers with at least one child aged 0-14 years. "Non-natives" refers to all foreign-born people with no regards to nationality. Data on changes in the employment gap are not available for people with disabilities.

Source: OECD calculations based on OECD Employment database, OECD International Migration database and OECD Family database.

StatLink http://dx.doi.org/10.1787/888933881496

11.1. Young people with low skills

The successful engagement of young people in the labour market is crucial for their own economic prospects and well-being as well as for overall economic growth and social cohesion. However, low-skilled youth often struggle in the labour market. On average, the unemployment risk of 25-34-year-olds with below upper-secondary education is more than twice that of people of the same age who completed tertiary education (Figure 11.2). A few countries, in particular Colombia and Mexico, show the reverse pattern, but this is because there low-skilled youth tend to live in very poor households and have to work to survive given limited, if not inexistent, social assistance. A disproportionate number of young people with low educational attainment lost their job during the Great Recession. Their employment rates remain below their level before the crisis in the majority of OECD countries, while employment rates of young people with tertiary education are higher today than a decade ago (OECD, 2017[1]).

Beyond educational attainment, it is also the type of skills acquired and the proficiency in these skills that influence the probability of finding a job and how much it pays (OECD, 2014[2]). Young people with weak foundation skills – in literacy and numeracy – are more likely to be neither in employment nor in education or training (NEET). Moreover, evidence suggests that youth unemployment can have serious negative effects on earnings and employment opportunities even 20 years later (Schmillen and Umkehrer, 2017[3]). Prolonged periods without a job may lead young people into crime and reduce their civic engagement as well as their trust in society and other citizens, with large long-term consequences for social inclusion (Carcillo et al., 2015[4]).

Figure 11.2. Low-skilled young people are more likely to be unemployed

Unemployment rate of 25-34-year-olds by educational attainment, 2016

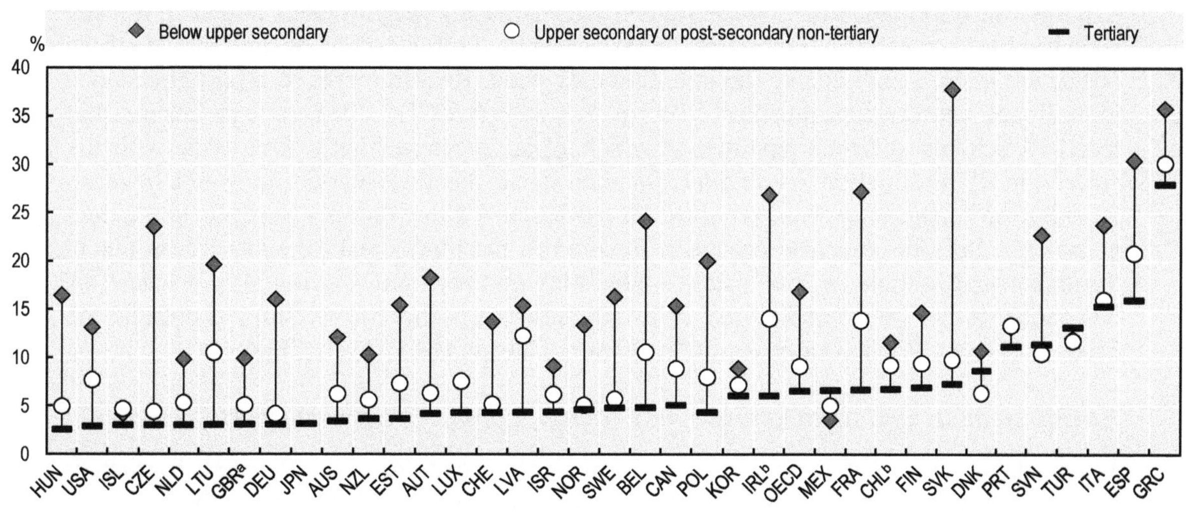

a) Data for upper-secondary attainment include completion of a sufficient volume and standard of programmes that would be classified as completion of intermediate upper-secondary programmes.
b) Year of reference differs from 2016.
Source: OECD (2017[1]), *Education at a Glance 2017: OECD Indicators,* http://dx.doi.org/10.1787/eag-2017-en.

StatLink http://dx.doi.org/10.1787/888933881515

The stark contrast in labour market outcomes between skilled and unskilled youth may increase in the future in the context of further rising levels of educational attainment and a growing demand for skills, unless policy responds to the challenge (see Chapter 14). Many of the jobs destroyed during the crisis are gone for good. It is thus essential that all young people are equipped with good foundation skills that will enable them to create and seize economic opportunities and learn new skills.

Fighting early school leaving is essential

According to the OECD Programme for International Student Assessment (PISA), almost one-in-five students does not reach the basic level of skills that is considered to be needed to function in today's societies. Students from low socio-economic backgrounds are twice as likely to be weak performers, indicating that social circumstances affect personal outcomes and are obstacles to achieving educational potential.

Failure to get an upper-secondary qualification is a major disadvantage in future life. To reduce the number of young people who leave school without an upper-secondary qualification, policies need to ensure that signs of disengagement are detected early and young people at risk of dropping out of school receive the support they need to complete their education.

Systematic monitoring of school performance helps identify at-risk youth

Strategies intervening at an early stage hold the best promise of keeping at-risk students in education. In most cases, dropping out of school is not a sudden, unexpected event, but the consequence of a longer process of gradual disengagement (Lyche, 2010[5]).

Schools can systematically monitor student attendance and performance and keep the key stakeholders – notably parents and social services – informed to ensure that troubled pupils are tracked and receive the attention they need. Requirements to report attendance to national education authorities, like in Norway (OECD, 2018[6]), can ensure that teachers, schools and municipalities take school absences seriously. One issue with the collection of information on regular attendance can be that schools may not have an incentive to report drop-outs promptly, in particular if their funding depends on student enrolment. Specific attention has to be devoted to the higher risk of school drop-out in disadvantaged schools by, for instance, attracting and retaining high-quality teachers, as has happened in Finland and Korea, or by strengthening school leadership, as through the Student Success Teacher programme in Ontario, Canada (OECD, 2012[7]).

At-risk students and their families may require comprehensive support

When absenteeism and poor school performance are caused, or aggravated, by factors beyond education (such as family problems, health concerns or drug abuse), these need to be addressed too.

If specialised support staff are in place in schools, they can quickly identify and address the challenges that a troubled young person may face. Trained psychologists or social workers can be an important first point of contact for students, parents and teachers when problems arise. Where schools lack the resources for such specialised staff, designated teachers with the appropriate training can help. Support networks outside schools (such as social, health or public employment services or non-governmental organisations) play an important role to address more severe and long-lasting problems that schools are incapable of dealing with on their own – see, for example, the headspace centres in Australia (OECD, 2015[8]) or the Educational Territories of Priority Intervention programme in Portugal (OECD, 2016[9]).

Vocational education and training can help smooth school-to-work transitions

Vocational education and training (VET) plays a dual role: it enables young people to develop a mix of general and job-specific skills and directly responds to the skill needs of the labour market. In a number of OECD countries, however, VET policies are often overshadowed by a stronger focus on academic education. Students and the general public tend to view VET as comparatively low status. Improvements to the quality of VET will be crucial to combat its negative image and achieve better outcomes for people transitioning from school to work.

Apprenticeships are an ideal way of providing relevant practical training

Apprenticeship programmes, where students combine classroom learning with practical training with an employer, typically for a period of several years, are often regarded as a good way of supporting young people who do not want to continue with formal education. Empirical research suggests that apprenticeships yield positive returns in terms of wages and job stability (Carcillo et al., 2015[4]). Learning in the workplace also allows young people to develop both "hard" skills on modern equipment and "soft" skills (such as teamwork, communication or negotiation skills) through real-world experience. Countries with a long tradition of apprenticeships are Austria, Germany and Switzerland.

In many OECD countries, the main challenge is not with the provision of quality training, but with the insufficient number of apprenticeship places offered by firms. The involvement of social partners in drawing up curricula is important to ensure that training meets the employers' needs. However, the financial burden in terms of wage and non-wage costs deters some companies from taking on apprentices. Accordingly, a number of countries have introduced financial incentives to make it more attractive for employers to create apprenticeship places. Australia and the United Kingdom, for example, directly subsidise employers taking apprentices; Canada and France grant tax credits. A number of countries have introduced a special sub-minimum wage for apprentices (OECD, 2016[9]).

Pre-apprenticeship programmes and career guidance play important roles

At-risk youth may lack the motivation and skills to find a position for an apprenticeship or, if they find one, to succeed in the programme; non-completion rates are high among apprentices in many countries (OECD, 2014[10]). At the same time, there is evidence that the least educated youth are also those who benefit the most from apprenticeship programmes (Céreq, 2011[11]). Some countries, including Austria and Germany, have created pre-apprenticeship programmes for disadvantaged youth who cannot find an employer. These programmes can prepare young people for VET programmes, by improving their skills, building motivation, familiarising them with work routine and giving them short spells of work experience.

Quality career guidance can boost education and training completion rates by improving the match between young people and their chosen path (OECD, 2016[9]). It can strengthen social mobility by informing young people of career paths that their family and social networks may not suggest and encourage them to choose careers that are more likely to see strong labour demand. Good practices in Finland illustrate that career guidance is of particular importance for young people considering VET programmes, including apprenticeships, as these affect career prospects more directly than general secondary education programmes (OECD, forthcoming[12]).

Activating unemployed and inactive youth

Public employment services play a key role in supporting unemployed and inactive young workers who have few skills and difficulty finding a job. For youth who have become marginalised, more specific outreach policies in collaboration with other youth services are important (OECD, 2010[13]). The appropriate intervention depends on the individual's employment barriers. Extensive profiling helps ensure that young people receive the type and intensity of support they need and that resources are spent effectively.

Activation programmes mix a range of interventions

In many countries, "education first" is the approach for early school-leavers who otherwise have little chance of finding quality employment. Social or public employment services work with the educational authorities to re-integrate them in mainstream schooling. Some countries, including Australia and Denmark, even tie eligibility for income support to a return to education (OECD, 2016[9]).

Comprehensive, full-time, second-chance educational programmes can be a suitable alternative for early school-leavers who are unable or unwilling to return to a standard school. Second-chance programmes, like the US Job Corps programme, combine catch-up courses in foundation skills, vocational classes, counselling and career guidance and often lead to an upper-secondary qualification. They have been shown to reduce benefit dependency and criminal activity and raise earnings in the long term (Schochet, Burghardt and McConnell, 2006[14]; Cohen and Piquero, 2015[15]). But such programmes should be well-targeted as they tend to be costly, requiring well-trained and highly motivated staff capable of providing intensive support and supervision.

Work experience programmes or short training courses with a strong practical component may be attractive policy options for the most disadvantaged youth. They can help regain self-esteem, build a work routine and prepare for later participation in education or training programmes. Even when such programmes do not improve employment prospects in the regular labour market (Kluve et al., 2016[16]; Card, Kluve and Weber, 2017[17]), they can be used to address social or health issues of disadvantaged youth.

Hiring subsidies for businesses have proven to be effective to improve young jobseekers' employment prospects. However, such subsidies should only target low-skilled, long-term unemployed jobseekers to reduce "deadweight", i.e. the risk that employers pocket the subsidy to recruit jobseekers whom they would have hired in any case (Cahuc, Carcillo and Zylberberg, 2014[18]).

Low-cost, low-intensity interventions, such as job-search assistance, counselling and short training courses (in resume writing and interview techniques), can be sufficient for youth with low barriers to labour market entry. They may also be useful for testing a young person's readiness for participating in more intensive activities.

Support for at-risk youth is often difficult to co-ordinate

Comprehensive support for young people with multiple barriers often requires different actors to work together, based on good policy co-ordination and cross-communication (OECD, 2015[19]). Common databases with client information accessible to government services at all levels can help, but they are frequently unavailable, due to privacy concerns or for political reasons.

Interesting policy initiatives to better co-ordinate support policies for young people exist in several OECD countries. Australia set up regional "partnership brokers" to strengthen local connections between schools, businesses, community groups and families (OECD, 2016[20]), Finland created one-stop shops (*Ohjaamos*) for different youth services (OECD, forthcoming[12]), and Norway integrated a range of different social and employment services under the umbrella of the Labour and Welfare Administration (OECD, 2018[6]).

11.2. People with care responsibilities

Care responsibilities can have a profound effect on the labour market situation of many workers. Although people with care responsibilities include both men and women, they tend more frequently to be women. Differences in the employment patterns of men and women emerge when they start a family or, typically later in life, care for partners or elderly parents. For example, compared with childless women, mothers tend to work fewer hours, earn less than men and more frequently stop working altogether. Overall, the labour market careers of women are disproportionately hampered by care responsibilities (OECD, 2012[21]; OECD, 2017[22]; OECD, 2018[23]).

Across the OECD, the gender gap in the employment rate of childless men and women is relatively small at 5 percentage points, but this gap grows to 23 percentage points when comparing men and women who have at least one child below age 14 (OECD, 2017[22]). In some instances, the reduction in paid work by mothers reflects choice and a preference for spending time with their children. Traditional attitudes towards women's work and family roles continue to play a role: on average across the OECD, almost two-thirds of all women think that mothers with young children should work, but mostly on a part-time basis (OECD, 2016[24]).

In many cases, however, people with care responsibilities do not choose to sacrifice paid work, but are constrained to do so. Finding affordable quality childcare or out-of-school-hours care may be a challenge, especially for low-income mothers with young children; access to paid leave benefits to care for children or dependants may not be available; and workplace measures are sometimes insufficiently flexible. Addressing barriers to combine work and care responsibilities will facilitate the pursuit of individual labour market aspirations and foster a more efficient use of the talent available in labour markets and society (OECD, 2007[25]).

Ensuring access to early childhood education and care

Since childcare commitments tend to affect the labour market behaviour of mothers more than that of fathers, early childhood education and care (ECEC) services are especially important for women's labour market opportunities. Investments in high-quality ECEC services also serve wider policy objectives, as participation in high-quality ECEC fosters cognitive and social development, particularly for children from disadvantaged backgrounds (OECD, 2013[26]; Havnes and Mogstad, 2015[27]; García et al., 2017[28]).

Subsidising ECEC is necessary to ensure that all parents have access to affordable care. All OECD governments help fund ECEC, spending 0.7% of GDP on average and more than 1% of GDP in the Nordic countries and France. These differences in the financial support for ECEC, together with differences in parental leave and attitudes towards non-parental care for young children, contribute to cross-country differences in the participation in ECEC services (Figure 11.3).

One in three children below age 3 participates in formal ECEC on average across OECD countries. Participation is highest in Denmark and Iceland and lowest in several Central and Eastern European countries, where lengthy parental leave entitlements often encourage parents to stay at home until their children enter pre-primary education. It is generally much higher among children aged 3-5; in most OECD countries more than 80% participate. Pre-primary education is frequently offered to all children as a statutory right from the age of 3, or participation is compulsory for one or two years before primary school. ECEC services for 3-5-year-olds are often heavily subsidised or even free.

Childcare costs are high for parents, reaching an average of 13% of the disposable income of a typical dual-earner couple with two children (OECD, 2017[22]). These high costs weaken incentives to work for second earners and single parents (Box 11.1), especially those with low potential earnings. Hence, children in low-income families make comparatively little use of ECEC services, even though the evidence suggests that they stand to gain the most in cognitive terms (OECD, 2016[29]). Lowering effective tax rates on working – by reducing childcare costs for low-income families or tax burdens on second earners or single parents – would encourage low-earning mothers with young children to work and increase the use of ECEC services.

Childcare issues continue when children enter pre-primary or primary school. Opening hours of schools are frequently not compatible with a full-time working week and school holidays are usually longer than annual leave entitlements for employees. Thus, working families with school-age children often need to find additional care solutions. Out-of-school-hours (OSH) services are well-developed in some countries: in Denmark, France, Hungary, Slovenia and Sweden, more than half of children aged 6-11 use OSH services during a typical week. National guidelines can provide local authorities with ideas on the type of activities to be offered, the qualifications needed for staff and carers and the structure of fees.

Figure 11.3. Participation in early childhood education and care services

Participation rates for 0-2-year-olds and 3-5-year-olds, 2014 or latest available year

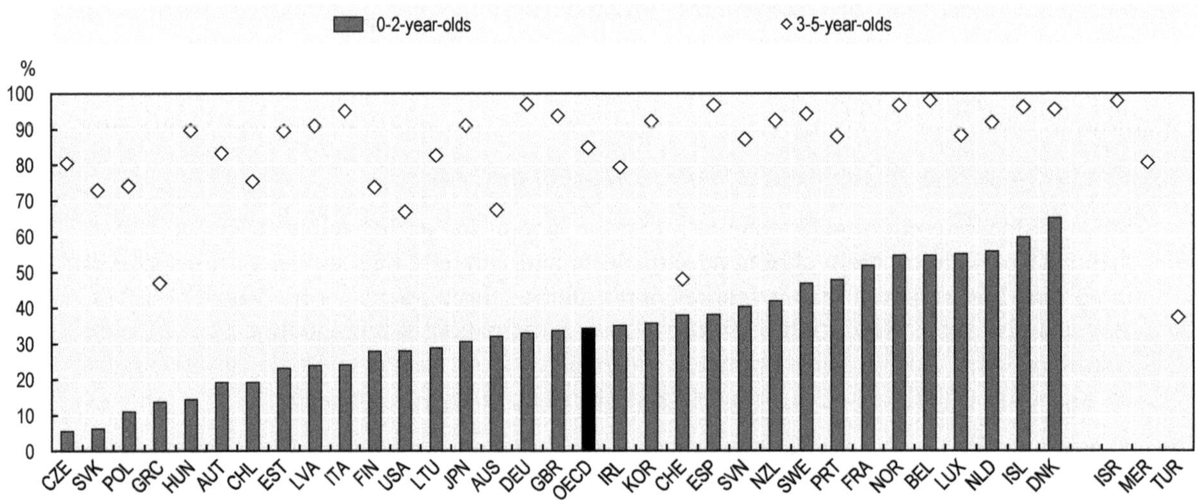

Note: Subject to some variation across countries, early childhood education and care (ECEC) services for 0-2-year-olds include centre-based services (e.g. nurseries or day-care centres and pre-schools, both public and private), organised family day-care and care services provided by (paid) professional childminders. ECEC services for 3-5-year-olds include pre-primary education and primary education.
Source: OECD Family Database, http://www.oecd.org/els/family/database.htm.

StatLink http://dx.doi.org/10.1787/888933881534

Towards a better sharing of unpaid work among parents

Women tend to do more unpaid work, including care work, than men. A disproportionate responsibility for unpaid work limits women's opportunities to enter and progress in the labour market. A comparison of countries suggests that more women participate in paid work when their male partners take on more housework. For example, gender gaps in unpaid work are smaller than one hour per day in Norway and Sweden, two countries that also have high full-time employment rates for women (OECD, 2018[30]).

Couples tend to be fairly egalitarian in their division of (unpaid) household labour before children are born, but with children women take on more unpaid work than men (OECD, 2017[31]). Fathers' leave, when taken around childbirth, can help correct this imbalance: fathers who take such leave are more likely to have an active role in childcare both early on and after they return to work (Huerta et al., 2013[32]). Fathers' leave is also good for women's labour market outcomes, since it helps reduce gender discrimination in the workplace and make it less likely that only women take care-related leave or part-time jobs (Rønsen and Kitterød, 2015[33]).

Attitudes also likely play a role. Nordic men, for instance, appear more gender-egalitarian in their opinion and behaviour than other men. More individuals believe that parental leave should be split equally between men and women in the Nordic countries than in all other OECD countries except France and Germany (OECD, 2017[31]). Fathers with a child of pre-school age want their partners to work about 35 hours per week in Finland and Sweden, while this is just 20-25 hours per week in "part-time work countries", including Germany, the Netherlands and the United Kingdom.

To encourage take-up of parental leave among men, a number of OECD countries have introduced individual parental entitlements to paid leave periods (Adema, Clarke and Frey, 2015[34]). Most common are "mummy and daddy quotas" in which specific portions of an overall parental leave period are reserved exclusively for each parent. Other options include "bonus periods", where a couple may qualify for some extra weeks of paid leave if both parents use a certain amount of shareable leave, and the provision of paid parental leave as an individual entitlement for each parent right from birth.

Box 11.1. Helping single parents match work and care commitments

The work-life balance issues for single parents – often mothers – are challenging as they have no partner with whom to share daily care responsibilities for children. At the same time, employment participation of single parents is often crucial to limit poverty risks for them and their children. It is thus important to address care and employment barriers for single parents simultaneously, in particular in light of their increasing numbers (OECD, 2011[35]).

In the Nordic countries, the overall policy stance is to provide the necessary support and facilitate labour market participation for all parents, regardless of their partnership status. Public policy provides a continuum of support to all parents with young children, especially during the pre-teen years (OECD, 2018[30]): paid parental leave is followed by the provision of affordable ECEC and OSH services during primary school. Persons without a job are expected to use the available employment services and actively engage in job search, and the tax-and-benefit system provides parents with broadly the same financial incentives to work as others.

In some other OECD countries, tax-and-benefit policies provide income support to single parents without expecting them to seek employment until their youngest child goes to secondary school and sometimes even later (OECD, 2007[25]). This was the policy stance in, for example, Australia, Ireland, New Zealand and the United Kingdom, until reforms over the past ten years introduced an expectation for parents on income support to look for work and strengthen their self-sufficiency.

Since the reform in the United Kingdom, single parents are expected to seek employment when they have a child aged 3 or over. The employment rate of single parents has increased from 57% in 2007 to 68% in 2017 (Rabindrakumar, 2018[36]), and poverty rates among single-parent families have fallen from 30% in 2007 to 22% in 2015. However, many single parents in work are trapped in low-paying jobs close to the poverty line, a situation that is often compounded by high childcare costs and little control over working hours to help reconcile work and care responsibilities. Furthermore, some single parents on income support moved to health-related benefits or were "disconnected" from work or benefit support, especially if they did not have a strong history of labour market attachment or a demonstrated skill set (Avram, Brewer and Salvatori, 2018[37]). To avoid such "disconnect" and associated poverty risks, it is crucial for policy to provide ample childcare support and effective training and skills policies and make integration in quality employment a reality for many single parents (OECD, 2011[38]; Ahn, 2015[39]).

Caring for elderly relatives

Care commitments for children are not the only source of work-family tensions. A rising number of older people require long-term care and – although formal care systems exist – many of those providing such care are informal carers, mainly family and friends (OECD, 2017[40]). Some of those caring for elderly relatives are likely to already have their own family care commitments as well as jobs, which is why they are sometimes referred to as the "sandwich generation".

Many older people who need elderly care services prefer to stay in their own homes as long as possible, retain their independence and remain part of their local community. While home care can lead to better outcomes for the elderly, it also means that informal carers, such as partners or adult children, take on an important role. It is hence important to enable workers to take time off for caregiving. Employees in most OECD countries are often entitled to flexible working hours or family-caregiver leave, although such arrangements are often short or apply only in case of very serious illness. Ensuring that workers can use them for a wide spectrum of caregiving situations and at short notice is important, as the needs they are designed to meet are often unpredictable.

Greater control over working hours

Flexible working arrangements cover a variety of practices that can improve efficiency of production processes and help workers make their work schedules fit better with care commitments. Measures include reduced working hours, flexible start and finishing times as well as more advanced options, such as the opportunity to work "compressed" weeks or telework from home. Flexible working arrangements can act as a complement to other parental support, for example by allowing parents to match working hours with childcare opening hours, but are particularly important when other support is underdeveloped.

On average across European countries, only 30-35% of employed parents report to have at least some control over their working time, with this proportion being highest in Denmark, Finland, the Netherlands, Norway and Sweden. Regular part-time work is the most common form of flexible working (OECD, 2016[41]).

Several OECD countries guarantee working parents access to at least some form of flexible working. Parents of young children have the option to work part-time, either through a statutory right to request reduced hours when children are young (in Austria, Finland, Slovenia and Sweden) or the possibility to take statutory parental leave part-time (in Denmark, Iceland, Korea and Poland). The Netherlands and the United Kingdom have introduced legislation that gives all workers (subject to firm size or contract history) a comprehensive statutory right to request changes to hours as well as other forms of flexible working, including the location of work. Nevertheless, the prevalence of part-time work in both countries also contributes to the persistence of gender pay gaps and limiting female career opportunities (OECD, 2012[21]).

11.3. Migrants

One-in-eight persons in the OECD was born abroad. Skills and labour market prospects vary widely among immigrants. Some are highly qualified, while others face difficulties in finding employment that pays a decent salary, which may be due to language barriers, no recognition of education degrees, discrimination and a lack of basic skills or relevant work experience. Getting policy right is important for helping these immigrants integrate in the labour market of their host country.

Given the diversity of the immigrant population, a range of policies matter. For those migrants who come with relatively high skills, the objective should be to make the most of their skills. For those migrants who are especially vulnerable, for example because they come for humanitarian reasons, the policy challenges are much broader and particularly acute. The first part of the section focuses on making the most of the skills of migrants and the second on addressing the needs of vulnerable migrants.

Making the most of the skills of migrants

Building host-country language skills is critical for successful integration

Evidence clearly suggests that some proficiency in the host-country language is an essential prerequisite for the social and labour market integration of migrants (OECD, 2018[42]). Poor knowledge of the host-country language can be self-perpetuating, since both networks and employment are important routes through which language skills can be built. Language proficiency is also a key ingredient for the acquisition of new skills relevant in the host-country labour market and the transferability of existing skills.

One tool which has proven effective in enhancing the efficiency of language acquisition is the combination of language instruction with vocational training. This helps build work-related language skills while gathering work experience in the host country. Australia pioneered on-the-job language training and co-funding of employer-based training, offering courses that entitle migrants to up to 200 hours of vocation-specific language tuition and 80 hours of work placements (OECD, 2016[43]).

Recognition of qualifications can help migrants better use their skills

Education acquired outside the OECD tends to be strongly discounted in the host-country labour market, often resulting in people being over-qualified for the work they do. This problem can, in part, be ascribed to the different quality of education systems in the origin and host countries and employer uncertainty regarding the value of the qualifications obtained abroad.

Integration policy can play an important role by providing an infrastructure that formally recognises and validates the value of foreign qualifications (OECD, 2017[44]). However, to be successful the outcomes of such procedures need to be accepted among employers. Sweden is one of the countries that have recently made progress in improving recognition processes. Programmes map and validate the skills of participants in their mother tongue, while at the same time offering language tuition alongside these activities (OECD, 2016[43]).

Beyond the recognition of formal qualifications, recognition of prior learning – which documents non-formal competences – may be particularly important for migrants who have acquired their job-related skills in a different context. Recognition of prior learning can also provide a quick and cost-effective way to identify individual needs for further training and prevent the duplication of training content. Finland's competence-based qualification system, for example, recognises vocational competencies, regardless of whether the person acquired them through work experience, studies or other activities. Employers understand the qualifications, as they can be obtained in the formal education system (OECD, 2018[45]).

Local labour market contact enables migrants to demonstrate their skills

Newly-arrived migrants often have little or no local labour market experience. This puts them at a disadvantage when it comes to demonstrating their suitability for a position. As a result, temporary apprenticeship or training programmes, that provide an opportunity to demonstrate skills, can be an important stepping stone into employment. This opportunity is likely to be especially valuable to migrants for whom information asymmetries due to unfamiliar qualifications tend to be larger.

For instance, Swedish employers hiring newly-arrived refugees can benefit from several subsidised employment schemes which have the objective of providing migrants with local labour market experience. Among these, "Step-in Jobs" is targeted particularly at newly-arrived humanitarian migrants. The programme, which provides a subsidy covering 80% of wage costs, is intended to ease transition into regular employment through building skills and experience. Requirements of the programme are that participants undertake language training alongside their work and that the employment contains an element of mentorship (OECD, 2016[43]).

Discrimination needs to be overcome to improve migrants' labour market access

Discrimination may also undermine the ability of the foreign-born to find work and put their skills to use. It occurs when employers prefer to hire candidates of a particular origin. Empirical studies which try to isolate the effect of discrimination on hiring from other factors suggest that, in many countries, migrants must send twice as many applications to be invited for a job interview than native-born people with an equivalent curriculum vitae (OECD, 2013[46]).

Most OECD countries have taken measures to combat discrimination. However, tackling discrimination through the courts can be a challenge, as past experience has proven. Anti-discrimination policy itself appears to raise awareness but not to reduce discrimination. Hence, besides anti-discrimination policy, several countries – including Belgium, France and the Netherlands – have introduced policies to incentivise diversity and harness corporate social responsibility. In addition, innovative recruitment methods, that for example simulate work situations, have been useful in addressing discrimination that stems from employer uncertainty regarding the productivity of migrant workers (OECD and UNHCR, 2018[47]).

Policy can help compensate for migrants' lack of local knowledge and networks

Widespread recruitment through informal means is another way through which foreign-born can be put at a disadvantage. Migrants, particularly those who have newly arrived, tend to have fewer contacts that are relevant to the labour market and less knowledge of how the labour market functions. Many vacancies, although not necessarily closed to migrants, may be filled in such a way that migrants have little opportunity to apply, irrespective of how well they are equipped for the job. The role of the public employment services, which match jobseekers with employers, is therefore particularly important for migrants. In addition, many OECD countries offer job-search training as part of early integration efforts and have adopted career mentoring schemes to provide migrants with access to networks (OECD, 2014[48]).

Addressing the needs of vulnerable migrants

Integration policies to help vulnerable migrants acquire basic skills

Integration represents a long-term investment, for the host country and the immigrants themselves. Depending on the educational institutions in the origin country, migrants bring with them quite diverse education backgrounds.

Across the OECD, around one-quarter of migrants are low-educated, a similar proportion as among the native-born. This aggregate, however, masks differences across countries. Australia, Canada, Ireland and the United Kingdom are characterised by large intakes of high-educated labour migrants, while in some other European countries the low-educated are over-represented among immigrants.

The integration process for those who arrive after school age but lack basic skills can be long. In recognition of this, several OECD countries provide adult education combined with long-term language training. Norway, in particular, focuses heavily on low-skilled humanitarian migrants in its integration efforts, requiring them, in exchange for income support, to take adult education classes to endow them with the basic skills needed to function in Norway. In addition, all humanitarian migrants above compulsory schooling age who require primary or lower-secondary education are entitled to dedicated, long-term adult education (OECD, 2016[49]).

Migrants arriving for humanitarian reasons often require additional support

Refugees, in particular, tend to face considerable barriers to integration. The reasons are manifold: those arriving for international protection migrate not because they want to but because they have to; they had little or no time to prepare for migration (for example to collect proof of qualifications or learn the language); their health may have worsened during a long journey; and they often had no contact with the host country before arrival.

The unique set of integration challenges for refugees is often reflected in low employment rates. In contrast to labour migrants who already have an employer upon arrival, refugees arrive without a job. In contrast to international students, refugees have no educational institution to provide them with a programme of daily activities and link them to their host country. In contrast to migrants who arrive to reunite with their family, refugees often have no family links to their host country and more limited networks through which they can orient themselves and access information. Hence, the employment support needs of refugees are distinct, not only in the type of these needs, but also in their intensity.

Most Scandinavian countries provide newly-arrived refugees with structured multi-year programmes that combine language and labour market training and civic integration courses. Programmes typically last two to three years, although their duration may be adjusted in line with the education levels of individual refugees. In Denmark, for example, illiterate refugees who do not possess basic skills may receive additional language training, which goes beyond the scope of the official three-year induction programme and lasts for up to five years (OECD, 2016[49]).

Family migrants and migrants with childcare responsibilities

Family migrants, many of whom arrive in their host country with no direct ties to the labour market, often experience particular difficulties integrating in the labour market and society. Many left their careers and homes to follow their spouse; others may migrate for humanitarian reasons or to reunite with family members who themselves are refugees (OECD, 2017[50]). Alongside their efforts to integrate, many family migrants must also juggle childcare responsibilities, which can compromise their involvement in early integration activities. As time passes, these migrants risk becoming increasingly distant from the labour market.

Family migrants are seldom in the spotlight of integration and activation measures. They rarely claim social assistance, in part due to the common requirement that they have a family member in the host country who is able to guarantee their living expenses. Yet, not integrating family migrants represents a lost resource and risks long-run consequences for the integration success of their children.

Integration programmes need to be compatible with childcare or employment, allowing migrant parents to learn the host-country language, participate in integration activities and work at the same time. In Germany, for instance, all integration courses aim to provide a childcare option if no other childcare is available. Integration courses also have a special track for mothers and migrant women that focuses on education and childcare (OECD, 2017[51]).

At the same time, migrants with care responsibilities should not be sent on an exclusively childcare-centred integration track that maintains their distance to the labour force. Active labour market programmes must be accessible to those with childcare duties, and early childhood education and care options should become more widely available and better known among migrant parents. Research has shown that labour market participation among foreign-born mothers has a pronounced impact on the outcomes of their children. For the native-born children of migrants, the effect of having had a working mother at age 14 on the probability of being employed when an adult is, at 9 percentage points, more than twice the effect for the children of native-born (OECD, 2017[52]).

Young migrants and children of poorly educated migrants

Young migrants face a number of challenges when they arrive in their host country. Besides orienting themselves in a new country, they must learn the language and integrate into school in time to catch up with their native-born peers. Research indicates that, while it takes children approximately two years to acquire communicative language skills, they can take up to seven years to develop the academic language used in school environments (OECD, 2015[53]). This is a challenge for all young migrants but even more so for those from countries with quite different education systems. Many, particularly those who arrive towards the end of compulsory schooling, struggle to qualify for further education, which often translates into lifelong difficulties to gain durable employment. Recognising this, in New Zealand where school is compulsory until age 16 and education is free until age 19, refugees are allowed to stay in high school until they are 20 or 21.

These challenges can be particularly acute for unaccompanied minors who, in addition, face a strong motivation to begin work and remit money to their family who, in many cases, has invested all its savings into funding the journey of the child. While a strong motivation to work is, in principle, a good premise for further integration, it can also risk preventing these minors from engaging in the longer-term integration investments that are necessary to build a resilient career (OECD, forthcoming[54]).

Alongside young migrants, the native children of migrants are also at greater risk of poor labour market outcomes. In many countries, particularly in Europe, children of migrants enter the labour market in greater numbers. Young people with two foreign-born parents now account for over 9% of all youth aged between 15 and 34 and 11% of those below the age of 15 (OECD, 2017[52]). The integration of these children, particularly those of low-educated parents, is a growing concern, given that the intergenerational transmission of disadvantages appears to be stronger among migrants than native-born. Increasing access to early childhood education with a specific focus on children with language obstacles not only allows parents to participate in the labour market but also provides high returns for the children. Many OECD countries have specific policies in place to help children of immigrants with language obstacles, often based on systematic language screening in pre-school and follow-up remedial training (OECD, forthcoming[55]).

11.4. People with disabilities

Disability is widespread: in the OECD, around 14% of the working-age population report to have a disability or chronic health condition hampering their daily life; one-third of them have a severe disability (OECD, 2003[56]; OECD, 2010[57]). Disability or chronic ill-health often develops over the lifetime, sometimes gradually, sometimes suddenly due to an accident or illness. The prevalence of disability therefore increases with age, which is a growing problem given the rapid ageing of populations in most OECD countries.

The large majority of persons with disabilities have significant work capacities and many of them have full work capacity. It is therefore concerning that the employment rate for persons with disabilities is only around half that of persons without disabilities and that their unemployment rate is twice as high. The employment disadvantage of persons with disabilities is smallest in Iceland, Sweden and Switzerland and largest in Hungary, the Slovak Republic and the United States (see Figure 11.1).

Low employment rates translate into low incomes for many persons with disabilities, despite the availability of disability benefits in most countries. One in seven persons with a disability lives in a household with an equivalised income of below 50% of the median, a common definition of poverty. This compares with an income-poverty rate of below 10% for persons without disabilities. The difference in poverty rates between persons with and without disabilities tends to be larger in countries where the employment gap is higher and income-support benefits for those not working are low.

At the same time, OECD countries struggle with the costs of their sickness and disability benefit programmes. On average, 6% of the working-age population receive a disability benefit, a similar number as 20 years ago (Figure 11.4). The fiscal cost of paying disability benefits to so many people is considerable. Average public spending on disability benefits is 2% of GDP, and in some countries it is as high as 4% of GDP. It often exceeds spending on unemployment benefits.

Figure 11.4. Disability benefit caseloads are rather high in many OECD countries

Disability-benefit recipients as a share of the working-age population (%)

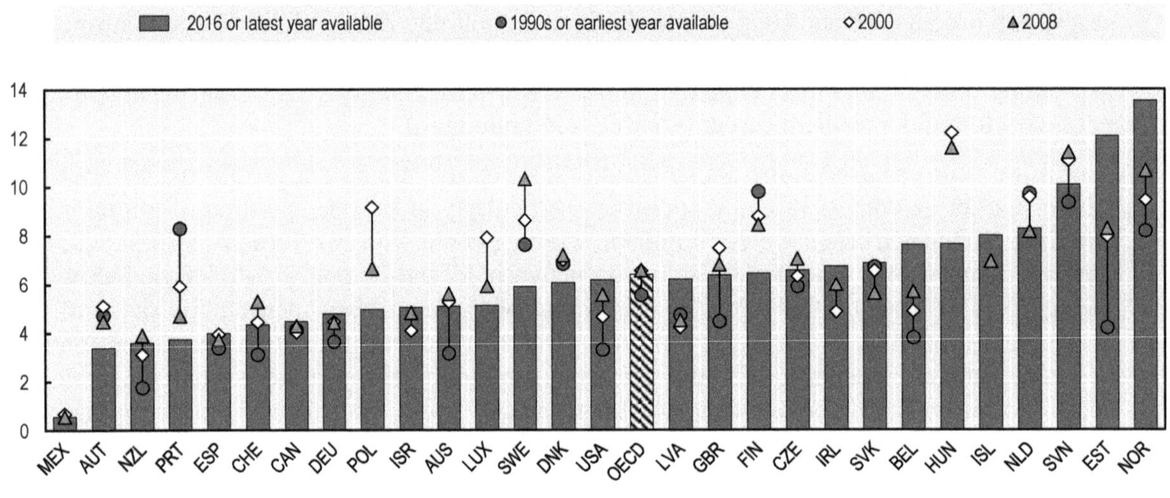

Source: Update of (OECD, 2010[57]), *Disability and Work: Breaking the Barriers: A Synthesis of Findings across OECD Countries*, https://doi.org/10.1787/9789264088856-en.

StatLink http://dx.doi.org/10.1787/888933881553

A growing "medicalisation" of disability policy

In many countries, disability benefits have become the benefit of last resort for people unable to stay in, or enter, the labour market. A number of policy developments have played a role:

- Reforms in several countries have restricted access to, and the maximum duration of, unemployment and social assistance benefit schemes, partly through stronger enforcement of labour market activation of jobseekers. This contributed to the decline in unemployment, and in particular long-term unemployment, in many OECD countries prior to the global financial crisis.
- Older workers – who often had been encouraged to retire several years before the legal retirement age – can no longer draw on some options previously available to leave the labour market prematurely, due to the retrenchment and phasing-out of early-retirement options and special unemployment retirement pathways.
- As a result, in many countries disability benefit systems, which overall have seen little change compared to reforms in other areas, have become the only benefit that can be received permanently and without any conditionality.

These developments have led to a "medicalisation" of labour market issues associated with disability. However, most persons with disabilities want to work and can work in ways compatible with their health condition. Supporting those people to gain and retain work is a "win-win" policy: it helps them avoid exclusion and have higher incomes while reducing benefit dependency. Due to the strong link between disability and age, policies addressing the employment of persons with disabilities will also affect, and be affected by, policies addressing the employment of older workers, the subject of the next section.

Towards an employment-oriented disability policy: What remains to be done?

A key question is whether disability should be treated as a health issue, to be addressed with special rules and programmes, or rather an employment issue, to be tackled with mainstream policies. Singling out disability as a special problem has distanced it from employment policy and lowered the employment expectation of both persons with disabilities and those helping them into work. All actors, including employers and public authorities, need to better recognise their mutual rights and responsibilities. A person with disability who seeks a job is in the first place a jobseeker, although possibly facing additional barriers to employment. This gives the employment focus in disability policy first-order importance.

Strengthening responsibilities and incentives

It is mainly the behaviour of five actors that affects the functioning of disability policy: the individuals with disabilities themselves, employers, public authorities, employment service providers and health professionals.

Persons with chronic health conditions or disabilities should be given a clear message that work in line with their capacity is expected and a prerequisite to receiving complementary benefits, if needed. Compulsory participation in rehabilitation programmes and job-search requirements in line with work capacity are both therefore important. Several countries have moved in this direction; examples are the introduction of the rehabilitation-before-benefit principle in German-speaking countries, work-focused interviews in the United Kingdom and unemployment benefits with adjusted job-search requirements for those with partial disabilities in Australia (OECD, 2010[57]).

Employers are important in several ways. They can help prevent disability, retain workers with disabilities and hire jobseekers with disabilities (see Chapter 9). To foster disability prevention and job retention, a better matching of responsibilities and incentives is required to strengthen employer action in preventing longer-term sickness absence (through co-payments for sickness benefits and rigorously enforced occupational health and safety regulations) and helping sick workers back into a job in the company (through a clear rehabilitation and return-to-work process). To foster job creation, wage subsidies and other incentives to hire workers with disabilities can be useful. The Netherlands is the country which has gone furthest on several of these aspects, thereby contributing to declining rates of sickness absence and disability benefit claims (OECD, 2014[58]). Sick leaves are very costly for Dutch employers who also have to make significant efforts to help people return to work and face a significant sanction if they fail to do so.

Public authorities have a key role in guiding people with disabilities through the system. They need to have effective tools and clear incentives to assess people's work capacity, direct them to the right service and, where appropriate, deliver services that help people into employment. Only few countries have so far tackled incentives of public authorities. One example is Denmark which has experimented with financial incentives for local job centres to stimulate labour market integration (OECD, 2013[59]).

Employment service providers need stronger incentives to bring people into sustainable employment. Traditionally, they are paid for every client they serve, irrespective of the actual outcome achieved. Paying for sustainable outcomes instead of managing caseloads could have a significant impact. Australia and the United Kingdom have developed their provider market in this direction, with increasing attention to longer-term employment outcomes and the degree of disadvantage of customers: the longer a customer stays in employment and the higher is the level of disadvantage, the higher is the payment which the provider will receive – see OECD (2014[60]; 2015[8]).

Health professionals are key actors as providers of sickness certificates and other capacity assessments, and as gatekeepers to the benefit system. Doctors influence their patients' future pathways and should be given the time, resources and incentives to provide information that promotes employment and a return to work, without undermining their patients' long-term health. Doctors often need better training and direction in understanding the value of work when evaluating their patients' health. Sickness absence guidelines in the Netherlands and Sweden are good examples of how the behaviour of doctors can be changed (OECD, 2013[61]; OECD, 2014[58]).

Moving from disability to employability

Disability benefit programmes have long been cash transfer schemes with little attention to the effect that they may have on employment, under the assumption that beneficiaries cannot be expected to work. This assumption is contradicted by the fact that most beneficiaries have at least some work capacity. In many countries, the case for a more unified scheme for all those who are able to work, including those with disabilities and partial work capacities, is strong. Turning disability benefits into an employment instrument requires an increased focus on a number of critical aspects (OECD, 2010[57]):

- A first step in the operation of a disability programme must be an assessment of persons' remaining work capacity and their barriers to work, not their disability. Time and effort of all actors must be used more effectively than in the past when a lot of time was invested in demonstrating the inability to work. Denmark, for example, has a comprehensive assessment process in which health issues play a relatively minor role (OECD, 2013[59]). The United Kingdom has moved in this direction as well, including by changing the name of the benefit programme to signal the shift in focus (OECD, 2014[60]).
- A second aspect is to award disability payments on a transitory basis, as is common for sickness and unemployment benefits, and to reassess entitlements and work capacity regularly. Disability payments are increasingly provided for a temporary period, at least initially, but they often become permanent because reassessments of entitlements are not very rigorous. Countries also tend to "grandfather" beneficiaries in case of system reform. The Netherlands and the United Kingdom are exemptions worth mentioning as they tend to reassess all entitlements when work capacity assessment methods and criteria are changed.
- A third aspect is support to facilitate the transition back to work. The return to work may be gradual, in line with a person's improving work capacity. Austria and Finland are two countries that have recently introduced the option of a gradual return to work for people receiving health-related benefits.
- A fourth aspect is that disability schemes must be designed so that working, or working more hours, always pays. Also here, more and more countries, including Ireland and the Netherlands, are lowering the high effective marginal tax rates that many of those moving from benefits back into work face.

Providing the right services at the right time

More people with disabilities could work if they were given the right supports at the right time. Countries invest more in rehabilitation and employment measures than they used to. Nevertheless, on average, OECD countries spend only 5% of their total disability-related spending on labour market programmes for persons with disabilities, while the remainder is used for out-of-work benefits. For comparison, the share going to labour market activation is as high as one-third for unemployment-related spending. Moreover, services must be provided in a timely, tailored and integrated way.

Providing services in a timely way means providing services as early as possible because re-employment chances decline quickly with the duration of time people have been away from the labour market or between the completion of education and entry into the labour market. Early action is essential in general and for persons with disabilities in particular. Data for a number of countries show that after six months of absence only few people return to the labour market successfully (OECD, 2015[62]). Switzerland is probably the country with the largest shift to early identification and action, which has considerably reduced the number of disability benefit claims (OECD, 2014[63]).

Providing services in a tailored way means adapting services to the actual needs of people through systematic profiling and engagement, with active case management for those who are more in need and quick referral to adequate services and supports. The shift to such type of individually-tailored services in some OECD countries makes, at the same time, a strong case for the unification of systems and services.

Providing services in an integrated way means identifying complementary (such as health, skills or social) barriers that a jobseeker may face. All these barriers should be addressed concurrently as doing so sequentially – such as first addressing any health issues before providing any employment support – just delays the process and reduces re-employment chances. Integrating services requires much-improved cross-agency co-ordination and co-operation, especially between the benefit authority and employment service, including through information exchange and clarity about responsibilities and funding issues. Countries like Belgium, Denmark and Sweden have gone furthest in this regard (Arends et al., 2014[64]; OECD, 2015[62]).

11.5. Older workers

Increasing employment rates among older workers requires measures that improve both incentives to continue working and employment opportunities at old age. Older workers are a diverse group. Many do well in the labour market and enjoy working, while others are trapped in poor-quality jobs or even struggle to find and hold on to jobs. Pension policies, together with other social policies concerning health and the labour market, need to reflect this diversity so as to prevent societies from ageing unequally, as is recognised in the OECD Recommendation of the Council on Ageing and Employment Policies (OECD, 2015[65]) and the OECD Action Plan for Preventing Ageing Unequally (OECD, 2017[66]).

Inequalities in skills and health affect older cohorts disproportionately because the risks of skill obsolescence and reduced work capacity due to health problems tend to rise with age. Promoting the employability of workers throughout their working lives – with a view of maintaining employment opportunities at an older age – is a key requirement for longer, rewarding careers. In a context of ageing populations, mobilising more fully the potential labour force and sustaining high productivity at old age are essential. This in turn requires a healthy workforce with relevant skills.

Changing work and retirement patterns

Over the past decade, many OECD and emerging market economies have undergone substantial pension reforms, often under the pressure of population ageing and financial sustainability concerns. The most visible change has been made in raising pension ages. On average in the OECD, the pension age will increase from 64.3 in 2016 to 65.8 by 2060 for male workers entering the labour force at age 20, and from 63.4 to 65.5 for female workers. In recent reforms, "age 67" has become the new "65" and several countries are going even further. In Denmark, for example, the pension age is due to increase gradually from 65 to 67 years over 2019-22 and subsequently will be linked to changes in life expectancy.

Setting a legal norm does not mean that all people actually work up to these higher ages. Many workers leave the labour market well before reaching the pension age. However, effective retirement ages have been increasing in most countries over the past decade. On average in the OECD, men left the workforce two years later in 2016 than in 2006, and women nearly one and a half years later (Figure 11.5). But several countries still have considerable scope to close the gap between pension ages and effective retirement ages and to further increase the pension age. For instance, at current policy settings full-career workers entering the labour market at age 20 today will still be able to retire with a full pension before 65 in France, Greece, Luxembourg and Slovenia.

While pension reforms face strong resistance in many countries, calls for more flexible retirement rules are re-surfacing in the public debate (OECD, 2017[67]). People differ in their preferences on how and when to move from work to retirement. Some want to stop working earlier because of health issues, to pursue other interests or to care for elderly relatives or grandchildren. Others are able and motivated to work longer, perhaps for the income or the social interactions that work brings, or simply because they like their job. A recent survey suggests that for two-thirds of EU citizens combining a part-time job and a partial pension is more appealing than retiring fully.

Real choice in making the retirement decision means that postponing retirement should be sufficiently rewarding to compensate for lost pension years, while retiring a few years before the normal retirement age should not be overly penalised. Importantly, people need clear information on the benefits that they can expect to receive under each scenario to make informed choices and, in particular, to ensure that the size of their pension is adequate. For instance, Chile, the Czech Republic, Estonia, Italy, Mexico, Norway, Portugal, the Slovak Republic and Sweden offer flexible retirement options that: i) allow combining work and pensions after the retirement age, with no limit on earnings; ii) reward postponing retirement; and iii) do not overly penalise retiring early. Overall, the financial incentive structure in these countries encourages people to remain in work longer, thereby reducing the risk of poverty for retirees.

Enhancing job quality to make the most of a diverse workforce

Job quality influences people's sense of engagement and well-being at work and beyond. Compelling evidence indicates that poor work environments can have a profound impact on an individual's physical and mental health. Job quality affects the retirement decisions of older workers, since jobs that are more enjoyable and support good health are likely to translate into longer working lives (Cazes, Hijzen and Saint-Martin, 2015[68]).

The determinants of working conditions and work organisation are primarily an issue for businesses, but policies and institutions can provide employers with incentives and tools to improve them. Many of these policies, such as safety-at-work regulations or well-designed sickness schemes, are similar to the ones that have the objective of disability prevention discussed in the previous section.

Figure 11.5. Contrasting the effective retirement age with the legal pension age

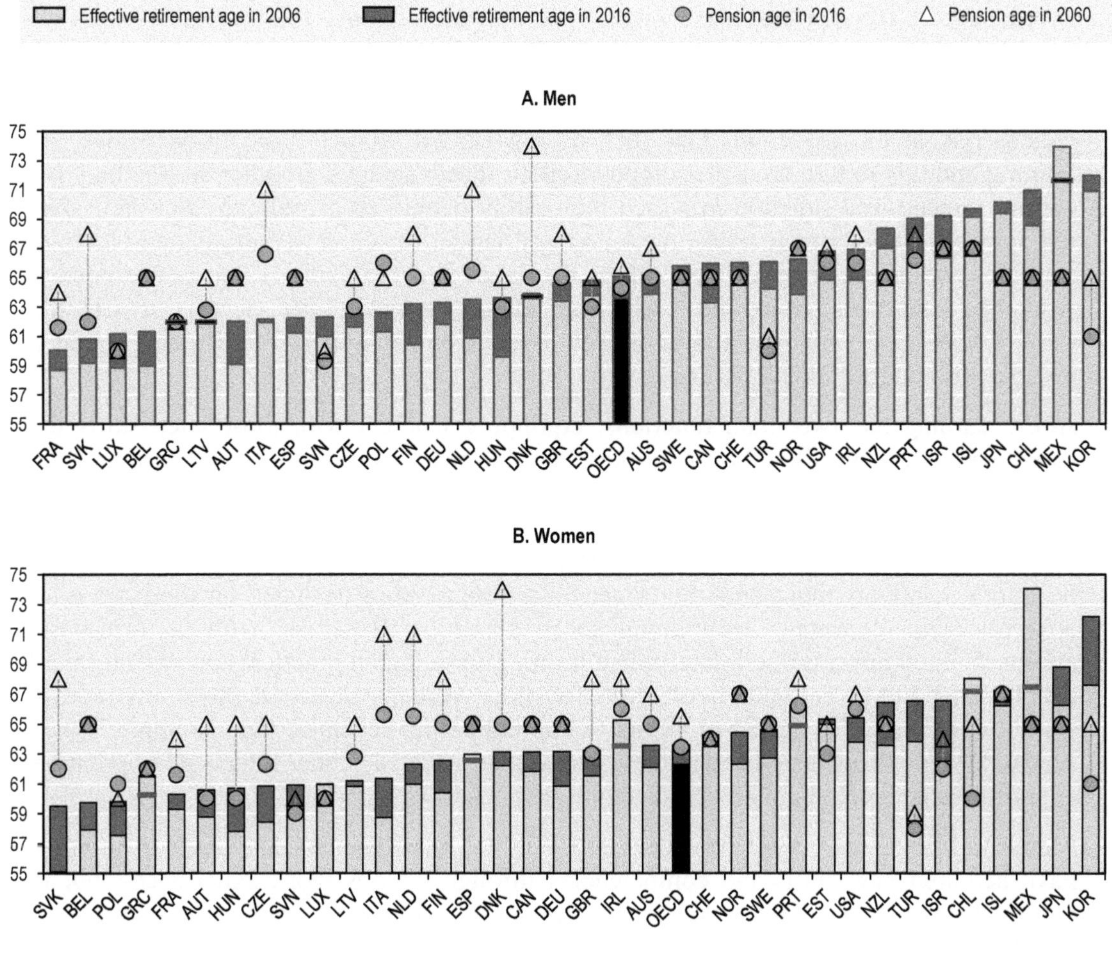

Source: OECD (2017[67]), *Pensions at a Glance 2017: OECD and G20 Indicators*, http://dx.doi.org/10.1787/pension_glance-2017-en.

StatLink http://dx.doi.org/10.1787/888933881572

Good practices by employers in managing a diverse workforce with workers of different ages should be encouraged through initiatives that provide guidance on, for example, how to promote sharing of knowledge across age groups, how to adjust work responsibilities and working-time arrangements to better balance professional and family responsibilities and how to create a good work environment, in general and especially for older workers. Examples of such initiatives can be found in Denmark and Germany, where programmes are in place that combine practical guidelines and financial incentives for employers to promote well-being at work, in particular for older workers (OECD, forthcoming[69]).

Flexible working time arrangements help particularly older women who would otherwise be more likely to retire early to care for their grandchildren, parents or other relatives. The employment barriers of older women are often inherited from problems conciliating work and family responsibilities at a younger age. Recent research by Saint-Martin, Inanc and Prinz (forthcoming[70]) finds that workplace flexibility generally benefits both individuals – by reducing stress at home and work, thus reducing absenteeism – and employers – by lowering costly worker turnover and increasing productivity, although changing workplace practices may give rise to short-term costs.

Investing in effective skill development strategies over the life course

Workers who maintain and upgrade their competencies by undertaking training during their working life fare better in the labour market when older. Yet, workforce groups at greater risk in the labour market, such as low-skilled workers, generally receive less training and this in turn tends to compound their disadvantages. In other words, they risk getting trapped in a situation in which they rarely benefit from training, and their skills remain weak or deteriorate over time, making it harder for them to participate in learning activities and possess marketable skills as they age. This problem is often exacerbated by workers, sometimes from the early age of 45, having little access to training. Governments and employer and employee associations should take concerted action to reverse this pattern (OECD, 2017[40]).

Adult learning has two main functions: equipping workers with job-related skills that match employers' needs and raise workers' productivity, employability and earnings; and helping people acquire adequate foundation skills (for example in numeracy or literacy) which are essential to support lifelong learning, even if they may have less immediate returns. The appropriate skill mix evolves over the work life, with job-related skills becoming relatively more important over time. Programmes designed on the basis of an apprenticeship concept – combining short classroom sessions with a firm-based approach – and informal, self-determined training focusing on practical and relevant work problems tend to be particularly effective for older workers. Countries have only recently started to promote the access of adults to apprenticeship schemes. One example is New Zealand Apprenticeships, a programme introduced in 2014, under which all apprentices enjoy the same level of government support, regardless of age (OECD, 2017[40]).

Many mid-career and older workers, whose initial qualifications may appear outdated, have acquired new skills and competencies through various work experiences, but no certificates to prove it. This makes formal validation systems for skills and competencies, which render them transparent to employers and establish an appropriate basis for further learning, particularly important for older workers. In case of job loss, the recognition of prior learning and validation of acquired experience can play crucial roles to help workers find a quality job that matches their actual competences and skills. The experiences of Portugal and the United Kingdom show how the recognition, validation and certification of acquired skills can help improve the employability of mid-career and older workers, especially when combined with additional training measures (OECD, forthcoming[69]).

Removing barriers to retain and hire older workers

Some older people are less productive, due to their age and health, and require in-work benefits or social protection. The higher likelihood of reduced work capacity or declining productivity among the elderly may make some employers hesitant to retain or hire older workers. Public policy can help overcome this in four main ways: affirmative action (including through information campaigns and guidelines); coercive action (in the form of anti-age discrimination laws); specific support for older workers with low productivity and few employment prospects; and measures to facilitate job mobility (OECD, 2017[40]).

Affirmative and coercive actions tend to be mutually reinforcing. Anti-age discrimination legislation gives a strong message that discrimination should not be tolerated, but it may only be effective when accompanied with public awareness campaigns and guidelines that help employers implement good employment practices with respect to age diversity and make older workers themselves aware of their rights. Information campaigns should also have as an objective to change some of the priors that potential employers may have of older workers (such as lack of motivation or inability to adapt to new technologies).

Anti-age discrimination laws will be powerful if enforcement is not necessarily dependent on the initiative of individuals deprived of their rights. Victims often face strong barriers to bring a case before court, with legal action being costly and complex and the outcome uncertain. Hence, enforcement by specific agencies, mandated to investigate companies and take – even in the absence of individual complaints – legal action against employers operating discriminatory practices, can play an important role. One example is the US Equal Employment Opportunity Commission, which is granted extensive powers (OECD, 2008[71]). Since its establishment in the 1960s, the commission has been at the forefront of the fight against discrimination. In particular, it has the authority to investigate charges of discrimination against employers, to settle the charge where discrimination is found, and to file a lawsuit to protect the rights of individuals and the interests of the public if the settlement procedure has not reached a successful conclusion.

Additional support is also necessary to help employers retain or hire disadvantaged older workers, i.e. those with low productivity and few employment prospects. This is essential to prevent early withdrawal from the labour market and reduce poverty risks at old age. Several countries introduced wage-subsidy and in-work benefit schemes to strike a better balance between older workers' productivity and the cost of employing them. These schemes are designed, over a certain period of time, to incentivise firms to employ older workers.

Nevertheless, packages of placement, training and counselling measures targeted at disadvantaged older workers may be more effective than wage subsidies alone. For instance, Germany's "Perspective 50 Plus" employment pacts for older workers in the regions, which ran from 2005 to 2015, placed great emphasis on intensive counselling for the older unemployed. Another example is Canada's Targeted Initiative for Older Workers programme which supports older jobseekers, typically between ages 55 and 64, who live in small, vulnerable communities, helping them regain a place in the labour market and improve their employability.

Policy-makers also need to strike the right balance between protecting older workers' jobs and increasing their mobility. Greater mobility requires hiring more jobseekers over a certain age and increasing older workers' willingness and ability to change jobs. Special employment protection rules for older workers can be counterproductive; they may reduce hiring chances and firms may seek to avoid penalties through early retirement arrangements. Ultimately, the best form of employment protection for older workers is to improve their employability and increase the range of job opportunities open to them.

Conclusion

This chapter reviewed policy options to enhance the prospects for five groups of workers who tend to face disadvantages in the labour market: low-skilled young people, people with care responsibilities, migrants, persons with disabilities and older workers. Each group faces unique challenges; nevertheless several common lessons can be drawn.

Designing policy in an employment-oriented way

One of the main reasons why employment rates for disadvantaged workers are low is that policy is insufficiently employment-oriented. For example, persons with partial work capacity should receive stronger incentives to stay in or return to work. Retirement rules should make it more rewarding for older individuals to stay in the labour market. Early contacts with the labour market, in particular for low-skilled youth and newly-arrived migrants, can be essential to avoid a lifetime out of decent work. In some countries, this requires a change in the mindsets of policy-makers and individuals, away from social protection towards an employment-oriented social policy.

Preventing exclusion through early intervention

Early intervention is crucial to avoid a lifetime out of work or in poor-quality jobs. The way governments deal with supporting the upbringing of young children may be the most vivid example in this respect. Mothers who, following birth, stay out of work for too long tend to become detached from the labour market, which substantially reduces their labour market prospects. Early education and care and low effective tax rates on second earners are two ways to support young mothers, and they are at the same time likely to benefit the cognitive development of young children. As the chapter discusses, similar considerations arise for each group of disadvantaged workers.

Intervening against discrimination

Women, migrants, persons with disabilities and older workers tend to be affected by discriminatory practices. They are often paid lower wages than others with similar competences and less likely to be offered a job or promotion. Such practices are sometimes in breach of anti-discrimination legislation, but policy initiatives need to go beyond relying on law enforcement processes which can be cumbersome and entail uncertain outcomes for the individuals concerned. Combining enforcement of regulation with suitable financial incentives and information campaigns that encourage employers to hire, promote and retain these workers holds the best promise of reducing discrimination.

Packaging measures

For all five groups of disadvantaged workers, no one policy exists that can eradicate their disadvantages. To make reforms for enhancing the inclusion of disadvantaged workers in the labour market a success, policies need to be combined into coherent packages. It is the combination of stronger work incentives, continued skills development during work life and health-friendly human resource policies that may allow older workers to retire later. Similarly, to help young mothers return to work swiftly, affordable childcare, not overly excessive tax rates on second earners' incomes, greater flexibility of working hours and a stronger engagement of fathers at home may all be required. Another example are low-skilled unemployed or inactive youth requiring comprehensive support in the form of training courses, job-search assistance, employer subsidies and career guidance. Making different agencies work together to meet the specific needs of each person is one of the most difficult challenges to be overcome if people from disadvantaged groups are to be able to fulfil their labour market potential.

Note

[1] Employment gaps are even larger for low-skilled youth.

References

Adema, W., C. Clarke and V. Frey (2015), "Paid Parental Leave: Lessons from OECD Countries and Selected U.S. States", *OECD Social, Employment and Migration Working Papers*, No. 172, OECD Publishing, Paris, http://dx.doi.org/10.1787/5jrqgvqqb4vb-en. [34]

Ahn, H. (2015), "Economic well-being of low-income single-mother families following welfare reform in the USA", *International Journal of Social Welfare*, Vol. 24/1, pp. 14-26, http://dx.doi.org/10.1111/ijsw.12095. [39]

Arends, I. et al. (2014), "Mental Health and Work: Achieving Well-integrated Policies and Service Delivery", *OECD Social, Employment and Migration Working Papers*, No. 161, OECD Publishing, Paris, http://dx.doi.org/10.1787/5jxsvvn6pq6g-en. [64]

Avram, S., M. Brewer and A. Salvatori (2018), "Can't work or won't work: Quasi-experimental evidence on work search requirements for single parents", *Labour Economics*, Vol. 51, pp. 63-85, https://www.ifs.org.uk/publications/8399. [37]

Cahuc, P., S. Carcillo and A. Zylberberg (2014), *Labor economics*, MIT Press, Boston, MA, https://mitpress.mit.edu/books/labor-economics-second-edition. [18]

Carcillo, S. et al. (2015), "NEET Youth in the Aftermath of the Crisis: Challenges and Policies", *OECD Social, Employment and Migration Working Papers*, No. 164, OECD Publishing, Paris, http://dx.doi.org/10.1787/5js6363503f6-en. [4]

Card, D., J. Kluve and A. Weber (2017), "What works? A meta analysis of recent active labor market program evaluations", *Journal of the European Economic Association*, Vol. 16/3, pp. 894–931. [17]

Cazes, S., A. Hijzen and A. Saint-Martin (2015), "Measuring and Assessing Job Quality: The OECD Job Quality Framework", *OECD Social, Employment and Migration Working Papers*, No. 174, OECD Publishing, Paris, http://dx.doi.org/10.1787/5jrp02kjw1mr-en. [68]

Céreq (2011), *Développer l'apprentissage ? Constats, limites et propositions*, Bref n° 293-2 octobre 2011, Bulletin de recherche emploi-formation du Céreq, http://www.cereq.fr/publications/Cereq-Bref/Developper-l-apprentissage-Constats-limites-et-propositions. [11]

Cohen, M. and A. Piquero (2015), "Benefits and costs of a targeted intervention program for youthful offenders: The YouthBuild USA offender project", *Journal of Benefit-Cost Analysis*, Vol. 6/03, pp. 603-627, https://papers.ssrn.com/sol3/papers.cfm?abstract_id=1154055. [15]

García, J. et al. (2017), *Quantifying the Life-cycle Benefits of a Prototypical Early Childhood Program*, National Bureau of Economic Research, Cambridge, MA, http://dx.doi.org/10.3386/w23479. [28]

Havnes, T. and M. Mogstad (2015), "Is universal child care leveling the playing field?", *Journal of Public Economics*, Vol. 127, pp. 100-114, http://dx.doi.org/10.1016/J.JPUBECO.2014.04.007. [27]

Huerta, M. et al. (2013), "Fathers' Leave, Fathers' Involvement and Child Development: Are They Related? Evidence from Four OECD Countries", *OECD Social, Employment and Migration Working Papers*, No. 140, OECD Publishing, Paris, http://dx.doi.org/10.1787/5k4dlw9w6czq-en. [32]

Kluve, J. et al. (2016), "Do Youth Employment Programs Improve Labor Market Outcomes? A Systematic Review", http://ftp.iza.org/dp10263.pdf (accessed on 28 May 2018). [16]

Lyche, C. (2010), "Taking on the completion challenge: A literature review on policies to prevent dropout and early school leaving", *OECD Education Working Papers*, No. 53, OECD Publishing, Paris, http://dx.doi.org/10.1787/5km4m2t59cmr-en. [5]

OECD (2018), *Investing in Youth: Norway*, OECD Publishing, Paris, http://dx.doi.org/10.1787/9789264283671-en. [6]

OECD (2018), *Is the Last Mile the Longest? Economic Gains from Gender Equality in Nordic Countries*, OECD Publishing, Paris, http://dx.doi.org/10.1787/9789264300040-en. [30]

OECD (2018), *OECD Employment Outlook 2018*, OECD Publishing, Paris, http://dx.doi.org/10.1787/empl_outlook-2018-en. [23]

OECD (2018), *Skills on the move: Migrants in the Survey of Adult Skills*, OECD Publishing, Paris, https://dx.doi.org/10.1787/9789264307353-en. [42]

OECD (2018), *Working Together: Skills and labour market integration of immigrants and their children in Finland*, OECD Publishing, Paris, https://dx.doi.org/10.1787/9789264305250-en. [45]

OECD (2017), *Catching Up? Intergenerational Mobility and Children of Immigrants*, OECD Publishing, Paris, http://dx.doi.org/10.1787/9789264288041-en. [52]

OECD (2017), *Dare to Share: Germany's Experience Promoting Equal Partnership in Families*, OECD Publishing, Paris, http://dx.doi.org/10.1787/9789264259157-en. [31]

OECD (2017), *Education at a Glance 2017: OECD indicators*, OECD Publishing, Paris, http://dx.doi.org/10.1787/eag-2017-en. [1]

OECD (2017), *International Migration Outlook 2017*, OECD Publishing, Paris, http://dx.doi.org/10.1787/migr_outlook-2017-en. [50]

OECD (2017), *Making Integration Work: Assessment and recognition of foreign qualifications*, OECD Publishing, Paris, http://dx.doi.org/10.1787/9789264278271-en. [44]

OECD (2017), *Making Integration Work: Family Migrants*, OECD Publishing, Paris, http://dx.doi.org/10.1787/9789264279520-en. [51]

OECD (2017), *Pensions at a Glance 2017: OECD and G20 Indicators*, OECD Publishing, Paris, http://dx.doi.org/10.1787/pension_glance-2017-en. [67]

OECD (2017), *Preventing Ageing Unequally*, OECD Publishing, Paris, http://dx.doi.org/10.1787/9789264279087-en. [40]

OECD (2017), *Preventing Ageing Unequally - Action Plan*, OECD, Paris, https://www.oecd.org/social/C-MIN-2017-6-EN.pdf. [66]

OECD (2017), *The Pursuit of Gender Equality: An Uphill Battle*, OECD Publishing, Paris, http://dx.doi.org/10.1787/9789264281318-en. [22]

OECD (2016), *Be Flexible! Background brief on how workplace flexibility can help European employees to balance work and family*, OECD Publishing, Paris, https://www.oecd.org/els/family/Be-Flexible-Backgrounder-Workplace-Flexibility.pdf. [41]

OECD (2016), *Investing in Youth: Australia*, OECD Publishing, Paris, http://dx.doi.org/10.1787/9789264257498-en. [20]

OECD (2016), *Making Integration Work: Refugees and others in need of protection*, Making Integration Work, OECD Publishing, Paris, http://dx.doi.org/10.1787/9789264251236-en. [49]

OECD (2016), *Society at a Glance 2016: OECD Social Indicators*, OECD Publishing, Paris, http://dx.doi.org/10.1787/9789264261488-en. [9]

OECD (2016), *Walking the tightrope: Background brief on parents' work-life balance across the stages of childhood*, OECD Publishing, Paris, http://www.oecd.org/social/family/Background-brief-parents-work-life-balance-stages-childhood.pdf. [24]

OECD (2016), *Who uses childcare? Background brief on inequalities in the use of formal early childhood education and care (ECEC) among very young children*, OECD, Paris, http://www.oecd.org/els/family/Who_uses_childcare-Backgrounder_inequalities_formal_ECEC.pdf (accessed on 21 February 2018). [29]

OECD (2016), *Working Together: Skills and Labour Market Integration of Immigrants and their Children in Sweden*, OECD Publishing, Paris, http://dx.doi.org/10.1787/9789264257382-en. [43]

OECD (2015), *Fit Mind, Fit Job: From evidence to practice in mental health and work*, OECD Publishing, Paris, http://dx.doi.org/10.1787/9789264228283-en. [62]

OECD (2015), *Immigrant Students at School: Easing the Journey towards Integration*, OECD Publishing, Paris, http://dx.doi.org/10.1787/9789264249509-en. [53]

OECD (2015), *Integrating social services for vulnerable groups: Bridging sectors for better service delivery*, OECD Publishing, Paris, http://dx.doi.org/10.1787/9789264233775-en. [19]

OECD (2015), *Mental Health and Work: Australia*, OECD Publishing, Paris, http://dx.doi.org/10.1787/9789264246591-en. [8]

OECD (2015), *Recommendation of the Council on Ageing and Employment Policies*, OECD, Paris, https://www.oecd.org/els/emp/Ageing-Recommendation.pdf. [65]

OECD (2014), *G20-OECD-EC Conference on quality apprenticeships for giving youth a better start in the labour market*, OECD Publishing, Paris. [10]

OECD (2014), *International Migration Outlook 2014*, OECD Publishing, Paris, http://dx.doi.org/10.1787/migr_outlook-2014-en. [48]

OECD (2014), *Mental Health and Work: Netherlands*, OECD Publishing, Paris, http://dx.doi.org/10.1787/9789264223301-en. [58]

OECD (2014), *Mental Health and Work: Switzerland*, OECD Publishing, Paris, http://dx.doi.org/10.1787/9789264204973-en. [63]

OECD (2014), *Mental Health and Work: United Kingdom*, Mental Health and Work, OECD Publishing, Paris, http://dx.doi.org/10.1787/9789264204997-en. [60]

OECD (2014), *OECD Employment Outlook 2014*, OECD Publishing, Paris, http://dx.doi.org/10.1787/empl_outlook-2014-en. [2]

OECD (2013), *International Migration Outlook 2013*, OECD Publishing, Paris, http://dx.doi.org/10.1787/migr_outlook-2013-en. [46]

OECD (2013), *Mental Health and Work: Denmark*, OECD Publishing, Paris, http://dx.doi.org/10.1787/9789264188631-en. [59]

OECD (2013), *Mental Health and Work: Sweden*, OECD Publishing, Paris, http://dx.doi.org/10.1787/9789264188730-en. [61]

OECD (2013), *PISA 2012 Results: Excellence through Equity (Volume II): Giving Every Student the Chance to Succeed*, PISA, OECD Publishing, Paris, http://dx.doi.org/10.1787/9789264201132-en. [26]

OECD (2012), *Closing the Gender Gap: Act Now*, OECD Publishing, Paris, http://dx.doi.org/10.1787/9789264179370-en. [21]

OECD (2012), *Equity and quality in education: Supporting disadvantaged students and schools*, OECD Publishing, Paris, http://dx.doi.org/10.1787/9789264130852-en. [7]

OECD (2011), *Doing Better for Families*, OECD Publishing, Paris, http://dx.doi.org/10.1787/9789264098732-en. [38]

OECD (2011), *The Future of Families to 2030*, OECD Publishing, Paris, http://dx.doi.org/10.1787/9789264168367-en. [35]

OECD (2010), *Off to a good start? Jobs for youth*, Jobs for youth/Des emplois pour les jeunes, OECD Publishing, Paris, http://dx.doi.org/10.1787/9789264096127-en. [13]

OECD (2010), *Sickness, Disability and Work: Breaking the Barriers: A Synthesis of Findings across OECD Countries*, OECD Publishing, Paris, http://dx.doi.org/10.1787/9789264088856-en. [57]

OECD (2008), *OECD Employment Outlook 2008*, OECD Publishing, Paris, http://dx.doi.org/10.1787/empl_outlook-2008-en. [71]

OECD (2007), *Babies and Bosses - Reconciling Work and Family Life: A Synthesis of Findings for OECD Countries*, OECD Publishing, Paris, http://dx.doi.org/10.1787/9789264032477-en. [25]

OECD (2003), *Transforming Disability into Ability: Policies to Promote Work and Income Security for Disabled People*, OECD Publishing, Paris, http://dx.doi.org/10.1787/9789264158245-en. [56]

OECD (forthcoming), *Identifying ways of raising effective retirement ages: Impact of the wage-skill relationship on the labour demand for older workers*, OECD Publishing, Paris. [69]

OECD (forthcoming), *Investing in Youth: Finland*, OECD Publishing, Paris, https://www.oecd-ilibrary.org/employment/investing-in-youth_24126357. [12]

OECD (forthcoming), *Making Integration Work: Effective language training*, OECD Publishing, Paris. [55]

OECD (forthcoming), *The challenges and policy responses facing OECD countries in the integration of unaccompanied minors*, OECD Publishing, Paris. [54]

OECD and UNHCR (2018), *Engaging with employers in the hiring of refugees: A 10-point multi-stakeholder action plan for employers, refugees, governments and civil society*, OECD Publishing, Paris, http://www.oecd.org/els/mig/UNHCR-OECD-Engaging-with-employers-in-the-hiring-of-refugees.pdf. [47]

Rabindrakumar, S. (2018), *One in four: A profile of single parents in the UK*, Gingerbread. [36]

Rønsen, M. and R. Kitterød (2015), "Gender-Equalizing Family Policies and Mothers' Entry into Paid Work: Recent Evidence From Norway", *Feminist Economics*, Vol. 21/1, pp. 59-89, http://dx.doi.org/10.1080/13545701.2014.927584. [33]

Saint-Martin, A., H. Inanc and C. Prinz (forthcoming), "Job quality, health and productivity: An evidence-based framework for analysis", *OECD Social, Employment and Migration Working Papers*. [70]

Schmillen, A. and M. Umkehrer (2017), "The scars of youth: Effects of early-career unemployment on future unemployment experience", *International Labour Review*, Vol. 156/3-4, pp. 465-494. [3]

Schochet, P., J. Burghardt and S. McConnell (2006), *National Job Corps study and longer-term follow-up study: Impact and benefit-cost findings using survey and summary earnings records data*, Mathematica Policy Research, Princeton, NJ, https://wdr.doleta.gov/research/FullText_Documents/National%20Job%20Corps%20Study%20and%20Longer%20Term%20Follow-Up%20Study%20-%20Final%20Report.pdf. [14]

Chapter 12. Managing self-employment, new forms of work, and the platform economy

After providing an overview of trends in self-employment, own-account and platform work, this chapter provides a comprehensive policy discussion of how to address the challenges of some of these "new" forms of work – covering labour market regulation, social protection, tax, social dialogue and skills. The objective of policy makers should be to balance innovation, entrepreneurship and flexibility, on the one hand, with job quality and worker rights and protections, on the other. The latter is important not only from a worker perspective, but also to ensure a level playing field between competing firms.

The statistical data for Israel are supplied by and under the responsibility of the relevant Israeli authorities. The use of such data by the OECD is without prejudice to the status of the Golan Heights, East Jerusalem and Israeli settlements in the West Bank under the terms of international law.

Introduction

Recent innovations in technology and business models have led to the emergence of the "platform economy" and new ways of working more generally. From an employment perspective, these developments have been interesting because they have promoted more flexible forms of employment, which have been a boon to employers as well as many workers.

However, there are also concerns that these new forms of work offer individuals little or no employment protection, reduced social protection, poor working conditions (including pay), and put them in a weak bargaining position vis-à-vis employers and clients. This is not only a challenge for the workers themselves, but can also create an uneven playing field if firms try and get a competitive advantage simply by evading their dues and responsibilities. A key policy challenge is therefore to promote innovation, entrepreneurship and flexibility, on the one hand, while improving job quality and worker rights and protections, on the other.

The platform economy has brought renewed attention to these issues, but they are by no means new. Many workers like hairdressers, plumbers and gardeners share characteristics with platform workers and face comparable challenges. Several countries have seen increases in the number of solo self-employed (or own-account workers) as a result of tax and regulatory incentives embedded in their systems, rather than as a consequence of technological change. The general, structural rise in service-sector jobs has been a further driver behind these trends.

This chapter focuses on these non-standard forms of work and, in particular, on the grey area between self- and dependent employment. After providing an overview of trends in self-employment, own-account and platform work (section 12.1), the chapter provides a comprehensive policy discussion – covering employment regulation, social protection, tax, social dialogue and skills (section 12.2). The final section concludes.

12.1. Stylised facts

Trends in self-employment, own-account and platform work

The emergence of new forms of work is closely tied to the advent of the platform economy. Capturing the extent of platform work through existing household and labour force surveys has, until recently, been impossible. Various *ad hoc* attempts exist, though differences in terms of platform definition, time period covered, and survey methodology have made it difficult to compare estimates. For example, some surveys cover only income from labour platforms (i.e. technologies that allow users to sell their labour, such as chauffeuring others or doing remote data entry), while others also include income from capital platforms (i.e. technologies that allow users to sell or rent property, such as apartments or used goods). Data sources include face-to-face surveys, phone surveys, online surveys, administrative data such as tax records or bank data, and, more recently, new questions added to labour force and household surveys. Overall, the best evidence indicates that platform work still only represents a small share of overall employment (less than 1%) (Katz and Krueger, 2016[1]; Farrell and Greig, 2016[2]; Jackson, Looney and Ramnath, 2017[3]; Statistics Canada, 2017[4]; Statistics Finland, 2018[5]). There is some indication that it has grown fast, but there are also signs that this growth may have levelled off in recent times (Farrell and Greig, 2016[6]).

It is important to stress that platform work is not in and of itself a form of employment, but rather refers to the means through which the work is obtained and (sometimes) carried out. In theory, platform workers could be engaged in any kind of employment relationship. In practice, many are (rightly or wrongly) classified as self-employed and, in particular, as independent contractors (or own-account workers/solo self-employed). Many of these workers will face similar challenges to platform workers and it is, therefore, of interest to look at this group of workers more broadly – also because the rise in solo self-employment in some countries has been driven by policy decisions (tax and regulatory incentives) rather than by technology. While there has been no clear trend across the OECD on average in the share of own-account workers in total employment between 1995 and 2016 (Figure 12.1), there have been substantial increases in some countries like the Netherlands, the Slovak Republic and the United Kingdom.

Figure 12.1. Share of own-account workers in total employment

1958, 2005, 2016

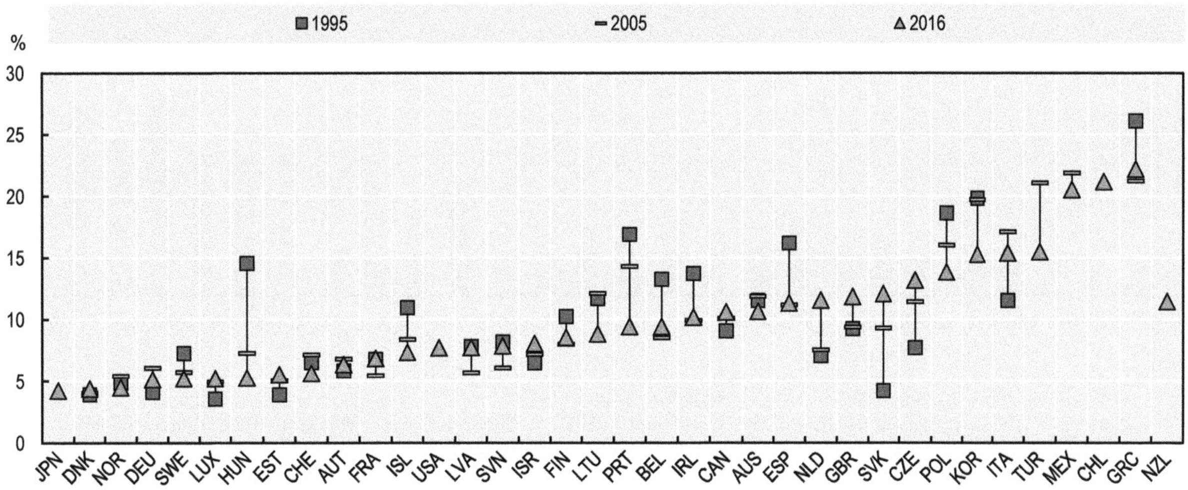

Note: Data are for 1996 (instead of 1995) for Hungary and Switzerland; 1997 (instead of 1995) for Estonia, Czech Republic and Poland; 1998 (instead of 1995) for Latvia, Lithuania and the Slovak Republic; 2006 (instead of 2005) for Turkey; and 2015 (instead of 2016) for New Zealand.
Source: OECD Gender - Entrepreneurship database.

StatLink http://dx.doi.org/10.1787/888933881591

Own-account work is a particular challenge in cases where individuals are financially dependent on a single employer. These are the so-called economically "dependent" self-employed who earn most of their income from just one client. The reason these are a group of interest to policy makers is that they tend to be in a vulnerable position vis-à-vis their client and may need special protections put in place (especially since they will not have access to the usual benefits and protections that employees do). Only a few countries have official (legal) definitions of dependent self-employment and, where these exist, they tend to differ. For example, in Spain, the *trabajador autónomo económicamente dependiente* (economically dependent self-employed, or "TRADE") covers own-account workers who depend on a single client for at least 75% of their income. In Portugal, an individual is considered dependent self-employed when at least 80% of their yearly income comes from one single client (*regime dos trabalhadores independentes e que prestam serviços maioritariamente a uma entidade contratante*). Estimating the extent of dependent self-employment is further complicated by the fact that standard labour force and household surveys do not permit the identification of such workers. Based on the European Working Conditions Survey, Figure 12.2 looks at changes between 2010 and 2015 in dependent self-employment, defined as those own-account workers who generally do not have more than one client. It shows that in around two thirds of countries, dependent self-employment has risen over this time period.

Figure 12.2. Share of own-account workers who generally do not have more than one client

2010 and 2015

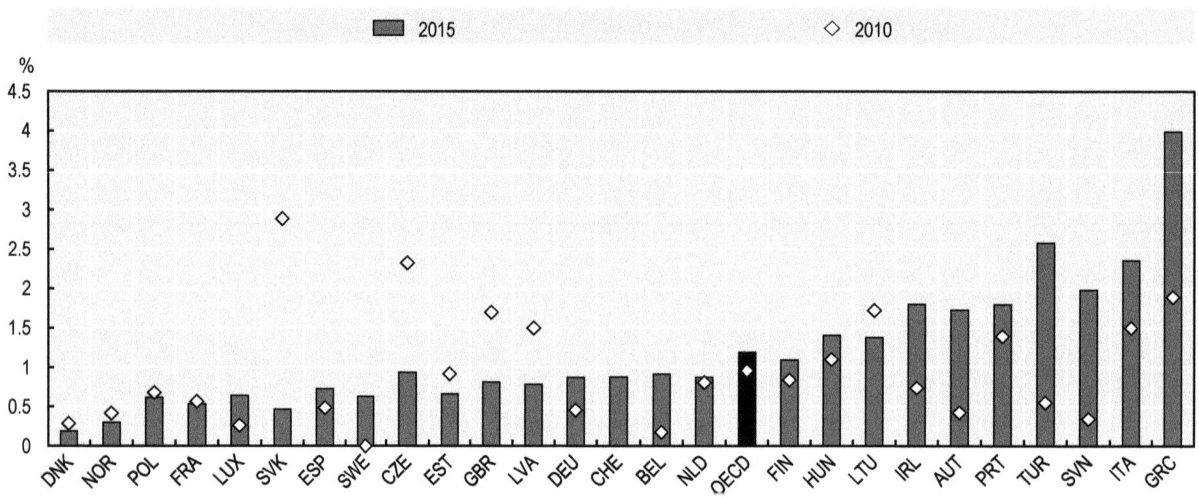

Note: The OECD average refers to 25 EU countries plus Turkey.
Source: OECD calculations based on Eurofound (2010), "5th European Working Conditions Survey (EWCS)" and Eurofound (2015), "6th European Working Conditions Survey (EWCS)".

StatLink http://dx.doi.org/10.1787/888933881610

A closely related, but distinct, concept is that of false self-employment. The exact definition of false self-employment will also vary from country to country, depending on the legal tests in place to determine employment status. In most countries, economic dependency on a single client (i.e. dependent self-employment) will not be sufficient for a person to be considered to be falsely self-employed. Indeed, one can be financially dependent on one client, while still being genuinely self-employed. In general, for an employment relationship to be labelled as false self-employment, there also needs to be an element of control by the client/employer so that the individual has little freedom to decide over working hours, the way work is carried out, the place of work, etc. In other words: the characteristics of the employment relationship must closely mirror those of an employer-employee relationship. Estimates of false self-employment are also difficult to obtain, and international comparisons are even more tricky because definitions of what it means to be an employee will vary significantly. Figure 12.3 nonetheless makes an attempt at estimating the extent to which own account workers who generally only have one client also cannot change at least two of the following: i) the order of their tasks; ii) their method of work; and iii) the speed or rate of work. The graph suggests that this share has increased in the majority of EU countries.

Figure 12.3. Share of own-account workers who generally do not have more than one client and have little control over how their work is carried out

2010 and 2015

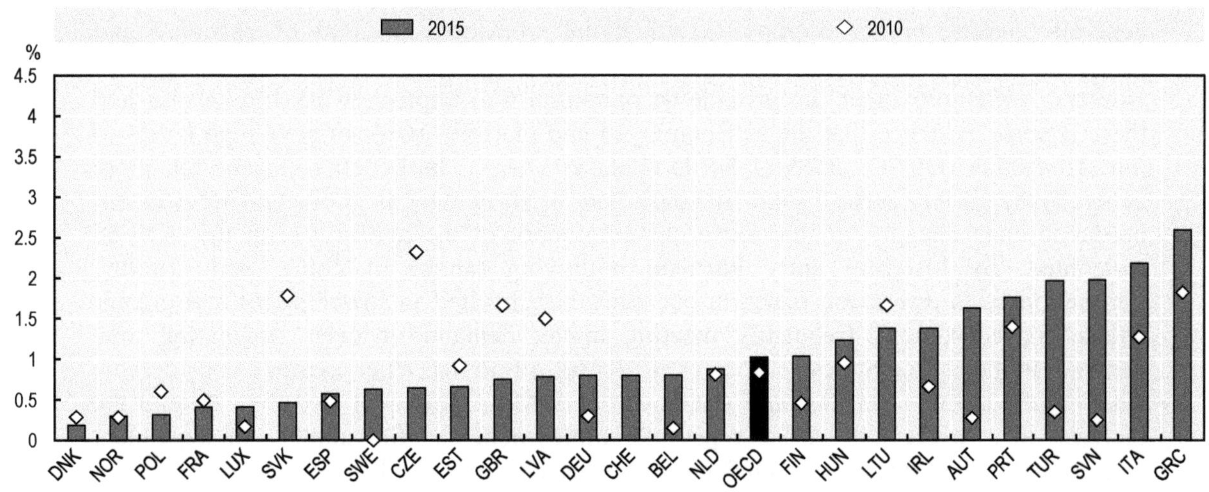

Note: The OECD average refers to 25 EU countries plus Turkey.
Source: OECD calculations based on Eurofound (2010), "5th European Working Conditions Survey (EWCS)" and Eurofound (2015), "6th European Working Conditions Survey (EWCS)".

StatLink http://dx.doi.org/10.1787/888933881629

What has driven these trends?

Firms are constantly trying to find new business models and ways of producing goods and services more cheaply. In some cases, this has resulted in an increased use of non-standard employment arrangements, outsourcing, and a shift of the costs, risks and responsibilities from employers onto workers. Technology has further promoted this trend by facilitating the outsourcing not only of jobs, but also of individual tasks, as it has significantly lowered the transaction costs involved in doing so and made it possible even for small and medium enterprises to outsource. Technology has also enabled individuals to have greater choice about where and when they work, and part of the increase in non-standard forms of work may reflect a desire for more flexible ways of fitting work around other responsibilities. For example, there is some evidence that ride-hailing apps reduce barriers to entry in the labour market for women and that women drivers particularly value the flexibility that such apps offer (IFC, 2018[7]). Structural change more generally, and the shift to service-sector jobs in particular, have further contributed to this trend (OECD, 2015[8]).

However, significant differences across countries in the prevalence of, and trends in, self-employment and own-account work suggest that policy decisions, whether intentional or not, can amplify or dampen the emergence and/or rise of such forms of work. As one example, growth in self-employment has been facilitated by reforms on the regulatory or fiscal side which have generated very strong incentives for employers and workers to prefer self-employment over dependent employment. For example, forthcoming OECD research (Milanez and Bratta, forthcoming[9]) shows that, both in the Netherlands and the United Kingdom, differences in total employment costs between the self-employed and employees are large enough to shift employer-employee preferences towards self-employment.

Advantages and disadvantages

For firms, business models based on outsourcing work to self-employed workers generally means more flexibility to adjust the workforce in light of changing and sometimes unpredictable economic conditions, as well as significant cost savings. For workers, self-employment can provide an opportunity to improve work-life balance and there is some evidence that the self-employed and platform workers have high levels of job satisfaction (OECD, 2000[10]; Forde et al., 2017[11]). The benefits may be felt more generally by society as well (and by consumers in particular) as goods and services are produced more cheaply. In this sense, the emergence of the platform economy is to be welcomed. By lowering entry barriers, improving labour matching, and bringing transaction costs down, the platform economy has resulted in lower prices and greater choice for consumers, frequently meeting unmet demand or even stimulating new demand. In the United States, (Cohen et al., 2016[12]) find that Uber creates a considerable amount of consumer surplus, and (Hathaway and Muro, 2016[13]) find that, despite the increase in own-account workers, payroll employment (i.e. the number of dependent employees) in the "rides and rooms" industries has also increased.

However, excessive use of such business models may have adverse effects as well – on employers, workers and society as a whole. From the firm side, over-reliance on outsourced workers can gradually erode firm-specific skills, and it has been shown that non-standard employment results in lower investments in training (OECD, 2014[14]) which, in the long-run, results in lower productivity growth. Firms should also be concerned about having a level playing field on which to compete, and avoiding situations where less responsible firms are gaining a competitive edge simply because their business model is based on evading regulation and/or reducing their tax bill. In addition, such tax avoidance behaviour is likely to result in a larger tax bill for all other firms if unprotected workers end up having to rely on social assistance programmes which are financed through general taxation rather than social security contributions. The deliberate misclassification of workers as independent contractors is of particular concern and presents a significant challenge for government revenues. For example, in the United States, the Department of Labor has estimated that between 10-30% of self-employed workers are misclassified and that this could have a significant impact on tax revenue (Brumm, 2016[15]).

While self-employment may mean increased flexibility for workers as well, they are unlikely to reap the benefits if they have little bargaining power vis-à-vis their clients and/or intermediaries. The self-employed, particularly those without employees, earn, on average, much less than employees (OECD/EU, 2017[16]). Self-employment is also less secure than employment and considerable numbers of the self-employed exit before five years (OECD/EU, 2017[16]). Self-employment brings with it the opportunity for flexibility and autonomy, leading to greater levels of job and life satisfaction. The trade-off, however, is that their working conditions are characterised by long working hours and the potential for stress and health-related issues (OECD/EU, 2017[16]).

Emerging evidence for the platform economy suggests that, while pay varies enormously reflecting the heterogeneity of platform work, many platform workers earn very low wages, frequently well below national minimum wages (CIPD, 2017[17]; Lepanjuuri, Wishart and Cornick, 2018[18]; Forde et al., 2017[11]).

There are also concerns around health and safety and working hours (Quinlan, 2015[19]; Ticona and Mateescu, 2018[20]) – often reflecting the lack of regulation of platform work (Garben, 2017[21]). It has sometimes been argued that the increased flexibility offered by jobs in the platform economy could remove certain barriers to labour market participation and make it easier for traditionally underrepresented groups to find work (see evidence above about women and Uber). While there is as much heterogeneity in the types of workers as there is in the nature of platforms and platform work, on average, platform workers tend to be younger, male, more highly educated and more likely to be based in urban areas (Balaram, Warden and Wallace-Stephens, 2017[22]; Berg, 2016[23]; Farrell and Greig, 2016[2]; Bonin, 2017[24]; Huws, Spencer and Joyce, 2016[25]; Pesole et al., 2018[26]). With the exception of youth, therefore, it is not clear that the platform economy has yet delivered on the promise of helping to reduce gaps in employment rates for disadvantaged groups.

12.2. Policy response

While self-employment and entrepreneurship should be encouraged, policy makers need to ensure that job quality amongst those workers is maximised. They should also avoid situations in which own-account work is chosen purely on the basis of tax and/or regulatory incentives, as well as situations in which firms choose such forms of work in order to shift risks and responsibilities onto the shoulders of workers. In doing so, policy makers face some delicate trade-offs: how to tackle false self-employment without harming genuine entrepreneurship (Kautonen et al., 2010[27]); how to regulate without stifling innovation; how to promote job quality without affecting job quantity?

Policy makers can act on several fronts, including: employment regulation, skills, social dialogue, tax and social protection. The exact combination of reforms and interventions will depend on each country's specific challenges, their starting point, as well as national specificities. In addition, policy makers should be careful not to over-simplify the existing landscape. For example, platforms operate and treat their workers in diverse ways; taking a binary approach to regulation could create more problems than it solves.

Balancing incentives

Many individuals will prefer self-employment over dependent employment because it gives them more freedom, allows them to be their own boss, enables them to achieve a better work-life balance, or even allows them to earn more money. Similarly, many companies will choose to outsource some of their functions and activities because it makes business sense for them to do so. In most countries, the self-employed will pay fewer taxes and social security contributions than employees, which will reflect a number of factors, including that they receive less social protection in return, or that the government wishes to encourage entrepreneurship. On average, companies and individuals will balance these benefits against the cost of being self-employed and/or of outsourcing jobs.

However, a problem arises where incentives are so strong as to lead to an "inefficiently high" level of self-employment. This could lead to a misallocation of labour resources as well as to an undermining of social protection systems (particularly where lower-risk individuals choose to become self-employed and are allowed to opt out of parts of the social protection system, leaving only the "bad risks" behind and resulting in an increased reliance on social assistance). In addition, to the extent that the self-employed participate less in training, very high levels of self-employment could act as a drag on productivity. Moreover, where such incentives lead to false self-employment, this could have important consequences not only for individuals (in terms of employment protection, social protection, worker's voice, etc.) but also for firms who may face unfair competition from those who are trying to evade their dues and responsibilities.

Where strong fiscal and regulatory imbalances between employment forms exist, governments should aim to reduce them. Some countries have already done so. For example, a tax reform was introduced in the Czech Republic in 2004 to halt the spread of "false" self-employment. While it remains difficult to isolate the effect of policy reforms from other factors, the incidence of own-account work increased less in the Czech Republic than in the Slovak Republic during this period (OECD, 2008[28]). In Austria, concerns that independent contractors (*freie Dienstnehmer*) would be used by employers to evade taxes and regulations led the government to gradually integrate them into the social protection system and, since 2008, they pay the same social security contributions as standard employees.

A related measure which countries could take is to encourage hiring on standard contracts by making them more attractive relative to non-standard employment arrangements. This could be achieved by easing the obligations or enhancing the flexibility associated with standard contracts for employers. For example, as part of its 2015 labour market reform, Italy provided a temporary amnesty from fines to employers who would convert existing self-employed contracts into standard, open-ended employment ones (Williams and Lapeyre, 2017[29]).

Addressing worker classification

It is difficult, and perhaps not even desirable, to completely eliminate differences in tax and regulatory treatment between different employment forms, and so incentives for misclassification will always exist to some extent or other. Because of this, it is important that labour market regulation is clear about what constitutes various forms of employment; that employers and workers are aware of the legislation; and that the existing legislation is properly enforced.

In some cases, existing legislation might be adequate, but firms and workers might not be familiar with it. Government action should then focus on helping firms and workers identify employment relationships, for example by providing better guidance and information on contractual status. In the United States, the Department of Labor had published guidance in 2015 to help with the classification of employees and independent contractors. While this "Administrator's Interpretation" arguably took an expansive view of the employment relationship, it was consistent with court rulings on the matter. In June 2017, the guidance was withdrawn by the new administration.

Employment relationships are usually established by courts on the basis of the principle of "primacy of facts": regardless of how employers and workers describe the relationship between them in the contract, the determination of the existence of an employment relationship will be guided by the actual facts – i.e. it will be based on certain objective conditions being met. In particular, the extent of subordination and dependence of the worker on the employer will be assessed, based on a range of indicators which can vary from country to country but typically include: the worker's integration in the organisation; the extent to which the worker controls his/her conditions of work (including the place and time of work); who provides the tools, materials or machines; the regularity of payments; and the extent of financial dependence of the worker on the employer. In common law countries, judges base their rulings on certain tests developed by case law. In civil-law countries, these criteria will be enshrined in law and there will often be a presumption of an employment relationship if these criteria are met, with the burden of proof put on the employer to show that this is not the case.

In some cases, there may be a need to clarify, revise or update regulations, including definitions of employment relationships – e.g. what it means to be an employee, self-employed, or even an employer (e.g. in tripartite employment relationships and cases involving an intermediary, like a platform). For example, some countries have a very expansive definition of employee which covers independent contractors for certain purposes (e.g. Sweden, Canada). Other countries have several employment tests and/or definitions which vary across legal/policy areas (labour, tax, social protection), and this could contribute to possible confusion. In such cases, there may be a case for harmonising them. For example, in the United States, the tests for defining employee status range from the broadest "suffer or permit" test[1], passing through the hybrid[2] and the "ABC" tests[3], to the narrowest common law test[4] (Waas et al., 2017[30]).

An intermediate worker category may offer a solution to the classification issue, but it also has its problems. Some countries have a "third worker category" to capture all those workers who can be considered to fall somewhere in between an independent contractor and an employee, and to give this group access to a basic set of rights, benefits and protections. In most cases, the extension of rights to workers in this intermediate category relates to social protection while the termination of contracts remains strictly regulated by commercial law. Some examples include: the worker category in the United Kingdom; the "semi-subordinate" worker *(lavoro parasubordinato)* in Italy; and the "employee-like" persons *(arbeitnehmerähnliche Person)* in Germany. While France does not have a third worker category as such, the government has proposed to allow platforms to sign a charter which sets out their responsibilities towards workers, and the rights of the latter. In return, platforms would not risk having their workers be re-classified as employees. In effect, therefore, this solution would create a separate category of workers.

While such an intermediate category may help some own-account workers, it is not clear that a third category necessarily makes the classification issue any easier (De Stefano, 2016[31]). There is also a risk that some employees may lose their rights and protections by having their status downgraded into the third category. This happened to some employees in Italy who were shifted into the intermediate "semi-subordinate" category (Liebman, 2006[32]; Muehlberger, 2007[33]). To some extent, such downgrading could be prevented by tightening the criteria to be classified as an intermediate worker, but then there is a risk that these become too burdensome and time-consuming so that few workers end up being classified as such. This is the problem in Spain, where strict requirements to be classified as TRADE have resulted in few workers being classified as such. Finally, in the case of platform workers, the issue is complicated by the tripartite nature of the employment relationship which makes it unclear who the employer would be (if, indeed, there is an employer at all).

Even where existing legislation is adequate and workers/firms are well-informed, it might be difficult and costly for workers to challenge their employment status. Governments may then wish to make it easier/less costly for employment status to be challenged, for example by placing the burden of proof on the employer (rather than the employee), reducing court fees, reducing the risks to workers, and/or protecting workers against potential retaliation. While in most countries, it is up to the worker to challenge their employment status, in some countries the labour authority has some power to enforce compliance with labour laws – although this is usually limited and does not include the possibility of ordering a civil remedy or taking a claim to court without the consent of the aggrieved worker(s). In Australia, Chile, Poland, Spain and the United States, however, the labour authority can seek for a civil remedy on behalf of the aggrieved workers even in the absence of consent, particularly in cases where an important public interest is concerned. In Sweden, trade unions can take employers to court on behalf of the worker (Williams and Lapeyre, 2017[29]). Some platforms have tried to get workers to sign arbitration agreements under which they waive away the right to sue in court. In the United States, the National Labor Relations Board has ruled that such waivers violate labour law (Waas et al., 2017[30]).

In addition, governments may wish to strengthen the penalties for firms not complying with legislation. Indeed, where consequences of abuse are minimal, firms may have little incentive to correctly classify workers. Policy options include: requalification of the employment relationship; imposing retroactive payment of taxes and social security contributions; imposing greater penalties if firms continue to breach the law in repeated comparable cases; and extending the application of tribunal judgments beyond the plaintiffs and to the entire workforce in a similar situation. Such actions might be combined with efforts to strengthen the labour inspectorate's capacity to monitor and detect breaches, e.g. increased responsibilities and resources, innovative methods to inspect those working from home/on platforms, etc.

Regulating platform work

Another policy response is to attempt to regulate the use of new forms of work (in the same way as temporary work agency work and temporary contracts have been regulated in the past), which could restrict or even prohibit their use. Regulating platform work from a labour perspective is tricky since many workers may be genuinely self-employed and therefore do not have an employment contract. Most platform workers nonetheless sign terms of use with the platform and those could be the subject of regulatory intervention. For example, countries may want to ban arbitration agreements under which workers waive rights to litigation, or non-compete clauses which prohibit the individual from working for other platforms. But regulatory interventions are likely to have to come primarily from outside the labour domain, including in the fields of commercial, competition and tax policy, or even specific sectoral regulation (e.g. transport or accommodation). In some countries, decisions have been taken to ban certain platforms outright – often based on arguments of unfair competition. For example, the transportation network company Uber has been banned from (or has voluntary pulled out of due to legal restrictions) the following jurisdictions: Alaska, Oregon (except Portland) in the United States, Vancouver in Canada, Bulgaria, Denmark, Greece, Hungary, Italy, Germany, the Northern Territory in Australia, Japan, and Taiwan.[5] But such decisions should not be taken lightly, and the various trade-offs should be carefully considered. The example of temporary work agency (TWA) work in the past can be helpful, which was initially banned in many countries but which, with the development of appropriate regulation, provided numerous good job opportunities for individuals.

Improving working conditions

In order to improve working conditions among those in new forms of work, governments should first of all ensure that workers and employers are aware of their respective rights and responsibilities. For example, in Austria, many workers for the courier firm Foodora were unclear about the terms and conditions of their contracts (Johnston and Land-Kazlauskas, 2018[34]). Governments can run public information campaigns and/or require firms to provide workers with written statements on their employment status and the associated rights and protections. For example, in the United Kingdom, the government's response to the Taylor Review ("Good Work") (HM Government, 2018[35]) includes plans to ensure that all workers receive information from day one on their working relationship, and what rights they are entitled to.

Governments might also consider how various rights, benefits and protections could be extended to those in new forms of work. In many cases, labour laws, policies and institutions have been designed with the standard, open-ended full-time employee in mind. Extending these to, say, the self-employed is not always straightforward, and so one solution proposed has been to introduce an intermediate or third worker category which would provide access to some of these rights and protections (generally those that can easily be extended), but not others (those that are more difficult to extend). However, a better alternative might be to revisit each major labour law and policy individually (even those which, at first, seem more difficult to extend to non-standard workers) and carefully assess how it might be tailored to broaden coverage, where appropriate (Kennedy, 2016[36]). For example:

- *Pay*. For employees in standard employment arrangements, a legally-binding minimum wage can help to prevent exploitation and address in-work poverty. However, minimum wages typically do not cover independent workers, who are considered "businesses" and are often paid per task that they complete rather than remunerated by the hour. Yet many of these workers are price takers (i.e. are in a poor bargaining position) and earn very low wages. One possible option for addressing low pay among such workers would be to extend minimum wage legislation by requiring employers or clients to pay the equivalent of the minimum wage to individuals working on a piece rate basis. Other options include exemptions from competition law[6] to give independent workers collective bargaining rights (see below) or the extension/adaptation of homework legislation (which, in many countries, regulates pay) to the gig economy. In the Netherlands, the government announced that all self-employed with hourly earnings under a certain threshold (most likely around EUR 15-18) would automatically be re-classified as employees (unless they work for an employer for a short time and do not perform the employer/firm's core activities).
- *Working time*. Traditional concerns around working time have centered around the issue of excessive working hours. This is why labour legislation usually contains rules limiting working hours and requiring periods for rest and recuperation, including weekly rest and paid annual leave. Such legislation will not apply to the self-employed, who are their own boss. But, in cases, of dependent self-employment, there may be a need for governments to intervene. For instance, many own-account workers in the platform economy have limited ability to choose their hours of work (Lehdonvirta, 2018[37]). Fierce competition between workers on certain platforms means that they often need to remain on-call if they do not want to lose out when new gigs are advertised. While some platforms have introduced their own limits (e.g. CloudFactory sets upper and lower limits on the amount of work each worker can complete in a week) and workers have adopted their own, informal practices (Lehdonvirta, 2018[37]), governments may wish to consider how working time legislation (including rights

to annual leave) could be extended to such workers (see Box 12.1 for a related discussion on variable-hours and on-call contracts).

Box 12.1. Variable-hours and on-call contracts

While the focus of this chapter is on self-employed workers, several countries have faced challenges with so-called "variable-hours" or "on-call" contracts. These can be either permanent or fixed-term employment arrangements, but are characterised by the fact that working hours are neither predictable nor guaranteed. The employer and employee may agree a minimum number of guaranteed hours, and in some countries, there may be no guaranteed hours at all (so-called "zero-hour" contracts).

In recent years, there have been a number of reforms aimed at tempering the consequences of unpredictability in working hours on workers' overall earnings, earnings volatility, and their ability to plan ahead. This has particularly been the case for so-called "zero-hour" contracts. Reforms undertaken include: restricting the use of such contracts to situations where employers truly have a variable need for labour (Finland); requiring employers to provide information (such as the minimum number of hours) upfront or in the employment contract (Finland, Ireland and Norway); requiring advance notice of work schedules (Finland, Ireland, Netherlands, Norway and Oregon in the United States) or adjusting the contracted hours to reflect hours actually worked (Ireland); giving employees the right to request a more predictable contract after a certain period of time (UK, Australia); compensation in case workers are called in but sent home again without work (Ireland) or in case they are expected to remain available outside guaranteed hours (New Zealand); and introducing provisions for sick pay and for compensation in cases of termination of employment (Finland). In addition, in the United Kingdom, there was a recent public consultation on introducing a higher minimum wage for such types of contracts to discourage their (over-)use.

To a large extent, the concerns around variable-hours/on-call contracts derive from asymmetries in bargaining power between workers and employers. That is why some measures aim to strengthen the bargaining power of workers like, for example, the banning of exclusivity clauses (i.e. contract clauses which forbid workers from working for other employers – the United Kingdom and the Netherlands) or removal of obligations on the employee to accept work where the employer does not offer guaranteed hours (e.g. in New Zealand where firms must offer compensation for such availability). However, in some cases, countries have undermined the bargaining position of workers – for example, by expecting the unemployed to take up variable- (or zero-) hour contacts through activation measures.

- *Occupational Safety and Health.* Many new forms of work transfer responsibilities for occupational health and safety from the employer to individual workers, who often lack the training or resources to take appropriate measures to ensure that working conditions and the working environment are safe. Sometimes, strong competition between workers may result in corners being cut and unnecessary risks being taken while, at the same time, labour inspectorates are often not adequately prepared to deal with these new forms of employment (or may not even be able to intervene, since independent work is outside their remit). Regulations may therefore need to be adapted/clarified, and monitoring and control mechanisms strengthened and improved.

- *Anti-discrimination*. Because of its potential negative impact on inclusiveness, but also on productivity, countries have put in place measures to tackle discrimination on the basis of race, gender, religion, political opinion, socio-economic background, etc. The emergence of the platform economy has an ambiguous effect on the ability to protect workers from discrimination. To the extent that platforms promote anonymity they might help address discrimination. However, where such anonymity is not guaranteed, discrimination may be worse because of the lack of regulation and enforcement (see Edelman, Luca and Svirsky (2017[38]) for evidence of racial discrimination; Ajunma (2018) for agc discrimination; Galperin and Greppi (2017[39]) for geographical discrimination; and Galperin, Cruces and Greppi (2017[40]) for evidence of gender discrimination). Moreover, while algorithms may offer the promise of removing human judgment from decisions, there is some evidence that, in fact, they may reinforce human prejudice and embed biases of their own Sweeney (2013[41]). This emerging evidence suggests that governments should think carefully about how non-discrimination laws might be extended to online platforms. At the very least, increased transparency on the part of labour platforms in terms of publishing data on outcomes for various groups would shed light on the extent of any problems.

Improving working conditions in new forms of work will also require proper enforcement, which will oftentimes mean strengthening the labour inspectorate's capacity to monitor working conditions and ensure compliance in new forms of work (e.g. increased responsibilities and resources, innovative methods to inspect those working from home/on platforms) as well as making it easier for workers to take legal action over working conditions (e.g. reducing court costs, protecting workers against retaliation; greater penalties if firms continue to breach the law in repeated, comparable cases; permitting class-action lawsuits).

Strengthening social protection

Self-employed workers frequently have reduced access to social protection. There are two aspects to this. First, there is an issue of statutory access – i.e. they are formally excluded from certain aspects of social protection. However, even where the self-employed have statutory access, their effective protection may be reduced because they have difficulty in meeting eligibility criteria or contribution thresholds (effective access).

The challenges

In most countries, a sizeable part of the social protection system was designed with full-time, permanent, dependent employees in mind. While in some countries this may partly reflect a time when there was less diversity in employment arrangements, a key reason for a lack of coverage is that there are significant difficulties in covering certain types of non-standard workers. In particular, there are significant gaps when it comes to the self-employed (Spasova et al., 2017[42]). The gaps are particularly acute when it comes to unemployment benefits and protection against accidents at work and occupational injuries. A key reason for this is that there are significant moral hazard problems in providing social protection (and unemployment benefits in particular) to the self-employed. The self-employed do not meet several conditions that typically limit moral hazard in relation to unemployment benefits: fluctuations in demand for their services are hard to distinguish from voluntary idleness, as there is no employer to confirm a layoff; and job search efforts are even more difficult to monitor than for dependent employees. As a result, where they are covered by unemployment insurance, they often face more stringent conditions. In Sweden, self-employed workers have to close down their business before claiming benefits. In Austria, self-employed workers have six months to decide whether to opt into voluntary unemployment insurance upon starting their business – this decision is binding for eight years. In Belgium, only self-employed workers whose company went bankrupt, or who had such a low income from self-employment that either their social security contributions were waived or they did not reach a minimum earnings threshold (around EUR 13 000) for two years are entitled to benefits.

Even when the self-employed have statutory access to social protection, they may not in practice meet relevant eligibility requirements. While it is difficult to estimate with precision the number of individuals who do not meet these requirements, it is possible to identify those at risk of not qualifying because of their job or employment type. Such analysis indicates that, across the EU on average, 54.5%, 37.8% and 46.1% of the self-employed risk not being eligible for unemployment, sickness and maternity benefits, respectively (Matsaganis et al., 2016[43]). Even these figures appear relatively low, however. Indeed, recent OECD evidence suggests that fewer than one-in-three jobseekers receive unemployment benefits, on average across countries (OECD, 2018[44]). While relatively little is known about the extent to which platform workers are covered by social protection, the indications from the emerging research is that there are significant protection gaps in this sector (Forde et al., 2017[11]). The lack of social protection for non-standard workers is not just a concern for the workers themselves: a move towards more non-standard employment also risks eroding the contribution base of social protection systems and may have a negative impact on the government budget.

Improving social protection for the self-employed

The specific course of action to improve social protection for all workers, including the self-employed, will vary from country to country, depending on national specificities (including societal preferences), cost/benefit calculations, and options for financing. For instance, coverage gaps are not new and providing the exact same degree of social protection to everybody, independently of work status, may not be possible or even desirable.

In some cases, countries may be able to extend statutory access to existing social protection schemes to the self-employed. For example, in Norway, benefits for carers of dependent persons were extended in 2015 to also cover self-employed individuals. In Austria, the "new" self-employed (e.g. lecturers, artists, scientists, journalists, writers, etc. who perform work on the basis of a contract for services) have been covered by social protection (health, pensions and accidents) since the 1990s. Indeed, Austria is one of the countries with the most complete social protection coverage for self-employed workers. In France, platforms have been expected to cover workplace accident contributions since the start of 2018.

In cases where self-employed workers already have statutory access but coverage is low, effective access could be improved through parametric changes such as, for example, adjusting rules and thresholds of existing schemes/programmes (e.g. earnings/hours/minimum contribution thresholds; allowing for interrupted contributions periods) and changing how self-employed earnings are assessed (e.g. consider annual, not monthly earnings; flat contributions; etc.)[7] For example, during the recent economic and financial crisis, Portugal relaxed the contribution requirements for gaining access to regular unemployment insurance. More specifically, the necessary contributory history was lowered from 450 to 360 days over the past 24 months. The evidence suggests that, despite a significant increase in unemployment between 2011 and 2013, the coverage rate of unemployment benefits held up well (OECD, 2017[45]).

Where the challenges specific to self-employment are too great to extend existing social protection schemes, countries may wish to introduce specially designed schemes. For example, the German artists' insurance is a special scheme that offers artists and writers health, pensions and long-term care insurance (but not for unemployment). Membership is mandatory (although low-earning artists and those with high incomes or private insurance can be exempt). Qualifying writers and artists only pay employee social security contributions that make up half of the scheme's total budget; institutions that rely on the services of artists and writers (e.g. publishers, theatres, libraries or private companies), contribute proportionally to their use of artists' and writers' services, covering 30% of the overall cost. The remaining 20% is covered by a public subsidy, justified by private households' consumption of art and writing.[8] Such special schemes frequently target artists, but also farmers – e.g. the Farmers' Pension Insurance in Finland (also available to artists); the farmers' pension fund in Germany; and similar schemes exist in Greece and Poland.[9]

A closely related policy response (already discussed in one of the previous sections) is the creation of a third/intermediate worker category. Often, these categories are created to improve access to social protection – either to existing schemes (e.g. the extension of unemployment benefits to the self-employed in Portugal in 2012 – albeit with a different financing set-up) or to entirely new schemes (e.g. in Italy, a specific new scheme was introduced in 2015 (Bill no. 22) for 'dependent self-employed' persons working on co.co.pro. contracts, called DIS-COLL).

Given that some of the key challenges in covering self-employed workers relate to the payment of social security contributions, one option open to countries would be to increase reliance on universal benefits financed through general taxation (see also Chapter 8. This would extend coverage to all non-standard workers and dispose of the necessity to track entitlements across jobs and over the lifecycle. Some benefits – such as health insurance and maternity or parental leave – are already universal in a number of OECD countries. In some countries, like Australia and New Zealand, income replacement benefits are tax-financed (and means-tested) – although payments in such systems tend to be lower than in insurance-based ones.

Financing social protection through general taxation may weaken the link between what is paid and expected benefits (which could, in turn, encourage more tax evasion and/or reduce public support, making it more difficult to raise benefit levels). Therefore, moving away from social security contributions might be easiest in cases where the link between contributions and benefits is already weak. In France, for example, social charges are levied on personal capital income and there has been talk of introducing a "social" value-added tax (VAT) – (i.e. a VAT rate increase to finance the social security system). Moving to a social protection system financed more through general taxation would also have some other benefits (see Chapter 8 for a fuller discussion).

At the extreme, existing social protection could be replaced with a universal, unconditional public transfer (i.e. basic income). This would have the advantages of being simple and of leaving no one behind. But, as OECD work has demonstrated, an unconditional payment to everyone at meaningful but fiscally realistic levels would require tax rises as well as reductions in existing benefits, and would often not be an effective tool for reducing income poverty (OECD, 2017[46]). In addition, some disadvantaged groups would lose out when existing benefits are replaced by a basic income and the impact on work incentives is ambiguous. Currently, a number of countries are piloting different forms of a basic income (e.g. Canada, Finland, the Netherlands, Italy and Scotland). None of them are entirely universal or unconditional, but these experiments should be watched closely for their evaluation results.

Another option which countries may wish to consider is to enhance the portability of benefits so that entitlements are not lost when individuals move across social security systems or change employment status. One way of operationalising this would be to tie entitlements to individuals rather than to jobs. Such rights would be recorded in an individual account which could accommodate contract work and short-time, contingent employment and collect the entitlements of multiple job holders in one place. In Latvia, the social insurance system is fully individualised, as each person's contributions are registered on a separate account. In the United States, there are multiemployer plans in certain sectors (which tend to be the outcome of collective bargaining agreements and typically only apply if workers stay within the sector) and, for independent contractors and freelancers there are multiple employer welfare arrangements (MEWA) (Katz and Krueger, 2016[1]; Hill, 2015[47]). Such portability does not have to imply a move away from risk-sharing. Indeed, one can maintain a system which remains collective and allows for redistribution while just changing the way in which it is administered. In Belgium, self-employed workers who used to be employees keep their accumulated rights to unemployment benefits for a period of eight years.

The emergence of new forms of work and the platform economy in particular also calls for reforms in the administration of benefits. In particular, there are new challenges in monitoring work activity with platforms making it easier for individuals to combine the receipt of benefits with informal work in the platform economy.

Seeking fair taxation of self-employed income

As discussed above, differences in tax treatment between various employment forms can introduce incentives for individuals and/or employers to prefer certain forms of employment over others. For example, some countries offer tax credits against personal income tax to unincorporated self-employed workers (which are not available to standard employees); social security contribution liabilities may vary by employment form, for both individuals and firms; and some countries offer tax credits against corporate income tax to firms who employ workers of certain types.

The concept of tax neutrality in this context posits that countries' tax systems should not affect individuals' or firms' decisions with respect to employment form. However, because there are often also differences between employment forms in terms of access to social protection and employment regulation, tax neutrality may not necessarily be a desirable objective in and of itself. Instead, governments should seek to ensure that the package of benefits and protections which the self-employed are entitled to is commensurate with their tax and social security contributions so as to avoid choices of employment form purely based on differences in fiscal burdens. There are other reasons to question basic tax neutrality, such as the fact that the self-employed may take on greater entrepreneurial risk. In addition, effective tax incidence may vary by employment form.

In recent years, many countries have undertaken steps to bring platform workers into the tax system, including: simplifying procedures and automatic tax declarations; the introduction of special tax rates, cost deductions or thresholds; agreements with platforms to communicate the income of workers and/or withhold tax directly; better guidance and/or educational programmes/media campaigns to make platform workers aware of their tax obligations. For example, Uber in Estonia shares information on the financial transactions between customers and drivers so that the tax authorities can prefill drivers' tax forms (BEIS, 2017[48]). In Belgium, the government introduced a special regime for platform workers in 2016: workers earning up to EUR 5 000 annually (indexed) through platform work could report "miscellaneous income" and pay a 10% income tax instead of 33%.

Strengthening labour relations and worker's voice

Workers in new forms of employment may face specific barriers to collective representation. For example, competition law prohibits self-employed contractors from unionising and negotiating collectively. In the platform economy, workers on the same platform might not necessarily have any contact with one another if they are working alone and separated by different geographies, or even languages and legal contexts. In addition, given the triangular nature of work in the platform economy (employer-client-worker) and the fact that most workers are classified as self-employed, makes it difficult to determine who the counterpart for social dialogue and collective bargaining would be.

Yet labour relations can play an important role in improving working conditions for workers in non-standard forms of work. For example, temporary work agencies were initially perceived as disruptive as the platforms of today and were highly contested and even banned in a number of countries. However, through social dialogue, agencies found a way to be accepted and improve labour relations, as well as to co-define the regulation of the sector. Similarly, social partners are finding innovative ways of representing workers in new forms of work and strengthening their voice (Keune, 2013[49]) – and improvements in working conditions can be made even without formal union recognition and outside collective bargaining avenues (Johnston and Land-Kazlauskas, 2018[34]). For example, some unions have pursued legal strategies – like GMB, the union for professional drivers in the United Kingdom, which has challenged the employment status of drivers for ride-sharing apps; or the International Brotherhood of Teamsters in Seattle, which has pushed for new legislation which would extend collective bargaining rights to drivers for Transportation Network Companies. There have also been attempts at setting up:

- New unions (e.g. the New York Taxi Worker Alliance) and unaffiliated guilds (e.g. the Independent Drivers Guild)
- Special structures within existing unions (e.g. for the *parasubordinati* in Italy; for own-account workers (ZZP) in the Netherlands)
- Platform cooperatives (the Union Taxi Cooperative in Denver)
- Works councils (in Austria, Foodora app-based delivery workers have recently joined together to form a works council with the support of Vida, the Austrian union representing workers in the transport and services sector).

New technologies can help organise workers' voice, e.g. by enabling peer-to-peer exchange, sharing information, rating employers/clients, etc. (also sometimes referred to as "platform-based collective action"). For example, Turkopticon allows workers on Mechanical Turk to rate and review requesters; while Dynamo is a forum that helps them organise campaigns, but also to share information, collaborate and develop guidelines for academic requesters in setting wages and task design. Another website, Coworker.org, provides mechanisms for workers to communicate about their concerns and organise campaigns to change employer practices.

But there are limits to what can be achieved without union recognition and collective bargaining. This is why some governments are seeking to ensure the right to freedom of association and extend the right to collective bargaining where appropriate. In practice, this is not always straightforward because allowing the self-employed to collectively bargaining is against competition policy in most countries (Daskalova, 2017[50]). The general rationale behind such rules makes sense, as it is meant to protect consumers from price fixing and its negative consequences. However, in the case of certain categories of self-employed workers who are price takers, there may be an argument for improving their pay. There have been some interesting initiatives in this area:

- Canada introduced a dependent contractor category for purposes of collective bargaining eligibility under provincial labour laws. This covers workers who are legally independent but economically dependent on a single employer.
- In the United States, the Seattle City Council, following lobbying by the Teamster Union, unanimously approved an ordinance in 2015 which granted ride-hailing drivers the right to unionise and, therefore, bargain collectively.
- In Ireland, in 2017, the Parliament adopted the Competition Amendment Act which introduces exemptions from competition law for certain self-employed workers – in particular freelance performers – allowing them to bargain collectively. The Act also allows for trade unions to ask for other categories of workers to be added to the exemption list, provided this would have no or minimal impact on competition in the category within which they work. It is unclear at this stage whether the Irish decision will be judged to be in breach of European Competition Law (O'Loughlin, 2017[51]).

Promoting investments in skills

Self-employment brings additional complications for skills policy since workers in such types of employment are less likely to receive training.

Adjustments may be needed to existing training mechanisms to make them accessible to individuals regardless of their employment status. Countries should make sure that existing training schemes cover non-standard workers as well, including the self-employed. In France, for example, a recent decree stipulates that platforms which determine the characteristics of work and set remuneration will, under certain conditions, have to reimburse workers for fees paid to validate acquired experience (Donini et al., 2017[52]). Provision of education and training might also be made more flexible such that adults can overcome time constraints and care responsibilities which act as barriers to participation. As pointed out by the Taylor Review in the United Kingdom (BEIS, 2017[48]), work has become more flexible, but training and skills policies have struggled to keep pace with such increases in flexibility. In particular, countries may wish to facilitate shorter/different pathways to training (e.g. blended learning, distance provision, Massive Open Online Courses (MOOCs), Stackable/Modular and Micro-Credentials) – while being careful that these do not disadvantage low-skilled workers with poor digital skills (National Academies of Sciences, Engineering, 2017[53]).

But addressing the challenge posed by self-employment might also require the development of new instruments for incentivising investments in training (such as personal training accounts, or lifelong training rights) as well as mechanisms to allow the portability of training rights between employers. In France, for example, individual training accounts (*Compte Personnel de Formation - CPF)* cover all working age individuals, including the self-employed. Full-time workers CPFs are credited with EUR 500 per year up to a maximum of EUR 5 000 (EUR 800 and EUR 8 000, respectively, for the low-skilled.

The platform economy offers the promise of new job opportunities – however governments should make sure that individuals have the digital skills required to find work via platforms. According to the Survey of Adult Skills, nearly half of adults in the OECD lack basic digital skills (OECD, 2013[54]). It is perhaps not surprising, therefore, that, on average platform workers are found to be higher-skilled than the average worker. Some governments are already taking steps to help individuals find work opportunities in the platform economy. The San Francisco Office of Economic and Workforce Development (OEWD) partnered with Samaschool to launch a pilot programme (*Bridge to Employment*) that provides support to aspiring gig economy workers. The goal is to help individuals take advantage of gig economy work opportunities to gain experience, develop skills, and earn additional income.

Improving data collection

One key challenge to developing evidence-based policy responses to the rise in non-standard forms of employment is that robust and up-to-date data on the number of workers and their characteristics are often lacking. For example, it is still not clear how many workers are active on platforms and dependent self-employment remains very difficult to identify in most existing data sources. Governments should therefore aim to improve the data available to policy-makers, including by: clarifying definitions (e.g. what does it mean to be a platform worker?); updating existing household and labour force surveys (e.g. by adding and/or adjusting questions); using administrative data sources (like tax and social security data) and linking them to survey data where possible; partnering with the private sector to obtain and analyse platform/employer data; and developing new data collection exercises (e.g. through special surveys or data crawling).

Conclusion

While the rise in self-employment and own-account work is by no means a universal trend across OECD countries, the issue of dependent self-employment and worker misclassification, as well as the protection and job quality of self-employed workers more generally, is receiving increased policy attention in many countries – and this has been partly driven by the emergence of the platform economy. The challenge for policy makers is to put in place policies and institutions which simultaneously promote entrepreneurship and flexibility, on the hand, and job quality and worker rights and protections, on the other. This chapter has reviewed some of the policy options open to countries to achieve this. It is important to repeat that achieving this goal is likely to require action on various fronts. For example, in ensuring adequate social protection for workers in non-standard forms of work, policy makers may need to consider the issues of worker classification and taxation, in addition to reviewing social protection systems. Solutions may therefore require a whole-of-government approach if they are to be successful.

Notes

[1] The Fair Labor Standards Act (FLSA) defines the term "employ" to include the words "suffer or permit to work". Suffer or permit to work means that if an employer requires or allows individuals to work the latter will be considered employees.

[2] Courts frequently use the "economic realities test" or a hybrid of the common-law control test (see below) and the economic realities test to determine independent contractor status. In addition to the degree of control the employer exercises, the latter takes into account the degree to which the workers are economically dependent on the business.

[3] The ABC test is used in some states to determine whether a person is an employee or an independent contractor for the purpose of determining state unemployment tax. Some courts using this test look at whether a worker meets three separate criteria to be considered an independent contractor: i) is the worker free from the employer's control and direction in carrying out the work?; ii) does the work take place outside the usual course of the business and off its site?; and iii) is the worker usually engaged in an independent trade, occupation, profession or business.

[4] The common-law control test (or sometimes also called the 20-factor or right-to-control test) is used by the Inland Revenue Service to determine whether a worker is an employee for tax purposes. The test involves a great degree of subjectivity, and even with all the facts, it may still be difficult to say whether the services rendered were performed as an employee. Finding that a worker is an employee is a finding that the person was subject to control over when, where, and how (the means and methods) to perform the work. This finding does not mean the control is actually exercised—only that the employer has the right to exercise it.

[5] https://en.wikipedia.org/wiki/Uber_protests_and_legal_actions.

[6] Another option to explore is applying competition law to address monopsony power where this might exist. A growing body of research indicates that labour markets are frequently characterised by monopsonistic power, with potentially negative impacts on wages and employment (Azar, Marinescu and Steinbaum, 2017[59]; Marinescu and Rathelot, 2018[58]; Manning and Petrongolo, 2017[57]; Benmelech, Bergman and Kim, 2018[60]).

[7] The self-employed have fluctuating earnings. This is because they are paid at irregular intervals, because there are time-lags between work and payment, and/or because demand for their services is erratic (ISSA, 2012[54]). Paying regular contributions on a monthly basis might therefore be difficult for them.

[8] Indeed, one key challenge with providing social protection to the self-employed is that many have very low earnings and cannot afford to pay both employee and employer social security contributions. The government could subsidise schemes for the self-employed, but this raises concerns about equal treatment and may create adverse incentives for both employers and employees. If jobs have to be heavily subsidised, it raises the question of whether there is a social benefit which justifies such a subsidy. Where they exist, such schemes are therefore often limited to occupations that are thought to create special value for the public, such as the arts.

[9] In some countries, the self-employed have set up their own schemes. For example, in the Netherlands, some self-employed have created a "bread fund" (*broodfonds*) where they agree to provide each other with an income if they are unfit for work. There are now 170 of these bread funds in the Netherlands (Kremer, Went and Knottnerus, 2017[55]).

References

Azar, J., I. Marinescu and M. Steinbaum (2017), "Labor Market Concentration", *NBER Working Paper Series*, No. 24147, National Bureau of Economic Research, Cambridge, MA, http://www.nber.org/papers/w24147.pdf (accessed on 23 August 2018). [59]

Balaram, B., J. Warden and F. Wallace-Stephens (2017), *Good Gigs - A fairer future for the UK's gig economy*, RSA, https://www.thersa.org/globalassets/pdfs/reports/rsa_good-gigs-fairer-gig-economy-report.pdf (accessed on 31 May 2018). [22]

BEIS (2017), *Good work: the Taylor review of modern working practices*, Department for Business, Energy & Industrial Strategy, https://www.gov.uk/government/publications/good-work-the-taylor-review-of-modern-working-practices (accessed on 04 June 2018). [48]

Benmelech, E., N. Bergman and H. Kim (2018), "Strong Employers and Weak Employees: How Does Employer Concentration Affect Wages?", No. 24307, National Bureau of Economic Research, Cambridge, MA, http://dx.doi.org/10.3386/w24307. [60]

Berg, J. (2016), "Income security in the on-demand economy: Findings and policy lessons from a survey of crowdworkers", International Labour Office, http://www.ilo.org/wcmsp5/groups/public/---ed_protect/---protrav/---travail/documents/publication/wcms_479693.pdf (accessed on 01 June 2018). [23]

Bonin, H. (2017), *The Incidence of Platform Work in Germany*, http://www.oecd.org/els/soc/7_Bonin_The_Incidence_of_Platform_Work_in_Germany.pdf (accessed on 31 May 2018). [24]

Brumm, F. (2016), *Making Gigs Work The new economy in context*, University of Illinois - Urbana Champaign, https://blogs.illinois.edu/files/6232/430823/98170.pdf (accessed on 01 June 2018). [15]

CIPD (2017), *To Gig or Not to Gig? Stories from the Modern Economy*, https://www.cipd.co.uk/Images/to-gig-or-not-to-gig_2017-stories-from-the-modern-economy_tcm18-18955.pdf (accessed on 01 June 2018). [17]

Cohen, P. et al. (2016), "Using Big Data to Estimate Consumer Surplus: The Case of Uber", *NBER Working Paper*, No. 22627, National Bureau of Economic Research, Cambridge, MA, http://dx.doi.org/10.3386/w22627. [12]

Daskalova, V. (2017), "Regulating the New Self-Employed in the Uber Economy: What Role for EU Competition Law?", *Discussion paper*, No. 2017-028, TILEC, https://papers.ssrn.com/sol3/papers.cfm?abstract_id=3009120 (accessed on 29 January 2018). [50]

De Stefano, V. (2016), "The rise of the «just-in-time workforce»: On-demand work, crowdwork and labour protection in the «gig-economy»", *Conditions of Work and Employment Series*, No. 71, International Labour Organization, http://www.ilo.org/wcmsp5/groups/public/---ed_protect/---protrav/---travail/documents/publication/wcms_443267.pdf (accessed on 06 June 2018). [31]

Donini, A. et al. (2017), "Towards collective protections for crowdworkers", *Transfer: European Review of Labour and Research*, Vol. 23/2, pp. 207-223, http://dx.doi.org/10.1177/1024258916688863. [52]

Edelman, B., M. Luca and D. Svirsky (2017), "Racial Discrimination in the Sharing Economy: Evidence from a Field Experiment", *American Economic Journal: Applied Economics*, Vol. 9/2, pp. 1-22, http://dx.doi.org/10.1257/app.20160213. [38]

Farrell, D. and F. Greig (2016), *Paychecks, Paydays, and the Online Platform Economy*, JPMorgan Chase Institute, https://www.jpmorganchase.com/corporate/institute/document/jpmc-institute-volatility-2-report.pdf (accessed on 31 May 2018). [2]

Farrell, D. and F. Greig (2016), *The Online Platform Economy - Has Growth Peaked?*, JPMorgan Chase Institute, https://www.jpmorganchase.com/corporate/institute/document/jpmc-institute-online-platform-econ-brief.pdf (accessed on 22 August 2018). [6]

Forde, C. et al. (2017), *The Social Protection of Workers in the Platform Economy*, European Parliament, http://www.europarl.europa.eu/RegData/etudes/STUD/2017/614184/IPOL_STU(2017)614184_EN.pdf (accessed on 04 June 2018). [11]

Galperin, H., G. Cruces and C. Greppi (2017), "Gender Interactions in Wage Bargaining: Evidence from an Online Field Experiment", *SSRN*, http://dx.doi.org/10.2139/ssrn.3056508. [40]

Galperin, H. and C. Greppi (2017), "Geographical Discrimination in Digital Labor Platforms", https://annenberg.usc.edu/sites/default/files/2017/11/27/Geographical%20Discrimination%20Galperin%20%26%20Greppi.pdf (accessed on 01 June 2018). [39]

Garben, S. (2017), *Protecting Workers in the Online Platform Economy: An overview of regulatory and policy developments in the EU*, European Agency for Safety and Health at Work, Luxemburg, http://dx.doi.org/10.2802/918187. [21]

Hathaway, I. and M. Muro (2016), *Tracking the gig economy: New numbers*, Brookings, https://www.brookings.edu/research/tracking-the-gig-economy-new-numbers/ (accessed on 11 June 2018). [13]

Hill, S. (2015), *New Economy, New Social Contract*, New America, https://static.newamerica.org/attachments/4395-new-economy-new-social-contract/New%20Economy,%20Social%20Contract_UpdatedFinal.34c973248e6946d0af17116fbd6bb79e.pdf (accessed on 04 June 2018). [47]

HM Government (2018), *Good Work*, https://assets.publishing.service.gov.uk/government/uploads/system/uploads/attachment_data/file/679767/180206_BEIS_Good_Work_Report__Accessible_A4_.pdf (accessed on 01 June 2018). [35]

Huws, U., N. Spencer and S. Joyce (2016), *Crowd Work in Europe*, http://www.uni-europa.org/wp-content/uploads/2016/12/2016-12-Crowd-work-in-Europe.pdf (accessed on 31 May 2018). [25]

IFC (2018), *Driving Toward Equality: Women, Ride-Hailing, and the Sharing Economy*, https://www.ifc.org/wps/wcm/connect/ec101088-8a12-4994-9918-14455b8e2cd9/00418+IFC+DTE+Report_Complete_Layout+Final2-pxp.pdf?MOD=AJPERES (accessed on 01 June 2018). [7]

ISSA (2012), *Handbook on the extension of social security coverage to the self-employed - Social Protection and Human Rights*, ISSA, http://socialprotection-humanrights.org/resource/handbook-on-the-extension-of-social-security-coverage-to-the-self-employed/ (accessed on 01 June 2018). [55]

Jackson, E., A. Looney and S. Ramnath (2017), "The Rise of Alternative Work Arrangements: Evidence and Implications for Tax Filing and Benefit Coverage", *Working Papers*, No. 114, Office of Tax Analysis, https://www.treasury.gov/resource-center/tax-policy/tax-analysis/Documents/WP-114.pdf (accessed on 31 May 2018). [3]

Johnston, H. and C. Land-Kazlauskas (2018), "Organizing on-demand: Representation,voice, and collective bargaining in the gig economy", *Conditions of Work and Employment Series*, No. 94, International Labour Office, http://www.ilo.org/wcmsp5/groups/public/---ed_protect/---protrav/---travail/documents/publication/wcms_624286.pdf (accessed on 01 June 2018). [34]

Katz, L. and A. Krueger (2016), "The Rise and Nature of Alternative Work Arrangements in the United States", *NBER Working Paper Series*, No. 22667, NBER, http://www.nber.org/papers/w22667.pdf (accessed on 31 May 2018). [1]

Kautonen, T. et al. (2010), "Involuntary self- employment" as a public policy issue: a cross-country European review", *International Journal of Entrepreneurial Behavior & Research*, Vol. 16/2, pp. 112-129, http://dx.doi.org/10.1108/13552551011027002. [27]

Kennedy, J. (2016), *Three Paths to Update Labor Law for the Gig Economy*, Information Technology & Innovation Foundation, http://www2.itif.org/2016-labor-law-gig-economy.pdf (accessed on 01 June 2018). [36]

Keune, M. (2013), "Trade union responses to precarious work in seven European countries", *International Journal of Labour Research*, Vol. 5/1, pp. 59-78, https://dare.uva.nl/search?identifier=80f6596c-efad-416c-bf1a-6836fde562e9 (accessed on 04 June 2018). [49]

Kremer, M., R. Went and A. Knottnerus (2017), *For the Sake of Security. The Future of Flexible Workers and the Modern Organisation of Labour | Investigation | The Netherlands Scientific Council for Government Policy*, WRR, https://english.wrr.nl/publications/investigation/2017/05/01/for-the-sake-of-security (accessed on 08 June 2018). [56]

Lehdonvirta, V. (2018), "Flexibility in the Gig Economy: Managing Time on Three Online Piecework Platforms", *New Technology, Work and Employment*, https://papers.ssrn.com/sol3/papers.cfm?abstract_id=3099419 (accessed on 01 June 2018). [37]

Lepanjuuri, K., R. Wishart and P. Cornick (2018), *The Characteristics of Those in the Gig Economy*, Department for Business, Energy and Industrial Strategy, http://www.natcen.ac.uk/media/1543748/The-characteristics-of-those-in-the-gig-economy.pdf (accessed on 01 June 2018). [18]

Liebman, S. (2006), *Employment situations and workers' protection - Italy*, ILO, http://ilo.org/ifpdial/areas-of-work/labour-law/WCMS_205366/lang--en/index.htm (accessed on 05 June 2018). [32]

Manning, A. and B. Petrongolo (2017), "How Local Are Labor Markets? Evidence from a Spatial Job Search Model", *American Economic Review*, Vol. 107/10, pp. 2877-2907, http://dx.doi.org/10.1257/aer.20131026. [57]

Marinescu, I. and R. Rathelot (2018), "Mismatch Unemployment and the Geography of Job Search", *American Economic Journal: Macroeconomics*, Vol. 10/3, pp. 42-70, http://dx.doi.org/10.1257/mac.20160312. [58]

Matsaganis, M. et al. (2016), *Non-Standard Employment and Access to Social Security Benefits*, European Commission, http://ec.europa.eu/social/BlobServlet?docId=15687&langId=en. [43]

Milanez, A. and B. Bratta (forthcoming), "Taxation of Non-standard Work", *Tax Policy Working Paper*. [9]

Muehlberger, U. (2007), "Work on the Border Between Employment and Self-Employment", in *Dependent Self-Employment*, Palgrave Macmillan UK, London, http://dx.doi.org/10.1057/9780230288782_2. [33]

National Academies of Sciences, Engineering, A. (2017), *Information Technology and the U.S. Workforce*, National Academies Press, Washington, D.C., http://dx.doi.org/10.17226/24649. [53]

O'Loughlin, K. (2017), *Irish Equity wins legislation to recommence collective bargaining for freelance performers in Ireland!*, http://fia-actors.com/no_cache/media/news/news-detail/article/irish-equity-wins-legislation-to-recommence-collective-bargaining-for-freelance-performers-in-ireland/ (accessed on 04 June 2018). [51]

OECD (2018), *OECD Employment Outlook 2018*, OECD Publishing, Paris, http://dx.doi.org/10.1787/empl_outlook-2018-en. [44]

OECD (2017), *Basic income as a policy option: Can it add up?*, OECD Publishing, http://www.oecd.org/employment/future-of-work.htm (accessed on 04 June 2018). [46]

OECD (2017), *Labour Market Reforms in Portugal 2011-15: A Preliminary Assessment*, OECD Publishing, Paris, http://dx.doi.org/10.1787/9789264269576-en. [45]

OECD (2015), *In It Together: Why Less Inequality Benefits All*, OECD Publishing, Paris, http://dx.doi.org/10.1787/9789264235120-en. [8]

OECD (2014), *OECD Employment Outlook 2014*, OECD Publishing, Paris, http://dx.doi.org/10.1787/empl_outlook-2014-en. [14]

OECD (2013), *OECD Skills Outlook 2013: First results from the survey of adult skills*, OECD Publishing, Paris, https://doi.org/10.1787/9789264204256-en. [54]

OECD (2008), *OECD Employment Outlook 2008*, OECD Publishing, Paris, http://dx.doi.org/10.1787/empl_outlook-2008-en. [28]

OECD (2000), *OECD Employment Outlook 2000: June*, OECD Publishing, Paris, http://dx.doi.org/10.1787/empl_outlook-2000-en. [10]

OECD/EU (2017), *The Missing Entrepreneurs 2017: Policies for Inclusive Entrepreneurship*, OECD Publishing, Paris, http://dx.doi.org/10.1787/9789264283602-en. [16]

Pesole, A. et al. (2018), *Platform Workers in Europe,*, Publications Office of the European Union, http://dx.doi.org/10.2760/742789. [26]

Quinlan, M. (2015), *The effects of non-standard forms of employment on worker health and safety*, International Labour Office, Geneva, http://www.ilo.org/wcmsp5/groups/public/---ed_protect/---protrav/---travail/documents/publication/wcms_443266.pdf (accessed on 14 June 2018). [19]

Spasova, S. et al. (2017), *Access to social protection for people working on non-standard contracts and as self-employed in Europe*, European Commission, http://ec.europa.eu/social/BlobServlet?docId=17683&langId=en. [42]

Statistics Canada (2017), *The sharing economy in Canada*, http://www.statcan.gc.ca/daily-quotidien/170228/dq170228b-eng.pdf (accessed on 01 June 2018). [4]

Statistics Finland (2018), *Around 0.3 per cent of Finns earned at least a quarter of their income through digital platforms in 2017*, http://www.stat.fi/til/tyti/2017/14/tyti_2017_14_2018-04-17_tie_001_en.html (accessed on 01 June 2018). [5]

Sweeney, L. (2013), "Discrimination in Online Ad Delivery", http://dataprivacylab.org/projects/onlineads/1071-1.pdf (accessed on 01 June 2018). [41]

Ticona, J. and A. Mateescu (2018), *How Domestic Workers Wager Safety in the Platform Economy*, https://www.fastcompany.com/40541050/how-domestic-workers-wager-safety-in-the-platform-economy (accessed on 14 June 2018). [20]

Waas, B. et al. (2017), *Crowdwork – A Comparative Law Perspective*, http://www.hugo-sinzheimer-institut.de/fileadmin/user_data_hsi/Veroeffentlichungen/HSI_Schriftenreihe/Waas_Liebman_Lyubarsky_Kezuka_Crowdwork.pdf (accessed on 01 June 2018). [30]

Williams, C. and F. Lapeyre (2017), "Dependent self-employment: Trends, challenges and policy responses in the EU", *Employment Working Paper*, No. 228, ILO, http://ilo.org/wcmsp5/groups/public/---ed_emp/documents/publication/wcms_614176.pdf (accessed on 01 June 2018). [29]

Part IV. Resilient and adaptable labour markets

Chapter 13. Nurturing labour market resilience

Labour market developments following the global financial crisis of 2008-09 differed starkly across countries. This partly reflects cross-country differences in the size and the nature of the underlying economic shocks. However, cross-country differences in labour market resilience, i.e. an economy's capacity to limit fluctuations in employment and to ensure a rapid rebound, also played a role. This chapter discusses how counter-cyclical macroeconomic policies, state-dependent employment and social policies as well as structural policies can strengthen labour market resilience.

The statistical data for Israel are supplied by and under the responsibility of the relevant Israeli authorities. The use of such data by the OECD is without prejudice to the status of the Golan Heights, East Jerusalem and Israeli settlements in the West Bank under the terms of international law.

Introduction

The global financial crisis of 2008-09 and the slow pace of the subsequent recovery in many countries has highlighted the importance of labour market resilience, i.e. limiting fluctuations in employment and ensuring a quick rebound in the wake of economic shocks. Labour market resilience is crucial not only to limit short-term social costs but also to support labour market and economic performance in the medium to long term. In particular, resilient labour markets reduce the degree to which increases in cyclical unemployment translate into structural unemployment, lower labour force participation and lower wage growth.

Labour market resilience in the wake of the Great Recession has differed widely across countries, which partly reflects differences in the size and the nature of the initial economic shock. In a number of countries, including Germany and Japan, employment losses were limited and short-lived, with employment back around pre-crisis levels within 2-3 years. In some other countries, such as a number of Southern European countries, employment losses were large and more persistent. While some countries experienced only transitory declines in external demand, others were additionally hit by financial, sovereign debt and balance of payments crises. For instance, Germany and Japan only experienced deep but short-lived declines in exports, whereas a number of euro area countries, such as Greece, Italy and Spain, were additionally hit by banking crises, sovereign debt crises and sudden capital flow reversals.

Yet cross-country differences in labour market resilience also reflect differences in macroeconomic policy as well as structural policy and institutional settings. The monetary and fiscal policy response to the initial economic shock differed widely across countries, contributing to cross-country differences in the size and the duration of output losses (OECD, 2010[1]). Even when accounting for cross-country differences in output losses, there were large cross-country differences in labour market outcomes. In some countries, the labour market adjusted to the fall in aggregate demand mainly through the employment margin whereas in others the number of hours worked or wages declined. To some extent, these differences in margins of adjustment reflect structural policy and institutions (OECD, 2017[2]).

The remainder of the chapter is structured as follows. Section 13.1 documents labour market resilience across OECD countries and Section 13.2 discusses the role of public policies and institutions.

13.1. Labour market resilience during and after the crisis of 2008-09

Labour market resilience in this chapter is defined as the capacity of the labour market to limit persistent deviations in employment from pre-crisis trends in the aftermath of adverse output shocks (i.e. recessions).[1] This definition encompasses the avoidance of excessive fluctuations in labour market outcomes as well as the swiftness of the rebound.

There were large differences in output developments across OECD countries in the wake of the economic and financial crisis (Figure 13.1, Panel A). In countries with annualised output per capita losses of 12% or more, including Estonia, Greece and Latvia, cumulative losses over the period 2008-15 amount to at least a year of lost income. Several other countries either were little affected by the Great Recession (e.g. Israel) or partially made up for output losses relative to trend in the wake of the Great Recession through above-trend growth in later years (e.g. Germany).

Figure 13.1. Persistent deviations of output and unemployment from pre-crisis crisis trends

2008-15

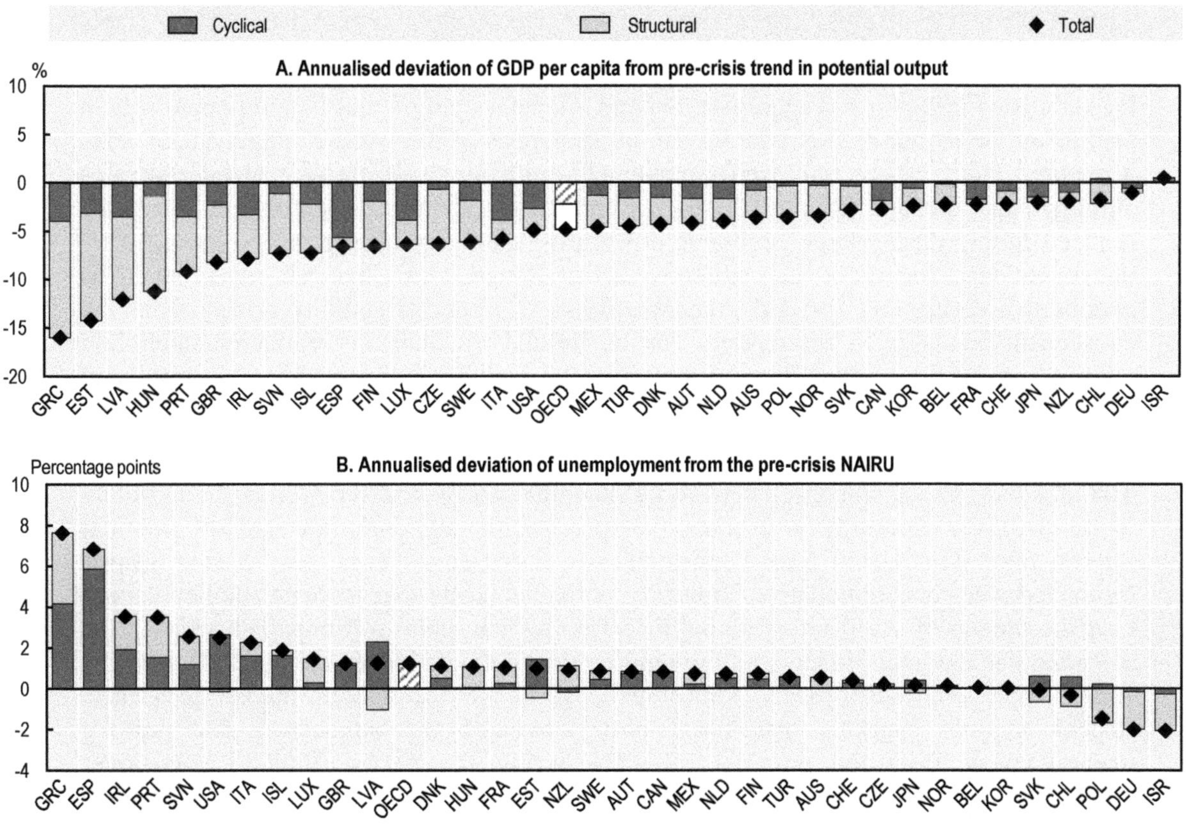

Note: The total height of the bars in Panel A denotes the annualised deviation of output from the pre-crisis trend in potential output, with the part in grey denoting the deviation of potential output from the pre-crisis trend in potential output. The total height of the bars in Panel B denotes the deviation of the unemployment rate from the pre-crisis NAIRU, with the part in grey denoting the deviation of the NAIRU from the pre-crisis NAIRU.

Source: OECD (2017[3]), "Labour market resilience: The role of structural and macroeconomic policies", in *OECD Employment Outlook 2017*, https://doi.org/10.1787/empl_outlook-2017-6-en.

StatLink http://dx.doi.org/10.1787/888933881648

Differences in output developments – which reflected differences in the nature and the size of the initial economic shock and differences in the macroeconomic policy response – accounted for around half of the differences in labour market resilience. Countries with large deviations of output per capita from pre-crisis trends such as Greece, Spain and Ireland, which were hit by major banking, sovereign debt and balance of payment crises, typically experienced large deviations of unemployment from the pre-crisis rate (Figure 13.1, Panel B). The opposite was true for countries with small deviations of output per capita from the pre-crisis trend, such as Germany and Japan that experienced transitory declines in external demand. However, differences in output developments cannot fully account for differences in labour market developments, suggesting that policies and institutions that affect the different margins of labour market adjustment also played a role (OECD, 2017[3]).

13.2. Policy lessons from the global crisis

This section discusses the lessons from the global crisis for macro-economic policies, state-contingent employment and social policies and structural labour market policies.

The role of macroeconomic policies

By stabilising inflation and aggregate demand, monetary policy plays an important role in stabilising the labour market and preventing hysteresis in the wake of aggregate shocks. Monetary policy can be deployed immediately, with rapid effects on real interest rates and aggregate demand (Ramey, 2016[4]). Even when short-term interest rates cannot be reduced further during large economic downturns, monetary easing can be provided by unconventional measures that directly affect longer-term interest rates, such as quantitative easing and forward guidance. Risks to financial stability arising from the consequent increases in asset prices can be limited by financial regulation, including micro- and macro-prudential measures such as well-designed bank stress tests and adequate capital ratios. To further limit such risks, monetary support needs to be gradually scaled back as economic conditions normalise.

The monetary policy response needs to be accompanied by counter-cyclical fiscal policy to be effective, especially in a context of persistently low inflation and low nominal interest rates (OECD, 2016[5]). Persistently low inflation over the past decade despite prolonged, very accommodative, monetary policy suggests that monetary policy cannot bear the burden of stabilisation alone. Fiscal policy can help to mitigate shocks via the so-called automatic stabilisers and through the use of discretionary measures. During the Great Recession, fiscal policy contributed significantly to labour market resilience. Recent analysis suggests that fiscal policy reduced the annualised deviation of unemployment from the pre-crisis NAIRU during the period 2008-15 from over 4 to about 1 percentage point for the OECD as a whole (OECD, 2017[2]), although there were marked differences across countries (Figure 13.2).

The automatic fiscal stabilisers need to be allowed to operate and could be strengthened in a number of countries by making expenditure on social and labour market programmes, such as unemployment insurance and active labour market programmes, more contingent on aggregate economic conditions (see below). During deep economic downturns, the automatic fiscal stabilisers can be complemented with timely and high-quality discretionary measures – preferably with a focus on measures such as public investment that both add to demand and raise the long-term growth potential of the economy. Lags in the implementation of such discretionary measures can to some extent be addressed by identifying projects well before the economic downturn so that a pool of rapidly implementable projects is available when it is most needed (OECD, 2015[6]).

Fiscal policy is particularly effective during economic downturns and when initial levels of public debt are low (Auerbach and Gorodnichenko, 2012[7]; Auerbach and Gorodnichenko, 2013[8]; Ilzetzki, Mendoza and Végh, 2013[9]). Collective action across economies would bring additional gains (OECD, 2016[5]). At the same time, public debt needs to be kept at prudent levels during economic upturns to enhance the space available for fiscal support during downturns (OECD, 2010[11]). In this light, counter-cyclical fiscal rules that have sufficient flexibility to permit temporary fiscal support during large downturns but require building fiscal buffers during upturns are preferable to rules with a narrow focus on the headline fiscal balance or government debt.

Figure 13.2. Fiscal policy contributed to labour market resilience in most countries

Annualised deviation of unemployment from the pre-crisis NAIRU, 2008-15

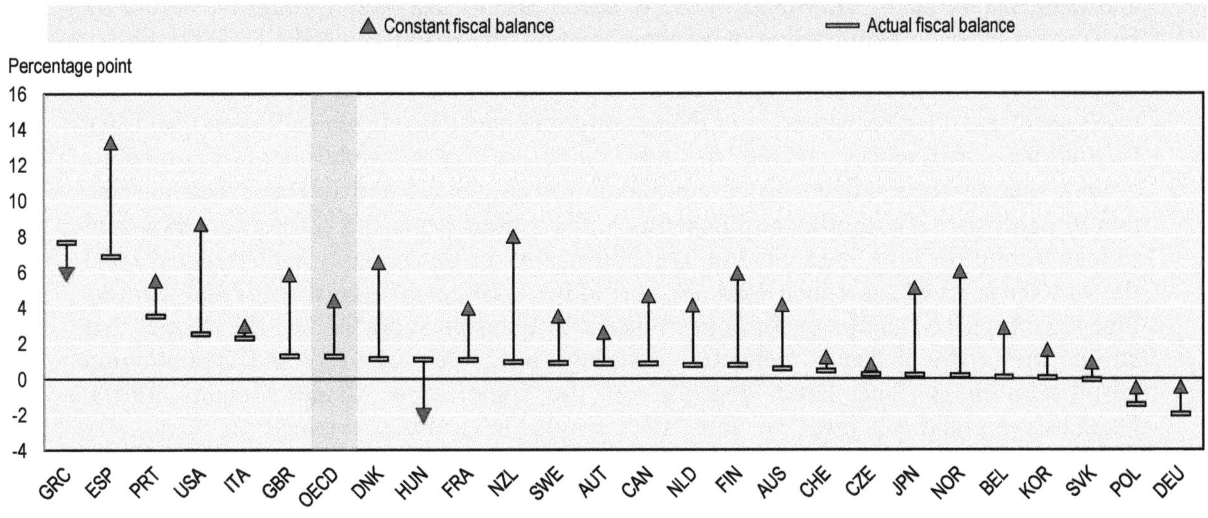

Note: "Actual fiscal balance" refers to the annualised deviation of unemployment from the pre-crisis NAIRU as reported in Figure 13.1. "Constant fiscal balance" refers to the econometrically estimated deviation of unemployment from the pre-crisis NAIRU that would have obtained in the absence of any changes in the headline fiscal balance since the start of the economic and financial crisis.
Source: OECD (2017[3]), "Labour market resilience: The role of structural and macroeconomic policies", in *OECD Employment Outlook 2017*, https://doi.org/10.1787/empl_outlook-2017-6-en.

StatLink http://dx.doi.org/10.1787/888933881667

The role of state-dependent employment and social policies

Employment and social policies are partly needs-driven and thus contain an element of state-dependency. A key question is to what extent it is desirable to further increase their responsiveness to changes in the business cycle, so as to both enhance their effectiveness during economic downturns and strengthen automatic fiscal stabilisation. This sub-section discusses the role of short-time work schemes for preserving jobs in times of crisis, the role of unemployment benefit schemes for consumption smoothing and supporting aggregate demand and the role of activation policies for helping people who lose their jobs return to work.

Short-time work schemes preserve jobs in times of crisis, but can become an obstacle to structural change in good times

An important lesson from the global crisis is the positive role of well-designed short-time work programmes in mitigating the unemployment costs of deep economic downturns. Short-time work (STW) programmes are public schemes that are intended to preserve jobs at firms temporarily experiencing low demand by encouraging work-sharing, while also providing income-support to workers whose hours are reduced due to a shortened workweek or temporary lay-offs. A crucial aspect of all STW schemes is that the contract of an employee with the firm is maintained during the period of STW or the suspension of work. The main purpose of STW schemes is to avoid "excessive" layoffs, that is, the permanent dismissal of workers during an economic downturn whose jobs would be viable in the longer-term. In an environment where firms are risk-neutral and they can fully insure their employees, excessive layoffs are effectively ruled out (Burdett and Wright, 1989[10]). However, in an environment where firms are financially constrained, as during a credit crunch, a well-designed STW scheme may help to increase welfare (Braun and Brügemann, 2014[11]). Moreover, STW schemes may also help to improve equity by sharing the burden of adjustment more equally across the workforce (OECD, 2009[12]).

Twenty-five OECD countries operated a STW programme during the global financial crisis, with considerable variation in their institutional design (Hijzen and Venn, 2011[13]). Institutional differences relate to the range of permissible hours reductions ("work-sharing requirements"), the conditions for employers and workers that must be met to participate ("eligibility requirements"), the actions firms and workers are expected to take during (or after) participation ("conditionality or behavioural requirements") and the way the costs of short-time work are shared between governments, firms and workers ("generosity"). The challenge for policy makers is to design short-time work schemes that strike the right balance between ensuring adequate take-up and maintaining cost-effectiveness. The latter depends on the importance of deadweight effects, i.e. subsidies paid to preserve jobs that would have been retained anyway, and displacement effects, i.e. subsidies paid to preserve jobs that are unviable even in the long-run, slowing the process of reallocation.

There is now considerable evidence that short-time work helped preserving jobs in the aftermath of the global financial crisis (Hijzen and Martin, 2013[14]; Hijzen and Venn, 2011[13]; Cahuc and Carcillo, 2011[15]; Boeri and Bruecker, 2011[16]). The largest impact was observed in Germany, Italy and Japan (Figure 13.3). Results based on firm-level data typically yield more mixed results due to the difficulty of accounting for selection into short-time work programmes (Bellmann, Gerner and Upward, 2012[17]; Boeri and Bruecker, 2011[16]; Calavrezo, Duhautois and Walkowiak, 2010[18]). When a credible research design is available, firm-level studies confirm the positive role of short-time work on employment in the early phase of the crisis (Cahuc, Kramarz and Nevoux, 2018[19]). Yet the continued use of STW during the recovery is also likely to have exerted a negative influence on the strength of the recovery by limiting job creation and output growth (Hijzen and Martin, 2013[14]; Cahuc, Kramarz and Nevoux, 2018[19]). Their use should therefore be cut back during good times to avoid that that they undermine the efficient reallocation of resources and thereby productivity growth.

Figure 13.3. Short-time work schemes preserved jobs during the Great Recession

Number of jobs preserved during the crisis of 2008-09

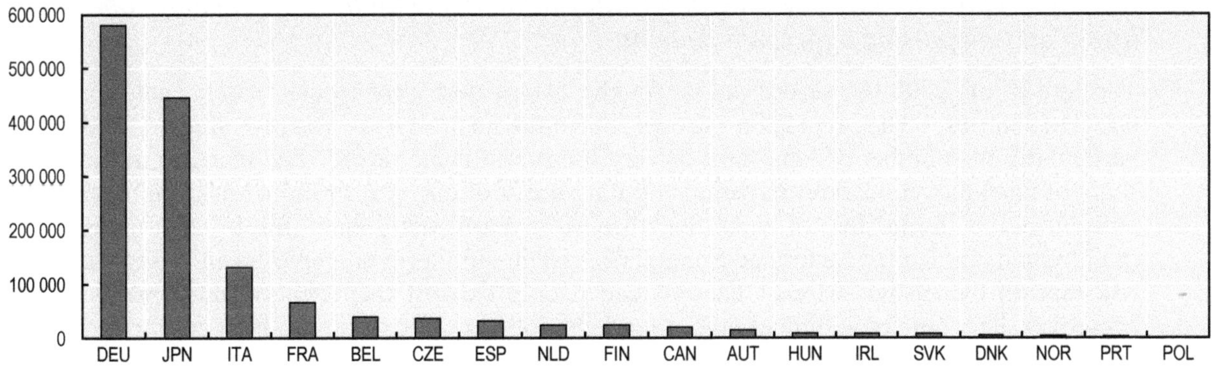

Source: Hijzen and Martin (2013[14]), "The role of short-time work schemes during the global financial crisis and early recovery: A cross-country analysis", *IZA Journal of Labor Policy*, Vol. 2/1, p. 5, http://dx.doi.org/10.1186/2193-9004-2-5.

StatLink http://dx.doi.org/10.1787/888933881686

To ensure that short-time work schemes can be deployed rapidly, it is desirable to design them when business conditions are normal. Short-time work schemes that were introduced from scratch in response to the 2008-09 recession typically had only limited take-up and therefore not much of an impact, while schemes that pre-dated the 2008-09 crisis typically had higher levels of take-up (OECD, 2010[20]). This may reflect firms' lack of familiarity with new schemes or simply the fact that that they became operational too late when the need for them had largely subsided. Evidence for France suggests that programme familiarity is indeed a very important determinant of take-up (Cahuc, Kramarz and Nevoux, 2018[19]). This highlights the importance of providing clear and easily accessible information on the modalities of their use.

Another possibility may be to establish a dormant state-contingent scheme which can be triggered in times of crisis. Sweden, which did not have a public short-time work scheme during the crisis, adopted such a scheme in 2013. It can be triggered in the event of a deep economic crisis with the agreement of the government and the social partners and is strictly time-limited (Ibsen, 2013[21]). The advantage of this dormant scheme is that it can be scaled up more quickly than entirely new schemes. Moreover, the strong presence of the social partners in Swedish workplaces is likely to greatly facilitate its roll-out.[2]

The institutional design of short-time work schemes can also help ensure that such schemes are mainly used in times of crisis and phased out rapidly when the economy recovers. One option is to temporarily relax eligibility and conditionality conditions or increase the generosity of public subsidies during times of crisis, while tightening conditions and reducing generosity in good times. Most countries with a short-time work scheme in place before the crisis took measures to temporarily increase their attractiveness (OECD, 2009[12]). Other measures that can help to ensure that the use of short-time work is temporary are to limit the maximum duration for which short-time work subsidies are available and to target them at firms with temporary difficulties. More generally, firms should be required to share the cost of short-time work, which is the case in about half the countries with a short-time work scheme in place (Hijzen and Venn,

2011[13]), so that they only have incentives to participate if they genuinely want to preserve jobs and expect the situation to improve..

Income-support policies are crucial for alleviating financial hardship among job losers and supporting aggregate demand

The crisis of 2008-09 served as a tough "stress test" for social safety nets in OECD countries. The recession drove unemployment rates sharply higher and particularly the number of long-term or very long-term unemployed. The increase in the share of unemployed workers experiencing long spells of one year or more has been most pronounced in a number of countries that were particularly hard hit by the crisis (e.g. Ireland, the United States and Spain). The rise in long-term unemployment raises the risk that an increasing share of unemployed people exhaust their benefit entitlements. Moreover, in countries with dual labour markets, job losses are likely to be concentrated on workers with flexible work arrangements (e.g. temporary contracts, temporary agency workers, own-account workers), who are less likely to be eligible to unemployment insurance benefits, either because they do not meet minimum contribution requirements or because they are formally excluded. Minimum contribution requirements may also be too high for unemployed youth and other recent labour market entrants without recent work experience.

The effectiveness of social safety nets in supporting the incomes of the unemployed and in providing a stabilising response to the decline in aggregate demand therefore is likely to differ importantly across countries (Price, Dang and Botev, 2015[22]; OECD, 2010[20]). Countries with universal systems of means-tested benefits (e.g. Australia, New Zealand and the United Kingdom) in principle provide income support to all job-losers suffering from financial hardship, but can involve large falls in incomes and weak automatic stabilisers. Countries with comprehensive two-tier systems of unemployment insurance and social assistance (e.g. Denmark, Norway and Sweden) provide the most effective support for the unemployed and tend to have strong automatic stabilisers. However, generous income support systems also carry the risk of undermining work incentives if not properly embedded in an effective activation strategy based on a rigorous mutual obligations framework.

To strengthen unemployment benefits' impact on short-term stabilisation, while limiting their effects on work incentives, there may be a case for temporarily increasing generosity during downturns. Costs of unemployment insurance in terms of reduced work incentives and benefits in terms of consumption smoothing vary over the business cycle (see Chapter 9). During economic slumps, aggregate consumption can drop dramatically in the absence of sufficient benefits, while the behavioural costs of insurance is limited by the lack of job opportunities. Inversely, during economic booms, these behavioural costs can be large if generous benefits prevent too many people from accepting job offers (Schmieder, von Wachter and Bender, 2012[23]; Kroft and Notowidigdo, 2016[24]; Mitman and Rabinovich, 2015[25]).[3]

Consistent with the argument for state-contingent unemployment insurance, the majority of OECD countries took additional measures in response to the 2008-09 crisis to strengthen social safety nets for the unemployed. These typically focused on addressing coverage gaps by temporarily relaxing eligibility rules or extending the maximum duration of unemployment benefits. A number of countries, including Canada, Chile and the United States, have (semi-) automatic rules that temporarily increase the maximum duration of unemployment benefits when the unemployment rate exceeds a threshold. In order to facilitate a return to work, extensions in maximum duration of unemployment benefits should be accompanied with an intensification of activation measures, in particular where activation systems are currently underdeveloped. As discussed below, since scaling up activation systems temporarily is not straightforward, the risks in terms of more persistent unemployment in the case of large extensions needs to be weighed carefully.

Unemployment benefits need to be combined with effective activation policies within a strictly enforced mutual obligations framework by which government support is conditional on benefit recipients' active job search and/or participation in programmes that promote their job prospects (Chapter 9). While the number of job opportunities is depressed in times of crisis, it is important to maintain as much as possible the mutual-obligations approach. It is equally important that access to early retirement and disability benefits is not relaxed. Failing to maintain the integrity of the mutual-obligations approach or alleviating pressures on the labour market by moving unemployed people in disability and early retirement can have long-lasting effects on the effective supply of labour, with serious consequences for economic growth and the sustainability of public finances. For instance, looser job search requirements in unemployment insurance and relaxed health criteria for disability insurance have been found to have lowered effective retirement ages in the aftermath of past recessions (OECD, 2009[12]).

To maintain effective re-employment and training support to all unemployed jobseekers , public employment services need to scale up their capacity significantly during deep recessions (OECD, 2009[12]). Increasing capacity requires additional financial resources. This would also help to strengthen the counter-cyclicality of fiscal policy. However, in practice financial resources on active labour market policies only respond modestly to changes in the number of clients (Box 13.1). A particularly effective way of increasing spending on activation during downturns would be to base such increases on pre-defined rules. In Australia, Denmark and Switzerland, for instance, spending on activation is adjusted according to the government's official unemployment forecasts (OECD, 2009[12]). However, scaling up capacity is not just a matter of financial resources; it also requires recruiting additional staff and extending programme capacity. A key question is whether this can be done quickly enough and whether service quality can be maintained in the process. One possible way of alleviating capacity constraints may be to involve private providers in the delivery of re--employment and training services. However, the challenge of doing so effectively should not be underestimated, since it can take several years to fine-tune and requires rigorous performance management by the public authorities (OECD, 2005[26]).

Box 13.1. The modulation of active labour market policies over the business cycle

Spending on active labour market programmes (ALMPs) responded only weakly to the rise in unemployment following the Great Recession (Figure 13.4). A 1% increase in the number of unemployed was associated with a 0.4% increase in active labour market spending. While this was almost twice as high as during previous crisis episodes, the less than proportional increase in spending still resulted in a sharp decline in resources per jobseeker. According to OECD (2012[27]), the value of resources per unemployed person declined by 20% between 2007 and 2010 on average across the OECD. A more significant increase is likely to be necessary to preserve the mutual-obligations ethos of activation regimes. This is particularly important in countries with relatively generous unemployment benefits and a strong emphasis on activation policies to maintain work incentives as well as in countries where the generosity of unemployment benefits is low, but has been temporarily extended in response to the increase in needs following the crisis.

Figure 13.4. The responsiveness of spending on labour market programmes to changes in unemployment

Elasticity of spending with respect to the number of unemployed, OECD average

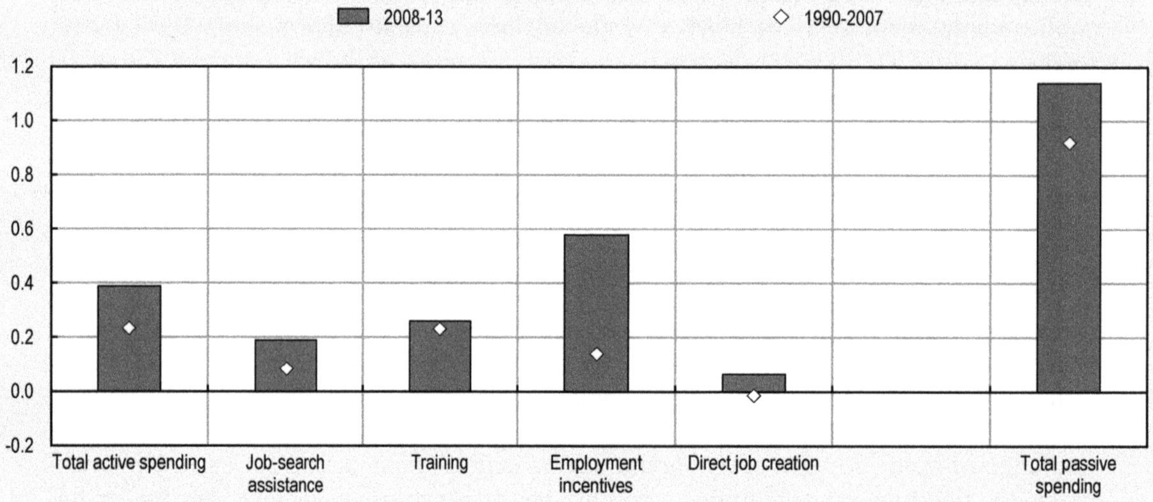

Source: OECD (2017[31]), "Labour market resilience: The role of structural and macroeconomic policies", in *OECD Employment Outlook 2017*, https://doi.org/10.1787/empl_outlook-2017-6-en.

StatLink http://dx.doi.org/10.1787/888933881705

Linking budgets for spending on labour market programmes to labour market conditions raises a number of practical policy questions about implementation, including whether changes should be adopted on an ad hoc or automatic basis. Automatic rules may provide an effective instrument to make ALMP spending more responsive to the business cycle by allowing for a timelier, more predictable, and more transparent response. However, automatic rules also have their drawbacks. They involve an element of rigidity in the way policy responds to changing circumstances, since they are inherently informed by past events and could thus prove to be sub-optimal in new circumstances. An alternative could be semi-automatic mechanisms that trigger a policy adjustment under pre-specified conditions, but that allow for policy discretion in the design of the adjustment. A number of OECD countries already have automatic or quasi-automatic rules to make active labour market spending more responsive to labour market conditions, including Australia, Denmark and Switzerland.

A particular difficulty is that it may be not be straightforward to translate funding increases into higher capacity in the short run.[1] Countries with more generous benefits, and that rely more heavily on the mutual-obligations approach, probably have the strongest incentives in maintaining resources per unemployed approximately constant during periods of high cyclical unemployment. Moreover, these are more likely to be countries that have the necessary infrastructure in place to translate funding increases into increased capacity quickly, while maintaining service quality. The difficulty of scaling up the capacity for labour market programmes may explain why spending on hiring subsidies ("employment incentives"), which are easy to expand, increased more strongly than spending on other categories of active labour market spending.

[1] This may explain why the presence of automatic rules for active labour market spending did little to stem the decline in resources available per unemployed jobseeker during the crisis.

During economic downturns, the focus of active labour market policies may need to shift from core job-search assistance to training. As labour demand declines, the caseload of public employment services counsellors increases while fewer job opportunities become available, which can make a focus on placing unemployed people in jobs less effective. Moreover, recessions reduce the opportunity cost of time spent in training (Lechner and Wunsch, 2009[28]) and often speed up structural change, thereby raising the need for workers to acquire new skills and change occupations. Therefore, during economic downturns, active labour market policies may need to focus on assigning workers to appropriate training schemes. These programmes should preferably be designed and evaluated well before the crisis hits in order to take medium- and long-term labour market needs into account. As a last resort, public employment schemes may provide a way of keeping hard-to-place job seekers connected to the labour market (Gregg and Layard, 2009[29]) although the evidence suggests that such programmes are costly and have had little success in getting workers permanent jobs in the open labour market.

There is also a case for supporting job creation by temporarily scaling up employment subsidies during economic downturns (OECD, 2010[20]). These can take the form of stock subsidies, such as reductions in social security contributions, or explicit subsidies to new hires (gross hiring subsidies) or only to new hires associated with net job creation (net hiring subsidies). Stock subsidies can help boost employment, but they are expensive and involve deadweight losses by subsidising jobs that would have existed without the subsidy. Gross hiring subsidies entail smaller deadweight losses and are thus more cost effective, but they risk being "gamed" by businesses that raise labour turnover rather than net hiring to pocket the subsidy. Recent empirical evidence from France and the United States suggests that temporary gross hiring subsidies can be a cost-effective way of supporting employment during recessions, but that effectiveness may rapidly decline during economic upturns as the subsidies may push up wages rather than employment (Cahuc, Carcillo and Le Barbanchon, 2018[30]; Neumark and Grijalva, 2017[31]). The most cost-effective way of subsidising employment during downturns are net hiring subsidies, the drawback being that such schemes are complex, and typically difficult to administer for governments as well as firms (contributing to low take-up).

The role of structural policies and institutions

Structural policies can play an important role in shaping the way the labour market responds to economic downturns, including the way the cost of adjustment is shared between firms and workers as well as between different groups of workers. This sub-section focuses mainly on the role of collective bargaining and employment protection legislation, but also touches briefly on the role of several other structural policies and institutions.

Collective bargaining can help adjusting to temporary shocks by facilitating working time reductions

Well-designed collective bargaining systems can promote labour market resilience by facilitating adjustments in wages and working time. Working time adjustments have a much greater potential for shock absorption than wage adjustments, but are only effective in the context of temporary shocks.[4]

Coordination between bargaining units (firms and/or industries) can promote good labour market outcomes by providing room for adjustment to changes in macro-economic conditions (OECD, 2017[2]). Countries with effective wage coordination include those with predominantly sector-level bargaining, notably the Nordic countries, Austria, Germany, the Netherlands and Switzerland as well as Japan. One way to achieve effective coordination is peak-level bargaining based on the presence of national confederations of unions and employers that provide guidance to bargaining parties at lower levels. Another possibility is pattern bargaining where a leading sector sets the targets – usually the manufacturing sector exposed to international trade – and others follow. A precondition for a well-functioning co-ordination of wage bargaining is to have strong and representative employer and employee organisations (OECD, 2018[32]). Wage co-ordination requires a high level of trust in and between the social partners, the availability of objective and shared information on the labour market situation, as well as well-functioning mediation bodies (Ibsen, 2016[33]).

Another example of how countries with predominantly sector-level bargaining can enhance labour market resilience is by providing flexibility within the framework of sector-level agreements at the firm level to allow for adjustments in working time and wages under certain conditions, including through the use of opt-out clauses in the case of economic hardship. An example of such mechanisms is Germany, where sectoral wage agreements provide room for employer-initiated reductions in working time. These agreements typically specify a band around the standard working week, within which employers can vary working hours while maintaining hourly pay (OECD, 2010[20]). This is intended to provide employers with an improved ability to adapt to temporary variations in product demand while providing a high level of employment security. According to Bach et al. (2009[34]), such employer-initiated reductions in working time accounted for approximately 40% of the reduction in working time during the recession of 2008-09. Similar arrangements also played an important role in limiting job losses in Sweden (Ibsen, 2013[21]).

To avoid excessive job losses and weak job recoveries employment protection rules need to be balanced across contract types

An adequate level of employment protection provisions for regular workers can promote labour market resilience by preserving job matches that are at risk of being suppressed but are viable in the medium term. However, excessively strict employment protection risks becoming counter-productive by increasing incentives for the use of temporary contracts in good times that are also easier to terminate in a downturn (Blanchard and Landier, 2002[35]; Boeri, 2011[36]; Cahuc, Charlot and Malherbet, 2016[37]). This can amplify job cuts in the wake of economic downturns and slow the creation of jobs associated with regular contracts in a recovery (OECD, 2012[27]; 2017[2]).[5]

The challenge for public policy is to design employment protection that strikes the right balance between preserving viable job matches while avoiding labour market segmentation (Chapters 7 and 10). This could be achieved by avoiding excessively high levels of advance notice and ordinary severance pay for workers on regular contracts. Judicial uncertainty related to layoffs of workers on regular contracts could be reduced by defining unfair dismissals narrowly, focusing on false reasons, reasons unrelated to work, discrimination and prohibited grounds. At the same time, there may be room to tighten the regulations governing the use of temporary contracts while strengthening enforcement.

Non-labour market structural policies

Structural policies beyond the labour market can support labour market resilience by limiting output fluctuations, thereby reducing the burden on macroeconomic policies (OECD, 2017[38]). A sound legal and judicial infrastructure based on high-quality institutions enhances both growth and resilience, including by promoting the diversification of funding sources away from the banking sector and towards capital markets. By contrast, financial market liberalisation and capital openness tend to raise growth but also tend increases the risk of banking and currency crises, which may to some extent be mitigated by effective and coordinated prudential financial policies.

Conclusion

This chapter has highlighted that labour market resilience plays a key role in limiting the social costs of economic downturns and the extent to which cyclical changes in employment adversely affect labour market and economic performance in the medium to long term. It has emphasised that counter-cyclical monetary and fiscal policies can be highly effective in cushioning the impact of adverse economic shocks on labour market outcomes, but that a forceful policy response during downturns requires building up fiscal buffers during upturns. A number of structural policies and institutions can help containing fluctuations in employment and promoting a rapid rebound. Adequate social benefits do not only support people who lose their jobs during downturns, but also contribute to stabilising aggregate demand. Active labour market policies can promote a rapid return to work as economic conditions normalise, while short-time work schemes can prevent people from losing their jobs in the first place by promoting adjustments in hours worked rather than employment. A level of employment protection for regular workers that limits labour market segmentation can limit large employment losses for non-regular workers during downturns and can promote the creation of regular jobs during the recovery.

If well designed, policies and institutions that enhance labour market resilience are also conducive to good structural labour market outcomes. As a matter of fact, countries with highly resilient labour markets typically also performed well in terms of low average pre-crisis unemployment rates (OECD, 2012[27]). Vigorous counter-cyclical macroeconomic policies can help countries prevent becoming stuck in low-growth traps characterised by weak investment, high unemployment, as well as low wage and productivity growth (OECD, 2016[5]). Unemployment benefits with broad coverage that provide workers with sufficient financial resources and time to look for a job that matches their skills do not necessarily reduce work incentives, especially during periods of depressed aggregate demand. If combined with adequate activation measures in a strictly enforced mutual obligations framework, such benefits can even contribute to more productive job matches. Well-designed short-term work schemes can prevent productive job matches from being dissolved, thereby preserving workers' skills and labour productivity in the medium term. Similarly, a level of employment protection for regular workers that prevents labour market segmentation can promote labour productivity, including by strengthening incentives to invest in workers' skills (Bassanini, Nunziata and Venn, 2009[39]).

Notes

[1] The analysis does not distinguish between the sources of output fluctuations (e.g. demand, supply or financial shocks).

[2] Apart from being familiar with the modalities of the public short-time work schemes, the social partners also have gained useful experience during the crisis with the use of private short-time work arrangements that do not rely on public subsidies (Ibsen, 2013[21]). These private arrangements are made possible through the use of hard-ship clauses in sectoral collective agreements.

[3] This argument does also imply that the aggregate elasticity of benefit extensions on unemployment is smaller than its elasticity for individuals due to the competition for jobs between job seekers (Landais, 2015[41]; Landais, Michaillat and Saez, 2018[43]). However, whether this is the case has been the subject of some controversy in the literature (Hagedorn, Manovskii and Mitman, 2015[42]).

[4] By contrast, permanent shocks typically require that aggregate wages adjust in line with aggregate productivity.

[5] Similarly, Sutherland and Hoeller (2013[40]) show that strict employment protection provisions for regular workers are associated with higher persistence of recessions and lower productivity growth, which partly reflects adverse effects on resource reallocation and skill matching.

References

Auerbach, A. and Y. Gorodnichenko (2013), "Fiscal Mulpliers in Recession and Expansion", in Alesina, A. and F. Giavazzi (eds.), *Fiscal Policy after the Financial Crisis*, University of Chicago Press, https://www.nber.org/chapters/c12634. [8]

Auerbach, A. and Y. Gorodnichenko (2012), "Measuring the Output Responses to Fiscal Policy", *American Economic Journal: Economic Policy*, Vol. 4/2, pp. 1-27, http://dx.doi.org/10.1257/pol.4.2.1. [7]

Bach, H. et al. (2009), *IAB Kurzbericht Die Krise wird deutliche Spuren hinterlassen Rezession überwunden?*, http://doku.iab.de/kurzber/2009/kb2009.pdf. [34]

Bassanini, A., L. Nunziata and D. Venn (2009), "Job protection legislation and productivity growth in OECD countries", *Economic Policy*, Vol. 24/58, pp. 349-402, http://dx.doi.org/10.1111/j.1468-0327.2009.00221.x. [39]

Bellmann, L., H. Gerner and R. Upward (2012), "The Response of German Establishments to the 2008-2009 Economic Crisis", *OECD Social, Employment and Migration Working Papers, No. 137*, http://dx.doi.org/10.1787/5k8x7gwmb3jc-en. [17]

Blanchard, O. and A. Landier (2002), "The Perverse Effects of Partial Labour Market Reform: Fixed-Term Contracts in France", *The Economic Journal*, Vol. 112/480, pp. 214-244, https://www.jstor.org/stable/pdf/798373. [35]

Boeri, T. (2011), "Institutional Reforms and Dualism in European Labor Markets", *Handbook of Labor Economics*, Vol. 4, pp. 1173-1236, http://dx.doi.org/10.1016/S0169-7218(11)02411-7. [36]

Boeri, T. and H. Bruecker (2011), "Short-time work benefits revisited: some lessons from the Great Recession", *Economic Policy*, Vol. 26/68, pp. 697-765, http://dx.doi.org/10.1111/j.1468-0327.2011.271.x. [16]

Braun, H. and B. Brügemann (2014), "Welfare Effects of Short-Time Compensation", *IZA Discussion Paper*, No. 8597, http://ftp.iza.org/dp8597.pdf. [11]

Burdett, K. and R. Wright (1989), "Unemployment Insurance and Short-Time Compensation: The Effects on Layoffs, Hours per Worker, and Wages", *Journal of Political Economy*, Vol. 97/6, pp. 1479-1496, http://dx.doi.org/10.1086/261664. [10]

Cahuc, P. and S. Carcillo (2011), "Is Short-Time Work a Good Method to Keep Unemployment Down?", *Nordic Economic Policy Review*, Vol. 1/1, pp. 133-165, http://ftp.iza.org/dp5430.pdf. [15]

Cahuc, P., S. Carcillo and T. Le Barbanchon (2018), "The Effectiveness of Hiring Credits", *The Review of Economic Studies*, http://dx.doi.org/10.1093/restud/rdy011. [30]

Cahuc, P., O. Charlot and F. Malherbet (2016), "Explaining the spread of temporary jobs and its impact on labor turnover", *International Economic Review*, Vol. 57/2, pp. 533-572, http://dx.doi.org/10.1111/iere.12167. [37]

Cahuc, P., F. Kramarz and S. Nevoux (2018), "When Short-Time Work Works", *IZA Disucssion Paper*, No. 11673, http://ftp.iza.org/dp11673.pdf. [19]

Calavrezo, O., R. Duhautois and E. Walkowiak (2010), *Short-Time Compensation and Establishment Exit: An Empirical Analysis with French Data*, http://repec.iza.org/dp4989.pdf. [18]

Gregg, P. and R. Layard (2009), *A Job Guarantee*, http://cep.lse.ac.uk/textonly/_new/staff/layard/pdf/001JGProposal-16-03-09.pdf. [29]

Hagedorn, M., I. Manovskii and K. Mitman (2015), "The Impact of Unemployment Benefit Extensions on Employment: The 2014 Employment Miracle?", *NBER Working Papers*, No. 20884, http://www.nber.org/papers/w20884.pdf. [42]

Hijzen, A. and S. Martin (2013), "The role of short-time work schemes during the global financial crisis1 and early recovery: a cross-country analysis", *IZA Journal of Labor Policy*, Vol. 2/1, p. 5, http://dx.doi.org/10.1186/2193-9004-2-5. [14]

Hijzen, A. and D. Venn (2011), "The Role of Short-Time Work Schemes during the 2008-09 Recession", *OECD Social, Employment and Migration Working Papers*, No. 115, OECD Publishing, Paris, http://dx.doi.org/10.1787/5kgkd0bbwvxp-en. [13]

Ibsen, C. (2016), "The Role of Mediation Institutions in Sweden and Denmark after Centralized Bargaining", *British Journal of Industrial Relations*, Vol. 54/2, pp. 285-310, http://dx.doi.org/10.1111/bjir.12142. [33]

Ibsen, C. (2013), *Short-time work in Sweden*, http://www.eurofound.europa.eu/eiro/2012/03/articles/se1203019i.htm. [21]

Ilzetzki, E., E. Mendoza and C. Végh (2013), "How big (small?) are fiscal multipliers?", *Journal of Monetary Economics*, Vol. 60/2, pp. 239-254, http://dx.doi.org/10.1016/j.jmoneco.2012.10.011. [9]

Kroft, K. and M. Notowidigdo (2016), "Should Unemployment Insurance Vary with the Unemployment Rate? Theory and Evidence", *The Review of Economic Studies*, Vol. 83/3, pp. 1092-1124, http://dx.doi.org/10.1093/restud/rdw009. [24]

Landais, C. (2015), "Assessing the welfare effects of unemployment benefits using the regression kink design", *American Economic Journal: Economic Policy*, Vol. 7/4, http://dx.doi.org/10.1257/pol.20130248. [41]

Landais, C., P. Michaillat and E. Saez (2018), "A Macroeconomic Approach to Optimal Unemployment Insurance: Theory", *American Economy Journal: Economic Policy*, Vol. 10/2, pp. 152-81, http://dx.doi.org/10.1257/pol.20150088. [43]

Lechner, M. and C. Wunsch (2009), "Are Training Programs More Effective When Unemployment Is High?", *Journal of Labor Economics*, Vol. 27/4, pp. 653-692, http://dx.doi.org/10.1086/644976. [28]

Mitman, K. and S. Rabinovich (2015), "Optimal unemployment insurance in an equilibrium business-cycle model", *Journal of Monetary Economics*, Vol. 71, pp. 99-118, http://dx.doi.org/10.1016/j.jmoneco.2014.11.009. [25]

Neumark, D. and D. Grijalva (2017), "The employment effects of state hiring credits", *ILR Review*, Vol. 70/5, pp. 1111-1145, http://dx.doi.org/10.1177/0019793916683930. [31]

OECD (2018), *OECD Employment Outlook 2018*, OECD Publishing, Paris, http://dx.doi.org/10.1787/empl_outlook-2018-en. [32]

OECD (2017), "Labour market resilience: The role of structural and macroeconomic policies", in *OECD Employment Outlook 2017*, OECD Publishing, Paris, http://dx.doi.org/10.1787/empl_outlook-2017-6-en. [3]

OECD (2017), *OECD Employment Outlook 2017*, OECD Publishing, Paris, http://dx.doi.org/10.1787/empl_outlook-2017-en. [2]

OECD (2017), "Resilience in a time of high debt", in *OECD Economic Outlook, Volume 2017 Issue 2*, OECD Publishing, Paris, http://dx.doi.org/10.1787/eco_outlook-v2017-2-3-en. [38]

OECD (2016), *OECD Economic Outlook, Volume 2016 Issue 2*, OECD Publishing, Paris, http://dx.doi.org/10.1787/eco_outlook-v2016-2-en. [5]

OECD (2015), *OECD Economic Outlook, Volume 2015 Issue 1*, OECD Publishing, Paris, http://dx.doi.org/10.1787/eco_outlook-v2015-1-en. [6]

OECD (2012), *OECD Employment Outlook 2012*, OECD Publishing, Paris, http://dx.doi.org/10.1787/empl_outlook-2012-en. [27]

OECD (2010), *OECD Economic Outlook, Volume 2010 Issue 1*, OECD Publishing, Paris, http://dx.doi.org/10.1787/eco_outlook-v2010-1-en. [1]

OECD (2010), *OECD Employment Outlook 2010: Moving Beyond the Jobs Crisis*, http://www.oecd.org/employment/emp/48806664.pdf (accessed on 25 October 2018). [20]

OECD (2009), *OECD Employment Outlook 2009: Tackling the Jobs Crisis*, OECD Publishing, Paris, http://dx.doi.org/10.1787/empl_outlook-2009-en. [12]

OECD (2005), *OECD Employment Outlook 2005*, OECD Publishing, Paris, http://dx.doi.org/10.1787/empl_outlook-2005-en. [26]

Price, R., T. Dang and J. Botev (2015), "Adjusting fiscal balances for the business cycle: New tax and expenditure elasticity estimates for OECD countries", *OECD Economics Department Working Papers*, No. 1275, OECD Publishing, Paris, http://dx.doi.org/10.1787/5jrp1g3282d7-en. [22]

Ramey, V. (2016), *Macroeconomic Shocks and Their Propagation*, National Bureau of Economic Research, Cambridge, MA, http://dx.doi.org/10.3386/w21978. [4]

Schmieder, J., T. von Wachter and S. Bender (2012), "The Effects of Extended Unemployment Insurance Over the Business Cycle: Evidence from Regression Discontinuity Estimates Over 20 Years", *The Quarterly Journal of Economics*, Vol. 127/2, pp. 701-752, https://doi.org/10.1093/qje/qjs010. [23]

Sutherland, D. and P. Hoeller (2013), "Growth-promoting Policies and Macroeconomic Stability", *OECD Economics Department Working Papers*, No. 1091, OECD Publishing, Paris, http://dx.doi.org/10.1787/5k3xqsz7c8d2-en. [40]

Chapter 14. Promoting adaptable labour markets

Sustaining good labour market performance in a context of rapid technological progress, deepening globalisation and demographic change requires policies that make labour markets more adaptable. Such policies include: i) framework conditions that promote the efficient reallocation of workers across jobs, firms, industries and regions; ii) adult learning systems that are responsive to changes in labour market needs, provide strong incentives for learning and link training rights to workers rather than jobs; and iii) effective employment and social policies to help displaced workers regain suitable jobs quickly.

The statistical data for Israel are supplied by and under the responsibility of the relevant Israeli authorities. The use of such data by the OECD is without prejudice to the status of the Golan Heights, East Jerusalem and Israeli settlements in the West Bank under the terms of international law.

Introduction

Globalisation, technological progress and demographic change are having a profound impact on labour markets. New jobs are being created in expanding businesses, industries and regions and being destroyed in declining ones, with the nature of many jobs rapidly changing as well. Labour markets will need to become more adaptable to ensure that productivity gains are passed on to workers, while mitigating the risks of higher structural unemployment, lower job quality, skills mismatches and rising inequalities.

Adaptability requires policies that promote the efficient redeployment of workers from low-performing to higher-performing businesses and industries and regions – while also helping workers to take full advantage of new opportunities. These include product market policies that do not unduly constrain the entry and orderly exit of firms, as well as labour market and housing policies that promote the mobility of workers across businesses and regions. Such reallocation-friendly policies need to be accompanied by policies that allow workers to acquire the skills to succeed in tomorrow's labour markets and policies to (re)develop declining regions.

But the efficient redeployment of workers and the provision of labour market-relevant skills cannot, on their own, prevent rapid economic change from causing significant hardship to some workers. Supporting displaced workers will require targeted policies that help them get back to work quickly and limit the extent to which adversely-affected regions fall behind. Early intervention measures related to job-search assistance and re-training are key to avoid that displaced workers become trapped in long-term unemployment and benefit exhaustion. Moreover, specific policies are needed to support workers in declining regions. This requires maintaining high-quality local public services in lagging regions, but it may in some cases additionally require targeted interventions in the areas of activation and skills policies.

The remainder of this chapter is structured as follows. Section 14.1 discusses the role of product, labour and housing market policies in promoting the efficient reallocation of workers across jobs, firms, industries and regions in the face of structural economic change. Section 14.2 highlights the need for responsive, effective and worker-centred adult learning systems that enable workers deal with rapidly changing skill needs. Section 14.3 examines how policies targeted at displaced workers and lagging regions can support the most vulnerable workers to adapt to structural change..

14.1. Promoting the reallocation of workers across jobs, firms and regions

Adapting to rapid economic and technological change triggered by digitalisation, globalisation and demographic change puts a premium on the reallocation of workers and firms to growing sectors and regions.

Keeping entry barriers low to favour the emergence of innovative firms

Business dynamism is a key driver of job creation and productivity growth. Young firms account for an important share of job creation across OECD economies and disproportionately contribute to productivity growth since they tend to be more innovative and productive than existing firms (Foster, Haltiwanger and Syverson, 2008[1]; Criscuolo, Gal and Menon, 2014[2]; Haltiwanger, Jarmin and Miranda, 2013[3]) (Figure 14.1). For example, young firms tend to have a competitive advantage in radical innovation, whereas large incumbent firms tend to focus more on incremental innovation since adopting radical organisational changes and taking large risks is often more difficult for them. In addition, the entry of young firms generally strengthens competition, which can stimulate the productivity growth of existing firms. Overall, multi-factor productivity (MFP) growth over the 2000s was weaker in sectors that recorded larger declines in the share of young firms (Adalet McGowan et al., 2015[4]).

Figure 14.1. Young firms account for an important share of job creation

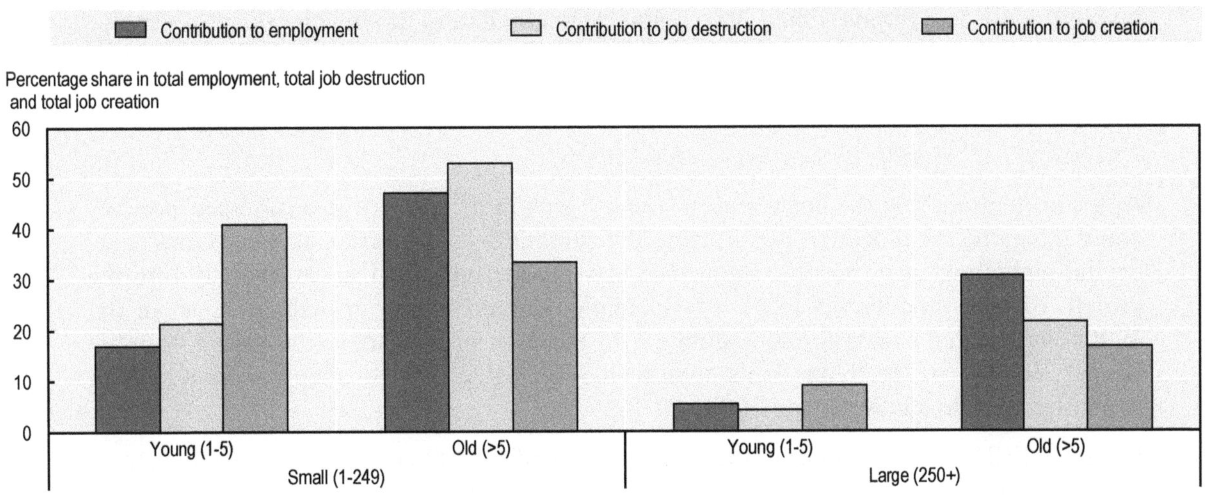

Source: Criscuolo et al. (2014[2]), "The Dynamics of Employment Growth: New Evidence from 18 Countries", *OECD Science, Technology and Industry Policy Papers*, No. 14, http://dx.doi.org/10.1787/5jz417hj6hg6-en.

StatLink http://dx.doi.org/10.1787/888933881724

A source of concern is that business dynamism has tended to decline in a number of OECD countries over the past decades (Calvino, Criscuolo and Menon, 2015[5]). The causes of this decline are not fully understood yet. It may relate to global technological and economic trends, such as the rise in information and communication technologies (ICT) and the increasing market power of the largest firms in some industries and countries. It is also likely to reflect policy-induced rigidities that complicate the entry and growth of new firms.[1]

A range of product market policies can promote the emergence of young innovative firms and the reallocation of resources to high-productivity firms. The evidence suggests that flexible product markets – as measured by the OECD product market regulation indicators – are associated with higher productivity growth and a more efficient reallocation of resources towards high-productivity firms (Arnold, Nicoletti and Scarpetta, 2011[6]). This may reflect lower barriers to the creation and growth of new firms related to lower administrative burdens on start-ups, less burdensome sector-specific regulations (e.g. in retail) or less demanding licensing requirements. Moreover, competition-friendly product market regulation may promote the diffusion of innovation in the economy (Andrews, Criscuolo and Gal, 2016[7]) and the adoption of digital technologies (Andrews, Nicoletti and Timiliotis, 2018[8]).

The evidence further suggests that strict employment protection rules and financial constraints may limit reallocation to the most productive businesses (Chapter 7). In particular, strict employment protection rules have been found to be negatively associated with the propensity of high-productivity firms to be larger than less-productive ones (Andrews and Cingano, 2014[9]; Haltiwanger, Scarpetta and Schweiger, 2014[10]). Since intangible capital is more difficult to collateralise than physical capital, young and innovative firms may have difficulties to access financing (Demmou, Stefanescu and Arquie, 2018[11]; Brassell and Boschmans, 2018[12]). Policies can address such financing constraints by encouraging equity-financing (which in many countries remains less favourable for tax purposes than debt financing), stimulating the development of venture capital markets and standing ready to provide public financing or co-financing to young innovative firms in case of market failures.

Ensuring the smooth exit of inefficient firms

Apart from promoting the entry and post-entry growth of innovative businesses, policies could strengthen reallocation by ensuring the smooth exit of inefficient ones. Otherwise, capital and labour may become trapped in low-productivity businesses, thereby limiting growth of high-productivity ones. For example, low economic growth in Japan in the 1990s was related – among other things – to the high prevalence of so-called "zombie firms", i.e. low productivity firms that would typically exit in a competitive market (Caballero, Hoshi and Kashyap, 2008[13]).

Recent OECD analysis suggests that in a number of OECD countries the prevalence of zombie firms has risen between 2003 and 2013 (Adalet McGowan, Andrews and Millot, 2017[14]). Subsequent research has shown that, apart from being less productive than other firms, zombie firms reduce the growth opportunities of healthier firms and their access to credit (so-called "zombie congestion"), which hinders their employment and investment (Adalet McGowan, Andrews and Millot, 2017[14]; Andrews and Petroulakis, 2017[15]). This zombie congestion particularly penalises the growth of young firms, which makes it even more damaging for the economy as young firms tend to be more innovative.

Insolvency policies can play a key role in reducing the prevalence of zombie firms and fostering the efficient reallocation of resources in the economy. Recent OECD research shows that insolvency regimes that delay the liquidation or restructuring of weak firms reduce productivity growth (Adalet McGowan, Andrews and Millot, 2017[16]; Adalet McGowan, Andrews and Millot, 2017[17]). The design of insolvency regimes varies significantly across countries, in particular with respect to the treatment of failed entrepreneurs, the availability of preventative and streamlining tools and ease of corporate restructuring (Figure 14.2), suggesting significant room for policy improvement in many countries.

Apart from insolvency policies, the health of the financial sector is an important determinant of zombie firm prevalence (Andrews and Petroulakis, 2017[15]). Indeed, there is empirical evidence that zombie firms are more likely to be connected to weak banks, suggesting that the zombie firm problem may partly stem from bank forbearance. This highlights the importance of sound financial regulations to ensure healthy banking systems and reinforces the case for diversifying corporate financing away from bank lending towards market-based debt and equity financing. This could, for instance, be achieved by reducing the debt bias in corporate tax systems and encouraging the development of venture capital markets (Andrews, Adalet McGowan and Millot, 2017[18]).

The exit of inefficient firms can have adverse effects on employment in the short term and at the local level. Recent OECD research suggests that active labour market policies (ALMPs) and low labour taxes can mitigate such costs, as they tend to boost the re-employment probability of displaced workers (Andrews and Saia, 2017[19]; OECD, 2018[20]). ALMPs appear to be particularly effective in bringing displaced workers back to work when administrative entry barriers in product markets are low (see also Section 14.3 below).

Figure 14.2. OECD indicator of insolvency regimes

2016

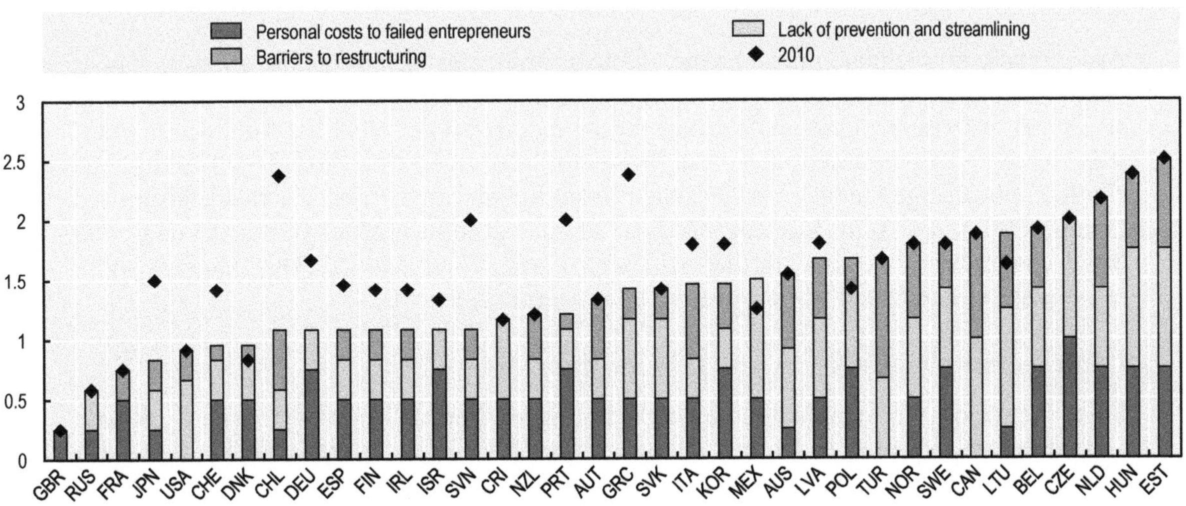

Note: Higher values indicate higher barriers to restructuring. The stacked bars correspond to three subcomponents of the insolvency indicator in 2016. The diamond corresponds to the value of the aggregate insolvency indicator based on these three subcomponents in 2010.

Source: Adalet McGowan and Andrews (2018[21]), "Design of insolvency regimes across countries", *OECD Economics Department Working Papers*, No. 504, http://dx.doi.org/10.1787/d44dc56f-en.

StatLink http://dx.doi.org/10.1787/888933881743

Enhancing geographical mobility to foster efficient reallocation

Rapid economic change can have diverging effects on local labour markets. The evidence suggests, for instance, that increased trade integration of a number of high-income OECD countries with China led to highly localised job losses (Autor, Dorn and Hanson, 2016[22]; Malgouyres, 2016[23]; OECD, 2017[24]), with newly created jobs concentrated in other geographic areas. Similarly, regions with high initial shares of routine jobs have seen declines in low- and middle-skill employment (Autor and Dorn, 2013[25]), whereas the creation of high-skilled jobs in knowledge-intensive services (especially ICT) tends to be concentrated in other regions (Sorbe, Gal and Millot, 2018[26]).

Geographic mobility would allow workers to benefit from the opportunities triggered by globalisation and rapid technological change despite geographic mismatches between job destruction and creation. This could be achieved by a range of policies that promote residential mobility, such as: i) taxing housing property (e.g. by taxing imputed rents) rather than real estate transactions; ii) ensuring a good responsiveness of housing supply to changes in demand and prices (e.g. through appropriate land use and planning regulations) to avoid that housing prices in job-rich areas become unaffordable for workers trying to move in; iii) avoiding unjustified support to homeownership (such as the tax deductibility of mortgage interest) since homeownership can be an obstacle to mobility; iv) avoiding rent controls, which tend to lockin tenants and weaken incentives for construction; and v) carefully designing social housing schemes to make sure that they do not create barriers to mobility (Andrews, Caldera Sánchez and Johansson, 2011[27]; Caldera Sánchez and Johansson, 2011[28]). The empirical evidence suggests that making residential mobility easier can increase the re-employment probabilities for workers displaced by firm exit (Andrews and Saia, 2017[19]). Geographic mobility could also be promoted by better recognition of skills and qualifications across regions and countries.

14.2. Building more responsive, effective and worker-centred adult learning systems

As a result of technological change, globalisation and demographic change, labour markets are experiencing profound structural changes in their occupational and industrial structures, with far-ranging implications for the required types of skills. Automation alone may lead to the destruction of one-in-seven jobs over the next 15-20 years and significantly change the way many of the remaining jobs are carried out (Nedelkoska and Quintini, 2018[29]). Adult learning needs to be scaled up to enable workers to deal with these changes and avoid a further widening of skill imbalances. This requires more responsive, effective and worker-centred adult learning systems.

Adult learning is key to address skill imbalances

Since the majority of people affected by changing skill needs is already in the workforce and adults are expected to work for longer, adult learning is a key issue to ensure that workers and firms can harness the opportunities while addressing the challenges associated with the future of work. This will require a significant upscaling of adult learning systems in all countries in combination with specific measures targeted at those lacking basic skills. On average across OECD countries, almost one quarter of adults lack basic numeracy skills and an even larger share of adults have no or very limited digital skills that are needed to navigate and solve problems in everyday life (Chapter 3). Improving the skills of these adults will be crucial to protect them against the potentially negative effects of automation and globalisation. Yet, despite the importance of life-long learning for adults with low skills, workers with low skills or in jobs at high risk of automation are much less likely to participate in adult learning than workers with high skills or workers whose jobs are safe (Chapter 10). In addition, low-skilled adults are disproportionately employed in non-standard forms of work, which tend to be associated with additional barriers to training (Chapter 12).

In the absence of effective adult learning systems, there is a risk that rapid structural change leads to growing imbalances between skill supply and demand. While some imbalances are unavoidable, especially in periods of rapid transition, persistent imbalances can have significant costs for individuals, companies and society at large. They are associated with negative labour market outcomes for individuals, including lower wages and job satisfaction, and hamper companies' innovation and technology adoption. According to the OECD Skills for Jobs database (OECD, 2017[30]), countries differ considerably in the extent to which the supply of skills adapts to changing skill needs (see Box 14.1 for details). Large skill imbalances, associated with intense occupational shortages and surpluses, tend to be especially prevalent in countries such as Greece, Iceland and Spain, while they are relatively modest in countries such as France, the Netherlands, Norway and Switzerland (OECD, 2018[31]). Moreover, occupational imbalances have been widening during the last decade, as evidenced by intensified skill shortages in high-level cognitive and soft skills, and by growing surpluses in routine and physical skills (Figure 14.3). The risk of automation is likely to further amplify these trends in the future (Nedelkoska and Quintini, 2018[29]).

Skill imbalances and skills mismatches are closely intertwined. Skill shortages can lead to under-qualification, as employers facing recruitment difficulties may lower hiring requirements to fill their vacancies. Skill surpluses may give rise to over-qualification as job-seekers are more likely to accept job offers below their skill level. On average across the OECD, approximately 36% of workers are mismatched, with approximately equal shares reporting that that they are overqualified (17%) – i.e. that they had higher qualifications than required to perform their jobs – and under-qualified (19%) – i.e. that they had lower qualifications than required to perform their jobs (see Chapter 7 for further details).

Figure 14.3. Skill imbalances have tended to widen over the last decade

OECD unweighted average of skills imbalances, index, 2004 and 2014

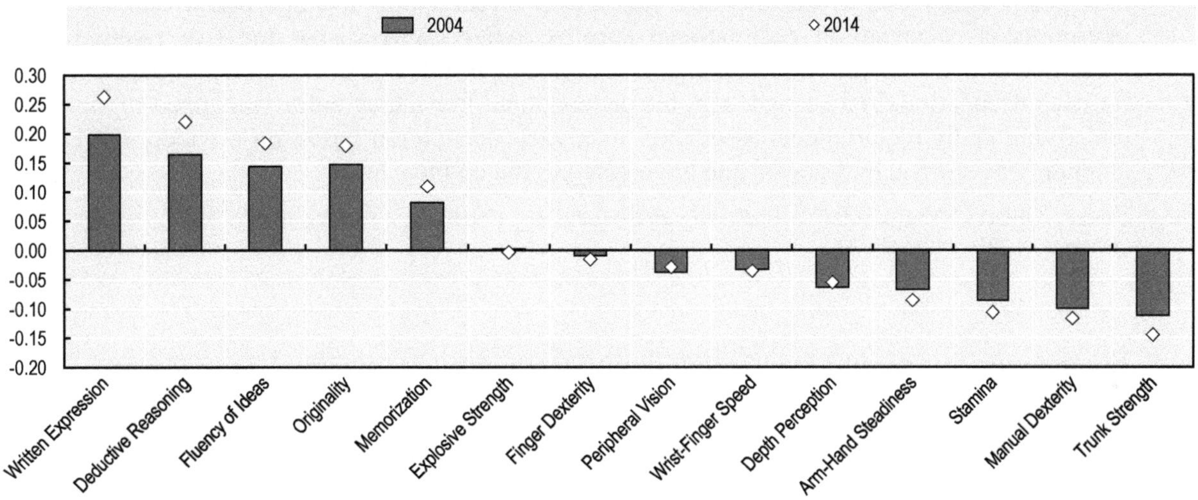

Notes: A value of one corresponds to the maximum skill shortage observed across OECD countries and skills dimensions. A positive value indicates means a skill shortage and a negative value indicates a surplus. Skills are ordered by the intensity of shortages in 2014.
Source: *OECD Skills for Jobs Database* (2018), www.oecdskillsforjobsdatabase.org (accessed on 26 October 2018).

StatLink http://dx.doi.org/10.1787/888933881762

Scaling up adult learning

While there are significant benefits from investing in adult learning for firms and individuals, there are various reasons why there is a shortfall of such investments in many countries and particularly among disadvantaged groups and in small and medium-sized enterprises. These include imperfect information on costs and benefits, financial constraints, and various labour market imperfections that break the link between those who invest in adult training and those who benefit from it. For example, workers with a weak bargaining position may not be able to fully capitalise on their investments in adult learning. Employers may face similar problems in a context where workers are increasingly mobile across firms. Governments at the national and the local levels thus need to ensure that adult learning is: i) responsive to changing skill needs; ii) effective in the sense of benefits exceeding costs; and iii) sufficiently worker-centred by linking adult learning to individuals rather than to jobs. Specific measures to encourage adult learning among disadvantaged groups are also needed and are discussed in Chapter 10 on labour market inclusiveness.

Box 14.1. The OECD Skills for Jobs Database

The *OECD Skills for Jobs Database* is a key instrument for assessing and anticipating skill needs. It documents the evolution of skills imbalances in terms of shortages and surpluses. To this end, the OECD Skills for Jobs Database makes use of detailed performance indicators by occupation and a taxonomy of skill requirements by occupation. The degree of "labour market pressure" for each occupation in each country is assessed by five performance measures which compare an occupation's long-term path in terms of wages, working time, employment, unemployment and under-qualification with the country average. Above-average performance on each of these outcomes is interpreted as a signal of occupational shortage whereas below-average performance is interpreted as a signal of occupational surplus. After standardising the five relative performance measures, they are aggregated into a single index of occupational imbalance for each occupation. In a second step, the occupational imbalance index is mapped to the underlying skills requirements associated with each occupation based on a widely-used taxonomy developed by O*NET and aggregated to the country level.

Source: OECD (2018$_{[311]}$), *OECD Skills for Jobs Database* (2018), www.oecdskillsforjobsdatabase.org (accessed on 26 October 2018).

Promote the responsiveness of adult learning systems to changing labour market needs

Ensuring that skill supply aligns with skill demand requires responsive demand-driven adult education and training systems (OECD, 2016$_{[32]}$). A precondition to achieve this is to have in place robust systems and tools for assessing and anticipating skill needs, combined with effective mechanisms and procedures which ensure that such information feeds into policy-making, lifelong guidance and the education and training choices of individuals. One promising way that can help achieve this is to couple high-quality information on the skills needs of employers with information on education and training options and their potential benefits for career advancement in terms of job opportunities and pay. Online tools and databases are ideal for disseminating such information as widely as possible among all possible stakeholders, including prospective students, trainers as well as career and skills councillors.

A demand-driven adult learning system also thrives on close links between the world of education and training on the one hand and the world of work on the other. Such links can be strengthened by vocational education and work-based learning programmes. Apprenticeship programmes, where students of all ages combine classroom learning with practical training with an employer for a period of several years, such as in Austria, Germany and Switzerland, are often regarded as best practice. Vocational education and work-based learning programmes tend to be most effective where employer and trade union involvement is strong and co-operation well-developed. More generally, social partners should be closely involved in the development and implementation of the government's policy agenda at the national level with respect to adult learning by allowing them to take part in permanent advisory bodies, specific working groups or ad hoc consultations in relation to adult learning policy, as well as at the local level, as numerous successful examples illustrate (Box 14.2).

Box 14.2. Examples of local skills development programmes

The development of better local labour market information is critical to help individuals, employers, and policy makers to make well-informed decisions about skills development and training. In the United States, the Workforce Intelligence Network (WIN) in southeast Michigan illustrates how to join-up local actors to build a strong local labour market information system and improve matching between job seekers and employers (OECD, 2014[33]). The mission of the organisation is to cultivate a comprehensive and cohesive talent system to ensure that employers find the workers they need. WIN brings together key partners in workforce development such as community colleges, four-year postsecondary institutions, K-12 schools, economic development organisations, government, community based organisations, and employers. WIN has developed a data dashboard and produces quarterly labour market reports, which publicise job market data related to employer demand, preferred credentials, and labour force fluctuations.

Initiatives as the local level play a critical role in reaching out to employers to promote awareness and participation in apprenticeship training. Local apprenticeship hubs in Manchester and Leeds (the United Kingdom) have been successful in coordinating the range of government actors involved in apprenticeship programmes to provide a "one-stop" offer to local employers (OECD/ILO, 2017[34]). Taking a decentralised approach to apprenticeships can be particularly effective in bringing on board local small and medium enterprises (SME) who often face unique barriers. In Ireland, the state-funded support body Skillnet has been effective in actively supporting and working with businesses to address their current and future skills needs. The programme funds 65 training networks which operate locally, supporting over 14 000 companies and 50 000 trainees. Member companies actively participate in determining their own training needs and how, when and where training will be provided (OECD, 2014[33]).

Strategic local partnerships can also help to adapt employment and skills programmes to the changing nature of work at the local level. Under the Workforce and Innovation Opportunity Act (WIOA) in the United States, for instance, local workforce investment boards – representing private sector employers, labour unions, non-profit organisations, and government agencies - are required to develop a local plan to provide a coordinated response to current and future workforce development challenges. The City of New York has further developed Industry Partnerships which, focusing on a specific sector, are designed to work collaboratively with a diverse set of stakeholders – including employers, community-based organisations, organised labour, philanthropy, government, training providers and educational institutions. The Industry Partnerships identify the most pressing needs that employers have for qualified talent, then revise or design training curricula with employer input or develop other solutions to address those needs (City of New York, 2017[35]).

Financial incentives for participants and providers can be used for steering adult learning investments towards in-demand skills. For instance, the Higher Education Funding Council of England (HEFCE) distributes public funds to higher education institutions to promote specific skill policy objectives, like the development of facilities related to science, technology, engineering and math (STEM) training. Financial incentives can also focus on workers in jobs at high risk of automation or unemployed workers whose skills have become obsolete. Training programmes yield the most successful employment outcomes when they are tied closely to the needs of the labour market (OECD, 2017[36]). This can be done by directing public resources to training activities that address clearly identified labour market needs or take the form of more market-driven forms of targeting by providing subsidies to employers for hiring and training (see also discussion below).

Promote the cost-effectiveness of adult learning

To ensure that firms and workers have strong incentives to invest in adult training it needs to be cost-effective, which depends on the value of adult learning for workers and firms as well as its costs.

The value of adult education and training to firms and workers depends crucially on its quality, but also on the extent to which the skills acquired through training and education are recognised by employers. Yet clear and well-defined quality assurance systems tend to be rare (Broek and Zoetermeer, 2013[37]). In large part, this is related to the diversity and considerable number of actors involved in the provision of adult learning. To assess the effectiveness of adult learning, regular and systematic quality assessments are needed based on the monitoring of learning and labour market outcomes or impact evaluations. To ensure high quality standards and promote an effective demand for adult learning, it is crucial that quality assessments are disseminated widely and effectively. This requires establishing minimum standards through licencing, certification and labelling systems. Ideally, such standard-setting is complemented with the provision of high-quality public information on the effectiveness of individual training and education providers based on the learning and labour market outcomes of past students. Beyond the formal provision of training and education, skills certification programmes also have a role to play by ensuring that less formal forms of adult training are also formally recognised.

The costs of adult learning can be an important barrier, especially among firms and workers with limited financial resources of their own, and hence provides an argument for the use of financial incentives (OECD, 2017[38]). Financial incentives targeted at individuals can be useful to stimulate the acquisition of portable skills and to promote adult learning among vulnerable groups. Those targeted at employers can be useful to promote the acquisition of more directly work-related skills, particularly in SMEs. In general, the effectiveness of financial incentives tends to be enhanced when they contain an element of co-financing since this reduces the risk that training is subsidised that would have been undertaken anyway or has little social value (OECD, 2006[39]). Moreover, direct subsidies typically allow for a better targeting than general tax incentives. However, both direct subsidies and general tax incentives risk becoming very expensive for the public purse if adult learning is supposed to be scaled up radically. Financial incentives that rely on more important contributions from individuals and employers are less likely to hit fiscal constraints, but may require a system based on mandatory contributions to ensure that sufficient resources are mobilised (e.g. individual saving accounts for training, training levies). A collective system may also help to ensure that SMEs and vulnerable workers have the financial resources to invest in adult learning. In a number of countries, the social partners have implemented sectoral initiatives to promote adult learning based on a system of pooled resources (e.g. Finland, the Netherlands).

Make adult training worker-centred by linking it to individuals rather than jobs

The changing organisation of work may further call for a re-think of the rights and duties of workers, firms and government in the management and provision of adult learning. In a world of work organised around long-term employer-employee relationships, workers and firms generally have strong incentives to invest in training. However, the incentives for workers and firms to invest in adult learning may be weakened in a changing world of work, where there is great uncertainty about the skills required by employers in the future, and where work is less stable and more often organised through non-standard work relationships. With workers being increasingly mobile and often combining several jobs at the same time, employer incentives for adult learning may be weak. Moreover, due to the rise of platform and independent contract work, an increasing share of the workforce may no longer have an employer who is responsible for the provision of training and may lack the information, advice and counselling required to pursue training on its own. This calls for training rights and incentives that are available to all individuals regardless of their employment status.

As a result of these developments, there has been a renewed interest from policy makers in individual learning accounts (ILAs). ILAs can take different forms, including: i) individual savings accounts where time credits or financial resources for training are accumulated over time; and ii) voucher schemes which provide entitlements to direct government payments for training, sometimes with a contribution from the participant. ILAs have existed for some time, although rarely universal and country-wide. The original motivation for their use was mainly to create a "market" for adult learning, while empowering individuals to make their own career choices by choosing training courses offered by competing providers. The current interest in ILAs is slightly different and lies in their potential to attach training rights to individuals rather than jobs, and therefore their ability to make training rights portable between jobs and available to all irrespective of employment status. This could help to increase participation in lifelong training for non-standard workers.

A number of countries have individual training accounts systems or conducted experiments to assess their effectiveness (OECD, 2017[40]). In France, for instance, an individual training account (*Compte Personnel de Formation*, CPF) was introduced at the beginning of 2015. In that scheme, employees – and since January 2018 all working-age adults including own-account workers and unemployed persons– get time credits for training in their individual accounts based on hours worked during the year. Accumulated training credits can only be used at the initiative of the individual and are strictly personal in the sense that they remain valid even when changing employer or becoming unemployed, ensuring potentially strong incentives to individuals to train throughout their lives.[2] Studies for the United States further suggest that the effectiveness of individual training accounts is strengthened when coupled with advice and counselling (OECD, 2017[38]). While individual training accounts can be part of a broader strategy to scale up adult learning, they tend to be used only sporadically by individuals with low skills, suggesting that additional measures are needed to enhance their participation in adult learning (see Chapter 10).

14.3. Supporting displaced workers

While promoting reallocation and investing in adult learning is key to make labour markets more adaptable to structural change, it is unavoidable that some workers get displaced from their jobs as their employers are forced to cut back their operations or shut down completely. The cost of job displacement (contract termination of permanent workers with long job tenure due to economic reasons) in terms of foregone income can be large. In some countries, including Germany, Portugal and the United Kingdom, earnings in the year of dismissal fall by 30% on average, with incomes remaining below pre-displacement levels for a long time and even after workers are re-employed. To reduce the costs of job displacement, effective employment and social policies are needed (OECD, 2018[41]). To the extent that job losses are concentrated in specific regions – in many cases compounding the challenges of lagging regions – there may be a need for additional measures at the regional level.

Employment policies for displaced workers

The main focus of policies for displaced workers should be on early intervention measures and effective activation polices.

Early intervention measures have proved particularly effective

A crucial difference between displaced workers and most other groups served by the public employment service is that it is often possible to initiate re-employment services during the notice period prior to displacement. Rapid response services, for example by setting up a temporary public employment service office in factories that will soon close, facilitate the timely delivery of re-employment services. Such early interventions can speed up the adjustment process and achieve better outcomes by starting the process before workers become unemployed. Employers typically view job applications from workers who are still employed more favourably and labour market prospects tend to deteriorate the longer a worker is unemployed. Although such early interventions can be effective, they are not used as widely as would be desirable, as they are often limited to workers affected by mass layoffs.

The extent to which employers and unions are actively involved in the planning and provision of re-employment services to displaced workers can be important for the effectiveness of early interventions. In Sweden, the job security councils, which are operated by the social partners, demonstrate the feasibility of offering early intervention measures to all displaced workers, including those affected by individual or small-scale layoffs, when employers and unions are actively engaged (OECD, 2015[42]). Employment protection rules can help establish an appropriate level of employer engagement by requiring employers to respect a minimum period of advance notice for layoffs. Governments can then ensure that notified workers are the focus of outreach activities by the public employment services or that workers are required to register with the public employment service as soon as they are notified. The latter can help ensure that early intervention measures are not limited to workers who are displaced through mass layoffs, but also reach those affected by individual dismissal.

An effective activation strategy is essential

An effective national activation strategy to get people into work provides a solid foundation for promoting the rapid re-employment of displaced workers. But policy also needs to take into account the specific barriers to re-employment confronting displaced workers (e.g. obsolete skills and the lack of recent job-search experience), specific advantages (e.g. a history of stable employment and strong labour force attachment) as well as the specific local circumstances (e.g. displacement frequently concentrated in economically declining regions).

While all displaced workers should benefit from prompt access to basic job-search services, some will require more intensive re-employment services or retraining. One key challenge is to identify this smaller group rapidly and offer them intensive services when these are most effective rather than after a long period of unemployment as is commonly the case. Another important challenge is to ensure that all groups of displaced workers have equal access to re-employment help, including those who do not immediately qualify for unemployment benefits, for example, because severance pay is treated as compensation. This requires decoupling participation in re-employment services from the receipt of public income support. Moreover, a pragmatic mix of general activation policies and programmes specifically targeted at displaced workers usually works best (OECD, 2018[20]).[3]

Local employment services can play a critical role in strategies to facilitate structural change and support displaced workers, but they require flexibility and capacity to take a stronger leadership role. The OECD Reviews on Local Job Creation have shown that allowing greater room for manoeuvre to local employment services is a difficult challenge for governments. The awarding of greater flexibility must therefore be accompanied by guarantees regarding the accountability of decision-making and the efficiency of service delivery. This crucially requires putting in place a rigorous performance management system and ensuring that local employment services have adequate skills and sufficient resources. It also requires ensuring that front-line staff have good local labour market information and strong contacts with employers so they can become quickly aware of new employment opportunities as they arise.

Income-support policies for displaced workers

Income-support policies play a crucial role in alleviating the costs of job displacement, in the form of lost labour income during unemployment and potentially also lower earnings upon re-employment. To the extent that technological developments are such that significant groups of displaced workers are at risk of very long-term unemployed in the absence of sufficient work opportunities for all people, resulting in elevated "technological unemployment", a more fundamental rethink of social protection may be required. However, based on the OECD's current assessment of the speed of automation over the next 15-20 years, such a prospect is neither likely nor inevitable since the risk of technological unemployment depends crucially on the extent to which new opportunities can be created and workers can adapt their skills to the changing world of work.

Income-support policies alleviate the costs of displacement

Compared with other groups of unemployed people, displaced workers tend to have relatively high benefit entitlements in most countries, because their employment histories are generally more stable than those of many other unemployed people. Nonetheless, benefits only provide compensation for a proportion of earnings losses, with large differences across countries. During the first year of unemployment, the average net replacement rate is 19% in the United States and 75% in Denmark. Earnings losses are especially large for workers experiencing a long spell of unemployment or becoming re-employed at a significantly lower wage or part-time. To avoid that displaced workers experiencing long spells of unemployment are left without income-support it is crucial that social-assistance benefits are available for those who have exhausted their unemployment benefit entitlements. Apart from addressing financial hardship, high coverage social and unemployment benefits also provide a contact point for public employment and social services through which appropriate support measures can be taken to overcome barriers to work (see Chapter 9 for a more in-depth discussion).

An important question in the context of displaced workers is whether wages of re-employed workers should be topped up to compensate for part of the earnings losses due to displacement through the use of wage insurance schemes. Evaluations of two small wage insurance schemes in Canada and the United States suggest that wage insurance mitigates the income declines of displaced workers, but does not speed up re-employment (Bloom et al., 2001[43]; Wandner, 2016[44]). Other pilot studies of wage insurance schemes would be of considerable value, in light of the effect that job displacement has on worker well-being.

Income support policies to deal with elevated structural unemployment

In the unlikely event that automation and digitalisation significantly raise structural unemployment due to the absence of sufficient job opportunities, more far-ranging measures may be needed to provide adequate income support.

To ensure that all workers receive at least some income support a number of countries are experimenting with various forms of basic income schemes. A universal, unconditional "no-questions-asked" public transfer would be simple and have the advantage that no one is left without support. But an unconditional payment to everyone at a meaningful level would most likely require tax rises as well as reductions in existing benefits and would not be an effective tool to reduce poverty (OECD, 2017[45]; Hanna and Olken, 2018[46]). At constant social spending, the implied basic income would in most countries be well below the current level of social assistance. In addition, some disadvantaged groups would lose out when existing benefits are replaced by a basic income, illustrating the downsides of social protection without any form of targeting at all.

Another option to deal with high levels of structural unemployment may be to make use of job guarantees – i.e. the promise of a job to anyone willing and able to work at some minimum wage rate. Compared to basic income schemes, job guarantees fit better with the philosophy of "mutual obligations", whereby society's responsibility to support those in need is matched by the individual's duty to contribute something in return. Job guarantees also have the advantage over basic income schemes that they go beyond the provision of income and, by providing a job, help individuals to stay connected with society, build self-esteem, as well as develop skills and competencies. However, past experience with public sector employment programmes has shown that they have negligible effects on the post-programme outcomes of participants, and therefore are best considered as a form of income-support rather than a policy to promote self-sufficiency and need to be tightly targeted to those with limited resources of their own.

Policies to support lagging regions

To the extent that job displacement is concentrated in specific regions, additional measures are needed to support lagging regions.[4] At a minimum, limiting regional inequalities requires that high-quality public services, including public education, public health, public transport and public employment services, are maintained in lagging regions. In some cases, additional public investments in education, transport and infrastructure are needed to strengthen a region's competitiveness and facilitate the diffusion of innovation and good practices across regions, industries and firms (Moretti, 2012[47]; OECD, 2018[48]). Such policies require the cooperation of the national, regional and local governments to enhance the capacity of regional and local governments to effectively administer and implement large-scale investment projects, education and employment programmes. It also requires well-established and transparent procedures for the selection of such projects and the way they are awarded to private contractors.

But preventing displaced workers in lagging regions from further falling behind also requires place-based employment and social policies. These should tackle the social problems associated with the local concentration of unemployment, social exclusion and poverty, through: i) the provision of easily accessible anti-poverty programmes; ii) the establishment of community centres and the use of urban regeneration projects; and iii) retraining, work experience or entrepreneurship programmes that help displaced workers move into new activities or towards other regions with suitable job opportunities. Some regions may need to raise specific support for linguistic minorities and promote the acquisition of new skills and trades for indigenous people whose traditional ways for maintaining their livelihoods are being eroded in an increasingly modern and interconnected world.

Conclusion

Sustaining good labour market performance and inclusive growth in a context of rapid technological progress, deepening globalisation and demographic change require that labour markets are adaptable, i.e. that worker and firms can absorb, adapt to and make the most of the opportunities while being able to deal with the challenges associated with a changing world of work. Many of the policies and institutions that have been discussed in this Volume implicitly reflect the need for adaptable labour markets since adaptability is crucial for achieving good labour market performance in a rapidly changing economic context. This chapter explicitly discusses key policies to strengthen adaptability.

- *Promote the efficient reallocation of workers across jobs, firms, industries and regions*. Adapting to digitalisation, globalisation and demographic change requires that innovative businesses are not held back by overly burdensome product market regulations, especially administrative barriers to firm entry, and lack of financing. At the same time, effective insolvency regimes and more balanced financial systems that do not favour debt over equity financing could promote the exit or re-structuring of the least productive ones. Removing excessively restrictive employment protection rules and reforming housing policies that reduce geographic mobility would prevent workers from becoming trapped in low-productivity businesses and regions and allow them to move where the best jobs are.
- *Building more responsive, effective and worker-centred adult learning systems*. Rapidly changing skill needs require giving greater priority to adult learning. Yet few countries have fully effective learning systems and existing systems tend to widen rather than reducing skill gaps: in all OECD countries workers most at risk of automation are least likely to participate in adult learning. Without appropriate action, there is a significant risk that workers without basic skills become unemployed, are pushed into dead-end jobs or leave the labour force altogether. To meet this challenge countries urgently need to invest in effective adult learning

systems. Such systems should be responsive to changes in labour market needs, meet high quality and transparency requirements, incentivise workers and firms to invest in adult learning and be sufficiently worker-centred by linking training rights to workers rather than jobs.

- *Support displaced workers through the use of effective employment and social policies*. While technological change creates new opportunities, it also implies considerable turbulence in labour markets, associated with firm closures, mass layoffs and dismissals. Job displacement tends to be painful for those involved, in terms of lost income during unemployment, but often also leaves long-lasting scars to worker careers. To alleviate the cost of job displacement – both in the short-term but also in the long-term as a result of scarring effects – it is crucial that displaced workers return to work as quickly as possible. This requires effective activation strategies as discussed in Chapter 9, but also early intervention measures during the notice period. Income-support policies are key to alleviate the costs of job displacement during unemployment but potentially also during re-employment through the use of wage insurance schemes.

Notes

[1] Ideally, young firms should grow rapidly or exit (so-called "up-or-out" dynamics) to avoid creating a large mass of small low-productivity firms (Calvino, Criscuolo and Menon, 2015[5]).

[2] The CPF is currently being reformed, amongst other by expressing training accounts in euros instead of hours.

[3] Many targeted programmes focus on workers who are adversely affected by higher import competition; the two most prominent examples are the Trade Adjustment Assistance in the United States and the European Globalisation Adjustment Fund in the European Union.

[4] For example, OECD (2018[48]) finds that the risk of automation differs considerably across regions within countries.

References

Adalet McGowan, M. and D. Andrews (2018), "Design of insolvency regimes across countries", *OECD Economics Department Working Papers*, No. 1504, OECD Publishing, Paris, http://dx.doi.org/10.1787/d44dc56f-en. [21]

Adalet McGowan, M. et al. (2015), *The Future of Productivity*, OECD, Paris, https://www.oecd.org/eco/OECD-2015-The-future-of-productivity-book.pdf. [4]

Adalet McGowan, M., D. Andrews and V. Millot (2017), "Insolvency Regimes, Technology Diffusion and Productivity Growth: Evidence from Firms in OECD Countries", *OECD Economics Department Working Papers*, No. 1425, OECD Publishing, Paris, http://dx.doi.org/10.1787/36600267-en. [17]

Adalet McGowan, M., D. Andrews and V. Millot (2017), "Insolvency regimes, zombie firms and capital reallocation", *OECD Economics Department Working Papers*, No. 1399, OECD Publishing, Paris, http://dx.doi.org/10.1787/5a16beda-en. [16]

Adalet McGowan, M., D. Andrews and V. Millot (2017), "The Walking Dead? Zombie Firms and Productivity Performance in OECD Countries", *OECD Economics Department Working Papers*, No. 1372, OECD, http://dx.doi.org/10.1787/18151973. [14]

Andrews, D., M. Adalet McGowan and V. Millot (2017), "Confronting The Zombies: Policies For Productivity Revival", *OECD Economic Policy Paper*, No. 21, OECD Publishing, Paris, https://doi.org/10.1787/f14fd801-en. [18]

Andrews, D., A. Caldera Sánchez and Å. Johansson (2011), "Housing Markets and Structural Policies in OECD Countries", *OECD Economics Department Working Papers*, No. 836, OECD Publishing, Paris, http://dx.doi.org/10.1787/5kgk8t2k9vf3-en. [27]

Andrews, D. and F. Cingano (2014), "Public policy and resource allocation: evidence from firms in OECD countries", *Economic Policy*, Vol. 29, pp. 253-296. [9]

Andrews, D., C. Criscuolo and P. Gal (2016), "The Best versus the Rest: The Global Productivity Slowdown, Divergence across Firms and the Role of Public Policy", *OECD Productivity Working Papers*, No. 5, OECD, Paris, http://dx.doi.org/10.1787/24139424. [7]

Andrews, D., G. Nicoletti and C. Timiliotis (2018), "Digital technology diffusion: A matter of capabilities, incentives or both?", *OECD Economics Department Working Papers*, No. 1476, OECD Publishing, Paris, http://dx.doi.org/10.1787/7c542c16-en. [8]

Andrews, D. and F. Petroulakis (2017), "Breaking the Shackles: Zombie Firms, Weak Banks and Depressed Restructuring in Europe", *OECD Economics Department Working Papers*, No. 1433, OECD Publishing, Paris, http://dx.doi.org/10.1787/0815ce0c-en. [15]

Andrews, D. and A. Saia (2017), "Coping with creative destruction: Reducing the costs of firm exit", *OECD Economics Department Working Papers*, No. 1353, OECD Publishing, Paris, http://dx.doi.org/10.1787/bbb44644-en. [19]

Arnold, J., G. Nicoletti and S. Scarpetta (2011), "Regulation, resource reallocation and productivity growth", *Nordic Economic Policy Review*, Vol. 2. [6]

Autor, D. and D. Dorn (2013), "The growth of low-skill service jobs and the polarization of the US Labor Market", *American Economic Review*, http://dx.doi.org/10.1257/aer.103.5.1553. [25]

Autor, D., D. Dorn and G. Hanson (2016), "The China Shock: Learning from Labor-Market Adjustment to Large Changes in Trade", *Annual Review of Economics*, Vol. 8, http://dx.doi.org/10.1146/annurev-economics-080315-015041. [22]

Bloom, H. et al. (2001), "Testing a financial incentive to promote re-employment among displaced workers: The Canadian Earnings Supplement Project (ESP)", *Journal of Policy Analysis and Management*, Vol. 20/3, pp. 505-523. [43]

Brassell, M. and K. Boschmans (2018), "Fostering the Use of Intangibles to Strengthen SME Access to Finance", *OECD SME and Entrepreneurship Papers*, No. forthcoming, OECD. [12]

Broek, S. and B. Zoetermeer (2013), *Developing the adult learning sector Quality in the Adult Learning Sector (Lot 1) Final report (Open Call for tender EAC/26/2011)*, Panteia, http://arhiv.acs.si/porocila/Quality_in_the_Adult_Learning_Sector-final_report.pdf (accessed on 15 November 2018). [37]

Caballero, R., T. Hoshi and A. Kashyap (2008), "Zombie Lending and Depressed Restructuring in Japan", *American Economic Review*, Vol. 98/5, pp. 1943-1977, http://dx.doi.org/10.1257/aer.98.5.1943. [13]

Caldera Sánchez, A. and Å. Johansson (2011), "The Price Responsiveness of Housing Supply in OECD Countries", *OECD Economics Department Working Papers*, No. 837, OECD Publishing, Paris, http://dx.doi.org/10.1787/5kgk9qhrnn33-en. [28]

Calvino, F., C. Criscuolo and C. Menon (2015), "Cross-country evidence on start-up dynamics", *OECD Science, Technology and Industry Working Papers*, No. 2015/6, OECD Publishing, Paris, http://dx.doi.org/10.1787/5jrxtkb9mxtb-en. [5]

City of New York (2017), *WIOA Local Plan for New York*, https://goo.gl/forms/wo2IKLWpkq9sL1653. [35]

Criscuolo, C., P. Gal and C. Menon (2014), "The Dynamics of Employment Growth: New Evidence from 18 Countries", *OECD Science, Technology and Industry Policy Papers*, No. 14, OECD Publishing, Paris, http://dx.doi.org/10.1787/5jz417hj6hg6-en. [2]

Demmou, L., I. Stefanescu and A. Arquie (2018), "Labour productivity growth and finance: The role of intangible assets", *OECD Economics Department Working Papers*, No. forthcoming, OECD. [11]

Foster, L., J. Haltiwanger and C. Syverson (2008), "Reallocation, Firm Turnover, and Efficiency: Selection on Productivity or Profitability?", *American Economic Review*, Vol. 98/1, pp. 394-425, http://dx.doi.org/10.1257/aer.98.1.394. [1]

Haltiwanger, J., R. Jarmin and J. Miranda (2013), "Who creates jobs? Small versus large versus young", *The Review of Economics and Statistics*, Vol. XCV, http://dx.doi.org/10.1162/REST_a_00288. [3]

Haltiwanger, J., S. Scarpetta and H. Schweiger (2014), "Cross country differences in job reallocation: The role of industry, firm size and regulations ☆", Vol. 26, pp. 11-25, http://dx.doi.org/10.1016/j.labeco.2013.10.001. [10]

Hanna, R. and B. Olken (2018), *Universal Basic Incomes vs. Targeted Transfers: Anti-Poverty Programs in Developing Countries*, http://www.nber.org/data-appendix/w24939 (accessed on 27 August 2018). [46]

Malgouyres, C. (2016), "The Impact of Chinese Import Competition on the Local Structure of Employment and Wages: Evidence from France", *Banque de France Working Papers*, No. 603, https://ideas.repec.org/p/bfr/banfra/603.html (accessed on 23 July 2018). [23]

Moretti, E. (2012), *The new geography of jobs*, Houghton Mifflin Harcourt, https://books.google.fr/books/about/The_New_Geography_of_Jobs.html?id=mxFMI7XWMzEC&source=kp_book_description&redir_esc=y (accessed on 29 October 2018). [47]

Nedelkoska, L. and G. Quintini (2018), "Automation, skills use and training", *OECD Social, Employment and Migration Working Papers*, No. 202, OECD Publishing, Paris, http://dx.doi.org/10.1787/2e2f4eea-en. [29]

OECD (2018), "Back to work: Lessons from nine country case studies of policies to assist displaced workers", in *OECD Employment Outlook 2018*, OECD Publishing, Paris, http://dx.doi.org/10.1787/empl_outlook-2018-8-en. [20]

OECD (2018), *Job Creation and Local Economic Development 2018: Preparing for the Future of Work*, OECD Publishing, Paris, http://dx.doi.org/10.1787/9789264305342-en. [48]

OECD (2018), *OECD Employment Outlook 2018*, OECD Publishing, Paris, http://dx.doi.org/10.1787/empl_outlook-2018-en. [41]

OECD (2018), *OECD Skills for Jobs Database*, http://www.oecdskillsforjobsdatabase.org (accessed on 26 October 2018). [31]

OECD (2017), "Basic Income as a Policy Option", https://www.oecd.org/els/soc/Basic-Income-Policy-Option-2017-Brackground-Technical-Note.pdf (accessed on 29 October 2018). [45]

OECD (2017), *Financial Incentives for Steering Education and Training*, Getting Skills Right, OECD Publishing, Paris, http://dx.doi.org/10.1787/9789264272415-en. [38]

OECD (2017), *Getting Skills Right: France*, Getting Skills Right, OECD Publishing, Paris, http://dx.doi.org/10.1787/9789264284456-en. [40]

OECD (2017), *Getting Skills Right: Good Practice in Adapting to Changing Skill Needs: A Perspective on France, Italy, Spain, South Africa and the United Kingdom*, Getting Skills Right, OECD Publishing, Paris, http://dx.doi.org/10.1787/9789264277892-en. [36]

OECD (2017), *Getting Skills Right: Skills for Jobs Indicators*, Getting Skills Right, OECD Publishing, Paris, http://dx.doi.org/10.1787/9789264277878-en. [30]

OECD (2017), "How technology and globalisation are transforming the labour market", in *OECD Employment Outlook 2017*, OECD Publishing, Paris, http://dx.doi.org/10.1787/empl_outlook-2017-7-en. [24]

OECD (2016), *Skills Matter: Further Results from the Survey of Adult Skills*, OECD Publishing, Paris, https://www.oecd-ilibrary.org/docserver/9789264258051-en.pdf?expires=1528454178&id=id&accname=guest&checksum=3F8691BC71E74034089E48F5909F120D (accessed on 08 June 2018). [32]

OECD (2015), *Back to Work: Sweden: Improving the re-employment prospects of displaced workers*, OECD Publishing, Paris, http://dx.doi.org/10.1787/9789264246812-en. [42]

OECD (2014), *Employment and Skills Strategies in the United States*, OECD Publishing, Paris, https://doi.org/10.1787/9789264209398-en. [33]

OECD (2014), *Employment and Skills Strategies in the United States*, OECD Reviews on Local Job Creation, OECD Publishing, Paris, https://dx.doi.org/10.1787/9789264209398-en. [49]

OECD (2006), *OECD Employment Outlook 2006*, OECD Publishing, Paris, https://doi.org/10.1787/empl_outlook-2006-en. [39]

OECD/ILO (2017), *Engaging Employers in Apprenticeship Opportunities: Making It Happen Locally*, OECD Publishing, Paris, http://dx.doi.org/10.1787/9789264266681-en. [34]

Sorbe, S., P. Gal and V. Millot (2018), "Can productivity still grow in service-based economies? Preliminary evidence and scoping for further research", *OECD Economics Department Working Papers*, No. forthcoming, OECD, Paris. [26]

Wandner, S. (2016), "Wage insurance as a policy option in the United States", *Upjohn Institute Working Papers*, No. 16-250, Upjohn Institute for Employment Research, Kalamazoo, MI. [44]

Part V. Implementing the OECD Jobs Strategy

Chapter 15. The political economy of reforms

Many OECD countries undertook important structural reforms in the wake of the global financial and economic crisis. Despite the long-run improvements in well-being that such reforms are likely to bring, they often face strong opposition, particularly in the case of labour market reforms. This chapter describes the factors that make reform happen and the policies that can help support the reform process. Good economic times are the best time for reforms, since then their benefits materialise more quickly. In practice, however, reforms are often undertaken in downturns, when the perceived urgency of reforms, but also their short-term costs are greater. Another political economy consideration is that many reforms create winners and losers in the labour market and affect the distribution of income. Appropriate design and complementary policies can mitigate these potential downsides of reforms to enhance political support.

Introduction

The political economy of reforms is an integral component of the new OECD Jobs Strategy, in recognition of the fact that, without proper design and implementation, policy reforms for stronger and more inclusive labour markets and economies may not achieve their stated goals. Choosing the right opportunity to create support for a reform and to maximise its benefits is important for policy-makers, politicians and, most importantly, for citizens.

Over the past decades, OECD countries have adopted and implemented reforms in a wide range of areas, including labour markets, product markets and financial markets. Most of these reforms have had important consequences for various aspects of labour market performance: employment, job quality, inclusiveness, and resilience and adaptability. Reforms took place in different countries at different times. The period after the outburst of the global financial and economic crisis saw a particularly high number of reforms, especially in the European countries that were hit hardest.

Many reforms involve winners and losers, which can weigh on the political support for reforms. Those who may lose out tend to have strong incentives to lobby against the reform. Sometimes, losses are concentrated within a specific industry, region or group of workers. Countries have therefore frequently combined economy-wide policies with measures dedicated to cushioning the impact on certain industries, regions or workers. Labour market reforms tend to be particularly contentious, as they often affect large parts of the population and so create many potential winners and losers.

Another reason that may make it difficult to get reforms passed is that reforms can give rise to significant short-term costs despite being welfare-enhancing in the longer term. As the chapter shows, for some reforms this is especially likely to be the case when they are undertaken in an economic downturn. The transitional costs of such reforms can be mitigated through appropriate design and complementary policies.

The remainder of this chapter is organised as follows. Section 15.1 briefly describes the context within which governments in OECD countries have been undertaking reforms. Section 15.2 defines ten guiding principles for promoting a pro-active reform agenda and its implementation. Section 15.3 focuses on the short-term challenges of reforms and the policy choices that can help mitigate them. Section 15.4 discusses the issue of winners and losers of reform and how those who may lose out can stand in the way of reform initiatives. The chapter concludes with final remarks highlighting the most important insights.

15.1. A good time for reform?

The global economy, a decade after the onset of the global financial crisis, is enjoying fairly strong and widespread economic growth, even if some large emerging market economies are facing headwinds. The positive economic outlook should be conducive to the successful implementation of required labour market and other structural reforms. In many countries, reforms are needed to confront an array of challenges (see Chapter 2 for a more detailed discussion): productivity growth has been at historically low rates over the past 10-15 years. Real wage growth has been lower still. Inequality is at record-highs, and vulnerable groups face weak prospects in the labour market. Megatrends, such as digitalisation and globalisation, carry opportunities, but also risks for some groups of workers.

During the crisis, deep reforms were undertaken, including in southern euro area countries with a macroeconomic adjustment programme. Recently, reform efforts have diminished, with some notable exceptions (for example France). In part, this is to be expected given that in the countries where reforms were most needed they have been made and some time is needed to assess whether they have the desired impact. The slowdown in reform activity may also be related with reform fatigue or a decline in the perceived urgency of required reforms. Nevertheless, one-third of OECD countries implemented, or were in the process of implementing, an important reform last year in one or more areas of labour market policy (social assistance, minimum wages, collective bargaining systems, gender inclusion, integration of immigrants and minorities, activation policies and labour market regulations) – see OECD (2018[1]).

The counter-cyclicality of reform activity over the past decade – high during the crisis years and low during years of comparatively strong global growth – suggests that policy has been more reactive than pro-active. Such a pattern, which is not unique to the past ten years (Drazen and Easterly, 2001[2]), may not be ideal for several reasons. As will be illustrated below, the short-term challenges of reforms tend to be larger in bad than good economic times. Reforms undertaken in bad economic times may also be driven more by urgent needs rather than long-term well-being considerations. Further, the preparation of reforms takes time which may not be available in the face of a short-term emergency. The next section discusses options for politicians and other policy-makers to support the development of a more pro-active reform agenda.

15.2. Guiding principles for the design and implementation of a pro-active reform agenda

Initiatives for reforms to promote well-being often run into opposition, preventing their implementation. This is because many, if not all, reforms involve transitional or distributional costs. Labour market reforms tend to be especially contentious, since, in contrast to regulatory changes in a particular sector for example, they tend to affect all parts of the economy and a larger share of the population. Looking at the history of structural reforms and subsequent performance, ten lessons for the successful design and implementation of reforms can be drawn (Tompson, 2009[3]; Caldera Sánchez, de Serres and Yashiro, 2016[4]):

1. *Electoral mandate for reform*

   An electoral mandate for the government to reform is important. Without approval by the electorate, reforms tend to succeed only when their benefits become very rapidly visible, which is rarely the case for major reforms. The exception may be, as mentioned earlier, times of crises which can create opportunities for "reform surprises", as governments may have no choice other than to reverse course. Another, external force for reform arises for countries that become or are members of an economic union or international organisation. Accession countries in Eastern Europe adopted major reforms before and after joining the European Union (Duval, Furceri and Miethe, 2018[5]). However, without an electoral mandate, there is a risk that such reforms lack sufficient ownership and are (partially) unwound once the immediate need for them has dissipated.

2. *Leadership*

   Strong leadership, by an individual policy-maker or an institution in charge of the reform, is critical. It should, however, not be equated with unilateral action by the government. While unilateral action is sometimes the only way forward, successful leadership usually means winning consent, rather than securing compliance. This is in particular the case for labour market reforms that are facilitated by tripartite discussions between the government and the social partners. Such reforms may be led by a strong government, but are more likely to achieve the desired outcomes when the social partners are closely involved. The "wage moderation" in Germany in the 2000s probably owes much to a common understanding between the government and the social partners that the country's external competitiveness should improve (Bofinger, 2017[6]).[1]

3. *Effective communication*

   Effective communication, also through the social media, is essential. Successful reforms are usually accompanied by co-ordinated efforts to persuade voters and stakeholders of the need for reform and, in particular, to communicate the costs of no reform. When, as is often the case, the costs of the status quo are opportunity costs, they tend to be politically "invisible", making the challenge all the greater. It is typically fairly clear who will pay the price for a reform – which firms are likely to come under pressure and which jobs may be at risk – whereas it is not obvious who pays for the status quo: it is difficult to identify firms that have never entered the market or sectors that have not developed or the workers whom they would have employed.

4. *Reform commitment*

   Reform commitment is closely connected with effective communication, but goes beyond it. Announcing a reform early and committing credibly to it can help bring forward the gains from the reform. For example, announcing product market reforms in advance can trigger an immediate response by firms, increasing investment and output even before the reform is actually implemented (Adjemian et al., 2008[7]). In the area of labour market reforms, announcing future employment protection legislation reforms early can increase hiring as firms anticipate lower costs of layoff procedures, while avoiding an immediate rise of dismissals as existing rules continue to apply (International Monetary Fund, 2016[8]). In downturns, this can be an effective way to limit temporary declines in employment due to such reforms (OECD, 2016[9]).

5. *A solid evidence base*

   Policy design must be underpinned by solid research and analysis. An evidence-based and analytically sound case for a reform serves both to improve the quality of policy and to enhance prospects for reform adoption. The impact of economic analysis also depends on the source: research presented by authoritative, non-partisan institutions commanding trust across the political spectrum tends to have a greater effect. The United Kingdom is one among several countries with a history of influential, independent bodies (comprising, for example, the Institute for Fiscal Studies, the National Institute of Economic and Social Research or the Office for Budget Responsibility). Building such institutions can take time, as their effectiveness depends greatly on their reputation. When a reform is passed, it is important to ensure that it is fully implemented, effectively enforced and rigorously evaluated. This requires investing in data collection, if data to monitor compliance and outcomes are not available, and strengthening evaluation mechanisms to assess the effects of reforms. To enable credible impact evaluations, they should be planned at the design stage of the policy reform.

6. *Packaging reforms*

Policies are often more effective when they are combined in coherent packages to enhance synergies and reduce their transitional or distributional costs (OECD, 2016[9]). For instance, interventions to help workers facing severe barriers to employment may be most effective when they simultaneously involve the design of taxes and benefits (including unemployment and in-work benefits), active labour market policies and minimum wage floors. In a modelling exercise, Cacciatore et al. (2016[10]) find that unemployment benefit, product market and employment protection reforms boost gross domestic product (GDP), employment and wages faster when they are combined than when the reforms are undertaken in isolation.

7. *Sequencing reforms*

In certain cases, outcomes might be enhanced if reforms are sequenced, for example when product market reforms precede labour market reforms (Blanchard and Giavazzi, 2003[11]). Reforming product markets first can, by lowering rents in product markets, reduce the incentives of workers to fight for a share of these rents and thus resistance to labour market reforms. Another argument for gradualism is that, as governments have a limited amount of political capital, it is best if they allocate it to one reform at a time. However, too long a time lag between reforms may not be desirable either. In the case of New Zealand's reforms during the 1980s and 1990s, a significant time lag (of five years) between the product and labour market reforms reduced the potential overall gains from these reforms (Caldera Sánchez, de Serres and Yashiro, 2016[4]).

8. *Time*

Successful structural reforms take time. Many successful reforms take two years or more to prepare and adopt. This time for framing a specific reform is often preceded by a multi-year period of "pre-work", in which problems and proposals are debated and studied. By contrast, less successful reforms are sometimes undertaken in response to an immediate pressure. While governments should be ready to use political "windows of opportunity" when they open up, doing so may create problems if it leads to excessive haste. It is also not unusual for reforms to take several attempts, as can, for example, be observed in the legislative process of the United States. Blocked, reversed or limited early reforms need not be seen as failures: they may play a role in undermining the status quo. Successful labour market reforms have often followed earlier setbacks, which helped set the stage for subsequent, sometimes far-reaching reforms.

9. *Overcoming short-term challenges of reforms*

Structural reforms, especially when undertaken in a downturn, as is often the case, may face short-term challenges, for example by pressuring employment or wages. Such costs can fuel people's resistance to reform and hence make politicians less inclined to undertake the reform in the first place. Complementary macroeconomic and structural policies can help mitigate, or even completely offset, these transitional costs. The issue of short-term reform challenges is important and complex and so the following section is devoted to it.

10. *Winners and losers of reforms*

    Reforms may create winners and losers and also change the distribution of wages and income in the economy. This is likely to be especially the case for labour market reforms, which involve larger parts of the population than more narrow policy initiatives. Those who may lose out, even when in a minority, can have a potent voice and may stifle reform efforts at an early stage. In some cases, but not always, monetary transfers that compensate for such losses in absolute or relative income may be adequate. Another option to reduce reform resistance is to implement a reform gradually through the use of so-called "grandfather clauses". Section 15.4 explores these issues in more detail.

15.3. Short-term challenges of reforms

A large body of research indicates that many reforms of product and labour markets have the potential to improve productivity growth and, possibly, employment over a longer time span. Yet, reforms may face short-term challenges, especially during an economic downturn.

Besides specific factors relevant in the context of each reform, as will be discussed below, other, more general factors can dampen the short-term benefits from structural reforms in a downturn. For example, the number of households and firms with liquidity or credit constraints may be higher, reducing the scope to bring forward reform-driven income gains. For those with no liquidity or credit constraints, the precautionary motive to save in the face of reforms is likely to be stronger in a period of heightened economic uncertainty. Also, in an environment where macroeconomic policy does not, or cannot, respond to lower inflation and external demand is weak, certain reforms, including those that affect wage dynamics, may further depress demand, by increasing real interest rates and dampening consumption and investment.

This section focuses on the short-term challenges of reforms in unemployment benefits, activation spending, product markets and employment protection, the areas where most evidence has been accumulated. These reforms should not, however, be viewed as an exhaustive set of measures for which short-term challenges as regards policy adoption and implementation are relevant. Another caveat is that the focus is on the short-term effects on total employment and output, while the reforms affect many aspects of labour market performance, as the other chapters in this Volume discuss. The section also cites examples of cases in which packages of reforms in different policy areas can alleviate short-term challenges and therefore improve the political feasibility of reforms.

Reforms of unemployment benefits and activation spending

Unemployment benefit reforms may increase or decrease replacement rates, or they may widen or tighten eligibility. Reforms that reduce overly generous income replacement rates appear to increase employment relatively quickly, possibly because they promote job search and hires (Bouis et al., 2012[12]). Such reforms are also found to be associated with stronger investment and output growth. However, the empirical analysis suggests that reducing the generosity of unemployment income support can have negative short-run effects in bad economic times, i.e. when output and employment are substantially below potential (see also the discussion on state-contingent unemployment benefits in Chapter 13). Thus, cutting the level or duration of unemployment benefits in a downturn could run the risk of making the labour market situation temporarily worse, so that these reforms may be met with increased political opposition. A decrease in unemployment benefits could also have the side effect of increasing inflows into social assistance and disability benefit schemes.

Countries with short unemployment benefit entitlements, or tight eligibility rules, and strong fiscal positions could consider temporarily extending the levels or the duration of benefits during a downturn. In the United States, for example, unemployment insurance is automatically extended in bad economic times. The increased generosity makes measures to contain moral hazard through strict enforcement of job-search requirements particularly important. However, these policies are costly and therefore especially hard to implement in countries with large government debt or fiscal imbalances. Insofar as other structural reforms may temporarily increase unemployment, a higher generosity of unemployment benefits can help cushion the rise in unemployment. Italy and Portugal are two countries that reformed dismissal regulations during the euro area crisis. As part of a package of reforms, they also reinforced the unemployment benefit systems, with higher benefits or extended coverage, to better support those potentially affected by job losses.

Increases in public spending on active labour market policies are found to raise output and employment over the medium term (International Monetary Fund, 2016[8]; OECD, 2017[13]). The effects are more pronounced in bad economic times, potentially reflecting larger fiscal multipliers in recessions. They become smaller, but remain when such a spending reform is implemented in a budget-neutral way. The experience from the Great Recession tells a similar story. Countries with a strong activation approach (including Australia, Austria, Norway, Switzerland and the United Kingdom) had a relatively modest or short-lived rise in unemployment (OECD, 2013[14]). Stepping up activation spending can also help cushion negative effects that some other reforms undertaken in parallel may have on employment (Cournède, Denk and Garda, 2016[15]). Systems which receive more funding when the number of jobless rises perform especially well.

Higher activation spending in recessions can be achieved through discretionary measures or, as in Denmark, through automatic adjustments to changes in unemployment. Automatic adjustments tend to work better than discretionary measures, which are often difficult to implement because higher resources on activation compete with other budgetary pressures. Overall, there is a strong case for allocating more resources to active labour market policies in recessionary periods, both on economic and political grounds. The return on spending, in the form of higher income and employment, can be substantial, reducing the economic pain of many workers. In practice, the benefits from higher activation spending tend to be predicated on institutional contexts where an effective activation strategy is already in place. If this is not the case, the scope to rapidly scale up active labour market policies in the face of rising unemployment is limited, as fine-tuning these institutions often takes several years (OECD, 2015[16]). Chapter 9 discusses the conditions for a well-functioning activation system in more depth, including the role that private and not-for-profit agencies can play to enhance effectiveness and alleviate capacity constraints.

Reforms of product markets and employment protection legislation

Recent OECD research has studied the short-term employment effects of two broad reforms: those aimed at fostering competition in product markets (more precisely in the network industries versus the retail sector) and those affecting the rigidity of employment protection legislation. These reforms, if properly designed and implemented, enhance the efficiency in the allocation of labour to the most productive and rewarding uses and contribute to stronger productivity growth. Right after the reform, they nevertheless may face some challenges before their benefits unfold.

Several studies based on micro-data indicate that reforms in the retail sector tend to promote a reallocation of jobs, but entail no job losses, even in the short run (Bertrand and Kramarz, 2002[17]; Skuterud, 2005[18]; Viviano, 2008[19]; Sadun, 2015[20]). This result probably reflects the competitive situation in the retail industry, where deregulation often implies the fast entry of large competitors, while incumbents are too small to strategically anticipate entry by cutting staffing. Owners of small shops and their employees are frequently afraid of the ability of competing enterprises to open a store and quickly win a large share of the local market. They may therefore try to block market entry, as has happened in the United Kingdom, where some local authorities do not permit the opening of "big boxes" at the fringes of urban areas.

Regulatory reforms in network industries (energy, transport and communication) may have different effects to the ones for the retail sector. In network industries, regulation tends to give rise to more concentrated markets and shelter dominant players. The labour market may thus adjust to liberalisation through the immediate re-organisation of large incumbents and the gradual expansion of successful entrants. This could result in a temporary decline in employment (Bassanini and Cingano, 2018[21]).

Econometric estimations, based on sector-level data, confirm this line of reasoning. Lower entry barriers to network industries are found to lead to a temporary job loss which is at its maximum three years post-reform, but disappears afterwards (Panel A of Figure 15.1). Comparing results in business-cycle downturns with those in upturns shows that the initial negative employment effects only arise in bad times. In a related study that uses firm-level data, Gal and Hijzen (2016[22]) find that, in the first two years after a sector-specific deregulation reform, employment in large network industry firms declines or remains the same, whereas employment in large retail firms increases.

Employment protection legislation (EPL) governs the rules on the hiring and, especially, firing of workers. Flexibility-enhancing EPL reforms thus have the potential to improve job allocation, reduce labour market dualism and promote productivity (see Chapter 7). With respect to long-term employment, empirical studies suggest that reforms have no or a small positive effect. Immediately after the reform, however, employment may decline as firms wanting to dismiss workers can now do so at a lower cost, while other firms may take time to hire new workers. These issues were studied in the same sector-level empirical framework that was used above for reforms of network industries (OECD, 2016[9]).

The study finds that reforms of employment protection legislation that reduce dismissal costs are associated with short-term employment losses, but these are reversed within a few years on average (Panel B of Figure 15.1). These transitional losses are not sizeable when the reform is implemented in an economic upswing. Moreover, they are less acute in countries with significant labour market dualism, which are also the countries that experience the greatest benefits from reforms that lower the use of fixed-term contracts. A similar conclusion was reached by International Monetary Fund (2016[8]) and related micro-econometric studies (OECD, 2016[9]).

Figure 15.1. The temporary employment costs of regulatory reforms

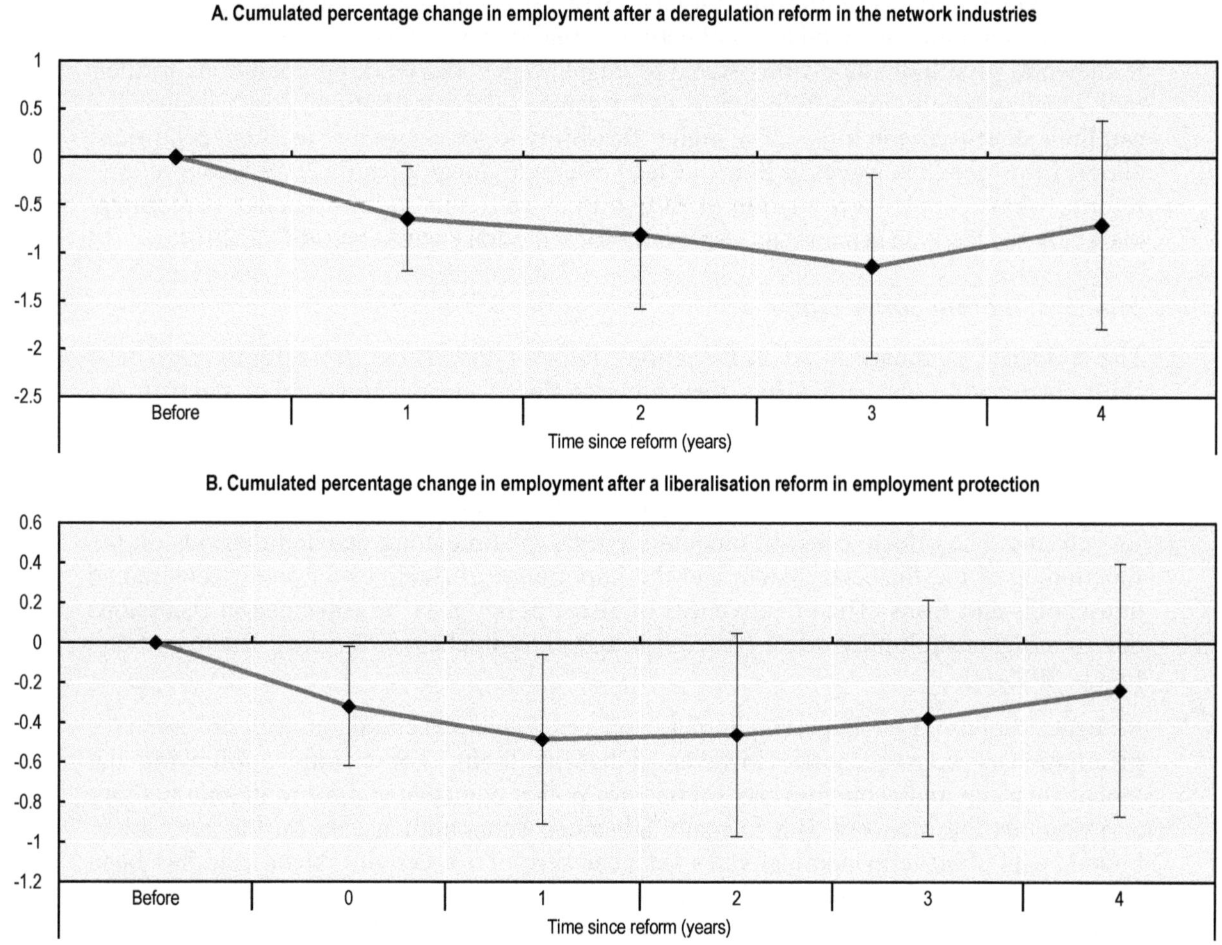

Note: The figures report point estimates and 90%-confidence intervals of the cumulated percentage change in employment due to reforms in network industry regulation (Panel A) and job dismissal regulation for regular contracts (Panel B). The estimates refer to a reform lowering the OECD indicator of entry barriers by one point (Panel A) and a reform lowering the OECD indicator of employment protection legislation by 0.2 points (Panel B).

Source: OECD (2016[9]), *OECD Employment Outlook 2016*, http://dx.doi.org/10.1787/empl_outlook-2016-en, using *EU-KLEMS Database*, *OECD Product Market Regulation Database* and *OECD Employment Protection Legislation Database*.

StatLink http://dx.doi.org/10.1787/888933881781

One way to avoid a spike in dismissals after a job dismissal reform is the introduction of "grandfather clauses". These clauses preserve entitlements of existing workers, for example by applying the new rules only to new hires. The limited available evidence, including from Portugal (OECD, 2017[23]), suggests that grandfather clauses help avoid the short-term negative effects of EPL reforms and can even have a small positive effect on employment in the short run. Grandfather clauses have, however, the downside of delaying the desired reform effects on allocative efficiency. Another way to cushion the impact of a flexibility-enhancing EPL reform is to accompany it with a simultaneous expansion of active labour market programmes, as discussed above.

Collective bargaining institutions also influence the short-term costs of EPL or other reforms. Co-ordination in wage bargaining helps negotiators take into account the macroeconomic effects of reforms (OECD, 2018[24]). In situations where some firms in a sector are hit more than others, collective bargaining systems that, within a sectoral framework, give individual firms scope to adapt wages and working conditions to their individual situation – often referred to as "organised decentralisation" (see Chapter 8) – can limit short-term job losses. The higher flexibility to set wages and working conditions allows firms to adjust wages or hours instead of employment. Spain's 2012 labour market reform, which coupled a relaxation of EPL with more flexibility in collective bargaining, markedly reduced job separations, especially for temporary workers (OECD, 2014[25]).

Macroeconomic policy support

The evidence summarised in this section suggests that structural reforms can have short-term costs, especially when they are introduced at an unfavourable stage in the business cycle. These short-term costs can undermine political support.

Demand-side (i.e. monetary and fiscal) policies are suited to mitigate a negative impact from reforms in the short run when demand is weak and hence to support public backing for reforms. The effectiveness of monetary policy in stimulating demand depends on the functioning of the financial system and the importance of liquidity- or credit-constrained households and firms. The effectiveness of fiscal policy may be enhanced in recessions due to a higher multiplier effect (Auerbach and Gorodnichenko, 2012[26]; Blanchard and Leigh, 2013[27]).[2]

Monetary policy is an important tool for ensuring that structural reforms do not have disinflationary consequences. However, it has its limits. For example, following the global financial and economic crisis monetary policy contributed a lot to sustain activity and promote the recovery. But in many advanced economies it also hit the zero lower bound, with short-term nominal rates set near zero. To a certain extent, this has been overcome through unconventional monetary policy, in particular central banks providing forward guidance on long-term nominal rates and buying up bonds of longer maturities.

It is in cases such as these, when monetary policy is at its limits, that fiscal policy can be especially powerful to mitigate the costs of structural reforms and garner political support. Fiscal policy also has the advantage of being able to target particular segments of workers affected by a reform, for example through active labour market policies. Generally, the effect on aggregate demand is likely to be stronger for government spending measures than tax cuts. Spending measures have a direct impact on aggregate demand, while tax reductions have a more muted effect since they may be saved because of, for instance, high uncertainty. In practice, fiscal stimulus measures can be designed on both the spending side and the tax side to have a rapid and substantial effect.

Among public spending measures, investment tends to be the most powerful instrument (Fournier and Johansson, 2016[28]; Hijzen et al., 2017[29]). In contrast to boosting current public expenditure, higher investment adds to the capital stock and so has not only a short-term demand effect but also a longer-term supply effect. In situations with little scope for additional monetary stimulus, an expansion in well-designed public investment projects can even pay for itself, i.e. raise output more than increase debt, thus reducing the public debt-to-GDP ratio (OECD, 2016[30]).

Some tax reductions can also be put in place to increase household disposable income and boost household spending in the short term. While in theory consumption should not respond much to temporary changes in taxes, as households are likely to smooth their consumption over their lifetime, the evidence suggests that temporary tax reductions can boost consumption in the short term. This is particularly the case for cuts in labour taxes or social security contributions targeted at lower-income workers, as spending by this group is closely tied to its disposable income due to liquidity constraints (de Mooij and Keen, 2012[31]).

The scope for expansionary fiscal policy may, however, be limited when long-run fiscal constraints are significant. During the early 2010s, several southern euro area countries faced difficulties to mitigate the short-term impacts of labour market and other reforms, due to lack of fiscal space. In such environments, the positive effect from a fiscal expansion could even be offset by the contractionary effect through adverse reactions in financial markets. These considerations underline the need to create fiscal space in good times to be able to use the fiscal lever for promoting demand when needed, not only to counteract a negative demand shock, but also to support the implementation of structural reforms.

15.4. Winners and losers of reforms

Structural reforms can make some people worse off, temporarily or permanently. A reform that removes licensing requirements for taxis in urban centres is likely to durably reduce incomes of incumbent taxi drivers. Increases in the retirement age reduce the time available for leisure of people who will need to work longer. Reforms that increase the flexibility of open-ended contracts reduce the job security of workers on these contracts (unless these workers continue to be entitled to their old protection rules through the grandfathering of the reform). Changes to the systems of unemployment insurance and social assistance alter the amount of benefits that persons receive or can expect to receive. Initiatives to modify a country's collective bargaining system can be politically particularly sensitive, as they often influence the pay of a large number of workers in the economy.

Most structural reforms create winners and losers. Losing out usually is associated with a move down in the wage distribution. A downward move in the wage distribution is likely to be especially painful when it comes with a decline in wages or wage growth. Reforms can also influence other aspects of job quality, such as job security and satisfaction. As insights from behavioural economics suggest, declines in job quality can be particularly salient to the people involved. The resistance to the reform by the individuals who are negatively affected by the reform can therefore be strong. In some cases, as in the taxi example, the weight of affected incumbent workers for political decision-making may be disproportionately high, given their ability to organise themselves better than the beneficiaries, who are more numerous, but individually gain less than those who lose out (Olson, 1971[32]; Boeri et al., 2006[33]).

Another example for reforms where losses are narrowly concentrated are sector-specific deregulations. For instance, in the past extensive regulation in network industries ensured that workers in these industries benefited from higher wages and stronger job security. The large liberalisation of network industries in nearly all OECD countries over the last 30 years has changed this situation dramatically, with workers in network industries losing out compared with other workers. Such considerations are not unique to network industries, but similarly arise in other regulated sectors (Jean and Nicoletti, 2015[34]).

To give an idea of the magnitudes involved, in the late 1980s, the average wage premium for network industry workers is estimated to have been 16% (Denk, 2016[35]), compared with workers who had similar characteristics but were employed in other sectors. Based on the data in the OECD Product Market Regulation Database, regulation in network industries declined strongly and in 2013 was 60% lighter than 30 years before. This liberalisation of network industries has reduced the average wage premium for network industry workers to an estimated 6% (Figure 15.2). Without deregulation, every year the incomes of network industry workers, relative to other workers, would have been up to about 10% higher.

Figure 15.2. Network industry regulation and wage premium for network industry workers

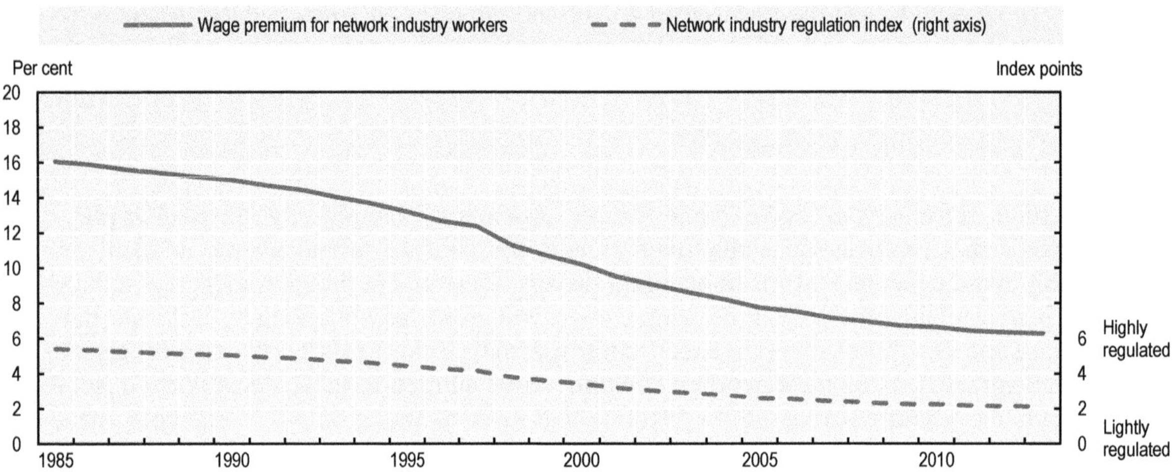

Note: The figure shows the average regulation of network industries in 21 OECD countries and the associated estimated wage premium for workers in this industry. The wage premium measures how much more workers in network industries earn compared with workers in other industries who have the same observable characteristics (such as age, gender and education). The simulations use the average estimate according to which one unit of the regulation index increases the labour earnings of network industry workers by 3.0%.
Source: Estimations based on Denk (2016[35]), "How Do Product Market Regulations Affect Workers? Evidence from the Network Industries", *OECD Economics Department Working Papers*, No. 1349, http://dx.doi.org/10.1787/5167d865-en, using Eurostat Structure of Earnings Survey, *OECD Product Market Regulation Database* and specific micro-data sources for Australia, Germany, Korea, Switzerland, the United Kingdom and the United States.

StatLink http://dx.doi.org/10.1787/888933881800

Compensation to people who are adversely affected by a reform has sometimes helped make structural reform happen (OECD, 2010[36]; Trebilcock, 2014[37]). It may be implicit, for example in the form of "flanking programmes" (such as re-employment services), as mentioned in the previous section, but can also involve monetary payments (Høj et al., 2007[38]).

From an economic point of view, compensation tends to be more justified when the reform creates a disadvantage that workers, or capital owners, could not anticipate at the time of their career, or investment, choice. An example are people who have recently acquired a firm or paid for a licence (for example for a taxi), not expecting a reform at the time of the purchase. Higher competition would reduce the value of the firm or licence, as previously expected rents were capitalised in their value. A similar case can arise for laid-off people who committed all their life to working for a protected utility giant in an industry that is being opened up to competition by other firms.

An important judgement in the context of compensation is whether the reform puts people at an unfair disadvantage relative to other workers. Workers adversely affected by higher import competition often fall in this category, which motivates programmes such as the Trade Adjustment Assistance in the United States. In other instances, however, reforms can reduce wages or job quality, but not in an unfair way, even if the reform was not expected. This is the case when regulatory reforms reduce large economic rents, while nevertheless leaving some rents. Compensations to people who lose out but continue to be advantaged, although to a lesser extent than before, can be unfair towards others funding the compensation to these workers or capital owners (Cournède et al., 2016[39]).

A further consideration is that reforms that lower the wage premium in regulated sectors do not necessarily decrease the wage growth of workers in the deregulated sectors, if the overall wage increase generated through higher economy-wide productivity offsets the fall in their relative wages. For the case of network industries, simulations suggest that the income-enhancing effects of past reforms in these industries have almost exactly offset the fall in the wage premium, so that network industry workers have experienced a relative, but no absolute decline in wage growth following the reform. It is not clear that workers should be compensated for the loss of their relative income status, which was due to regulation, even when they keep the same wage level.

Compensation can have the additional downside of encouraging behaviour that reduces efficiency. The anticipation of compensation may induce ex-ante rent-seeking and lower incentives to promote productivity (Kaplow, 2003[40]). Paying compensation could hence even harden resistance to reform, since incumbents may seek to maximise pay-outs. At least in principle, an arguably fairer and more efficient "compensation strategy" would be to reform product and labour markets very broadly rather than narrowly in certain sectors or segments. As illustrated above, this strategy can offset the relative losses in wage growth that workers may experience from greater competition in their sector with purchasing power gains from parallel reforms in other sectors (Blanchard and Giavazzi, 2003[11]; Gersbach, 2004[41]).

Conclusion

Labour market and other policy reforms have the potential to promote stronger and more inclusive labour markets and economies. Nevertheless, this has not made them universally popular or easy to enact. This chapter has shed new light on how a better preparation, design and timing of reforms can enhance their political feasibility and attractiveness. The most important lessons from the analysis can be summarised as follows.

Structural reforms are best undertaken during good economic times

Structural reforms are often undertaken when the status quo is no longer sustainable and thus in many cases during an economic downturn. However, the evidence clearly suggests that structural reforms tend to have the smallest – if any – side effect on employment when implemented in good times. For example, when demand for their products is high, relaxing job protection regulations will not entice firms to shed much of their workforce. Even when reforms temporarily depress domestic demand, a favourable climate in trading partners' economies can make the benefits from reform become visible more rapidly. The general message is that, when the economy does well, there is no time for complacency.

To ensure success, reforms require political leadership and broad support

Most structural reforms involve trade-offs and thus are not supported by everyone in society. At the same time, however, successful reforms require a critical mass of electoral and political support. Broad acceptance of the need to reform is often easier built in crisis situations. Generally, a strong leadership and evidence base, rigorous evaluation after the reform and effective communication (including by using new technologies) can help ensure success of a reform and continued support. Solid evidence and evaluation require investing in data collection, where the necessary data for monitoring compliance and outcomes are not available. Another element that facilitates the adoption and implementation of good reforms is high levels of co-operation and trust between the government, employers and workers.

Addressing their short-term challenges can help build support for reforms

Some structural reforms may entail labour market costs during the transition. Monetary and especially fiscal policies can help cushion potential short-term contractionary effects. In terms of fiscal policy, stepping up active labour market policies and temporarily increasing unemployment benefit levels or durations are likely to be most suited to both boost aggregate demand and support people who are most affected. Clever design can also help contain short-term costs. For example, in the context of job dismissal reforms, "grandfather clauses" that preserve old entitlements protect current jobs and avoid a spike in layoffs, but may delay the benefits of reform.

Policies that support those who may lose out can help make reform happen

To ensure political support and broad increases in well-being, governments may design reforms in a way that they embed compensatory elements for those who are most likely to be negatively affected. Compensation is often implicit, for example when it comes in the form of activation programmes, but sometimes it can also involve money transfers. As a general rule, compensation strategies are more likely to be warranted for reforms creating a disadvantage that workers did not foresee at the time they made their career choice. By contrast, reforms that remove privileges to certain firms or workers lead to incumbents losing out, but only insofar as they no longer benefit from unfair advantages. Compensatory payments are in these cases harder to justify, although they may still help make structural reform happen.

Notes

[1] Following the general election in 1998, the new government established the *Pact for Work, Education and Competitiveness*. Trade unions hoped that weaker wage growth would create jobs; employer associations saw the benefits of lower relative labour costs; and the government supported take-home pay and external competitiveness by reducing social security contributions financed with higher indirect taxes.

[2] Chapter 13 in this Volume discusses the roles of monetary and different fiscal policies for labour market resilience.

References

Adjemian, S. et al. (2008), "Variantes en univers incertain", *Economie & Prévision*, Vol. 183-184/2, pp. 223-238. [7]

Auerbach, A. and Y. Gorodnichenko (2012), "Measuring the Output Responses to Fiscal Policy", *American Economic Journal: Economic Policy*, Vol. 4/2, pp. 1-27, http://dx.doi.org/10.1257/pol.4.2.1. [26]

Bassanini, A. and F. Cingano (2018), "Before it gets better: The short-term employment costs of regulatory reforms", *ILR Review*. [21]

Bertrand, M. and F. Kramarz (2002), "Does entry regulation hinder job creation? Evidence from the French retail industry", *Quarterly Journal of Economics*, Vol. 117/4, pp. 1369-1413. [17]

Blanchard, O. and F. Giavazzi (2003), "Macroeconomic effects of regulation and deregulation in goods and labor markets", *Quarterly Journal of Economics*, Vol. 118/3, pp. 879-907. [11]

Blanchard, O. and D. Leigh (2013), "Growth forecast errors and fiscal multipliers", *American Economic Review*, Vol. 103/3, pp. 117-120. [27]

Boeri, T. et al. (eds.) (2006), *Structural reforms without prejudices*, Oxford University Press. [33]

Bofinger, P. (2017), "Hartz IV: die Lösung für die Probleme in der Währungsunion?", *Wirtschaftsdienst*, Vol. 97/6, pp. 404-408. [6]

Bouis, R. et al. (2012), "The Short-Term Effects of Structural Reforms: An Empirical Analysis", *OECD Economics Department Working Papers*, No. 949, OECD Publishing, Paris, http://dx.doi.org/10.1787/5k9csvk4d56d-en. [12]

Cacciatore, M. et al. (2016), "Short-term pain for long-term gain: Market deregulation and monetary policy in small open economies", *Journal of International Money and Finance*, Vol. 68, pp. 358-385. [10]

Caldera Sánchez, A., A. de Serres and N. Yashiro (2016), "Reforming in a difficult macroeconomic context: A review of the issues and recent literature", *OECD Economics Department Working Papers*, No. 1297, OECD Publishing, Paris, http://dx.doi.org/10.1787/5jlzgj45b3q0-en. [4]

Cournède, B., O. Denk and P. Garda (2016), "Effects of flexibility-enhancing reforms on employment transitions", *OECD Economics Department Working Papers*, No. 1348, OECD Publishing, Paris, http://dx.doi.org/10.1787/bd8e4c1f-en. [15]

Cournède, B. et al. (2016), *Enhancing economic flexibility: What is in it for workers?*, OECD Publishing, Paris, https://doi.org/10.1787/b8558a5b-en. [39]

de Mooij, R. and M. Keen (2012), "Fiscal devaluation and fiscal consolidation: The VAT in troubled times", in *Fiscal policy after the financial crisis*, National Bureau of Economic Research, Inc. [31]

Denk, O. (2016), "How Do Product Market Regulations Affect Workers? : Evidence from the Network Industries", *OECD Economics Department Working Papers*, No. 1349, OECD Publishing, Paris, http://dx.doi.org/10.1787/5167d865-en. [35]

Drazen, A. and W. Easterly (2001), "Do crises induce reform? Simple empirical tests of conventional wisdom", *Economics and Politics*, Vol. 13/2, pp. 129-157. [2]

Duval, R., D. Furceri and J. Miethe (2018), "The needle in the haystack: What drives labor and product market reforms in advanced countries?", *IMF Working Papers*, No. 18/101. [5]

Fournier, J. and Å. Johansson (2016), "The Effect of the Size and the Mix of Public Spending on Growth and Inequality", *OECD Economics Department Working Papers*, No. 1344, OECD Publishing, Paris, http://dx.doi.org/10.1787/f99f6b36-en. [28]

Gal, P. and A. Hijzen (2016), "The short-term impact of product market reforms: A cross-country firm-level analysis", *OECD Economics Department Working Papers*, No. 1311, OECD Publishing, Paris. [22]

Gersbach, H. (2004), "Structural reforms and the macroeconomy: The role of general equilibrium effects", in Solow, R. (ed.), *Structural reform and economic policy*, Palgrave Macmillan. [41]

Hijzen, A. et al. (2017), "Labour market resilience: The role of structural and macroeconomic policies", *OECD Economics Department Working Papers*, No. 1406, OECD Publishing, Paris. [29]

Høj, J. et al. (2007), "An empirical investigaton of political economy factors behind structural reforms in OECD countries", *OECD Economic Studies*, Vol. 2006/1, http://dx.doi.org/10.1787/eco_studies-v2006-art3-en. [38]

International Monetary Fund (2016), *World Economic Outlook: Too slow for too long*. [8]

Jean, S. and G. Nicoletti (2015), "Product market regulation and wage premia in Europe and North America: An empirical investigation", *International Economics*, Vol. 144, pp. 1-28. [34]

Kaplow, L. (2003), "Transition policy: A conceptual framework", *NBER Working Papers*. [40]

OECD (2018), *Economic Policy Reforms 2018: Going for Growth Interim Report*, OECD Publishing, Paris, http://dx.doi.org/10.1787/growth-2018-en. [1]

OECD (2018), *OECD Employment Outlook 2018*, OECD Publishing, Paris, http://dx.doi.org/10.1787/empl_outlook-2018-en. [24]

OECD (2017), *Labour Market Reforms in Portugal 2011-15: A Preliminary Assessment*, OECD Publishing, Paris, http://dx.doi.org/10.1787/9789264269576-en. [23]

OECD (2017), *OECD Employment Outlook 2017*, OECD Publishing, Paris, http://dx.doi.org/10.1787/empl_outlook-2017-en. [13]

OECD (2016), *OECD Economic Outlook, Volume 2016 Issue 2*, OECD Publishing, Paris, http://dx.doi.org/10.1787/eco_outlook-v2016-2-en. [30]

OECD (2016), *OECD Employment Outlook 2016*, OECD Publishing, Paris, http://dx.doi.org/10.1787/empl_outlook-2016-en. [9]

OECD (2015), *OECD Employment Outlook 2015*, OECD Publishing, Paris, http://dx.doi.org/10.1787/empl_outlook-2015-en. [16]

OECD (2014), *The 2012 Labour Market Reform in Spain: A Preliminary Assessment*, OECD Publishing, Paris, http://dx.doi.org/10.1787/9789264213586-en. [25]

OECD (2013), *OECD Employment Outlook 2013*, OECD Publishing, Paris, https://doi.org/10.1787/empl_outlook-2013-en. [14]

OECD (2010), *Making Reform Happen: Lessons from OECD Countries*, OECD Publishing, Paris, http://dx.doi.org/10.1787/9789264086296-en. [36]

Olson, M. (1971), *The logic of collective action: Public goods and the theory of groups*, Harvard University Press. [32]

Sadun, R. (2015), "Does planning regulation protect independent retailers?", *Review of Economics and Statistics*, Vol. 97/5, pp. 983-1001. [20]

Skuterud, M. (2005), "The impact of Sunday shopping on employment and hours of work in the retail industry: Evidence from Canada", *European Economic Review*, Vol. 49/8, pp. 1953-1978. [18]

Tompson, W. (2009), *The political economy of reform: Lessons from pensions, product markets and labour markets in ten OECD countries*, OECD. [3]

Trebilcock, M. (2014), *Dealing with losers: The political economy of policy transitions*, Oxford University Press. [37]

Viviano, E. (2008), "Entry regulations and labour market outcomes: Evidence from the Italian retail trade sector", *Labour Economics*, Vol. 15/6, pp. 1200-1222. [19]

Chapter 16. Boosting labour market performance in emerging economies

This chapter uses the Jobs Strategy framework to discuss how emerging economies can confront the dual challenge of low productivity and inclusiveness in a context of widespread informality. Pervasive informality implies that large parts of the workforce do not have access to social insurance or basic regulatory protections. It also limits the ability of the government to collect taxes and hence the resources at its disposal to confront the challenge of promoting inclusive growth. A comprehensive approach is needed that simultaneously promotes formality and reaches out to the most vulnerable.

Introduction

Promoting inclusive growth is a major policy challenge in emerging economies. Compared with the typical OECD economy, emerging economies generally exhibit much lower standards of living and higher levels of inequality. In addition, emerging economies also have to face up to pervasive labour informality. Widespread informality implies that large parts of the workforce are effectively beyond the reach of the government and do not have access to social insurance or regulatory protections. Moreover, informality limits the ability of the government to collect taxes and hence the resources at its disposal to promote inclusive growth.

This chapter uses the Jobs Strategy framework to discuss how emerging economies can enhance labour market performance, and more specifically, confront the dual challenge of low productivity and low inclusiveness, in a context of widespread informality. To this end, it focuses on emerging economies that have a link with the OECD, namely Argentina, Brazil, Chile, China, Colombia, Costa Rica, India, Indonesia, Mexico, Kazakhstan, Peru, the Russian Federation, South Africa, Thailand, Tunisia, and Turkey. Given the enormous diversity in this group of countries in terms of income, size, demography, and institutions, the nature of the challenges and the most appropriate policy responses may differ substantially and can only partially be reflected given the scope of this chapter.

The issues discussed in the chapter may not only be of interest to policy-makers in emerging economies, but also to those in more advanced economies. The advent of the platform economy, and associated rise in self-employment, has raised difficult questions about differences in regulatory treatment between dependent employees and self-employed. Emerging economies have been struggling with similar issues for a long time due to the importance of informal work. In recent years, this has resulted in the development of innovative social protection schemes that provide interesting insights also for more advanced economies.

The chapter is organised as follows. Section 16.1 describes the dual challenge of low productivity and inclusiveness in a context of pervasive informality. Section 16.2 discusses the role of policies and institutions for promoting productivity and formality, while Section 16.3 discusses how policies and institutions can promote inclusiveness without undermining formality. The final section concludes.

16.1. Key challenges

The emerging economies considered in this chapter share a dual challenge of (1) low productivity and (2) low labour market inclusiveness. For both these challenges, curbing informality plays a key role.

Economic development is lagging

Economic development is much lower in emerging economies than in the typical OECD country. The gap in gross domestic product (GDP) per capita between emerging economies and the OECD average varies between 40% (Turkey) and 87% (India) (Figure 16.1, Panel A). In other words, the average income in emerging economies is roughly two to ten times lower than that in the average OECD country.

Low economic development mainly reflects lagging productivity. Across the covered emerging economies, labour productivity is between 84% (India) and 18% (Turkey) below the OECD average (Figure 16.1, Panel A). All countries except Argentina, Mexico, and Turkey have experienced productivity convergence during the last few decades, as productivity growth has exceeded the OECD average (Figure 16.1, Panel B). However, the degree of productivity convergence has varied substantially, with particularly fast convergence in the East and Central Asian countries considered here.

Figure 16.1. Productivity levels are well below the OECD average, despite some catch-up in recent decades

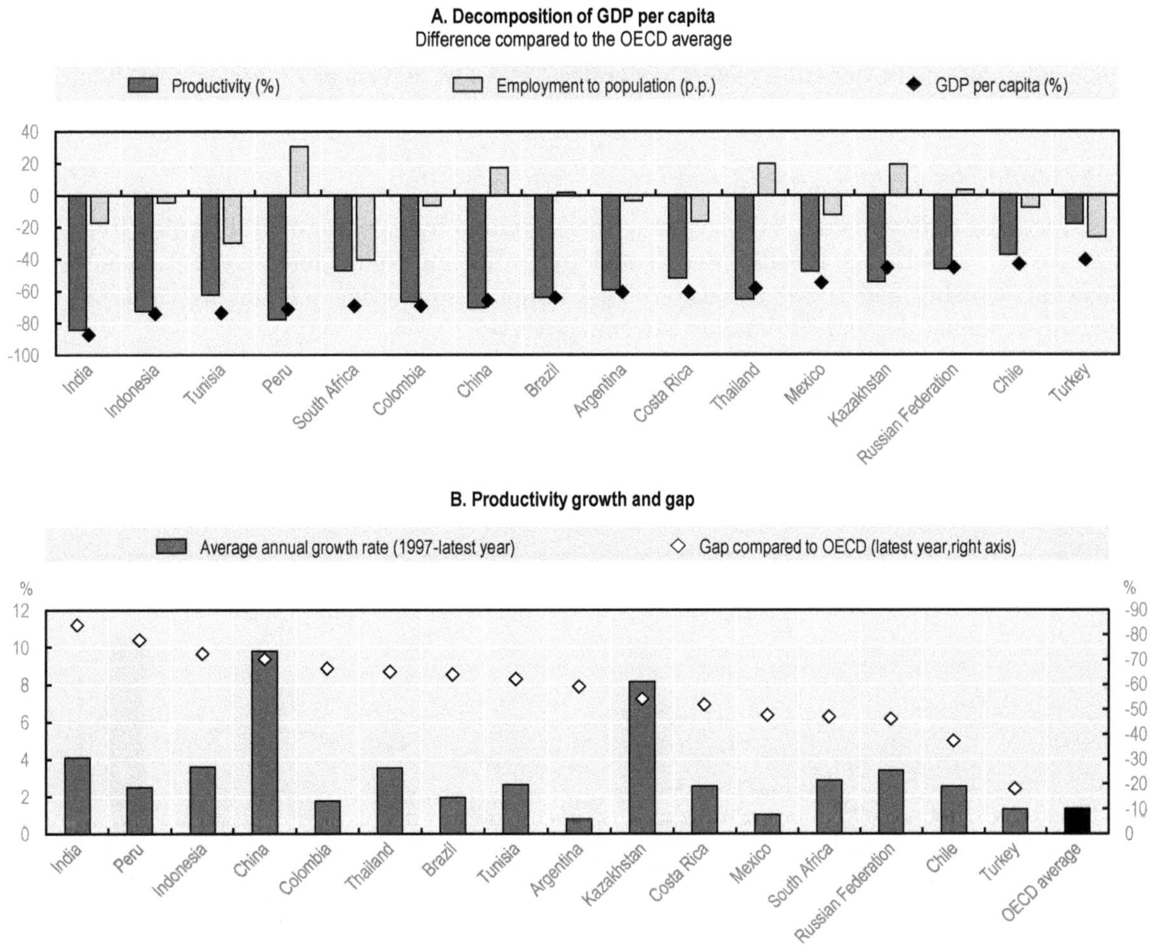

Note: Panel A: Data refer to 2017, except for Brazil, China, Costa Rica, India, the Russian Federation and South Africa (2016). Panel B: Data refer to 1997-2017 except for Brazil, China, Costa Rica, India, the Russian Federation and South Africa (1997-2016).

Source: OECD Compendium of Productivity indicators for OECD countries, Brazil, China, Colombia, Costa Rica, India, Indonesia, Russian Federation and South Africa; Word Bank, World Development indicators for Argentina, Kazakhstan, Peru, Thailand, and Tunisia.

StatLink http://dx.doi.org/10.1787/888933881819

To promote productivity in emerging economies, improvements are needed across the board in all firms, but particularly at the bottom of the productivity distribution. Compared with more advanced economies, the distribution of productivity across firms tends to be more dispersed, with a long fat tail of low-productivity firms (Bloom et al.,

2010[1]; Levy and López-Calva, 2016[2]; Bento and Restuccia, 2017[3]). Low-productivity work typically reflects the abundance of people with poor basic skills and the demand for low-quality goods and services by these same workers and their families (La Porta and Shleifer, 2014[4]).

In addition to boosting productivity, promoting economic development also requires raising employment, and particularly labour force participation. Bringing employment rates to OECD levels would reduce the gap in GDP per capita between emerging economies and the OECD on average by four to five percentage points (Figure 16.1, Panel A). This mainly requires boosting labour force participation, particularly among women (see Box 16.1). Unemployment tends to be less of an issue.[1] This is in part related to the fact that most workers can ill afford being unemployed for extended periods of time since unemployment benefit systems generally have low coverage or are non-existent (OECD, 2015[5]).

Jobs tend to be of poor quality and inclusiveness is low

A second key policy priority is to promote inclusiveness by ensuring that the gains from productivity growth are broadly shared and by protecting vulnerable workers against financial hardship and social exclusion. This requires supporting job quality, tackling excessive inequalities and eliminating extreme poverty.

Figure 16.2. Emerging economies exhibit low wages and high wage inequality

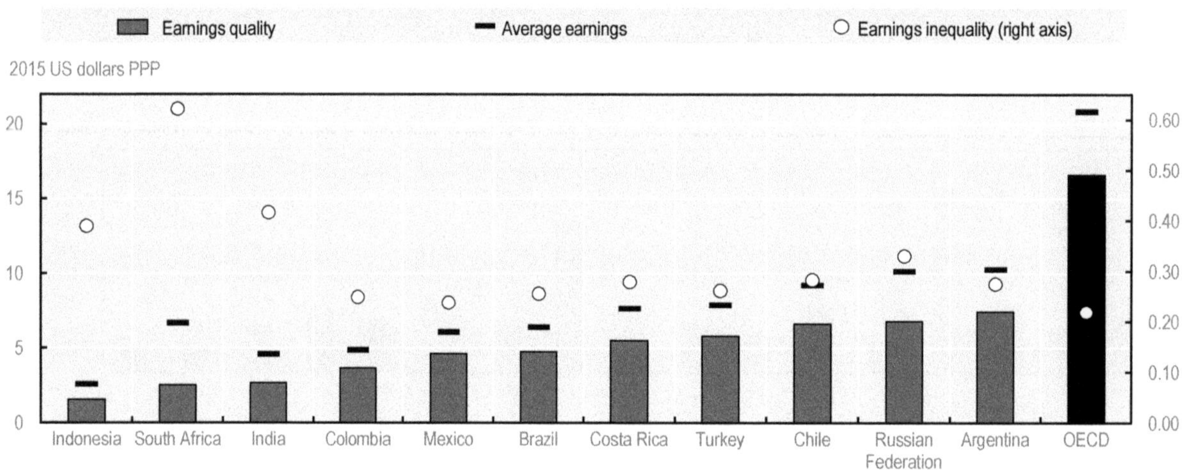

Note: Earnings quality is measured as the general mean of earnings with high inequality aversion, while earnings inequality is measured by the corresponding Atkinson inequality index. Calculations are based on gross hourly earnings for 2015 except for Costa Rica and Indonesia (2016), Argentina and the Russian Federation (2013) and India (2012). The OECD average is a simple average of earnings quality.

Source: OECD countries: *OECD Earnings Quality Database*; OECD Secretariat calculations based on Encuesta Permanente de Hogares (EPH) for Argentina, Pesquisa Nacional por Amostra de Domicilios (PNAD) for Brazil, Gran Encuesta Integrada de Hogares (GEIH) for Colombia, Encuesta Continua de Empleo (ECE) for Costa Rica, National Sample Survey (NSS) for India, Sakernas for Indonesia, Russia Longitudinal Monitoring Survey for the Russian Federation and National Income Dynamics Study (NIDS) for South Africa.

StatLink http://dx.doi.org/10.1787/888933881838

Job quality is a major concern in emerging economies. Lower earnings quality compared to the OECD average reflects both substantially lower average earnings and higher levels of earnings inequality (Figure 16.2). To an important extent, this results from the low levels and wide dispersion of productivity as discussed above. Workers in emerging economies also tend to be more vulnerable to labour market risks than their counterparts in more advanced economies (OECD, 2015[6]). In most emerging economies, this primarily reflects the risk of falling into extreme low pay.[2] The quality of the working environment is also generally lower in emerging economies compared with OECD countries. One indication of this is the higher incidence of working very long hours (OECD, 2015[6]).[3]

Box 16.1. Closing gender gaps in the labour markets of emerging economies

Gender gaps in labour force participation and education have shrunk, but progress is uneven

Over the past three decades, women throughout the emerging world have been catching up with men in a number of labour market outcomes. One of the most notable improvements has been an unprecedented increase in female labour force participation, but progress has been very uneven across emerging economies. The most significant improvements have been recorded in Latin America, particularly in Chile and Costa Rica, where the participation gap has fallen by 1 percentage point per year since the mid-1999s. The largest gaps remain in Tunisia, India, and Indonesia. Low-skilled women from poor families, however, continue to face substantial participation gaps throughout the world.

Gender gaps in educational attainments have also generally been shrinking in recent decades. Enrolment rates in primary and secondary education are almost identical for boys and girls, and in many countries women are now attending tertiary education more frequently than men. The most remarkable improvements have been recorded in Tunisia, China, Turkey, Indonesia, and India. However, girls' educational performance lags behind in mathematics and often in science, which, in conjunction with biased social norms regarding gender roles, results in a lower share of girls to study and work in STEM-related fields (science, technology, engineering, and mathematics). Average improvements in school attainment also hide the fact that girls from poorer families are still much less likely to be enrolled in school at all levels of education. Closing these remaining gaps in education is an important policy objective.

Women continue to hold worse jobs than men

Women tend to have lower-quality jobs than men in emerging economies. The sectors and occupations where women most typically work tend to be less productive and pay lower wages. This is related to the fact that women are more likely to have informal jobs than men. Moreover, a large share of working women (often the majority) are self-employed, and they typically own smaller, less successful, and more often informal businesses than men. Credit constraints, as well as gaps in financial literacy and business-related knowledge, are among the key drivers of gender gaps in entrepreneurship. As a result, the gender pay gap in emerging economies is even larger than in OECD countries. Most worryingly, wide gender pay gaps persist when comparing workers with the same level of education and in similar jobs. Women in emerging economies also have less secure jobs, facing higher risks of both unemployment and extreme low pay (OECD, 2015[6]).

A key driver of gender inequality in emerging economies continues to be the uneven distribution of household and family care between men and women. Action is required to promote flexible work arrangements, make parental leave more effective, and fight gender discrimination.

Source: This box has been prepared by Paolo Falco (OECD) based on OECD (2016[7]), "Closing gender gaps in the labour markets of emerging economies: The unfinished job", in *OECD Employment Outlook 2016*, https://doi.org/10.1787/empl_outlook-2016-8-en.

Labour market inclusiveness in emerging economies tends to be low (see Chapter 3). The low-income rate, i.e. the share of persons in households with a disposable income of less than half the median, tends to be high. While on average across the OECD, about one-in-ten people live in poor households, this ratio ranges from one-in-four in China to one-in-eight in the Russian Federation across emerging economies. Elevated low-income rates reflect both high pay inequality and high rates of inactivity among disadvantaged groups, such as youth and older workers with low skills. Income inequalities between men and women also remain large (Box 16.1).

At the same time, considerable progress has been made in eradicating extreme poverty rates in most emerging economies, although it remains a pressing policy concern in some. The percentage of the population living on less than USD 1.90 per day in 2011 purchasing power parity (PPP), the international extreme poverty line as used by the World Bank, is around 20% in India and South Africa, and remains between 3% and 7% in Brazil, Peru, Colombia, and Indonesia. Extreme poverty rates went down in all countries during the last few decades. Progress has been particularly impressive in China and Indonesia, where extreme poverty rates went down from around 45% in the mid-90s to 1% (China) and 7% (Indonesia) now (World Bank, 2016[8]).

Informality is pervasive

Weak productivity and limited inclusiveness are for an important part related to informality, where workers and firms are partially or fully outside the remit of regulation and do not contribute to social insurance.

Informal employment is persistently high among emerging economies, albeit with significant cross-country variation (Figure 16.3). Among the countries considered, informality rates range from about 30% in Chile to around 90% in India. Informality is common among very different groups of workers, including own-account workers, family workers and self-employed, but also unregistered wage employees in formal or informal firms (OECD, 2009[9]). In some cases, it reflects a subsistence strategy in the absence of opportunities for formal wage employment, while in others, it reflects a voluntary choice as workers opt out of formality to avoid having to pay social security contributions and taxes (Perry et al., 2007[10]; Meghir, Narita and Robin, 2015[11]).

Informality rates went down in all the emerging economies considered here, but only slowly. Informality tends to shrink as an economy develops. However, this is not an automatic process, as informality depends on many different factors, including the ability of successful formal firms to attract suitable workers (Díaz et al., 2018[12]). Moreover, rapid population growth, especially among the poor, can slow formalisation, as it sustains the supply of low-skilled informal workers and the demand for low-quality goods (La Porta and Shleifer, 2014[4]).[4]

Figure 16.3. Informality rates have only decreased slowly

Informally employed persons as a % of the working-age employment

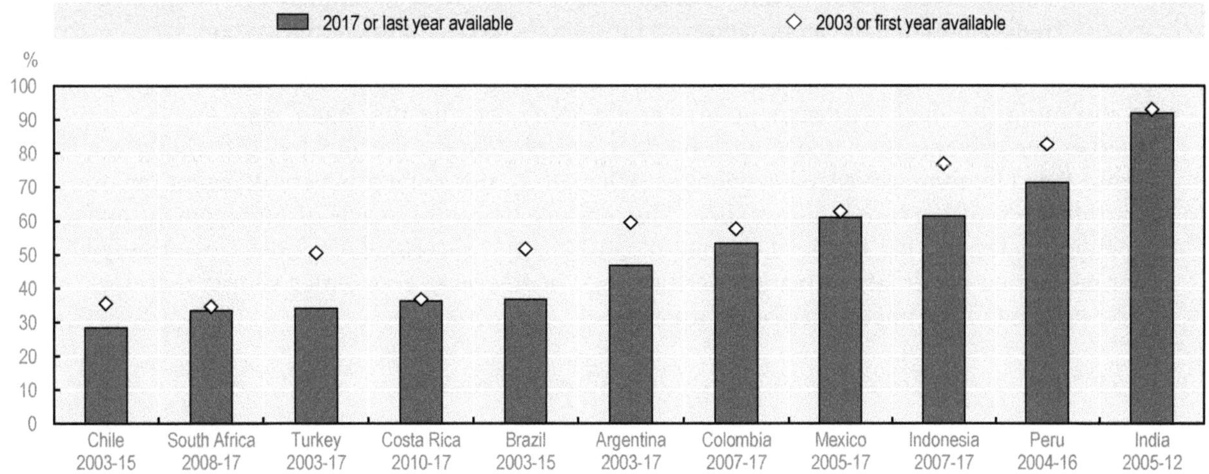

Note: Informality is defined to include: i) employees who do not pay social security contributions; and ii) self-employed who do not pay social security contributions or whose business is not registered.
Source: OECD calculations based on the Encuesta Permanente de Hogares (EPH) for Argentina, Pesquisa Nacional por Amostra de Domicilios (PNAD) for Brazil, the CASEN for Chile, Gran Encuesta Integrada de Hogares (GEIH) for Colombia, Encuesta Continua de Empleo (ECE) for Costa Rica, the National Sample Survey (NSS) for India, the Sakernas for Indonesia, Encuesta Nacional de Ocupación y Empleo (ENOE) for Mexico, Encuesta Nacional de Hogares (ENAHO) for Peru, the QLFS for South Africa and the HLFS for Turkey.

StatLink http://dx.doi.org/10.1787/888933881857

High and persistent informal employment represents a major policy concern and greatly complicates the challenge of promoting strong productivity growth and more inclusive labour markets.

- Informality is associated with low productivity and hinders productivity growth. Informal firms are highly overrepresented in the bottom of the size and productivity distribution (Hsieh and Klenow, 2009[13]; Li and Rama, 2015[14]; OECD, 2018[15]). Informal firms tends to be small since this allows them to stay under the radar of enforcement agencies and minimise the risk of detection. However, this also tends to hold down productivity growth as it prevents them from reaching an efficient scale of production and limits their access to credit. Moreover, informality can provide a source of unfair competition to formal firms and thereby weaken incentives for formal-sector development.[5]

- Informality is closely related to low labour market inclusiveness, not least because large portions of the workforce are left unprotected from statutory or collectively agreed labour standards as well as social insurance.[6] Moreover, mobility rates between informal and formal employment tend to be relatively low, suggesting that the job-quality gap associated with informal work can be highly persistent over time (Bosch and Esteban-Pretel, 2012[16]; Cruces, Ham and Viollaz, 2012[17]; OECD, 2015[6]).[7] Finally, persons from groups associated with a weaker labour market position, such as low-skilled youth, women or older workers, are much more likely to work informally than others (OECD, 2008[18]).

- Informality limits the capacity of the state to collect taxes and hence the resources that can be used to promote inclusive growth, through for example public investment in infrastructure and education and the development of labour market programmes (Besley and Persson, 2014[19]). It also limits the degree of redistribution that can be achieved through the taxes-and-benefits system.

In sum, promoting labour market performance in emerging economies requires confronting the dual challenge of low productivity, on the one hand, and low labour market inclusiveness, on the other. While these challenges are not too different from those faced by more advanced economies (Chapter 2), the context is very different due to the presence of pervasive informality. This greatly limits the reach of employment and social policies and the financial resources available for government action. Any strategy for promoting better labour market performance in emerging economies should therefore take account of the importance of informality.

16.2. Promoting productivity growth and tackling informality

Tackling informality requires a comprehensive strategy that simultaneously addresses all the main factors that drive it. Past experience suggests that narrow reforms that focus on only one specific element affecting formality tend to have only modest effects (Bruhn and McKenzie, 2014[20]). A comprehensive approach to tackling informality should focus on the following elements: i) the development of relevant skills and their efficient use in the labour market; ii) lowering the costs of formality while enhancing its benefits; iii) improving the efficiency of enforcement.

Attaining a skilled workforce and reducing skill mismatch

A skilled workforce is a major determinant of economic and labour market performance (Gennaioli et al., 2013[21]). Differences in human capital account for about half of the difference in GDP per capita between Latin-American countries and OECD countries (Hanushek and Woessmann, 2012[22]). The importance of a skilled workforce reflects both the greater likelihood that skilled workers are employed, as well as their tendency to be more productive in their jobs. Skills also facilitate the dissemination of productivity-enhancing technologies and can thereby help lagging firms to catch up with the technological frontier.

Skill development is also very important for reducing informality. For example, in Colombia, skill upgrading explains two thirds of the reduction in informality from 70% in 2007 to 62% in 2017 (IMF, 2018[23]).[8] Formal work necessitates higher productivity and more skilled workers to compensate for the costs of social security contributions, personal income taxes and complying with regulatory requirements. It is therefore not surprising that low-skilled workers are overrepresented in informal work and typically have weak prospects of moving to formal work (OECD, 2015[24]; Cruces, Ham and Viollaz, 2012[17]).

Improving educational enrolment and the quality of education

While emerging economies have made impressive progress in expanding coverage of basic education, enrolment rates of secondary and tertiary education need to be improved to promote the further upskilling of the workforce.[9] In addition, the overall quality of the educational system requires further attention. According to the Programme for International Student Assessment (PISA), the average level of skills among high-school students in emerging economies remains well below the OECD average and improvements over time have been modest.

Poor educational outcomes can be ameliorated by ensuring that sufficient financial resources are available for public spending on education, by enhancing the collection of taxes and addressing informality. Governments in emerging economies tend to spend less as a share of GDP on education than OECD countries. This reflects lower public spending overall rather than a lower spending priority for education, since emerging economies tend to devote a larger share of their public budget to education than more advanced economies.

Fiscal constraints highlight the importance of making spending more effective. This can be done by promoting early childhood education, in particular among children in poor households since this increases the motivation for further study and its effectiveness (Heckman, 2006[25]; Kugler et al., 2018[26]). Other cost-effective measures include providing information about school quality and returns to schooling, promoting teacher quality, and using digital technologies in the provision of education services (Ganimian et al., 2016[27]; World Bank, 2018[28]).

Tackling pervasive skill mismatch

While improving the supply of skills is critical, it is equally important that the skills provided by the education system correspond to the skills that are required by firms and that the labour market matches workers to jobs in which they can put their skills to their best possible use. Skill mismatches prevent firms and workers from reaching their full potential, resulting in lower productivity, wages and job satisfaction (Mcgowan and Andrews, 2015[29]; OECD, 2017[30]). Moreover, mismatches lower the returns to education, and therefore, the incentives for workers to invest in education (Levy and López-Calva, 2016[2]).

Skill mismatch tends to be high in emerging economies. In each of the emerging economies for which suitable data are available, skill mismatch exceeds the average level in the OECD (Figure 16.4). Moreover, with the exception of South Africa, overqualification tends to be relatively more important than underqualification, in contrast to OECD countries where underqualification tends to be somewhat more important on average.

Figure 16.4. Skill mismatches are high in emerging economies

Percentage of mismatched workers

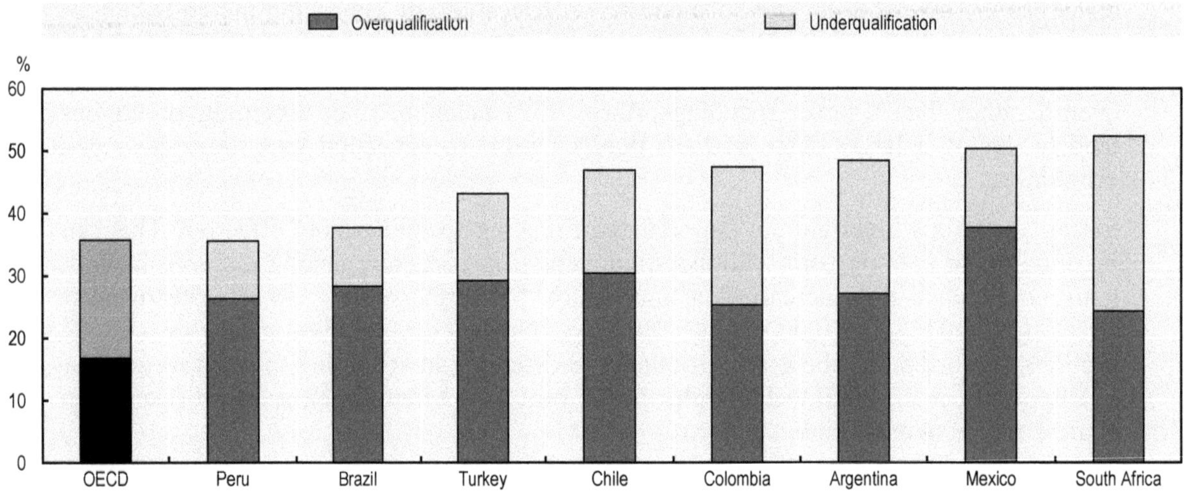

Note: Mismatch is calculated as the share of individuals with a higher (overqualification) or lower (underqualification) level of qualification than the modal level in his/her occupation.
Source: OECD Skills for Jobs Database, 2018, https://stats.oecd.org/Index.aspx?DataSetCode=MISMATCH.

StatLink http://dx.doi.org/10.1787/888933881876

Skill mismatch can be reduced by ensuring that the educational system provides the skills needed by employers, the labour market allows for an efficient matching between workers and firms and worker skills are fully used in the workplace.

To ensure that students leave the educational systems with the skills required by formal employers, it is essential to strengthen the links between the world of education and the world of work. One promising way of doing this is by combining classroom learning with workplace training, including through the use of apprenticeships. This not only promotes skill acquisition and ensures that training programmes correspond to employer needs, but also provides youth with valuable work experience in formal firms (OECD, 2015[24]). The Colombian *Jovenes en Acción* programme, for instance, which combines classroom training with an internship in the formal sector, increased the probability of working formally and raised earnings up to ten years after programme completion (Attanasio et al., 2015[31]; OECD, 2016[32]).

Reducing skill mismatch also requires an efficient matching of worker skills with firm needs. This requires good information about the skills of workers and the available job opportunities. Skills accreditation programmes, such as the *Recognition of Prior Learning programme* in South Africa (OECD, 2017[33]), can help providing better information about worker skills, while information about job vacancies can be disseminated through online platforms or the public employment services, including towards disadvantaged groups. Efficient skills matching also requires that workers can easily move across jobs and firms can adjust their workforce in line with emerging challenges and opportunities. Among other things, this requires sufficiently flexible product markets and employment protection regulations, coupled with effective employment and social policies that support workers rather than their jobs (see discussion below).

Another way of reducing mismatch is to promote the use of skills in the workplace by investing in the competences of entrepreneurs and promoting the use of high performance management and work practices (Bloom et al., 2013[34]; Bloom et al., 2018[35]). This is also likely to support formal-sector development since better skilled managers can deal more easily with the administrative processes that come with formality.[10] Moreover, high-performance management and work practices are likely to be more effective in formal firms since they tend to be part of a long-term strategy based on stable employer-employee relationships.

Lowering the costs of formality while enhancing its benefits

Promoting productivity growth crucially requires a business-friendly environment in which formal jobs can flourish. This includes a legal system that enforces property rights and contracts in a fair and timely manner (Quatraro and Vivarelli, 2015[36]). Having the legal power to demand that contracts are upheld is a major advantage of being in the formal sector and should be guaranteed by the government. An effective judiciary is also key for productivity growth, as it allows formal firms to access credit, reduces uncertainty to foreign investors, and supports the participation in global value chains (Perry et al., 2007[10]).

In many emerging economies, stringent product market rules hold back competition, productivity growth and the creation of formal jobs (Koske et al., 2015[37]). Barriers to entrepreneurship, trade and investment tend to be considerably higher in emerging economies than in more advanced OECD countries. They tend to protect incumbents against competition from outsiders by imposing high administrative hurdles to potential entrants. State control, as reflected by high shares of public ownership in the market sector, also tends to be more important. Pro-competitive reforms can promote productivity growth by: improving the operational efficiency of firms and the efficient allocation of resources (OECD, 2016[38]); enhancing institutional quality by reducing the scope for rent-seeking behaviour and corruption (Rijkers, Arouri and Baghdadi, 2016[39]); and fostering formal-sector job creation by reducing the administrative costs of registering or running a business.

Labour taxes should be kept moderate as they can represent a substantial cost for the creation of formal jobs, particularly of low-skilled ones (Cano-Urbina, 2015[40]; Bosch and Esteban-Pretel, 2012[16]; Frölich et al., 2014[41]). While labour tax rates tend to be similar or lower on average than in OECD countries, they tend to be much higher for low-wage workers (OECD, 2015[5]). This reflects a much greater reliance on social security contributions, which tend to be proportional to income, as opposed to personal income taxes, which tend to be more progressive. This has potentially important implications not only for labour market inclusiveness, but also the attractiveness of being formal. To the extent that there is a strong link at the individual level between social security contributions and entitlements, a significant labour tax wedge may not have important implications for the choice between working formally or informally. However, incentives to work formally tend to be weakened if: i) social security has a significant redistributive component, ii) the social security system does not provide value for money due to poor management; or iii) workers do not value entitlements because they are short-sighted.[11] To strengthen the incentives of working formally, one possibility could be to reinforce the link between entitlements and contributions. Another is to promote incentives for formality among low-wage workers by making labour taxes more progressive. This can be achieved through the use of exemptions from social security contributions for low-wage workers or by relying more strongly on general taxation, including progressive personal income taxes.

Labour market regulation has traditionally been a popular instrument for governments in emerging economies to ensure adequate working conditions, but it should be used carefully to avoid unnecessarily adding to the cost of formal employment. While the design of occupational and safety regulations should be driven primarily by considerations over the wellbeing of workers rather than their costs to firms, this is less obvious in other regulatory areas. Indeed, employment protection regulations and statutory minimum wages could be considerably lightened in certain emerging economies, provided that effective social-assistance and unemployment-insurance systems are in place.[12] Such an approach is likely to increase the attractiveness of formality to firms by reducing payroll and dismissal costs, while at the same time provide more effective protection to workers and their families (see Section 16.3).

Enhancing compliance through enforcement, social dialogue and social norms

Tackling informality also requires enhancing compliance with regulations through an effective judiciary, well equipped labour inspectorates and the involvement of the social partners. Compliance can also be enhanced through the establishment of social norms that promote a responsible business conduct.

The effective enforcement of labour, tax and social security regulations is essential for combatting informal employment. In most emerging economies, this requires additional resources for labour inspectorates since labour inspectors tend to be few and their training insufficient.[13] At the same time, limited resources can often be used more efficiently by applying risk-assessment methods to target non-complying firms and workers, such as small firms and firms in the service sector (OECD, 2008[18]). To avoid the risk that enforcement further worsens the position of already vulnerable workers in the labour market (Ulyssea, 2010[42]; Ulyssea, 2018[43]; Almeida and Carneiro, 2012[44]), it should not be overly harsh, by balancing sanctions in case of non-compliance with technical assistance to help workers and firms navigate administrative processes.

Collective bargaining and social dialogue can play a key role in ensuring that labour market regulations and labour standards are upheld. Trade unions as well as other forms of collective worker representation are well placed to raise instances of non-compliance and provide a voice to workers. However, unionisation rates tend to be very low in emerging economies (OECD, 2018[45]). This partly reflects the fact that the rights of freedom of association and collective bargaining are often not well respected. Governments should make greater efforts to protect these rights and to promote constructive social dialogue more generally.

Social norms can contribute to compliance with labour laws by promoting the responsible business conduct of firms. The OECD Guidelines for Multinational Enterprises are the most encompassing government-supported instrument to promote the responsibility of employers for the quality of employment conditions and industrial relations in their business operations and supply chains (see Chapter 7). Among other things, they commit governments to encourage multinational enterprises to contribute to the effective abolition of child and forced labour, tackle discrimination, promote the right of worker representation, enhance health and safety in the workplace, and mitigate the adverse effects of collective layoffs.

16.3. Protecting workers

Productivity growth is a necessary but not a sufficient condition for broadly shared increases in living standards. It is equally important that vulnerable workers are protected against financial hardship and social exclusion by effective social protection systems.[14] When considering different options for strengthening social protection due consideration should be given to the possible effects of taxes and benefits on work incentives, notably those for formal work.

Strengthening social protection

Social protection in emerging economies is generally much weaker than in more advanced OECD countries. It is also largely focused on formal workers, leaving an important share of the population vulnerable to poverty and economic shocks.

Weak social protection in part reflects low social spending. Overall public social expenditure as a share of GDP falls well short of the average level in the OECD, and is even half that level in some emerging economies (OECD, 2016[46]). This is partly related to the pervasiveness of informality and the constraints that this places on the ability to collect taxes. Given the difficulty of expanding the budget for public social expenditures in the short-term, a strong targeting of social expenditures towards the most vulnerable is needed (OECD, 2015[5]).

However, contributory social insurance programmes account for the bulk of public social expenditures in emerging economies, while their coverage, by definition, is limited to formal workers (OECD, 2010[47]).[15] As a result, the impact of social insurance benefits on the income distribution tends to be regressive, whereas such benefits typically have a strong inequality-reducing effect in more advanced economies (Causa and Hermansen, 2017[48]). Even among formal workers, the effectiveness of social insurance tends to be limited due to the combination of patchy coverage, and low levels of benefits or, in some countries, the complete absence of key programmes such as unemployment insurance.

Non-contributory social assistance benefits can make a potentially important contribution to alleviating financial hardship in emerging economies since they can be targeted at those who need it most, including informal workers. In practice, however, the effectiveness of social assistance in rolling back poverty is often limited, due to a combination of insufficient resources, resulting in benefits that are not sufficiently high to lift families out of poverty, as well as poor targeting, due to the difficulty of means-testing in emerging economies.[16]

Strengthening labour market inclusiveness requires reinforcing social assistance in countries where informality remains pervasive and existing programmes are not sufficiently effective in addressing financial hardship. Strengthening social insurance is also important to protect formal workers against labour market risks and to avoid that adverse career events drive people into informality.

Protecting the most vulnerable against financial hardship

Various approaches to social assistance have emerged

The principal objective of social assistance is to reduce poverty, tackle social exclusion and promote economic development by focusing on poor segments of the population irrespective of their labour market status. During the past twenty years, there has been a proliferation of large-scale, and sometimes innovative, cash transfers (CT) programmes in emerging economies.[17] One can differentiate three broad classes (Barrientos, 2016[49]):

- Unconditional cash transfers (UCT), usually targeted to poor households with older household members. Examples of UCTs beyond old-age pensions include the Chinese Di Bao system which seeks to provide a guaranteed minimum income for all households and South Africa's Child Support Grant which provides income support to caregivers of children. UCT programmes do not impose any conditions beyond being below the income (or wealth) threshold.
- Conditional cash transfers (CCT) programmes, which provide income support to poor household that comply with certain behavioural requirements in relation to education or health (e.g. school attendance, vaccinations, health clinic visits). Apart from reducing poverty, CCTs also seek to promote equal opportunities and long-term economic growth by investing in the education and health of children. Examples include *Bolsa Familia* in Brazil – currently the largest CCT in operation worldwide – and *Prospera* in Mexico (formerly known as *Oportunidades*).
- Integrated anti-poverty programmes, which combine income support to the poor with interventions that seek to address the structural causes of poverty. This recognises the need for a comprehensive approach to tackling the often multiple barriers to durably moving out of poverty.[18] The best known example is *Chile Solidario* which combines income support with personal counselling and access to social services (e.g. education, employment, healthcare, housing and justice).

Cash transfers do not need to entail negative employment effects

CTs typically play a significant effect in reducing financial hardship among benefit recipients. The evidence suggests that households receiving social benefits have higher incomes and increase their consumption (Bastagli et al., 2016[50]). This means that the effect of benefit receipt is not fully offset by adverse effects on work incentives and that benefits play a potentially important role in alleviating liquidity constraints (Banerjee et al., 2017[51]).

However, CTs tend to have modest effects on reducing poverty and inequality. This reflects a combination of low benefit generosity – benefits typically do not exceed 20% of the average wage (OECD, 2011[52])[19] – and poor targeting due to the use of proxy-means tests (OECD, 2010[47]). Inaccurate targeting tends to give rise to significant errors of exclusion, i.e. eligible households who not receive income support, in some cases well over 50% of potential beneficiaries, implying that financial hardship in many cases remains unaddressed. Errors of inclusion, i.e. non-eligible households who receive benefits, tend to be smaller, but remain far from negligible, raising important questions about the efficiency of public spending (OECD, 2010[47]; Soares, Ribas and Osório, 2010[53]; Golan, Sicular and Umapathi, 2017[54]; Larrañaga, Contreras and Ruiz-Tagle, 2012[55]).

CTs in emerging economies typically do not generate strong negative employment effects for a number of reasons (OECD, 2011[52]; Banerjee et al., 2017[51]; Banerjee et al., 2017[51]).[20] First, benefit recipiency is not conditional on labour market status, as tends to be the case in more advanced OECD countries. CTs are typically seen as a complement to subsistence incomes rather than a response to joblessness. This means that joblessness is generally not a condition for eligibility.[21] Second, the use of crude and infrequent means tests to determine initial and continued benefit eligibility for CTs in emerging economies implies that additional income is not immediately taxed away as a result of benefit withdrawal. Third, levels of transfers are generally low and recipient households are typically very poor.[22] This means that work incentives are likely to remain relatively strong. There may even be positive labour market effects when benefits alleviate financial barriers to labour force participation among very poor households.[23]

While loose means tests and low benefits limit potentially adverse labour market effects, they also limit the effectiveness of CTs in reducing poverty. One way of increasing policy effectiveness without inducing significant labour market effects may be to make use of graduated benefits which only gradually decline as income rises (OECD, 2011[52]). The main drawback of such an approach is that it would require a shift from proxy-means tests towards means-tests based on regular income declarations, which are more demanding in terms of administrative capacity and may be costly to operate. Given the difficulties involved with targeting, an alternative option could be to move towards a universal basic income (UBI), i.e. an unconditional benefit for everyone irrespective of income or labour market status. While this would address the issue of horizontal equity that results from inaccurate targeting, benefits would be too low to significantly alleviate financial hardship among the poor without substantial additional fiscal resources (Hanna and Olken, 2018[56]).

Address poverty at it roots and promote long-term labour market outcomes

Conditional cash transfers can make a potentially important contribution to the inter-generational transmission of poverty and long-term labour market outcomes through their impact on education and health. The evidence shows positive effects of varying extents on school attendance, child nutrition and height for age (Narayan et al., 2018[57]). Evidence on long-term labour market effects remains scarce as children among recipient households are only starting to make their way to the labour market now, but typically point to small positive effects (Millán et al., 2019[58]; Kugler and Rojas, 2018[59]; Behrman, Parker and Todd, 2011[60]). However, CCT programmes have been criticised for falling short of their promises as a result of a weak enforcement of conditionality and poor-quality education and health services (OECD, 2011[52]; Fiszbein et al., 2009[61]).

A growing awareness of the need for a comprehensive approach to tackle the social problems that drive poverty and enhance the long-term effectiveness of CCTs has contributed to the development of integrated anti-poverty programmes that combine income support with a range of social services. While evaluations of *Chile Solidario* during its initial period of operation suggest that the programme did not yield significant employment effects (Carneiro, Galasso and Ginja, 2018[62]; Galasso, 2011[63]; Larrañaga, Contreras and Ruiz-Tagle, 2012[55]), the programme has been redesigned to enhance its effectiveness and similar programmes have been developed elsewhere. For example, in Argentina *Seguro de Capacitacion y Empleo* (SCE) was established in 2006 to provide employment services to recipients of the CCT *Plan Jefes*. Evaluation results suggest that this increased formal employment and wages (López Mourelo and Escudero, 2017[64]). In Mexico, *Prospera,* which replaced *Oportunidades* in 2014, systematically registers benefit recipients with the public employment services to support poor households in getting a foothold in the labour market (OECD, 2017[65]).

Protecting formal workers against the consequences of job loss

Even though social assistance can provide an important backstop for displaced workers, it is also important that effective income support policies are available for workers who are displaced from formal jobs to provide them with the necessary time and resources to search for a new formal job and to avoid that they are pushed into informal work.

Support for displaced workers tends to be job-oriented

Income support to formal-sector job losers generally takes two forms: unemployment insurance (UI) and severance pay (SP). UI represents a worker-oriented approach to job displacement by alleviating the impact of job loss on consumption during the period of unemployment and to provide workers with the means to search for a suitable job. By contrast, SP represents a more job-oriented approach in the sense that it tends to reduce the risk of unemployment directly through the use of a firing penalty.[24] Moreover, UI represents a collective approach based on the pooling of risks across individuals and firms. This reduces the cost of insurance and allows for redistribution. By contrast, SP provides a more individualised approach, as firms are held directly responsible for the costs of their layoff behaviour.[25]

Severance pay represents the main source of income support to job losers in emerging economies, in contrast to more advanced OECD economies where unemployment insurance tends to be much more important. As an illustration, Figure 16.5 juxtaposes the value of income support during the first year of unemployment that is available to eligible job losers from either UI or SP.[26] In the emerging economies considered here, except South Africa and the Russian Federation, SP represents the main source of income support. Some emerging economies do not have a universal UI system at all and, where it exists, coverage tends to be very low, particularly among the most vulnerable, as a result of strict eligibility requirements or short maximum durations. By contrast, in all non-emerging OECD economies except Lithuania, the value of income support from UI exceeds (or equals) that from SP. They all have universal UI systems in place, while about half do not impose any mandatory SP requirements.

The importance of SP in emerging economies reflects to an important extent legal traditions (Botero et al., 2004$_{[66]}$), but is also related to the difficulty of providing UI effectively in a context of widespread informality and weak administrative capacity. Workers at low risk of job loss may opt out of the system by working informally ("adverse selection"). Moreover, benefit recipients often have the possibility of working informally while receiving benefits, reducing incentives to look actively for another formal job ("moral hazard").

Because of the difficulties in providing UI in a context of widespread informality, employment protection has sometimes been considered as a low-cost alternative to unemployment insurance in emerging economies (Heckman and Pages, 2004$_{[67]}$). However, the emphasis on job security rules is unlikely to be ideal for providing effective protection to formal-sector job losers, nor for promoting formal-sector development and productivity.Despite being a legal requirement, in practice severance payments are rarely made in emerging economies due to widespread non-compliance, particularly in the case of vulnerable workers with a weak bargaining position (World Bank, 2019$_{[68]}$).There is a risk, moreover, that overly strict employment protection rules push workers from low-skilled jobs into informal ones (Betcherman, 2015$_{[69]}$). Finally, strict employment protection hampers the efficient allocation of resources, and hence productivity growth.

Figure 16.5. Severance pay represents the main form of unemployment compensation in emerging economies

Value of income support in number of months of previous earnings, 2013

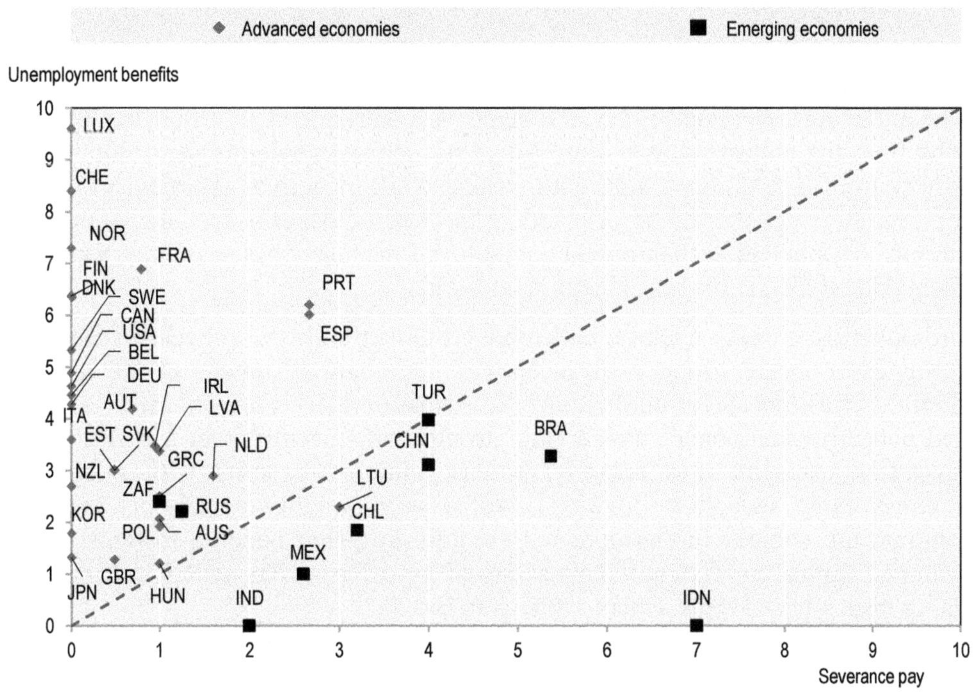

Note: Income support for 12 months of unemployment for dismissals without just cause of workers with four years of tenure in previous job. Severance pay: total value of severance pay for workers in previous job for four years divided by previous monthly wage; Unemployment insurance: maximum duration in months for workers with four years of contributions times the average replacement rate over the benefit duration period. Systems based on individual saving accounts are also taken into account.

Source: OECD tax and benefits models; *OECD/IAB Employment Protection Database*, 2013 update, www.oecd.org/employment/protection; and Social Security Programs Throughout the World, https://www.ssa.gov/policy/docs/progdesc/ssptw.

StatLink http://dx.doi.org/10.1787/888933881895

Strengthening unemployment insurance for workers

To provide more effective support to displaced workers from formal jobs, UI systems should be designed or redesigned so as to minimise the unintended effects of benefit receipt on incentives to work formally, while maximising support to cash-strapped job losers in their search for quality work in a context of widespread informality and significant administrative constraints. This can be achieved by giving individuals more responsibility for the cost of unemployment benefits through the use of individual unemployment saving accounts (IUSA), collective UI schemes with limited benefit generosity, or a combination of the two.

IUSAs provide self-insurance against the risk of unemployment based on mandatory savings by the employee, employer, or both. They preserve strong work incentives, as unemployed workers can make withdrawals from their own personal savings accounts under certain modalities to support their income and assist them in their job-search. IUSAs can also strengthen incentives for working formally since social security contributions are less likely to be perceived as a tax on labour and more likely as a delayed payment. The main drawback of IUSA systems relates to their potential to provide adequate protection to vulnerable workers due to the lack of risk pooling; i.e. those most likely to exhaust their accounts as a result of frequent and/or long-lasting spells of unemployment.

A second possibility is to complement IUSAs with a small collective UI system to provide income support to job losers who have no or insufficient savings in their individual savings accounts. Such a scheme was introduced in Chile in 2001. While benefits from the collective fund were found to increase unemployment durations more than those from IUSAs, consistent with weaker work incentives (Hartley, van Ours and Vodopivec, 2011[70]), this could also reflect the role of benefits for alleviating liquidity constraints that prevent cash-strapped unemployed persons from searching for a job that fits their skills (OECD, 2011[52]; Chetty, 2008[71]).

A third option is to make use of a collective UI system only, with benefit schedules that are designed to ensure strong work incentives. The main advantage of this approach is that it allows for (more) risk-pooling and redistribution than is possible with no or only a limited collective component. Preserving strong work incentives in a context of weak administrative capacity may require, at least initially, benefits with relatively low replacement rates and short durations. Addressing liquidity constraints that lead to sub-optimal job choices furthermore may require targeting benefits towards job losers with limited resources. This could be achieved by offering flat benefit schedules, as in China, or means-tested replacement rates, as in Brazil.[27]

Gradually develop public employment services

Efforts to strengthen collective unemployment insurance schemes should be accompanied by investments in employment policies to minimise the risk of benefit dependency, facilitate the return to work and limit skills mismatch.

The role of the public employment services depends on the specific features of the UI system. In countries with a relatively short maximum duration of benefits, such as Brazil, activation may be light, by mainly focusing on the administration of initial benefit eligibility and the provision of job-brokering services. In countries where benefits are available for a relatively long duration, such as China and the Russian Federation, the public employment services may need to play a more important role, including by monitoring and enforcing continued eligibility and engaging in the development of individual action plans.

While investing in public employment services is important, it is equally important to tread cautiously and complement investments in the PES with investments in administrative capacity. The evidence on the effectiveness of more elaborate employment programmes, including training, is not encouraging (Kluve, 2016[72]; McKenzie, 2017[73]; Hirshleifer et al., 2016[74]). While to some extent this may reflect the role of insufficient treatment intensity related to limited resources, weak administrative capacity related to, for instance the coordination of benefit administration and re-employment services, is also likely to play an important role.

Conclusions

This chapter uses the Jobs Strategy framework to discuss how emerging economies can confront the dual challenge of low productivity and inclusiveness in a context of widespread informality. Informality complicates this dual challenge by holding back productivity growth, leaving large parts of the workforce without social insurance and basic regulatory protection, and by limiting fiscal space to invest in measures that can support inclusive growth. The main message of this chapter is that governments in emerging economies should concentrate more directly on workers by providing them with the skills to succeed in the labour market and protecting the most vulnerable against financial hardship. The current focus on the protection of well-paid formal jobs through the combination of rigid product market regulations, strict employment protection rules and high minimum wages risks being counterproductive, with adverse consequences for productivity, formality and inclusiveness. More specifically, the chapter provides the following messages:

- *Invest in skills.* Investing in skills is critical for raising productivity, reducing inequality and promoting formal employment. More needs to be done to ensure that education is accessible and affordable to everyone, including children from disadvantaged backgrounds. The quality of educational systems deserves particular attention since too many students enter the labour market without the skills that are needed in formal jobs. Poor-quality education not only does little to enhance career prospects in the formal sector, it also represents a waste of financial resources and time and can lead to false expectations, particularly among the young, with potentially important consequences for trust in public institutions.
- *Strengthen social protection.* In emerging economies, social protection tends to be weak and mainly focused on formal workers. More should be done to protect poor families against financial hardship while addressing the roots of poverty. This requires investing in comprehensive social assistance systems in combination with employment, social and health services that tackle barriers to the gainful employment of working-age adults and promote the long-term labour market prospects of children. A better targeting of benefits to poor households would further increase policy effectiveness, but may also weaken work incentives. Benefit dependency can be avoided by allowing for benefit schedules that gradually decline with additional income. Similarly, to promote formal employment among low-wage workers, the financing of social insurance systems could be made more progressive or the importance of general taxation increased. In the longer term, a more integrated approach to social protection could be envisaged that provides social assistance and social insurance in a unified framework.
- *Provide more flexible product and labour markets.* Compared with OECD standards, product market regulations, employment protection rules and statutory minimum wages in emerging economies tend to be relatively strict, while at the same time leave large parts of the economy unregulated. This undermines productivity growth, formal sector development and, in the case of product market regulations, also institutional quality by increasing the scope for regulatory capture and corruption. Rather than relying on strict regulations, more attention should be given to addressing poverty through social assistance and supporting workers who have been displaced from formal jobs through unemployment insurance. At the same time, to promote a good environment for firms and adequate labour standards for workers, governments should enhance compliance with existing labour and product market regulations through an effective judiciary, well-equipped labour inspectorates and constructive social dialogue.

Notes

[1] The main exception is South Africa where about 1 in 4 active persons are unemployed (OECD, 2015[6]).

[2] In a number of emerging economies, such as urban China, urban Colombia and Peru, high shares of fixed-term work among wage employees further add to vulnerability (OECD, 2015[24]).

[3] Apart from reflecting a poor quality of the working environment, this could also reflect the role of low hourly wages for the need to put in long working hours to make a decent living.

[4] The average annual change in formality rates shown here correlate negatively with the compound annual growth rate in real GDP per capita (-0.5) and positively with population growth (0.2).

[5] On average across the emerging economies considered here, competition from the informal sector is reported as the biggest obstacle faced by formal firms (World Bank Enterprise Surveys, http://www.enterprisesurveys.org/)

[6] More specifically, informality tends to be associated with i) lower wages, reflecting both low worker productivity and the absence of binding wage floors; ii) less secure work, due to a higher risk of job loss and the lack of social protection; and iii) a lower quality of the work environment, related to poor health and safety, long working hours and limited training opportunities (OECD, 2015[24]).

[7] In China and Colombia, most outflows from informal jobs are to unemployment and inactivity, implying that informal work does not work well as a stepping stone to formal work (OECD, 2015[24]).

[8] Also almost half of the regional variation in informality can be attributed to access to good quality higher education (IMF, 2018[23]).

[9] Net enrolment rates in secondary and tertiary education are generally well below the OECD average in emerging economies, in particular in South Africa and Indonesia (UNESCO, 2018[77]).

[10] Managers in formal firms much more often have a college degree than their counterparts in informal firms (La Porta and Shleifer, 2014[4]).

[11] Providing informal workers with subsidised access to certain aspects of social security could also weaken incentives for formal work. For example, the provision of health insurance to informal workers in Colombia and Mexico has spurred an intense debate about its effects on formality (OECD, 2011[52]).

[12] *De jure* minimum wage relative to the median wage is relatively high in emerging economies such as Colombia, Turkey, Costa Rica, and Chile (see Chapter 8).

[13] The number of labour inspectors per 10 000 workers in emerging economies for the 10 countries for which there is data lies between 0.2 (Mexico) and 0.6 (South Africa), except for Chile (1.7) which is the only country above the average of 0.9 for 25 OECD countries (ILOSTAT, https://www.ilo.org/ilostat).

[14] This is not just a social concern, but also has implications for efficiency. Financial hardship may generate liquidity constraints that impede effective job search, with adverse consequences for labour force participation and skill mismatches (OECD, 2011[52]). It may also reduce investments in human capital, with negative consequences for economic growth in the long-term (Cingano, 2014[76]).

[15] This largely reflects the role of contributory schemes for health and pensions, while contributory schemes for unemployment, disability and sickness tend to be considerably smaller, if present at all.

16 Public spending on social assistance ranges from less than 1% in Thailand, Costa Rica, Tunisia, China, and Indonesia, to 3-4% of GDP in Colombia, South Africa, and Chile (World Bank ASPIRE, datatopics.worldbank.org/aspire).

17 For the countries for which data are available, on average about 70% of social assistance is spent on cash transfers including social pensions, and about 30% on in-kind transfers and subsidised public services, with large differences across countries (World Bank ASPIRE, datatopics.worldbank.org/aspire).

18 The approach is similar in spirit as the OECD activation strategy in relation to joblessness (see Chapter 9).

19 UCT programmes targeted at the elderly often are considerably more generous than other CT programmes.

20 There are social assistance programmes that target unregistered workers, which creates incentives to remain or become informal. An example is the introduction of the Argentinian child allowance scheme, *Asignación Universal por Hijo* (AUH), whose introduction led to large negative effects on labour market formalisation among programme beneficiaries (Garganta and Gasparini, 2015[79]).

21 The increasing emphasis on social assistance to working families in OECD countries could be seen as convergence to the practice in emerging economies (see Chapter 10).

22 In programmes with more generous (and less targeted) benefits, negative employment effects tend to be more important. OECD evidence indicates that the South African *Old Age Pension*, covering more than 80% of the elderly population offering twice the median per capita income, reduced employed in households with an OAP recipient (OECD, 2011[52]).

23 For example, OECD evidence in the context of South African *Child Support Grant* suggests that benefits can promote labour force participation among mothers with young children in very poor households (OECD, 2011[52]).

24 In a perfectly competitive labour market, mandated severance pay between employer and employee in the case of dismissal has no impact on dismissal behaviour since its costs will be fully offset by lower wages (Lazear, 1990[78]). However, this is unlikely to be the case in practice due to the presence of wage rigidities and financial market imperfections. Moreover, severance pay tends to come with other aspects of employment protection such as the complexity of dismissal procedures and the definition of unfair dismissal that affect layoff behaviour.

25 By increasing firing costs for employers, SP may help to reduce "excessive turnover" of workers whose job matches have temporarily become unprofitable and it can strengthen incentives to invest in firm-specific human capital. See Chapter 7 for further details.

26 Note that the figure only takes account of the generosity of income support and not of actually receiving income support which may have important implications in practice.

27 Declining benefit schedules as in the Russian Federation can also contribute to maintaining good work incentives over the unemployment spell.

References

Almeida, R. and P. Carneiro (2012), "Enforcement of Labor Regulation and Informality", *American Economic Journal: Applied Economics*, Vol. 4/3, pp. 64-89, http://dx.doi.org/10.1257/app.4.3.64. [44]

Attanasio, O. et al. (2015), "Long Term Impacts of Vouchers for Vocational Training: Experimental Evidence for Colombia", *NBER Working Paper*, No. 21390, http://dx.doi.org/10.3386/w21390. [31]

Banerjee, A. et al. (2017), "Debunking the Stereotype of the Lazy Welfare Recipient: Evidence from Cash Transfer Programs", *The World Bank Research Observer*, Vol. 32/2, pp. 155-184, http://dx.doi.org/10.1093/wbro/lkx002. [51]

Barrientos, A. (2016), *Social Assistance In Developing Countries*, Cambridge University Press, http://admin.cambridge.org/sb/academic/subjects/politics-international-relations/political-economy/social-assistance-developing-countries (accessed on 23 August 2018). [49]

Bastagli, F. et al. (2016), *Cash Transfers: What Does The Evidence Say? A Rigorous Review Of Programme Impact And Of The Role Of Design And Implementation Features*, Overseas Development Institute, http://www.odi.org/sites/odi.org.uk/files/resource-documents/10749.pdf (accessed on 05 September 2018). [50]

Behrman, J., S. Parker and P. Todd (2011), "Do Conditional Cash Transfers for Schooling Generate Lasting Benefits?", *Journal of Human Resources*, Vol. 46/1, pp. 93-122, http://dx.doi.org/10.3368/jhr.46.1.93. [60]

Bento, P. and D. Restuccia (2017), "Misallocation, Establishment Size, and Productivity", *American Economic Journal: Macroeconomics*, Vol. 9/3, pp. 267-303, http://dx.doi.org/10.1257/mac.20150281. [3]

Besley, T. and T. Persson (2014), "Why Do Developing Countries Tax So Little?", *Journal of Economic Perspectives*, Vol. 28/4, pp. 99-120, http://dx.doi.org/10.1257/jep.28.4.99. [19]

Betcherman, G. (2015), "Labor Market Regulations: What do we know about their Impacts in Developing Countries?", *The World Bank Research Observer*, Vol. 30/1, pp. 124-153, http://dx.doi.org/10.1093/wbro/lku005. [69]

Bloom, N. et al. (2013), "Does Management Matter? Evidence from India", *The Quarterly Journal of Economics*, Vol. 128/1, pp. 1-51, http://dx.doi.org/10.1093/qje/qjs044. [34]

Bloom, N. et al. (2010), "Why Do Firms in Developing Countries Have Low Productivity?", *American Economic Review: Papers & Proceedings*, Vol. 100/2, pp. 619-623, http://dx.doi.org/10.1257/aer.100.2.619. [1]

Bloom, N. et al. (2018), "Do Management Interventions Last? Evidence from India", *World Bank Policy Research Working Papers*, No. 8339, http://dx.doi.org/10.1596/1813-9450-8339. [35]

Bosch, M. and J. Esteban-Pretel (2012), "Job Creation And Job Destruction In The Presence Of Informal Markets", *Journal of Development Economics*, Vol. 98/2, pp. 270-286, http://dx.doi.org/10.1016/J.JDEVECO.2011.08.004. [16]

Botero, J. et al. (2004), "The Regulation of Labor", *The Quarterly Journal of Economics*, Vol. 119/4, pp. 1339-1382, http://dx.doi.org/10.1162/0033553042476215. [66]

Bruhn, M. and D. McKenzie (2014), "Entry Regulation and the Formalization of Microenterprises in Developing Countries", *The World Bank Research Observer*, Vol. 29/2, pp. 186-201, http://dx.doi.org/10.1093/wbro/lku002. [20]

Cano-Urbina, J. (2015), "The Role Of The Informal Sector In The Early Careers Of Less-Educated Workers", *Journal of Development Economics*, Vol. 112, pp. 33-55, http://dx.doi.org/10.1016/J.JDEVECO.2014.10.002. [40]

Carneiro, P., E. Galasso and R. Ginja (2018), "Tackling Social Exclusion: Evidence from Chile", *Unpublished*, http://www.ucl.ac.uk/~uctppca/cs_jan12_2018.pdf (accessed on 29 August 2018). [62]

Causa, O. and M. Hermansen (2017), "Income Redistribution Through Taxes And Transfers Across Oecd Countries", *OECD Economics Department Working Papers*, No. 1453, http://dx.doi.org/10.1787/bc7569c6-en. [48]

Chetty, R. (2008), "Moral Hazard versus Liquidity and Optimal Unemployment Insurance", *Journal of Political Economy*, Vol. 116/2, pp. 173-234, http://dx.doi.org/10.1086/588585. [71]

Cingano, F. (2014), "Trends in Income Inequality and its Impact on Economic Growth", *OECD Social, Employment and Migration Working Papers*, No. 163, OECD Publishing, Paris, http://dx.doi.org/10.1787/5jxrjncwxv6j-en. [75]

Cruces, G., A. Ham and M. Viollaz (2012), "Scarring Effects Of Youth Unemployment And Informality Evidence From Brazil", *Unpublished*, http://conference.iza.org/conference_files/worldb2012/viollaz_m8017.pdf (accessed on 05 September 2018). [17]

Díaz, J. et al. (2018), "Pathways to Formalization: Going beyond the Formality Dichotomy", No. 11750, IZA, http://www.iza.org (accessed on 15 September 2018). [12]

Fiszbein, A. et al. (2009), *Conditional Cash Transfers Reducing Present And Future Poverty*, World Bank. [61]

Frölich, M. et al. (eds.) (2014), *Social Insurance, Informality, And Labor Markets : How To Protect Workers While Creating Good Jobs*, Oxford University Press. [41]

Galasso, E. (2011), "Alleviating Extreme Poverty In Chile: The Short Term Effects Of Chile Solidario", *Estudios de Economía*, Vol. 38/1, pp. 101-127, https://scielo.conicyt.cl/pdf/ede/v38n1/art05.pdf (accessed on 29 August 2018). [63]

Ganimian, A. et al. (2016), "Improving Education in Developing Countries: Lessons From Rigorous Impact Evaluations", *Review of Educational Research*, Vol. 86/3, pp. 719-755, http://dx.doi.org/10.3102/0034654315627499. [27]

Garganta, S. and L. Gasparini (2015), "The Impact Of A Social Program On Labor Informality: The Case Of Auh In Argentina", *Journal of Development Economics*, Vol. 115, pp. 99-110, http://dx.doi.org/10.1016/J.JDEVECO.2015.02.004. [78]

Gennaioli, N. et al. (2013), "Human Capital and Regional Development", *The Quarterly Journal of Economics*, Vol. 128/1, pp. 105-164, http://dx.doi.org/10.1093/qje/qjs050. [21]

Golan, J., T. Sicular and N. Umapathi (2017), "Unconditional Cash Transfers in China: Who Benefits from the Rural Minimum Living Standard Guarantee (Dibao) Program?", *World Development*, Vol. 93, pp. 316-336, http://dx.doi.org/10.1016/J.WORLDDEV.2016.12.011. [54]

Hanna, R. and B. Olken (2018), "Universal Basic Incomes vs. Targeted Transfers: Anti-Poverty Programs in Developing Countries", *NBER Working Paper*, No. 24939, http://www.nber.org/data-appendix/w24939 (accessed on 27 August 2018). [56]

Hanushek, E. and L. Woessmann (2012), "Schooling, educational achievement, and the Latin American growth puzzle", *Journal of Development Economics*, Vol. 99/2, pp. 497-512, http://dx.doi.org/10.1016/J.JDEVECO.2012.06.004. [22]

Hartley, G., J. van Ours and M. Vodopivec (2011), "Incentive Effects Of Unemployment Insurance Savings Accounts: Evidence From Chile", *Labour Economics*, Vol. 18/6, pp. 798-809, http://dx.doi.org/10.1016/j.labeco.2011.06.011. [70]

Heckman, J. (2006), "Skill Formation And The Economics Of Investing In Disadvantaged Children", *Science*, Vol. 312/5782, pp. 1900-1902, http://dx.doi.org/10.1126/science.1128898. [25]

Heckman, J. and C. Pages (2004), *Law and Employment*, University of Chicago Press, http://dx.doi.org/10.7208/chicago/9780226322858.001.0001. [67]

Hirshleifer, S. et al. (2016), "The Impact of Vocational Training for the Unemployed: Experimental Evidence from Turkey", *The Economic Journal*, Vol. 126/597, pp. 2115-2146, http://dx.doi.org/10.1111/ecoj.12211. [74]

Hsieh, C. and P. Klenow (2009), "Misallocation and Manufacturing TFP in China and India", *Quarterly Journal of Economics*, Vol. 124/4, pp. 1403-1448, http://dx.doi.org/10.1162/qjec.2009.124.4.1403. [13]

IMF (2018), "Colombia : Selected Issues", *IMF Staff Country Reports* No. 18/129, https://www.imf.org/en/Publications/CR/Issues/2018/05/29/Colombia-Selected-Issues-45899 (accessed on 05 September 2018). [23]

Kluve, J. (2016), "A Review of the Effectiveness of Active Labour Market Programmes with a Focus on Latin America and the Caribbean", *ILO Research Department Working Paper*, No. 9, https://www.ilo.org/wcmsp5/groups/public/@dgreports/@inst/documents/publication/wcms_459117.pdf (accessed on 23 August 2018). [72]

Koske, I. et al. (2015), "The 2013 Update of the OECD's Database on Product Market Regulation: Policy Insights for OECD and Non-OECD Countries", *OECD Economics Department Working Papers*, No. 1200, http://www.oecd.org/eco/workingpapers (accessed on 05 September 2018). [37]

Kugler, A. et al. (2018), "Long-Term Direct and Spillover Effects of Vocational Training: Experimental Evidence from Colombia 1", *Unpublished*, https://lacer.lacea.org/bitstream/handle/123456789/61291/lacea2016_effects_vocational_training.pdf?sequence=1 (accessed on 18 September 2018). [26]

Kugler, A. and I. Rojas (2018), "Do CCTs Improve Employment and Earnings in the Very Long-Term? Evidence from Mexico", *NBER Working Paper*, http://dx.doi.org/10.3386/w24248. [59]

La Porta, R. and A. Shleifer (2014), "Informality and Development", *Journal of Economic Perspectives*, Vol. 28/3, pp. 109-126, http://dx.doi.org/10.1257/jep.28.3.109. [4]

Larrañaga, O., D. Contreras and J. Ruiz-Tagle (2012), "Impact Evaluation of Chile Solidario: Lessons and Policy Recommendations", *Journal of Latin American Studies*, Vol. 44/02, pp. 347-372, http://dx.doi.org/10.1017/S0022216X12000053. [55]

Lazear, E. (1990), "Job Security Provisions and Employment", *The Quarterly Journal of Economics*, Vol. 105/3, p. 699, http://dx.doi.org/10.2307/2937895. [77]

Levy, S. and L. López-Calva (2016), "Labor Earnings, Misallocation, and the Returns to Education in Mexico", *IDB Working Paper*, No. IDB-WP-671, http://dx.doi.org/10.2139/ssrn.2956686. [2]

Li, Y. and M. Rama (2015), "Firm Dynamics, Productivity Growth, and Job Creation in Developing Countries: The Role of Micro- and Small Enterprises", *The World Bank Research Observer*, Vol. 30/1, pp. 3-38, http://dx.doi.org/10.1093/wbro/lkv002. [14]

López Mourelo, E. and V. Escudero (2017), "Effectiveness of Active Labor Market Tools in Conditional Cash Transfers Programs: Evidence for Argentina", *World Development*, Vol. 94, pp. 422-447, http://dx.doi.org/10.1016/J.WORLDDEV.2017.02.006. [64]

Mcgowan, M. and D. Andrews (2015), "Skill Mismatch and Public Policy in OECD Countries", *OECD Economics Department Working Paper Series*, No. 1210, https://www.oecd.org/eco/growth/Skill-mismatch-and-public-policy-in-OECD-countries.pdf (accessed on 06 June 2018). [29]

McKenzie, D. (2017), "How Effective Are Active Labor Market Policies in Developing Countries? A Critical Review of Recent Evidence", *The World Bank Research Observer*, Vol. 32/2, pp. 127-154, http://dx.doi.org/10.1093/wbro/lkx001. [73]

Meghir, C., R. Narita and J. Robin (2015), "Wages and Informality in Developing Countries", *American Economic Review*, Vol. 105/4, pp. 1509-1546, http://dx.doi.org/10.1257/aer.20121110. [11]

Millán, T. et al. (2019), "Long-Term Impacts of Conditional Cash Transfers: Review of the Evidence", *The World Bank Research Observer*, https://www.parisschoolofeconomics.eu/docs/macours-karen/molina-et-al-long-term-impacts-of-cct-review-of-the-evidence-2018july09.pdf (accessed on 05 September 2018). [58]

Narayan, A. et al. (2018), *Fair Progress? Economic Mobility across Generations around the World*, World Bank Group, Washington DC, https://openknowledge.worldbank.org/bitstream/handle/10986/28428/211210ov.pdf?sequence=9 (accessed on 05 July 2018). [57]

OECD (2018), *OECD Compendium of Productivity Indicators 2018*, OECD Publishing, Paris, http://dx.doi.org/10.1787/pdtvy-2018-en. [15]

OECD (2018), "The Role Of Collective Bargaining Systems For Good Labour Market Performance", in *OECD Employment Outlook 2018*, OECD Publishing, http://dx.doi.org/10.1787/empl_outlook-2018-7-en. [45]

OECD (2017), *Building an Inclusive Mexico: Policies and Good Governance for Gender Equality*, OECD Publishing, Paris, https://www.oecd-ilibrary.org/docserver/9789264265493-en.pdf?expires=1537261648&id=id&accname=ocid84004878&checksum=97B84377ADE61F755D216EB204B5949B (accessed on 18 September 2018). [65]

OECD (2017), *Getting Skills Right: South Africa*, Getting Skills Right, OECD Publishing, Paris, http://dx.doi.org/10.1787/9789264278745-en. [33]

OECD (2017), *OECD Skills Outlook 2017: Skills and Global Value Chains*, OECD Publishing, Paris, http://dx.doi.org/10.1787/9789264273351-en. [30]

OECD (2016), *Closing gender gaps in the labour markets of emerging economies: The unfinished job*, OECD Publishing, Paris, https://doi.org/10.1787/empl_outlook-2016-8-en. [7]

OECD (2016), *OECD Reviews of Labour Market and Social Policies: Colombia 2016*, OECD Publishing, http://dx.doi.org/10.1787/9789264244825-en. [32]

OECD (2016), *Society at a Glance 2016: OECD Social Indicators*, OECD Publishing, Paris, http://dx.doi.org/10.1787/9789264261488-en. [46]

OECD (2016), *The Future Of Productivity*, OECD Publishing, https://www.oecd.org/eco/OECD-2015-The-future-of-productivity-book.pdf (accessed on 06 June 2018). [38]

OECD (2015), "Enhancing Job Quality In Emerging Economies", in *OECD Employment Outlook 2015*, OECD Publishing, http://dx.doi.org/10.1787/empl_outlook-2015-en (accessed on 24 August 2018). [24]

OECD (2015), *In It Together: Why Less Inequality Benefits All*, OECD Publishing, Paris, http://dx.doi.org/10.1787/9789264235120-en. [5]

OECD (2015), *OECD Employment Outlook 2015*, OECD Publishing, Paris, http://dx.doi.org/10.1787/empl_outlook-2015-en. [6]

OECD (2011), *The Labour Market Effects of Social Protection Systems in Emerging Economies*, OECD Publishing, http://dx.doi.org/10.1787/empl_outlook-2011-en (accessed on 23 August 2018). [52]

OECD (2010), *The Global Crisis in Emerging Economies: The Jobs Impact and Policy Response*, OECD Publishing, http://www.oecd.org/els/emp/48806694.pdf (accessed on 23 August 2018). [47]

OECD (2009), *Is Informal Normal? Towards More and Better Jobs in Developing Countries*, OECD Publishing, http://www.oecd.org/dev/inclusivesocietiesanddevelopment/isinformalnormaltowardsmoreandbetterjobsindevelopingcountries.htm (accessed on 05 September 2018). [9]

OECD (2008), "Declaring Work Or Staying Underground: Informal Employment In Seven OECD Countries", in *OECD Employment Outlook 2008*, OECD Publishing, http://www.oecd.org/els/emp/oecdemploymentoutlook2008.htm (accessed on 05 September 2018). [18]

Perry, G. et al. (2007), *Informality*, World Bank, http://dx.doi.org/10.1596/978-0-8213-7092-6. [10]

Quatraro, F. and M. Vivarelli (2015), "Drivers of Entrepreneurship and Post-entry Performance of Newborn Firms in Developing Countries", *The World Bank Research Observer*, Vol. 30/2, pp. 277-305, http://dx.doi.org/10.1093/wbro/lku012. [36]

Rijkers, B., H. Arouri and L. Baghdadi (2016), "Are Politically Connected Firms More Likely to Evade Taxes? Evidence from Tunisia", *The World Bank Economic Review*, Vol. 30/Supplement_1, p. lhw018, http://dx.doi.org/10.1093/wber/lhw018. [39]

Soares, F., R. Ribas and R. Osório (2010), "Evaluating The Impact Of Brazil'S Bolsa Família: Cash Transfer Programs In Comparative Perspective", *Latin American Research Review*, Vol. 45/2, pp. 173-190, http://pdfs.semanticscholar.org/6ddd/6db8c49fe528a9a3d718e880ccb01b0e34c43.pdf. [53]

Ulyssea, G. (2018), "Firms, Informality, and Development: Theory and Evidence from Brazil", *American Economic Review*, Vol. 108/8, pp. 2015-2047, http://dx.doi.org/10.1257/aer.20141745. [43]

Ulyssea, G. (2010), "Regulation of Entry, Labor Market Institutions and the Informal Sector", *Journal of Development Economics*, Vol. 91/1, pp. 87-99, http://dx.doi.org/10.1016/J.JDEVECO.2009.07.001. [42]

UNESCO (2018), *UNESCO Data*, http://uis.unesco.org/node/334718 (accessed on 05 September 2018). [76]

World Bank (2019), *World Development Report 2019: The Changing Nature of Work*, World Bank, http://www.worldbank.org/en/publication/wdr2019 (accessed on 05 September 2018). [68]

World Bank (2018), *World Development Report 2018: Learning to Realize Education's Promise*, World Bank, http://www.worldbank.org/en/publication/wdr2018 (accessed on 05 September 2018). [28]

World Bank (2016), *Poverty and Shared Prosperity 2016: Taking on Inequality*, World Bank, Washington DC, https://openknowledge.worldbank.org/bitstream/handle/10986/25078/9781464809583.pdf (accessed on 05 September 2018). [8]

Chapter 17. Going national: Implementing the OECD Jobs Strategy

This chapter provides guidance for developing country-specific policy recommendations from the broad policy principles of the new OECD Jobs Strategy. To this end, it provides an illustrative procedure to identify countries' main policy challenges and develops broad policy packages to address them. It also highlights the importance of considering countries' initial conditions – in terms of the state of the business cycle, fiscal and administrative capacity, past reforms, preferences and demography – for tailoring policy recommendations to country specific priorities, capabilities and needs.

The statistical data for Israel are supplied by and under the responsibility of the relevant Israeli authorities. The use of such data by the OECD is without prejudice to the status of the Golan Heights, East Jerusalem and Israeli settlements in the West Bank under the terms of international law.

Introduction

The new *OECD Jobs Strategy* provides a comprehensive set of policy recommendations organised around: i) the quantity and quality of jobs; ii) labour market inclusiveness; and iii) resilience and adaptability. Using the new *Jobs Strategy* Dashboard, this chapter maps these guidelines to country-specific labour market contexts by identifying countries' main policy challenges and presenting examples of policy packages to address them.

Countries' policy challenges are based on underperformance on one dimension of the Dashboard *relative* to other dimensions, implying that there can be large differences in *absolute* performance between countries sharing the same challenge. There can also be large differences between countries in terms of business cycle conditions; fiscal and administrative capacity; past reforms; social preferences and demography that need to be accounted for when developing country-specific policy recommendations. The examples of broad policy packages developed here should thus be seen as a starting point for more granular and nuanced country-specific recommendations.

The remainder of the chapter is structured as follows. Section 17.1 situates the chapter in the overall context of the new *OECD Jobs Strategy* and describes an illustrative procedure to derive country-specific policy recommendations. Section 17.2 develops broad policy packages that address the main policy challenges emerging from this procedure. Section 17.3 emphasises a range of additional factors that will have to be taken into account to tailor policy packages to country-specific circumstances.

17.1. An illustrative procedure of how to identify policy challenges

To assist countries with the implementation of the new OECD Jobs Strategy, this chapter describes an illustrative procedure for translating its general recommendations into country-specific ones. To this end, it identifies country-specific performance challenges using the dashboard of the new OECD Jobs Strategy (Chapter 3) and presents elements of broad policy packages to address them. These challenges and policy packages constitute a starting point for formulating fully-fledged country-specific reform strategies, which also should fully take account of the country-specific context, such as past reforms and social preferences (Figure 17.1).

Figure 17.1. Developing country-specific reform recommendations

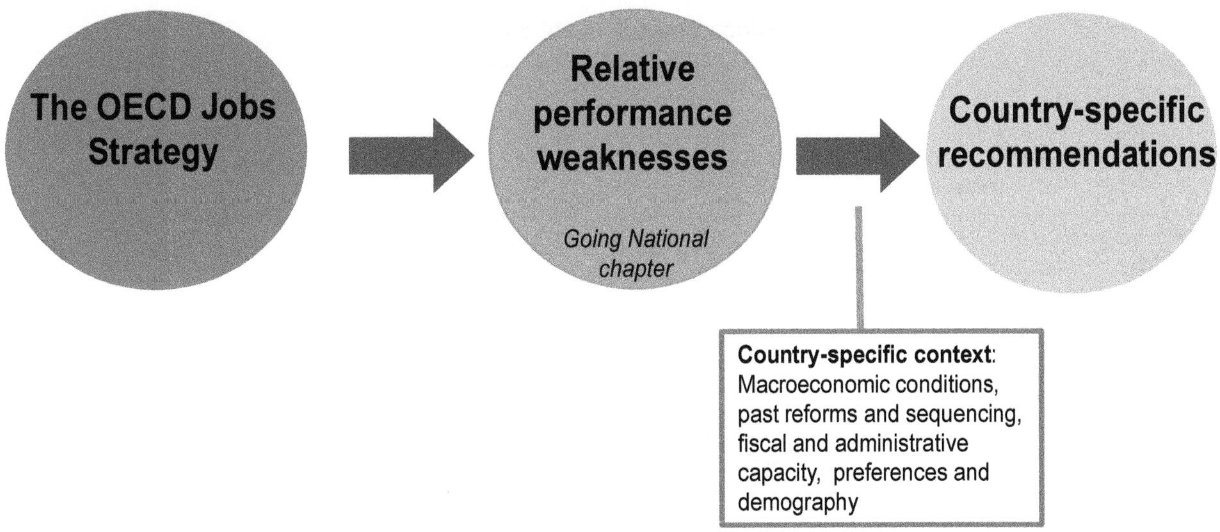

The OECD Jobs Strategy dashboard describes labour market performance using indicators of job quantity, job quality and inclusiveness (Panel A) as well as indicators of framework conditions for resilience and adaptability (Panel B). As an illustration of how the dashboard and the analysis of the Jobs Strategy could be used to identify policy challenges, this chapter presents areas of largest underperformance relative to other areas (*relative* performance), with each country being assigned one challenge from Panel A of the dashboard and one from Panel B.[1] While this procedure allows establishing performance priorities for all countries, there may be large differences in *absolute* performance even among countries sharing the same challenge. For instance, countries with job quantity as the main challenge may include countries with below-average performance in job quantity as well as countries with above-average performance (if they are performing even better on job quality and inclusiveness). While this procedure allows for an easy identification of country-specific challenges in all countries, it can easily be amended in the context of specific countries, by taking account of a broader set of challenges or selecting them differently between policy objectives.

Figure 17.2. An illustrative diagnostic process to identify policy challenges

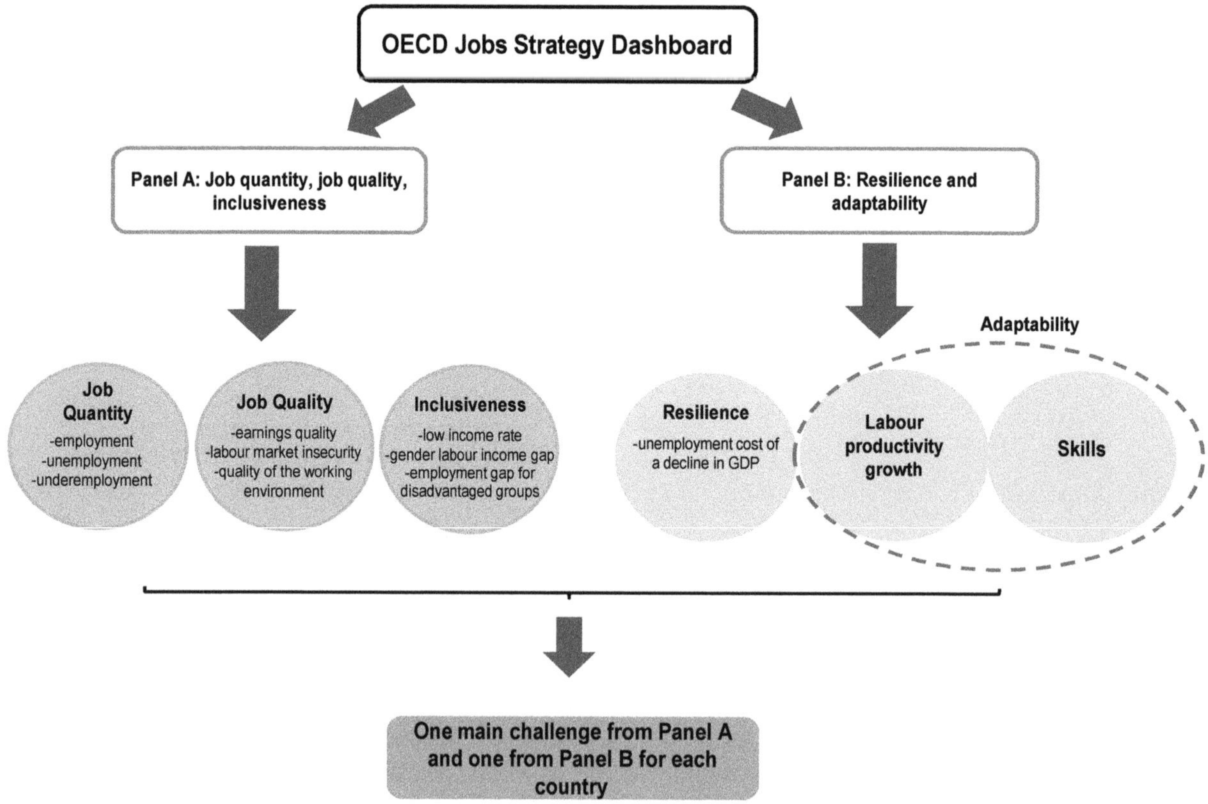

17.2. Identification of policy challenges and examples of broad policy packages

Broad performance areas

On average, countries with job quantity as a performance challenge also do worse than the OECD average in terms of job quality and inclusiveness (Figure 17.3). Countries with inclusiveness as the main challenge perform around the OECD average in terms of job quantity and job quality, whereas countries with job quality as the main challenge typically outperform the OECD average in job quantity and inclusiveness. Regarding the performance areas of Panel B, countries with a challenge in one area tend to outperform the OECD average in other areas.

Figure 17.3. Identifying policy challenges by broad performance area

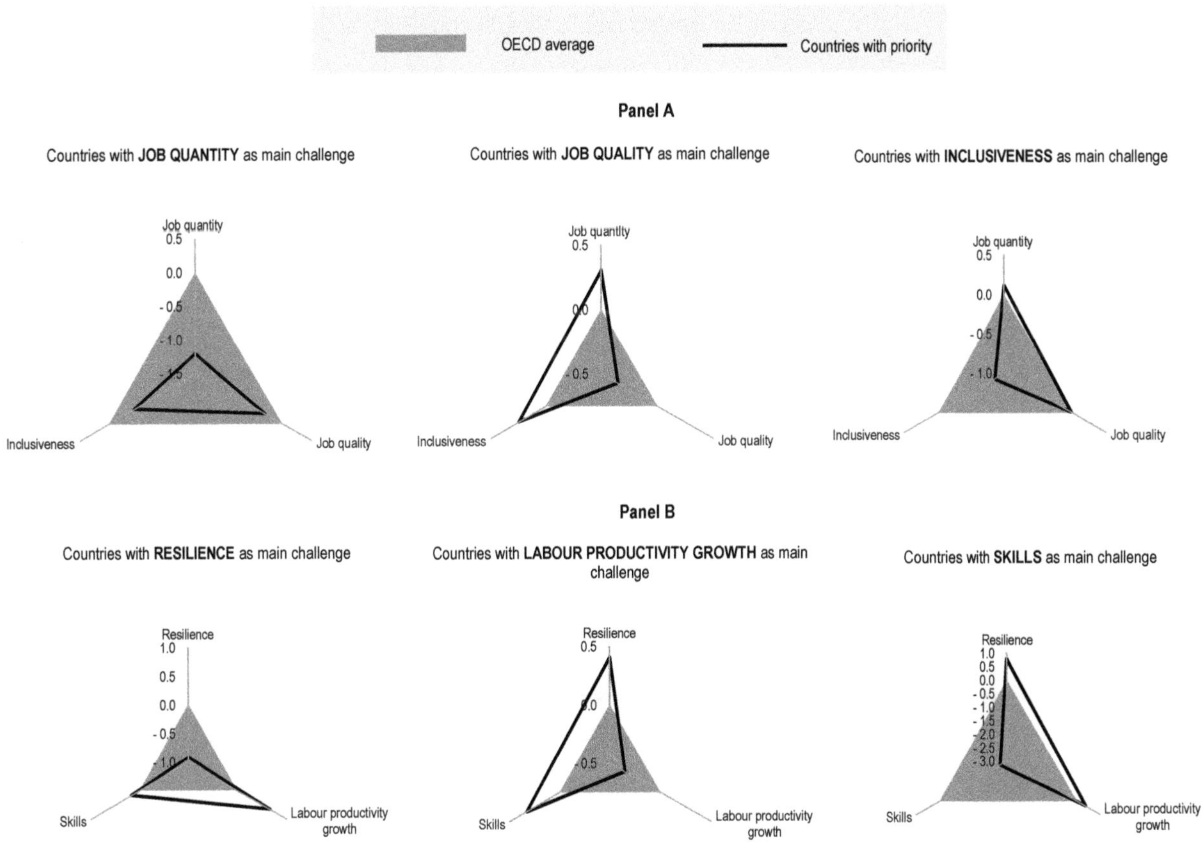

Note: The blue triangle indicates the average performance of OECD countries (see Chapter 3, Table 3.1 for details on the indicators). The black line indicates the average performance of countries with the same performance challenge. All indicators have been standardised and rescaled so that a higher score indicates better outcomes.

StatLink http://dx.doi.org/10.1787/888933881914

Dissecting policy challenges by broad performance areas

Even countries with the same challenge based on *relative* performance can differ importantly in terms of *absolute* performance (Figure 17.4). For instance, Denmark performs *relatively* worse in job quantity than in job quality or inclusiveness but performs above the OECD average in job quantity (it does well in terms of *absolute* performance), whereas other countries with job quantity as the main challenge, such as Greece, Italy and Spain, perform well below the OECD average.

Relative performance across the sub-indicators of job quantity, job quality and inclusiveness may also differ significantly across countries even for countries with the same broad challenge (Figure 17.5). For instance, Canada, China, Japan, Korea and the United States share inclusiveness as broad performance challenge, but differ importantly in terms of *relative* performance across sub-indicators. In Canada, China and the United States, weak relative performance is mainly driven by high rates of low-income households, whereas in Japan and Korea, this is driven by relatively large gender gaps.

Figure 17.4.Large differences in *absolute* performance for countries with the same policy challenge

Standard deviations across OECD countries

A. Job quantity, quality and inclusiveness

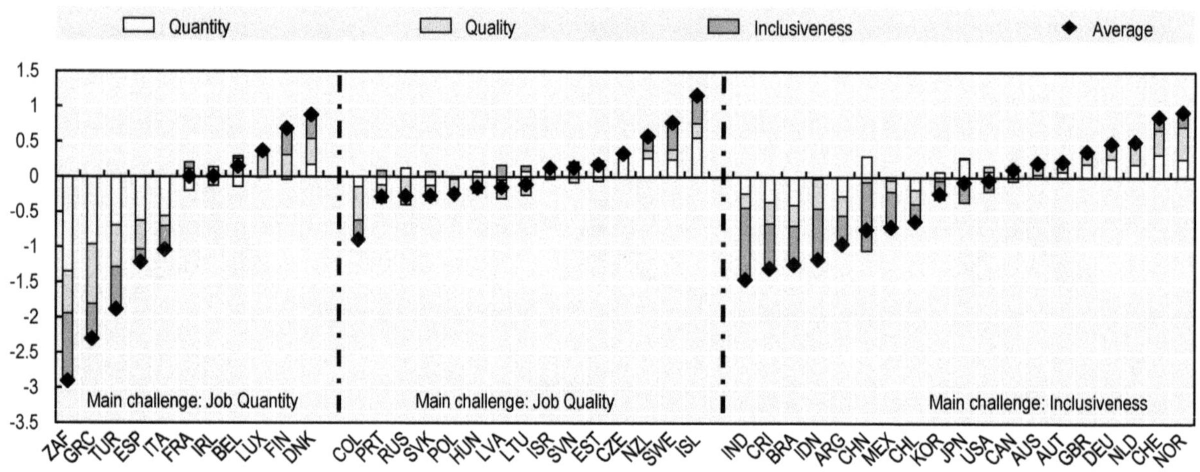

B. Resilience and adaptability

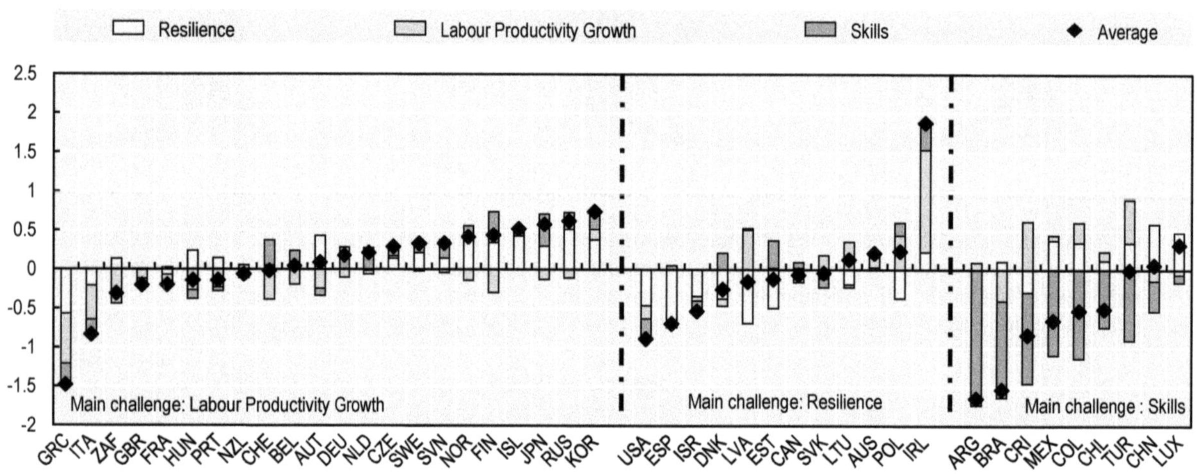

Note: The figure shows contributions to overall *absolute* performance in Panel A and B of the Dashboard. *Absolute* performance is standardised based on the OECD average, with units on the vertical axis denoting standard deviations. On the horizontal axis, countries are sorted by main challenge and in ascending order of absolute performance (i.e. from the worst to the best performers).

StatLink http://dx.doi.org/10.1787/888933881933

Figure 17.5. Large differences in disaggregate relative performance for countries with the same policy challenge

Standard deviations across OECD countries

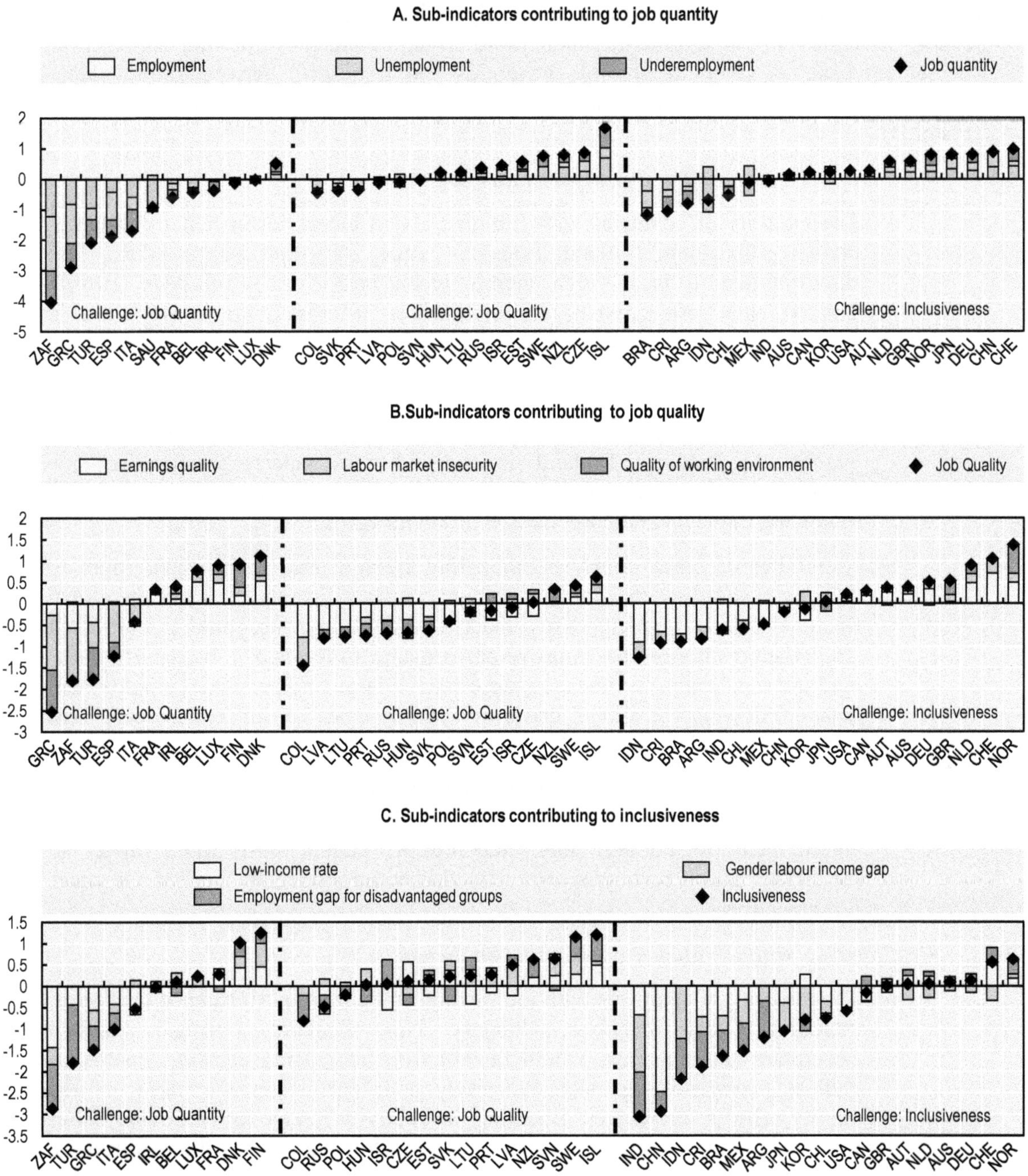

Note: The figures shows contributions to *absolute* performance in job quantity, job quality and inclusiveness. *Absolute* performance is standardised based on the OECD average for each sub-indicator, with units on the vertical axis denoting standard deviations. In each panel, countries are sorted in ascending order of *absolute* performance in each main dimension (i.e. from the worst to the best performer).

StatLink http://dx.doi.org/10.1787/888933881952

Elements of broad policy packages to address country-specific challenges

This sub-section presents a number of examples of broad policy packages to address country-specific challenges. Given large differences in *absolute* performance and in the economic and institutional context between countries sharing the same broad challenges, these policy packages should again be seen only as broad illustrations. Country-specific reform strategies would require a much more in-depth analysis. In this sub-section, special emphasis is given to possible synergies and trade-offs between policy areas related to job quantity, job quality, inclusiveness (Panel A) and resilience and adaptability (Panel B):

- *Countries with job quantity as the main challenge*
    - The majority of countries with job quantity as broad performance challenge, including Belgium, Finland, France, Greece, Italy and South Africa, also share the need to tackle high unemployment and foster *productivity growth.* This typically reflects weak job performance in terms of job creation and in some cases also weak labour force participation. Policies that promote job creation and productivity growth are likely to be mutually reinforcing. In Belgium, France and Greece, for instance, overly strict product market and employment protection rules may limit both productivity growth and job quantity. In Belgium, Finland, France and Italy underperformance on job quantity may also reflect high non-wage labour costs, which calls for reviewing the level and composition of labour taxes.
    - A number of other countries, including Ireland and Spain, have room to enhance *resilience*. Poor job performance partly reflects a legacy of the global financial crisis. In many cases, macroeconomic and structural policies that strengthen resilience also improve performance in terms of job quantity in the medium run. Spain, for instance, experienced large and persistent employment losses following the global crisis of 2008-09 and the subsequent euro area crises which had not been fully reversed 2017.
    - A few countries, including Turkey, need to enhance effective labour supply and improve *skills*. Lack of relevant skills represents a major barrier to employment. In Turkey, poor outcomes in student skills often reflect an inefficient use of resources which is also compounded by limited resources for education.
- *Countries with job quality as the main challenge*
    - The majority of countries with job quality as the main performance challenge, including Czech Republic, Hungary, New Zealand, Portugal, Russian Federation and Slovenia, would benefit from increasing earnings quality as well as *productivity growth.* Relatively poor performance in terms of job quality reflects low wages. Boosting productivity is key for achieving better working conditions, including higher wages. However, this is likely to require important structural reforms since these countries also underperform in terms of productivity *growth.* These can include reforms that reduce barriers to entry and exit of firms where they are particularly high such as in Slovenia, and the Russian Federation as well as making better use of R&D tax incentives and subsidies to promote the faster diffusion of innovation from leading to lagging firms (New Zealand and Portugal). However, on their own, such reforms are unlikely to achieve high levels of job quality. In some countries, such as

Hungary and the Russian Federation, additional measures may be needed to promote job quality, for instance in the areas of occupational health and safety and social dialogue.

- Most other countries, including Estonia, Israel, Latvia, Lithuania, Slovak Republic and Poland, may need to combine measures to promote job quality, especially earnings quality, with measures to strengthen *resilience*. Policies to promote resilience, including a sound macroeconomic policy framework, can have the added benefit of raising job security by limiting employment losses during economic downturns and ensuring a rapid rebound. In turn, policies to promote job quality may have the added benefit of strengthening resilience. Estonia, Israel, Latvia and Poland, for instance, would benefit both in terms of resilience and job quality from strengthening social dialogue.

- *Countries with inclusiveness as the main challenge*
  - The majority of countries with inclusiveness as the main performance challenge would benefit from also promoting *labour productivity growth*, including Austria, Germany, Japan, Korea, Netherlands, Norway, Switzerland and the United Kingdom. Indeed, even though most of these countries perform above average in many important areas of job quantity, job quality and inclusiveness, they could do even better if they improved gender equality in the labour market. Depending on the nature of gender inequalities (see Chapter 10), this could be achieved by strengthening access to affordable, high-quality child care to promote female participation; enhancing work-life balance; promoting a more equal sharing of parenting responsibilities; and reducing labour supply distortions in the tax and transfer system. To promote labour productivity growth, Austria, Germany, Japan and Korea could reduce barriers to entry in services, such as professional licencing requirements, which would have the additional benefit of reducing barriers to work for low-qualified workers, thereby raising inclusiveness.
  - Most emerging market economies have much room to improve inclusiveness and ***skills***, including Argentina, Brazil, Chile, China, Costa Rica, Mexico and South Africa. Providing access to high-quality education is crucial to create equal opportunities for all segments of the population. In many emerging market economies, this could, for instance, be achieved by improving both educational enrolment and quality. Another way of improving skills and promoting inclusiveness in these countries would be to reduce high levels of informality, which could be achieved by increasing the benefits of formality, decreasing the cost of formalisation and improving enforcement methods.
  - In a number of English-speaking countries, such as Australia, Canada and the United States, there is scope to promote inclusiveness, with a particular focus on reducing the low-income rate, and to strengthen *resilience.* In Canada and the United States, the share of the working-age population with low disposable income is large compared with the OECD average. This could be addressed by raising investment in skills, strengthening social safety nets and developing a comprehensive activation strategy, which would have the added benefit of strengthening the automatic fiscal stabilisers and thereby strengthen resilience. To address gender gaps in labour income, which are high in all countries in all of these countries, full-day childcare and primary education could be extended and taxes for second earners be reduced.

17.3. Integrating the country-specific context

While the above policy options provide illustrative examples, they do not yield operational country-specific policy recommendations. Apart from accounting for the magnitude of performance gaps, such operational recommendations require accounting for a range of other country-specific factors, including: macroeconomic conditions; fiscal and administrative capacity; past reforms, synergies and sequencing; social preferences; and demographic conditions.

Macroeconomic conditions and policies

Reaping the full benefits of reforms takes time. Product and labour market reforms significantly raise economic and labour market performance in the long run (Boeri, Cahuc and Zylberberg, 2015[1]). But structural reforms often involve significant reallocation of resources across firms and sectors that can result in short-term costs, notably in the labour market (Chapter 15).

The short-term effect of structural reforms depends on the state of the business cycle. For instance, reforms to employment protection have positive effects on employment and output when implemented during cyclical upswings, but can exacerbate shortfalls in employment during periods of slack (see Chapter 15 for more detailed discussion). A possible reason is that while in good times these reforms may spur hiring by reducing the cost of future dismissal, in periods of slack they may trigger instantaneous layoffs. By contrast, labour tax reductions or increases in public spending on activation have larger effects on output and employment during periods of slack (IMF, 2016[2]; OECD, 2017[3]).

Supportive macroeconomic policies can limit the short-term costs of structural reforms and promote their political viability. They can, for instance, enhance the positive effect of labour and product market reforms on employment in the short-run (IMF, 2016[2]). Moreover, supportive fiscal policy can be used to compensate the losers of reform (Høj et al., 2006[4]).

Fiscal and administrative capacity

Limited capacity to raise fiscal revenues can be a barrier to reform. Emerging market economies typically collect taxes of between 12 to 32% of GDP, while the average for advanced countries is around 35% (Figure 17.6). This suggests that countries with limited fiscal capacity face more difficulties to find the resources needed to adopt and implement reforms, especially in the areas of job quality and inclusiveness that often require raising social spending. For instance, Northern European countries such as Sweden and Denmark with strong fiscal capacity can implement relatively generous public income support and employment programmes to promote job quality whereas this is not the case in most emerging market economies. More generally, countries with limited fiscal capacity may need to prioritise reforms that are budget neutral, such as adjusting both taxes and expenditure to raise work incentives, rather than reforms that require financing high up-front costs, such as increasing spending on activation or strengthening the social safety net (IMF, 2012[5]).

Figure 17.6. Tax revenue varies widely across countries

Tax revenue as % of GDP, 2016

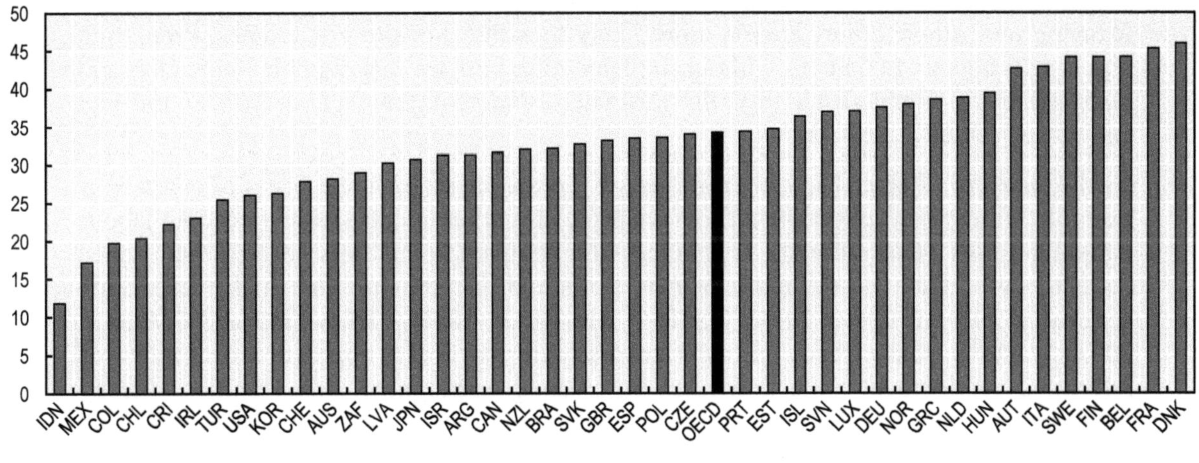

Note: Data refers to 2016 for all countries except for Australia and Japan (2015). OECD average is the unweighted average of the countries included in the graph.
Source: *OECD Tax Revenue Database*, 2018, https://stats.oecd.org/Index.aspx?DataSetCode=REV.

StatLink http://dx.doi.org/10.1787/888933881971

Limited administrative capacity can be another barrier to reform. For instance, in many emerging market economies large informal sectors evade taxation and labour market rules. In these countries, labour market security needs to be promoted by other means than public income support and employment programmes, including by increasing the use of mandatory self-insurance based on individual saving accounts for those who can afford it and by providing a redistributive component for those who cannot rely on individual savings. The Chilean unemployment insurance system of individual unemployment saving accounts (*Régimen de Seguro de Cesantía*) in combination with a Solidarity Fund (*Fondo de Cesantía Solidario*) provides an interesting example of self-insurance combined with income support in the event of job loss for the poor (OECD, 2011[6]). Similarly, in countries such as Greece, Italy, Spain and Turkey, limited administrative capacity can hamper the effective implementation and delivery of active labour market programmes.

In addition to improving fiscal and administrative capacity, stepping up the public administration's transparency, accountability, capacity and professionalism — including at the local level — and improving the business environment are preconditions for successfully implementing reforms. In emerging market economies such as Colombia, Costa Rica and Mexico the capacity of the public sector is weak, both in terms of human and financial resources, corruption remains widespread and the rule of law is weak (Kaufmann, Kraay and Zoido-Lobaton, 1999[7]). These factors hinder the effective implementation of policies (Chapter 16). In these countries, policy action should aim at being particularly simple, transparent and easily accountable. For instance, this may imply erring on the side of less conditionality and less targeting of social benefits while limiting their generosity.

Past reforms, synergies and sequencing

When synergies between policies exist, combining and coordinating them produces better outcomes than implementing them separately. For example, a country that simultaneously implements reforms in the areas of education, activation and innovation rather than focusing on a single policy area is more likely to achieve positive outcomes. Promoting higher educational attainment without implementing policies that support innovation and skills matching might result in skills mismatch, underemployment, dissatisfaction and emigration (OECD, forthcoming[8]).

As discussed in Chapter 15, some reforms are a prerequisite for the success of others. For example, ideally it would be better to have product market liberalisation preceding labour market reforms. The rationale is that pro-competitive product market reforms reduce market power, facilitate the entry of new firms and, in turn, promote higher economic activity and labour demand (IMF, 2016[2]; Høj et al., 2006[4]; Blanchard and Giavazzi, 2003[9]).[2] As a consequence, product market reforms could improve the chances of reforming employment protection rules by creating employment opportunities, thereby reducing the incentives for incumbent workers to protect their jobs (Koeniger and Vindigni, 2003[10]; Dias Da SIlva, Givone and Sondermann, 2078[11]).

Activation and social protection measures can complement each other, as there are important synergies between income or in-kind support on the one hand ("passive policies") and activation measures ("active policies") on the other (Chapter 9). Usually, incentives operating through existing social protection measures (i.e. threat of benefit withdrawal, bonus payments or different forms of sanction) can encourage participation in activation-related programmes. Similarly, a system of effective income support payments makes it much easier to target activation measures such as training, or job search assistance (OECD, 2015[12]). Such targeting can, in turn, create the fiscal space and the political support that is needed to ensure adequate support for families who need it most. For this reason, the effectiveness of active policy measures might be more limited in countries with lower levels of social benefits or where benefits can only be received for a short duration of time. As a consequence of this complementarity, policy adjustments in one area often indicate a need for reviewing provisions in the other. For instance, to maintain a balance between rights and responsibilities, extensions of unemployment benefit duration or coverage may need to be accompanied by measures to maintain the activation approach for a growing number of benefit recipients. The Nordic countries, for example, have achieved high employment rates despite high social benefits by imposing strict eligibility and job search requirements.

Labour market reforms that raise labour supply, such as activation policies, will boost employment when the extra supply gets absorbed by rising labour demand. Activation policies can be expected to work best if they are embedded in a comprehensive policy framework that facilitates job creation and dynamic labour markets. For instance, reforms that increase wage flexibility as well as product and capital market reforms that encourage job growth can enhance the effectiveness of activation policies. Additionally, the effectiveness of active labour market policies is enhanced by lower entry barriers in product markets and higher public sector efficiency (Andrews and Saia, 2016[13]).

Preferences for redistribution and social dialogue

Preferences for redistribution vary substantially across countries (Alesina, Giuliano and Alesina, 2009[14]). Countries with strong preferences for redistribution (e.g. the Nordic countries) typically promote inclusiveness through the tax and transfer system (Causa and

Hermansen, 2017[15]). Where the tax and transfer system is less redistributive, inclusiveness could be promoted by investing in the education to provide equality of opportunity and/or by direct interventions in market outcomes. Such interventions include supporting earnings at the lower end of the income distribution by using minimum wages and activation policies that facilitate re-employment.

Specific country preferences towards social dialogue and collective bargaining, rather than state- and market-oriented approaches, are another element that need to be taken into account when developing country-specific recommendations. For example, in some countries, collectively-agreed wage floors are used to ensure that workers at the bottom of the wage ladder also benefit from economic growth. By contrast, in the absence of collective bargaining agreements, the same policy objective may be achieved by using statutory minimum wages. For example, Australia does not have sector level bargaining, but sets industry-level minimum wages that vary according to occupation through a system of wage regulation *(Modern Awards)*.

In countries with strong social dialogue, social partners may partly substitute for the government in providing integrated packages of labour market policies, such as training and retraining opportunities as well as career guidance and information to foster mobility. For instance, *Jobs Security Councils* (JSCs) in Sweden provide an example of continuous and tailored re-employment services for displaced workers that are provided by the social partners (i.e. employer federations in close collaboration with union federations), rather than by the public employment services or other public actors (Chapter 14).

Demographic factors: Ageing and migration

Declines in fertility rates and increases in life expectancy are leading to population ageing in many OECD countries, which is raising the old-age dependency ratio (the ratio of older people to the working-age population and shifting the composition of the workforce from young to older workers (Figure 17.7). Countries with ageing populations are also likely to face shortages of qualified labour, which have implications for potential growth and the sustainability of social insurance systems (IMF, 2018[16]; OECD, 2017[17]). Population ageing is also likely to lead to important changes in industrial and occupational structure as consumer tastes change, with demand likely to shift from durable goods towards services.

In countries with rapidly ageing populations, such as Germany, Italy, Japan and Slovenia, it is important to strengthen skills, workplace and activation policies that allow, support and encourage people to continue working at older ages as well as policies promoting female labour force participation and the integration of disadvantaged groups, including migrants. Pension reform needs to go together with skills policies that focus on adapting the skills of individuals to changing labour market needs. In this context, it will be particularly important for governments to design high-quality, life-long, learning systems that will permit adults to regularly update, upgrade, and acquire new skills and competences in order to stay employed and/or find new employment. A comprehensive activation strategy for older workers requires a combination of rewarding work at an older age, removing disincentives on the side of employers to hiring and retaining older workers and improving the employability of older workers. Reducing labour taxes for older workers and policies that improve the job-matching process can encourage individuals to keep working or seek employment.

By contrast, in many emerging market economies with a young and growing workforce (e.g. India, Mexico, Saudi Arabia), the challenge will be to harness the full potential of the demographic dividend, ensuring that youth have the skills necessary to be gainfully employed and make a contribution to economic growth. Skills and educational policies, in these countries, should focus on providing high-quality initial education to all individuals, particularly by increasing educational attainment and by reducing school dropout rates, while ensuring youth are provided with skills that are needed in formal jobs. Additionally, these countries should focus on ensuring a smooth transition from school to work, for example by improving the capacity of the public employment services to reach out to youth, by strengthening family-friendly policies, and by providing youth with adequate income support.

Figure 17.7. The old-age dependency ratio will almost double in the next 35 years on average

Number of people older than 65 years per 100 people of working age (20-64), 2015-50

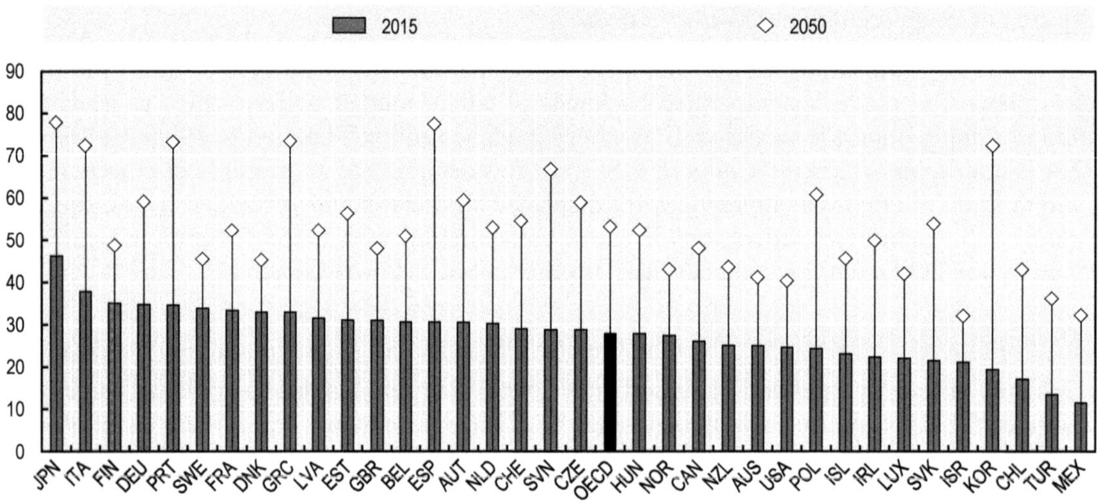

Note: The projected old-age dependency ratios differ based on the sources used. This report is based on UN data for comparison reasons. The largest differences are the following: according to Eurostat the old-age dependency ratio (65+/20-64) would increase by 39 and 19 percentage points between 2015 and 2050 in Spain and Austria, respectively, against 47 and 29 points with UN data. On the other hand, it would increase in Latvia by 33 points based on Eurostat against only 21 points with UN data.

Source: OECD (2017[18]), *Pensions at a Glance 2017: OECD and G20 Indicators*, https://doi.org/10.1787/pension_glance-2017-en.

StatLink http://dx.doi.org/10.1787/888933881990

In conjunction with other policies, migration can make a significant contribution to address demographic imbalances across countries and regions. In most OECD countries, immigration can help address shortages, but in many cases there is also a need for accompanying integration policies (Chapter 11). This mainly relates to migrants coming for reasons other than employment, such as family (including accompanying family of workers) or humanitarian reasons. Indeed, such non-labour migration accounts for the bulk of immigration to most OECD countries. An example of good practice in integration is Sweden, where tailor-made introduction courses combining language and other training as well as work experience, are provided for refugees to facilitate stepwise integration into the labour market. In order to encourage employers to provide migrants with initial labour market experience, employers hiring newly-arrived refugees are able to benefit from a number of subsidised employment schemes (OECD, 2016[19]). Countries with high shares of low-educated migrants may also need to review their educational policies to ensure equal opportunities for children of these immigrants in terms of schooling as a precondition to avoid marginalisation in adulthood. In this context, increasing access to early childhood education with a specific focus on children with language obstacles is particularly important.

Conclusions

This chapter has provided guidance on how to bring the policy recommendations of the new *OECD Jobs Strategy* to the national level. It has provided an illustration on how performance challenges could be identified for each country, by focusing on *relative* performance weaknesses (weaknesses in one area of labour market performance relative to another). Additionally, the chapter provides a set of broad policy packages to address the main policy challenges. Even for countries with potentially similar broad priorities, disaggregate performance gaps and the country-specific context differ significantly. Finally, the chapter has highlighted a range of other factors that need to be accounted for to develop operational country-specific policy recommendations, including macroeconomic conditions; fiscal and institutional capacity; past reforms; sequencing; social preferences; as well as demography.

Notes

[1] All indicators are standardised (mean zero and standard deviation of one), with negative numbers representing areas of underperformance. For countries that are performing above average in all the dimensions, priorities are established as areas where performance is weaker (i.e. indicators where the country scores closer to the average). The indicators used for the country-specific diagnostic process are: summary indicators of job quantity, job quality, inclusiveness, resilience and two measures of adaptability (labour productivity growth and student skills). This set of indicators is widely available across countries and allows a general assessment of countries' labour market performance and of their ability to face the opportunities and the challenges of the future of work.

[2] Product market reforms should also be prioritised because they have the highest short-term gains, they boost output regardless of overall economic conditions and because they do not weigh on public finances (IMF, 2016[2]).

References

Alesina, A., P. Giuliano and A. Alesina (2009), "Preferences for Redistribution", *NBER Working Paper Series*, National Bureau of Economic Research, Cambridge, MA, http://www.nber.org/papers/w14825. [14]

Andrews, D. and A. Saia (2016), "Coping with creative distruction: reducing the costs of firm exit", *OECD Economics Department Working Papers*, No. 1353, OECD, Paris. [13]

Blanchard, O. and F. Giavazzi (2003), "Macroeconomic Effects of Regulation and Deregulation in Goods and Labor Markets", *The Quarterly Journal of Economics*, Vol. 118/3, pp. 879-907, http://dx.doi.org/10.1162/003355303360698450. [9]

Boeri, T., P. Cahuc and A. Zylberberg (2015), "The Costs of Flexibility-Enhancing Structural Reforms", *OECD Economics Department Working Papers,*, No. 1264, OECD, Paris, https://www.oecd-ilibrary.org/economics/the-costs-of-flexibility-enhancing-structural-reforms_5jrs558c5r5f-en. [1]

Causa, O. and M. Hermansen (2017), "Income redistribution through taxes and transfers across OECD countries", *OECD Economics Department Working Papers*, No. No. 1453, OECD, Paris, https://www.oecd-ilibrary.org/economics/income-redistribution-through-taxes-and-transfers-across-oecd-countries_bc7569c6-en. [15]

Dias Da SIlva, A., A. Givone and D. Sondermann (2078), "When do countries implement structural reforms?", *Working Paper Series*, No. 2078, European Central Bank, http://dx.doi.org/10.2866/0417. [11]

Høj, J. et al. (2006), "The Political Economy of Structural Reform", *OECD Economics Department Working Papers*, No. 501, OECD, https://www.oecd-ilibrary.org/economics/the-political-economy-of-structural-reform_881353527404. [4]

IMF (2018), "Chapter 2: Labor Force Participation in Advanced Economies: Drivers and Prospects", in *World Economic Outlook: Cyclical Upswing, Structural Change.*, International Monetary Fund, https://www.imf.org/en/Publications/WEO/Issues/2018/03/20/world-economic-outlook-april-2018. [16]

IMF (2016), "Chapter 3. Time for a Supply-Side Boost? Macroeconomic Effects of Labor and Product Market Reforms in Advanced Economies", in *IMF World Economic Outlook (WEO): Too Slow for Too Long, April 2016*, http://www.imf.org/en/Publications/WEO/Issues/2016/12/31/Too-Slow-for-Too-Long. [2]

IMF (2012), "Fiscal Policy and Employment in Advanced and Emerging Economies", IMF , Washington, DC, https://www.imf.org/external/np/pp/eng/2012/061512.pdf (accessed on 12 July 2018). [5]

Kaufmann, D., A. Kraay and P. Zoido-Lobaton (1999), "Governance matters", *Policy Research Working Paper*, No. WPS 2196, World Bank, Washington, DC, http://documents.worldbank.org/curated/en/665731468739470954/Governance-matters. [7]

Koeniger, W. and A. Vindigni (2003), "Employment Protection and Product Market Regulation", *IZA Working papers*, No. No. 880, IZA. [10]

OECD (2017), "Labour market resilience: The role of structural and macroeconomic policies", in *OECD Employment Outlook 2017*, OECD Publishing, Paris, http://dx.doi.org/10.1787/empl_outlook-2017-6-en. [3]

OECD (2017), *Pensions at a Glance 2017: OECD and G20 Indicators*, OECD Publishing, Paris, http://dx.doi.org/10.1787/pension_glance-2017-en. [18]

OECD (2017), *Preventing Ageing Unequally*, OECD Publishing, Paris, http://dx.doi.org/10.1787/9789264279087-en. [17]

OECD (2016), *Working Together: Skills and Labour Market Integration of Immigrants and their Children in Sweden*, OECD Publishing, Paris, http://dx.doi.org/10.1787/9789264257382-en. [19]

OECD (2015), "Activation policies for more inclusive labour markets", in *OECD Employment Outlook 2015*, OECD Publishing, Paris, http://dx.doi.org/10.1787/empl_outlook-2015-7-en. [12]

OECD (2011), "The Labour Market Effects of Social Protection Systems in Emerging Economies", in *OECD Employment Outlook 2011*, OECD Publishing, Paris, http://dx.doi.org/10.1787/empl_outlook-2011-4-en. [6]

OECD (forthcoming), *OECD Skills Strategy*, OECD Publishing, Paris. [8]

ORGANISATION FOR ECONOMIC CO-OPERATION AND DEVELOPMENT

The OECD is a unique forum where governments work together to address the economic, social and environmental challenges of globalisation. The OECD is also at the forefront of efforts to understand and to help governments respond to new developments and concerns, such as corporate governance, the information economy and the challenges of an ageing population. The Organisation provides a setting where governments can compare policy experiences, seek answers to common problems, identify good practice and work to co-ordinate domestic and international policies.

The OECD member countries are: Australia, Austria, Belgium, Canada, Chile, the Czech Republic, Denmark, Estonia, Finland, France, Germany, Greece, Hungary, Iceland, Ireland, Israel, Italy, Japan, Korea, Latvia, Lithuania, Luxembourg, Mexico, the Netherlands, New Zealand, Norway, Poland, Portugal, the Slovak Republic, Slovenia, Spain, Sweden, Switzerland, Turkey, the United Kingdom and the United States. The European Union takes part in the work of the OECD.

OECD Publishing disseminates widely the results of the Organisation's statistics gathering and research on economic, social and environmental issues, as well as the conventions, guidelines and standards agreed by its members.

OECD PUBLISHING, 2, rue André-Pascal, 75775 PARIS CEDEX 16
(81 2018 82 1 P) ISBN 978-92-64-30880-0 – 2018

www.ingramcontent.com/pod-product-compliance
Ingram Content Group UK Ltd.
Pitfield, Milton Keynes, MK11 3LW, UK
UKHW051456290926
15471UKWH00008B/1237

9 789264 308800